The Production of Reality

Sixth Edition

For Peter Kollock (1959–2009). May your spirit of mindfulness live on in these words.

The Production of Reality

Essays and Readings on Social Interaction

Sixth Edition

Jodi O'Brien

Seattle University

Los Angeles | London | New Delhi
Singapore | Washington DC | Melbourne

FOR INFORMATION:

SAGE Publications, Inc.
2455 Teller Road
Thousand Oaks, California 91320
E-mail: order@sagepub.com

SAGE Publications Ltd.
1 Oliver's Yard
55 City Road
London, EC1Y 1SP
United Kingdom

SAGE Publications India Pvt. Ltd.
B 1/I 1 Mohan Cooperative Industrial Area
Mathura Road, New Delhi 110 044
India

SAGE Publications Asia-Pacific Pte. Ltd.
3 Church Street
#10-04 Samsung Hub
Singapore 049483

Acquisitions Editor: Jeff Lasser
Editorial Assistant: Alexandra Croell
Production Editor: Bennie Clark Allen
Copy Editor: Sarah J. Duffy
Typesetter: C&M Digitals (P) Ltd.
Proofreader: Sue Schon
Indexer: Terri Morrissey
Cover Designer: Candice Harman
Marketing Manager: Johanna Swenson
eLearning Editor: Gabrielle Piccininni

Copyright © 2017 by SAGE Publications, Inc.

Library of Congress Cataloging-in-Publication Data

Names: O'Brien, Jodi, editor.

Title: The production of reality : essays and readings on social interaction/ Jodi O'Brien.

Description: Sixth edition. | Los Angeles : SAGE, [2017] | Includes index.

Identifiers: LCCN 2015042924 | ISBN 9781452217833 (pbk. : alk. paper)

Subjects: LCSH: Social psychology.

Classification: LCC HM1033.O27 2017 | DDC 302—dc23 LC record available at http://lccn.loc.gov/2015042924

This book is printed on acid-free paper.

16 17 18 19 20 10 9 8 7 6 5 4 3 2 1

CONTENTS

PREFACE TO THE SIXTH EDITION

In my class syllabus for a course in social psychology, I make this statement:

> The main goal of this course is that you understand how we become social creatures and how, through our everyday interactions with one another, we make and remake ourselves and our social worlds. One important implication of the ideas covered in this course is that if we understand how it is that we participate in the construction of our own realities, then we can take a more active and purposeful approach toward making this the sort of world in which we want to live.

During the production of this book, I was reminded of a scene in the film *Annie Hall,* wherein Woody Allen's character, Alvy Singer (as a young man), reports that he is depressed because he has read that the universe is expanding. As the universe expands, it changes shape. Consequently, what we think we know about it changes as well—whatever we think we know today may change tomorrow. Believing that this will eventually mean "the end of everything," the young Alvy refuses to do his homework: "What's the point?" he sighs.

Indeed, what's the point in learning anything if, in fact, everything that we learn now will be invalid later on?

WHAT'S THE POINT?

The Production of Reality was initially compiled to provide students with a social psychology text that was useful and relevant to their everyday lives. One thing that you will probably learn in your sojourn through higher education, if you haven't already, is that there are many voices, many points of view, and many ways of learning and knowing. Diversity and complexity are hallmarks of life in the new millennium. Our social universe is continually expanding, and as it expands, so too does our stockpile of knowledge. Even more profound is the fact that the more we learn about our social universe, the more it changes shape. How do we make sense of this shifting and complexity? This is one of the most significant questions of our times. Several relatively new fields of study (for example, cultural studies) have emerged in the past few decades with the aim of exploring this particular question. Scholars in established disciplines—such as anthropology, communications, English, history, law, philosophy, women's and gender studies, and even geography—have also taken up this question. The commonality across disciplines of the themes of global expansion, diversity, and complexity is a sign of the importance of this inquiry. It is an exciting time to be a part of this intellectual dialogue.

Sociologists and social psychologists have been exploring for more than a century to map patterns of human social behavior. As sociologists, we know a great deal about patterns—how to look for them, how to read them, and how to interpret the consequences. In particular, sociologists have a lot to contribute regarding structured relations of power. *Structured* is the operative word in this phrase. Sociologists and social psychologists know a great deal about structure and the ways in which it matters in everyday life. To make sense of our own lives, we need an understanding of the underlying patterns and material conditions that make up the particular cultural milieu in which we live. Racism, for example, is a persistent problem in U.S. society. The tools for understanding and potentially eradicating racism can be forged through an understanding of *why* and *how* people, even self-professed nonracists, are stuck in a social groove that produces patterns of racism. These grooves or ruts are what sociologists mean when we talk about social patterns and social structures.

THE LOGIC OF THE BOOK

This book is organized as a combination of essays and readings. The *essays* introduce relevant themes and concepts and raise questions intended to awaken you to the mysteries of human social life. These essays constitute the theoretical logic of the book. The *readings* have been selected to illustrate and elaborate various aspects of social interaction that are described in the essays. The readings span several decades and represent many different voices and points of view. Some of the readings are considered sociological classics—articles that every well-educated student should be familiar with. Some of the language and examples used by the authors of some of these older pieces may seem outdated and even offensive. I encourage you to read these selections as a form of social history as well as social theory. In other words, ask yourself what it was that was different about the times in which these authors wrote. Can you be critical and still comprehend why the ideas might have been groundbreaking at the time they were written? The contemporary readings include research studies, narrative essays, and some fiction. It is likely that different readings will resonate for different readers. As you read these diverse selections, consider why it is that certain types of writing and particular themes seem more or less appealing to you. What does your own response as a reader indicate about your social biography?

NEW EMPHASES FOR THE SIXTH EDITION

The Production of Reality is about human behavior, or social psychology. The intent in each edition has been to ground social psychology in the experiences of students and to provide an understanding of the forces that shape our feelings, thoughts, and actions. In recent years, inquiries into the relationship between the body, brain, and behavior have become popular. Old questions such as "Is behavior determined mostly by nature or biology?" have resurfaced. New research into the nature/nurture binary offers some promising new directions for understanding human experience. At the same time, some of this research reflects troubling histories of racism, sexism, and other social hierarchies that, historically, have been justified through "laws of nature" arguments. This edition includes a sharper focus on the nature/nurture research trend. Additional new material takes up contemporary experiences that reflect our changing global world, including the proliferation of wearing the head scarf (hijab) in Western cultures and transgender experiences in the United States.

MANY QUESTIONS, YOUR OWN ANSWERS

The general intent of this book is to immerse you in the puzzles and issues of contemporary social psychology and to provide a framework for constructing your own understanding of the social world. Toward this end, many questions are posed, and you are invited to reflect on them in light of the concepts and theories presented in the book. As you will discover in reading this text, there are no absolute or final answers to the most important human questions. This is because we are constantly creating new ways of understanding ourselves and our social worlds. Through our ability to think and communicate, we are expanding our social universe. The material in this text is intended to provide you with a framework for understanding this creative social-psychological process (as well as for avoiding some of the pitfalls that appear when we fail to recognize our own involvement in the process). It can be useful to approach this material as a set of building blocks that you can assemble and reassemble to construct a framework for making sense of your own life.

If you (unlike Woody's character Alvy) are willing to do your homework, I am confident that your own universe of knowledge will expand in useful and profound ways.

ACKNOWLEDGMENTS

The creation of any product is always a collective enterprise. There are many who have helped to shape this book. The members of the SAGE production staff continue to be creative, helpful, and encouraging allies in my efforts to push beyond the boundaries of the traditional textbook. Thanks especially to Jeff Lasser, Alex Croell, Bennie Allen, and Sarah Duffy for shepherding this book along so expertly.

My commitment to bridging the gap between teaching and scholarship has been fostered by role models such as Hubert (Tad) Blalock, Howard Becker, Fred Campbell, Karen Cook, and Judy Howard. Over the course of my career, my commitment has been continuously renewed through interactions with colleagues who struggle valiantly in the quest to provide relevant and useful knowledge for students. I am repeatedly impressed with the dedication of these teacher-scholars. I am also tremendously grateful for the honest and constructive comments from the reviewers of this book. For the current edition, these reviewers included the following: Todd Migliaccio, Sacramento State University; Doug Maynard, University of Wisconsin; Michelle Durden, California State University Sacramento; Liza L. Kuecker, Western New Mexico University; Michelle Dietert, Texas A&M University Central Texas; Sara Pollak Levine, Fitchburg State University; Mark Horowitz, University of Texas at Brownsville; Monika Ardelt, University of Florida; Jerome Rabow, CSUN and UCLA; Robert J. Alexander, William Paterson University and Kean University; Kristi M. Fondren, Marshall University.

Much of my thinking as it developed in this book is the result of generous conversations with students. I thank them for sharing their intellectual passion and for trusting me to be open to learning from them. I am fortunate to have several friends and colleagues who are always responsive to my requests for feedback or my need for inspiring company. They include Michele Berger, Mark Cohan, Wendy Chapkis, Carly Chillmon, Mako Fitts, Gabriella Gutierrez y Muhs, Pierrette Hondagneu-Sotelo, Kevin Krycka, Tom Linneman, Kari Lerum, Rachel Luft, Nancy Naples, Peter Nardi, David Newman, Ken Plummer, Rich Serpe, Cecilia Ridgeway, Beth Schneider, Arlene Stein, Eve Shapiro, Pepper Schwartz, Judy Taylor, Verta Taylor, France Winddance Twine, and Christine Williams. Carol Lombardi, who copyedited the third edition, gets credit for the Woody Allen reference. Steve Rutter, the founder of Pine Forge Press and the person responsible for the original version of this book, is a true visionary in the field of textbook production. I am honored to have his friendship. Thanks especially to my good buddy Val Jenness for always reminding me that laughter really is the best medicine. As always, thanks to Ron Obvious just for being there and to Sabina Neem for constantly reminding me to lean back.

Jodi O'Brien

SAGE Publications gratefully acknowledges the following reviewers:

Robert J. Alexander, *William Paterson University and Kean University*

Monika Ardelt, *University of Florida*

Michelle Dietert, *Texas A&M University Central Texas (TAMUCT)*

Michelle Durden, *California State University Sacramento*

Kristi M. Fondren, *Marshall University*

Mark Horowitz, *University of Texas at Brownsville*

Liza L. Kuecker, *Western New Mexico University*

Sara Pollak Levine, *Fitchburg State University*

Doug Maynard, *University of Wisconsin*

Todd Migliaccio, *Sacramento State University*

Jerome Rabow, *CSUN and UCLA*

PART I

INTRODUCTION

A father said to his double-seeing son, "Son, you see two instead of one."

"How can that be?" the boy replied. "If that were true, I would see four moons up there in place of two."

—Idries Shah (1972), *Caravan of Dreams*

I have come to see that knowledge contains its own morality, that it begins not in neutrality but in a place of passion within the human soul. Depending on the nature of that passion, our knowledge will follow certain courses and head toward certain ends.

—Parker Palmer (1993), *To Know as We Are Known*

WHAT IS REAL?

Jodi O'Brien

In rural villages, religious festivals are an important part of the local culture. A documentary film crew was around to record one of these events in another country. The film shows brightly colored decorations, music, dancing, and a variety of delicious and special foods made for the festival. The special treats are clearly a highlight for everyone, especially the children, who crowd around the stands. In the middle of one crowd of children waiting for a treat is a very large stone bowl. A large stone pillar rises out of the center of the bowl. The pillar seems alive. It is completely covered by shiny black beetles crawling around and over each other. The person in charge takes a tortilla, spreads some sauce on the inside, grabs a handful of live beetles, and fills the burrito with them, quickly folding the tortilla so that the beetles cannot escape. Playfully pushing the beetles back into the tortilla between bites, a gleeful child eats the burrito with relish. Would you be willing to try a beetle burrito? Is a strip of burnt cow muscle (also known as a steak) inherently any more or less desirable than a beetle burrito? If you had grown up in that village, would you be eating and enjoying beetle burritos? What does your answer have to say about the social and cultural origins of what seems like an almost biological trait—our tastes in food?

In his book *The Te of Piglet*, Benjamin Hoff (1992) recounts the following narratives, based on the writings of Chinese Taoist philosophers:

> A man noticed that his axe was missing. Then he saw the neighbor's son pass by. The boy looked like a thief, walked like a thief, behaved like a thief. Later that day, the man found his axe where he had left it the day before. The next time he saw the neighbor's son, the boy looked, walked, and behaved like an honest, ordinary boy.
>
> A man dug a well by the side of the road. For years afterward, grateful travelers talked of the Wonderful Well. But one night, a man fell into it and drowned. After that, people avoided the Dreadful Well. Later it was discovered that the victim was a drunken thief who had left the road to avoid being captured by the night patrol—only to fall into the Justice-Dispensing Well. (p. 172)

What sort of reality do these Chinese tales illustrate? Does the essence of the neighbor boy or the nature of the well change? Or do people's perceptions change? Consider occasions when your perceptions of someone or something may have been influenced by your own momentary experiences. Is it possible that reality depends on how you look at something? How much does your point of view depend on your own interests?

Consider further: A group of employees from a local business gathers every night after work to share drinks and conversation. They express dissatisfaction with the conditions of their job and the unethical behavior of the boss. Several of them recall occasions of being mistreated or harassed. As the evening progresses, they become emboldened by this sharing of experience and some of them even threaten to confront the boss. The next day, life resumes as usual at work. The employees all go about their jobs with competence. In the presence of the boss, everyone is quiet and respectful. The status quo prevails. Think about the difference between the late-night and workday activities of these people. What is the source of the disparity between the behaviors in each setting? Are these people being any more or less truthful in either situation? Why do we often remain silent in the face of injustice? What forces compel people to change their circumstances?

These scenarios all focus on the intersection between social expression and individual perceptions, tastes, and behaviors. In each case, a taken-for-granted body of cultural knowledge influences individual action. Children in some villages consume beetles with gusto, whereas others might look on in horror. Yet we all feel that our own personal tastes are reasonable.

People's reactions to the world depend on how they define the situation. The definition of the situation can differ from moment to moment, depending on what the person is inclined to see. Someone's actions may appear perfectly reasonable in one situation and completely unreasonable in another. Indeed, a great deal of human behavior appears unreasonable and illogical if viewed out of context.

In 1956, anthropologist Horace Miner published a study of a peculiar people called the Nacirema. Miner was especially interested in the culture's obsession with a daily body ritual that was typically performed in secret and required a special room or "shrine" and substantial medicines and potions:

> While each family has at least one such shrine, the rituals associated with it are not family ceremonies but are private and secret. The rites are normally only discussed with children, and then only during the period when they are being initiated into these mysteries. I was able, however, to establish sufficient rapport with the natives to examine these shrines and to have the rituals described to me.
>
> The focal point of the shrine is a box or chest which is built into the wall. In this chest are kept the many charms and magical potions without which no native believes he could live. These preparations are secured from a variety of specialized practitioners. The most powerful of these are the medicine men, whose assistance must be rewarded with substantial gifts. However, the medicine men do not provide the curative potions for their clients, but decide what the ingredients should be and then write them down in an ancient and secret language. This writing is understood only by the medicine men and by the herbalists who, for another gift, provide the required charm.

Beneath the charm-box is a small font. Each day every member of the family, in succession, enters the shrine room, bows his head before the charm-box, mingles different sorts of holy water in the font, and proceeds with a brief rite of ablution. The holy waters are secured from the Water Temple of the community, where the priests conduct elaborate ceremonies to make the liquid ritually pure (p. 503).

Miner was particularly fascinated with the "mouth rituals" of the Nacirema. He notes:

In the hierarchy of magical practitioners, and below the medicine men in prestige, are special-ists whose designation is best translated "holy-mouth-men." The Nacirema have an almost pathological horror of and fascination with the mouth, the condition of which is believed to have a supernatural influence on all social relationships. Were it not for the rituals of the mouth, they believe that their teeth would fall out, their gums bleed, their jaws shrink, their friends desert them, and their lovers reject them. They also believe that a strong relationship exists between oral and moral characteristics. For example, there is a ritual ablution of the mouth for children which is supposed to improve their moral fiber.

The daily body ritual performed by everyone includes a mouth-rite. Despite the fact that these people are so punctilious about care of the mouth, this rite involves a practice which strikes the uninitiated stranger as revolting. It was reported to me that the ritual consists of inserting a small bundle of [bristles] into the mouth, along with certain magical powders, and then moving the bundle in a highly formalized series of gestures. (p. 504)

The astute reader eventually realizes that Nacirema is "American" spelled backward and that the odd rituals that Miner is describing are everyday bathroom practices such as teeth brushing. (How many of us have been threatened with that moral enhancing "ritual ablution of the mouth" for children, otherwise known as having your mouth washed out with soap?)

Miner's intent is to parody the tendency to think of our own practices and beliefs as natural and normal and the routines of other groups and cultures as peculiar and perhaps even revolting. Even the language we use to describe everyday cultural patterns reflects a familiarity that we often take for granted. "Mouth-rite" and "holy mouth men" convey very different impressions than teeth-brushing and dentist. We are *embedded* in our own cultural beliefs and practices to such an extent that it's often difficult to see how arbitrary or bizarre these practices might seem from the outside. This book is an exploration of this cultural embeddedness (what will later be referred to as cultural "mindlessness") and its consequences for understanding ourselves and others.

"REALNESS"

Cultural beliefs and practices include rules about what is "real" and what is "not real." These rules are often taken for granted and usually we follow them without being aware of them. These rules are not necessarily based on logic or sensory perception. The study of culture and behavior involves figuring out these rules and making them explicit.

This book is about how human beings learn and conform to cultural rules of reality in various situations. These rules enable us to organize and to make sense of our experiences and to share our understanding with others.

When people interact with one another, they do so according to shared cultural rules. The result of this interaction is a set of meaningful patterns that we think of as society. It is important to note that these rules are constructed by human beings and that they are meaningful only within a specific social context. In other words, behavior is contextually meaningful. Taken out of context, many behaviors appear contradictory, silly, or even immoral. For instance, how is it that you know to modulate your voice to a whisper in certain spaces, or the difference between when to hug and when to shake hands in a social situation. Why is "making fun of someone" funny in some settings and cruel in others? Where do we draw the line, or, more importantly, how do we know what the line is? How do people know what to expect and what to do in different contexts, especially in situations that may appear contradictory? How do we learn the rules, lines, and boundaries of reality? The ability to distinguish between contexts and to behave in accordance with social expectations is a defining feature of humanness. It is also the main subject of this book.

REALITY IS ACHIEVED
THROUGH SYMBOLIC INTERACTION

The production of meaningful realities occurs through human interaction. In other words, we *practice* social reality every time we interact with others. Human culture is achieved through interactions among individuals who share highly complex, richly nuanced definitions of themselves and the situations in which they participate. We *learn* to be human, and our learning depends on and is achieved through interactions with other humans. The basis for meaningful human behavior is in our capacity for language—not just definitions and grammar, but metaphor. Consider, for example, a computer that is directed to translate the sentence "The spirit is willing but the flesh is weak" into Russian. The computer has the necessary vocabulary and grammar to make this translation, but it translates the phrase as "The vodka is good but the meat is rotten." The computer provides a literal translation, but the translation does not convey the intended meaning of the phrase (Scheff, 1990). One of the most remarkable aspects of human behavior is our ability to learn, share, and create nuanced, metaphorical meaning. This nuanced comprehension is what enables us to engage in very complex behavior and to know the difference between various cultural rules and contexts, for instance, the difference between a "holy mouth man" and a "dentist."

The focus in this book is on how we learn these cultural rules and the ways in which we practice them through our everyday interactions. According to many social psychologists, these interactions form the basis of human existence. The aim is to demonstrate how humans learn to participate in culture and ultimately to produce and reproduce themselves and their various cultures. We will explore a number of questions: What cognitive and emotive capacities are necessary for people to be able to engage in meaningful social interaction? How is social behavior affected by a disruption of these processes? How do interactional dynamics shape our behavior and our sense of who we are and what we can do? How do these processes contribute to the production of culture? How is it possible that, through our own behavior, we may be perpetuating cultural systems that we oppose ideologically (e.g., racism)? The general aim is to explore the social foundations of mind, self, and culture. The framework for this exploration is a theoretical perspective known as symbolic interactionism.

Symbolic Interactionism

There are several different forms of social psychology. This book is written according to a subfield of social psychology known as *symbolic interactionism*. Each of the many approaches to the study of human social behavior has strengths and limitations, and I encourage you to become familiar with them. Through many years of teaching and study, I have come to appreciate symbolic interactionism as a perspective that offers one of the most useful frameworks for understanding human behavior in a social context. In other words, this perspective provides excellent tools for understanding the complexity of our own behavior.

For instance, have you ever wondered why you feel so strongly about something in one situation and completely different in another, or why your self-esteem seems to blossom in some circumstances and shrivel in others? The symbolic interactionist perspective provides the tools for understanding how we can simultaneously have what seems to be a stable personality and also be constantly shifting in our experiences, values, and points of view. At the social level, symbolic interactionism provides a framework for understanding how society can also seem to be both stable and constantly in flux. Most importantly, this perspective invites us to wake up to the ways in which we ourselves create and perpetuate social routines that may or may not be good for us. In short, symbolic interactionism portrays humans as active co-creators in both individual and social experience. To the extent that we become aware of these processes, we are better equipped to participate in our own liberation.

Three points are noteworthy regarding symbolic interactionism in contrast to other social-psychological perspectives:

1. Symbolic interactionism gives primacy to the social situation over individual psychology. In other words, behavior is assumed to be organized primarily in response to social factors.

2. The focus of study is on observable behavior, but the cause of this behavior is assumed to be non-observable processes of individual interpretation. In other words, behavior is based on subjective interpretation of the social environment instead of being a direct response to objective stimuli.

3. Symbolic interactionism uses *interpretive* methodologies. The researcher attempts to take the perspective of the subject and to interpret the context in which the behavior takes place. In other words, the researcher tries to "look over the

shoulder" of the subject or group of interest. Some of the methods used to gather information about human relations include fieldwork, interviews, and participant observation. The aim is to understand how humans see and enact their own beliefs and ideals and to trace the implications of these beliefs and actions.

The organization of this book is intended to provide you with a tool kit for understanding self and society. These tools or topics include language and self-awareness, symbolic communication and socialization, self-development, interaction with others, and the production of social life. I use the metaphor of *production* to illustrate that social life is something we create together. The first basic tenet of symbolic interactionism is that society is socially constructed. What this means is that through our engagement with others we are constantly generating cultural meaning and rules. Each of the sections of this book will explore aspects of this process.

CONCLUSION: SO, WHAT'S REAL?

What is reality anyway? Nothin' but a collective hunch.

—Trudy the bag lady

According to the symbolic interactionist perspective, truth and reality are determined by the context in which they are practiced. Does this mean that anything goes? Far from it. Reality may differ across social groups, but within each group, a taken-for-granted system of knowledge establishes boundaries about what is real, true, and right. A central line of inquiry in symbolic interactionism is uncovering what these boundaries consist of and how groups and cultures produce and reproduce their systems of knowledge through their interactions. For instance, symbolic interactionists have noted that people living in modern, Western cultures act as if their reality is based on a "natural" truth (things are the way they are because nature intended them to be that way). Other cultures might have a faith-based reality (things are the way they are because a transcendent god intends them to be that way). These realities include complex, culturally specific rules for how one can know things. Thus, people in one society may believe in the existence of germs that cause illness. They may invest considerable resources to develop the technology necessary to "see" and "control" these germs. In another culture, people may invest similar resources to perfect ceremonies and rituals to "see" and "communicate with" the spirits that control health and well-being.

Cultural rules about what is real are often contradictory as well. It is fascinating to observe human behavior and culture to see the ways in which seemingly contradictory systems of reality exist side by side. For instance, in the United States, systems of rationality and Christianity often coexist, despite some apparent contradictions. Even so, contradictory belief systems have rules for navigating the contradictions. For example, it is considered normal for the president of the United States to make statements such as "one nation under God" in speeches. But if the president were to say that he or she was leading the country based on "visions" received from God, people might question the president's abilities. Similarly, citing your religious beliefs as a basis for not dating someone is considered reasonable, but these same beliefs are unacceptable as a reason for not paying taxes. Knowing which cultural rules apply in specific contexts is considered "common sense" or "what everybody knows."

In place of the question "What is real?" try asking, "What are some of the beliefs and practices that make up commonsense realities? What are the implications and consequences of these realities? How do different realities depict the world and the place of humans in it?" These questions remind us to scrutinize our own rules of interaction and their implications for self and society. To do so, we must step out of our cultural embeddedness and make the "taken for granted" explicit. One of the major strengths of the symbolic interactionist perspective is that it encourages us to see how we ourselves are authors and actors in the human story and, ideally, to take responsibility for the scripts we produce and the parts we play.

At the same time, this perspective also teaches us the tenacity of cultural rules for shaping individual lives and for creating and recreating differences and hierarchies among people. Beliefs and practices about power, authority, and morality may be cultural in origin, but they are real in their consequences. Paradoxically, those who hold the most cultural power are sometimes the least aware of their privilege or the ways in which taken-for-granted interactional practices work to their favor. For example, employers are much less likely to be aware of unfair working conditions than employees. The status quo prevails not because employees are cowardly or content with unjust conditions, but because conventional workplace beliefs and practices are likely to result in punishment (e.g., dismissal from the job) if they speak up. Employers are typically socialized to perceive such action as "insubordinate" and trained to "reduce conflict" by getting rid of "troublemakers." Symbolic interactionism provides a perspective for analyzing the larger cultural context that gives rise to and supports these sorts of beliefs and practices and for understanding how, even when we're theoretically opposed to such practices, we may end up reinforcing them through our behavior.

ORGANIZATION OF THE BOOK

The basic components for understanding self and society are *symbols, the social self, interaction,* and *social patterns.* The materials in this book are organized to present a picture of society as the product of human interactions based on the use of shared social symbols that are incorporated into human conduct through cognitive-emotive processes. In other words, self-development is a process of learning cultural scripts for who we can be, what we can do, and what is important and desirable. These scripts reflect a preexisting social structure. As we learn them and engage in interactions with one another, we enact, reproduce, and potentially change this structure.

Part I introduces some of these basic components and explores the general idea of socially constructed realities.

In Part II, the focus is on the ways our thoughts and feelings reflect cultural learning and values as well as distinct, private, personal experiences. For symbolic interactionists, the key to this puzzle is the *symbol,* an abstract representation of something that may or may not exist in a tangible form. For example, *table* is the symbolic representation of a class of objects constructed from hard substances and designed to serve certain purposes. *Guilt* symbolizes a feeling that you are probably familiar with, but it has no actual, physical referent. Complex combinations of symbols used for communication are known as *language.* Through language, humans are able to identify meaningful symbols, understand cultural expectations, and incorporate these expectations into conscious, reflexive behavior. Language is the encyclopedia and the map of human culture. It is also through language that humans generate, preserve, and alter social structure.

The focus of Part III is the process of socialization, or the way in which humans learn social rules and routines and cultural values. One of the questions that drive the discussion in this section is that of how different people with relatively similar backgrounds and experiences come to have different ideas and expectations and to behave in different ways. The concept of *reference groups* provides a useful and intriguing answer to this question and illustrates the ways in which people organize and evaluate their own behavior in terms of the expectations of specific groups or ideas of groups.

The focus of Part IV is the social self. The first emphasis is on the way in which we learn, through our capacity for language, to recognize our own actions as aspects of an entity we call "self." The second emphasis is on the interactional or social aspects of self-development. Through our interactions with others, we learn to attach meaning to our own behavior, feelings, and thoughts and to assemble this meaning into a coherent pattern that becomes a stable self. This section also explores some of the ways in which self-image is shaped and influenced by social contexts, including and computer-mediated environments.

The topic of Part V is social interaction. Social relationships, such as love or power, are given meaning and come to life when they are acted out by members of a social group. These patterns are discernible in the encounters of everyday life, such as conversations. Basic interaction requires people to project an image of what part they wish to play, what part they want others to play, and how they intend to define the situation. For an interaction to proceed smoothly, the actors must agree on a definition of the situation and perform it together. Even arguments, as we will discuss, hold to a particular definition of the situation ("this is a fight") and follow specific rules of interaction. In addition to defining situations, people negotiate how they will define themselves and others.

The social construction of reality is the focus of Part VI. In this section, we begin to put together the ideas and concepts from the previous sections to develop a theory of the production and reproduction of social realities. The key point of this section is that realities are social constructs that exist through shared expectations about how the world is organized. These realities are quite fragile, because they depend on the participation of people who are socialized to comprehend and perform patterns and rituals that follow highly structured (but often unrecognized) rules of interaction. Ironically, these implicit rules can be made explicit by violating them and forcing interaction to a confused halt. We discuss several "violations" as a way of demonstrating how to "see" the rules of interaction. An important question in this section is why certain patterns of reality endure so well, given that they are based on such fragile dynamics.

The Epilogue is an essay on the implications of this material for living a meaningful life. Once we wake up to the mindless patterns of everyday routine, how do we practice staying awake and remain connected to ourselves and others in a meaningful, liberated way? And how do we grapple with multiple perspectives and contradictions. Social life is dynamic and complex, and our understanding of who we are and of what is meaningful is forged through the process of wrestling with everyday contradictions.

References and Suggestions for Further Reading

Hoff, B. (1992). *The te of Piglet*. New York, NY: Penguin.

Miner, H. (1956). Body ritual among the Nacirema. *American Anthropologist, 58,* 503–507.

Palmer, P. (1993). *To know as we are known*. San Francisco, CA: Harper.

Scheff, T. (1990). *Discourse, emotion, and social structure*. Chicago, IL: University of Chicago Press.

Shah, I. (1972). *Caravan of dreams*. Baltimore, MD: Penguin.

THE NATURE OF HUMANNESS

Jodi O'Brien

Who are you? What are you? What makes you human? How do you explain your various tastes, preferences, ideals, and beliefs? Various branches of the social and natural sciences have different perspectives on the nature of humanness. There are also a variety of theological perspectives on what it means to be human. Each of these perspectives focuses on different aspects of the human experience, for example, our physiological ability to use tools due to an opposable thumb, or our ability to communicate, or our ability to conceive of and orient ourselves toward the existence of a higher being.

Recent developments in the fields of biotechnology, genetic engineering, and neurology, as well as computer-mediated communications, also contribute to conversations about the nature of humanness. Current debates about stem cell research; genetic social engineering; and the "realness" of online, computer-mediated relationships indicate that our definitions of humanness are always in flux. For instance, what are the implications of artificial limbs and organs or cloning on how we understand humanness in relationship to the body? How do we determine the realness of human relationships conducted entirely through electronic social media? The rules for deciding what is human and who is "real" shift and change in response to contemporary social, cultural, and technological developments. One persistent debate is whether human behavior is shaped primarily by biology or social environment: the nature/nurture debate.

NATURE VERSUS NURTURE—A FALSE BINARY

You may have participated in conversations in which people argue about whether certain behaviors are determined primarily by your genetic makeup or your cultural environment. Those who take a social constructionist perspective argue that humans are born "blank slates" and that society "writes on us," thereby forming our impressions and experiences. The socio-biological perspective holds that we have certain predetermined traits that exist as part of our bio-genetic makeup. The various perspectives, nature or nurture, have been employed politically throughout recent history to make the case for social hierarchies such as intelligence and race (the idea that people from specific racial backgrounds are naturally smarter), eugenics (certain people, by nature of their biology, are not fully human), criminal behavior, mental illness, and gender and sexual deviance.

As an undergraduate student, I studied biology with considerable enthusiasm. One of the first things we learned in our biology courses was the dictum: Nature doesn't determine, nature hints. The theories that we studied as budding biologists instructed us to think of the human organism in relation to its material and environmental surroundings. For instance, an infant born with a genetic propensity for great height may not actually grow to above average, or even normal, height if fed a very poor diet. Height is a function of both nature and nurture. The human genome project is an attempt to chart the DNA territory of humans. This has been a vast undertaking. Throughout the project, many of the most highly regarded scientists involved have continually reminded us that just because we can now map genetic combinations, it does not necessarily mean that we understand how the genes actually operate in shaping the complexity of human life. Again, they remind us of the dictum: Nature only hints. For instance, genetic researchers can now identify a gene for Parkinson's disease quite easily. However, the likelihood that the disease will manifest actively in persons who carry the gene is less than 50%. What other factors influence the likelihood that someone carrying the gene may actually develop the disease? Geneticists have been among the most consistent in saying that the rest of the story involves a complex interaction of environmental factors, which may include diet, health patterns, stress, and other cultural-material influences.

Thoughtful, well-trained biological and genetic scientists tend to agree that human behavior is a *complex combination* of nature and nurture. Nature and nurture are not opposing positions in a debate that can be settled rhetorically. They are interrelated processes that, together, constitute human behavior.

THE CASE OF GENDER

Biologist Anne Fausto-Sterling is an expert on gender development. She is one of several cutting-edge scientists leading the way in integrating biological and socio-cultural theories of human behavior. She describes the relationship between nature and nurture as a "dynamic system." As she remarks on her website,

> I believe that both sex and gender are in part social constructs. But they take place in the body, and so are simultaneously biological. Dynamic systems theories link the social—which impinges on the developing body—to the body itself. Cultural experience has physiological effects.

In other words, we are not merely blank slates; we have bodies and we experience the world through our bodies. At the same time, our bodies do not arrive preformed; rather, the body "acquires nervous, muscular and emotional responses as a result of a give and take with its physical, emotional and cultural experiences."

Think, for instance, of the simple case of wearing high-heeled shoes. The musculature and gait of people who regularly wear high-heeled shoes will develop accordingly. Although a bit trite, this example illustrates the dynamic between social behavior and the experience of our bodies. More sophisticated research looks at the ways in which repeated cultural experiences form neural networks that shape our perceptions and emotional responses. For example, from the moment they are born, infants are exposed to cultural gender expectations: They are dressed in particular colors and fabrics, offered gender-specific toys, and, perhaps most notably, encouraged when they behave in ways that are consistent with cultural gender rules. Much of this cultural coaching is unconscious but so pervasive that even the most gender-aware parents have difficultly avoiding culturally imposed gender expectations. As an experiment, spend a day doing something very minor that is gender atypical for you; for instance, sit with your legs spread wide apart or cross your legs (depending on your usual behavior), and pay attention to how you feel in your body.

Fausto-Sterling is especially interested in gender variance. In her research she takes note of the many variations that exist among individuals who are trying to fit into a system that offers only two gender choices (female/male). Biologically, there is ample evidence that people vary along a spectrum; there are variations on chromosomal structures. Rather than the presumed XY and XX, there are at least five documented variations. Do you know what your chromosomal structure is, or do you just assume it matches the gender you consider yourself to be? There are individuals who have sex characteristics that resemble both female and male (inter-sex). In other words, from a biological perspective, nature may be hinting that the penis/vagina gender binary we assume to be natural (as rooted in reproductive propensity) is actually insufficient to account for the full range of natural possibilities. For Fausto-Sterling, sex and gender are best conceptualized as points in a multidimensional space.

Imagine you had a box of blocks with at least five shapes and you were required to sort them all into two piles. What would you do? Most likely you'd find a particular characteristic and use that as your sorting rule. Perhaps some of the shapes look more roundish to you and some seem squarish. You can sort them into two piles of roundish and squarish, but you will still see the variation within each pile. For instance, where did you decide to place the star-shaped block? Over time, and the more you emphasize the binary you've created, the more likely you will come to see it that way (and to overlook the variation). You may even forget that you originally determined this categorical scheme yourself and come to see it as something "natural." This illustration is overly simplistic but provides some insight into the fascinating and richly complicated connections between bodies and social processes. Researchers in fields such as biology, evolutionary psychology, evolutionary linguistics, and neurology are increasingly exploring the dynamic interplay between the physical body and the cultural scripts that we use to understand, guide, and direct our bodies. This is a new frontier with much yet to be discovered. For our purposes here there are several noteworthy points from the work of Fausto-Sterling and other researchers in these areas:

- We experience the world through our bodies.
- But we use cultural categories to classify and make sense of bodies (including classifications such as gender and race).
- These categories do not necessarily represent the full variation that exists in nature.
- Our bodies are not entirely preformed, but develop in relation to socio-developmental categories, processes, and experiences.

In this society we are born into a culture that immediately groups infants into gender categories according to specific gender rules. There are only two gender rules: They are fixed for life and we have to have one. For many people, the body-experience-identity relationship will be more or less congruent. In this case, they will have no reason to question their assigned gender category. But others may experience *contradictory embodiment* (I don't feel like the boy I'm supposed to be because I have a penis) or *contradictory identity-experience* (I don't feel comfortable doing the girl things I'm supposed to want to do). There are several variations on the possibility of contradictory body-experience-identity, but we're usually not aware of the variation because of the social forces that work to erase variation and reinforce the binary. For instance, in the case of inter-sex infants, well-intentioned parents and medical practitioners typically determine that the child will be raised female or male and perform surgery to make the body conform to the binary choice. In other words, the variation is surgically "corrected."

To return to our original question, are these variations best explained by nature or nurture? The answer is both. Gendered bodies reflect cultural categories that may be based on a limited binary—there is more variation than we are aware of because we shoehorn people into one of two categories, and for the most part, people learn to fit. Many people develop into comfortable representations of the expected gender rules; others do not. Recently, with wider recognition of transgender and gender queer experiences, this has begun to change. As cultural scripts shift in recognition of this variation, we might expect to see more of the multidimensionality that constitutes the body-experience-identity. Much of this will depend on the social ability to stretch beyond binary thinking and not simply explain the variation away as an abnormality.

Historically in the United States, people whose experiences did not line up with expected gender categories struggled to make sense of themselves and their feelings. When they did not conform to expected categories, they were considered "deviant." For many years, the legal system reinforced this gender binary classification by punishing people who did not wear the right clothing (until the 1970s gender nonconformity, including cross-dressing, was a punishable offense in several states). Another social system, medicine, reinforced the legal system by labeling gender nonconformity as a mental illness (gender dysphoria). According to medical practitioners, people who didn't feel they belonged to their assigned gender category could receive treatment (in the form of hormones and surgery) only if they followed a particular medical protocol that involved successfully "passing" as the other gender for at least a year.

This example demonstrates that the nature/nurture debate is a false dichotomy and redirects attention to the ways in which social categories are used to classify and give meaning to bodies. Social systems such as education, law, religion, and medicine give legitimacy to these categories by drawing attention to "deviance" and reinforcing conformity. One of the paradoxes of the gender case is that the *social system of science* uses the logic of "nature" to justify social classifications and hierarchies. People who do not "fit" are "abnormal" (and have historically been turned over to medical systems for "treatment"). This is what social theorist Michel Foucault refers to as *truth regime*. In the case of gender, a social classification scheme is reinforced using the language and authority of science.

"Nature or nurture?" is the wrong question to consider, both scientifically and socially. Genuine scientific curiosity and observation lead us to recognize that classifying bodies by a sex/gender binary is a social activity and that there is clearly more variation than the binary allows for. Is this nature or nurture? The social constructivist approach transcends this question by operating in tandem with biological research in exploring the range and implications of contradictory embodiment within social systems. This approach conflates the "commonsense" presumption of a gender binary with "natural order" and uses systems such as medicine and law to support the "naturalness" of this binary.

A Socio-Bio Zeitgeist?

This is an exciting time to be studying human behavior, and social psychologists have much to learn from emerging studies in fields such as biology and neurology. Many sociologists and psychologists have embraced the turn toward biological explanations of human behavior. The challenge is to avoid falling back into the "truth trap" of the question: Is it nature or nurture? The nature/nurture debate is based on a false dichotomy that separates bodies from culture and/or neglects the existence of embodied experience. Fields of study that aim to integrate these perspectives are likely to be the most useful and informative in the near future. Social constructionist perspectives (which include symbolic interactionism) contribute to these studies by focusing on the following:

- how we use social categories to make sense of our bodies, feelings, and experiences (see Parts III and IV on social identities)
- how we use these social categories and scripts to organize our interactions with others (see Part V on social interaction)
- how we reinforce these categories through patterns of language and interaction (see Parts V and VI)
- the systems and perspectives we use to give legitimacy to certain behaviors and practices over others (see Part VI on the production of reality)

Thoughtful students of human behavior recognize the need to integrate biological and social studies. Social constructivists are recognizing the need to adapt the "blank slate" metaphor and to *embody* human social experience. There is significant new research that demonstrates the links between cells and molecules (systems biology), the development of motor skills in infants (developmental psychology), and the development of neural pathways or networks that enable routine (largely mindless) behavior (neurology). These studies contribute to a richer understanding of language development and the corresponding ability to engage in social identification and routines without prior direct experience (e.g., vicarious learning and socialization). They also help us understand deeply entrenched social prejudices such as unconscious bias (e.g., racist and sexist behavior even when we don't intend it).

There is a common misunderstanding that a socially constructed reality implies that we can simply change reality. Symbolic interactionism is the study of deeply ingrained, typically mindless social beliefs and practices that shape our behavior in certain, predictable patterns. Our embodied experiences reflect neural networks, physiological development, and hormonal processes. How we recognize and make sense of these experiences is a social process. And the meaning we give to our experiences further shapes neurological and physiological development. It's a dynamic process, and one of the lessons of social psychology is that, for the most part, we are largely unaware of any of these processes and how they affect our everyday lives.

By way of conclusion, here are a few examples of integrated research programs that are leading to new insights about human behavior. One particularly influential line of research that combines these perspectives is the study of teenagers and social development, especially with regard to crime. Studies in neurology indicate that the areas of the brain associated with the judgment necessary to fully engage in expected social behavior are not completely developed in teenagers, which leads to excessively poor decisions in certain situations, especially in the company of other youth. At the same time, researchers are also asking what types of social circumstances facilitate the development and exercise of better judgment. This approach holds promise for more comprehensive ways of working with youth, especially those caught up in the juvenile justice system.

Another example is the expanding understanding of forms of autism. For many years, autism has been viewed as a devastating curse that isolated the afflicted individual from society. From a social development perspective, individuals with autism were unable to participate in social life because they were unresponsive to the environmental cues and patterns that are taken for granted as a basis of normality. Eventually, delineations were made that classified individuals on an *autism spectrum* depending on how responsive they were to the social environment. From this perspective some individuals were perceived as high functioning and given more opportunities for social engagement, which resulted in increased social functioning. More recently, and due in part to input from those diagnosed with autism, there has been a major shift in the labeling of autism as a disability. Instead, many now recognize autism as an alternative form of neurological processes. *Neuroatypicality* is an emerging idea that suggests that there are different ways the brain operates. The new language of neuroatypicality reflects changing social perceptions that are linked to new ways of understanding the brain and human development. An integrated neuro-social approach provides new insights in brain functioning and invites us to question what we consider "typical" or "normal" human social interaction. (See "Shared

Meaning Is the Basis of Humanness," on p. 74, on the changing perceptions of the congenitally deaf from "retarded" to different language users.)

Similarly, research in evolutionary psychology explores the roots of hate. Psychologist James Waller and his colleagues have suggested the idea of *universal reasoning circuits* to explain the persistence among human societies to form groups of insiders and outsiders and to construct elaborate systems of hate regarding the "other." Social psychologists are well aware of the insider/outsider phenomenon, but the underlying reasons for the tenacity of xenophobia are not well understood. Waller uses integrated socio-biological research of this sort to help us better understand entrenched racism and its unconscious roots.

Another example comes from evolutionary linguistics. One of the questions that has long interested linguists and social psychologists, not to mention anyone who wants a web post to go viral, is why some ideas, tunes, images, and so on get lodged in the collective mindset. In Reading 4, linguist Susan Blackmore makes the case for memes as analogous to adaptive genes, where some find root in the collective conscious and spread, while others do not. Social constructionists study how it is that certain ideas and belief systems take hold and persist even in the face of considerable contradictory evidence (see Part VI). Research such as Blackmore's expands this inquiry into questions about how specific ideas prevail and are widely employed.

The material in this book focuses primarily on the social influences on human development and behavior. However, a full understanding of the richness of human life involves knowledge of both the physical and cultural aspects of our experiences. For that matter, we should probably consider spiritual knowledge as well. As you develop your understanding of social psychology, keep in mind that it's one aspect of a much larger puzzle. See if you can formulate questions that take into account the connections between nature and nurture rather than falsely separate them.

The study of social psychology through the perspective of symbolic interactionism will enable you to understand both the significance and the entrenchment of the cultural patterns that shape our lives and our choices.

References and Suggestions for Further Reading

Bonnie, R. J., Johnson, R. L., Chemers, B. M., & Schuck, J. (2013). *Reforming juvenile justice: A developmental approach.* Washington, DC: National Research Council.

Fausto-Sterling, A. (2012). *Sex/gender: Biology in the social world.* New York, NY: Routledge. (Website: http://www.annefaustosterling.com)

Sacks, O. (1989). *Seeing voices: A journey into the world of the deaf.* Berkeley: University of California Press.

Waller, J. (2002). *Becoming evil: How ordinary people commit genocide and mass killing.* New York, NY: Oxford University Press.

PERSPECTIVES ON SOCIAL BEHAVIOR

Jodi O'Brien

Social psychology is the study of the relationship between the individual and the rules and patterns that constitute society. Most sociologists and psychologists agree that human behavior is shaped to some extent by physiological, biological, neurological, and even metaphysical processes that are beyond the scope of social psychology. However, social psychologists emphasize that the majority of the activities people engage in and encounter in others on a day-to-day basis constitute *social* behavior—behavior that is both influenced by and expressed through social interaction. Some of the questions that social psychologists ask are: How does a person become socialized? What are the implications of human socialization for the transmission of culture? How does human action contribute to the production and reproduction of cultural and social institutions? Underlying these questions is the question: How do we *know* things?

HOW DO WE KNOW? *EPISTEMOLOGY*

It is the theory that determines what we can observe.

—Albert Einstein

How do we "know" things? How do we discover "truth"? Epistemology is the study of how we know things. Different groups and cultures have different ways of determining truth, such as faith, tradition, and science. Science is a dominant way of knowing in contemporary Western societies. Can the methods of science uncover the "real" truth? Sociologist Earl Babbie (1986) suggests that truth is a matter of agreement based on shared rules of what is real (see Reading 3). This holds for scientific claims of truth as well as for superstitious beliefs. For a long time, scientists believed in a universal truth and sought the underlying natural patterns that would reveal this truth. The metaphor that guided their inquiries was that of a watch or clock. They saw the universe as a grand watch ticking merrily away. The scientist's job was to take it apart piece by piece in order to figure out how this amazing machine worked. It's probably no historical accident that this perspective developed alongside the rise of industrial mechanization in the 18th and 19th centuries.

In the 20th century, however, physicists, including Werner Heisenberg and Albert Einstein, began to question the possibility of a universal, objective truth. They observed that different experiments designed to address the same question yielded different results depending on how the question was asked. For example, when light was hypothesized to be composed of waves, the experiments produced a pattern that suggested it was waves. But when light was hypothesized to be made up of particles, the tests revealed a pattern of particles. Was it possible that light was both wave and particle, both energy and matter, at the same time? Heisenberg concluded that the experimental process itself interacts with reality, that there is no completely objective stance from which to view truth (Biggs & Peat, 1984). That is, scientists shape the outcome to some extent by their interaction with the phenomenon. Even scientific interpretations are based on preexisting perspectives, or "pre-theories." This led Einstein to make his often-quoted remark, "It is the theory that determines what we can observe."

These observations set the stage for the contemporary debate between those who practice science with the goal of discovering and verifying truth (sometimes referred to as *positivism*) and those who argue that truth is relative—in the case of science, relative to the theories themselves (*constructivism*). That is, theories do not reflect "natural" reality. They are a social construction. The philosophy underlying positivism is that natural laws govern the universe and that these laws can be known. The philosophy underlying what came to be known as constructivism is that any order we perceive in nature is the product of our own perspectives for organizing the "facts," or theories. In other words, our theories do not simply verify or refute reality; they actually interact with the observed phenomenon to construct a truth that reflects the original perspective.

The Social Constructivist Perspective

The material in this book is based on a constructivist perspective. According to this perspective, knowledge, including scientific knowledge, is *subjective*. It is the product of the context within which it was constructed. Humans do not experience the world in its natural state. We do not gather and observe facts that interpret themselves; rather, the selection and interpretation of data are based on classification schemes constructed by the observer. No matter how logical and insightful these schemes are, they influence how we make sense of the data and how we arrive at conclusions about truth.

The case of Copernicus, who was able to convince some of his fellow astronomers in the 1500s that the earth revolved around the sun rather than the other way around, is an example of the relationship between scientific discovery and sociohistorical context. During the time of Copernicus, most people believed that the sun and all other planets known to exist in the heavens circled the earth. This belief was based on mathematical calculations made by Ptolemy in the 2nd century CE. Several of Copernicus's contemporaries suspected, based on years of charting the movement of the planets, that the earth might actually revolve around the sun. However, the language of the day (the dominant system of thought characterizing the historical epoch) incorporated Ptolemy's scheme of mathematics because it supported the Catholic theology that the earth was the center of the universe and humans the center of all things. Most mathematical calculations, the predominant method for charting the movement of celestial bodies, were based on this theory and in turn supported it.

Copernicus was successful in launching a scientific revolution not because he gathered new empirical evidence that demonstrated conclusively the earth's movement around the sun, but because he developed a mathematical statement that suggested this to be the case. He used the perspective of the time, with a slightly new twist, to advance an alternative theory. The lesson is that existing systems of thought can be used either to affirm or to alter a particular version of scientific truth. The accuracy of a scientific proposition is assessed by the prevailing standards of the time. These standards are also shaped by perspectives. Copernicus was able to reach his colleagues by using the shared language of their knowledge to cast new light on an old question. He met with resistance from the church, however, because his observations did not coincide with another, very powerful perspective of the day. A century later, even with the evidence of his telescope to back him up, Galileo was still made to recant similar assertions that the earth revolved around the sun when the church found them to be "incorrect" according to its standards.

A more recent example from paleontology shows how existing classification schemes shape scientific discoveries. In the book *It's a Wonderful Life*, evolutionary biologist, paleontologist, and natural history essayist Stephen Jay Gould (1989) tells the story of the Burgess Shale. This limestone quarry, which was formed more than 530 million years ago, supported more life forms than can be found in the oceans today. The Burgess Shale was discovered by modern paleontologists in 1909. According to Gould, its discovery could have changed our entire understanding of biological evolution. However, the first discoverers classified every fossil according to a preexisting taxonomy, which consisted of only two categories: worms and arthropods. This scheme supported the two dominant perspectives in the study of human evolution: the hierarchical "ladder of progress" theory (that humans are the ultimate goal/result of evolution) and the "inverted cone" theory (which holds that creatures evolve with increasing diversity and complexity). Gould points out that the first taxonomists were unable to "see" the richness of the Burgess Shale because they were "trapped by history. . . . The familiar iconographies of evolution are all directed toward reinforcing a comfortable view of human inevitability and superiority. The comfortably familiar becomes a prison of thought" (p. 1).

An alternative classification scheme might have enabled paleontologists to see evidence for a different set of theories. For example, a more recent theory, which acknowledges the rich diversity of the species fossilized in the Burgess Shale, does not assume the superiority of human evolution. Instead, its model is based on the image of an "incredibly prolific bush," in which branches occupied by particular species either break off, branch out, or continue. From this theoretical vantage point, human evolution is an awesome improbability, not an inevitable truth.

So the Burgess Shale fossils were first classified according to theories that assumed the superior nature of the human species, a theme prevalent in the early part of the 20th century. More recently, the fossils have been reclassified, this time according to theories that question assumptions of human superiority. Which perspective is correct? Symbolic interactionists would say that both are correct according to the criteria for scientific research holding sway when the classification schemes were developed. The two classifications of the Burgess Shale are consistent with the perspectives of their respective dates of publication.

This story illustrates that evidence is inevitably classified and interpreted. The theories that shape the process of classification and interpretation determine the picture of reality that emerges, because these systems of thought provide a lens through which to collect, organize, and interpret the information. The implication, then, is that scientific knowledge is not a direct representation of the natural world but is based on systems of thought that are culturally and historically bound. Thus, theoretical perspectives generally reflect the prevalent paradigms of thought that characterize a particular culture at a particular time in its history.

ASSUMPTIONS ABOUT HUMAN NATURE AND SOCIETY

All theoretical perspectives are based on assumptions—unquestioned beliefs used as a foundation on which to construct a theory. Every theory must have a starting point, a point at which some central ideas are fixed for the purpose of pursuing the implications of the ideas. Proponents of various perspectives do not necessarily believe that these assumptions are true. They realize that such assumptions allow them to construct and solve puzzles. In order to comprehend and evaluate a social theory, we need to know the assumptions on which the theory is based.

In addition, no program of study can pursue every possible line of thought. Therefore, different perspectives scrutinize specific aspects of the social story. Each theory allows us to observe details that might otherwise go unnoticed. Microbiologists, for instance, focus primarily on the cellular structure of the physical body in order to construct theories about how organisms behave; psychologists focus on the internal thoughts and impulses of individuals; sociologists emphasize groups of individuals. Each type of research gives primary emphasis to different units of analysis: cells, individuals, and groups.

Researchers sometimes become so focused on their own unit of analysis that they forget it is part of a larger picture. Thus, you will note (even in this book) statements such as "The most interesting aspects of behavior are social." It would be just as easy to say that the most interesting aspects of behavior are biological or spiritual. The noteworthy point is that different perspectives give primacy to different aspects of behavior. To effectively evaluate a perspective, we need to mentally locate the primary focus within its larger context—such as the cell within the organ of the body from which it was taken or individual psychology within a social context.

The debate about human nature and its relationship to society centers around two questions: What can be assumed about the human creature in order to build theories of behavior and society? Which aspects of behavior should be the primary focus in the study of the relationship between the individual and society? Social psychologists have addressed these questions from a variety of perspectives. Here we discuss three—utilitarianism, behaviorism, and the cognitive/interpretive perspective—before sketching the basic premises of symbolic interactionism.

Utilitarianism

Several philosophers in the 17th, 18th, and 19th centuries (such as Thomas Hobbes, Jeremy Bentham, John Stuart Mill, and Adam Smith) were interested in new forms of government that would provide peace and order for as many people as possible. These thinkers lived in times characterized by the upheaval and rapid changes forged by the industrial revolution. They were also reacting to social structures in which the many were ruled by a privileged few.

In theorizing about alternative forms of government, these philosophers began with the assumption, based on the writings of Aristotle, that humans have a rational nature. They postulated that the human creature is intelligent and self-interested and is thus motivated to achieve its desires in a pragmatic way. Conflict arises because, in the attempt to satisfy their own desires and pursue scarce resources, people often exploit and injure others.

Hobbes suggested that, because they are reasonable and know what is in their own best interest, people cooperate with laws that provide order for all. In other words, humans are not dumb brutes who need to be ruled by an intelligent few (as Niccolò Machiavelli, among others, had argued), but reasonable beings who govern themselves because they desire order. Without laws and order, each person has to be constantly alert to the possibility of attack. Such alertness and defense require a lot of energy and personal resources. Therefore, rational individuals would be willing to give up some degree of freedom, such as the right to harm others, in order to have a government to protect them.

A corresponding assumption of utilitarianism is that a person will pursue the course of action that is most likely to produce the greatest returns for the least cost. Behavior is therefore the result of cost/benefit analysis in the pursuit of desired ends.

From the utilitarian perspective, society consists of two or more individuals exchanging resources that have some value to each. How available a resource is and who holds the resource determine the structure of society. For example, if you own a small forest in an area where there is little wood, others may very well want to exchange something they own for some of your wood. One neighbor may offer you sheep in return for firewood. Another might offer wine in exchange for lumber. If you already have enough sheep of your own, you will probably opt to exchange your wood for wine. When you convert the trees from your forest into lumber, others may approach you to purchase lumber as well. If these exchanges are profitable, you might become a major producer of lumber over time. But to continue exchanging lumber for wine if another neighbor offered you a better deal for your wood would not be rational. The key point is that these exchange relationships are rational; they're based on the law of supply and demand and on rules of trade that promote free exchange.

Utilitarianism is a pillar of modern Western thought. For example, the discipline of economics is based on the utilitarian assumption that humans are rational beings who calculate risks, costs, and benefits and make decisions accordingly. A major branch of political science is also founded on this tradition. Social psychologists whose research is based on the utilitarian perspective address such questions as how social order is possible among people with competing interests and how people establish power over others to get what they want. This tradition is known as *rational choice theory* in sociology and as *exchange theory* in social psychology.

All these versions of utilitarianism assume that people behave rationally to maximize the attainment of their desires at minimal cost. What their desires are often remains untold, although frequently these desires are assumed to include some form of material rewards and power. The key point is that these theories assume that individual action is rational. In these versions of utilitarianism, it is also assumed that social institutions emerge from rational exchange relationships. In other words, institutions exist and operate as they do because they meet the needs of rational human beings.

The utilitarian tradition does not attempt to explain how humans become rational calculators; it simply assumes that they are. One theoretical implication of utilitarianism is that those individuals who fail to act rationally will not be successful competitors in the exchange market. Because they are not successful, they will not exist as observable cases for a researcher to study. Therefore, theoretically speaking, the perspective needn't be concerned with nonrational actors, because such actors, if they did exist, would eventually be weeded out of society. Another implication is that society is very fluid and changes constantly with the redistribution of tangible resources. One noteworthy contribution of utilitarian theory is the idea that we can figure out what people value by looking at what sorts of choices they make. This notion, which economists refer to as *revealed utility*, holds that we can know what a person *really* values only when the person has to make a choice. When making a choice, people deliberate, and this process of deliberation reveals their preferences and values. Thus, there are no real values independent of choice-making actions.

The following theoretical perspectives derive from utilitarianism but specifically address questions of individual psychology. Behaviorism, which is closely related to utilitarianism, makes even fewer assumptions about human nature than its theoretical predecessor. The cognitive/interpretive perspective and symbolic interactionism, on the other hand, offer more complex theories of the individual and make different initial assumptions about human nature.

Behaviorism

Behaviorism is a school of thought generally associated with B. F. Skinner, who assumed behavior to be hedonistic. In other words, humans and other animals seek pleasure and avoid punishment. This logic is similar to utilitarianism, except that it incorporates no assumptions about rational behavior. Organisms, including humans, simply become conditioned by particular stimuli and learn to behave in a manner that produces positive results and avoids negative ones.

Humans are socialized through a process that teaches them that certain actions are accompanied by punishments and certain actions are followed by rewards, or positive reinforcement. For example, if a child is repeatedly spanked for throwing food, the child will learn to associate the conduct with punishment and will avoid this behavior. When the child is rewarded for a behavior, such as successful toilet training, the child will repeat the behavior and thus become socialized to engage in acceptable behavior. In short, a person's behavior is predicted by the person's reinforcement history.

— This relationship between the environment and behavior is often referred to as the stimulus-response relationship. A stimulus is anything in a person's environment that provokes an action (response). The environment includes internal physiology as well as external forces. Stimuli usually exist in a tangible form, such as food or money, although some researchers also recognize less tangible stimuli, such as approval or affection.

— According to behaviorism, human action can be, and often is, irrational or neurotic. Neurotic behavior is the result of conditioned responses to stimuli that may not actually be associated with the outcome but that the actor associates with the desired outcome because of prior conditioning. For example, an animal that has been trained (conditioned) by electric shock not to venture beyond specific boundaries will continue to stay within these boundaries, even when the electric shock is removed. Humans often engage in superstitious behaviors (such as wearing a lucky sweater for exams) in the neurotic belief that certain actions and outcomes are correlated. That is, if a person *perceives* a connection between a particular action and outcome, he or she will persist in the behavior in hopes of producing (or avoiding) the anticipated response.

Behaviorism and its derivative, *social learning theory*, constitute one building block in most of the predominant social psychology theories. The theories differ, however, with regard to whether a particular stimulus will produce the same response in all subjects. Some behaviorists think that all people desire certain universal or objective resources and that all avoid certain punishments. Something is said to be objective if its effect is independent of the subject's comprehension of it; it is universal if it produces the same response in all subjects. The pain of fire, for example, can be considered objective and universal. Pain typically results for all who come into contact with a flame, regardless of their opinions or thoughts about fire.

On the other hand, money, which many assume to be a universal motivator, may have little or no effect on subjects who do not consider it to be important. In other words, the effect of money as a potential stimulus to action depends on a person's *subjective* interpretation of the stimulus. Let's say that a researcher places a subject in a situation where she is predicted to cheat an acquaintance in order to get money. If the subject wants to be seen as a good person more than she wants the money, she may respond in a manner that contradicts the researcher's predictions. Behavior based on subjective perceptions can be predicted only if the researcher knows what the person values. Determining individual values and desires is difficult to do.

Nonetheless, all variants of social psychology depend in some way on the assumption that behavior is based on the desire to gain rewards and avoid punishments. However, just what these rewards and punishments are and how the researcher should figure them out is a complex puzzle.

Behaviorism does not offer much of a picture of society. It assumes preexisting socialized beings who socialize the next generations through conditioned stimulus-response patterns. (How the first humans became socialized and why they valued certain things are questions that are addressed by evolutionary anthropologists and biologists, among others.) The primary emphasis in behaviorism is on the individual's reinforcement history—in other words, the patterns of learning achieved through the application of particular rewards and punishments. Why, for example, humans in each culture prefer to wear particular types of clothing and why some costumes convey different impressions and are accorded more prestige than others is not a story that can be told from the behaviorist perspective. The story that can be told is how people learn that they must wear clothes if they wish to avoid punishment, such as being spanked or jailed, and that certain clothes bring rewards, such as popularity and dates.

This perspective offers the possibility that one might construct an "ideal" society and train people to behave in a manner that supports its ideals. In *Walden Two*, which was very influential during the 1970s, Skinner (1976) illustrates the construction of a utopian society based on *behavioral engineering*. His premise is that with the right reinforcement schedule (that is, behavioral engineering), people can be taught to engage in socially desirable activities and to avoid socially undesirable actions.

Freud and the Unconscious

Although we do not offer a full review here, the theories of Freud are a useful point of comparison. In contrast to the behaviorists, Sigmund Freud and his followers argue that behavior is largely the result of *unconscious* desires and impulses that arise in the human psyche. From this perspective, Skinner's utopian society is doomed to failure, because people can never be perfectly socialized. Unconscious desires and impulses, such as sexuality and aggression, counteract the effects of even the most careful behavioral conditioning. Thus, the Freudian perspective sees humans as nonrational and unlikely to act on a reasonable calculation of costs and benefits—quite the opposite of the utilitarian view. Freudians believe that most behavior is an attempt to arrive at some tolerable compromise between the impulses that surge through our unconscious and the desire to live within the boundaries established by our social community.

Freud was one of the first researchers to direct his attention to the human unconscious. In so doing, he unlocked a black box previously ignored by most students of human social behavior. Behaviorists discount the distinction between the conscious and the unconscious. They prefer to focus on the link between an observable stimulus and an observable response. In conversation with a Freudian, a behaviorist might say that unconscious impulses are simply a form of stimulus—in this case, an internal rather than an external stimulus. The important feature for the behaviorist is what happens to a person when he or she acts on impulse. Is the behavior punished and thereby eventually extinguished, or is it rewarded and therefore repeated?

Freud might not have disagreed with this analysis, but he wanted to document what human impulses and drives consist of and how the contradictions inherent in these forces are reconciled through human development. That is, his agenda was to demonstrate that civilization is the product of our attempt to temper and harness our unruly impulses. Social institutions exist to bring some modicum of order where there would otherwise be only the chaos of beasts raping and murdering one another. At the same time, although we may become socialized, we may never be fully reconciled to the "rules" of society.

The Cognitive/Interpretive Perspective

Another perspective that offers a more complex view of human beings than that assumed by the utilitarians or the behaviorists is the cognitive/interpretive approach. In addition to examining the human psyche, it examines human thought processes, or *cognition*.

Many researchers who agree with the basic proposition of behaviorism—that behavior is the result of learning which actions produce punishments and which ones produce rewards—also conclude that most forms of stimuli are subjective rather than objective. In other words, the way a person responds to a stimulus depends on how the person *interprets* the stimulus. For example, a person who is hugged will respond differently if the hug is interpreted as an aggressive clinch or a show of affection. Same stimulus, different subjective interpretations, different responses.

Cognitive social psychologists believe that *interpretation*—(or thought) intervenes between the stimulus and response. The thought processes include paying attention to certain information, storing it, and later recalling it. That is, according to most variants of this perspective, behavior is the result of an individual's selective interpretation of the stimulus. For example, it's not likely that you would drool in anticipation if offered a burrito filled with live beetles. But some people, as discussed in the essay "What Is Real?" (pp. 2–10, Part I), consider a tortilla filled with beetles a delicacy and would respond with enthusiasm. Again, same stimulus, different subjective interpretations, different responses. (This process of interpretation is covered in detail in Part II.)

Another element of the cognitive/interpretive perspective concerns the question of whether humans are capable of rational thought. In a major research program conducted over the past three decades, two cognitive social psychologists, Daniel Kahnemann and Amos Tversky, have explored this question (Tversky, Kahnemann, & Slovic, 1982). One assumption of rationality is that if you prefer A to B and B to C, then you should prefer A to C. Tversky and colleagues decided to test this assumption, known as *transitivity*. In one experiment, people were asked to select panty hose from a variety of styles and colors. The experiments demonstrated that people who preferred panty hose A to panty hose B and panty hose B to panty hose C did not necessarily prefer A to C. In fact, after having selected A in the choice between A and B and B in the choice between B and C, many participants selected C when given a choice between A and C. In other words, someone who claims to prefer nylon to wool and wool to cotton will presumably prefer nylon to cotton as well. But Tversky and colleagues demonstrated that this is not necessarily the case. Many people who preferred nylon to wool and wool to cotton selected cotton in the choice between cotton and nylon.

In another study, a group of researchers observed that even the ability to perform complex mathematical calculations depends on context (Lave, 1988). Women who performed poorly on written math exams were tested on the same skills while grocery shopping. These women performed very rational calculations while shopping for the best bargains. Conversely, men who performed well on written math tests but whose wives generally did the shopping did not fare well in locating bargains at the grocery store. The same cognitive skill operated differently in different contexts.

Another assumption of rationality that has not held up to experimental scrutiny is decision making based on the laws of probability. Consider this test: A researcher holds 100 cards that contain short biographical statements taken from 30 engineers and 70 lawyers. The following card is selected at random and read: "Bob is in his middle 40s. He enjoys mathematical puzzles, dislikes social gatherings, and likes to build model trains." Is Bob a lawyer or an engineer? Most people guess that he is an engineer. Yet, based on probability, the most rational guess is that he is a lawyer. The tendency to guess Bob's profession based on types of behavior or activities associated with certain professions is a form of stereotyping, which is very different from applying the laws of rational probability.

Social cognition is the manner in which people impose preexisting categories of thought—schemas—on the stimuli in their environment and use these categories to select what to pay attention to, how to interpret the information, and whether to store it in and recall it from memory. In one study of schemas, subjects were shown a film of a woman and a man having a celebration dinner. Half the subjects were told that the woman was a librarian; the others were told that she was a waitress. When asked later to recall details from the film, the subjects recalled information consistent with role schemas, for example, that the librarian wore glasses and mentioned a trip to Europe or that the waitress liked to bowl and drink beer. The subjects not only recalled information consistent with their pre-established stereotypes, but actually made up information that affirmed these schemas as well. For example, subjects reported that the waitress ate a hamburger. Those believing her to be a librarian reported that she ate roast beef. But in the film, she ate neither (Cohen, 1981).

The implication is not that people lie or make things up but rather that perception is influenced by social categories and is a constructive as well as interpretive process. This perspective also implies that society "exists" in the structure of a person's thoughts.

But if social institutions are individually relative, then how do human groups come to have the shared perceptions and interpretations necessary for communication and the transmission of culture? The cognitive/interpretive perspective theorizes that our social group is the source of our shared schemas. The untold story is how the ideas of "society" get into human minds and influence individual perceptions to begin with. We have placed the term *society* in quotes here to underscore another point regarding the cognitive conception of society—the idea that society is somehow "out there," independent of human actors but able to shape and direct human thought. In addition, because of its emphasis on human thought processes, the cognitive/interpretive perspective has not focused much on actual human behavior. It assumes that thoughts somehow predict behavior. However, without a more developed idea of the relationship between thought and behavior, this perspective cannot easily explain how human actions lead to social patterns.

Symbolic Interactionism

The foregoing theoretical traditions each have a different view of human nature and focus on different aspects of the relationship between the individual and society. The utilitarian tradition depicts human beings as rational calculators, and thus the primary lines of inquiry are the implications of the exchange of goods between rational actors and the effect of these economic exchanges on the structure of society. Behaviorists view the human being as the sum of a history of rewards and punishment. Each person learns to pursue certain lines of action and to avoid others. Social behavior within any particular group is the result of this conditioned learning. Theoretically it should be possible, according to this perspective, to engineer different types of social behavior that would result in alternative types of societies. Utilitarians and behaviorists emphasize observable actions and are interested in the effects of these actions on the social environment. In contrast, Freudians and cognitive/interpretivists focus on internal processes. Freudians are interested in how unconscious impulses are dealt with in the process of socializing the human into a healthy adult. Cognitive/interpretivists focus on human thought. For them, a central line of inquiry is how people make sense of the stimuli they encounter, that is, how they perceive and deal with the environment in an organized fashion.

This book presents social psychology from the perspective of *symbolic interactionism*. This perspective depicts the production of society as an ongoing process of negotiation among social actors. Like the cognitive/interpretive perspective, symbolic interactionism suggests that the potential for society exists in the minds of people who share common expectations about reality. Society is enacted in momentary, situational encounters among humans. In other words, there is no society independent of the human mind and human expressions of culture. The implication, in a strict theoretical sense, is that humans exist as embryonic potential and that anything the mind can conceive is possible. However, symbolic interactionists point out that humans limit these possibilities by creating and maintaining social boundaries that make life orderly and predictable.

Two main points are worth underlining. One is that stable patterns of interaction among human beings can be observed. These patterns, which include relationships of power, affection, exchange, and so forth, give meaning to social existence—they constitute social structure. The second point is that, enduring as these patterns may seem, they are fragile in that they require constant coordination by and shared understanding from the people involved to maintain them. The tacit compliance of each of the participants is what makes social patterns endure.

Pragmatism

Symbolic interactionism shares with utilitarianism the assumption that humans are motivated to make practical use of the things they encounter in their environment (including other people). According to the symbolic interactionist, people may not necessarily be rational, but they are pragmatic. Humans attempt to mold the environment to their own ends. Symbolic interactionists assume that the ends a person desires and the means he or she employs to achieve these ends are based on socially constructed meanings. Anthropologists—who also study human groups—have long debated whether human interactions should be viewed primarily as an exchange of utilities or as an exchange of socially meaningful symbols. The difference between symbolic interactionists and utilitarians is that the latter focus on the exchange of tangible resources that have some intrinsic utility, whereas the former focus on the exchange of symbolically meaningful items and actions. From the utilitarian perspective, the value of an item used in exchange is in its potential use—for example, as food or currency. Symbolic interactionists would view an item used in exchange in terms of the symbolic gesture it communicates, such as a show of respect, friendship, or solidarity. They consider exchange to be one line of action that occurs within the more general ceremony constituting social life. From the symbolic interactionist perspective, the exchange of utilities would not be possible without the underlying trust that exists among those who share the same social expectations.

Deliberation

Unlike utilitarians, symbolic interactionists make no assumptions about rationality, except insofar as rationality constitutes one set of cultural rules (in modern culture, we are *expected* to be rational). Another significant feature that symbolic interactionism shares with utilitarian theory is the assumption that deliberations—pragmatic choices—*reveal* something about what people value and how they make sense of their circumstances. For instance, if you are deliberating between reading this text and going to a movie with friends, ask yourself whether your decision to read the text is based on your desire to enhance your knowledge (one type of motivation) or your desire to get a good grade on an exam (an altogether different motivation). You may in fact be influenced by both forms of motivation. The point is that you can probably learn more about yourself by focusing on the sorts of deliberations you make than you can by simply responding to a question such as "Do you value education?" When you deliberate and make pragmatic decisions, you are doing so in accordance with your own understanding and valuation of a particular context.

This deliberative process also shares common assumptions with behaviorism. When you deliberate, you are considering possible rewards and punishments and weighing the pros and cons. This is actually a cognitive-emotive process, but it reflects your particular *reinforcement history.* What do you perceive to be rewarding or punishing? What has occurred to you in the past, and what systems of belief do you hold that lead you to these particular assessments?

Symbolic interactionism is similar to behaviorism in emphasizing that human action is motivated by a desire to seek rewards and avoid punishments. However, symbolic interactionists study the *interactional context*; that is, they study how participants in an interaction negotiate the meaning of the situation to get one another to respond in a desirable way. The emphasis on meaning negotiated through interaction is a more social focus than the individual stimulus-response patterns studied by behaviorists.

Symbolic interactionists acknowledge (in concert with Freudians) that humans are bundles of drives and impulses. Both theories emphasize the manner in which humans learn to observe, comment on, and direct their own impulses. Deliberation can be seen as an internal conversation in which we consider how to bring our behavior in line with the expectations of others (a specific reference group).

The symbolic interactionist portrays humans as creatures who are reasonable and pragmatic in the pursuit of rewards and the avoidance of punishment. People learn which behaviors produce which outcomes by observing their own actions and others' reactions. The point to underscore is that symbolic interactionism focuses on subjective interpretations of events that occur in an interactional context. The assumption is that, whether we are dealing with someone face to face or having an internal dialogue with an imagined other, most human activity involves evaluating how to respond to others in specific contexts. *In this regard, symbolic interaction is the most social of the social psychologies.*

The important questions of study from this perspective are what meaning people give to a social context and how they negotiate and enact this meaning through interaction with others. For this reason, symbolic interactionists talk of "performing reality." Society consists of an ongoing, negotiated performance of socially meaningful interactions.

Reading Notes for Understanding Symbolic Interactionism

The following reading notes are drawn from the experiences of teachers and students who have used this material. Readers sometimes fall into the traps of *individualism, psychologism*, and *reification*.

Individualism

We see ourselves in terms of our relationships to other people (social roles), and we evaluate ourselves in terms of cultural expectations. Even when we are resisting, we are resisting specific cultural values. One cherished social role in modern Western society is the image of strong individuals who do not allow society to influence their actions and beliefs. Consider for a moment how you may have learned about this image. Ironically, individualism is a culturally learned value. If you think about it, you will recall many sources of learning about the desirability of being distinctly individual, the "leader of the pack," the "lone hero." When was the last time you saw a movie that featured a group or community as the star? If you grew up in Western society, chances are you learned that the individual is the most important social unit in most situations. This ideal is usually associated with the belief that you achieved your uniqueness independently of any social influences.

There is evidence that average people act in accordance with this belief. Social psychologists demonstrated some years ago that people are inclined to attribute observed behaviors to individual agency rather than to social or environmental factors. For example, if someone performs poorly on an exam, the cause is likely to be seen as lack of intelligence or lack of studying—that is, as individual ability or choice. The likelihood that poor performance might be due to the exam's cultural bias (a social factor), which might make it difficult for some people to interpret the questions, is often not considered to be a valid explanation. Similarly, if one person is observed hitting another, we are likely to assume that the person is angry or hostile, has a short temper, and lacks self-control. We will probably assume that the behavior is connected to certain personality traits. The possibility that the person was induced to act aggressively through the dynamics of the situation often doesn't enter into our assessment. This tendency to assume individual responsibility over social forces is known as the *fundamental attribution error.* People are more likely to attribute behaviors to individual personality and character traits than to social context.

In recent years, some researchers have suggested that the fundamental attribution error is a U.S. phenomenon (e.g., Hewstone, 1983). People in other cultures do not tend to make such individualistic judgments when trying to explain things. This tendency underscores the U.S. cultural attitude that single, individual actions are the primary forces shaping the world. Several observers and critics have also noted that the myth of individualism pervades the U.S. study of social behavior and organizations. The criticism is that individual psychology and development, not environmental factors (particularly social context), are presumed to explain social behavior. European social psychologists criticize their counterparts in the United States for this imbalance between individual psychology and social context.

From the perspective of symbolic interaction, you will learn that the relationship between individual personality and social values is a *dynamic and ongoing process.* You learn possible ways of seeing yourself and evaluating your own behavior from your family and other significant cultural sources, but as your sense of self develops, you also make choices about the ways in which you wish to respond to these possibilities. In this way, you are both uniquely you and a product of your cultural environment. Similarly, your own choices and actions will contribute to the maintenance of cultural values and patterns, or, depending on some of the choices you make, your actions may disrupt cultural patterns. When you consider the effects of such actions at the collective level, you will begin to see how many individuals supposedly acting on their own impulses and desires can collectively actually reinforce or change society. Recognizing that you are shaped by cultural forces does not take away from your individuality. In fact, students of social psychology often find that they have a better sense of themselves once they learn to identify the cultural influences that are shaping how they think and feel. Individualism, the belief that you are not influenced by cultural factors, is one of the cultural myths that a thoughtful social psychologist learns to recognize as incorrect and even misleading in the quest for understanding human behavior.

Psychologism

Social psychologists who study human cognition note that each of us has a tendency to interpret information in terms of its specific relevance to our own experiences. This information-processing bias is termed *psychologism* (or the self-consensus bias). Psychologism, when coupled with the ideal of individualism, makes it difficult for students to comprehend theories that pertain to the social group. The tendency is to interpret and evaluate the information offered by these theories in terms of individual psychology and experience. Readers tend to ask, "Does the theoretical perspective match my personal situation?"

Many people view theories that emphasize group knowledge and socialization as antithetical to their own individuality. But this separation of individual and group is based on a false dichotomy. As we discuss throughout this book, there is no possibility of the concept of the individual (including individual rights, feelings, and so forth) without the social group.

Remember that you do not have to deny personal experience in order to explore the implications of group knowledge. The question to ask yourself is "How might collective meanings and social interactions shape how I see the world and how I act?" What humans do in interaction with others may or may not be harmonious with their private thoughts. However, and this is the point to emphasize, whether or not people accept or believe in their own public actions, these actions are observable by others and come to be real in their consequences.

Reification

Reification means to treat an abstract concept as if it were real, independent of human activity. For example, people tend to think of IQ as a real thing that exists inside our brains and shapes our intelligence. In fact, IQ is simply a score derived from a battery of tests that are not meaningful beyond their direct application. In spite of this, parents and educators often act as if IQ is real and make decisions accordingly. Similarly, people sometimes treat sociological concepts—for example, norms—as if they were physical structures that exist somewhere in a state of nature and "do" things to humans. When a concept is reified, or given a life of its own, we tend to forget the extent to which our own beliefs and actions contribute to the construction and perpetuation of the processes described by the concept. Thus students are inclined to write papers in which they make claims such as "Society causes people to be poor."

It's more than a little bit ironic that we tend to think of ourselves as individuals who are entirely free of social influence and, at the same time, see many social forces and their consequences for other people as if the forces had a life of their own. This way of thinking reflects a kind of social illiteracy. We fail to see just how firmly entrenched certain social "rules" are and how they shape our personal lives, and at the same time fail to see how our own behavior reflects and contributes to the perpetuation of these social forces. The false separation of the individual and society deters us from a comprehensive and complex understanding of the ways in which we are both products of and producers of society.

Symbolic interactionism offers a way to reconcile the false separation of the individual and society. The perspective teaches us that social reality is the product of coordinated activity among real individuals. The puzzle is how abstract concepts are communicated, shared, and reproduced and how they take on patterns of stability that make them appear real. The enduring, stable character of social interaction is what we come to know, in a reified way, as society.

CONCLUSION

Symbolic interactionism is conducted at the intersection of individuals and society. From this perspective, it is not possible to make sense of one without incorporating the other. The challenge for symbolic interactionism has been to represent society in a way that avoids reification—in other words, to model social patterns and relationships as the products of ongoing individual activity. At the same time, symbolic interactionism must account for the observation that existing social patterns do influence and constrain individual actions. The ultimate aim of symbolic interactionism, as presented in this book, is to place the individual and society on the same level and to analyze the reciprocal relationships between individual action and social patterns and institutions. Social life is conceived as a dynamic web of reciprocal influences among members of a social group. This web is made up of the interactions of individuals. Individuals spin and re-spin the web. At the same time, they are influenced by the existing patterns of previously spun strands.

Symbolic interactionism is unique in the study of both psychology and sociology in that it is the only perspective that assumes an active, expressive model of the human actor and treats individual and social phenomena at the same level of analysis. In gaining an understanding of this perspective, think in terms of process and feedback. This viewpoint is admittedly more complicated than representing social life in terms of simple dichotomies and cause-and-effect reasoning. However, in reality individual existence and social patterns are mutually constitutive—the relationship between the individual and society is reciprocal. Symbolic interactionism offers a rich story about human behavior and its social consequences. We think you will find this story to be instructive and relevant to your personal life and the social world in which you are a participant.

REFERENCES AND SUGGESTIONS FOR FURTHER READING

Babbie, E. (1986). *Observing ourselves: Essays in social research.* Belmont, CA: Wadsworth.

Biggs, J., & Peat, D. (1984). *Looking glass universe: The emerging science of wholeness.* New York, NY: Simon & Schuster.

Cohen, C. (1981). Person categories and social perception: Testing some boundaries of the processing effects of prior knowledge. *Journal of Personality and Social Psychology, 40,* 441–452.

Gould, S. J. (1989). *It's a wonderful life: The Burgess Shale and the nature of history.* New York, NY: Norton.

Hewstone, M. (Ed.). (1983). *Attribution theory: Social and functional extensions.* Oxford, UK: Basil Blackwell.

Kuhn, M., & McPartland, T. (1954). An empirical investigation of self-attitude. *American Sociological Review, 19,* 68–76.

Lave, J. (1988). *Cognition in practice: Mind, mathematics, and culture in everyday life.* New York, NY: Cambridge University Press.

Skinner, B. F. (1976). *Walden two.* New York, NY: Macmillan.

Tversky, A., Kahnemann, D., & Slovic, P. (Eds.). (1982). *Judgment under uncertainty: Heuristics and biases.* New York, NY: Cambridge University Press.

REALITY AS A COLLECTIVE HUNCH

Most of us know that different cultures have distinct values and beliefs. Everyday life also consists of patterns of thinking, organizing time, and making sense of things in ways that differ across cultures and between groups of people. The readings in this section illustrate some of the differences in how people perceive everyday reality.

"Islands of Meaning" is written by sociologist Eviatar Zerubavel. In this essay, he gives many examples to illustrate the ways we carve up our lives with respect to divisions such as time and geography. We tend to think of these divisions as natural, but Zerubavel demonstrates that these divisions are actually social creations that are so entrenched that we come to think of them as natural.

"The Search for Signs of Intelligent Life in the Universe" is a selection from a popular Broadway play written by Jane Wagner and performed by Lily Tomlin. In this excerpt, the character Trudy the bag lady ponders the meaning of life and the arbitrariness of cultural rules for what is real.

"Truth, Objectivity, and Agreement" is a thought-provoking essay written by social methodologist Earl Babbie. Babbie wants readers to understand that everyone, even scientists, interprets information based on preexisting ideas. This subjectivity is a fact of human experience. Scientists deal with their own subjectivity by creating rules for observation and by using explicit theoretical starting points. One implication is that there is no "objective" truth. Truth is a matter of intersubjective agreement about what is being observed and how to observe it.

The section concludes with a discussion by evolutionary linguist Susan Blackmore on social memes and what they indicate about our capacity for collective knowing.

READING QUESTIONS

1. As you read the articles in this section, think of examples of cultural rules that you take for granted and assume to be fixed in nature.

2. What does it mean to say that cultural rules are arbitrary?

3. Consider your relationship to time. Do you think people's rhythms have been altered by the invention of digital clocks that carve time into units of seconds versus analog clocks that signal only, say, quarter hours? What about people who organize time in terms of the sun only?

4. Spend a day thinking of yourself as an anthropologist from Mars. What do you see when you look at your world from the perspective of an outsider?

5. Think of some examples of intersubjective agreement. Why do we believe the intersubjective truths proposed by some groups and not others?

6. Do you think you have to be similar to members of a culture to understand them (e.g., do you have to be a priest to understand a culture of priests)? Or is it possible to devise methods that would enable you to "put yourself in another's shoes" or "look over their shoulder" to gain insight into their worldviews and experiences?

7. What methods do you currently use in your own life when you're trying to understand someone else?

REALITY AS A COLLECTIVE HUNCH

1

Islands of Meaning

Eviatar Zerubavel

(1991)

In the beginning . . . the earth was unformed and void . . . and God divided the light from the darkness. And God called the light Day, and the darkness He called Night.[1]

The very first act of the Creation was one of dividing. It was through being separated from one another that entities began to emerge. The first day was thus spent on dividing the light from the darkness while the next two were dedicated to separating the waters under the heaven from those above it as well as from the dry land.[2] Indeed, according to Genesis, the first three days of the Creation were devoted exclusively to making distinctions.

Like most cosmogonies, the biblical story of the Creation is an allegorical account of the process through which we normally create order out of chaos. These theories of the origin of the universe almost invariably describe the formation of essences (the heavens, the earth, life) out of a boundless, undifferentiated void.[3] Distinctions, they all tell us, are at the basis of any orderliness.

Separating entities from their surroundings is what allows us to perceive them in the first place. In order to discern any "thing," we must distinguish that which we attend from that which we ignore. Such an inevitable link between differentiation and perception is most apparent in color-blindness tests or camouflage, whereby entities that are not clearly differentiated from their surroundings are practically invisible.[4] It is the fact that it is differentiated from other entities that provides an entity with a distinctive meaning[5] as well as with a distinctive identity that sets it apart from everything else.

The way we cut up the world clearly affects the way we organize our everyday life. The way we divide our surroundings, for example, determines what we notice and what we ignore, what we eat and what we avoid eating. By the same token, the way we classify people determines whom we trust and whom we fear, whom we marry and whom we consider sexually off limits. The way we partition time and space likewise determines when we work and when we rest, where we live and where we never set foot.

Indeed, our entire social order is a product of the ways in which we separate kin from nonkin, moral from immoral, serious from merely playful, and what is ours from what is not. Every class system presupposes a fundamental distinction between personal features that are relevant for placing one in a particular social stratum (for example, occupation, color of skin, amount of formal education) and those that are not (for example, sexual attractiveness, height, intelligence), and any society that wishes to implement a welfare or retirement policy must first distinguish the well-to-do from the needy and those who are fully competent to work from those who are "too old." By the same token, membership in particular social categories qualifies us for, or disqualifies us from, various benefits, exemptions, and jobs.[6] It is the need to distinguish "us" from "them" that likewise generates laws against intermarriage, and the wish to separate mentally the "masculine" from the "feminine" that leads to the genderization of professions and sports.

It is boundaries that help us separate one entity from another: "To classify things is to arrange them in groups . . . separated by clearly determined lines of demarcation. . . . At the bottom of our conception of class there is the idea of a circumscription with fixed and definite outlines."[7] Indeed, the word *define* derives from the Latin word for *boundary*, which is *finis*. To define something is to mark its boundaries,[8] to surround it with a mental fence that separates it from everything else. As evidenced by our failure to notice objects that are not clearly differentiated from their surroundings, it is their boundaries that allow us to perceive "things" at all. These lines play a critical role in the construction of social reality, since only with them do meaningful social entities (families, social classes, nations) emerge out of the flux of human existence. Examining how we draw them is therefore critical to any effort to understand our social order. It also offers us a rare glimpse into the not-so-orderly world that underlies our social world, the proverbial chaos that preceded the Creation.

Boundaries are normally taken for granted[9] and, as such, usually manage to escape our attention. After all, "Nothing evades our attention so persistently as that which is taken for granted. . . . Obvious facts tend to remain invisible."[10] In order to make them more "visible," we must suspend our usual concern with what they separate and focus instead on the process by which we cut up the world and create meaningful

entities. In short, we must examine how we actually separate entities from one another, whether it be humans from animals, work from hobby, official from unofficial, or vulgar from refined.

The way we cut up the world in our mind manifests itself in how we construct age, gender, and ethnicity as well as in how we arrange food in supermarkets and books and movies in bookstores and video stores. It is manifested as well in how we divide our homes into separate rooms, and in our sexual taboos. Conventional metaphors such as *closed, detached*, and *clear-cut* similarly reveal how we experience reality as made up of insular entities, while our need to keep such discrete islands of meaning neatly separate from one another is evident from our gut response to ambiguous creatures.

The way we draw lines varies considerably from one society to another as well as across historical periods within the same society. Moreover, their precise location, not to mention their very existence, is often disputed and contested within any given society. Nonetheless, like the child who believes the equator is a real line[11] or the racist who perceives an actual divide separating blacks from whites, we very often experience boundaries as if they were part of nature. . . .

Things assume a distinctive identity only through being differentiated from other things, and their meaning is always a function of the particular mental compartment in which we place them. Examining how we draw lines will therefore reveal how we give meaning to our environment as well as to ourselves. By throwing light on the way in which we distinguish entities from one another and thereby give them an identity, we can explore the very foundations of our social world, which we normally take for granted.

At a time when political and moral distinctions are constantly blurred—when the international order we have regarded for nearly half a century as a given is virtually collapsing and our definitions of work, art, and gender are in flux—the very notion of a social order is being questioned. At such a point it is therefore critical for us to understand the actual process by which we establish boundaries and make distinctions. How we draw these fine lines will certainly determine the kind of social order we shall have.

* * * * *

The first man who, having enclosed a piece of ground, bethought himself of saying "This is mine," and found people simple enough to believe him, was the real founder of civil society.[12]

We transform the natural world into a social one by carving out of it mental chunks we then treat as if they were discrete, totally detached from their surroundings. The way we mark off islands of property is but one example of the general process by which we create meaningful social entities. . . .

CHUNKS OF SPACE

The perception of supposedly insular chunks of space is probably the most fundamental manifestation of how we divide reality into islands of meaning. Examining how we partition space, therefore, is an ideal way to start exploring how we partition our social world.

The way we carve out of ecological continuums such as continents and urban settlements supposedly insular countries and neighborhoods is a classic case in point.[13] Despite the fact that Egypt and Libya or Chinatown and Little Italy are actually contiguous, we nevertheless treat them as if they were discrete. Not only does it represent that state as a discrete three-dimensional chunk jutting out of a flat backdrop, it also portrays both the Missouri River and the Rocky Mountains as if they indeed broke off at its borders.

Spatial partitions clearly divide more than just space. The lines that mark off supposedly insular chunks of space often represent the invisible lines that separate purely mental entities such as nations or ethnic groups from one another, and crossing them serves to articulate passage through such mental partitions. That is why we attribute such great symbolic significance to acts such as trespassing[14] or crossing a picket line and regard the crossing of the Red Sea by the ancient Israelites coming out of Egypt as an act of liberation. That is also why the Berlin Wall could represent the mental separation of democracy from communism and why opening the border between Austria and Hungary in 1989 could serve as a symbolic display of the spirit of glasnost.

Often abstract and highly elusive, mental distinctions need to be concretized. Wearing different sets of clothes, for example, helps substantiate the mental distinction between business and casual or ordinary and festive, just as color coding helps us mentally separate different types of information we put in our notebooks, calendars, or files. Choosing among different variants of a language (such as the one used for speeches and the one used for intimate conversations) likewise helps express the mental contrast between the formal and the informal.[15] In a similar manner, we often use differentiation in space to reinforce mental differentiation. Partitioning our home into separate rooms, for example, helps us compartmentalize our daily activity into separate clusters of functions (eating, resting, playing, cleaning) as well as mentally separate culture (study) from nature (bathroom)[16] or the formal (living room) from the informal (family room). Along similar lines, separate aisles in music stores help reinforce the mental separation of classical and popular music, just as separate floors of department stores help us keep the worlds of men and women separate in our mind. In a similar manner, we express discontinuities among supposedly separate bodies of information by relegating them to separate drawers, newspaper sections, and library floors; and keep different categories of food separate in our mind by assigning them to separate pages of restaurant menus, chapters of cookbooks, aisles of supermarkets, and sections of the refrigerator. Similar forms of zoning help give substance to the mental contrasts between even more abstract entities such as the sacred and the profane,[17] the permitted and the forbidden,[18] the dangerous and the safe, and the good and the evil.[19]

The mental role of spatial partitions is also evident from the way neighborhood boundaries graphically outline rather elusive social class differences.[20] Even more revealing is the way separate bathrooms in the army help articulate status differences between officers and soldiers. The conspicuous absence of doors from rooms we define as public likewise highlights the role of spatial partitions in keeping the private and public spheres separate.[21] "A lock on the door," notes Virginia Woolf in her aptly titled study of privacy and selfhood, *A Room of One's Own*, "means the power to think for oneself."[22] It is the realization that the definition of our selfhood is at stake that makes us so sensitive to the symbolism of having the license to close the door to our room or office.

BLOCKS OF TIME

The way we divide time is evocative of the manner in which we partition space. Just as we cut supposedly discrete chunks like countries and school districts off from ecological continuums, we also carve seemingly insular segments such as "the Renaissance" or "adolescence" out of historical continuums. Such discontinuous experience of time is quite evident from the way we

isolate from the flow of occurrences supposedly freestanding events such as meetings, classes, and shows, some of which we further subdivide into smaller though still discrete particles— meals into courses, baseball games into innings.[23] It is also manifested in our ability to create stories with beginnings and ends as well as in the way we break down novels, sonatas, and plays into chapters, movements, and acts.

In a similar manner, we isolate in our mind supposedly discrete blocks of time such as centuries, decades, years, months, weeks, and days, thus perceiving actual breaks between "last week" and "this week"[24] or "the fifties" and "the sixties." That is why many of us may not carry over sick days from one year to the next and why officials try to use up their entire budget before the end of the fiscal year. A similar discontinuity between successive tax years also leads some couples to plan the births of their offspring for December, even to the point of inducing those that would naturally have occurred in January.

Central to such discontinuous perception of time is our experience of beginnings, endings, and "turning points." Most revealing in this regard is the sense of conclusion we experience as a performance, picnic, or season is coming to an end,[25] the radical change we expect at the turn of a century or a millennium or even between two contiguous decades, and the experience of a "fresh" start (or "turning over a new leaf") often associated with the beginning of a "new" year. Even in services that operate around the clock, night staff are often expected to allow the day ("first") shift a fresh start with a "clean desk."[26] A pregnant friend of mine who came back to the same clinic that had handled her previous pregnancy within the same year was asked to provide her entire medical history all over again, as she would now be considered a "new" case.

Temporal differentiation helps substantiate elusive mental distinctions. Like their spatial counterparts, temporal boundaries often represent mental partitions and thus serve to divide more than just time. For example, when we create special "holy days," we clearly use time to concretize the mental contrast between the sacred and the profane.[27] In a similar manner, we use it to give substance to the equally elusive contrast between the private and the public domains, using, for example, the boundary of the workday to represent the mental partition between being "on" and "off" duty.[28] Groups likewise use the way they periodize their own history to highlight certain ideological distinctions, as evident, for example, in the Zionist use of "the Exile"[29] or the American use of "the Great Depression" or "Vietnam" as discrete historical eras. The boundaries of the Sabbath, the workday, and "the Vietnam era" clearly represent major mental discontinuities. Like neighborhoods, drawers, and wings of museums, what they define are clearly more than mere chunks of time.

FRAMES

Temporal differentiation often entails an experience of discontinuity among different sorts of reality as well. Transitions from televised news to commercials or from live coverage to replay, for example, obviously involve more than just breaks in time. Along similar lines, warmup and "real" jumps in long-jump competitions are clearly anchored not only within two distinct blocks of time but also within two separate realms of experience, as are comments made before meetings begin and those included in the official minutes.[30]

Spatial differentiation often entails similar experiential discontinuity. The knight on the chessboard and the glass of water on the table are obviously situated not only within two distinct chunks of space but also within two separate "realities." That is also true of what occurs on and off the stage or inside and outside the picture frame.

Crossing the fine lines separating such experiential realms from one another involves a considerable mental switch from one "style" or mode of experiencing to another, as each realm has a distinctive "accent of reality."[31] At the sound of the bell that signals the end of a boxing match, as brutal punches are instantly transformed into friendly hugs, our entire sense of what is real is dramatically altered. That also happens, of course, when actors enter the stage and are immediately transformed into fictional characters. Picture frames similarly remind viewers that they cannot smell the flowers or eat the apples they see in pictures,[32] as pictorial space is "a structure altogether different from the real space we experience. Within actual space an object can be touched, whereas in a painting it can only be looked at; each portion of real space is experienced as part of an infinite expanse, but the space of a picture is experienced as a self-enclosed world. . . . [The work of art] builds a sovereign realm."[33]

It is precisely that quality that makes frames the ideal prototype of all boundaries delineating the various realms of our experience,[34] those mental lines that separate ordinary reality from the "worlds" of art, dream, play, and symbolism as well as off-the-record from official statements, parenthetical from ordinary remarks,[35] the metaphoric from the literal, satire from sheer slander, commentary from pure coverage, parody from plagiarism, and maneuvers from actual war. Framing is the act of surrounding situations, acts, or objects with mental brackets[36] that basically transform their meaning by defining them as a game, a joke, a symbol, or a fantasy. Play, for example, is actually "a name for contexts in which the constituent acts have a different sort of relevance . . . from that which they would have had in non-play. . . . The essence of play lies in a partial denial of the meanings that the actions would have had in other situations."[37]

A frame is characterized not by its contents but rather by the distinctive way in which it transforms the contents' meaning. The way framing helps de-eroticize what we normally consider sexual is quite suggestive of the remarkable transformational capacity of frames. The party frame, for example, allows even perfect strangers to hold one another while moving together in a pronounced rhythmic fashion (though only while the music is playing).[38] In a similar manner, in the context of art, respectability is granted to otherwise obscene literary passages and poetic metaphors as well as to nude modeling and photography,[39] just as the play frame helps de-eroticize games such as "house" and "doctor." Ordinary sexual meanings are likewise antisepticized by science, which allows genital display in anatomy books, and medicine, which de-eroticizes mouth-to-mouth resuscitation and gynecological examinations.[40]

In cutting chunks of experience off from their surroundings, frames obviously define not only different but also separate realms of experience. In delineating a space which the viewer cannot enter, picture frames, for example, "[cut] the artist's statement off from the room in which it is hung,"[41] thus visually articulating an experiential cleavage between ordinary reality and the artistic realm.[42] Supposedly bounded, experiential realms do not spill over into one another,[43] and the "reality" of any object is therefore always confined to the boundaries of the particular frame within which it is situated. That is why it is so difficult to prolong a dream after waking up or to sustain an erotic experience when someone knocks on the door, as well as why we normally do not hold others responsible for any harm they may have caused us in our fantasies. Along similar lines, terrified as we are by Captain Hook, Darth Vader, or the Wicked Witch of the West when we read about them or watch them on the screen, we nonetheless know that they can never step out of the fictional frames in which they belong and therefore cannot really hurt us.

Picture frames also make us disregard the wall surrounding the picture.[44] Like them, all frames basically define parts of our perceptual environment as irrelevant, thus separating that which we attend in a focused manner from all the out-of-frame experiences[45] that we leave "in the background" and ignore. Thus, for example, when we play checkers, the material of which the pieces are made is considered totally irrelevant to the game and, therefore, out of frame. In fact, when a piece is missing, we often replace it with a coin, totally disregarding the latter's ordinary monetary value. Likewise, within an erotic context, we normally perceive others as attractive or not, ignoring ordinary distinctions based on social class, status, or ethnic origin.[46]

Moreover, frames make us ignore entire acts or objects despite their obvious physical presence in the situation. At concerts, for example, we usually disregard such acts as replacing a mouthpiece or wiping spittle off one's horn, which are clearly not part of the framed performance in which they are visually embedded. We likewise ignore "background" activity such as nail biting or doodling at meetings and routinely skip page numbers and translators' notes when reading books.[47] And just as we exclude from the game frame such accidents as unintentionally knocking a piece off the chessboard (in sharp contrast to removing deliberately a captured piece), we also instruct jurors to ignore "unacceptable" evidence presented to them.

The experiential discontinuity between what is situated "inside" and "outside" frames also applies to human objects, as mere presence at a social situation may not always guarantee inclusion in the frame surrounding it.[48] In social gatherings, full-fledged participants are often surrounded by a mental partition[49] that keeps mere bystanders practically "out of focus." (Such discontinuity becomes apparent when we poke fun at those who laugh at jokes that were not addressed to them or when cardplayers scold kibitzers who offer unsolicited advice: "Who asked you, anyway?")[50] Cabdrivers, waiters, stenographers, and children are often assigned such out-of-frame status. So are technicians installing equipment at rock concerts, attendants who clean after the animals at circuses, food vendors at sports events, and photographers at weddings, all of whom are clearly situated outside the entertainment frame that surrounds everyone else. Despite their obvious physical presence at these situations, they are considered "non-persons"[51] and thus relegated to the out-of-frame "background." That is also why we sometimes fail to notice the very presence of those we assume do not understand the language we speak or the topic we discuss.[52]

CHUNKS OF IDENTITY

The manner in which we isolate supposedly discrete "figures" from their surrounding "ground" is also manifested in the way we come to experience ourselves.[53] It involves a form of mental differentiation that entails a fundamental distinction between us and the rest of the world. It is known as our sense of identity.

The most obvious form of identity is the experience of an insular self that is clearly cut off from one's surrounding environment,[54] a self with "clear and sharp lines of demarcation" that we experience as autonomous and "marked off distinctly from everything else."[55] Such self presupposes the experience of some "ego boundary"[56] that marks the "edge" of our personhood,[57] the point where we end and the rest of the world begins. Such boundary is at the heart of the fundamental experiential separation of what is "inside" the self from what lies "outside" it.[58]

The experience of a self presupposes some "psychological division from the rest of the world."[59] It is a product of a long process that begins when, as infants, we psychologically disengage ("hatch") from our initial "symbiotic" relationship with our most immediate other, usually our mother.[60] As a result of such process of individuation, we withdraw from a somewhat fluid reality into one where the self as well as other individuals with sharp and firm contours seem to emerge as discrete entities that are clearly separate from their environment.[61]

The self is but one particular focus of identity. There are many other answers to the existential question of where we end and the rest of the world begins, and they all involve supposedly bounded clusters of individuals (a family, a profession, a political party, a nation) who experience themselves collectively—and are usually perceived by others—as insular entities[62] clearly separate from everyone else. In short, we experience ourselves not only as "I" but also collectively as "we," that is, as liberals, baseball fans, Muslims, women, humans. It is such perceptions of social clusters as discrete entities that lead us to regard a marriage between a Christian and a Jew or an Armenian and a Pole as "mixed."

The experience of such discrete entities presupposes a perception of some boundaries surrounding them.[63] Even a couple going steady experiences some clear partition separating them from others around them.[64] Such fine mental lines help us perceive a fundamental discontinuity between insiders and outsiders, those included in a social cluster and those who are left outside its confines. Only in relation to those lines do sentiments such as fidelity, loyalty, or patriotism, for example, evolve, and only in relation to them do we learn whom we can trust and of whom we should beware, who is available to us as a sexual partner and whom we must avoid. These are the boundaries that basically define the mental entities we come to experience as "us" and "them." They constitute the basis of our sense of identity and determine much of the scope of our social relations.

MENTAL FIELDS

Early in life, space is the only mode available for organizing a self.[65] Indeed, our individuation begins with the development of locomotor functions such as crawling, which allow us to literally withdraw from others.[66] Later we establish some nonspatial sense of selfhood,[67] actualizing our separateness by acts such as saying no[68] and experiences such as ownership of toys, yet the basic way in which we experience the self and its relations with others remains spatial nonetheless. We thus associate selfhood with a psychological "distance" from others[69] and experience privacy (including its nonspatial aspects, such as secrecy) as having some "space" for ourselves or as a "territory" of inaccessibility surrounding us.[70] We experience others as being "close" to or "distant" from us and portray our willingness or unwillingness to make contact with them using topological images such as "opening up" (or "reaching out") and being "closed" (or "removed").[71] We also use the image of "penetration" to depict the essence of the process of becoming intimate.[72]

Similar spatial imagery captures our experience of groups as bounded, "closed"[73] entities that one almost literally "enters" and "exists."[74] We thus "*incorporate*" members into, "expel" them from, and assign them "central" or "marginal" places in groups. We also use images such as "*extra*marital" (or "*out of* wedlock"), "mobility,"[75] and "knows his place"; perceive actual social "distance"[76] between blacks and whites or senior and junior executives; and mentally locate "distant" relatives in terms of the number of "steps" they are "removed" from us.[77] Such mental geography has no physical basis but we experience it as if it did.

We likewise use spatial images to depict supposedly discrete chunks of professional jurisdiction (boundary, turf, territory, arena)[78] as well as knowledge. We thus perceive academic disciplines

as surrounded by mental "walls"[79] and works as lying on the "fringes" of sociology or outside our "area" of expertise, and regard those whose interest does not transcend the confines of their "field" as "limited" or "narrow minded." Similar spatial imagery seems to underlie our perception of the *extra*curricular, *extra*judicial, and esoteric as well as of insular "domains" such as work, religion, or art.

Somewhat similar is our experience of the fine mental lines that separate acceptable from unacceptable behavior—the assertive from the rude, the funny from the crude. We basically "confine [ourselves] to a particular radius of activity and . . . regard any conduct which drifts outside that radius as somehow inappropriate or immoral. . . . Human behavior can vary over an enormous range, but each community draws a symbolic set of parentheses around a certain segment of that range and limits its own activities within that narrower zone."[80] Our quasi-spatial experience of such "normative outlines" of society[81] is quite evident from our use of verbs such as "*trans*gress" or "*ex*ceed" (which literally mean to step or go beyond), prefixes such as "over-" (as in "*over*ambitious"), "*out-*" (as in "outlaw"), or "extra-" (as in "*extra*vagant"), and metaphors such as "line of decency"[82] or "limits of authority."

In a somewhat similar manner, we also "enter" conversations, go "out of" business, portray breakthroughs as the crossing of a Rubicon[83] or a forbidden frontier,[84] and can appreciate a cartoon depicting someone reaching a line demarcated by the sign "Boundary of Self Respect."[85] Similar spatial imagery also underlies such concepts as "*extra*ordinary," "*out*standing," or "*ex*otic."

Spatial metaphors pervade much of our thinking.[86] In a wide variety of contexts, we use them to depict purely mental relations among entities. In fact, we basically experience reality as a "space"[87] made up of discrete mental fields delineated by mental "fences"[88] that define[89] and separate them from one another. Given the significance of proximity in perceptual grouping (the closer things are to one another, the more we tend to perceive them as a single entity[90]), we use closeness as a metaphor for conceptual similarity,[91] essentially seeing difference in terms of mental distance.[92] We thus consider similar mental items as belonging "together"[93] and different ones as being "worlds apart," and we may even try to locate an item "exactly halfway" between two others.[94]

A foremost prerequisite for differentiating any entity from its surrounding environment are exceptionally strong intra-entity relations.[95] A mental field is basically a cluster of items that are more similar to one another than to any other item. Generating such fields, therefore, usually involves some lumping. As we group items in our mind (that is, categorize the world), we let their similarity outweigh any differences among them. As a result we perceive mental fields as relatively homogeneous lumps and regard their constituent items as functionally interchangeable variants ("allo-" variants) of a single unit of meaning.[96] Even when we notice differences among them, we dismiss them as totally irrelevant[97]—"making no difference"—and consequently ignore them.

Thus, despite the obvious differences among them, we regard the prefixes of the adjectives "*in*accurate," "*im*proper," "*dis*honest," and "*un*usual" as functionally equivalent variants of a single morpheme.[98] We regard them as basically "the same" because no confusion of meaning is likely to occur if one of them is substituted for another (that is, if we say "disaccurate" or "unproper"). Nor do we normally attribute much significance to the difference between right-eye and left-eye winks, which we perceive as functionally interchangeable variants of a single gesture,[99] or between a kiss and an affectionate look, which we often substitute for each other as tokens of intimacy.[100] Along similar lines, we usually

ignore the obvious difference between 490- and 540-millimicron-long light waves, regarding both as variants of the color "green,"[101] and casually substitute pretzels for potato chips as party snacks. And though clearly aware of the difference between thirty-one- and twenty-eight-day blocks of time, we nonetheless regard both as structurally equivalent variants of the unit "month"[102] and expect identical monthly paychecks for January and February. Along similar lines, we usually perceive conventional historical periods as relatively homogeneous stretches, often lumping together events that occurred centuries apart from one another yet within the same "period" (as in "the Middle Ages").[103]

In a similar manner, we establish social clusters in our mind by regarding all cluster members as similar and ignoring all differences among them, as when we lump together all those whose income falls below a certain "poverty line" as an undifferentiated lot—"the poor." We generally tend to downplay differences within our own group as well as among others,[104] as evident from the extremely broad categories ("Orientals") in which we lump those who came to America[105] or from various catchall categories for outsiders, such as the ancient Greek "barbarian," the Armenian *odar*,[106] the Gypsy *gadjo*, or the Jewish *goy*.

Ignoring intracluster differences and regarding all cluster members as basically "the same" often results in stereotypes, as when racists claim that all blacks are lazy or that all Orientals look alike. Nonetheless, without some lumping, it would be impossible ever to experience any collectivity, or mental entity for that matter. The ability to ignore the uniqueness of items and regard them as typical members of categories is a prerequisite for classifying any group of phenomena. Such ability to "typify"[107] our experience is therefore one of the cornerstones of social reality.

RITUAL TRANSITIONS

Most of the fine lines that separate mental entities from one another are drawn only in our own head and, therefore, totally invisible. And yet, by playing up the act of "crossing" them, we can make mental discontinuities more "tangible." Many rituals, indeed, are designed specifically to substantiate the mental segmentation of reality into discrete chunks. In articulating our "passage" through the mental partitions separating these chunks from one another, such rituals, originally identified by Arnold Van Gennep as "rites of passage,"[108] certainly enhance our experience of discontinuity.

The various rites we perform when we cross the equator, tropic of Cancer, or arctic circle[109] are perfect cases in point. In dramatizing our passage through these imaginary lines that exist only on maps, they certainly make them more "tangible" (somewhat like the road sign Welcome to Massachusetts). In a similar manner, we also dramatize the mental discontinuity between the public and private domains by knocking on the door before entering a room as well as by altering our appearance, as in the following caricature of a stereotypical return home, "from 'a hard day at the office': a banal scene in which the social passage is signified by the man successively removing his hat . . . taking off his jacket, stripping away his tie (exaggerated gesture), opening his shirt collar. . . . A whole set of statements about the contrast between [home] and the 'larger world' is going on."[110] Along similar lines, soldiers coming home even for a few hours often change into civilian clothes just to actualize their "exit" from the military world. Lowering their voices on entering church similarly helps congregants substantiate the mental separation of the sacred from the profane, whereas the ritual apology ("I beg your pardon") we offer on entering each

other's "personal space" likewise promotes our experience of an insular self.

In a similar manner, weddings substantiate the boundaries of the family, whose crossing transforms people into spouses and in-laws. They also signal, of course, the crossing of the mental partition that separates marriage from singlehood, just like puberty rites[111] (or modern equivalents such as obtaining a driver's license or going for the first time to an R-rated film), which dramatize the transition from childhood to adulthood. (The fact that we rarely celebrate divorces and usually articulate second weddings considerably less than first ones suggests that entering marriage entails a much greater break in identity than exiting or reentering it.) In dramatizing the moments of entering and exiting it, birth and death rituals[112] likewise substantiate the experience of life as a discrete block of time (as well as the mental contrast between life and nonlife). The need to substantiate the way we segment time into discrete blocks also accounts for the holidays we create to commemorate critical transition points between historical epochs[113] as well as for the rituals we design to articulate significant changes in our relative access to one another—greetings, first kisses, farewell parties, bedtime stories.[114] Changes of lighting or background music likewise signal transitions among successive segments of theatrical performances, films,[115] rock concerts, and circus shows, whereas ritual switches from sitting to standing help to "punctuate" religious services[116] and demarcate featured solos in jazz.

The ritual of raising the curtain before the beginning of a show[117] and the almost obligatory "once upon a time" or "and they lived happily ever after"[118] that signal crossings of the line separating fairy tales from "real" life similarly serve to substantiate the boundaries of frames.[119] So do the ritual glove touch or kickoff that prefaces sports events, the suspension of meter that signals the dissolution of the poetic frame,[120] and the caption "The End" that used to announce the conclusion of films. (Within films, conventional cues such as soft focus, overexposure, change from color to black and white, and suspension of background music often signal transitions from characters' here and now into their memories, fantasies, or dreams.) Along similar lines, organ preludes are often used to announce a religious frame,[121] "soft" music (and candlelight) a romantic frame, and dance music (and hors d'oeuvres) a party.

By switching from one language to another or even from standard to colloquial speech, we often articulate transitions from formality to informality or from just talking to quoting.[122] In a similar manner, speakers often clear their throats to announce the conclusion of their informal introductory remarks (just as chairpersons use gavels to announce the formal parts of meetings), change their tone to signal diversions from the general thrust of their talk to "parenthetical" remarks, and sit down to announce the beginning of the more informal question-and-answer part.[123] Children likewise use a change of voice to "enter" the make-believe frame[124] and the ritual call "Time" to exit from a game in order to tie a loose shoelace or get a drink.

Along similar lines, by punishing deviants who transgress its moral boundaries, society not only forces us to see that such lines do indeed exist but also demarcates their precise "location." Like weddings, funerals, and bedtime stories, punishment is a ritual that dramatizes the act of crossing some mental partition. In substantiating the mental segmentation of human behavior into acceptable and unacceptable, it serves to "locate and publicize"[125] moral edges:

> The deviant is a person whose activities have moved outside the margins of the group, and when the community calls him to account for that vagrancy it is making a statement about the nature and placement of its boundaries. . . . Members of a community inform one another about the placement of their boundaries by participating in the confrontations which occur when persons who venture out to the edges of the group are met by policing agents. . . . Whether these confrontations take the form of criminal trials, excommunication hearings, courts-martial, or even psychiatric case conferences, they [demonstrate] where the line is drawn. . . . Morality and immorality meet at the public scaffold, and it is during this meeting that the line between them is drawn. . . . Each time the community moves to censure some act of deviation, then, and convenes a formal ceremony to deal with the responsible offender, it . . . restates where the boundaries of the group are located.[126]

Moral boundaries remain a meaningful point of reference, of course, only as long as society indeed curbs all attempts to transgress them.[127] When society fails to punish deviants who venture beyond the limit of what it defines as acceptable, members will wonder whether such a line really exists.

Only the need to announce crossings of frame boundaries prompts us to indent quotations like the one above on a page of text[128] and only the need to substantiate an insular self compels us to say grace before we ingest parts of the environment into our body through the act of eating. Substantiating the insularity of conventional chunks of space, time, and identity is likewise the only reason for the rites we perform around doorsills,[129] the birthday cards[130] and New Year midnight kisses with which we "punctuate" life as well as history, and the various initiation rites (such as baptism, adoption, and naturalization) by which we dramatize the incorporation of new members into religious communities, families, or nations. Such rituals of "passage" are all products of some basic need to substantiate in our acts the mental discontinuities we perceive in our mind. As such, they play a major role in our ability to think analytically.

NOTES

1. Genesis 1:1–5.

2. Ibid., 6–10.

3. See, for example, Paul Seligman, *The Apeiron of Anaximander* (London: Athlone Press, 1962).

4. Gyorgy Kepes, *Language of Vision* (Chicago: Paul Theobald, 1951 [1944]), p. 45; Wolfgang Köhler, *Gestalt Psychology* (New York: New American Library, 1947), pp. 84, 93.

5. See also Ferdinand de Saussure, *Course in General Linguistics* (New York: Philosophical Library, 1959 [1915]), pp. 116–22; Michel Foucault, *The Order of Things* (New York: Vintage, 1973 [1966]), p. 144.

6. Paul Starr, "Social Categories and Claims in the Liberal State," in Mary Douglas, ed., *How Classification Works* (Edinburgh: Edinburgh University Press, forthcoming).

7. Emile Durkheim and Marcel Mauss, *Primitive Classification* (Chicago: University of Chicago Press, 1963 [1903]), p. 4. See also Karl W. Deutsch, "Autonomy and Boundaries according to Communications Theory," in Roy R. Grinker, ed., *Toward a Unified Theory of Human Behavior* (New York: Basic Books, 1956), pp. 278–79; Anatol Rapoport, "Statistical Boundaries," in *Toward a Unified Theory of Human Behavior*, p. 308. In Hebrew, the words for *classifying* (*sivug*) and *boundary* (*syag*) indeed derive from the same root.

8. Kenneth Burke, *A Grammar of Motives* (Berkeley: University of California Press, 1969 [1945]), p. 24. See also Gottlob Frege, "Logic in Mathematics," in *Post-humous Writings* (Chicago: University of Chicago Press, 1979 [1914]), pp. 155, 179, 195, 229, 241; Joan Weiner, "The Philosopher Behind the Last Logicist," in Crispin Wright, ed., *Frege—Tradition and Influence* (Oxford: Basil Blackwell, 1984), p. 72n.

9. Don Handelman, "The Ritual Clown: Attributes and Affinities," *Anthropos* 76 (1981):340.

10. Gustav Ichheiser, *Appearances and Realities* (San Francisco: Jossey-Bass, 1970), p. 8.

11. See also Henning Henningsen, *Crossing the Equator* (Copenhagen: Munksgaard, 1961), pp. 99–101.

12. Jean Jacques Rousseau, "A Discourse on the Origin of Inequality," in *The Social Contract and Discourses* (New York: E. P. Dutton, 1950 [1754]), p. 234.

13. See also Robert C. Tryon, *Identification of Social Areas by Cluster Analysis* (Berkeley: University of California Press, 1955), p. 71.

14. Barry Schwartz, "The Social Psychology of Privacy," *American Journal of Sociology* 78 (1968):747.

15. Charles A. Ferguson, "Diglossia," *Word* 15 (1959):325–40.

16. Stanley J. Tambiah, "Animals Are Good to Think and Good to Prohibit," *Ethnology* 8 (1969): 423–59; Pierre Bourdieu, "The Berber House," in Mary Douglas, ed., *Rules and Meanings* (Harmondsworth, England: Penguin, 1973 [1971]), pp. 98–110.

17. Robert Hertz, "The Pre-eminence of the Right Hand: A Study in Religious Polarity," in Rodney Needham, ed., *Right and Left* (Chicago: University of Chicago Press, 1973 [1909]); Barry Schwartz, *Vertical Classification* (Chicago: University of Chicago Press, 1981).

18. Kurt Lewin, *Principles of Topological Psychology* (New York: McGraw-Hill, 1936), p. 44.

19. Helms, *Ulysses' Sail*, pp. 22–31.

20. Gerald D. Suttles, *The Social Order of the Slum* (Chicago: University of Chicago Press, 1968), pp. 13–38, 225; Albert Hunter, *Symbolic Communities* (Chicago: University of Chicago Press, 1982 [1974]), pp. 84, 88.

21. See also Schwartz, "The Social Psychology of Privacy," pp. 747–49.

22. Virginia Woolf, *A Room of One's Own* (San Diego: Harcourt Brace Jovanovich, 1957 [1929]), p. 110. See also Woolf, pp. 4, 109; Christopher Alexander et al., *A Pattern Language* (New York: Oxford University Press, 1977), pp. 669–71.

23. On such segmentation of everyday life, see Kenneth L. Pike, *Language in Relation to a Unified Theory of the Structure of Human Behavior* (The Hague: Mouton, 1967 [1954]), pp. 73–82; Roger G. Barker and Herbert F. Wright, *Midwest and Its Children* (Hamden, Conn.: Archon, 1971 [1955]), pp. 225–73; Roger G. Barker, ed., *The Stream of Behavior* (New York: Appleton-Century-Crofts, 1963).

24. Zerubavel, *The Seven-Day Circle*, pp. 121–29. See also Zerubavel, pp. 102–6 and Zerubavel, *Patterns of Time in Hospital Life*, pp. 98–101. That is why nurses can take four-day blocks off only if no more than two of these days are within "the same" week

(*Patterns of Time in Hospital Life*, p. 21; *The Seven-Day Circle*, pp. 128–29).

25. See also Barbara H. Smith, *Poetic Closure* (Chicago: University of Chicago Press, 1968), pp. 2–4.

26. Zerubavel, *Patterns of Time in Hospital Life*, pp. 31–32.

27. Zerubavel, *Hidden Rhythms*, pp. 101–37; Zerubavel, *The Seven-Day Circle*, pp. 118–20.

28. Zerubavel, *Hidden Rhythms*, pp. 138–66.

29. Yael Zerubavel, "The Last Stand: On the Transformation of Symbols in Modern Israeli Culture," (Ph.D. diss., University of Pennsylvania, 1980), pp. 301–21; Yael Zerubavel, "Collective Memory and Historical Metaphors: Masada and the Holocaust as National Israeli Symbols" (paper presented at the meetings of the Association for Jewish Studies, Boston, December 1987).

30. See also Roy Turner, "Some Formal Properties of Therapy Talk," in David Sudnow, ed., *Studies in Social Interaction* (New York: Free Press, 1972), pp. 367–96.

31. Alfred Schutz, "On Multiple Realities," in *Collected Papers* (The Hague: Martinus Nijhoff, 1973 [1945]), vol. 1, pp. 230–31. See also William James, *The Principles of Psychology* (Cambridge: Harvard University Press, 1983 [1890]), pp. 920–23.

32. See also Gregory Bateson, "A Theory of Play and Fantasy," in *Steps to an Ecology of Mind* (New York: Ballantine, 1972 [1955]), pp. 187–88; Marion Milner, *The Suppressed Madness of Sane Men* (London: Tavistock, 1987), pp. 80–81, 225–26.

33. Georg Simmel, "The Handle," in Kurt H. Wolff, ed., *Georg Simmel, 1858–1918* (Columbus: Ohio State University Press, 1959 [1911]), p. 267.

34. Bateson, "A Theory of Play and Fantasy," pp. 184–92; Erving Goffman, *Frame Analysis* (New York: Harper Colophon, 1974).

35. See also Goffman, ibid., pp. 496–559; Erving Goffman, *Forms of Talk* (Philadelphia: University of Pennsylvania Press, 1981), pp. 144–57, 173–86, 226–327.

36. Schutz, "On Multiple Realities," p. 233; Goffman, *Forms of Talk*, pp. 251–69.

37. Gregory Bateson, *Mind and Nature* (New York: E. P. Dutton, 1979), p. 125.

38. See also Georg Simmel, "Sociability: An Example of Pure, or Formal Sociology," in Kurt H. Wolff, ed., *The Sociology of Georg Simmel* (New York: Free Press, 1950 [1917]), pp. 47–53.

39. Goffman, *Frame Analysis*, pp. 77–78; Murray S. Davis, *Smut* (Chicago: University of Chicago Press, 1983), pp. 216–19.

40. Joan P. Emerson, "Behavior in Private Places: Sustaining Definitions of Reality in Gynecological Examinations," in Hans P. Dreitzel, ed., *Recent Sociology No. 2* (London: Macmillan, 1970), pp. 74–97; Davis, *Smut*, pp. 219–24.

41. Goffman, *Frame Analysis*, p. 412.

42. Rudolf Arnheim, *Art and Visual Perception* (Berkeley: University of California Press, 1967 [1954]), p. 231; Edward T. Cone, *Musical Form and Musical Performance* (New York: W. W. Norton, 1968), p. 15; Meyer Schapiro, "On Some Problems in the Semiotics of Visual Art: Field and Vehicle in Image-Signs," *Semiotica* 1 (1969):224; Boris Uspensky, *A Poetics of Composition* (Berkeley: University of California Press, 1973), p. 143; Rudolf Arnheim, *The Power of the Center* (Berkeley: University of California Press, 1982), pp. 50–52, 63.

43. Schutz, "On Multiple Realities," pp. 230–33.

44. Bateson, "A Theory of Play and Fantasy," p. 187.

45. Goffman, *Frame Analysis*, pp. 201–46.

46. Davis, *Smut*, pp. 29–30.

47. Michel Butor, "The Book as Object," in *Inventory* (New York: Simon & Schuster, 1968), pp. 50–51; Goffman, *Frame Analysis*, pp. 227–30. See also Erving Goffman, *Behavior in Public Places* (New York: Free Press, 1963), pp. 43, 50–53; Goffman, *Frame Analysis*, p. 220.

48. Goffman, *Frame Analysis*, pp. 224–25; Goffman, *Forms of Talk*, pp. 131–40.

49. See, for example, Erving Goffman, *Encounters* (Indianapolis: Bobbs-Merrill, 1961), pp. 65–66; Harland G. Bloland, "Opportunities, Traps, and Sanctuaries: A Frame Analysis of Learned Societies," *Urban Life* 11 (1982):87ff.

50. See also Goffman, *Encounters*, pp. 63–64.

51. Erving Goffman, *The Presentation of Self in Everyday Life* (Garden City, N.Y.: Anchor, 1959), pp. 151–53; Goffman, *Behavior in Public Places*, p. 84; Goffman, *Frame Analysis*, p. 207.

52. Our assumption, however, may be false. Traveling in Europe and speaking together in Hebrew, my wife and I were once surprised on a bus by the woman sitting in front of us, who turned and asked us in Hebrew something about the weather. It was a subtle hint designed to remind us that "nonpersons" may interact with us in a far more "focused" way than we realize.

53. Heinz Werner, *Comparative Psychology of Mental Development* (New York: International Universities Press, 1957 [1940]), pp. 452–53; Witkin et al., *Psychological Differentiation*, p. 5; Herman A. Witkin, "Psychological Differentiation and Forms of Pathology," *Journal of Abnormal Psychology* 70 (1965):319.

54. Victor Tausk, "On the Origin of the 'Influencing Machine' in Schizophrenia," in Robert Fliess, ed., *The Psychoanalytic Reader* (New York: International Universities Press, 1948 [1919]), vol. 1, p. 68; Witkin et al., *Psychological Differentiation*, p. 14; Witkin, "Psychological Differentiation and Forms of Pathology," pp. 320–21.

55. Sigmund Freud, *Civilization and Its Discontents* (New York: W. W. Norton, 1962 [1930]), p. 13.

56. Tausk, "On the Origin of the 'Influencing Machine.'"

57. Paul Federn, "The Ego as Subject and Object in Narcissism," in *Ego Psychology and the Psychoses* (London: Imago Publishing Co., 1953 [1928]), p. 285.

58. Paul Federn, "Ego Psychological Aspect of Schizophrenia," in *Ego Psychology and the Psychoses*, p. 225. See also Tausk, "On the Origin of the 'Influencing Machine,'" p. 69; Jean Piaget, *The Construction of Reality in the Child* (New York: Basic Books, 1954), p. 281; Ernst Prelinger, "Extension and Structure of the Self," *Journal of Psychology* 47 (1959):13–23; Witkin et al., *Psychological Differentiation*, p. 134.

59. Nancy Chodorow, *The Reproduction of Mothering* (Berkeley: University of California Press, 1978), p. 68. See also Otto Fenichel, *The Psychoanalytic Theory of Neurosis* (New York: W. W. Norton, 1945), pp. 35–36.

60. Margaret S. Mahler and Kitty La Perriere, "Mother-Child Interaction during Separation-Individuation," in Margaret S. Mahler, *Separation-Individuation* (New York: Jason Aronson, 1979 [1965]), p. 36; Margaret S. Mahler, "On the First Three Subphases of the Separation-Individuation Process," in *Separation-Individuation*, pp. 121–22; Margaret S. Mahler et al., *The Psychological Birth of the Human Infant* (New York: Basic Books, 1975), pp. 52–54, 63.

61. Arthur Koestler, *The Act of Creation* (New York: Macmillan, 1964), p. 292.

62. Donald T. Campbell, "Common Fate, Similarity, and Other Indices of the Status of Aggregates of Persons as Social Entities," *Behavioral Science* 3 (1958):17–18. See also Reuben Hill, *Families Under Stress* (Westport, Conn.: Greenwood, 1971 [1949]), pp. 3–5; Fredrik Barth, *Ethnic Groups and Boundaries* (Boston: Little, Brown, 1969), p. 9.

63. See, for example, Kurt Koffka, *Principles of Gestalt Psychology* (New York: Harbinger, 1935), p. 665; Hill, *Families Under Stress*, pp. 3–5; Kai T. Erikson, *Wayward Puritans* (New York: John Wiley, 1966), pp. 11, 13, 196; Richard Handler, *Nationalism and the Politics of Culture in Quebec* (Madison: University of Wisconsin Press, 1988).

64. Mark Krain, "A Definition of Dyadic Boundaries and an Empirical Study of Boundary Establishment in Courtship," *International Journal of Sociology of the Family* 7 (1977): 120. See also Erving Goffman, *Relations in Public* (New York: Harper Colophon, 1972), pp. 19–23.

65. Sigmund Freud, *The Ego and the Id* (New York: W. W. Norton, 1962 [1923]), p. 16; Stanley R. Palombo and Hilde Bruch, "Falling Apart: The Verbalization of Ego Failure," *Psychiatry* 27 (1964):250, 252, 256.

66. Mahler and La Perriere, "Mother-Child Interaction," p. 36; Margaret S. Mahler, "On Human Symbiosis and the Vicissitudes of Individuation," in *Separation-Individuation*, pp. 85–86; Mahler, "On the First Three Subphases," pp. 124–25; Mahler et al., *The Psychological Birth of the Human Infant*, p. 72; Louise J. Kaplan, *Oneness and Separateness* (New York: Touchstone, 1978), pp. 191–98.

67. See, for example, James, *Principles of Psychology*, pp. 280–83.

68. Kaplan, *Oneness and Separateness*, p. 200.

69. Werner, *Comparative Psychology of Mental Development*, p. 452.

70. Georg Simmel, "The Secret and the Secret Society," in Kurt H. Wolff, ed., *The Sociology of Georg*

Simmel (New York: Free Press, 1950 [1908]), pp. 321–22; Goffman, *Relations in Public*, pp. 38–39; Eviatar Zerubavel, "Personal Information and Social Life," *Symbolic Interaction* 5 (1982):102–5.

71. See also Lewin, *Principles of Topological Psychology*; Maria A. Rickers-Ovsiankina, "Social Accessibility in Three Age Groups," *Psychological Reports* 2 (1956):283–94; Maria A. Rickers-Ovsiankina and Arnold A. Kusmin, "Individual Differences in Social Accessibility," *Psychological Reports* 4 (1958):391–406; Prelinger, "Extension and Structure of the Self."

72. Irwin Altman and Dalmas A. Taylor, *Social Penetration* (New York: Holt, Rinehart and Winston, 1973).

73. Max Weber, *Economy and Society* (Berkeley: University of California Press, 1978 [1925]), pp. 43–46; Campbell, "Common Fate," p. 22.

74. Arnold Van Gennep, *The Rites of Passage* (Chicago: University of Chicago Press, 1960 [1908]), pp. 103, 113.

75. Pitirim A. Sorokin, *Social and Cultural Mobility* (New York: Free Press, 1964 [1927]), p. 133. See also Sorokin, pp. 1–10; Pierre Bourdieu, "The Social Space and the Genesis of Groups," *Theory and Society* 14 (1985):723–44.

76. Georg Simmel, "The Stranger," in Kurt H. Wolff, ed., *The Sociology of Georg Simmel* (New York: Free Press, 1950 [1908]), pp. 402–8; Robert E. Park, "The Concept of Social Distance," *Journal of Applied Sociology* 8 (1924):339–44.

77. See, for example, Ward H. Goodenough, "Yankee Kinship Terminology: A Problem in Componential Analysis," in Stephen A. Tyler, ed., *Cognitive Anthropology* (New York: Holt, Rinehart and Winston, 1969 [1965]), pp. 269–71; David M. Schneider, *American Kinship* (Chicago: University of Chicago Press, 1980), pp. 23, 73.

78. Eliot Freidson, *Doctoring Together* (Chicago: University of Chicago Press, 1980 [1975]), pp. 69–85; Carol L. Kronus, "The Evolution of Occupational Power: An Historical Study of Task Boundaries between Physicians and Pharmacists," *Sociology of Work and Occupations* 3 (1976):3–37; Andrew Abbott, *The System of Professions* (Chicago: University of Chicago Press, 1988).

79. Margaret Mead, "Crossing Boundaries in Social Science Communications," *Social Science Information* 8 (1969):7.

80. Erikson, *Wayward Puritans*, p. 10.

81. Ibid., p. 12.

82. "Next: R-Rated Record Albums?" *Newsweek*, August 26, 1985, p. 69.

83. "Botha Goes Slow," *Newsweek*, August 26, 1985, p. 27.

84. Elihu Katz and Daniel Dayan, "Contests, Conquests, Coronations: On Media Events and Their Heroes," in Carl F. Graumann and Serge Moscovici, eds., *Changing Conceptions of Leadership* (New York: Springer-Verlag, 1986), p. 139.

85. *Newsday*, January 30, 1986, Part 2, p. 19.

86. Mark Johnson, *The Body in the Mind* (Chicago: University of Chicago Press, 1987).

87. Fred Attneave, "Dimensions of Similarity," *American Journal of Psychology* 63 (1950):516–56; Charles E. Osgood et al., *The Measurement of Meaning* (Urbana: University of Illinois Press, 1957), pp. 86, 89–97; Foucault, *The Order of Things*, pp. xviii–xix, xxii; Richard Beals et al., "Foundations of Multidimensional Scaling," *Psychological Review* 75 (1968):132; Samuel Fillenbaum and Amnon Rapoport, *Structures in the Subjective Lexicon* (New York: Academic Press, 1971), p. 4; J. Douglas Carroll and Myron Wish, "Multidimensional Perceptual Models and Measurement Methods," in Edward C. Carterette and Morton P. Friedman, eds., *Handbook of Perception, vol. 2: Psychophysical Judgment and Measurement* (New York: Academic Press, 1974), pp. 425–26; Eugene Hunn, "Toward a Perceptual Model of Folk Biological Classification," *American Ethnologist* 3 (1976):515; Robert Darnton, *The Great Cat Massacre and Other Episodes in French Cultural History* (New York: Vintage, 1985), p. 192; Frederick L. Bates and Walter G. Peacock, "Conceptualizing Social Structure: The Misuse of Classification in Structural Modeling," *American Sociological Review* 54 (1989):569n.

88. Anthony F. Wallace and John Atkins, "The Meaning of Kinship Terms," *American Anthropologist* 62 (1960):67.

89. The Hebrew words for *fence (gader)* and *definition (hagdara)* indeed derive from the same root.

90. Max Wertheimer, "Untersuchungen zur Lehre von der Gestalt," *Psycholo. Forsch.* 4 (1923): 301–50.

91. See also Werner, *Comparative Psychology of Mental Development*, pp. 222–25.

92. See, for example, Attneave, "Dimensions of Similarity"; Osgood et al., *The Measurement of Meaning*, pp. 89–97; Warren S. Torgerson, *Theory and Methods of Scaling* (New York: John Wiley, 1958), pp. 250, 260ff; Werner S. Landecker, "Class Boundaries," *American Sociological Review* 25 (1960):873; Roger N. Shepard, "The Analysis of Proximities: Multidimensional Scaling with an Unknown Distance Function," *Psychometrika* 27 (1962): 126; R. E. Bonner, "On Some Clustering Techniques," *IBM Journal of Research and Development* 8 (1964):22–32; Warren S. Torgerson, "Multidimensional Scaling of Similarity," *Psychometrika* 30 (1965):379–93; Peter M. Blau and Otis D. Duncan, *The American Occupational Structure* (New York: John Wiley, 1967), pp. 67–75, 152–61; Beals et al., "Foundations of Multidimensional Scaling," p. 127; Jack B. Arnold. "A Multidimensional Scaling Study of Semantic Distance," *Journal of Experimental Psychology* 90 (1971):349–72; Fillenbaum and Rapoport, *Structures in the Subjective Lexicon*; Abraham A. Moles, *Théorie des Objets* (Paris: Éditions Universitaires, 1972), pp. 59–61, 74; Stephen K. Reed, "Pattern Recognition and Categorization," *Cognitive Psychology* 3 (1972):382–407; Peter H. A. Sneath and Robert R. Sokal, *Numerical Taxonomy* (San Francisco: W. H. Freeman, 1973), p. 119; Carroll and Wish, "Multidimensional Perceptual Models," p. 393; Robert R. Sokal, "Classification: Purposes, Principles, Progress, Prospects," *Science* 185 (1974):1119; Victor Turner, "Metaphors of Anti-Structure in Religious Culture," in *Dramas, Fields, and Metaphors* (Ithaca: Cornell University Press, 1975 [1974]), p. 294; Alfonso Caramazza et al., "Subjective Structures and Operations in Semantic Memory," *Journal of Verbal Learning and Verbal Behavior* 15 (1976): 103–17; Hunn, "Toward a Perceptual Model," p. 515; Carol L. Krumhansl, "Concerning the Applicability of Geometric Models to Similarity Data: The Interrelationship between Similarity and Spatial Density," *Psychological Review* 85 (1978): 445–63; Edward E. Smith and Douglas L. Medin, *Categories and Concepts* (Cambridge: Harvard University Press, 1981), p. 105.

93. See, for example, Kurt Goldstein and Martin Scheerer, "Abstract and Concrete Behavior: An Experimental Study with Special Tests," *Psychological Monographs* 53 (1941), #2, pp. 59–60, 75–82, 103–7, 128.

94. Foucault, *The Order of Things*, p. 136.

95. Köhler, *Gestalt Psychology*, p. 93; Federn, "Ego Psychological Aspect of Schizophrenia," p. 222; Talcott Parsons, *The Social System* (New York: Free Press, 1964 [1951]), p. 482; Campbell, "Common Fate," pp. 18–20; Bonner, "On Some Clustering Techniques," p. 22; Smith, *Poetic Closure*, pp. 23–24; Robert R. Sokal, "Clustering and Classification: Background and Current Directions," in J. Van Ryzin, ed., *Classification and Clustering* (New York: Academic Press, 1977), p. 7; Smith and Medin, *Categories and Concepts*, pp. 110–11.

96. See also Jerome S. Bruner et al., *A Study of Thinking* (New York: John Wiley, 1956), pp. 2–4; Stephen C. Johnson, "Hierarchical Clustering Systems," *Psychometrika* 32 (1967):242; Yehudi A. Cohen, "Social Boundary Systems," *Current Anthropology* 10 (1969): 109–11.

97. Foucault, *The Order of Things*, p. 140.

98. On "allomorphs," see Pike, *Language in Relation to a Unified Theory*, pp. 164, 176–77, 206; Dwight Bolinger, *Aspects of Language* (New York: Harcourt, Brace & World, 1968), pp. 58–63. On their functional phonological analogues, "allophones," see Roman Jakobson, *Six Lectures on Sound and Meaning* (Cambridge: MIT Press, 1978 [1942]), pp. 28–33; Pike, *Language in Relation to a Unified Theory*, pp. 44–46, 325–28; Mario Pei, *Glossary of Linguistic Terminology* (New York: Columbia University Press, 1966), p. 10; Bolinger, *Aspects of Language*, pp. 43–44.

99. See Ray L. Birdwhistell, *Kinesics and Context* (Philadelphia: University of Pennsylvania Press, 1970), pp. 166, 193–95, 229.

100. Murray S. Davis, *Intimate Relations* (New York: Free Press, 1973), pp. 76–77.

101. Umberto Eco, *A Theory of Semiotics* (Bloomington: Indiana University Press, 1976), p. 77.

102. See also Zerubavel, *Patterns of Time in Hospital Life*, p. 4.

103. See also Y. Zerubavel, "The Last Stand," p. 309.

104. Henri Tajfel, *Human Groups and Social Categories* (Cambridge, England: Cambridge University Press, 1981), pp. 115–16, 121, 133, 243.

105. See also Richard Williams, *Hierarchical Structures and Social Value* (Cambridge, England: Cambridge University Press, 1990).

106. Howard F. Stein, *Developmental Time, Cultural Space.* Norman: University of Oklahoma Press, 1987), p. 6.

107. Berger and Luckmann, *The Social Construction of Reality*, pp. 30–34, 54–58; Schutz and Luckmann, *The Structures of the Life-World*, pp. 73–79, 238–41.

108. Van Gennep, *The Rites of Passage.*

109. Henningsen, *Crossing the Equator.*

110. Marshall Sahlins, *Culture and Practical Reason* (Chicago: University of Chicago Press, 1976), pp. 181–82n.

111. Van Gennep, *The Rites of Passage*, pp. 65–88.

112. Ibid., pp. 50–64, 146–65; Robert Hertz, "A Contribution to the Study of the Collective Representation of Death," in *Death and the Right Hand* (Aberdeen, Scotland: Cohen and West, 1960 [1907]), pp. 80–86; Michael C. Kearl, *Endings* (New York: Oxford University Press, 1989), p. 95.

113. Y. Zerubavel, "Collective Memory and Historical Metaphors."

114. Goffman, *Relations in Public*, pp. 73–94; Davis, *Intimate Relations*, pp. 56ff; Stuart Albert and William Jones, "The Temporal Transition from Being Together to Being Alone: The Significance and Structure of Children's Bedtime Stories," in Bernard S. Gorman and Alden E. Wessman, eds., *The Personal Experience of Time* (New York: Plenum, 1977), p. 131. See also Emanuel A. Schegloff and Harvey Sacks, "Opening up Closings," *Semiotica* 8 (1973):289–327; Stuart Albert and Suzanne Kessler, "Processes for Ending Social Encounters: The Conceptual Archaeology of a Temporal Place," *Journal for the Theory of Social Behavior* 6 (1976):147–70; Goffman, *Forms of Talk*, p. 130.

115. See also John Carey, "Temporal and Spatial Transitions in American Fiction Films," *Studies in the Anthropology of Visual Communication* 1 (1974):45.

116. Pike, *Language in Relation to a Unified Theory*, p. 76.

117. On ways of invoking or suspending the theatrical frame before the introduction of the curtain, see William Beare, *The Roman Stage* (London: Methuen, 1964), p. 179; Elizabeth Burns, *Theatricality* (New York: Harper Torchbooks, 1973), p. 41.

118. Michel Butor, "On Fairy Tales," in *Inventory* (New York: Simon & Schuster, 1968 [1960]), p. 213.

119. For a general discussion of "metamessages," see Gregory Bateson et al., "Toward a Theory of Schizophrenia," in *Steps to an Ecology of Mind* (New York: Ballantine, 1972 [1956]), p. 222; Bateson, "A Theory of Play and Fantasy."

120. Smith, *Poetic Closure*, pp. 24–25. See also pp. 50–95, 98–150, 158–66, 172–86.

121. Cone, *Musical Form and Musical Performance*, p. 13.

122. Jan-Peter Blom and John J. Gumperz, "Social Meaning in Linguistic Structure: Code-Switching in Norway," in John J. Gumperz and Dell Hymes, eds., *Directions in Sociolinguistics* (New York: Holt, Rinehart and Winston, 1972), pp. 425–26; John J. Gumperz, *Discourse Strategies* (Cambridge, England: Cambridge University Press, 1982), p. 76.

123. Goffman, *Forms of Talk*, p. 176.

124. Holly Giffin, "The Coordination of Meaning in the Creation of a Shared Make-Believe Reality," in Inge Bretherton, ed., *Symbolic Play* (Orlando, Fla.: Academic Press, 1984), p. 86.

125. Erikson, *Wayward Puritans*, p. 11.

126. Ibid., pp. 11–13.

127. Ibid., p. 13.

128. Butor, "The Book as Object," pp. 54–55.

129. H. Clay Trumbull, *The Threshold Covenant* (New York: Charles Scribner's Sons, 1906), pp. 3–12, 25–28, 66–68.

130. Vered Vinitzky-Seroussi, "Classification of Special Days and Specific People" (paper presented at the annual meeting of the Midwest Modern Language Association, Kansas City, November 1990). See also Esther Lavie, "Age as an Indicator for Reference in the Construction of Social Contexts" (Ph.D. diss., Tel-Aviv University, 1987), pp. 242–81.

REALITY AS A COLLECTIVE HUNCH

2

The Search for Signs of Intelligent Life in the Universe

Jane Wagner

(1986)

Here we are, standing on the corner of
"Walk, Don't Walk."
You look away from me, tryin' not to catch
my eye,
   but you didn't turn fast enough, *did* you?

You don't like my *raspy* voice, do you?
I got this *raspy* voice
'cause I have to yell all the time
'cause nobody around here ever
LISTENS to me.

You don't like that I scratch so much: yes, and
excuse me,
   I scratch so much
   'cause my neurons are
   on *fire*.

And I admit my smile is not at its Pepsodent best
   'cause I think my
   caps must've somehow got
   osteoporosis.

And if my eyes seem to be twirling around
like fruit flies—
   the better to see you with, my dears!
   Look at me,
   you mammalian-brained LUNKHEADS!

I'm not just talking to myself. I'm talking to
you, too.

And to you
and you
and you
and you and you and you!

I know what you're thinkin'; you're thinkin'
I'm crazy.
   You think I give a hoot? You people
   look at my shopping bags,
   call me crazy 'cause I save this junk. What
should we call the
   ones who
   buy it?

It's my belief we all, at one time or another,
   secretly ask ourselves the question,
   "Am *I crazy*?"
   In my case, the answer came back: A resound-
ing
   YES!

You're thinkin': How does a person know if
they're crazy
   or not? Well, sometimes you don't know.
Sometimes you
   can go through life suspecting you *are*
   but never really knowing for sure. Sometimes
you know for sure
   'cause you got so many people tellin' you
you're crazy
   that it's your word against everyone else's.

Another sign is when you see life so clear sometimes
    you black out.
This is your typical visionary variety
    who has flashes of insight
    but can't get anyone to listen to 'em
    'cause their insights make 'em sound so *crazy!*

In my case,
    the symptoms are subtle
    but unmistakable to the trained eye. For instance,
        here I am,
        standing at the corner of "Walk, Don't Walk,"
        waiting for these aliens from outer space to show up.
    I call that crazy, don't you? If I were sane,
    I should be waiting for the light like everybody else.

They're late
    as usual.

You'd think,
    as much as they know about time travel,
    they could be on time *once* in a while.

I could kick myself.
    I told 'em I'd meet 'em on the corner of "Walk, Don't Walk"
        'round lunchtime.
    Do they even know what "lunch" means?
    I doubt it.

And " 'round." Why did I say " 'round"? Why wasn't I more
    specific? This is so typical of what I do.

Now they're probably stuck somewhere in time, wondering
    what I meant by
    " 'round lunchtime." And when they get here, they'll be

dying to know what "lunchtime" means. And when they
    find out it means going to Howard Johnson's for fried
    clams, I wonder, will they be just a bit let down?
    I dread having to explain
    tartar sauce.

This problem of time just points out
    how far apart we really are.
    See, our ideas about time and space are different
    from theirs. When we think of time, we tend to think of
    clock radios, coffee breaks, afternoon naps, leisure time,
    halftime activities, parole time, doing time, Minute Rice, instant
    tea, mid-life crises, that time of the month, cocktail hour.
    And if I should suddenly
    mention *space*—aha! I bet most of you thought of your
    closets. But when they think of time and space, they really think
        of
    Time and Space.

They asked me once my thoughts on infinity and I told 'em
    with all I had to think about, infinity was not on my list
    of things to think about. It could be time on an ego trip,
    for all I know. After all, when you're pressed for time,
    infinity may as well
    not be there.
    They said, to them, infinity is
    time-released time.
    Frankly, infinity doesn't affect
    me personally one way or the other.

You think too long about infinity, you could go stark raving mad.

But I don't ever want to sound negative about going crazy.

I don't want to overromanticize it either, but frankly,
goin' crazy was the *best* thing ever happened to me.
I don't say it's for everybody;
some people couldn't cope.

But for me it came at a time when nothing else seemed to be
working. I got the kind of madness Socrates talked about,
"A divine release of the soul from the yoke of custom and convention." I refuse to be intimidated by
reality anymore.
After all, what is reality anyway? Nothin' but a collective hunch. My space chums think reality was once a
primitive method of
crowd control that got out of hand.
In my view, it's absurdity dressed up
in a three-piece business suit.

I made some studies, and
reality is the leading cause of stress amongst those in
touch with it. I can take it in small doses, but as a lifestyle
I found it too confining.
It was just too needful;
it expected me to be there for it *all* the time, and with all
I have to do—
I had to let something go.

Now, since I put reality on a back burner, my days are
jam-packed and fun-filled. Like some days, I go hang out
around Seventh Avenue; I love to do this old joke:

I wait for some music-loving tourist from one of the hotels
on Central Park to go up and ask someone.
"How do I get to Carnegie Hall?"
Then I run up and yell,
"Practice!"
The expression on people's faces is priceless. I never
could've done stuff like that when I was in my *right* mind.
I'd be worried people would think I was *crazy*.
When I think of the fun I missed,
I try not to be bitter.

See, the human mind is kind of like...
a piñata. When it breaks open,
there's a lot of surprises inside. Once you get the piñata
perspective, you see that losing your mind can be a peak experience.

I was not always a bag lady, you know.
I used to be a designer and creative consultant. For big
companies!
Who do you think thought up the color scheme for Howard Johnson's?
At the time, nobody was using
orange and aqua
in the same room together.
With fried clams.

Laugh tracks:
I gave TV sitcoms the idea for canned laughter.
I got the idea, one day I heard voices
and no one was there.

Who do you think had the idea to package panty hose
in a plastic goose egg?

One thing I personally don't like about panty hose:

When you roll 'em down to the ankles the way I like 'em, you
can't walk too good. People seem amused, so what's a little
loss of dignity? You got to admit:
It's a look!

The only idea I'm proud of—

my umbrella hat. Protects against sunstroke, rain and
muggers. For *some* reason, muggers steer clear of people
wearing umbrella hats.

So it should come as no shock . . . I am now creative consultant to
these aliens from outer space. They're a kinda cosmic
fact-finding committee. Amongst other projects, they've been
searching all over for Signs of Intelligent Life.

It's a lot trickier than it sounds.

We're collecting all kinds of data
about life here on Earth. We're determined to figure out,
once and for all, just what the hell it all means.
I write the data on these Post-its and then we study it.
Don't worry, before I took the consulting job, I gave 'em my whole
psychohistory.

I told 'em what drove *me* crazy was my *last* creative consultant
job, with the Ritz Cracker mogul, Mr. Nabisco. It was
my job to come up with snack inspirations to increase sales.
I got this idea to give Cracker Consciousness to the entire
planet.

I said, "Mr. Nabisco, sir! You could be the first to sell the
concept of munching to the Third World. We got an untapped
market here! These countries got millions and millions of
people don't even know where their next *meal* is *coming* from.
So the idea of eatin' *between* meals is somethin' just never
occurred to 'em!"

I heard myself sayin' *this!*
Must've been when I went off the deep end.
I woke up in the nuthouse. They were hookin' me up.
One thing they don't tell you about shock treatments, for
months afterwards you got
flyaway hair. And it used to *be* my best feature.

See, those shock treatments gave me new electrical circuitry
(frankly, I think one of the doctors' hands must've been wet).
I started having these time-space continuum shifts, I guess
you'd call it. Suddenly, it was like my central nervous system
had a patio addition out back.
Not only do I have a linkup to extraterrestrial
channels. I also got a hookup with humanity as a whole.
Animals and plants, too. I used to talk to plants all the time;
then, one day, they started talking back. They said,
"Trudy,
shut up!"

I got like this . . .
built-in Betamax in my head. Records anything.

It's like somebody's using my brain to dial-switch
through humanity. I pick up signals that seem
to transmit
snatches of people's lives.
My umbrella hat works as a satellite dish. I
hear this
sizzling sound like white noise. Then I know it's
trance time.
That's how I met my space chums. I was in
one of my trances,
watching a scene from someone's life, and I
suddenly sense
others were there
watching with me.

Uh-oh.
I see this skinny
punk kid.
Got hair the color of
Froot Loops and she's wearin' a T-shirt says
"Leave Me Alone."
There's a terrible family squabble going on.
If they're listening to each other,
they're all gonna get their feelings hurt.

I see glitches—
Now I see this dark-haired actress
on a Broadway stage. I know her. I see her all
the time outside
the Plymouth Theater, Forty-fifth Street . . .

Dial-switch me outta this!
I got enough worries of my own.
These trances are entertaining but distracting,
especially since
someone *else* has the remote control, and if
the pause button
should somehow get punched, I could have a
neurotransmitter
mental meltdown. Causes "lapses of the
synapses." I forget
things. Never underestimate the power of the
human mind to

forget. The other day, I forgot where I put my
house keys—
looked everywhere, then I remembered
I don't have a house. I forget more important
things, too.
Like the meaning of life.
I forget that.
It'll come to me, though.
Let's just hope when it does,
I'll be in . . .

My space chums say they're learning so much
about us
since they've begun to time-share my trances.
They said to me, "Trudy, the human mind
is so-o-o strange."
I told 'em, "That's nothin' compared to the
human genitals."
Next to my trances they love goin' through my
shopping bags.
Once they found this old box of Cream of
Wheat. I told 'em, "A
box of cereal." But they saw it as a picture of
infinity. You know
how on the front is a picture of that guy holding up a box of
Cream of Wheat
and on *that* box is a picture of that guy holding up a box of
Cream of Wheat
and on *that* box is a picture of that guy holding up a box of
Cream of Wheat
and on *that* box is a picture of that guy holding up a box of
Cream of Wheat . . .

We think so different.

They find it hard to grasp some things that
come easy to us,
because they simply don't have our frame of
reference.

I show 'em this can of Campbell's tomato soup.
I say,
"This is soup."
Then I show 'em a picture of Andy Warhol's painting
of a can of Campbell's tomato soup.
I say,
"This is art."

"This is soup."

"And this is art."

Then I shuffle the two behind my back.

Now what is this?

No,
this is soup
and *this is art!* . . .

Hey, what's this?

"Dear Trudy, thanks for making our stay here so jam-packed and
fun-filled. Sorry to abort our mission—it is not over,
just temporarily scrapped.

We have orders to go to a higher bio-vibrational plane.

Just wanted you to know, the neurochemical imprints of our
cardiocortical experiences here on earth will remain with us
always, but what we take with us into space that we cherish the
most is the 'goose bump' experience."
Did I tell you what happened at the play? We were at the back

of the theater, standing there in the dark,
all of a sudden I feel one of 'em tug my sleeve,
whispers, "Trudy, look." I said, "Yeah, goose bumps. You
definitely
got goose bumps. You really like the play that much?" They said
it wasn't the play
gave 'em goose bumps,
it was the audience.

I forgot to tell 'em to watch the play; they'd been watching
the *audience*!

Yeah, to see a group of strangers sitting together in the dark,
laughing and crying about the same things . . . that just knocked
'em out.
They said, "Trudy,
the play was soup . . .
the audience . . .
art."

So they're taking goose bumps
home with 'em.
Goose bumps!
Quite a souvenir.

I like to think of them out there
in the dark, watching us.
Sometimes we'll do something and they'll laugh.
Sometimes we'll do something and they'll cry.
And maybe one day we'll do something so magnificent,
everyone in the universe will get
goose bumps.

REALITY AS A COLLECTIVE HUNCH

3

Truth, Objectivity, and Agreement

Earl Babbie

(1986)

In conventional instruction in scientific methods, students are taught that a scientist begins with a question, specifies the exact meanings of the elements contained in the question, and designs experiments that reveal the relationships among those elements. By this process, a taxing question gets displaced by a definitive answer; ignorance gives way to knowledge.

Still, the image of scientists finding answers to questions misrepresents the nature of the enterprise, at least in social science. An instructive way to begin is by recognizing that everything we know today is likely to be overturned at some point in the future. It is ironic that we understand how human knowledge has been developing throughout human history (and presumably throughout human prehistory) and yet assume that what we know today is pretty much beyond that process.

Whenever we reach an answer to some question about human social life, our possession of that answer is likely to have an impact on the nature of social life itself, possibly to the extent of invalidating the answer. The "bandwagon effect" in the arena of public opinion is one example. Social researchers conduct surveys to answer the question, "What percentage of voters will vote for Candidate X?" If a large majority of those polled say they will vote for candidate X, the report of that result encourages others to vote the same way. If only a small minority say they will vote for Candidate X, the poll results shift additional voters away from that candidate.

Two points emerge from all this:

- Our knowledge is tenuous. Anything we "know" today may be overturned by new discoveries tomorrow.
- Anything we learn about human social life can have an impact on what we are studying, even to the extent of invalidating what we learned in the first place.

Our normal way of responding to questions is to answer them, thus closing the lines of inquiry they represent. Or if we think questions can't be answered, logic suggests that we avoid them altogether. For a social researcher, a more powerful method is appropriate- to hold them as *open questions* and to continue asking them even when no definitive answers seem possible. The purpose of this is to keep lines of inquiry open.

Perhaps the greatest contribution can be made by keeping questions open when everyone else seems to feel they have been answered. The power of social research, then, lies more in the realm of questions than in the realm of answers.

We should also open up similar questions in the area of social research. These include, among others:

- Can we ever be truly objective? Does truth even exist? Is reality just a matter of agreement?

- Do social researchers observe and study people's attitudes or actually create them?
- Is social science really scientific? Is it perhaps the first science?

Science is often portrayed as a search for the truth about reality. That sounds good, but what is *truth*? What is *reality*? Look those words up in a good dictionary, such as the *Oxford English Dictionary,* and you'll find definitions like "the quality of being true" and "the quality of being real." Beyond these basic tautologies are some additional definitions (from the *OED*):

Truth:

- Conformity with fact; agreement with reality
- Agreement with a standard or rule; accuracy, correctness
- Genuineness, reality, actual existence
- That which is in accordance with fact
- That which is true, real, or actual; reality

Reality:

- The quality of . . . having an actual existence
- Correspondence to fact; truth
- Real existence

Definitions of the words *true* and *real* are similar:

True:

- Consistent with fact; agreeing with reality; representing the thing as it is
- Agreeing with a standard, pattern, or rule; exact, accurate, precise, correct, right
- Consistent with, exactly agreeing with
- Conformable to reality; natural
- In accordance with reality

Real:

- Having an objective existence; actually existing as a thing

- Actually present or existing as a state or quality of things; having a foundation in fact; actually occurring or happening
- Consisting of actual things

These definitions point to the inherent circularity of language, which is inevitable as long as we use words to define words. In this case, things are true if they're real and real if they're true. The relationship between truth and reality can also be seen in the preponderance of words dealing with agreement: *conformity, accordance, correspondence, consistent with, representing.*

Here's a useful way of seeing the relationship between truth and reality: It is possible to make statements about reality; those that agree with (conform to, are consistent with, represent) reality are true. None of this tells us what truth or reality is, however. It only tells us about their relationship to one another.

Other words in the definitions we've seen may clarify the meanings of truth and reality—words such as *actual, existence,* and *fact.*

Actuality:

- The state of being actual or real; reality, existing objective fact

Actual:

- Existing in act or fact; really acted or acting; carried out; real

Factual:

- Pertaining to or concerned with facts; of the nature of fact, actual, real

Fact:

- Something that has really occurred or is actually the case
- Truth attested by direct observation or authentic testimony; reality

Existence:

- Actuality; reality
- Being; the fact or state of existing

Exist:

- To have place in the domain of reality, have objective being

By now, the incestuous circularity of language is getting a little annoying. Consider this abbreviated search for truth:

Truth is "That which is real; **reality.**"

Reality is "Having an actual **existence.**"

Existence is "**Actuality;** reality."

Actuality is "Existing objective **fact.**"

Fact is "**Truth** attested by direct observation."

In addition to the circularity of these relatively few words defining each other, let's take a cue from the definitions of *exist* and *existence* and add the term *being*.

Being:

- Existence
- That which exists or is conceived as existing

Be:

- To have or take place in the world of fact; to exist, occur, happen
- To have place in the objective universe or realm of fact, to exist
- To come into existence
- To be the case or the fact

For the most part, these new words simply add to the circularity of definitions that is becoming very familiar in this exercise. . . .

From time to time throughout these definitions, and now in the definition of *be*, the quality of objectivity has appeared as part of the background of a definition. In these cases, *real* does not just have existence, it has "objective existence"; *actuality* is not just a matter of fact but of "objective fact." Now, to *be* is to have a place in the "objective universe." Implicit in these uses is the contrast between objectivity and subjectivity.

Subjectivity:

- The quality or condition of viewing things exclusively through the medium of one's own mind or individuality
- The character of existing in the mind only

Subjective:

- Relating to the thinking subject, proceeding from or taking place within the subject; having its source in the mind

In stark contrast, *objective* is defined this way:

Objective:

- That which is external to the mind

The truth about *truth* eventually comes down to the recognition that we know most of the world through our minds. Moreover, we recognize that our individual minds are not altogether reliable. We have colloquial phrases such as "a figment of your imagination," and we realize that people often "see what they want to see." Simply put, the subjective realm refers to the possibly inaccurate perceptions and thoughts we have through the medium of our minds, yours and mine, whereas the objective realm refers to that which lies outside and is independent of our minds. We often term that objective realm *reality,* and term *true* a statement that accurately describes reality.

A couple of snags lie hidden in this construction of objectivity. First, neither you nor I, perceiving reality through our subjective minds, can know whether we perceive it accurately or not. The following scene should make the matter painfully clear.

Imagine that you are sitting in a room that has a small window with a view into another room. A light located in the other room can be turned on or off. Reality in this illustration is simply whether the light is on or off in the other room. Truth is a function of your ability to say accurately whether the light is on or off.

At first impression, nothing could be simpler. I turn the light on in the other room, and you say, "The light is on." I turn it off, and you say, "The light is off." This would be a model of objectivity.

The defect in this model is that your mind and its subjectivity have not been taken into account. But imagine that the small window before you has two shutters. The first shutter has a picture of the other room with the light on, and the second has a picture of the room with the light off. Sometimes the first shutter will close your view of the other room, sometimes the second shutter will, and sometimes there won't be any shutter—but you'll never know.

Now when I ask you whether the light is on in the other room, you will answer based on what you see, but what you see may be the open window or it may be one of the shutters. If you see one of the shutters, the scene you see may correspond with the real condition of the room or it may not.

Relating this illustration to real life, however, you would not be conscious of the possibility that you were looking at a shutter; instead, you would think that what you perceived was reality. You would feel sure that you knew the truth about whether the light was on or off because you saw it with your own eyes. And even if you became aware of the existence of the shutters, you couldn't be sure of reality because you still wouldn't know if what you were seeing was the other room or one of the shutters.

The point of this illustration is that you have no way out. In the normal course of life, you cannot be sure that what you see is really there. But there's a bigger problem than this. Given the subjectivity of your mind, you can't be sure there is *anything* out there at all. In the two-room illustration, maybe there is no window and no other room—only two shutters. Maybe it's all in your mind. How could you ever know?

The answer to both of these dilemmas is the same. If you can't be sure that what your mind tells you is true, you can at least gain some confidence in that regard if you find that my mind has told me the same thing. You say the light is on, and I say the light is on: case closed. Now you may feel doubly sure you know the light is on, not to mention that there's a window, a room, and a light.

Ultimately, our only proof of objectivity is intersubjectivity, and some dictionaries even define *objectivity* that way. When different subjects—with their individual, error-prone subjectivities—report the same thing, we conclude that what they report is objective, existing, actual, factual, real, and true.

Thus, the basis of truth is agreement. Basically, things are true if we agree they are. When Copernicus first said that the earth revolved around the sun, few people agreed; *today*, most people agree. We say that this view is not only true today but was true when Copernicus first expressed it, and was even true before Copernicus. But we say all that today when virtually everyone agrees with the view. Moreover, if all the world's astronomers were to announce a new discovery showing the sun revolved around the earth, we'd soon be saying that Copernicus was wrong and that the sun had always revolved around the earth, even before Copernicus.

When you think about the past history of agreements that were eventually overturned, you won't find much basis for confidence in what you and I now agree to be so. . . . [M]ost of what we "know" today will be thrown out as inaccurate tomorrow.

Where does science figure in all this? What about social science? Don't they offer an exception to this? Aren't they a dependable channel to the truth?

Ultimately, science—social or otherwise—also operates on the basis of agreement: in this case, agreement among fellow scientists. But there are some differences. Scientists recognize that knowledge is continually changing. They know that what they know today may be replaced tomorrow. In fact, the goal of science is to keep changing the truth.

Scientists are aware of the power of subjective biases and are explicitly committed to avoiding them in their research. Social researchers have an advantage in this respect, since bias itself is a subject matter for social science. On the other hand, social researchers have a disadvantage in that their subject matter—religion and politics, for example—is more likely to provoke personal biases than is the subject matter of the natural sciences.

For scientists, observation is a conscious and deliberate activity, whereas it is generally casual and semiconscious for most people in normal life. Thus, you might mistakenly recall that your best friend wore a blue dress yesterday, when it was really green. If you had been recording dress colors as part of a research project, however, you wouldn't have made that mistake.

Moreover, scientists have developed procedures and equipment to aid them in making observations. This also avoids some of the mistakes we make in casual observations. For example, scientists are explicit about the basis for their agreements. Rules of proof are contained within the system of logic prevailing at the time.

More important, perhaps, in the context of this essay, scientists are explicit about the intersubjective nature of truth. Peer review is an established principle: Scientists review each other's work to guard against errors of method or reasoning. Scientific journals perform what is called a gatekeeper function in this regard.

Articles submitted for publication are typically circulated among independent reviewers—other scientists knowledgeable in the area covered by the article. Unless the reviewers agree that the article represents a sound and worthwhile contribution to the field, it will not be published.

Scientists are by no means above error, however. Being human, they are susceptible to all the human foibles that afflict nonscientists. Though the scientific enterprise commits them to keeping an open mind with regard to truth, individual scientists can grow attached to particular views.

To understand the nature of science, it is essential to recognize that scientific knowledge at any given time is what scientists agree it is. Because scientific proof is fundamentally based on agreement among scientists, scientific knowledge keeps changing over time. It is probably unavoidable that we see this evolution of scientific knowledge over time as a process through which we get closer and closer to the truth. This view cannot be verified, however. All we can know for sure is that what we know keeps changing.

We can't even bank on views that haven't changed for a long time. Bear in mind, for example, that the idea that the earth was stationary and the sun moved was accepted much longer than our current view has been. Years ago, when I was living in a house on the slopes of a volcano in Hawaii, I took comfort in knowing that the volcano hadn't erupted for 25,000 years and hence probably wouldn't ever erupt again. Then I learned that its previous period of dormancy had been longer than that.

In the case of scientific knowledge, changes are generally occurring faster, not slower, than in the past. . . . [W]hat we learn about social life is often changed by just having the knowledge we've gained. On the whole, then, we'd do better simply to settle for the thrill of discovery than to worry about whether what we've discovered is the ultimate truth or simply a new and currently useful way of viewing things.

REALITY AS A COLLECTIVE HUNCH

4

Strange Creatures: The Meme Machine

Susan Blackmore

(2000)

We humans are strange creatures. There is no doubt that our bodies evolved by natural selection just as other animals' did. Yet we differ from all other creatures in many ways.

On the one hand, we are obviously animals comparable with any others. We have lungs, hearts and brains made of living cells; we eat and breathe and reproduce. Darwin's theory of evolution by natural selection can successfully explain how we, along with the rest of life on this planet, came to be here, and why we all share so many characteristics. On the other hand, we behave quite differently from other animals. Now that biology has so successfully explained much of our similarity with other creatures we need to ask the opposite question. What makes us so different? Could it be our superior intelligence, our consciousness, our language, or what?

A common answer is that we are simply more intelligent than any other species. Yet the notion of intelligence is extremely slippery, with interminable arguments about how to define it, how to measure it, and to what extent it is inherited. Research in artificial intelligence (AI) has provided some nice surprises for those who thought they knew what makes human intelligence so special.

In the early days of AI, researchers thought that if they could teach a computer to play chess they would have reproduced one of the highest forms of human intelligence. In those days the idea that a computer could ever play well, let alone beat a Grand Master, was unthinkable. Yet now most home computers come with passable chess programmes already installed, and in 1997 the program *Deep Blue* beat World Champion Garry Kasparov, ending unquestioned human supremacy at the game. Computers may not play chess in the same way as humans, but their success shows how wrong we can be about intelligence. Clearly, what we thought were human beings' most special capabilities may not be.

If intelligence does not provide simple answers, perhaps consciousness might. Many people believe that human consciousness is unique and is responsible for making us human. Yet scientists cannot even define the term 'consciousness'. Everyone knows what their own consciousness is like but they cannot share that knowledge with anyone else. This troublesome fact—the subjectivity of consciousness—may explain why for most of this century the whole topic of consciousness was more or less banned from scientific discussion. Now at last it has become fashionable again, but scientists and philosophers cannot even agree on what an explanation of consciousness would look l ike. Some say that the 'Hard Problem' of subjectivity is quite different from any other scientific problem and needs a totally new kind of solution, while others are sure that when we fully understand brain function and behaviour the problem of consciousness will have disappeared.

Some people believe in the existence of a human soul or spirit that transcends the physical brain and explains human uniqueness. With the decline in religious belief fewer and fewer people intellectually accept that view, yet most of us continue to think of ourselves as a little conscious 'me' inside our brain; a 'me' who sees the world, makes the decisions, directs the actions and has responsibility for them.

As we shall see later, this view has to be wrong. Whatever the brain is doing it does not seem to need help from an extra, magical self. Various parts of the brain carry on their tasks independently of each other and countless different things are always going on at once. We may feel as though there is a central place inside our heads into which the sensations come and from which we consciously make the decisions. Yet this place simply does not exist. Clearly, something is very wrong with our ordinary view of our conscious selves. From this confused viewpoint we cannot say with certainty that other animals are not conscious, nor that consciousness is what makes us unique. So what does?

WHAT MAKES US DIFFERENT?

What makes us different is our ability to imitate.

Imitation comes naturally to us humans. Have you ever sat and blinked, or waved, or 'goo gooed', or even just smiled, at a baby? What happens? Very often they blink too, or wave, or smile back at you. We do it so easily, even as an infant. We copy each other all the time. Like seeing, it comes so effortlessly that we hardly think about it. We certainly do not think of it as being something very clever. Yet, as we shall see, it is fantastically clever.

Certainly, other animals do not take naturally to it. Blink, or wave, or smile at your dog or cat and what happens? She might purr, wag her tail, twitch, or walk away, but you can be pretty sure she will not imitate you. You can teach a cat, or rat, to beg neatly for its food by progressively rewarding it, but you cannot teach it by demonstrating the trick yourself—nor can another cat or rat. Years of detailed research on animal imitation has led to the conclusion that it is extremely rare. Though we may think of mother cats as teaching their kittens to hunt, or groom, or use the cat door, they do not do it by demonstration or imitation. Parent birds 'teach' their babies to fly more by pushing them out of the nest and giving them the chance to try it than by demonstrating the required skills for them to copy.

Perhaps more telling is that we do not have separate words for radically different kinds of learning. We use the same word 'learning' for simple association or 'classical conditioning' (which almost all animals can do), for learning by trial and error or 'operant conditioning' (which many animals can do), and for learning by imitation (which almost none can do). I want to argue that the supreme ease with which we are capable of imitation, has blinded us to this simple fact—that *imitation* is what makes us special.

IMITATION AND THE MEME

When you imitate someone else, something is passed on. This 'something' can then be passed on again, and again, and so take on a life of its own. We might call this thing an idea, an instruction, a behaviour, a piece of information . . . but if we are going to study it we shall need to give it a name.

Fortunately, there is a name. It is the 'meme'.

The term 'meme' first appeared in 1976, in Richard Dawkins's bestselling book *The Selfish Gene*.

At the very end of the book he asked an obvious, if provocative, question. Are there any other replicators in addition to genes on our planet? The answer, he claimed, is 'Yes'. Staring us in the face, although still drifting clumsily about in its primeval soup of culture, is another replicator—a unit of imitation.

As examples, he suggested 'tunes, ideas, catch-phrases, clothes fashions, ways of making pots or of building arches'. He mentioned scientific ideas that catch on and propagate themselves around the world by jumping from brain to brain. He wrote about religions as groups of memes with a high survival value, infecting whole societies with belief in a God or an afterlife. He talked about fashions in dress or diet, and about ceremonies, customs, and technologies—all of which are spread by one person copying another. Memes are stored in human brains (or books or inventions) and passed on by imitation.

In a few pages, Dawkins laid the foundations for understanding the evolution of memes. He discussed their propagation by jumping from brain to brain, likened them to parasites infecting a host, treated them as physically realised living structures, and showed how mutually assisting memes will gang together in groups just as genes do. Most importantly, he treated the meme as a replicator in its own right.

If Dawkins is right then human life is permeated through and through with memes and their consequences. Everything you have learned by imitation from someone else is a meme. But we must be clear what is meant by the word 'imitation', because our whole understanding of memetics depends on it. Dawkins said that memes jump from 'brain to brain via a process which, in the broad sense, can be called imitation'. I will also use the term 'imitation' in the broad sense. So if, for example, a friend tells you a story and you remember the gist and pass it on to someone else then that counts as imitation.

You have not precisely imitated your friend's every action and word, but something (the gist of the story) has been copied from her to you and then on to someone else. This is the 'broad sense' in which we must understand the term 'imitation'. If in doubt, remember that something must have been copied.

Everything that is passed from person to person in this way is a meme. This includes all the words in your vocabulary, the stories you know, the skills and habits you have picked up from others and the games you like to play. It includes the songs you sing and the rules you obey. So, for example, whenever you drive on the left (or the right!), eat curry with lager or pizza and coke, whistle the theme tune from *Neighbours* or even shake hands, you are dealing in memes. Each of these memes has evolved in its own unique way with its own history, but each of them is using your behaviour to get itself copied.

Take the song 'Happy Birthday to You'. Millions of people—probably thousands of millions of people the world over—know this tune. Indeed, I only have to write down those four words to have a pretty good idea that you may soon start humming it to yourself. Those words affect you, probably quite without any conscious intention on your part, by stirring up a memory you already possess. And where did that come from? Like millions of other people you have acquired it by imitation. Something, some kind of information, some kind of instruction, has become lodged in all those brains so that now we all do the same thing at birthday parties. That something is what we call the meme.

Memes spread themselves around indiscriminately without regard to whether they are useful, neutral, or positively harmful to us. A brilliant new scientific idea, or a technological invention, may spread because of its usefulness. A song like Jingle Bells may spread because it sounds OK, though it is not seriously useful and can definitely get on your nerves. But some memes are positively harmful—like chain letters and pyramid selling, new methods of fraud and false doctrines, ineffective slimming diets and dangerous medical 'cures'. Of course, the memes do not care; they are selfish like genes and will simply spread if they can.

MEMES OF THE NEW AGE

One day in 1997, a young student came to interview me for his media project. After several predictable questions he said 'Dr. Blackmore, you are well known for your theory that alien abductions are really a form of sleep paralysis. Well I have experienced sleep paralysis *and* I have been abducted by aliens, and I can tell you they are not the same thing at all.'

It was my turn to ask the questions. Over many hours he told me of multiple abductions, starting when he was five years old and continuing into his adulthood. He told of aliens landing in the fields outside his house, of their visits to his bedroom and of operations they performed on him inside their spaceship. To top it all he showed me a tiny metallic object that the alien creatures had implanted in the roof of his mouth and which he had removed after two weeks of discomfort. Would I, with my 'closed mind' on UFOs, be prepared to analyse it scientifically?

Naturally I said yes. My own sceptical view of abductions was open to test by just this kind of object. There have been thousands of claims that people have been abducted, and several well-known academics prepared to support them. The stories are fairly consistent, and the people who tell them are known to be of at least average intelligence and education, and generally psychologically healthy. But absolutely no convincing physical evidence has ever been provided, unless you count some stained clothing and a few previous 'implants'. But you never know, this one might be it—every scientist's dream—an object of unimaginable consequence—a piece of technology from an alien civilisation. Of course I wanted to analyse it.

The analysis was simple and so was the answer. The mysterious object, though it looked very much like other 'implants' under the electron microscope, turned out to be made of dental amalgam. The young man was partly disappointed and partly relieved, but as far as I know he is still convinced that he has been abducted, even though he is not now so frightened of the creatures implanting more objects in his body.

So what is going on? Accusing these people of either making up their incredible stories, or suffering delusions, is unfair when many of them (and I have met many) appear perfectly ordinary, sane people. They have clearly been frightened by something that has happened to them, and are convinced that aliens are to blame.

ALIEN ABDUCTION AS A MEMEPLEX

I suggest that the aliens are a memeplex; a memeplex consisting of the idea of four-foot high skinny, large-headed creatures with big black eyes, an image of the ships they come in and the operations they perform, their intentions in visiting our planet, and all the other details we are fed through the media. Interestingly, the alien intentions vary with the group you favour. Followers of John Mack are inclined to the ecologically friendly type of alien who is coming to warn us of impending catastrophe, while followers of the Jacobs' school are abducted as part of an alien breeding programme making half-human-half-alien babies to invade our planet.

The memetic approach to alien abductions is to ask why these ideas should propagate so successfully, when they are not true. There is no mystery about why true and useful ideas should propagate successfully—they do so because people want and can use them. So memetics does not provide much advantage over other ways of looking at the world when it comes to understanding the success of good scientific theories or accurate news. However, memetics does help when it comes to explaining the spread of untrue, bizarre, and even harmful ideas. One such is alien abduction.

One key to alien abduction experiences is the phenomenon of sleep paralysis. During dreaming sleep most of our muscles are paralysed so that we do not act out our dreams. By the time we wake up this paralysis has usually worn off and we know nothing about it (unless experimenters intervene). However, the mechanism that keeps waking and dreaming apart can sometimes fail, especially in people who work shifts or have very disrupted sleep. Sometimes people wake up, can look around and think clearly, and yet are quite unable to move. Common sensations accompanying the paralysis include buzzing and humming noises, vibrations of the body or bed, a powerful sense that there is somebody or something in the room with you, and strange lights floating about. Since sexual arousal in dreams is common this can also persist into the paralysis. Sometimes, people feel as though they are being touched or pulled or even lifted from their bodies. If you recognize the symptoms, and can keep your cool, the best response is to relax and wait; the paralysis wears off within a minute or two. If you try to struggle you only make matters worse.

If you have no idea what is going on, the experience can be terrifying, and a natural reaction is to blame someone or something, or to seek an explanation. In previous periods of history and different cultures, various 'explanations' have been available. The incubus and succubus of medieval times were evil spirits sent to tempt the wicked into sexual activity. Until the early twentieth century, people in the south of England blamed witches for what they called 'hag-riding,' and even today there are people in Newfoundland who have been visited by the 'Old Hag' who comes at night to sit on their chests and stop them breathing. Kanashibari in Japan, Kokma in St. Lucia, and the Popobawa in Zanzibar are just some of the other current sleep paralysis myths. These myths are all successful memes.

Our culture is now full of stories of outer space, spaceships, UFOs, and sinister aliens. If you suffer from sleep paralysis and do not know what it is, your mind supplies the most readily available 'answer'. Once you start to think about aliens in a terrified and paralysed state, the aliens will seem all the more real. No wonder people think they have been abducted.

This explanation is supported by evidence that abductees suffer sleep disturbances, including sleep paralysis, more often than control groups. I would expect, although it has not been tested, that people who understand the psychological basis of sleep paralysis are unlikely to have abduction experiences, because they already have a better explanation for their experience.

Some people have only faint memories of disturbing experiences and are left wondering what happened. If they come across a hypnotist who specialises in 'recovering memories' of alien abduction then they are encouraged to relive the experience again and again until the story they tell comes to be indistinguishable from a real memory and is full of details of the aliens and their craft.

But this is not the whole story. The myth of abduction is a successful set of memes for other reasons too. For one thing, it is extremely hard to test, which has protected it from being demolished. The aliens, after all, are so clever that they can slip in through your ceiling without disturbing the plaster, whisk you away, do their wicked experiments and put you back, all without anyone else seeing you, or them. They are also adept at suppressing your memories of the abduction, and you may be left only with a fragment of uncertain memory and a tiny unexplained scar on your leg or nose. It may take an experienced hypnotist (who has plenty of experience with other abductees and knows just what questions to ask) to bring your full 'memory' back. The aliens are rarely captured on radar or successfully photographed because they have such advanced technology. And if you want to know why no government has evidence of alien landings, well you know the answer—there's a conspiracy. Governments do, of course, have whole spaceships and even frozen alien bodies in store but they employ lots of people to ensure the evidence is concealed and the public is never allowed to know. If you wonder why none of these employees has ever let on, this just proves how powerful the conspiracy is. Interestingly, evidence that might appear to be *against* the myth, such as demonstrating that a claimed implant is really a filling, has almost no effect. Strong believers quite rightly point out that one piece of negative evidence cannot disprove their beliefs, and non-believers never thought it was an implant in the first place.

The abduction memeplex has been enormously successful and we can now see why. First it serves a genuine function. That is, it provides an explanation for a scary experience. I suspect that if my student had known about sleep paralysis before he had his first abduction experience, it never would have turned into an abduction experience. Second, the idea appeals in modern American (and to a lesser extent European) culture. Humans, like many of their primate relatives, have evolved to defer to high-status males and to be afraid of them. God thrives on this natural tendency but so too do the more modern wonderful beings, who use the trappings of our scientific world and prey on genuine fears of technology. Third, the idea is promoted by television companies who have viewers eager to watch sensational programmes, and participants eager to tell their

amazing, unique, fantastic, first-hand, real-life stories and to feel very special (and possibly even get rich) by doing so. And finally, the idea is more or less irrefutable, and protected by a more or less plausible conspiracy theory.

Just how good the protection is will determine how long the memeplex lasts. Like a virus, it will spread to infect as much of the susceptible population as it can reach and then, like a virus, stop spreading. Because its only genuine function depends on people being ignorant about sleep paralysis, the dissemination of scientific understanding of sleep may undermine it. Also, as many people ask for concrete evidence and none is forthcoming, the claims may eventually wear thin. Since this kind of television feeds on novelty and surprise, the producers will not keep asking abductees to come and tell their amazing stories forever. This particular memeplex, although successful, has a limited life. Others look a bit more secure.

DEATH AND THE TRUTH TRICK

Research shows that people of all ages and backgrounds have somewhat similar experiences when they come close to death and are revived. Although most experience nothing, those who do report experiences tend to describe going down a dark tunnel toward a bright light, leaving the body and viewing their body from above, travelling to a beautiful place where beings of light await them, occasionally experiencing scenes from their life replayed all at once, and finally having to make a difficult decision to return to ordinary life. Normally, the experience is happy and peaceful, although occasionally it can be hellish. Above all, it feels absolutely real—'realer than real'. I have had this experience myself (although I was not close to death) and it was vivid, beautiful, absolutely realistic, and had a dramatic effect on my life. Reports from as long as two thousand years ago and from many different cultures suggest that the basic experience is common to humans everywhere and can affect them profoundly.

The core features of this complex experience can be understood in terms of what is going on in a brain under stress. For example, the surprisingly positive emotions are probably due to the brain releasing endorphins (morphine-like chemicals) under stress. Fear and stress also result in widespread random firing of neurons throughout the brain which, depending on where it occurs, has different effects. For example, stimulation of the temporal lobes (which can be done experimentally) can induce floating and flying sensations, memory flashbacks, and feelings of religious significance. Perhaps most interesting is the origin of the tunnel. Cells throughout the visual system are organised so that many are devoted to the centre of the visual field and far fewer to the periphery. So when all the cells fire randomly, the effect is like a bright light in the middle fading out toward the edges, or bands and lines in spirals and rings. This may be the origin of the near-death tunnel as well as the tunnels that are common in Shamanistic drawings and certain drug experiences.

Some near-death experiencers are happy to find rational explanations, but many reject them. They know they saw Jesus. He was as real as real can be. They know that they have a spirit that left their body, travelled down the tunnel and went to heaven. And they know their experience is proof of life after death.

What is interesting from the memetic point of view is that Christians typically see Jesus while Hindus meet Hindu deities. Some people encounter 'beings' of no particular religion, but there is no recorded case in which a religious person has met a deity from a different religion. Some Christians even meet St. Peter at his pearly gates, while Hindus are more likely to be judged by Chitragupta who has their names written in

his great book. Americans are likely to go along with the heavenly beings they meet while Indians are more likely to resist when they meet Yamraj, the King of the Dead, or his messengers, the Yamdoots, who have come to take them away. Americans are likely to meet their mothers but Indians rarely encounter female figures.

The experienced 'realness' of the visions leads many people who have them to reject any naturalistic explanation at all, and in the scientific literature the debate is dichotomised between those who are convinced that near-death experiences (NDEs) are evidence of life after death and those, like myself, who are not. In fact, the experience cannot be evidence of life after death because all the people who described the experiences were still alive. Nor can any naturalistic explanation, however full and satisfying, prove there is *no* life after death. So the argument is ultimately sterile. But from the memetic point of view this is not the issue. Instead, we should ask a different question—why are NDE memes so successful?

The answer is similar to that for abductions. The NDE story serves real functions. First, there are underlying brain states that predispose certain kinds of experience when people come close to death and which cry out for explanation. These are interpreted with the memes available to that person at the time, whether those memes come from television, science, or their religious upbringing. The classic NDE story also serves another function in reducing fear of death and providing reassurance about the meaning and purpose of life. Fear of death is a far more potent motivator than fear of sleep paralysis, and the desire for life after death an excellent hook for NDE memes. Memes do not need to be true to be successful.

They do, however, *claim* to be true. Natural selection has generally equipped us to choose ideas that are true over those that are false. Our perceptual systems are designed to provide as accurate a model of the external world as possible. Our capacity to think and solve problems is designed to give true rather than false answers, so in general, true memes should thrive better than false ones. But this provides an opportunity for deception—for truth mimicry. First, false claims can sneak into memeplexes under the protection of true ones. We might call this the 'truth trick'. Second, memes can simply *claim* to be true—or even 'The Truth'. So, for example, UFO believers claim that the conspiracy is suppressing The Truth. NDEers claim to have Seen The Truth with their own eyes. And believers in God and life after death know The Truth. This is a slightly different version of the 'truth trick', for it need have no element of validity at all.

Finally, NDE memes use the 'altruism trick'. People who come close to death and survive are often changed by the experience, becoming more caring of others and less concerned with themselves. The limited evidence available suggests that this change is a function of simply facing up to death, not of having a near-death experience, but when NDEers behave altruistically this helps spread their NDE memes—'I'm a nice person, I'm not so selfish now, believe me. I really did go to heaven'. Wanting to agree with this honestly nice person helps spread the memes. And if the NDE survivor really does help you, then you may take on the NDE memes as a way of returning the kindness. Thus, NDE memes spread, and among them is the idea that people who have had NDEs behave more altruistically.

The Christian version of NDEs depends heavily on the idea that only good people go to heaven. Having a beautiful NDE implies you are a good person and should be believed. This also means that people who have hellish NDEs are less likely to report them, and their memes will do less well (not to mention the fear and loneliness they must feel if they cannot talk about their experiences). Disbelievers in life after death and researchers who pursue brain-based explanations are treated as nasty people who, if only they were nicer, would come to The Truth—another tactic that gives heavenly NDE memes the edge. No one wants to share the beliefs of a nasty person.

If we have to set naturalistic explanations against heavenly ones, then a memetic viewpoint is far more compatible with the former. But memetics cannot settle this impossible issue one way or the other. What it can do is explain why powerful myths spread through whole cultures and provide a shape for some of the most profound experiences of people's lives. These strange experiences are, like all our experiences, dependent on a brain state that has been shaped by both genes and memes. I suggest we will come to understand them better when we stop trying to draw a line between 'real' and 'unreal' experiences, and ask how particular experiences are created by natural and memetic selection.

From alien abductions and near-death experiences we can glimpse a general formula for certain kinds of successful memeplex. Take a highly emotional naturally occurring human experience with no satisfactory explanation, provide a myth that appears to explain it, and include a powerful being or unseen force that cannot easily be tested. As optional extras include other functions such as social coercion (the Old Hag gets you when you do wrong), reduction of fear (you'll live forever in heaven), use the altruism trick (good people have this experience or believe this myth) or the truth trick (this explanation is The Truth).

Until recently, no one designed such memeplexes on purpose. They were designed by memetic selection. We may imagine that hundreds of thousands of myths and stories have been invented over the millennia and passed on by thousands and millions of people. The few that survived were the ones that had all the good tricks to aid their recall and propagation. Modern culture is the legacy of thousands of years of memetic evolution.

PART II

LANGUAGE AND SELF-AWARENESS

SHARED MEANING IS THE BASIS OF HUMANNESS

Jodi O'Brien

Imagine that you have just been kicked in the knee. How do you respond? Your immediate physical response is probably an upward jerk of the leg. Perhaps a rush of air and a surprised gasp escape your lips. In a behaviorist's terms, the blow to the knee is considered the stimulus, and your direct, physical response is your jerking leg and cry of pain. This physical response to the stimulus of being kicked is the same for most humans.

In addition to this physiological response, you are likely to have reactions that are not as predictable. How do you respond to the person who kicked you? You may kick the person in return. You may apologize for being in the way. You may flee. Your response to the person who kicked you depends on how you *interpret* the incident. Do you perceive it to be an act of aggression, an accident, a playful joke? Your interpretation of the incident is in turn based on the situation and the cues you pick up from the person who kicked you. If you are in a crowded space and the kicker smiles apologetically, you are likely to interpret the act as an accident and to respond accordingly. If you have been reading quietly in an empty room and the kicker glares at you menacingly, you are more likely to interpret the kick as an act of aggression rather than as an accident.

Symbolic interactionists are interested in the process of assigning meaning to actions and in the responses that follow. The meaning that you assign to being kicked determines how you will respond to the kicker and, in turn, how the kicker will respond to you. That is, how you *perceive* the incident will determine how you *feel* about it and your subsequent course of action. This perception will also be the basis for how you store the event in your memory and recall it later.

A jerk of the knee and a cry of pain may be predictable, universal, physical responses. However, there is nothing inherent in the interpretation that can be placed on the event. To symbolic interactionists, the most interesting aspects of human behavior are those that take place when we assign meaning to our own actions or interpret the actions of others. Although it is possible to chart direct stimulus-response patterns in human behavior, symbolic interactionists maintain that these patterns are of limited interest in understanding human behavior and social institutions. Most noteworthy behavior involves a process of *interpretation* between stimulus and response. Thus, the interesting question for the student of human behavior is not what the objective stimulus is (for example, the blow to the knee) but what *meaning* the receiver of the kick assigns to the stimulus (how the blow is perceived). It is the process of assigning meaning that determines how people feel and act.

Symbolic interactionists claim that symbolic activity mediates between stimulus and response. This essay explores the implications of being symbol-using creatures who interpret the world. We will also discuss human thought as a process of symbolic gestures achieved through the acquisition of language. From this perspective, social behavior is a manifestation of shared patterns of symbolic meaning.

Physical reality seems to recede in proportion as man's symbolic activity advances. (p. 99, Reading 6)

This quote is taken from the writings of a well-known philosopher, Ernst Cassirer (see Reading 6). Cassirer claims that humans do not respond directly to the physical universe. Rather, we perceive our environment selectively (are you paying attention to your feet right now, or just the words on this page?) and then we think about what we perceive. As Cassirer notes, "instead of dealing with the things themselves man is in a sense constantly conversing with himself" (p. 9, Reading 6). For Cassirer, humans do not exist in a direct state of nature; rather we exist in worlds in our head, worlds made up of commonly understood meaning, symbols, and conversations with ourselves. Cassirer is also considering that, like all animals, we have the capacity to respond directly to the physical world (you still flinch when you touch a thorny object), but that as our species has evolved in symbol use, we are less and less attuned to the natural world (we don't hear or see at the same frequency as many animals do, we can't sense changing weather patterns, and so forth). In short, we are less likely to *exist* in nature and increasingly likely to *think* about it. Thinking is a symbolic activity.

To exist in a state of nature is to be nonconscious, nonreflective, and nonsymbolic. In such a state, the organism is propelled directly by the forces of nature, which include internal physiology and the external environment. In contrast, the symbolic creature is able to comprehend, comment on, and organize behavior in accordance with abstract representations. This does not necessarily imply that humans are superior to animals, nor does it suggest that we do not have an animal form (biologically and physiologically). The point is that most noteworthy human activity is symbolic (abstracted from a direct state of nature). Thus, the symbolic interactionist focuses on human behavior and culture *primarily* as expressions of meaningful symbol systems.

A comparison with elephants illustrates this point. When elephants meet, one places its trunk in the mouth of the other. Body temperature and fluids in the mouth indicate whether each elephant is in a state of arousal or aggression or is passive. This encounter triggers the appropriate response—copulating, fighting, fleeing, or traveling together. The elephants, as far as we can tell, do not think about this encounter; they do not interpret the event and assign meaning to it. They simply engage in a series of stimulus-response behaviors with each other in a direct state of nature.

The difference between humans and elephants is that humans do not respond directly to the physical environment. Rather, humans impose symbolic interpretations on experiences and draw conclusions based on these interpretations. It is true that we are attuned to odors and other physiological manifestations of our fellow humans and that we may experience these directly rather than through a process of interpretation. But most of our responses to others are determined by our *interpretation* of various cues. These cues include physiological features, gestures, and accessories and adornments, such as clothing and other symbolically meaningful items.

Those of you who have driven across a border into another country know that it is the duty of border guards to ascertain whether you are bringing merchandise into (or out of) the country in violation of international or national laws. These guards cannot read your mind, nor can they experience directly whether you are telling the truth when you claim not to be carrying illicit goods. The guards infer your intentions based on symbolic cues, such as the type of car you are driving, your ethnicity and gender, and the style of your clothes and hair. In other words, the guards guess at your integrity based on their symbolic interpretation of you and the situation. Similarly, the police officer who stops a motorist cannot experience directly whether the accosted driver will be hostile or compliant. The officer makes inferences—guesses—based on available symbolic cues.

Consider the process of cue interpretation you engage in when you are trying to figure out if the person across the room is flirting with you. In such a situation, you have no direct knowledge of the person's actual mood or intentions. Is this someone who is a potential date? If you approach, will the person be hostile or receptive? Before making a move, you will assess the situation and consider many cues and will probably discuss the cues with a group of friends before deciding to act. All of this is interpretive behavior.

Social psychologists are interested in the signs people use to make inferences and the reliability of these signs for predicting the intentions of others. This predictability is not a function of directly reading the "natural" world. Rather, it is the product of the symbolic codes through which we assign meaning to objects. Human behavior is not determined directly from our encounters with the physical world. Our bodies are physical entities that exist in the physical world, but our experience of our own bodies, of other people, and of things in our environment is anchored in the internal conversation that constitutes our conscious thought.

Symbolic Meaning: It's the Name, Not the Thing

Herbert Blumer is credited with first use of the term *symbolic interactionism* to define the approach to the study of human behavior and society that we have been discussing (Fine, 1990). Blumer (1969), who was a sociologist at the University of California, Berkeley, suggested three basic premises:

1. Humans act toward a thing on the basis of the meaning they assign to the thing.

2. Meanings are socially derived, which is to say that meaning is not inherent in a state of nature. There is no absolute meaning. Meaning is negotiated through interaction with others.

3. The perception and interpretation of social symbols are modified by the individual's own thought processes. (p. 2)

Naming (Assigning Meaning)

When we make sense of a person, space, or occasion, we attach meaning to it. This process is known as *naming*. Naming has three elements: a label, a cognitive-emotive evaluation, and a recommended course of action. The conceptual names we have for persons, spaces, and things include each of these three components. Consider a round, hollow tube made of glass with a single closed end. We can label it a glass. But *glass* is a fairly abstract term, and we might each be imagining a different type of glass. Let's say that we further narrow the meaning of the label by imposing additional classifications—for example, the glass has a stem attached. This description suggests a wineglass, which we may evaluate subjectively as, perhaps, an elegant sort of glass or a decadent sort of glass. Regardless of the specific glass that each of us has in mind, we are in agreement as to its general purpose. That is, we know the recommended course of action toward the object that we have labeled a glass: It is a container from which we can drink.

Philosophers, linguists, and cognitive social psychologists agree that to name something is to know it. This process of object identification is central to human perception and appraisal. Humans name things and then respond according to the implications carried by the name. They do not respond to the essential nature of the thing itself. Thus, we say that human behavior involves not just a response to a stimulus but a process—naming—that mediates between stimulus and response.

Try the following exercise. Work up some saliva in your mouth. How does it feel? Now spit it into a glass. How does it look? Now drink it up. Most of you will probably respond to this last request with some hesitation. Yet I have simply asked you to reabsorb a substance that, in fact, you naturally generate and swallow continually all through the day. Why did you hesitate? Probably because you have an aversion to spit. This aversion is not a direct response to the natural essence of the substance. It is an aversion to the *name,* not the thing. Your reaction is based on your idea of spit—a symbolic process whereby you have conceptualized bodily fluids that have left the body as repulsive. The name *spit* implies an evaluative response ("Yuck!") and a course of action (avoidance). You do not respond directly to the nature of the fluid. Instead, you assign meaning to the fluid and respond to that meaning. Cassirer reminds us of the words of the Greek philosopher Epictetus: "What disturbs [people] are not things, but their opinions and fancies about things."

Symbols and Signifying

Emotional and behavioral responses to environmental stimuli are shaped by this naming process. Thus, behavior differs not in response to a particular stimulus but in response to the meaning that human actors assign to the stimulus. Consider Jane Wagner's "The Search for Signs of Intelligent Life in the Universe" (Reading 2). In this story, Trudy the "bag lady" is giving lessons about earth life to some "space chums." She attempts to explain the difference between a can of Campbell's soup and Andy Warhol's painting of a can of Campbell's soup. "This is soup, this is art." Warhol's rendering of the can of soup is not merely a stand-in image for the soup itself; rather, as art it constitutes a class of meaning unto itself. In contemplating the painting, a person doesn't consider whether the actual soup tastes good; instead, the person evaluates the worth of the painting based on what he or she knows about art. *Soup* and *art* are both abstract ideas, although each term conjures a different meaning. These different meanings imply different lines of action or responses toward the object. Similarly, the "conversation" we are now having, in which we are removed from one another's immediate presence, would not be possible if we did not share the abstract ideas of *book, reading,* and a similar symbolic system called *written English.*

What are these symbols that we use to assign meaning to our experiences? Symbols are abstract representations. Brand names are a form of symbolic representation that even young children are familiar with. Many parents are familiar with the exasperation of trying to locate, not to mention pay for, a pair of shoes that a teenager insists he or she *must* have. It's often the case that the materials and construction of the desired brand differ little from those of other brands, but the brand itself stands for something—in this case, being hip or cool—and in a social world, the brand makes all the difference.

Consider another example: A rectangular piece of cloth with red and white horizontal stripes and a blue square in the upper left-hand corner filled with white stars has significance beyond this physical description—it is a symbol, an abstract representation, of the United States of America.

A flag is a symbol not only of the nation "for which it stands," but also of the social convention of dividing the world into mutually exclusive geopolitical units known as nations. The U.S. flag not only stands for what is considered uniquely American, but also symbolizes a *distinction* from other nations. To be American is also to *not be* Russian, for example. Thus, a symbol defines both what something is and what it is not. The essence of the item you hold in your hands at this moment is tree pulp (assuming you are reading this as an actual book and not electronically) flattened and pressed into connected sheets with splotches of ink all over them. Most likely you do not think of the item this way, but rather as a book with abstract symbols in the form of written language for you to absorb. It is also likely that you do not consider the book as a source of toilet paper, although in its natural state, these pages have properties similar to those of the materials in toilet paper.

The study of semiotics and sociolinguistics is the study of the cultural systems of meaning that are conveyed through symbolic representation. Roland Barthes (1964/1967), for example, has studied food symbolism. All societies have cultural systems that *signify* what foods can be eaten and what foods should be excluded, how certain foods are supposed to be grouped (for example, breakfast, lunch, dinner, or appetizers, main courses, desserts), and the various rituals of use (table manners, picnics, feasts). Trudy's space chums have difficulty comprehending the distinction between "soup" and "art" because they do not share the symbolic understanding whereby an apparently similar material image is *assigned* to entirely different domains of meaning (food/art). In both examples, the symbolic system *signifies* how things are supposed to be grouped (classified) and how we are supposed to feel about them. Thus,

Naming = assigning symbolic meaning to things/persons/events

Symbolic meaning = a sign system that conveys messages regarding how to feel about and respond to the thing/person/event

Harlem Renaissance artist and writer Langston Hughes wrote a story called "That Powerful Drop" (Reading 5) to illustrate the significance of symbolic meaning within specific cultural contexts. In the story, Hughes's characters ponder the significance of "Negro blood." Physiologically, there is no difference between White and Black blood. However, in the context of this story—Southern states in the 1950s—identifying certain people as having "Negro blood" conveys the symbolic message that Black blood is less desirable and more problematic than White blood. Technically speaking, the characters in the story cannot see one another's blood, nor can most of us most of the time. It's not the blood per se, but the idea of what the blood stands for—in this case, skin hues and phenotypical characteristics such as nose and other facial features that are presumed to signify one's standing as a human being in relation to other human beings. This racial marker is mutually understood by people who share a cultural system of meaning premised on racial differentiation and prejudice. In another culture in which differentiation is based more on class position than on race, the phenotypical characteristics associated with "blood" might be less noticeable, but people's accents—do they sound educated or not?—might be highly notable and symbolically significant in creating social hierarchies.

Symbols, Experience, and Culture

Because symbols are abstractions, we can use them to transcend the concrete environment and to have experiences that are not rooted in time and space. Abstraction also allows us to remember, fantasize, plan, and have vicarious experiences. When we imagine something, we formulate an image, a symbolic representation, of something that is not present in the immediate state of nature. Remembering is a similar activity. When we fantasize and make plans, we are manipulating symbolic images. Vicarious experience allows us to learn by observing the actions of others; we need not experience everything ourselves to comprehend what someone else is experiencing. This is a key element in individual survival and in the transmission of culture.

Without symbol systems, human experience and culture would not be possible. To comprehend the significance of the human ability to engage in symbolic abstraction, consider how much time you spend in the presence of your intimate friends versus how much time you spend thinking, remembering, fantasizing, and planning about them. Ask yourself if it would be possible for you to experience love for someone if you could not imagine (represent conceptually) the person when he or she was not actually physically present. A great deal of human symbolic activity involves learning to sort and group people into social roles (for example, stranger, teacher, judge, soldier, priest). Culturally specific expectations are associated with different social roles. For example, we think, feel, and behave very differently with friends than we do with grandparents.

In 1970 a case study titled "Yes, Father-Sister" (Reading 7), neurologist Oliver Sacks describes a woman who has lost the ability to recognize and name people according to recognized social groups. She has a neurological disorder associated with language processing that has left her without "any 'center' to the mind." She is no longer able to comprehend or express symbolic *meaning*. All social roles are the same for her and can be interchanged at will. Thus, someone in her presence can be "Father," "Sister," or "Doctor" at any given moment. Imagine how disconcerting it would be if one of your parents called you indiscriminately "child," "parent," "lover," "salesclerk." People who are unable to engage in appropriate symbolic activity are trapped on islands, isolated from meaningful relationships. They are unable to access and express the cultural "script" that others share and find significant.

THE SOURCE OF SYMBOLIC
SYSTEMS OF MEANING: LANGUAGE

The primary way humans use symbols is through language. Language is a system of symbols that allows humans to communicate and share meaning. Language gives humans the capacity to become social creatures—which is to say, the capacity to comprehend and to participate in culture.

The basic unit of language is the word. Words are symbols that denote the meaning of something. Words can be conveyed through writing, speech, and sign. The power of words to represent the range of human activity can be seen in the following exercise: Try listing words for as many emotions as you can think of. Then read your list to someone else. Chances are that the person will comprehend the states of being that each word suggests. Now, select an emotion word that is well understood among those who share your language and attempt to communicate this emotion to someone simply by touching their arm (no fair trying to write out the name). General emotions such as anger, lust, and fright may possibly be communicated by touch. However, it is likely that the list of emotion words that you generated conveys a much wider range of emotion and greater emotional subtlety than you can communicate effectively without resorting to words. Does this exercise show that there are more emotions than there are ways of expressing them? No. It implies that there are as many emotions as there are words for describing them.

Words give meaning to our experiences. In many instances, a physiological state of arousal is meaningless and may even go unnoticed until the experience has been named.

Consider, for example, a young woman who, while traveling by plane, experiences a queasy stomach and sweaty palms. She is unable to ascertain whether she is experiencing airsickness or attraction to the person sitting next to her. Both experiences entail the same physiological responses, but different courses of action are deemed appropriate, depending on whether she labels the experience *nausea* or *love*.

Meaning consists not only of isolated words or names, but also of the additional ideas and experiences associated with particular words. An instructive exercise is to note words that have parallel definitions but carry very different connotations. *Bachelor* and *spinster* are one example. They are defined, respectively, as the male and female state of being unmarried. But *spinster* raises much less attractive images in the minds of most people than does the term *bachelor.* Language comprehension involves much more than just knowing words. Meaningful communication is based on shared understanding of a *cluster of meanings* associated with particular words. Recall the discussion of naming—words are the basis of naming and provide not only identification of objects, but also instructions for how to feel and respond to objects and situations that we encounter.

Language and Social Behavior

Language, thought, and social behavior are closely related. We interact with each other by observing ourselves and steering our behavior according to our interpretations of the expectations of others. This process is internal; we *talk* with ourselves about how to name situations, how to name our role in the situation, and how to assign meaning to others in the situation. We determine recipes for action based on the meaning we assign to the situation and experience feelings about the situation depending on how we have defined it. Without language, we would be unable to assign meaning to our own actions or to bring our actions in line with the expectations of our culture. We would be unsocialized.

Language and Socialization

Much research has been done on the relationship between language acquisition and human development. Researchers are particularly interested in the few documented cases of "feral children"—children raised in isolation from adult human interaction. In the 1940s, sociologist Kingsley Davis described the case of a young girl who was subjected to extreme isolation during crucial developmental years (Reading 8). In presenting her case, Davis pursued the hypothesis that social intercourse is necessary for the development of language and intellectual activity. Without exposure to language, children do not achieve the ability to engage in normal human activities. According to Davis's study of Anna and a parallel case, Isabelle, interaction with others is a key to kick-starting language acquisition and corresponding socialization. The question Davis couldn't fully address was whether there was a cut-off age for language acquisition. At the time he was writing in the 1940s, it was generally believed that if children did not have normal exposure to language within the first few years of life, their cognitive-emotive behavior would be limited.

Further evidence was reported in 1974 by linguist Sue Curtiss and her colleagues at UCLA. The case involved a young girl, Genie, who was discovered at age 14 living in horrendous circumstances of neglect. She had been kept hidden in an attic tied to a child's potty chair with almost no human engagement for most of her 14 years. At the time she was taken into protective custody Genie appeared physically to be around 6 years old and had the cognitive development of a 2- to 3-year-old. Within months of proper care and many skilled people working with her, she had progressed to the level of 4–5 years old and was eventually able to move to foster care, where she became part of the family and continued to develop language and emotional skills. When Curtiss and her colleagues wrote their progress report 3 years later, they noted that

> [Genie's] language acquisition so far, despite the tragic isolation that she has suffered, despite the lack of linguistic input, despite the fact that she had almost no language for the first fourteen years of her life, Genie is equipped to learn language and she is learning it. No one can predict how far she will develop linguistically or cognitively. The progress so far, however, has been remarkable, and a tribute to the human capacity for intellectual development. (p. 544)

Further information about the relationship between language and social behavior comes from studies of people who have experienced damage to the language centers of the brain. The neurological disorders that result from such damage are referred to as *aphasia*. These disorders usually impair a person's ability to engage in normal social interactions. Recall the woman described by Oliver Sacks who could no longer recognize social roles and therefore responded to everyone as if they were anything that popped into her mind.

Other researchers have documented similar consequences of aphasia (see, e.g., Lindesmith, Strauss, & Denzin, 1991). In one tragic case, a well-known symphony conductor contracts a virus that impairs his neurological language center. As a result of this impairment, his conceptual memories are wiped out to the extent that he no longer recognizes his own wife. When she hugs him, his sense of smell and touch serve as triggers that remind him, briefly, who she is. Thus reminded, he sobs and clings to her and asks where she has been for so long. Minutes later, when she returns to his room from taking a break, the entire scene is played over again. Without the capacity for language, specifically the ability to formulate a concept of *wife* and retain all his memories of her as wife in his mind, the man simply doesn't know who she is. Together, these curious and often tragic cases suggest to neurologists, linguists, and social psychologists that the relationship between the brain, language, and social behavior is highly complex and also crucial for what we consider "normal" human behavior.

Language and Thought

As powerful as a single word may be in assigning meaning, the full power of language is in the relationships among words, or the *structure* of language. Words are juxtaposed in such a way as to convey one meaning rather than another. For example, the words *cat, dog,* and *chases* each suggest a particular meaning. The first two are nouns that denote certain types of four-legged mammals, and the third is a verb that names a particular action. Presumably we have a shared understanding of the general class of meaning to which these words refer. Now, consider the alignment of the words *dog chases cat* and *cat chases dog.* Do both combinations suggest the same event? Try writing other possible combinations of these three words. How many of these combinations make sense to you?

The structure of language, called *syntax,* comprises the rules of grammar. Syntax allows humans to combine words to create strings or clusters of meaning more complex than the meaning suggested by isolated words. The syntax of a language also permits us to convey entirely different meanings by recombining symbols, as in the example of *cat, dog,* and *chases.* Another interesting feature of syntax is that humans appear to learn and use the rules of language without necessarily being aware of what these rules are. For example, although most people can give an example of a yes-or-no question (for instance, "Is your car red?"), very few could state the formal rules for constructing such a sentence. Nevertheless, people recognize when the rules have been violated. (We will return to this simple but profound point in Part III in discussing the similarities between language syntax and "social grammar." As with rules of grammar, people are implicitly aware of the rules of interaction and recognize it when these rules have been violated, but they cannot state explicitly what these rules are.) Thus, the power of language derives from the human ability to employ rules to convey meaning without necessarily being aware of the rules. Humans are continually able to represent new meanings, and these novel combinations will be understood by others, provided that the combinations follow accepted syntactical structure.

Linguists refer to the ability to formulate novel but mutually understood statements as the *generative* property of language. Humans generate their own ideas and codes of meaning; in other words, language and meaning are not predetermined by nature. The extent of this generative ability is profound—it allows small children to formulate novel sentences (rather than just repeating preprogrammed speech) and nuclear physicists to develop abstract and complex theories.

Nonetheless, not all combinations of words are equally meaningful or likely to be generated. What is intriguing is that people can ascertain the difference between gibberish and mutually comprehensible strings of words.

The meaning of what is generated is determined by the underlying structure of the language, or the particular patterns of discourse. Different languages entail distinct patterns of meaning. These language patterns profoundly influence culture. In short, different languages provide different ways to make sense of ourselves, others, and our circumstances.

During the past few decades, social scientists have debated whether language shapes thought or thought comes before language. George Herbert Mead (see Reading 12) theorized that, in the process of learning language, the mind develops and becomes structured in a manner that reflects the individual's culture. Anthropologists, too, have pursued the claim that distinct languages cause people of different cultures to view and think about the world differently. For instance, many anthropologists demonstrate ways in which different cultures divide up time and space as expressed in their various languages. Some cultures express time in a nonlinear way as compared with Western linear conceptions, for example.

Think about what your relationship to time might be if you could refer only to the concepts of *now* and *not now* and had no notion of *past* or *future*.

Language: Innate or Socially Produced?

Scholars agree that language is a bedrock of human behavior and social life. There is disagreement, however, about whether the capacity for language is socially learned (nurture) or physiologically innate (nature). Linguists such as Noam Chomsky consider language an innate human ability. Chomsky (1972) has made a convincing case that the *deep structure* of language is more complex than anyone could learn through social contact alone. He argues instead that one feature of the human brain is an inborn *computational modality*. That is, humans are hardwired to comprehend and generate abstract representations and to piece together complex strings of words that require them to compute various possible lines of meaning and association. This activity is so complex and so unavailable to general consciousness that, according to Chomsky and his supporters, it would be impossible for children to perform the incredible mental gymnastics required to communicate if the brain were not hardwired for language.

One of Chomsky's students, Steven Pinker, author of the popular book *The Language Instinct* (1994), offers a simple but noteworthy illustration of the computational modality using these three statements:

Ralph is an elephant.

Elephants live in Africa.

Elephants have tusks.

Pinker continues thus:

Our inference-making device [innate computational processor] . . . would deduce "Ralph lives in Africa" and "Ralph has tusks." This sounds fine but isn't. Intelligent you, the reader, knows that the Africa Ralph lives in is the same Africa that all the other elephants live in, but that Ralph's tusks are his own. (p. 79)

Pinker's point is that people make this distinction on the basis of common sense, but there is nothing in the words themselves that conveys this common sense; thus, the meaning is not logically explicit. The fact that people can make the distinction without hesitation is, for Pinker, a demonstration that people know things independently of the words used to express them. Thus, the way people think about and structure understanding precedes the language they use to express this understanding. Language itself contains so many ambiguities and oversimplifications that humans must have a larger organizing structure in mind before speaking; otherwise, we would be unable to fill in the blanks and sort through the ambiguities with such unconscious ease.

Rather than debate the nature/nurture aspects of language, there is a more useful and accurate (albeit more complex) way to think about human behavior. Chomsky is probably correct, in part—the aptitude for abstraction and linguistic computation is innate; it is a fundamental property of humanness. But what is the *source* of the conceptual abstractions that the mental processors are acting on? This puzzle is the untold story in contemporary linguistics.

Let's return to Ralph the elephant. If humans were preprogrammed with information, infants would be born knowing all there is to know about elephants, Africa, and tusks. Clearly, this is a silly speculation. Let's assume, then, that we comprehend the distinction between the sharing of one Africa by many elephants and the possession of tusks by single elephants because we have realized a distinction between being physically located in a space and possessing physical traits. Our ability to generalize these experiential observations and to incorporate them in language is the *natural, innate* computational element that Chomsky refers to.

Language, Thought, and Social Interaction

Our capacity for the abstraction and computation necessary to process language may be innate, but the actual content is *learned* through social contact. What Chomsky and colleagues can't tell us, as observers trying to make sense of human behavior, is the *significance* of Ralph in particular and of elephants, tusks, and Africa in general. This significance—people's attitudes, feelings, and behavior toward such strings of words—is determined by the context in which the words appear and the attributes people have learned to associate with these contexts. This is a social process. That is, the human capacity for the abstraction and computation necessary to process language may be innate, but the actual content is learned through social contact. Adults use language to teach children not necessarily *how* to think about, say, elephants, tusks, or Africa, but *what* to think about these things—and subsequently, how to respond. People don't need to be taught how to respond physiologically—for example, *what* to do physically when kicked in the knee. But the range of possible *social* responses to being kicked that occur to people, and their understanding of the appropriateness and consequences of a given response, are the result of having been taught, through language, what they should think about the incident. The name that we assign to an experience acts as a sort of shorthand that shapes our subsequent thoughts about how to respond to the situation. In this way, language, experience, and thought continually interact—they are mutually interconnected in a dynamic system loop.

A helpful (but limited) analogy is the relationship between computer hardware and software. Here, the human brain is the hardware and language the software. Humans are born with brain hardware that enables us to engage in complex, computational, abstract, representational thought, but the content—*what* we process—is input by others who provide us with meaningful ideas through the activity of language. In the same way that a computer cannot operate in a fully functional manner without being switched on and fed some software, there is considerable evidence that children who are not exposed to language fail to develop normal conceptual abilities.

Oliver Sacks (1989) explores this issue in his book about the congenitally deaf, *Seeing Voices*. On the basis of several case studies, Sacks asserts that those born without hearing are endowed with the same intellectual capacity as those who can hear. But in an oral-based culture, the congenitally deaf, in the absence of aural stimulation, fail to develop conceptual thought. The cognitive hardware of the congenitally deaf child may be in perfect working order, but the hearing impairment (deficient perceptual hardware) gets in the way of the necessary start-up. The child's language ability never really gets turned on. For this reason, many deaf children are mistakenly assumed to be developmentally disabled. However, when a congenitally deaf infant is exposed to sign language, the child not only proceeds along a normal course of cognitive development, but actually begins to communicate in sign earlier than hearing infants learn to talk. Some specialists suggest that the ability for communication is switched on before the infant's vocal cords are physically ready for speech. Signing infants don't have to wait for their vocal cords to develop.

"Feral children"—children raised in isolation—such as Anna and Genie described earlier, are often assumed to be developmentally disabled. The capacity for abstract thought may be innate, but in order to develop this capacity, children must be exposed to language-based social interaction. When children are isolated from social interaction, they are effectively denied access to the "switch" (language-based interaction) and the "software" (a specific language) through which conceptual thought develops. The implication is that humans require social stimulation and exposure to abstract symbol systems—language—in order to embark on the conceptual thought processes that characterize our species. Thus, human experience is given meaning and is organized through language, and the ability to form complex strings of words and to communicate verbally is innate. But the source of the meaning assigned to the words is social.

Experience and Conceptualization

In the late 1600s, the philosophers Gottfried Leibnitz and John Locke are said to have exchanged letters in which they debated the following question: Imagine a man who is born blind. How will he learn the difference between the concepts *triangle, square,* and *circle*? Like all children, he can be given blocks to play with. The "platonic solids" consist of blocks that are triangular, cubed, and round. The blind man could learn to tell the difference through his sense of touch. He could *feel* each one and be told the name, and then, whenever someone mentioned the name (for example, *triangle*), he would have an *idea* of what the triangle was. Now here is the question: What would happen if the man were suddenly able to see, and the three different blocks were set in front of him? Would he be able to *see* the difference and name them accordingly, or would he still have to *feel* each one? According to Locke, the man would not necessarily be able to *see* the different shapes. His *conceptual* understanding of the shapes would be based in his *experience* of touch. Leibnitz disagreed. He believed that the man would be able to conjecture what each was, based on the concept that he held in his mind (a concept that was rooted in the experience of touch, not sight).

One question that interests sociolinguists is what is the connection between experience, perception, and conceptualization. In the title case from his well-known book *The Man Who Mistook His Wife for a Hat,* Oliver Sacks (1987) describes a man who has retained his ability for abstraction but has lost the "commonsensical" meaning used in ordinary, day-to-day conversation. While trying to figure out what is wrong with the man, Sacks holds up a glove and asks him what he sees. The man studies it for a bit and then declares that it appears to be "some sort of container with five out-pouchings." Technically, this is an accurate description of the item. But is it meaningful? Sacks notes that seeing is a matter of conceptualization, not just sensory perception. We use our conceptual knowledge to make sense of what our senses are seeing. *Meaningful* concepts resonate with experience. A "glove" is really not the same thing as "a continuous surface unfolded on itself with five out-pouchings." The implication is that we learn conceptual meaning *in context.* Socially meaningful concepts reflect specific experiences—experiences that are visceral and imbued with feeling. Thus, when studying how children learn to assign meaning to concrete things in their environment, we have to take into account both the social content and the context of experience.

The Russian linguist and social psychologist Lev Vygotsky wrote extensively on the relationship between language and thought during the 1920s, but his writings have been available in English only since 1960 (e.g., Vygotsky, 1961). Writing independently of the North American debate regarding linguistic determinism, Vygotsky, like his fellow Eastern European social scientists, was inclined to see a mutual relationship between individual neurological-cognitive processes and social learning.

According to Vygotsky (1961), children make sense of their environment by grouping things (persons and objects) that seem, through their own experiences, to be connected. The result is *complex thinking*—grouping seemingly related things into *complexes.* Concepts generated from the complexes stand in as abstract representations of meaningful relationships between concrete things and experiences. For instance, a child's experiential complex for the family dog might consist of "Ruffy, big, furry, tail, bite." Conceptual thinking replaces the complex when the child learns the general name for the complex— *dog.* Initially, the child may attempt to interchange the specific name, *Ruffy,* with the general name, *dog.* She may also experience fear whenever she hears of a dog, because her complex or cluster includes the experience *bite.*

Comprehending a parent's explanation that "the dog will bite you only if you pull its tail" is an illustration of the child's ability to generalize based on abstract thinking. It is also an illustration of the child's ability to learn vicariously through language. The child needn't experiment with pulling the tail of every dog that she encounters to gain an understanding of the conceptual relationship between tail pulling and biting. Rather, she uses the words to formulate a more general idea and to encode both the specific experience and her general interpretation of it in her memory. Thus, she begins to develop a lexicon of experientially based, but socially influenced, names complete with evaluative action codes ("Dogs might bite, so beware").

Vygotsky (1961) bridges individual and social-cognitive linguistics through his idea of "pseudo-concepts," generalizations that are like concepts but that are actually complexes.

In the experimental setting, the child produces a pseudo-concept every time he surrounds a sample with objects that could just as well have been assembled on the basis of an abstract concept. For instance, when the sample is a yellow triangle and the child picks out all the triangles in the experimental material, he could have been guided by the general idea or concept of a triangle. Experimental analysis shows, however, that in reality the child is guided by concrete, visible likeness and has formed only an associative complex limited to a certain kind of perceptual bond. Although the results are identical, the process by which they are reached is not at all the same as in conceptual thinking.

Pseudo-concepts predominate over all other complexes in the child's thinking for the simple reason that in real life complexes corresponding to word meanings are not spontaneously developed by the child. The lines along which a complex develops are predetermined by the meaning a given word already has in the language of adults. . . . This language, with its stable, permanent meanings, points the way that a child's generalizations will take. The adult cannot pass on to the child his mode of thinking. He merely supplies the ready-made meaning of a word, around which the child forms a complex. . . . The pseudo-concept serves as the connecting link between thinking in complexes and thinking in concepts. Verbal intercourse with adults becomes a powerful factor in the intellectual development of the child. (pp. 67–69)

In other words, in normal cognitive development, children operate at the nexus of practical experience and pre-established concepts. Even as they are forming experience-based groupings of things in their environment, children are learning to use ready-made words that are based on conceptualizations that are already socially established. Thus, both the child's individual experiences and social influence, through preexisting language, play a role in the development of language and cognition. The resulting conceptual knowledge is a combination of experience and social learning. Concrete experiences enable the child to *comprehend* in an embodied, fully feeling way, but without preexisting language, the child would not be able to transcend the immediate experience and make sense of it in a more general way.

LANGUAGE, THOUGHT, AND CULTURE

We can discuss language and cognitive structure from one additional angle. Chomsky and others, in their zeal to make the point that humans have an innate capacity for representational computation, have rejected the notion that the particular language of a culture determines the way in which members of the culture classify persons, objects, and events. Many social scientists disagree and argue instead that language categories do in fact structure the way in which individuals perceive, organize, evaluate, feel about, and respond to their experiences and environments.

Language, as we have already noted, has evaluative and emotive components that make up concepts. Concepts, as Vygotsky details, do not necessarily emerge through direct experience but, rather, are handed down to us through social intercourse with other members of our culture. These concepts shape the way we focus on, categorize, evaluate, respond to, and remember people, objects, and events; in other words, language *does* structure perception and experience.

Consider the following string of words: *Race is not biologically significant; it is only skin deep.* When considered from a physiological perspective, this statement may indeed be correct. But is it representative of social reality as you know it? The words *Black* and *White* carry an entire history of meaning in the United States and shape, to a large extent, the way in which Americans are inclined to see, evaluate, and remember others. In short, race in the United States is hugely socially significant.

In learning the customs and belief systems of their culture, people learn to classify humans in a variety of ways. They learn that humans can be big, small, short, tall, fat, thin, brown, white, and so forth, and each of these "names" includes emotive-evaluative components and behavioral cues that reflect cultural categories and hierarchies.

Let us stress the point one more time—left to themselves, free of preexisting cultural influence, children would develop complexes that reflect their particular experience with their environment. The meaning that they would attach to words (that is, the abstract concepts and names that emerge from complexes) would thus accurately portray the world as they experienced it. Note that this path of learning leads to a process of stereotyping—if the child is bitten by a big fluffy animal that she later comes to name *dog*, she may, through experience, later presume that all such creatures are scary. In other words, her conceptual notion would stand in for real experience and would shape her response to such creatures. However, as generations of social scientists have demonstrated, children do not learn in a vacuum. More likely, they begin forming complex associations between named objects, people, and spaces by asking, "What's that?" The concepts given to them by others contain preconceived associations that reflect shared cultural evaluations. For example, a child who has no direct experience with lions can still learn to identify a picture of one—and, importantly, the child will absorb whatever emotive-evaluative-behavioral cues are expressed by the adults explaining what a lion is. Thus, a child can become scared by the *thought* of a lion without ever encountering one, because he or she has been taught that lions are scary.

This process of naming has serious implications for the structure of society. For instance, without ever having encountered a Mexican American before, an Anglo-American middle-class employer can find herself wondering whether a young "Mexican-looking" job candidate from Texas is likely to be "illegal." The sources of such a stereotype are subtle and varied. The employer may not even be aware that she is evaluating the candidate on the basis of a preconceived stereotypical framework. Her response is based on a cultural representation and may have no connection to her direct experience or the abilities of the prospective employee. But her naming process includes a prejudgment that will shape her response prejudicially.

By studying the way in which names are associated with other emotive-evaluative words, we can learn a great deal about the way in which culture, through language, shapes the thoughts of individuals. The power of language is not simply in words but in the manner in which words can be combined to create clusters of meaning. These associations, which we often take as common sense, reflect social divisions, not natural ones.

Categorization

The process of naming is an act of categorization. To categorize is to impose conceptual categories of meaning on things. Categories group things in a way that makes them related and gives them order. Cognitively, this is a very efficient operation, similar to a mental filing system (consider the system you use to organize your notes and materials for different classes so that you don't have to file through one big heap every time you need something). But categorization also presents problems. In her book *Mindfulness* (1990), Harvard psychologist Ellen Langer (Reading 9) describes these cognitive processes of categorization and some of the pros and cons of this amazing human ability. For instance, when we meet someone new, we classify the person according to cues such as type of clothing, posture, age, and so on. Based on these cues, we make an immediate assessment based on categorical associations (e.g., White, well-dressed, older, gray hair = gentleman = safe). We do this in the blink of an eye and largely without thinking about it. This ability for categorical associative thinking enables us to move quickly and efficiently through our daily encounters.

We navigate our way through life by making categorical assessments and responding to the information contained in the category as we have previously learned it. For the most part, this serves us well. We can be efficient in our thinking, and we don't have to experience everything directly in order to know what the situation requires of us. When you enter a classroom, for example, the category *classroom* implies a particular set of behaviors and expectations. You fall into a behavioral response that is routine, or mindless. However, if you entered what you *thought* was a classroom and heard music and saw people drinking and dancing, your mind would be triggered into a more aware, or mindful state, and you would begin searching for additional cues to make sense of the situation. The way in which we learn to recognize and define social situations is discussed in more detail in Part V. For now, the point is that our ability to make categorical assessments is a product of learning language—when we learn a word or an idea, we learn it as part of a categorical cluster of meanings.

The downside of this process is that we tend to get stuck or trapped in previously learned categories. This can lead to what Langer calls "mindlessness," or behavior that is based on unconscious or semiconscious routine. Mindlessness occurs when we rely on a few symbolic cues to fill in all the blanks. In Reading 9, Langer offers many interesting examples of mindlessness. The dangers of mindlessness include the omission of other relevant features of the event, object, or person in question and the perpetuation of stereotypes. For example, elderly people or persons with physical disabilities are often assumed to be mentally deficient as well because, stereotypically, it is common to categorically associate physical slowness or inability with mental slowness.

Stereotypes and Default Assumptions

All languages suggest categorical relationships based on notable symbols. In the absence of specific information, people use these general word-based categories to impose meaning on other people, things, and events and to form judgments that they then rely on to guide their behavior. A border guard, in the absence of any other information, may see a male motorist with a shaved head and five earrings in one ear and infer, based on categorical associations among clusters of symbols, that the person is a punk who is trying to smuggle drugs into the country. We all have a tendency to make these types of inferences. What is your general image of the border guard? Where did you get this information? Your ability to envision a border guard, even if you have personally never encountered one, is a process of stereotyping. You conjure up the image based on a classification scheme. Chances are that the border guard you imagine is based on a stereotype. This stereotype is most likely White, male, wearing some type of uniform, and carrying a gun.

Douglas Hofstadter (1986) is another scholar who writes about stereotypical thinking. He discusses what he calls *default assumptions.* Default assumptions are preconceived notions about the likely state of affairs—what we assume to be true in the absence of specific information. Given no other information, when I mention "secretary," you are likely to assume the secretary is female, because female and secretary are associated stereotypically. In the absence of specific details, people rely on the stereotype as a default assumption for filling in the blanks. Default assumptions have a tendency, in Hofstadter's words, to "permeate our mental representations and channel our thoughts" (p. 137). For instance, given the words *cat, dog,* and *chases,* you are likely to think first of a dog chasing a cat.

This line of thought reflects a default assumption that, all else being equal, the dog is more likely to chase the cat than the other way around. Default assumptions are based on prior experience and knowledge of circumstances. They are useful in that people cannot always afford the time it would take to consider every theoretical possibility that confronts them.

Nonetheless, it is possible that default assumptions are wrong. How might we know if we are wrong? Do we change our default assumptions if the facts of the situation prove us wrong? If, for example, the motorist with the shaved head does not have drugs in the car, will the border guard revise her categorical expectations regarding the association between a male with a shaved head and earrings, and drug use? Or will she reaffirm these general expectations with an account to herself of why this particular incident was different? She may decide that the person does, in fact, have drugs in the car but she was simply unable to find them. Thus, the general category shaved head = punk = drugs is confirmed. Furthermore, the category may now be associated with deviousness as well.

Default assumptions are only one type of language-based categorization. Hofstadter is particularly interested in race-based and gender-based categorization and default assumptions. For instance, if you hear that your school basketball team is playing tonight, do you assume it's the men's team? Most people would assume so unless a qualifier were added to provide specific information. In this case, the qualifier would be "the *women's* basketball team is playing tonight." Hofstadter means to show us that language is a powerful reflection of cultural associations and stereotypes. These associations are revealed in the way we use language. The phrase "my Black doctor" reflects the cultural assumption that, all else being equal, the speaker knows that his audience does not expect the physician to be Black. He adds a qualifier, *black,* to offset the expected default assumption. Similarly, consider the practice of hyphenation in racial and ethnic labeling.

Anglo-Americans rarely refer to themselves as such. Rather, the default assumption, in the absence of a qualifier such as Japanese American, is that an American is Anglo and White. The qualifier is considered unnecessary, because it is assumed to be the default. One of the problems with default assumptions such as these is that, in addition to being taken for granted, the categorical associations tend to include notions such as "normal" and sometimes even "culturally desirable." In other words, they reflect cultural hierarchies.

Hofstadter (1986) offers another exercise for finding culture embedded in language. He refers to these as "language asymmetries" (p. 103). Consider the following terms: *Mr., Mrs.,* and *Miss.* Presumably each is the polite form of address for someone you don't know well. Why are there two terms for women and only one for men? "Well," you might respond, "it's because the Miss/Mrs. lets you know if a woman is married or not." Correct. But why is there no corresponding distinction for men? The asymmetry suggests that a woman's marital status is significant information, whereas a man's marital status is not. Indeed, in modern Western culture marital status is one of the most important bits of information about a woman. This is reflected in the prominence of language that provides this information. In recent years, the term *Ms.* has come into use as an attempt to balance this asymmetry and deemphasize a woman's marital status. However, many professional organizations still instruct their employees to use *Mrs.* as the more "appropriate" or "polite" form of address when talking with a woman of marriageable age. Clearly this particular language pattern is deeply engrained in our cultural mind.

To emphasize the arbitrariness of these entrenched linguistic patterns, Hofstadter wrote a satire (Reading 11) in which he explores the implications of racial pronouns (Black/White) and descriptive forms of address that reflect the employment status of Black Americans. The resulting essay is provocative and may even be considered offensive. As you read it, consider similarly offensive linguistic patterns that go unnoticed (and that we may even defend) because they have become mindless.

Conclusions

By way of conclusion, consider the following statements. These are real headlines that linguist Steven Pinker (1994, p. 79) collected from various newspapers:

Child's Stool Great for Use in Garden

Stud Tires Out

Stiff Opposition Expected to Casketless Funeral Plan

Drunk Gets Nine Months in Violin Case

Iraqi Head Seeks Arms

Queen Mary Having Bottom Scraped

Columnist Gets Urologist in Trouble With His Peers

It's both mundane and amazing that we understand the double meanings and the underlying humor. The computational ability required to recognize these double entendres is innate and universal, but the content of each—or rather, its double content—and, more significantly, the fact that people find the phrases funny, is a consequence of social learning.

The complicated mental process that enables *generative grammar* is a universal human feature. But the lexicon of meanings available to individuals—the concepts through which they make sense of their experiences, encode these in memory, and feel about and act on them—derives from cultural learning. That is, we are interested in what is said, not said, and how it is said—what names do and don't exist and the evaluative-emotive components of those names. Different languages represent reality differently; particular languages highlight certain features of life and leave others in the haze of preconceived thought. Names/words/concepts reveal certain lines of action and possibilities to individual humans. In this way, although it may be theoretically possible for all humans to generate infinite and similar grammars and lexicons of meanings, it is not probable that members of a given culture will do so. And that which is unnamed is unknown. This idea has been summarized by the mathematician and philosopher Bertrand Russell: "Language serves not only to express thought but to make possible thoughts which could not exist without it."

The assertion that humans process all experience through socially constructed symbol systems has been a source of both caution and enthusiasm. This tension is expressed in the following quotation from a brooding poet in *Hyperion,* a science fiction novel:

> Words are the supreme objects. They are minded things. As pure and transcendent as any idea that ever cast a shadow into Plato's dark cave of our perceptions. But they are also pitfalls of deceit and misperception. Words bend our thinking to infinite paths of self-delusion, and the fact that we spend most of our mental lives in brain mansions built of words means that we lack the objectivity necessary to see the terrible distortion of reality which language brings. . . . [Yet] here is the essence of [humankind's] creative genius: not the edifices of civilization nor the bang-flash weapons which can end it, but the *words* which fertilize new concepts. . . . You see, in the beginning was the Word. And the Word was made flesh in the weave of the human universe. Words are the only bullets in truth's bandolier. (Simmons, 1990, pp. 190–191)

It is important to emphasize that the process of associating meaning with objects, persons, and events is an ongoing negotiation. In making sense of your world, you negotiate abstract meanings with others (interpersonal negotiation), and you negotiate with yourself to maintain a "fit" between your existing conceptual frameworks and concrete experience (intrapersonal negotiation). This negotiation is done through language. Even as you experience "unnamed" thoughts, emotions, and acts, you make sense of them by fitting them into the language categories available to you. For instance, if your culture has a category for *lover* that includes the default assumption that a pairing consists of one each of the two sexes, and you are paired with someone of the same sex, then you may find yourself without a name for this person when conversing with others who want to know about your attachments. Your experience may lead you to search for alternative names that stretch the category of *husband/wife* to include those who have same-sex partners. In this way, you are generating new concepts reflective of individual experience, but the fact that you have to search for a name for what you do or who you are is structured by the existing cultural classifications. Now, with the widening acceptance of marriage equality, many same-gender couples continue to use the terms *husband* and *wife* to refer to their partners. Consider the implications of adopting this culture-laden terminology for something as presumably radical as same-gender marriage. Some proponents of its use consider it a representation of their acceptance into one of this society's most significant institutions. Others consider if an offensive adaptation of an oppressively patriarchal institution and seek alternative language for their union. Regardless of which position you take, words are powerful cultural tools of belonging.

Meaning is not simply "out there"; it is something that is created and recreated through everyday interactions. The process reflects the complex interplay between individual experience and social structure. Individuals are constantly working to fit their individual thoughts and experiences into a form that can be expressed and shared with others. As you read the articles in this section, ask yourself the following: How do significant categories of language carve up my world? How do various concepts shape who I think I can be and what I think I can do? What are some of my default assumptions as a result of having absorbed the concepts of my culture? Am I aware that my language reflects a cultural value system?

References and Suggestions for Further Reading

Barthes, R. (1967). *Elements of semiology.* New York, NY: Hill & Wang. (Original work published 1964)

Blumer, H. (1969). *Symbolic interactionism.* Englewood Cliffs, NJ: Prentice Hall.

Brown, R. (1986). *Social psychology* (2nd ed.). New York, NY: Free Press.

Charon, J. (1989). *Symbolic interactionism* (3rd ed.). Englewood Cliffs, NJ: Prentice Hall.

Chomsky, N. (1972). *Language and the mind.* New York, NY: Harcourt Brace Jovanovich.

Curtiss, S., Fromkin, V., Krashen, S., Rigler, D., & Rigler, M. (1974). The linguistic development of Genie. *Language, 50,* 528–554.

Fine, G. (1990). Symbolic interactionism in the post-Blumerian age. In G. Ritzer (Ed.), *Frontiers of social theory* (pp. 117–157). New York, NY: Columbia University Press.

Hofstadter, D. (1986). *Metamagical themas: Questing for the essence of mind and pattern.* New York, NY: Bantam Books.

Langer, E. (1990). *Mindfulness.* Cambridge, MA: Da Capo Press.

Lee, D. (Ed.). (1980). *Wittgenstein's lectures, Cambridge 1930–1932.* Chicago, IL: University of Chicago Press.

Lindesmith, A. R., Strauss, A. L., & Denzin, N. K. (Eds.). (1991). *Social psychology* (7th ed.). Englewood Cliffs, NJ: Prentice Hall.

Mead, G. H. (1934). *Mind, self, and society.* Chicago, IL: University of Chicago Press.

Pinker, S. (1994). *The language instinct: How the mind creates language.* New York, NY: HarperPerennial.

Sacks, O. (1987). *The man who mistook his wife for a hat.* New York, NY: Harper & Row.

Sacks, O. (1989). *Seeing voices.* Berkeley: University of California Press.

Sapir, E. (1921). *Language.* New York, NY: Harcourt, Brace and World.

Simmons, D. (1990). *Hyperion.* New York, NY: Bantam.

Vygotsky, L. S. (1961). *Thought and language* (E. Hanfmann & G. Vahar, Trans.). Cambridge, MA: MIT Press.

SYMBOL USE, LANGUAGE, AND DEVELOPMENT

The readings in this section are illustrations of a basic component of symbolic interactionism. We respond to things, people, and situations in terms of the *meaning* they assign to the object, person, or event. We do not just respond to stimuli in our environment. We *interpret* the stimuli. Interpretation is an act of assigning meaning. The act of assigning a meaning or definition is known as *naming*. Language is the means for the process of making meaning and making sense of our environment. Language is an organized symbol system that enables us to think, imagine, learn vicariously, plan, direct our own behavior, and communicate with others. It is the basis of social life. Without language, individuals would not be able to learn or understand cultural expectations and would not be able to participate in social life. The study of the relationships among the brain, the mind, language, and culture is a fascinating area of research. The readings in this section illustrate some of the basic ideas that researchers agree on regarding language and social development.

"That Powerful Drop" is a brief excerpt from a story by Langston Hughes. Hughes was an artist and writer during the period in the 1920s known as the Harlem Renaissance. In this short story, the characters are pondering the significance of a "single drop of Negro blood." The story illustrates that it is the cultural meaning that matters, not the physical properties.

In the classic essay "A Clue to the Nature of Man," philosopher Ernst Cassirer describes humans as living in a symbolic world, a world of culturally created ideas, and not in a state of nature. He reminds us that it is our opinions and fancies of things that disturb (or delight) us, not the nature of the thing itself.

"Yes, Father-Sister" is a reading taken from the case files of the well-known neurologist Oliver Sacks. In this case, Sacks presents a woman who has lost the ability to name the people she encounters. She no longer recognizes the symbolic cues that enable her to place people into meaningful social categories.

"Final Note on a Case of Extreme Isolation" is a research note written by sociologist Kingsley Davis in 1947. Davis and his contemporaries were interested in the cases of children who had been raised in isolation from normal human interaction. When found, such children are considered more animal than human. They lack many of the basic signs of socialization that even severely developmentally delayed children raised in normal environments possess. Davis reviews the case of Anna and raises the question of whether it is possible for a child who is not exposed to human culture, especially language, by a certain age to ever become fully socialized.

READING QUESTIONS

1. Explain to someone the difference between responding to symbolic cues and responding directly to stimuli.

2. Practice slowing down your thinking in situations and see if you can catch yourself interpreting the situation.

3. When you encounter a stranger, what do you notice first in deciding what to think about the person?

4. Think of something that disturbs or frightens you. See if you can trace your feelings to your original experiences of naming. Is your fear or disgust based on direct experience, or is it based on an idea that you learned from someone else?

5. Consider how often you imagine or think about someone you love. If you had no language or ability for abstract thought, could you remember that person when he or she was not in your presence?

6. Think of an example of something that you've learned vicariously. How much of what you know is based on others telling you things?

7. The forms we use for expressing language influence us as much as the content of the language. Consider how your life might be different if you lived in a culture that had no written language. How would such a culture pass on learning and knowledge? Do you think people in such a culture would have stronger or weaker abilities to memorize?

SYMBOL USE, LANGUAGE, AND DEVELOPMENT

5

That Powerful Drop

Langston Hughes

(1953)

Leaning on the lamp post in front of the barber shop, Simple was holding up a copy of the *Chicago Defender* and reading about how a man who looks White had just been declared officially colored by an Alabama court.

"It's powerful," he said.

"What?"

"That one drop of Negro blood—because just *one* drop of Black blood makes a man colored. *One* drop—you are a Negro! Now, why is that? Why is Negro blood so much more powerful than any other kind of blood in the world? If a man has Irish blood in him, people will say, 'He's *part* Irish.' If he has a little Jewish blood, they'll say, 'He's *half Jewish*.' But if he has just a small bit of colored blood in him, BAM!—'*He's a Negro!*' Not, 'He's *part* Negro.' No, be it ever so little, if that blood is Black, '*He's a Negro!*' Now, this is what I do not understand—why our *one* drop is so powerful. Take paint—white will not make black *white*. But black will make white *black*. One drop of black in white paint—and the white ain't white no more! Black is powerful. You can have ninety-nine drops of White blood in your veins down South—but if that other *one* drop is Black, shame on you! Even if you look White, you're Black. That drop is really powerful. Explain it to me. You're colleged."

"It has no basis in science," I said, "so there's no logical explanation." . . .

SYMBOL USE, LANGUAGE, AND DEVELOPMENT

6

A Clue to the Nature of Man: The Symbol

Ernst Cassirer

(1944)

In the human world we find a new characteristic which appears to be the distinctive mark of human life. The functional circle of man is not only quantitatively enlarged; it has also undergone a qualitative change. Man has, as it were, discovered a new method of adapting himself to his environment. Between the receptor system and the effector system, which are to be found in all animal species, we find in man a third link which we may describe as the *symbolic system*. This new acquisition transforms the whole of human life. As compared with the other animals man lives not merely in a broader reality; he lives, so to speak, in a new *dimension* of reality. There is an unmistakable difference between organic reactions and human responses. In the first case a direct and immediate answer is given to an outward stimulus; in the second case the answer is delayed. It is interrupted and retarded by a slow and complicated process of thought. At first sight such a delay may appear to be a very questionable gain. Many philosophers have warned man against this pretended progress. "L'homme qui médite," says Rousseau, "est un animal dépravé": It is not an improvement but a deterioration of human nature to exceed the boundaries of organic life.

Yet there is no remedy against this reversal of the natural order. Man cannot escape from his own achievement. He cannot but adopt the conditions of his own life. No longer in a merely physical universe, man lives in a symbolic universe. Language, myth, art, and religion are parts of this universe. They are the varied threads which weave the symbolic net, the tangled web of human experience. All human progress in thought and experience refines upon and strengthens this net. No longer can man confront reality immediately; he cannot see it, as it were, face to face. Physical reality seems to recede in proportion as man's symbolic activity advances. Instead of dealing with the things themselves man is in a sense constantly conversing with himself. He has so enveloped himself in linguistic forms, in artistic images, in mythical symbols or religious rites that he cannot see or know anything except by the interposition of this artificial medium. His situation is the same in the theoretical as in the practical sphere. Even here man does not live in a world of hard facts, or according to his immediate needs and desires. He lives rather in the midst of imaginary emotions, in hopes and fears, in illusions and disillusions, in his fantasies and dreams. "What disturbs and alarms man," said Epictetus, "are not the things, but his opinions and fancies about the things."

From the point of view at which we have just arrived we may correct and enlarge the classical definition of man. In spite of all the efforts of modern irrationalism this definition of man as an *animal rationale* has not lost its force. Rationality is indeed an inherent feature of all human activities. Mythology itself is not simply a crude mass of superstitions or gross delusions. It is not merely chaotic, for it possesses a systematic or conceptual form.[1] But, on the other hand, it would be impossible to characterize the structure of myth as rational. Language has often been identified with reason, or with the very source of reason. But it is easy to see that this definition fails to cover the whole field. It is a *pars pro toto*; it offers us a part for the whole. For side by side with conceptual language there is an emotional language; side by side with logical or scientific language there is a language of poetic imagination. Primarily language does not express thoughts or ideas, but feelings and affections. And even a religion "within the limits of pure reason" as conceived and worked out by Kant is no more than a mere abstraction. It conveys only the ideal shape, only the shadow, of what a genuine and concrete religious life is. The great thinkers who have defined man as an *animal rationale* were not empiricists, nor did they ever intend to give an empirical account of human nature. By this definition they were expressing rather a fundamental moral imperative. Reason is a very inadequate term with which to comprehend the forms of man's cultural life in all their richness and variety. But all these forms are symbolic forms. Hence, instead of defining man as an *animal rationale*, we should define him as an *animal symbolicum*. By so doing we can designate his specific difference, and we can understand the new way open to man—the way to civilization.

NOTE

1. See E. Cassirer (1922), *Die Begriffsform im mythischen Denken*. Leipzig: B. G. Teubner.

SYMBOL USE, LANGUAGE, AND DEVELOPMENT

7

Yes, Father-Sister

Oliver Sacks

(1970)

Mrs. B., a former research chemist, had presented with a rapid personality change, becoming "funny" (facetious, given to wisecracks and puns), impulsive—and "superficial." ("You feel she doesn't care about you," one of her friends said. "She no longer seems to care about anything at all.") At first it was thought that she might be hypomanic, but she turned out to have a cerebral tumor. At craniotomy there was found, not a meningioma as had been hoped, but a huge carcinoma involving the orbitofrontal aspects of both frontal lobes.

When I saw her, she seemed high-spirited, volatile—"a riot" (the nurses called her)—full of quips and cracks, often clever and funny.

"Yes, Father," she said to me on one occasion.

"Yes, Sister," on another.

"Yes, Doctor," on a third.

She seemed to use the terms interchangeably.

"What *am* I?" I asked, stung, after a while.

"I see your face, your beard," she said. "I think of an Archimandrite Priest. I see your white uniform—I think of the Sisters. I see your stethoscope—I think of a doctor."

"You don't look at *all* of me?"

"No, I don't look at all of you."

"You realize the difference between a father, a sister, a doctor?"

"I *know* the difference, but it means nothing to me. Father, sister, doctor—what's the big deal?"

Thereafter, teasingly, she would say: "Yes, father-sister. Yes, sister-doctor," and other combinations.

Testing left-right discrimination was oddly difficult, because she said left or right indifferently (though there was not, in reaction, any confusion of the two, as when there is a lateralizing defect of perception or attention). When I drew her attention to this, she said: "Left/right. Right/left. Why the fuss? What's the difference?"

"*Is* there a difference?" I asked.

"Of course," she said, with a chemist's precision. "You could call them *enantio-morphs* of each other. But they mean nothing to *me*. They're no different for *me*. Hands . . . Doctors . . . Sisters . . .", she added, seeing my puzzlement. "Don't you understand? They mean nothing—nothing to me. *Nothing means anything* . . . at least to me."

"And . . . this meaning nothing . . . ," I hesitated, afraid to go on, "This meaninglessness . . . does *this* bother you? Does *this* mean anything to you?"

"Nothing at all," she said promptly, with a bright smile, in the tone of one who makes a joke, wins an argument, wins at poker.

Was this denial? Was this a brave show? Was this the "cover" of some unbearable emotion? Her face bore no deeper expression whatever. Her world had been voided of feeling and meaning. Nothing any longer felt "real" (or "unreal"). Everything was now "equivalent" or "equal"—the whole world reduced to a facetious insignificance.

I found this somewhat shocking—her friends and family did too—but she herself, though not without insight, was uncaring, indifferent, even with a sort of funny-dreadful nonchalance or levity.

Mrs. B., though acute and intelligent, was somehow not present—"de-souled"—as a person. I was reminded of William Thompson (and also of Dr. P.). This is the effect of the "equalization" described by Luria. . . .

POSTSCRIPT

The sort of facetious indifference and "equalization" shown by this patient is not uncommon—German neurologists call it *Witzelsucht* ("joking disease"), and it was recognized as a fundamental form of nervous "dissolution" by Hughlings Jackson a century ago. It is not uncommon, whereas insight is—and the latter, perhaps mercifully, is lost as the "dissolution" progresses. I see many cases a year with similar phenomenology but the most varied etiologies. Occasionally I am not sure, at first, if the patient is just "being funny," clowning around, or schizophrenic. Thus, almost at random, I find the following in my notes on a patient with cerebral multiple sclerosis, whom I saw (but whose case I could not follow up) in 1981:

She speaks very quickly, impulsively, and (it seems) indifferently . . . so that the important and the trivial, the true and the false, the serious and the joking, are poured out in a rapid, unselective, half-confabulatory stream. . . . She may contradict herself completely within a few seconds . . . will say she loves music, she doesn't, she has a broken hip, she hasn't. . . .

I concluded my observation on a note of uncertainty:

How much is cryptannesia-confabulation, how much frontal-lobe indifference-equalization, how much some strange schizophrenic disintegration and shattering-flattening?

Of all forms of "schizophrenia" the "silly-happy," the so-called "hebephrenic," most resembles the organic amnestic and frontal lobe syndromes. They are the most malignant, and the least imaginable—and no one returns from such states to tell us what they were like.

In all these states—"funny" and often ingenious as they appear—the world is taken apart, undermined, reduced to anarchy and chaos. There ceases to be any "center" to the mind, though its formal intellectual powers may be perfectly preserved. The end point of such states is an unfathomable "silliness," an abyss of superficiality, in which all is ungrounded and afloat and comes apart. Luria once spoke of the mind as reduced, in such states, to "mere Brownian movement." I share the sort of horror he clearly felt about them (though this incites, rather than impedes, their accurate description). They make me think, first, of Borges' "Funes," and his remark, "My memory, Sir, is like a garbage-heap," and finally, of the *Dunciad*, the vision of a world reduced to Pure Silliness—Silliness as being the End of the World:

Thy hand, great Anarch, lets the curtain fall;
And Universal Darkness buries All.

SYMBOL USE, LANGUAGE, AND DEVELOPMENT

8

Final Note on a Case of Extreme Isolation

Kingsley Davis

(1947)

Early in 1940 there appeared . . . an account of a girl called Anna.[1] She had been deprived of normal contact and had received a minimum of human care for almost the whole of her first six years of life. At this time observations were not complete and the report had a tentative character. Now, however, the girl is dead, and with more information available,[2] it is possible to give a fuller and more definitive description of the case from a sociological point of view.

Anna's death, caused by hemorrhagic jaundice, occurred on August 6, 1942. Having been born on March 1 or 6,[3] 1932, she was approximately ten and a half years of age when she died. The previous report covered her development up to the age of almost eight years; the present one recapitulates the earlier period on the basis of new evidence and then covers the last two and a half years of her life.

EARLY HISTORY

The first few days and weeks of Anna's life were complicated by frequent changes of domicile. It will be recalled that she was an illegitimate child, the second such child born to her mother, and that her grandfather, a widowed farmer in whose house her mother lived, strongly disapproved of this new evidence of the mother's indiscretion. This fact led to the baby's being shifted about.

Two weeks after being born in a nurse's private home, Anna was brought to the family farm, but the grandfather's antagonism was so great that she was shortly taken to the house of one of her mother's friends. At this time a local minister became interested in her and took her to his house with an idea of possible adoption. He decided against adoption, however, when he discovered that she had vaginitis. The infant was then taken to a children's home in the nearest large city. This agency found that at the age of only three weeks she was already in a miserable condition, being "terribly galled and otherwise in very bad shape." It did not regard her as a likely subject for adoption but took her in for a while anyway, hoping to benefit her. After Anna had spent nearly eight weeks in this place, the agency notified her mother to come to get her. The mother responded by sending a man and his wife to the children's home with a view to their adopting Anna, but they made such a poor impression on the agency that permission was refused. Later the mother came herself and took the child out of the home and then gave her to this couple. It was in the home of this pair that a social worker found the girl a short time thereafter. The social worker went to the mother's home and pleaded with Anna's grandfather to allow the mother to bring the child home. In spite of threats, he refused. The child, by then more than four months old, was next taken to another children's home in a near-by town. A medical examination at this time revealed that she had impetigo, vaginitis, umbilical hernia, and a skin rash.

Anna remained in this second children's home for nearly three weeks, at the end of which time she was transferred to a private foster-home. Since, however, the grandfather would not, and the mother could not, pay for the child's care, she was finally taken back as a last resort to the grandfather's house (at the age of five and a half months). There she remained, kept on the second floor in an attic-like room because her mother hesitated to incur the grandfather's wrath by bringing her downstairs.

The mother, a sturdy woman weighing about 180 pounds, did a man's work on the farm. She engaged in heavy work such as milking cows and tending hogs and had little time for her children. Sometimes she went out at night, in which case Anna was left entirely without attention. Ordinarily, it seems, Anna received only enough care to keep her barely alive. She appears to have been seldom moved from one position to another. Her clothing and bedding were filthy. She apparently had no instruction, no friendly attention.

It is little wonder that, when finally found and removed from the room in the grandfather's house at the age of nearly six years, the child could not talk, walk, or do anything that showed intelligence. She was in an extremely emaciated and undernourished condition, with skeleton-like legs and a bloated abdomen. She had been fed on virtually nothing except cow's milk during the years under her mother's care.

Anna's condition when found, and her subsequent improvement, have been described in the previous report. It now remains to say what happened to her after that.

LATER HISTORY

In 1939, nearly two years after being discovered, Anna had progressed, as previously reported, to the point where she could walk, understand simple commands, feed herself, achieve some neatness, remember people, etc. But she still did not speak, and, though she was much more like a normal infant of something over one year of age in mentality, she was far from normal for her age.

On August 30, 1939, she was taken to a private home for retarded children, leaving the county home where she had been for more than a year and a half. In her new setting she made some further progress, but not a great deal. In a report of an examination made November 6 of the same year, the head of the institution pictured the child as follows:

> Anna walks about aimlessly, makes periodic rhythmic motions of her hands, and, at intervals, makes guttural and sucking noises. She regards her hands as if she had seen them for the first time. It was impossible to hold her attention for more than a few seconds at a time—not because of distraction due to external stimuli but because of her inability to concentrate. She ignored the task in hand to gaze vacantly about the room. Speech is entirely lacking. Numerous unsuccessful attempts have been made with her in the hope of developing initial sounds. I do not believe that this failure is due to negativism or deafness but that she is not sufficiently developed to accept speech at this time. . . . The prognosis is not favorable. . . .

More than five months later, on April 25, 1940, a clinical psychologist, the late Professor Francis N. Maxfield, examined Anna and reported the following: large for her age; hearing "entirely normal"; vision apparently normal; able to climb stairs; speech in the "babbling stage" and "promise for developing intelligible speech later seems to be good." He said further that "on the Merrill-Palmer scale she made a mental score of 19 months. On the Vineland social maturity scale she made a score of 23 months."[4]

Professor Maxfield very sensibly pointed out that prognosis is difficult in such cases of isolation. "It is very difficult to take scores on tests standardized under average conditions of environment and experience," he wrote, "and interpret them in a case where environment and experience have been so unusual." With this warning he gave it as his opinion at that time that Anna would eventually "attain an adult mental level of six or seven years."[5]

The school for retarded children, on July 1, 1941, reported that Anna had reached 46 inches in height and weighed 60 pounds. She could bounce and catch a ball and was said to conform to group socialization, though as a follower rather than a leader. Toilet habits were firmly established. Food habits were normal, except that she still used a spoon as her sole implement. She could dress herself except for fastening her clothes. Most remarkable of all, she had finally begun to develop speech. She was characterized as being at about the two-year level in this regard. She could call attendants by name and bring in one when she was asked to. She had a few complete sentences to express her wants. The report concluded that there was nothing peculiar about her, except that she was feeble-minded—"probably congenital in type."[6]

A final report from the school made on June 22, 1942, and evidently the last report before the girl's death, pictured only a slight advance over that given above. It said that Anna could follow directions, string beads, identify a few colors, build with blocks, and differentiate between attractive and unattractive pictures. She had a good sense of rhythm and loved a doll. She talked mainly in phrases but would repeat words and try to carry on a conversation. She was clean about clothing. She habitually washed her hands and brushed her teeth. She would try to help

other children. She walked well and could run fairly well, though clumsily. Although easily excited, she had a pleasant disposition.

INTERPRETATION

Such was Anna's condition just before her death. It may seem as if she had not made much progress, but one must remember the condition in which she had been found. One must recall that she had no glimmering of speech, absolutely no ability to walk, no sense of gesture, not the least capacity to feed herself even when the food was put in front of her, and no comprehension of cleanliness. She was so apathetic that it was hard to tell whether or not she could hear. And all this at the age of nearly six years. Compared with this condition, her capacities at the time of her death seem striking indeed, though they do not amount to much more than a two-and-a-half-year mental level. One conclusion therefore seems safe, namely, that her isolation prevented a considerable amount of mental development that was undoubtedly part of her capacity. Just what her original capacity was, of course, is hard to say; but her development after her period of confinement (including the ability to walk and run, to play, dress, fit into a social situation, and, above all, to speak) shows that she had at least this capacity—capacity that never could have been realized in her original condition of isolation.

A further question is this: What would she have been like if she had received a normal upbringing from the moment of birth? A definitive answer would have been impossible in any case, but even an approximate answer is made difficult by her early death. If one assumes, as was tentatively surmised in the previous report, that it is "almost impossible for any child to learn to speak, think, and act like a normal person after a long period of early isolation," it seems likely that Anna might have had a normal or near-normal capacity, genetically speaking. On the other hand, it was pointed out that Anna represented "a marginal case, [because] she was discovered before she had reached six years of age," an age "young enough to allow for some plasticity."[7] While admitting, then, that Anna's isolation may have been the major cause (and was certainly a minor cause) of her lack of rapid mental progress during the four and a half years following her rescue from neglect, it is necessary to entertain the hypothesis that she was congenitally deficient.

In connection with this hypothesis, one suggestive though by no means conclusive circumstance needs consideration, namely, the mentality of Anna's forebears. Information on this subject is easier to obtain, as one might guess, on the mother's than on the father's side. Anna's maternal grandmother, for example, is said to have been college educated and wished to have her children receive a good education, but her husband, Anna's stern grandfather, apparently a shrewd, hard-driving, calculating farmowner, was so penurious that her ambitions in this direction were thwarted. Under the circumstances her daughter (Anna's mother) managed, despite having to do hard work on the farm, to complete the eighth grade in a country school. Even so, however, the daughter was evidently not very smart. "A schoolmate of [Anna's mother] stated that she was retarded in school work; was very gullible at this age; and that her morals even at this time were discussed by other students." Two tests administered to her on March 4, 1938, when she was thirty-two years of age, showed that she was mentally deficient. On the Stanford Revision of the Binet-Simon Scale her performance was equivalent to that of a child of eight years, giving her an I.Q. of 50 and indicating mental deficiency of "middle-grade moron type."[8]

As to the identity of Anna's father, the most persistent theory holds that he was an old man about seventy-four years of age at the time of the girl's birth. If he was the one, there is no indication of mental or other biological deficiency, whatever one may think of his morals. However, someone else may actually have been the father.

To sum up: Anna's heredity is the kind that *might* have given rise to innate mental deficiency, though not necessarily.

COMPARISON WITH ANOTHER CASE

Perhaps more to the point than speculations about Anna's ancestry would be a case for comparison. If a child could be discovered who had been isolated about the same length of time as Anna but had achieved a much quicker recovery and a greater mental development, it would be a stronger indication that Anna was deficient to start with.

Such a case does exist. It is the case of a girl found at about the same time as Anna and under strikingly similar circumstances. A full description of the details of this case has not been published, but in addition to newspaper reports, an excellent preliminary account by a speech specialist, Dr. Marie K. Mason, who played an important role in the handling of the child, has appeared.[9] Also the late Dr. Francis N. Maxfield, clinical psychologist at Ohio State University, as was Dr. Mason, has written an as yet unpublished but penetrating analysis of the case.[10] Some of his observations have been included in Professor Zingg's book on feral man.[11] The following discussion is drawn mainly from these enlightening materials. The writer, through the kindness of Professors Mason and Maxfield, did have a chance to observe the girl in April, 1940, and to discuss the features of her case with them.

Born apparently one month later than Anna, the girl in question, who has been given the pseudonym Isabelle, was discovered in November, 1938, nine months after the discovery of Anna.

At the time she was found she was approximately six and a half years of age. Like Anna, she was an illegitimate child and had been kept in seclusion for that reason. Her mother was a deaf-mute, having become so at the age of two, and it appears that she and Isabelle had spent most of their time together in a dark room shut off from the rest of the mother's family. As a result Isabelle had no chance to develop speech; when she communicated with her mother, it was by means of gestures. Lack of sunshine and inadequacy of diet had caused Isabelle to become rachitic. Her legs in particular were affected; they were so bowed that as she stood erect the soles of her shoes came nearly flat together, and she got about with a skittering gait.[12]

Her behavior toward strangers, especially men, was almost that of a wild animal, manifesting much fear and hostility. In lieu of speech she made only a strange croaking sound. In many ways she acted like an infant. "She was apparently utterly unaware of relationships of any kind. When presented with a ball for the first time, she held it in the palm of her hand, then reached out and stroked my face with it. Such behavior is comparable to that of a child of six months."[13] At first it was even hard to tell whether or not she could hear, so unused were her senses. Many of her actions resembled those of deaf children.

It is small wonder that, once it was established that she could hear, specialists working with her believed her to be feeble-minded. Even on nonverbal tests her performance was so low as to promise little for the future. Her first score on the Stanford-Binet was 19 months, practically at the zero point of the scale. On the Vineland social maturity scale her first score was 39, representing an age level of two and a half years.[14] "The general impression was that she was wholly uneducable and that any attempt to teach her to speak, after so long a period of silence, would meet with failure."[15]

In spite of this interpretation, the individuals in charge of Isabelle launched a systematic and skillful program of training. It seemed hopeless at first. The approach had to be through pantomime and dramatization, suitable to an infant. It required one week of intensive effort before she even made her first attempt at vocalization. Gradually, she began to respond, however, and, after the first hurdles had at last been overcome, a curious thing happened. She went through the usual stages of learning characteristic of the years from one to six not only in proper succession but far more rapidly than normal. In a little over two months after her first vocalization she was putting sentences together. Nine months after that she could identify words and sentences on the printed page, could write well, could add to ten, and could retell a story after hearing it. Seven months beyond this point she had a vocabulary of 1,500–2,000 words and was asking complicated questions. Starting from an educational level of between one and three years (depending on what aspect one considers), she had reached a normal level by the time she was eight and a half years old. In short, she covered in two years the stages of learning that ordinarily require six.[16] Or, to put it another way, her I.Q. trebled in a year and a half.[17] The speed with which she reached the normal level of mental development seems analogous to the recovery of body weight in a growing child after an illness, the recovery being achieved by an extra fast rate of growth for a period after the illness until normal weight for the given age is again attained.

When the writer saw Isabelle a year and a half after her discovery, she gave him the impression of being a very bright, cheerful, energetic little girl. She spoke well, walked and ran without trouble, and sang with gusto and accuracy. Today she is over fourteen years old and has passed the sixth grade in a public school. Her teachers say that she participates in all school activities as normally as other children. Though older than her classmates, she has fortunately not physically matured too far beyond their level.[18]

Clearly the history of Isabelle's development is different from that of Anna's. In both cases there was an exceedingly low, or rather blank, intellectual level to begin with. In both cases it seemed that the girls might be congenitally feeble-minded. In both a considerably higher level was reached later on. But the Ohio girl achieved a normal mentality within two years, whereas Anna was still marked inadequate at the end of four and a half years. This difference in achievement may suggest that Anna had less initial capacity. But an alternative hypothesis is possible.

One should remember that Anna never received the prolonged and expert attention that Isabelle received. The result of such attention, in the case of the Ohio girl, was to give her speech at an early stage, and her subsequent rapid development seems to have been a consequence of that. "Until Isabelle's speech and language development, she had all the characteristics of a feeble-minded child." Had Anna, who, from the standpoint of psychometric tests and early history, closely resembled this girl at the start, been given a mastery of speech at an earlier point by intensive training, her subsequent development might have been much more rapid.[19]

The hypothesis that Anna began with a sharply inferior mental capacity is therefore not established. Even if she were deficient to start with, we have no way of knowing how much so. Under ordinary conditions she might have been a dull normal or, like her mother, a moron. Even after the blight of her isolation, if she had lived to maturity, she might have finally reached virtually the full level of her capacity, whatever it may have been. That her isolation did have a profound effect upon her mentality, there can be no doubt. This is proved by the substantial degree of change during the four and a half years following her rescue.

Consideration of Isabelle's case serves to show, as Anna's case does not clearly show, that isolation up to the age of six, with failure to acquire any form of speech and hence failure to grasp nearly the whole world of cultural meaning, does not preclude the subsequent acquisition of these. Indeed, there seems to be a process of accelerated recovery in which the child goes through the mental stages at a more rapid rate than would be the case in normal development. Just what would be the maximum age at which a person could remain isolated and still retain the capacity for full cultural acquisition is hard to say. Almost certainly it would not be as high as age fifteen; it might possibly be as low as age ten. Undoubtedly various individuals would differ considerably as to the exact age.

Anna's is not an ideal case for showing the effects of extreme isolation, partly because she was possibly deficient to begin with, partly because she did not receive the best training available, and partly because she did not live long enough. Nevertheless, her case is instructive when placed in the record with numerous other cases of extreme isolation. This and the previous article about her are meant to place her in the record. It is to be hoped that other cases will be described in the scientific literature as they are discovered (as unfortunately they will be), for only in these rare cases of extreme isolation is it possible "to observe *concretely separated* two factors in the development of human personality which are always otherwise only analytically separated, the biogenic and the sociogenic factors."[20]

Notes

1. K. Davis (1940, January), "Extreme social isolation of a child," *American Journal of Sociology, 45*, 554–565.

2. Sincere appreciation is due to the officials in the Department of Welfare, Commonwealth of

Pennsylvania, for their kind cooperation in making available the records concerning Anna and discussing the case frankly with the writer. Helen C. Hubbell, Florentine Hackbusch, and Eleanor Mecklenburg were particularly helpful, as was Fanny L. Matchette. Without their aid neither of the reports on Anna could have been written.

3. The records are not clear as to which day.

4. Letter to one of the state officials in charge of the case.

5. Ibid.

6. Progress report of the school.

7. Davis (1940), p. 564.

8. The facts set forth here as to Anna's ancestry are taken chiefly from a report of mental tests administered to Anna's mother by psychologists at a state hospital where she was taken for this purpose after the discovery of Anna's seclusion. This excellent report was not available to the writer when the previous paper on Anna was published.

9. M. K. Mason (1942), "Learning to speak after six and one-half years of silence," *Journal of Speech Disorders, 7,* 295–304.

10. F. N. Maxfield (no date), "What happens when the social environment of a child approaches zero." Unpublished manuscript. The writer is greatly indebted to Mrs. Maxfield and to Professor Horace B. English, a colleague of Professor Maxfield, for the privilege of seeing this manuscript and other materials collected on isolated and feral individuals.

11. J. A. L. Singh & R. M. Zingg (1941), *Wolf-children and feral man.* New York: Harper & Bros., pp. 248–251.

12. Maxfield (no date).

13. Mason (1942), p. 299.

14. Maxfield (no date).

15. Mason (1942), p. 299.

16. Mason (1942), pp. 300–304.

17. Maxfield (no date).

18. Based on a personal letter from Dr. Mason to the writer, May 13, 1946.

19. This point is suggested in a personal letter from Dr. Mason to the writer, October 22, 1946.

20. Singh & Zingg (1941), pp. xxi–xxii, in a foreword by the writer.

CATEGORIZATION AND CULTURE

When we learn language, we also acquire a kind of social encyclopedia that provides us with an entire system of cultural knowledge. The way we talk about things shapes our experiences. Language directs our focus—what we pay attention to and what we ignore. Language also shapes our values and our perceptions. Language can be dissected and examined to reveal underlying cultural beliefs and value systems.

Ellen Langer is a psychologist who studies the ways in which we organize our understanding and experience through language-based categories. "Mindfulness and Mindlessness" is an excerpt from her book on the subject. In this selection, she describes the usefulness of categorical thinking and its relationship to cognitive efficiency (we don't have to think every thought anew all the time). She also illustrates some of the pitfalls of categorical thinking. The reading includes some memorable examples of the problems that can occur when we switch to "automatic pilot," or become mindless.

"Metaphors We Live By" is written by two psycholinguists, George Lakoff and Mark Johnson. They provide several illustrations of the ways in which metaphors shape our thinking and behavior. For example, the metaphor "time is money" leads us to organize our behavior in terms of "not wasting time," "saving time," and so forth. We even "spend" time with others.

Default assumptions are only one type of language-based categorization. Hofstadter is particularly interested in sex-based categorization. To stimulate discussion of sexism as a product of the relationship between language and thought, we have included a satire written by Hofstadter, "A Person Paper on Purity in Language," in which he draws an analogy between sex-based and race-based language differences.

READING QUESTIONS

1. According to Langer, what are some of the pros and cons of categorical thinking? Consider some examples of mindlessness in your own daily routines.

2. Make a list of some of the metaphors discussed by Lakoff and Johnson. Try inserting new words that convey a different meaning. For example, consider the expression "I'd like to *share* some time with you" rather than "*spend* some time with you."

3. Make a list of "language asymmetries" (see Part II, p. 91, and Reading 10 for definitions) and consider what underlying cultural values these asymmetries indicate.

4. Consider the use of the masculine *he* or *man* to refer to all people. Some people say that this "generic use" is perfectly acceptable because the terms "imply" women as well as men. Others argue that the term not only leaves out half the population, but also perpetuates an image of women as "auxiliary" and men as "central." Discuss this.

5. Discuss the cultural practice of women taking men's names when they marry. What cultural values does this practice convey?

9

Mindfulness and Mindlessness

Ellen Langer

(1990)

INTRODUCTION

> *I don't like the idea of a unitary subject;*
> *I prefer the play of a kaleidoscope: you*
> *give it a tap and the little bits of colored*
> *glass form a new pattern.*
>
> —Roland Barthes,
> *The Grain of the Voice*

One day, at a nursing home in Connecticut, elderly residents were each given a choice of houseplants to care for and were asked to make a number of small decisions about their daily routines. A year and a half later, not only were these people more cheerful, active, and alert than a similar group in the same institution who were not given these choices and responsibilities, but many more of them were still alive. In fact, less than half as many of the decision-making, plant-minding residents had died as had those in the other group. This experiment, with its startling results, began over ten years of research into the powerful effects of what my colleagues and I came to call *mindfulness,* and of its counterpart, the equally powerful but destructive state of *mindlessness.*[1] . . .

Social psychologists usually look for the ways in which behavior depends on context. When mindless, however, people treat information as though it were *context-free*—true regardless of circumstances. For example, take the statement:

Heroin is dangerous. How true is this for a dying individual in intolerable pain?

Once alerted to the dangers of mindlessness and to the possibility of bringing about a more mindful attitude by such deceptively simple measures as those used in the nursing home experiment, I began to see this double-edged phenomenon at work in many different settings. For instance, consider the events that led to the 1985 crash of an Air Florida plane that killed seventy-four passengers. It was a routine flight from Washington, D.C., to Florida with an experienced flight crew. Pilot and copilot were in excellent physical health. Neither was tired, stressed, or under the influence. What went wrong? An extensive examination pointed to the crew's pre-takeoff control checks. As the copilot calls out each control on his list, the pilot makes sure the switches are where he wants them to be. One of these controls is an anti-icer. On this day, the pilot and copilot went over each of the controls as they had always done. They went through their routine and checked "off" when the anti-icer was mentioned. This time, however, the flight was different from their experience. This time they were not flying in the usual warm southern weather. It was icy outside.

As he went through the control checks, one by one as he always did, the pilot appeared to be thinking when he was not.[2] The pre-takeoff routines of pilot and copilot have a lot in common with the tiresome safety demonstrations of flight attendants to experienced, glassy-eyed passengers. When we blindly follow routines or unwittingly carry out senseless orders, we are acting like automatons, with potentially grave consequences for ourselves and others.

WHEN THE LIGHT'S ON AND NOBODY'S HOME

Out of time we cut "days" and "nights," "summers" and "winters." We say what each part of the sensible continuum is, and all these abstract whats are concepts.

The intellectual life of man consists almost wholly in his substitution of a conceptual order for the perceptual order in which his experience originally comes.

—William James,
"The World We Live In"

Imagine that it's two o'clock in the morning. Your doorbell rings; you get up, startled, and make your way downstairs. You open the door and see a man standing before you. He wears two diamond rings and a fur coat, and there's a Rolls Royce behind him. He's sorry to wake you at this ridiculous hour, he tells you, but he's in the middle of a scavenger hunt. His ex-wife is in the same contest, which makes it very important to him that he win. He needs a piece of wood about three feet by seven feet. Can you help him? In order to make it worthwhile he'll give you $10,000. You believe him. He's obviously rich. And so you say to yourself, how in the world can I get this piece of wood for him? You think of the lumber yard; you don't know who owns the lumber yard; in fact you're not even sure where the lumber yard is. It would be closed at two o'clock in the morning anyway. You struggle but you

can't come up with anything. Reluctantly, you tell him, "Gee, I'm sorry."

The next day, when passing a construction site near a friend's house, you see a piece of wood that's just about the right size, three feet by seven feet—a door. You could have just taken a door off its hinges and given it to him, for $10,000.

Why on earth, you say to yourself, didn't it occur to you to do that? It didn't occur to you because yesterday your door was not a piece of wood. The seven-by-three-foot piece of wood was hidden from you, stuck in the category called "door."

This kind of mindlessness, which usually takes more humdrum forms—"Why didn't I think of Susan? She can unclog sinks"—could be called "entrapment by category." It is one of three definitions that can help us understand the nature of mindlessness. The other two, which we will also explain, are automatic behavior and acting from a single perspective.

TRAPPED BY CATEGORIES

We experience the world by creating categories and making distinctions among them. "This is a Chinese, not a Japanese, vase." "No, he's only a freshman." "The white orchids are endangered." "She's his boss now." In this way, we make a picture of the world, and of ourselves. Without categories the world might seem to escape us. Tibetan Buddhists call this habit of mind "The Lord of Speech."

We adopt sets of categories which serve as ways of managing phenomena. The most fully developed products of this tendency are ideologies, the systems of ideas that rationalize, justify, and sanctify our lives. Nationalism, communism, existentialism, Christianity, Buddhism—all provide us with identities, rules of action, and interpretations of how and why things happen as they do.[3]

The creation of new categories, as we will see throughout this book, is a mindful activity. Mindlessness sets in when we rely too rigidly on categories and distinctions created in the past (masculine/feminine, old/young, success/failure). Once distinctions are created, they take on a life of their own. Consider: (1) First there was earth. (2) Then there was land, sea, and sky. (3) Then there were countries. (4) Then there was Germany. (5) Now there is East Germany versus West Germany. The categories we make gather momentum and are very hard to overthrow. We build our own and our shared realities and then we become victims of them—blind to the fact that they are constructs, ideas.

If we look back at the categories of an earlier age, once firmly established, it is easier to see why new ones might become necessary. The Argentinean writer Jorge Luis Borges quotes from an ancient Chinese encyclopedia in which the animals are classified as "(a) belonging to the Emperor, (b) embalmed, (c) tame, (d) suckling pigs, (e) sirens, (f) stray dogs, (g) included in the present classification, (h) frenzied, (i) innumerable, (j) drawn with a very fine camel brush, (k) et cetera, (l) having just broken the water pitcher, (m) that from a long way off look like flies."[4] To be mindless is to be trapped in a rigid world in which certain creatures always belong to the Emperor, Christianity is always good, certain people are forever untouchable, and doors are only doors.

AUTOMATIC BEHAVIOR

Have you ever said "excuse me" to a store mannequin or written a check in January with the previous year's date? When in this mode, we take in and use limited signals from the world around us (the female form, the familiar face of the check) without letting other signals (the motionless pose, a calendar) penetrate as well.

Once, in a small department store, I gave a cashier a new credit card. Noticing that I hadn't signed it, she handed it back to me to sign. Then she took my card, passed it through her machine,

handed me the resulting form, and asked me to sign it. I did as I was told. The cashier then held the form next to the newly signed card to see if the signatures matched.

Modern psychology has not paid much attention to how much complicated action may be performed automatically, yet as early as 1896 Leon Solomons and Gertrude Stein looked into this question. (This was *the* Gertrude Stein who, from 1893 to 1898, was a graduate student in experimental psychology at Harvard University, working under William James.) They studied what was then called "double personalities" and which later came to be known as "split personalities," and proposed that the mindless performance of the second personality was essentially similar to that of ordinary people. Ordinary people also engage in a great deal of complex behavior without consciously paying attention to it. Solomons and Stein conducted several experiments in which they were their own subjects, demonstrating that both writing and reading could be done automatically. They succeeded in writing English words while they were otherwise caught up in reading an absorbing story. With much practice, they were even able to take dictation automatically while reading. Afterward, they were completely unable to recall the words they had written but were nevertheless quite certain they had written something. To show that reading could take place automatically, the subject read aloud from a book while a captivating story was read to him or her. Again they found that, after a lot of practice, they could read aloud unhampered while giving full attention to the story being read to them.

Solomons and Stein concluded that a vast number of actions that we think of as intelligent, such as reading and writing, can be done quite automatically: "We have shown a general tendency on the part of normal people, to *act,* without any express desire or conscious volition, in a manner in general accord with the *previous habits* of the person."[5]

An experiment I conducted in 1978 with fellow psychologists Benzion Chanowitz and Arthur Blank explored this kind of mindlessness.[6] Our setting was the Graduate Center at the City University of New York. We approached people using a copying machine and asked whether they would let us copy something then and there. We gave reasons that were either sound or senseless. An identical response to both sound and senseless requests would show that our subjects were not thinking about what was being said. We made one of three requests: "Excuse me, may I use the Xerox machine?"; "Excuse me, may I use the Xerox machine because I want to make copies?"; "Excuse me, may I use the Xerox machine because I'm in a rush?"

The first and second requests are the same in *content*—What else would one do with a copying machine except make copies? Therefore if people were considering what was actually being said, the first two requests should be equally effective. Structurally, however, they are different. The redundant request ("Excuse me, may I use the Xerox machine because I want to make copies?") is more similar to the last one ("Excuse me, may I use the Xerox machine because I'm in a rush?") in that both state the request and give a reason. If people comply with the last two requests in equal numbers, this implies attention to structure rather than conscious attention to content. That, in fact, was just what we found. There was more compliance when a reason was given—whether the reason sounded legitimate or silly. People responded mindlessly to the familiar framework rather than mindfully attending to the content.

Of course, there are limits to this. If someone asked for a very large favor or if the excuse were unusually absurd ("because an elephant is after me"), the individual would be likely to think about what was said. It is not that people don't hear the request the rest of the time; they simply don't think about it actively.

In a similar experiment, we sent an interdepartmental memo around some university offices. The message either requested or demanded the return of the memo to a designated room—and that was all it said.[7] ("Please return this immediately to Room 247," or "This memo is to be returned to Room 247.") Anyone who read such a memo mindfully would ask, "If whoever sent the memo wanted it, why did he or she send it?" and therefore would not return the memo. Half of the memos were designed to look exactly like those usually sent between departments. The other half were made to look in some way different. When the memo looked like those they were used to, 90 percent of the recipients actually returned it. When the memo looked different, 60 percent returned it.

When I was discussing these studies at a university colloquium, a member of the audience told me about a little con game that operated along the same lines. Someone placed an ad in a Los Angeles newspaper that read, "It's not too late to send $1 to _____," and gave the person's own name and address. The reader was promised nothing in return. Many people replied, enclosing a dollar. The person who wrote the ad apparently earned a good sum.

The automatic behavior in evidence in these examples has much in common with habit.[8] Habit, or the tendency to keep on with behavior that has been repeated over time, naturally implies mindlessness. However, as we will see . . . mindless behavior can arise without a long history of repetition, almost instantaneously, in fact.

ACTING FROM A SINGLE PERSPECTIVE

So often in our lives, we act as though there were only one set of rules. For instance, in cooking we tend to follow recipes with dutiful precision. We add ingredients as though by official decree. If the recipe calls for a pinch of salt and four pinches fall in, panic strikes, as though the bowl might now explode. Thinking of a recipe only as a rule, we often do not consider how people's tastes vary, or what fun it might be to make up a new dish.

The first experiment I conducted in graduate school explored this problem of the single perspective. It was a pilot study to examine the effectiveness of different requests for help. A fellow investigator stood on a busy sidewalk and told people passing by that she had sprained her knee and needed help. If someone stopped she asked him or her to get an Ace bandage from the nearby drugstore. I stood inside the store and listened while the helpful person gave the request to the pharmacist, who had agreed earlier to say that he was out of Ace bandages. After being told this, not one subject, out of the twenty-five we studied, thought to ask if the pharmacist could recommend something else. People left the drugstore and returned empty-handed to the "victim" and told her the news. We speculated that had she asked for less specific help, she might have received it. But, acting on the single thought that a sprained knee needs an Ace bandage, no one tried to find other kinds of help.

As a little test of how a narrow perspective can dominate our thinking, read the following sentence:

FINAL FOLIOS SEEM TO RESULT FROM YEARS OF DUTIFUL STUDY OF TEXTS ALONG WITH YEARS OF SCIENTIFIC EXPERIENCE.

Now count how many Fs there are, reading only once more through the sentence.

If you find fewer than there actually are (the answer is given in the notes),[9] your counting was probably influenced by the fact that the first two words in the sentence begin with F. In counting, your mind would tend to cling to this clue, or single perspective, and miss some of the Fs hidden within and at the end of words.

Highly specific instructions such as these or the request for an Ace bandage encourage mindlessness. Once we let them in, our minds snap shut like a clam on ice and do not let in new signals.

NOTES

1. E. Langer & J. Rodin (1976), "The effects of enhanced personal responsibility for the aged: A field experiment in an institutional setting," *Journal of Personality and Social Psychology, 34,* 191–198; J. Rodin & E. Langer (1977), "Long-term effects of a control-relevant intervention among the institutionalized aged," *Journal of Personality and Social Psychology, 35,* 897–902.

2. C. Gersick & J. R. Hackman (1990), "Habitual routines in task-performing groups," *Organizational Behavior and Human Decision Processes, 47,* 65–97.

3. C. Trungpa (1973), *Cutting through spiritual materialism,* Boulder & London: Shambhala.

4. T'ai P'ing (978), Kuang chi [Extensive records made in the period of peace and prosperity]; cited in J. L. Borges (1967), *Libro de los seres imaginarios,* Buenos Aires: Editorial Kiersa S. A., Fauna China, p. 88.

5. L. Solomons & G. Stein (1896), "Normal motor automation," *Psychological Review, 36,* 492–572.

6. E. Langer, A. Blank, & B. Chanowitz (1978), "The mindlessness of ostensibly thoughtful action: The role of placebic information in interpersonal interaction," *Journal of Personality and Social Psychology, 36,* 635–642.

7. Langer et al. (1978).

8. To understand the more complex relationship between automatic information processing and mindlessness, compare E. Langer (1989), "Minding matters," in L. Berkowitz (Ed.), *Advances in experimental social psychology* (pp. 137–173), New York: Academic Press; and W. Schneider & R. M. Schiffrin (1977), "Controlled and automatic human information processing: I. Detection, search, and attention," *Psychological Review, 84,* 1–66.

9. The correct answer is 8. A similar quiz was printed on the business card of the Copy Service of Miami, Inc.

10

Metaphors We Live By

George Lakoff and Mark Johnson

(1980)

The concepts that govern our thought are not just matters of the intellect. They also govern our everyday functioning, down to the most mundane details. Our concepts structure what we perceive, how we get around in the world, and how we relate to other people. Our conceptual system thus plays a central role in defining our everyday realities. If we are right in suggesting that our conceptual system is largely metaphorical, then the way we think, what we experience, and what we do every day is very much a matter of metaphor.

But our conceptual system is not something we are normally aware of. In most of the little things we do every day, we simply think and act more or less automatically along certain lines. Just what these lines are is by no means obvious. One way to find out is by looking at language. Since communication is based on the same conceptual system that we use in thinking and acting, language is an important source of evidence for what that system is like.

Primarily on the basis of linguistic evidence, we have found that most of our ordinary conceptual system is metaphorical in nature. And we have found a way to begin to identify in detail just what the metaphors are that structure how we perceive, how we think, and what we do.

To give some idea of what it could mean for a concept to be metaphorical and for such a concept to structure an everyday activity, let us start with the concept ARGUMENT and the conceptual metaphor ARGUMENT IS WAR. This metaphor is reflected in our everyday language by a wide variety of expressions:

ARGUMENT IS WAR

Your claims are *indefensible.*

He *attacked every weak point* in my argument.

His criticisms were *right on target.*

I *demolished* his argument.

I've never *won* an argument with him.

You disagree? Okay, *shoot!*

If you use that *strategy,* he'll *wipe you out.*

He *shot down* all of my arguments.

It is important to see that we don't just *talk* about arguments in terms of war. We can actually win or lose arguments. We see the person we are arguing with as an opponent. We attack his positions and we defend our own. We gain and lose ground. We plan and use strategies. If we find a position indefensible, we can abandon it and take a new line of attack. Many of the things we *do* in arguing are partially structured by the concept of war. Though there is no physical battle, there is a verbal battle, and the structure of an argument—attack, defense, counterattack, etc.—reflects this. It is in this sense that the ARGUMENT IS WAR metaphor is one that we live by in this culture; it structures the actions we perform in arguing.

Try to imagine a culture where arguments are not viewed in terms of war, where no one wins or loses, where there is no sense of attacking or defending, gaining or losing ground. Imagine a culture where an argument is viewed as a dance, the participants are seen as performers, and the goal is to perform in a balanced and aesthetically pleasing way. In such a culture, people would view arguments differently, experience them differently, carry them out differently, and talk about them differently. But we would probably not view them as arguing at all: They would simply be doing something different. It would seem strange even to call what they were doing "arguing." Perhaps the most neutral way of describing this difference between their culture and ours would be to say that we have a discourse form structured in terms of battle and they have one structured in terms of dance.

This is an example of what it means for a metaphorical concept, namely, ARGUMENT IS WAR, to structure (at least in part) what we do and how we understand what we are doing when we argue. *The essence of metaphor is understanding and experiencing one kind of thing in terms of another*. It is not that arguments are a subspecies of war. Arguments and wars are different kinds of things—verbal discourse and armed conflict—and the actions performed are different kinds of actions. But ARGUMENT is partially structured, understood, performed, and talked about in terms of WAR. The concept is metaphorically structured, the activity is metaphorically structured, and, consequently, the language is metaphorically structured.

Moreover, this is the *ordinary* way of having an argument and talking about one. The normal way for us to talk about attacking a position is to use the words "attack a position." Our conventional ways of talking about arguments presuppose a metaphor we are hardly ever conscious of. The

metaphor is not merely in the words we use—it is in our very concept of an argument. The language of argument is not poetic, fanciful, or rhetorical; it is literal. We talk about arguments that way because we conceive of them that way—and we act according to the way we conceive of things. . . .

In each of the examples that follow we give a metaphor and a list of ordinary expressions that are special cases of the metaphor. The English expressions are of two sorts: simple literal expressions and idioms that fit the metaphor and are part of the normal everyday way of talking about the subject.

THEORIES (AND ARGUMENTS) ARE BUILDINGS

Is that the *foundation* for your theory? The theory needs more *support*. The argument is *shaky*. We need some more facts or the argument will *fall apart*. We need to *construct* a *strong* argument for that. I haven't figured out yet what the *form* of the argument will be. Here are some more facts to *shore up* the theory. We need to *buttress* the theory with *solid* arguments. The theory will *stand* or *fall* on the *strength* of that argument. The argument *collapsed*. They *exploded* his latest theory. We will show that theory to be without *foundation*. So far we have put together only the *framework* of the theory.

IDEAS ARE FOOD

What he said *left a bad taste in my mouth*. All this paper has in it are *raw facts, half-baked ideas,* and *warmed-over theories*. There are too many facts here for me to *digest* them all. I just can't *swallow* that claim. That argument *smells fishy*. Let me *stew* over that for a while. Now there's a theory you can really *sink your teeth into*. We need to let that idea *percolate* for a while. That's *food for thought*. He's a *voracious* reader. We don't need to *spoon-feed* our students. He *devoured* the book. Let's let that idea *simmer on the back burner* for a while. This is the *meaty* part of the paper. Let that idea *jell* for a while. That idea has been *fermenting* for years.

With respect to life and death IDEAS ARE ORGANISMS, either PEOPLE or PLANTS.

IDEAS ARE PEOPLE

The theory of relativity *gave birth* to an enormous number of ideas in physics. He is the *father* of modern biology. Whose *brainchild* was that? Look at what his ideas have *spawned*. Those ideas *died off* in the Middle Ages. His ideas will *live on* forever. Cognitive psychology is still in its *infancy*. That's an idea that ought to be *resurrected*. Where'd you *dig up* that idea? He *breathed new life into* that idea.

IDEAS ARE PLANTS

His ideas have finally come to *fruition*. That idea *died on the vine*. That's a *budding* theory. It will take years for that idea to come to *full flower*. He views chemistry as a mere *offshoot* of physics. Mathematics has many *branches*. The *seeds* of his great ideas were *planted* in his youth. She has a *fertile* imagination. Here's an idea that I'd like to *plant* in your mind. He has a *barren* mind.

IDEAS ARE PRODUCTS

We're really *turning (churning, cranking, grinding) out* new ideas. We've *generated* a lot of ideas this week. He *produces* new ideas at an astounding rate. His *intellectual productivity* has decreased in recent years. We need to *take the rough edges off* that idea, *hone it down, smooth it out*. It's a rough idea; it needs to be *refined*.

IDEAS ARE COMMODITIES

It's important how you *package* your ideas. He won't *buy* that. That idea just won't *sell*. There is always a *market* for good ideas. That's a *worthless* idea. He's been a source of *valuable* ideas. I wouldn't *give a plugged nickel for that* idea. Your ideas don't have a chance in the *intellectual marketplace*.

IDEAS ARE RESOURCES

He *ran out of* ideas. Don't *waste* your thoughts on small projects. Let's *pool* our ideas. He's a *resourceful* man. We've *used up* all our ideas. That's a *useless* idea. That idea will *go a long way*.

IDEAS ARE MONEY

Let me put in my *two cents'* worth. He's *rich in* ideas. That book is a *treasure trove* of ideas. He has a *wealth* of ideas.

IDEAS ARE CUTTING INSTRUMENTS

That's an *incisive* idea. That *cuts right to the heart of* the matter. That was a *cutting* remark. He's *sharp*. He has a *razor* wit. He has a *keen* mind. She *cut* his argument *to ribbons*.

IDEAS ARE FASHIONS

That idea went *out of style* years ago. I hear sociobiology *is in* these days. Marxism is currently *fashionable* in western Europe. That idea is *old hat*! That's an *outdated* idea. What are the new *trends* in English criticism? *Old-fashioned* notions have no place in today's society. He keeps *up-to-date* by reading the New York Review of Books. Berkeley is a center of *avant-garde* thought. Semiotics has become quite *chic*. The idea of revolution is no longer *in vogue* in the United States. The transformational grammar *craze* hit the United States in the mid-sixties and has just made it to Europe.

UNDERSTANDING IS SEEING; IDEAS ARE LIGHT-SOURCES; DISCOURSE IS A LIGHT-MEDIUM

I *see* what you're saying. It *looks* different from my *point of view*. What is your *outlook* on that? I *view* it differently. Now I've got the *whole picture*. Let me *point something out* to you. That's an *insightful* idea. That was a *brilliant* remark. The argument is *clear*. It was a *murky* discussion. Could you *elucidate* your remarks? It's a *transparent* argument. The discussion was *opaque*.

LOVE IS A PHYSICAL FORCE (ELECTROMAGNETIC, GRAVITATIONAL, ETC.)

I could feel the *electricity* between us. There were *sparks*. I was *magnetically drawn* to her. They are uncontrollably *attracted* to each other. They *gravitated* to each other immediately. His whole life *revolves* around her. The *atmosphere* around them is always *charged*. There is incredible *energy* in their relationship. They lost their *momentum*.

LOVE IS A PATIENT

This is a *sick* relationship. They have a *strong, healthy* marriage. The marriage is *dead*—it can't be *revived*. Their marriage is *on the mend*. We're getting *back on our feet*. Their relationship is *in really good shape*. They've got a *listless* marriage. Their marriage is *on its last legs*. It's a *tired* affair.

LOVE IS MADNESS

I'm *crazy* about her. She *drives me out of my mind*. He constantly *raves* about her. He's gone *mad* over her. I'm just *wild* about Harry. I'm *insane* about her.

LOVE IS MAGIC

She *cast her spell* over me. The *magic* is gone. I was *spellbound*. She had me *hypnotized*. He has me *in a trance*. I was *entranced* by him. I'm *charmed* by her. She is *bewitching*.

LOVE IS WAR

He is known for his many rapid *conquests*. She *fought for* him, but his mistress *won out*. He *fled from* her *advances*. She *pursued* him *relentlessly*. He is slowly *gaining ground* with her. He *won* her hand in marriage. He *overpowered* her. She is *besieged* by suitors. He has to *fend* them *off*. He *enlisted the aid* of her friends. He *made an ally* of her mother. Theirs is a *misalliance* if I've ever seen one.

WEALTH IS A HIDDEN OBJECT

He's *seeking* his fortune. He's flaunting his *new-found* wealth. He's a *fortune-hunter*. She's a *gold-digger*. He *lost* his fortune. He's *searching for* wealth.

SIGNIFICANT IS BIG

He's a *big* man in the garment industry. He's a *giant* among writers. That's the *biggest* idea to hit advertising in years. He's *head and shoulders above* everyone in the industry. It was only a *small* crime. That was only a *little* white lie. I was astounded at the *enormity* of the crime. That was one of the *greatest* moments in World Series history. His accomplishments *tower over* those of *lesser* men.

SEEING IS TOUCHING; EYES ARE LIMBS

I can't *take* my eyes *off* her. He sits with his eyes *glued to* the TV. Her eyes *picked out* every detail of the pattern. Their eyes *met*. She never *moves* her eyes *from* his face. She *ran* her eyes *over* everything in the room. He wants everything *within reach of* his eyes.

THE EYES ARE CONTAINERS FOR THE EMOTIONS

I could see the fear *in* his eyes. His eyes were *filled* with anger. There was passion *in* her eyes. His eyes *displayed* his compassion. She couldn't *get* the fear *out* of her eyes. Love *showed in* his eyes. Her eyes *welled* with emotion.

EMOTIONAL EFFECT IS PHYSICAL CONTACT

His mother's death *hit* him *hard*. That idea *bowled me over*. She's a *knockout*. I was *struck* by his sincerity. That really *made an impression* on me. He *made his mark on* the world. I was *touched* by his remark. That *blew me away*.

PHYSICAL AND EMOTIONAL STATES ARE ENTITIES WITHIN A PERSON

He has a pain *in* his shoulder. Don't *give* me the flu. My cold has *gone from my head to my chest*. His pains *went away*. His depression *returned*. Hot tea and honey will *get rid of* your cough. He could barely *contain* his joy. The smile *left* his face. *Wipe* that sneer *off* your face, private! His fears *keep coming back*. I've got to shake off this depression—it keeps *hanging on*. If you've got a cold, drinking lots of tea will *flush it out* of your system. There isn't a *trace* of cowardice *in* him. He hasn't got *an honest bone in his body*.

VITALITY IS A SUBSTANCE

She's *brimming* with vim and vigor. She's *overflowing* with vitality. He's *devoid* of energy. I don't *have* any energy *left* at the end of the day. I'm *drained*. That *took a lot out of* me.

LIFE IS A CONTAINER

I've had a *full* life. Life is *empty* for him. There's *not much left* for him *in* life. Her life is *crammed* with activities. *Get the most out of* life. His life *contained* a great deal of sorrow. Live your life *to the fullest*.

LIFE IS A GAMBLING GAME

I'll *take my chances*. *The odds are against me*. I've got an *ace up my sleeve*. He's *holding all the aces*. It's a *toss-up*. If you *play your cards right*, you can do it. He *won big*. He's a real *loser*. Where is he when the *chips are down*? That's my *ace in the hole*. He's *bluffing*. The president is *playing it close to his vest*. Let's *up the ante*. Maybe we need to *sweeten the pot*. I think we should *stand pat*. That's *the luck of the draw*. Those are *high stakes*.

In this last group of examples we have a collection of what are called "speech formulas," or "fixed-form expressions," or "phrasal lexical items." These function in many ways like single words, and the language has thousands of them. In the examples given, a set of such phrasal lexical items is coherently structured by a single metaphorical concept. Although each of them is an instance of the LIFE IS A GAMBLING GAME metaphor, they are typically used to speak of life, not of gambling situations. They are normal ways of talking about life situations, just as using the word "construct" is a normal way of talking about theories. It is in this sense that we include them in what we have called literal expressions structured by metaphorical concepts. If you say "The odds are against us" or "We'll have to take our chances," you would not be viewed as speaking metaphorically but as using the normal everyday language appropriate to the situation. Nevertheless, your way of talking about, conceiving, and even experiencing your situation would be metaphorically structured. . . .

The most fundamental values in a culture will be coherent with the metaphorical structure of the most fundamental concepts in the culture. As an example, let us consider some cultural values in our society that are coherent with our UP-DOWN spatialization metaphors and whose opposites would not be.

"More is better" is coherent with MORE IS UP and GOOD IS UP.

"Less is better" is not coherent with them.

"Bigger is better" is coherent with MORE IS UP and GOOD IS UP.

"Smaller is better" is not coherent with them.

"The future will be better" is coherent with THE FUTURE IS UP and GOOD IS UP. "The future will be worse" is not.

"There will be more in the future" is coherent with MORE IS UP and THE FUTURE IS UP.

"Your status should be higher in the future" is coherent with HIGH STATUS IS UP and THE FUTURE IS UP.

These are values deeply embedded in our culture. "The future will be better" is a statement of the concept of progress. "There will be more in the future" has as special cases the accumulation of goods and wage inflation. "Your status should be higher in the future" is a statement of careerism. These are coherent with our present spatialization metaphors; their opposites would not be. So it seems that our values are not independent but must form a coherent system with the metaphorical concepts we live by. . . .

New Meaning

The metaphors we have discussed so far are *conventional* metaphors, that is, metaphors that structure the ordinary conceptual system of our culture, which is reflected in our everyday language. We would now like to turn to metaphors that are outside our conventional conceptual system, metaphors that are imaginative and creative. Such metaphors are capable of giving us a new understanding of our experience. Thus, they can give new meaning to our pasts, to our daily activity, and to what we know and believe.

To see how this is possible, let us consider the new metaphor LOVE IS A COLLABORATIVE WORK OF ART. This is a metaphor that we personally find particularly forceful, insightful, and appropriate, given our experiences as members of our generation and our culture. The reason is that it makes our experiences of love coherent—it makes sense of them. We would like to suggest that new metaphors make sense of our experience in the same way conventional metaphors do: They provide coherent structure, highlighting some things and hiding others.

Like conventional metaphors, new metaphors have entailments, which may include other metaphors and literal statements as well. For example, the entailments of LOVE IS A COLLABORATIVE WORK OF ART arise from our beliefs about, and experiences of, what it means for something to be a collaborative work of art. Our personal views of work and art give rise to at least the following entailments for this metaphor:

Love is work.

Love is active.

Love requires cooperation.

Love requires dedication.

Love requires compromise.

Love requires a discipline.

Love involves shared responsibility.

Love requires patience.

Love requires shared values and goals.

Love demands sacrifice.

Love regularly brings frustration.

Love requires instinctive communication.

Love is an aesthetic experience.

Love is primarily valued for its own sake.

Love involves creativity.

Love requires a shared aesthetic.

Love cannot be achieved by formula.

Love is unique in each instance.

Love is an expression of who you are.

Love creates a reality.

Love reflects how you see the world.

Love requires the greatest honesty.

Love may be transient or permanent.

Love needs funding.

Love yields a shared aesthetic satisfaction from your joint efforts.

Some of these entailments are metaphorical (e.g., "Love is an aesthetic experience"); others are not (e.g., "Love involves shared responsibility"). Each of these entailments may itself have further entailments. The result is a large and coherent network of entailments, which may, on the whole, either fit or not fit our experiences of love. When the network does fit, the experiences form a coherent whole as instances of the metaphor. What we experience with such a metaphor is a kind of reverberation down through the network of entailments that awakens and connects our memories of our past love experiences and serves as a possible guide for future ones.

Let's be more specific about what we mean by "reverberations" in the metaphor LOVE IS A COLLABORATIVE WORK OF ART.

First, the metaphor highlights certain features while suppressing others. For example, the active side of love is brought into the foreground through the notion of WORK both in COLLABORATIVE WORK and in WORK OF ART. This requires the masking of certain aspects of love that are viewed passively. In fact, the emotional aspects of love are almost never viewed as being under the lovers' active control in our conventional conceptual system. Even in the LOVE IS A JOURNEY metaphor, the relationship is viewed as a vehicle that is not in the couple's active control, since it can be *off the tracks, or on the rocks, or not going anywhere*. In the LOVE IS MADNESS metaphor ("I'm crazy about her," "She's driving me wild"), there is the ultimate lack of control. In the LOVE IS HEALTH metaphor, where the relationship is a patient ("It's a healthy relationship," "It's a sick relationship," "Their relationship is

reviving"), the passivity of health in this culture is transferred to love. Thus, in focusing on various aspects of activity (e.g., WORK, CREATION, PURSUING GOALS, BUILDING, HELPING, etc.), the metaphor provides an organization of important love experiences that our conventional conceptual system does not make available.

Second, the metaphor does not merely entail other concepts, like WORK or PURSUING SHARED GOALS, but it entails very specific *aspects* of these concepts. It is not just any work, like working on an automobile assembly line, for instance. It is work that requires that special balance of control and letting-go that is appropriate to artistic creation, since the goal that is pursued is not just any kind of goal but a joint aesthetic goal. And though the metaphor may suppress the out-of-control aspects of the LOVE IS MADNESS metaphor, it highlights another aspect, namely, the sense of almost demonic possession that lies behind our culture's connection between artistic genius and madness.

Third, because the metaphor highlights important love experiences and makes them coherent while it masks other love experiences, the metaphor gives love a new meaning. If those things entailed by the metaphor are for us the most important aspects of our love experiences, then the metaphor can acquire the status of a truth; for many people, love is a collaborative work of art. And because it is, the metaphor can have a feedback effect, guiding our future actions in accordance with the metaphor.

Fourth, metaphors can thus be appropriate because they sanction actions, justify inferences, and help us set goals. For example, certain actions, inferences, and goals are dictated by the LOVE IS A COLLABORATIVE WORK OF ART metaphor but not by the LOVE IS MADNESS metaphor. If love is madness, I do not concentrate on what I have to do to maintain it. But if it is work, then it requires activity, and if it is a work of art, it requires a very special *kind* of activity, and if it is collaborative, then it is even further restricted and specified.

Fifth, the meaning a metaphor will have for me will be partly culturally determined and partly tied to my past experiences. The cultural differences can be enormous because each of the concepts in the metaphor under discussion—ART, WORK, COLLABORATION, and LOVE—can vary widely from culture to culture. Thus, LOVE IS A COLLABORATIVE WORK OF ART would mean very different things to a nineteenth-century European Romantic and an Eskimo living in Greenland at the same time. There will also be differences within a culture based on how individuals differ in their views of work and art. LOVE IS A COLLABORATIVE WORK OF ART will mean something very different to two fourteen-year-olds on their first date than to a mature artist couple.

As an example of how the meaning of a metaphor may vary radically within a culture, let us consider some entailments of the metaphor for someone with a view of art very different from our own. Someone who values a work of art not for itself but only as an object for display and someone who thinks that art creates only an illusion, not reality, could see the following as entailments of the metaphor:

Love is an object to be placed on display.

Love exists to be judged and admired by others.

Love creates an illusion.

Love requires hiding the truth.

Because such a person's view of art is different, the metaphor will have a different meaning for him. If his experience of love is pretty much like ours, then the metaphor simply will not fit. In fact, it will be grossly inappropriate. Hence, the same metaphor that gives new meaning to our experiences will not give new meaning to his.

Another example of how a metaphor can create new meaning for us came about by accident. An Iranian student, shortly after his arrival in Berkeley, took a seminar on metaphor from one of us. Among the wondrous things that he found in Berkeley was an expression that he heard over and over and understood as a beautifully sane metaphor. The expression was "the solution of my problems"—which he took to be a large volume of liquid, bubbling and smoking, containing all of your problems, either dissolved or in the form of precipitates, with catalysts constantly dissolving some problems (for the time being) and precipitating out others. He was terribly disillusioned to find that the residents of Berkeley had no such chemical metaphor in mind. And well he might be, for the chemical metaphor is both beautiful and insightful. It gives us a view of problems as things that never disappear utterly and that cannot be solved once and for all. All of your problems are always present, only they may be dissolved and in solution, or they may be in solid form. The best you can hope for is to find a catalyst that will make one problem dissolve without making another one precipitate out. And since you do not have complete control over what goes into the solution, you are constantly finding old and new problems precipitating out and present problems dissolving, partly because of your efforts and partly despite anything you do.

The CHEMICAL metaphor gives us a new view of human problems. It is appropriate to the experience of finding that problems which we once thought were "solved" turn up again and again. The CHEMICAL metaphor says that problems are not the kind of things that can be made to disappear forever. To treat them as things that can be "solved" once and for all is pointless. To live by the CHEMICAL metaphor would be to accept it as a fact that no problem ever disappears forever. Rather than direct your energies toward solving your problems once and for all, you would direct your energies toward finding out what catalysts will dissolve your most pressing problems for the longest time without precipitating out worse ones. The reappearance of a problem is viewed as a natural occurrence rather than a failure on your part to find "the right way to solve it."

To live by the CHEMICAL metaphor would mean that your problems have a different kind of reality for you. A temporary solution would be an accomplishment rather than a failure. Problems would be part of the natural order of things rather than disorders to be "cured." The way you would understand your everyday life and the way you would act in it would be different if you lived by the CHEMICAL metaphor.

We see this as a clear case of the power of metaphor to create a reality rather than simply to give us a way of conceptualizing a preexisting reality. This should not be surprising. As we saw in the case of the ARGUMENT IS WAR metaphor, there are natural kinds of *activity* (e.g., arguing) that are metaphorical in nature. What the CHEMICAL metaphor reveals is that our current way of dealing with problems is another kind of metaphorical activity. At present most of us deal with problems according to what we might call the PUZZLE metaphor, in which problems are PUZZLES for which, typically, there is a correct solution—and, once solved, they are solved forever. The PROBLEMS ARE PUZZLES metaphor characterizes our present reality. A shift to the CHEMICAL metaphor would characterize a new reality.

But it is by no means an easy matter to change the metaphors we live by. It is one thing to be aware of the possibilities inherent in the CHEMICAL metaphor, but it is a very different and far more difficult thing to live by it. Each of us has, consciously or unconsciously, identified hundreds of problems, and we are constantly at work on solutions for many of them—via the PUZZLE metaphor. So much of our unconscious everyday activity is structured in terms of the PUZZLE metaphor that we could not possibly make a

quick or easy change to the CHEMICAL metaphor on the basis of a conscious decision.

Many of our activities (arguing, solving problems, budgeting time, etc.) are metaphorical in nature. The metaphorical concepts that characterize those activities structure our present reality. New metaphors have the power to create a new reality. This can begin to happen when we start to comprehend our experience in terms of a metaphor, and it becomes a deeper reality when we begin to act in terms of it. If a new metaphor enters the conceptual system that we base our actions on, it will alter that conceptual system and the perceptions and actions that the system gives rise to. Much of cultural change arises from the introduction of new metaphorical concepts and the loss of old ones. For example, the Westernization of cultures throughout the world is partly a matter of introducing the TIME IS MONEY metaphor into those cultures.

The idea that metaphors can create realities goes against most traditional views of metaphor. The reason is that metaphor has traditionally been viewed as a matter of mere language rather than primarily as a means of structuring our conceptual system and the kinds of everyday activities we perform. It is reasonable enough to assume that words alone don't change reality. But changes in our conceptual system do change what is real for us and affect how we perceive the world and act upon those perceptions.

The idea that metaphor is just a matter of language and can at best only describe reality stems from the view that what is real is wholly external to, and independent of, how human beings conceptualize the world—as if the study of reality were just the study of the physical world. Such a view of reality—so-called objective reality—leaves out human aspects of reality, in particular the real perceptions, conceptualizations, motivations, and actions that constitute most of what we experience. But the human aspects of reality are most of what matters to us, and these vary from culture to culture, since different cultures have different conceptual systems. Cultures also exist within physical environments, some of them radically different—jungles, deserts, islands, tundra, mountains, cities, etc. In each case there is a physical environment that we interact with, more or less successfully. The conceptual systems of various cultures partly depend on the physical environments they have developed in.

Each culture must provide a more or less successful way of dealing with its environment, both adapting to it and changing it. Moreover, each culture must define a social reality within which people have roles that make sense to them and in terms of which they can function socially. Not surprisingly, the social reality defined by a culture affects its conception of physical reality. What is real for an individual as a member of a culture is a product both of his social reality and of the way in which that shapes his experience of the physical world. Since much of our social reality is understood in metaphorical terms, and since our conception of the physical world is partly metaphorical, metaphor plays a very significant role in determining what is real for us. . . .

METAPHOR, TRUTH, AND ACTION

In the preceding section we suggested the following:

Metaphors have entailments through which they highlight and make coherent certain aspects of our experience.

A given metaphor may be the only way to highlight and coherently organize exactly those aspects of our experience.

Metaphors may create realities for us, especially social realities. A metaphor may thus be a guide for future action. Such actions will, of course, fit the metaphor. This will, in turn,

reinforce the power of the metaphor to make experience coherent. In this sense metaphors can be self-fulfilling prophecies.

For example, faced with the energy crisis, President Carter declared "the moral equivalent of war." The WAR metaphor generated a network of entailments. There was an "enemy," a "threat to national security," which required "setting targets," "reorganizing priorities," "establishing a new chain of command," "plotting new strategy," "gathering intelligence," "marshaling forces," "imposing sanctions," "calling for sacrifices," and on and on. The WAR metaphor highlighted certain realities and hid others. The metaphor was not merely a way of viewing reality; it constituted a license for policy change and political and economic action. The very acceptance of the metaphor provided grounds for certain inferences: there was an external, foreign, hostile enemy (pictured by cartoonists in Arab headdress); energy needed to be given top priorities; the populace would have to make sacrifices; if we didn't meet the threat, we would not survive. It is important to realize that this was not the only metaphor available.

Carter's WAR metaphor took for granted our current concept of what ENERGY is, and focused on how to get enough of it. On the other hand, Amory Lovins (1977) observed that there are two fundamentally different ways, or PATHS, to supply our energy needs. He characterized these metaphorically as HARD and SOFT. The HARD ENERGY PATH uses energy supplies that are inflexible, nonrenewable, needing military defense and geopolitical control, irreversibly destructive of the environment, and requiring high capital investment, high technology, and highly skilled workers. They include fossil fuels (gas and oil), nuclear power plants, and coal gasification. The SOFT ENERGY PATH uses energy supplies that are flexible, renewable, not needing military defense or geopolitical control, not destructive of the environment, and requiring only low capital investment, low technology, and unskilled labor. They include solar, wind, and hydroelectric power, biomass alcohol, fluidized beds for burning coal or other combustible materials, and a great many other possibilities currently available. Lovins' SOFT ENERGY PATH metaphor highlights the technical, economic, and sociopolitical *structure* of the energy system, which leads him to the conclusion that the "hard" energy paths—coal, oil, and nuclear power—lead to political conflict, economic hardship, and harm to the environment. But Jimmy Carter is more powerful than Amory Lovins. As Charlotte Linde (in conversation) has observed, whether in national politics or in everyday interaction, people in power get to impose their metaphors.

New metaphors, like conventional metaphors, can have the power to define reality. They do this through a coherent network of entailments that highlight some features of reality and hide others. The acceptance of the metaphor, which forces us to focus *only* on those aspects of our experience that it highlights, leads us to view the entailments of the metaphor as being *true*. Such "truths" may be true, of course, only relative to the reality defined by the metaphor. Suppose Carter announces that his administration has won a major energy battle. Is this claim true or false? Even to address oneself to the question requires accepting at least the central parts of the metaphor. If you do not accept the existence of an external enemy, if you think there is no external threat, if you recognize no field of battle, no targets, no clearly defined competing forces, then the issue of objective truth or falsity cannot arise. But if you see reality as defined by the metaphor, that is, if you do see the energy crisis as a war, then you can answer the question relative to whether the metaphorical entailments fit reality. If Carter, by means of strategically employed political and economic sanctions, forced the OPEC nations to cut the price of oil in half, then

you would say that he would indeed have won a major battle. If, on the other hand, his strategies had produced only a temporary price freeze, you couldn't be so sure and might be skeptical.

Though questions of truth do arise for new metaphors, the more important questions are those of appropriate action. In most cases, what is at issue is not the truth or falsity of a metaphor but the perceptions and inferences that follow from it and the actions that are sanctioned by it. In all aspects of life, not just in politics or in love, we define our reality in terms of metaphors and then proceed to act on the basis of the metaphors. We draw inferences, set goals, make commitments, and execute plans, all on the basis of how we in part structure our experience, consciously and unconsciously, by means of metaphor. . . .

Metaphors, as we have seen, are conceptual in nature. They are among our principal vehicles for understanding. And they play a central role in the construction of social and political reality. Yet they are typically viewed within philosophy as matters of "mere language," and philosophical discussions of metaphor have not centered on their conceptual nature, their contribution to understanding, or their function in cultural reality. Instead, philosophers have tended to look at metaphors as out-of-the-ordinary imaginative or poetic linguistic expressions, and their discussions have centered on whether these linguistic expressions can be *true*. . . .

We do not believe that there is such a thing as *objective* (absolute and unconditional) *truth,* though it has been a long-standing theme in Western culture that there is. We do believe that there are *truths* but think that the idea of truth need not be tied to the objectivist view. We believe that the idea that there is absolute objective truth is not only mistaken but socially and politically dangerous. As we have seen, truth is always relative to a conceptual system that is defined in large part by metaphor. Most of our metaphors have evolved in our culture over a long period, but many are imposed upon us by people in power—political leaders, religious leaders, business leaders, advertisers, the media, etc. In a culture where the myth of objectivism is very much alive and truth is always absolute truth, the people who get to impose their metaphors on the culture get to define what we consider to be true—absolutely and objectively true. . . .

AN EXPERIENTIALIST SYNTHESIS

What we are offering in the experientalist account of understanding and truth is an alternative which denies that subjectivity and objectivity are our only choices. . . . The reason we have focused so much on metaphor is that it unites reason and imagination. Reason, at the very least, involves categorization, entailment, and inference. Imagination, in one of its many aspects, involves seeing one kind of thing in terms of another kind of thing—what we have called metaphorical thought. Metaphor is thus *imaginative rationality*. Since the categories of our everyday thought are largely metaphorical and our everyday reasoning involves metaphorical entailments and inferences, ordinary rationality is therefore imaginative by its very nature. Given our understanding of poetic metaphor in terms of metaphorical entailments and inferences, we can see that the products of the poetic imagination are, for the same reason, partially rational in nature.

Metaphor is one of our most important tools for trying to comprehend partially what cannot be comprehended totally: our feelings, aesthetic experiences, moral practices, and spiritual awareness. These endeavors of the imagination are not devoid of rationality; since they use metaphor, they employ an imaginative rationality.

An experientialist approach also allows us to bridge the gap between the objectivist and subjectivist myths about impartiality and the possibility of being fair and objective. . . . [T]ruth is relative to understanding, which means that there is no absolute standpoint from which to obtain absolute objective truths about the world. This does not mean that there are no truths; it means only that truth is relative to our conceptual system, which is grounded in, and constantly tested by, our experiences and those of other members of our culture in our daily interactions with other people and with our physical and cultural environments. . . .

REFERENCE

Lovins, A. (1977). *Soft energy paths.* Cambridge: Ballinger.

CATEGORIZATION AND CULTURE

11

A Person Paper on Purity in Language

William Satire (alias Douglas R. Hofstadter)

(1985)

It's high time someone blew the whistle on all the silly prattle about revamping our language to suit the purposes of certain political fanatics. You know what I'm talking about—those who accuse speakers of English of what they call "racism." This awkward neologism, constructed by analogy with the well-established term "sexism," does not sit well in the ears, if I may mix my metaphors. But let us grant that in our society there may be injustices here and there in the treatment of either race from time to time, and let us even grant these people their terms "racism" and "racist." How valid, however, are the claims of the self-proclaimed "black libbers," or "negrists"—those who would radically change our language in order to "liberate" us poor dupes from its supposed racist bias?

Most of the clamor, as you certainly know by now, revolves around the age-old usage of the noun "white" and words built from it, such as *chairwhite, mailwhite, repairwhite, clergywhite, middlewhite, Frenchwhite, forewhite, whitepower, whiteslaughter, oneupwhiteship, straw white, whitehandle,* and so on. The negrists claim that using the word "white," either on its own or as a component, to talk about *all* the members of the human species is somehow degrading to blacks and reinforces racism. Therefore the libbers propose that we substitute "person" everywhere where "white" now occurs. Sensitive speakers of our secretary tongue of course find this preposterous. There is great beauty to a phrase such as

"All whites are created equal." Our forebosses who framed the Declaration of Independence well understood the poetry of our language. Think how ugly it would be to say "All persons are created equal," or "All whites and blacks are created equal." Besides, as any schoolwhitey can tell you, such phrases are redundant. In most contexts, it is self-evident when "white" is being used in an inclusive sense, in which case it subsumes members of the darker race just as much as fairskins.

There is nothing denigrating to black people in being subsumed under the rubric "white"— no more than under the rubric "person." After all, white is a mixture of all the colors of the rainbow, including black. Used inclusively, the word "white" has no connotations whatsoever of race. Yet many people are hung up on this point. A prime example is Abraham Moses, one of the more vocal spokeswhites for making such a shift. For years, Niss Moses, authoroon of the well-known negrist tracts *A Handbook of Nonracist Writing* and *Words and Blacks,* has had nothing better to do than go around the country making speeches advocating the downfall of "racist language" that ble objects to. But when you analyze bler objections, you find they all fall apart at the seams. Niss Moses says that words like "chairwhite" suggest to people—most especially impressionable young whiteys and blackeys— that all chairwhites belong to the white race. How absurd! It is quite obvious, for instance, that the chairwhite of the League of Black Voters is going to be a black, not a white. Nobody need think twice about it. As a matter of fact, the suffix "white" is usually not pronounced with a long "i" as in the noun "white," but like "wit," as in the terms *saleswhite, freshwhite, penwhiteship, first basewhite,* and so on. It's just a simple and useful component in building race-neutral words.

But Niss Moses would have you sit up and start hollering "Racism!" In fact, Niss Moses sees evidence of racism under every stone. Ble has written a famous article, in which ble vehemently objects to the immortal and poetic words of the first white on the moon, Captain Nellie Strongarm. If you will recall, whis words were: "One small step for a white, a giant step for whitekind." This noble sentiment is anything but racist; it is simply a celebration of a glorious moment in the history of White.

Another of Niss Moses' shrill objections is to the age-old differentiation of whites from blacks by the third-person pronouns "whe" and "ble." Ble promotes an absurd notion: that what we really need in English is a single pronoun covering *both* races. Numerous suggestions have been made, such as "pe," "tey," and others. These are all repugnant to the nature of the English language, as the average white in the street will testify, even if whe has no linguistic training whatsoever. Then there are advocates of usages such as "whe or ble," "whis or bler," and so forth. This makes for monstrosities such as the sentence "When the next President takes office, whe or ble will have to choose whis or bler cabinet with great care, for whe or ble would not want to offend any minorities." Contrast this with the spare elegance of the normal way of putting it, and there is no question which way we ought to speak. There are, of course, some yapping black libbers who advocate writing "bl/whe" everywhere, which, aside from looking terrible, has no reasonable pronunciation. Shall we say "blooey" all the time when we simply mean "whe"? Who wants to sound like a white with a chronic sneeze?

One of the more hilarious suggestions made by the squawkers for this point of view is to abandon the natural distinction along racial lines, and to replace it with a highly unnatural one along sexual lines. One such suggestion— emanating, no doubt, from the mind of a madwhite—would have us say "he" for male whites (and blacks) and "she" for female whites (and blacks). Can you imagine the outrage with which sensible folk of either sex would greet this "modest proposal"?

Another suggestion is that the plural pronoun "they" be used in place of the inclusive "whe." This would turn the charming proverb "Whe who laughs last, laughs best" into the bizarre concoction "They who laughs last, laughs best." As if anyone in whis right mind could have thought that the original proverb applied only to the white race! No, we don't need a new pronoun to "liberate" our minds. That's the lazy white's way of solving the pseudo-problem of racism. In any case, it's ungrammatical. The pronoun "they" is a plural pronoun, and it grates on the civilized ear to hear it used to denote only one person. Such a usage, if adopted, would merely promote illiteracy and accelerate the already scandalously rapid nosedive of the average intelligence level in our society.

Niss Moses would have us totally revamp the English language to suit bler purposes. If, for instance, we are to substitute "person" for "white," where are we to stop? If we were to follow Niss Moses' ideas to their logical conclusion, we would have to conclude that ble would like to see small blackeys and whiteys playing the game of "Hangperson" and reading the story of "Snow Person and the Seven Dwarfs." And would ble have us rewrite history to say, "Don't shoot until you see the *persons* of their eyes!"? Will pundits and politicians henceforth issue *person* papers? Will we now have egg yolks and egg *persons*? And pledge allegiance to the good old Red, *Person,* and Blue? Will we sing, "I'm dreaming of a *person* Christmas"? Say of a frightened white, "Whe's *person* as a sheet!"? Lament the increase of *person*-collar crime? Thrill to the chirping of bob*persons* in our gardens? Ask a friend to *person* the table while we go visit the *persons'* room? Come off it, Niss Moses—don't personwash our language!

What conceivable harm is there in such beloved phrases as "No white is an island," "Dog is white's best friend," or "White's inhumanity to white"? Who would revise such classic book titles as Bronob Jacowski's *The Ascent of White* or Eric Steeple Bell's *Whites of Mathematics?* Did the poet who wrote "The best-laid plans of mice and whites gang aft agley" believe that blacks' plans gang *ne'er* agley? Surely not! Such phrases are simply metaphors: Everyone can see beyond that. Whe who interprets them as reinforcing racism must have a perverse desire to feel oppressed.

"Personhandling" the language is a habit that not only Niss Moses but quite a few others have taken up recently. For instance, Nrs. Delilah Buford has urged that we drop the useful distinction between "Niss" and "Nrs." (which, as everybody knows, is pronounced "Nissiz," the reason for which nobody knows!). Bler argument is that there is no need for the public to know whether a black is employed or not. *Need* is, of course, not the point. Ble conveniently sidesteps the fact that there is a *tradition* in our society of calling unemployed blacks "Niss" and employed blacks "Nrs." Most blacks—in fact, the vast majority— prefer it that way. They *want* the world to know what their employment status is, and for good reason. Unemployed blacks want prospective employers to know they are available, without having to ask embarrassing questions. Likewise, employed blacks are proud of having found a job, and wish to let the world know they are employed. This distinction provides a sense of security to all involved, in that everyone knows where ble fits into the scheme of things.

But Nrs. Buford refuses to recognize this simple truth. Instead, ble shiftily turns the argument into one about whites, asking why it is that whites are universally addressed as "Master," without any differentiation between employed and unemployed ones. The answer, of course, is that in America and other Northern societies, we set little store by the employment status of whites. Nrs. Buford can do little to change that reality, for it seems to be tied to innate biological differences between whites and blacks. Many white-years of research, in fact, have gone into trying to understand why it is that employment status matters so much to blacks, yet relatively little to whites. It is true that both races have a longer life expectancy if employed, but of course people often do not act so as to maximize their life expectancy. So far, it remains a mystery. In any case, whites and blacks clearly have different constitutional inclinations, and different goals in life. And so I say, *Vive na différence!*

As for Nrs. Buford's suggestion that both "Niss" and "Nrs." be unified into the single form of address "Ns." (supposed to rhyme with "fizz"), all I have to say is, it is arbitrary and clearly a thousand years ahead of its time. Mind you, this "Ns." is an abbreviation concocted out of thin air: it stands for absolutely nothing. Who ever heard of such toying with language? And while we're on this subject, have you yet run across the recently founded *Ns.* magazine, dedicated to the concerns of the "liberated black"? It's sure to attract the attention of a trendy band of black airheads for a little while, but serious blacks surely will see through its thin veneer of slick, glossy Madison Avenue approaches to life.

Nrs. Buford also finds it insultingly asymmetric that when a black is employed by a white, ble changes bler firmly name to whis firmly name. But what's so bad about that? Every firm's core consists of a boss (whis job is to make sure long-term policies are well charted out) and a secretary (bler job is to keep corporate affairs running smoothly on a day-to-day basis). They are both equally important and vital to the firm's success. No one disputes this. Beyond them there may of course be other firmly members. Now it's quite obvious that all members of a given firm should bear the same firmly name—otherwise, what are you going to call the firm's products? And since it would be nonsense for the boss to change whis name, it falls to the secretary to change bler name. Logic, not racism, dictates this simple convention.

What puzzles me the most is when people cut off their nose to spite their faces. Such is the case with the time-honored colored suffixes "oon" and "roon," found in familiar words such as *ambassadroon, stewardoon,* and *sculptroon.* Most blacks find it natural and sensible to add those suffixes onto nouns such as "aviator" or "waiter." A black who flies an airplane may proudly proclaim, "I'm an aviatroon!" But it would sound silly, if not ridiculous, for a black to say of blerself, "I work as a waiter." On the other hand, who could object to my saying that the lively Ticely Cyson is a great actroon, or that the hilarious Quill Bosby is a great comedioon? You guessed it—authoroons such as Niss Mildred Hempsley and Nrs. Charles White, both of whom angrily reject the appellation "authoroon," deep though its roots are in our language. Nrs. White, perhaps one of the finest poetoons of our day, for some reason insists on being known as a "poet." It leads one to wonder, is Nrs. White *ashamed* of being black, perhaps? I should hope not. White needs Black, and Black needs White, and neither race should feel ashamed.

Some extreme negrists object to being treated with politeness and courtesy by whites. For example, they reject the traditional notion of "Negroes first," preferring to open doors for themselves, claiming that having doors opened for them suggest implicitly that society considers them inferior. Well, would they have it the other way? Would these incorrigible grousers prefer to open doors for whites? What do blacks want?

Another unlikely word has recently become a subject of controversy: "blackey." This is, of course, the ordinary term for black children (including teenagers), and by affectionate extension it is often applied to older blacks. Yet, incredible though it seems, many blacks—even teen-age blackeys—now claim to have had their "consciousness raised," and are voguishly skittish about being called "blackeys." Yet it's as old as the hills for blacks employed in the same office to refer to themselves as "the office blackeys." And for their superior to call them "my blackeys" helps make the ambiance more relaxed and comfy for all. It's hardly the mortal insult that libbers claim it to be. Fortunately, most blacks are sensible people and realize that mere words do not demean; they know it's how they are *used* that counts. Most of the time, calling a black—especially an older black—a "blackey" is a thoughtful way of complimenting bler, making bler feel young, fresh, and hirable again. Lord knows, I certainly wouldn't object if someone told me that I looked whiteyish these days!

Many young blackeys go through a stage of wishing they had been born white. Perhaps this is due to popular television shows like *Superwhite* and *Batwhite,* but it doesn't really matter. It is perfectly normal and healthy. Many of our most successful blacks were once tomwhiteys and feel no shame about it. Why should they? Frankly, I think tomwhiteys are often the cutest little blackeys—but that's just my opinion. In any case, Niss Moses (once again) raises a ruckus on this score, asking why we don't have a corresponding word for young whiteys who play blackeys' games and generally manifest a desire to be black. Well, Niss Moses, if this were a common phenomenon, we most assuredly *would* have such a word, but it just happens not to be. Who can say why? But given that tomwhiteys are a dime a dozen, it's nice to have a word for them. The lesson is that White must learn to fit language to reality; White cannot manipulate the world by manipulating mere words. An elementary lesson, to be sure, but for some reason Niss Moses and others of bler ilk resist learning it.

Shifting from the ridiculous to the sublime, let us consider the Holy Bible. The Good Book is of course the source of some of the most beautiful language and profound imagery to be found anywhere. And who is the central character of the Bible? I am sure I need hardly remind you; it is God. As everyone knows, Whe is male and white, and that is an indisputable fact. But have you heard the latest joke promulgated by tasteless negrists? It is said that one of them died and went to Heaven and then returned. What did ble report? "I have seen God, and guess what? Ble's female!" Can anyone say that this is not blasphemy of the highest order? It just goes to show that some people will stoop to any depths in order to shock. I have shared this "joke" with a number of friends of mine (including several blacks, by the way), and, to a white, they have agreed that it sickens them to the core to see Our Lord so shabbily mocked. Some things are just in bad taste, and there are no two ways about it. It is scum like this who are responsible for some of the great problems in our society today, I am sorry to say.

Well, all of this is just another skirmish in the age-old Battle of the Races, I guess, and we shouldn't take it too seriously. I am reminded of words spoken by the great British philosopher Alfred West Malehead in whis commencement address to my *alma secretaria,* the University of North Virginia: "To enrich the language of whites is, certainly, to enlarge the range of their ideas." I agree with this admirable sentiment wholeheartedly. I would merely point out to the overzealous that there are some extravagant notions about language that should be recognized for what they are: cheap attempts to let dogmatic, narrow minds enforce their views on the speakers lucky enough to have inherited the richest, most beautiful and flexible language on earth, a language whose traditions run back through the centuries to such deathless poets as Milton, Shakespeare, Wordsworth, Keats, Walt Whitwhite, and so many others. . . . Our language owes an incalculable debt to these whites for their clarity of vision and expression, and if the shallow minds of bandwagon-jumping negrists succeed in destroying this precious heritage for all whites of good will, that will be, without any doubt, a truly female day in the history of Northern White.

Post Scriptum

Perhaps this piece shocks you. It is meant to. The entire point of it is to use something that we find shocking as leverage to illustrate the fact that something that we usually close our eyes to is also very shocking. The most effective way I know to do so is to develop an extended analogy with something known as shocking and reprehensible. Racism is that thing, in this case. I am happy with this piece, despite—but also because of—its shock value. I think it makes its point better than any factual article could. As a friend of mine said, "It makes you so uncomfortable that you can't ignore it." I admit that rereading it makes even me, the author, uncomfortable!

Numerous friends have warned me that in publishing this piece I am taking a serious risk of earning myself a reputation as a terrible racist. I guess I cannot truly believe that anyone would see this piece that way. To misperceive it this way would be like calling someone a vicious racist for telling other people "The word 'nigger' is extremely offensive." If *allusions* to racism, especially for the purpose of satirizing racism and its cousins, are confused with racism itself, then I think it is time to stop writing.

Some people have asked me if to write this piece, I simply took a genuine William Safire column (appearing weekly in the *New York*

Times Magazine under the title "On Language") and "fiddled" with it. That is far from the truth. For years I have collected examples of sexist language, and in order to produce this piece, I dipped into this collection, selected some of the choicest, and ordered them very carefully. "Translating" them into this alternate world was sometimes extremely difficult, and some words took weeks. The hardest terms of all, surprisingly enough, were "Niss," "Nrs.," and "Ns.," even though "Master" came immediately. The piece itself is not based on any particular article by William Safire, but Safire has without doubt been one of the most vocal opponents of nonsexist language reforms, and therefore merits being safired upon.

Interestingly, Master Safire has recently spoken out on sexism in whis column (August 5, 1984). Lamenting the inaccuracy of writing either "Mrs. Ferraro" or "Miss Ferraro" to designate the Democratic vice-presidential candidate whose husband's name is "Zaccaro," whe writes:

> It breaks my heart to suggest this, but the time has come for *Ms.* We are no longer faced with a theory, but a condition. It is unacceptable for journalists to dictate to a candidate that she call herself *Miss* or else use her married name; it is equally unacceptable for a candidate to demand that newspapers print a blatant inaccuracy by applying a married honorific to a maiden name.

How disappointing it is when someone finally winds up doing the right thing but for the wrong reasons! In Safire's case, this shift was entirely for journalistic rather than humanistic reasons! It's as if Safire wished that women had never entered the political ring, so that the Grand Old Conventions of English—good enough for our grandfathers—would never have had to be challenged. How heartless of women! How heartbreaking the toll on our beautiful language!

A couple of weeks after I finished this piece, I ran into the book *The Nonsexist Communicator,* by Bobbye Sorrels. In it, there is a satire called "A Tale of Two Sexes," which is very interesting to compare with my "Person Paper." Whereas in mine, I slice the world orthogonally to the way it is actually sliced and then perform a mapping of worlds to establish a disorienting yet powerful new vision of our world, in hers, Ms. Sorrels simply reverses the two halves of our world as it is actually sliced. Her satire is therefore in some ways very much like mine, and in other ways extremely different. It should be read.

I do not know too many publications that discuss sexist language in depth. The finest I have come across are the aforementioned *Handbook of Nonsexist Writing,* by Casey Miller and Kate Swift; *Words and Women,* by the same authors; *Sexist Language: A Modern Philosophical Analysis,* edited by Mary Vetterling-Braggin; *The Nonsexist Communicator,* by Bobbye Sorrels; and a very good journal titled *Women and Language News.* Subscriptions are available at Centenary College of Louisiana, 2911 Centenary Boulevard, Shreveport, Louisiana 71104.

My feeling about nonsexist English is that it is like a foreign language that I am learning. I find that even after years of practice, I still have to translate sometimes from my native language, which is sexist English. I know of no human being who speaks Nonsexist as their native tongue. It will be very interesting to see if such people come to exist. If so, it will have taken a lot of work by a lot of people to reach that point.

One final footnote: My book *Gödel, Escher, Bach,* whose dialogues were the source of my very first trepidations about my own sexism, is now being translated into various languages, and to my delight, the Tortoise, a green-blooded male if ever there was one in English, is becoming *Madame Tortue* in French, *Signorina Tartaruga* in Italian, and so on. Full circle ahead!

PART III

PRODUCING SOCIAL IDENTITIES AND SOCIAL SCRIPTS

Social structure is an essential element of the reality of everyday life.

—Peter Berger and Thomas Luckmann (1966),
The Social Construction of Reality

To be aware of the idea of social structure and to use it with sensibility . . . is to possess a sociological imagination.

—C. Wright Mills (1959), *The Sociological Imagination*

LEARNING THE SCRIPT: SOCIALIZATION

Jodi O'Brien

As we discussed in the previous sections of this book, humans become social creatures through their ability to formulate language-based systems of meaning. We live in a symbolic universe rather than a direct state of nature. Humans organize their existence into a meaningful reality through symbols, and language is the primary form of symbol. One implication of this thesis is that *social order* exists in the human mind in the form of meaningful conceptual associations that organize each person's experiences and perceptions. This essay explores how this internal, cognitive system is learned, manifested, and reproduced among groups of people. The central theme of this essay, and the readings that follow, is that people *learn* cultural rules and social expectations. These rules and expectations take the form of *social routines*. As we learn these routines, they become part of our internal system of meaning, and we are able to respond to situations and experiences in ways that are consistent and comprehensible to others who share our culture.

WHAT IS SOCIALIZATION?

As a thought exercise, I ask the students in my classes to consider the difference between someone who is considered eccentric and someone who seems socially "off." By "off" we mean those people who don't seem to behave in a manner consistent with our expectations. Students struggle to explain the actual meaning of "off," but most everyone agrees that we know when we encounter someone who is "off." After some discussion, the students usually come to the conclusion that someone who is eccentric *knows* the rules, but *chooses* not to go along with them, whereas the person who is "off" doesn't seem to know or be able to act in accordance with the rules. What is the difference, and what does it mean to know social rules and to be able to choose to not to follow them?

Consider this related phenomenon: Can you give me an example of a yes-or-no question? (The preceding sentence is actually one such example.) Your answer is most likely "yes," and you could easily do so. Now, can you give me the grammatical rules for constructing a yes-or-no question? Unless you are an expert in English grammar, your answer is most likely to be "no."

As we discussed in the previous sections of the book, the grammatical complexity of language makes it seem miraculous that most all children are able to learn it with such ease. We all know our language—we can speak it, understand it, even have this conversation about what it is—but most of us don't actually know the rules for how it is constructed. When someone speaks "word salad" to you (i.e., forms a sentence that doesn't make sense) you know that the sentence is wrong, but you don't necessarily know the grammatical rules for *why* it is wrong. You know correct or incorrect language when you hear it, but you don't know why it is correct or incorrect. Think about that for a minute. The same logic applies to our understanding of social behavior. People who are similarly socialized share certain cultural expectations, and they know when these cultural expectations have been violated (i.e., when someone is "off"), but they can't necessarily explain the underlying rules. In this regard, social rules or expectations can be thought of as a form of *social grammar*. Language acquisition means that we not only know words, but also know the underlying structure for putting words together to form comprehensible meanings. This is grammar. Our capacity to use grammar (even if we don't know the underlying rules) enables us to form sentences and entire complexes of meaning that make sense to others, but seem spontaneous and original. Our capacity for social grammar has a similar effect: When we become socialized, we absorb an entire *structure* of social meaning and routine. It's our capacity for this social grammar that enables us to be spontaneously engaged in social interaction (we are not robots) while also behaving in ways that are meaningful and consistent for others.

Socialization is the process through which we learn not only cultural beliefs and social rules, but also the underlying *structure* or grammar that enables us to behave individually, organically, and seemingly spontaneously, while at the same time doing so in ways that make sense to ourselves and to others. An important point to keep in mind as you read the following material is that this is a *dynamic* process. We are always learning new ideas, new rules, and new routines, but we incorporate these into an existing structure of socialization so that they take on the qualities of order and consistency rather than chaos and instability.

SOCIAL LEARNING
AS A PROCESS OF INTERACTION

Social learning, or socialization, takes place through interaction with others. Child development scholars estimate that a child learns more in the first 5 years than in the entire remainder of life. It's no wonder that this is the case when you consider the extent of what the child has to learn in order to participate in human social life: language, a sense of self, cultural beliefs, attitudes and ideals, behavioral expectations, and so on. As I hope you will realize in reading the following material and the remainder of this book, the human capacity for learning and engaging in social action is an amazing thing.

Internalizing Society

Peter Berger and Thomas Luckmann are well-known social theorists, and their book *The Social Construction of Reality* (1966) has had considerable impact on sociology. In the early sections of their book, Berger and Luckmann focus on the question of how society gets into the individual (Reading 13). As they note, our everyday lives are shared with others, and it appears that our ability to get along, to comprehend one another, to share similar ideals and expectations, and to coordinate our activities is based on our ability to take on, or *internalize,* the feelings and attitudes of others. As they illustrate, when we see a toddler crying, we do not actually feel the toddler's pain, but we know from her crying that she is in distress. Our ability to read the signs of crying as a symbolic indication of distress and, further, to engage in a response of comforting the toddler indicates that we are capable of forming an *objective reality* out of shared, mutually understood signs and symbols.

Consider an older child who observes his crying sibling and asks, "Why is the baby crying?" The father explains that the baby is tired or hungry or is experiencing some related distress. Then the father comforts the baby. Observing this, the older child is likely to engage in similar actions of comforting when he next encounters the baby crying. (We've all seen very young children attempting to soothe an infant with utterances of "there, there" and similar cooing.) Through this process of observing, asking, and practicing, the child learns the meaning of pain and comforting and the relationship between the two. As he engages in comforting the infant, he is not just acting out a behavior, but also taking in the attitudes of a significant person in his environment (father) and experiencing these subjectively for himself. When his father praises him later for being a "good brother," the child further internalizes these attitudes as associated with an aspect of who he is, and he forms a web of understanding between certain events (baby crying = pain), appropriate attitude (concern), and expected response (comforting). As Berger and Luckmann emphasize, this entire process is very emotionally charged, and the subsequent praise ("good brother") by a significant other (father) has a strong impact on the way in which the child organizes and files this experience and, eventually, makes it a part of himself.

To be socialized means that we have internalized social attitudes and expectations, we can act in meaningful harmony with others in our social groups. But how exactly does this happen? And how is it that we can be simultaneously socialized and individual? One early thinker who made significant contributions to social psychological theories of the self and society is George Herbert Mead (Reading 12). Mead was a social philosopher writing and lecturing in Chicago in the early 1900s. Like his contemporary, Sigmund Freud, Mead was particularly interested in the connections between the development of mind and self, and the functioning of society. According to Mead, the human mind and self-awareness develop simultaneously in the process of learning language. For Mead, consciousness is the simultaneous awareness of our own feelings, impulses, and past behavior and the ability to "see" ourselves and direct our actions in accordance with social expectations. In this section, we look at Mead's theory of self-awareness and socialization. In the following section (Part IV) we explore Mead's ideas about the inner self.

"Self as Object"

Recall the discussion in Part II about language and the process of *naming*, or categorization. In the same way that children learn to group and make sense of their environment by attaching names and creating categories for things, people, and situations, they also learn to make sense of themselves as agents in the world. In other words, socialization begins when children become *aware* of their existence as an object in the world. In addition to learning concepts such as *dog, milk, toys,* and so forth, children develop the ability to recognize themselves as an object in the world and to conceptualize that object as *myself*. This ability requires a child to develop an inner eye or witness that is capable of observing the child's own behavior and recognizing that this behavior is associated with *self* and not something apart from self. Pause for a moment and observe your own inner eye or witness. Where is it located? How does it function? Without this ability to see your own behavior, and subsequently to name or categorize it, would you be able to exercise self-control?

When a child learns language and begins to develop the ability to conceptualize, she also learns to conceptualize her self. For Mead, children become aware of themselves as an object in the environment. As children learn the meaning of things, they begin to collect a set of self-object meanings by observing how others label or categorize them. Thus, the child not only learns the concept *ball*, but she learns the concept *bad girl* when she throws the ball in the house and someone scolds her. Very young children see themselves entirely as objects (similar to the way their parents see them) and tend to refer to themselves in the third person: "Ramon is a good boy," "Alex is sleepy," and so forth. They have learned to see themselves as objects and to attach meaning states such as *good* and *sleepy* to their objective being. In Mead's words, "the individual experiences himself as such, not directly, but only indirectly, from the particular standpoints of other individual members of the same social group" (p. 153, Reading 12). In other words, consciousness, or self-awareness, is the ability to see one's self as an object in the environment. But just who or what is doing the seeing?

"I" and "Me" and the "Generalized Other"

Mead uses the terms *I* and *me* to distinguish between the feelings, reactions, and behavior of the person as subject (*I*) and the internal socialized awareness, guidance, and evaluation of this behavior (*me*). In other words, the *me* is the "seer" that watches or observes the *I* and is able to guide and direct its impulses. This self-direction is usually done in accordance with socially learned ideals about how to behave. Children still learning this will sometimes engage in a willful behavior, such as pulling the cat's tail, and then, after a moment or two, exclaim, "Bad girl!" In this instance, the toddler is learning to link an impulse action (*I*) with her ability to observe the action (*me*) and evaluate it based on ideas learned from a significant other such as a parent.

Socialization is the process of taking on the attitudes, ideas, and values of the groups we belong to. As children gain self-awareness, they are learning to associate certain actions, social roles, and qualities with specific judgments or evaluations. Through this learning process, they are internalizing social meaning and values, and learning to guide and direct their behavior in accordance with these values. They are learning to take the position or attitude of the other. In Mead's words,

> To have self-consciousness one must have the attitude of the other in one's own organism as controlling the thing he is going to do. What appears in the immediate experience of one's self in taking that attitude is what we term the "me." It is that self which is able to maintain itself in the community. (p. 123)

In contrast, "the 'I' is the response of the individual to the attitude of the community and in reaction to it" (p. 123). For Mead, self-consciousness is, in large part, a conversation between the *I* and the attitudes of the community represented by the *me*. To the extent that the *me* is guiding behavior, we are engaging in socialized action.

An example I sometimes share with students, to their amusement, is my own behavior in the presence of a colleague who is completely bald. This colleague is much older than me and holds a high-ranking administrative position. For reasons I don't entirely understand, I often find myself wanting to rub his head when we sit together in meetings. In my mind, I can see myself reaching out to do this. At the same time, I can see how mortified everyone would be if I followed through on this action. Seeing all this in my mind enables me to resist the temptation to rub his head. Mead would describe the impulse to head-rub as the potential action of the *I*. The *me* is the overseer who observes the behavior and intentions of the *I* and brings them in line with cultural expectations: "You can't rub his head! That would be so embarrassing!"

Similar to the process of language acquisition, *primary socialization* is ceaseless and profoundly significant during the first years of human development. During this time, children internalize an entire encyclopedia of cultural attitudes and expectations. They do so through simultaneous development of self-awareness (*me*) whereby they learn to witness and to guide their own impulses in concert with these newly learned cultural expectations. For Mead, these internalized expectations are organized into a set of attitudes he calls the *generalized other*. It is this generalized other (voiced through the *me*) that we engage in internal dialogue with when we evaluate our own feelings, intentions, and actions. When we find ourselves saying, "Well, that's just the way it's done," or "People will be upset if I do that," we're responding to the *me*'s interpretation of the generalized other—our own internalization of social attitudes and expectations. We don't actually know who the "they" is that we're referencing; we just know that "they" have certain expectations, and we judge our own behavior in accordance with our perception of this generalized other, or "they." Although this illustration doesn't fully capture the nuance of Mead's theory, it can be helpful to think in terms of your *I* on trial while your *me* sits in judgment reading from the book of the generalized other.

¶Consider someone who says, "I feel so bad, I haven't cried at all about my mother's death." This seemingly simple statement reflects a very complicated process in which the person has internalized the social expectations for grief—especially grief regarding a parent—but upon observing herself not crying (a symbolic indication of grief), she "feels bad." In her internal dialogue, she notes her lack of tears and feels this as a judgment from the generalized other that her behavior is an inappropriate response to grief.

Imagine now that the woman shares her guilt with someone who has the status of a moral authority—for instance, a pastor or therapist. The therapist tells the woman not to worry, saying, "Many people are unable to cry when someone very close to them dies. It's a perfectly normal response." Upon hearing this, the woman is immediately relieved. Why? Because she has replaced the very general attitude of the generalized other with the more nuanced attitude of a specific moral authority. The potential impact is not only in the therapist's words, but in the social position the therapist holds as a moral authority. This presumed moral status is also an internalized social attitude. We learn to associate certain characteristics, including authority, morality, and so on, with specific social roles, such that typically we automatically or categorically associate authority with a police officer, morality with a priest, and so forth.

To summarize up to this point, the images and ideals you hold in your mind about proper behavior represent the attitudes and values of your immediate social community as passed on to you by significant people such as family members and, later, teachers, media, and so forth. These communal attitudes and expectations function as the generalized other (internalized social expectations) to give people an *ideal script* for acting the proper role in a situation. When you guide, direct, and evaluate your own behavior, you are engaging in an internal conversation. This conversation might be with generalized expectations ("Nice people don't pee on the sidewalk"), with your idea of the expectations of a particular group you associate yourself with ("I need a different haircut before I can show up for that party"), or with some specific person in your life ("My girlfriend is going to be so pissed if she catches me flirting this way"). According to Mead, these internal conversations represent an ongoing dialogue between the *I* and the attitudes of the generalized other as represented by the *me*.

Learning Social Roles and Identities

Much of our primary socialization includes learning the behavioral expectations for specific roles and identities. Mead called this stage of development the *play stage*. In the play stage, the child takes on the perceived attitudes of a social role or identity and acts it out. When children don costumes and engage in fantasy play, they are actually socializing one another in the expectations for cultural identities. In this way, they are learning what might be called the *scripts* that are associated with successful social engagement. Various events or situations have a script, and the script includes certain roles or identities as well as the attitudes and behavior associated with those identities. Accordingly, children play house and take on corresponding roles of parents, they play school and enact the roles of teacher and student, and so forth. Observe young children playing at these games, and you will note considerable negotiation about how a specific role is supposed to be played—what is the appropriate attitude, clothing, and so on. Children can be quite tyrannical about roles and rules in these games. This is because they are actually working very hard to learn and practice the meaning of various social roles and the attitudes, identities, situations, and expectations associated with these roles.

Socialization is a process of learning the gestures, cues, and expectations that enable us to engage in successful social performance of roles and identities (see Part V for a more extended discussion). When we become socialized into a role, we learn how to perform in ways that are consistent with the situation or event associated with that role. For instance, whenever you begin a new job, you learn basic skills of the trade, but you also learn how to convey the attitude associated with the job. New teachers, for example, may be masters of their area of knowledge, but they have to *practice* giving the impression that they are in charge of the class and in control of the situation. Just as young children overplay or insist on certain hyper-stylized behaviors in their fantasy games, a novice teacher may overdo the attempt to be seen as "in charge" and come across as too authoritative. Likewise, a junior employee who is invited to drinks with the boss for the first time may worry later that she appeared overeager in her attempts to convey an impression of interest and respect. Like all new skills, the ability to play the identity in a way that seems appropriate to our socialized understanding of the situation develops with practice. The more practiced we become, the less likely we are to judge our performance in accordance with attitudes of the generalized other, and the more likely we are to incorporate the evaluations and opinions of those who are significant to the situation. For instance, as I gained more teaching experience, I became less and less concerned with following some sort of internalized notion of *the* perfect teacher and more concerned with listening to the actual students in my classes for an evaluation of my teaching.

Sources of Socialization

This raises another interesting question regarding socialization. Where do the attitudes and expectations that we internalize come from? Primary socialization takes place largely under the influence of significant others. From these individuals we learn the basic knowledge of our society, and we internalize this knowledge as a coherent set of expectations, feelings, and attitudes. This means that our initial learning is shaped almost entirely by those who are nearest to us. This usually includes our parents and other close relatives. Once the child is initially socialized, additional sources become influential. These sources can be in the form of other people or, increasingly, through roles and identities as represented in media.

Initial socialization acts as a filter for these secondary sources, however. By the time they reach school, most children already have intricately socialized matrices of meaning and attitudes in the form of a generalized other that has been strongly etched by the attitudes of their primary significant others. They also have a well-developed self-awareness. Accordingly, all subsequent sources of socialization will be *filtered* through both the existing self-concept and the child's particular version of the generalized other. In other words, children are not robots simply taking in sources of social influence unaware; rather, they engage dynamically with these sources. As a child's self-awareness expands, so too does the capacity for processing multiple sources of social input. As self-awareness stretches to accommodate new experiences and influences, the internal conversation becomes more nuanced and sophisticated and reflects an increasingly diverse set of socialization sources. It's important to keep in mind, however, that we do not simply take in these sources and file them away to later exert influence over our behavior; we are in fact constantly engaging with new ideas and potential social learning through our internal conversations.

Parenthetically, and at the risk of editorializing, one implication of this is that in assessing the impact of various external sources of social influence (school curricula, television and related media), the pertinent issue is not the content itself, but the *quality of the internal conversation* the young person is engaged in *regarding* the content. Children actually have a tremendous capacity for complex thinking (contrary to popular belief). When they are allowed to grapple with complex moral issues, they demonstrate a refreshing ability to think about the situation in novel and intelligent ways. But this ability is also a function of socialization—a social learning process in which complex thinking is modeled for them, just as any other behavior or attitude is.

Accordingly, the most important question is not necessarily what is the content of social influence, but rather, how are we filtering it and talking about it to ourselves? I find it useful to pose this in terms of the question: Who or what are the audiences in your head? In addition to significant others, social psychologists use the concept of *reference group* to address the process of internal conversation. Reference groups are groups, real or fictional, that serve as a source of both social learning, similar to significant others, and internal assessment and evaluation. The following discussion looks at the ways in which reference groups are a source of information about attitudes and expectations, and also serve as an important internal witness and voice.

Social Learning Through Multiple Significant Others and Reference Groups

In 1966, sociologist Norman Denzin conducted a study on the "significant others of a college population." Denzin tracked the shifts that students went through during their college careers. He found that most traditionally aged freshmen remained strongly connected to their families and friends "back home." They talked with parents frequently, returned home for holidays and vacations, and were likely to discuss the material they were learning in terms of the beliefs and experiences of their parents and family. However, Denzin noted a distinct shift in students who were midway through their college careers. Sophomores and juniors talked more about their friends at school and were more involved in school-related activities and less interested in what was going on back home.

Denzin was particularly interested in the observation that students in this latter group expressed much more conflict, frustration, and disenchantment with their parents than those in the freshman class. The more advanced students seemed to be experiencing a conflict between the ideals and expectations of new role models (especially faculty, who were sometimes more liberal than the parents) and those of their family. By the senior year, Denzin observed that most students were strongly identified with their college peers, the faculty, and peer groups in the local region. These students expressed beliefs and commitments very similar to those of the faculty and were somewhat disdainful of the ideas they had held just a few years earlier.

According to Denzin, as the students became more identified with their college environment, their attachment to home shifted and, eventually, waned. This process of shifting identification was not always easy; students often experienced tremendous guilt, conflict, and ambivalence. Denzin's interpretation is that these feelings reflect the shift away from significant others whose values and behaviors we have grown accustomed to sharing. Exposure to new groups, new peers, and new environments leads to shifts in alliances and commitments, which in turn lead to shifts in our sense of self. As Denzin notes, the process, while inevitable, is not without some pain, conflict, and grief.

Although Denzin refers to them as the "significant others" of a college population, the shifting perspectives and attitudes that traditionally aged students are exposed to throughout their college years can be usefully understood in terms of reference groups. Sociologist Tamotsu Shibutani describes reference groups as *perspectives* that we adopt in accordance with our attachment to particular groups and the ideals they represent (see Reading 14). When observing our own behavior and imagining how it might appear to others, the "others" we have in mind are not the generalized other or specific significant others, but particular groups. Close association with a specific group (or our ideals of what that group stands for) may lead us to adopt perspectives that are consistent with the behaviors, values, and beliefs of that group. Consequently, when we are making sense of a particular situation, or formulating assessments and making decisions, we use the perspective represented by this group as our reference point. When people use phrases such as "speaking as a [Christian, Democrat, sociologist, etc.]," they are imagining themselves as members or representatives of a particular group and adopting the attitudes that they perceive to be consistent with this group.

Reference groups can be specific groups that we associate with regularly (such as a club, sports team, or church); they can be dispersed or abstract groups whose values we have adopted (social activists, community leaders, historical groups) or they can be imaginary groups whose ideals we have derived from television, film, literature, and other cultural sources. Evaluating self-actions from the perspective of the "woman who has it all" or the "honorable hero" are examples of using imagined reference groups for self-evaluation. Our associations with reference groups have a powerful influence on our self-assessments and the decisions we make. A strong identification with particular reference groups is a central factor in the organization of our goals, values, and behaviors. For instance, first-time, newly married people have little or no experience actually being husbands or wives, but the importance of their new social position leads them to identify strongly with these roles and, consequently, to make decisions in terms of what they think the *ideal* wife or husband might do. Major shifts in someone's behavior can usually be traced to the person's use of a particular reference group as a perspective for self-understanding and direction.

In Reading 15, sociologist Pamela Perry explores the development of distinctive perspectives regarding racial awareness and ethnic self-identification among students in two different high schools. Perry's ethnographic study revealed that White students in a predominantly White high school had little or no sense of ethnic self-identification. In contrast, White students in a multiracial high school had a strong ethnic awareness and well-articulated perspectives on race. Perry attributes these different perspectives to differences in reference groups between the two schools. In the multiracial school, race was more prevalent as a frame of reference and, accordingly, students had a more strongly developed understanding of different ethnicities; race served as a more significant reference group perspective than in the White school, where ethnicity was seen as undifferentiated and therefore insignificant as a self-referential category.

In another context, sociologist Yen Espiritu explores the differential socialization of young immigrant Filipina/os (Reading 16). She finds that immigrant families emphasize their own values and morality by contrasting it with what they perceive as the more loose moral behavior of White Americans, especially daughters. American girls who "sleep around" serve as a counter reference group whereby Filipino families elevate themselves morally above Whites who, historically, have colonized and oppressed them. This reading illustrates the power of the counter reference group in the socialization process: "We're not like them" is one way in which groups delineate their own values and practices.

Reference group perspectives also help to explain why people who engage in very similar behaviors may adopt different self-images and, consequently, lead very different lives. For instance, sexologists are interested in the gap between sexual behavior and sexual identification. Studies show repeatedly that a majority of people engage in sexual activity with someone of the same sex at some point in their lives. For example, many high school and college students report that they have sexually experimented with someone of the same gender. Yet not all of these individuals go on to identify as gay or lesbian. Thus, the social psychologist might ask how it is that bisexual *behavior* results in different sexual *identities.* One immediate answer might be that those who don't like the behavior don't continue it. However, this is countered by evidence that indicates that many people who have had same-sex experiences continue to seek them (or would if they had the opportunity); they just don't *identify* as gay or lesbian (or even as bisexual).

In a book called *Lesbian and Bisexual Identities,* sociologist Kristen Esterberg (1997) explores how women who have sex with other women *learn* to identify as either straight or lesbian. Esterberg uses case studies to map the path that women who are behaviorally bisexual take toward a particular sexual identity. The primary influences along this route are significant others and reference groups. Esterberg's case studies suggest that bisexual women who are strongly identified with a boyfriend and with extended family and friends who are actively supportive of this relationship tend to settle into an identity as "straight." Similarly, women who become involved with other women who identify not only as lesbian, but with a gay and lesbian community, tend to settle into lesbian identities. Repeated interaction with one perspective or another leads women whose behavior may be relatively similar to identify differently as lesbian or straight. This explanation suggests that sexual identities are fluid and shift over time depending on significant attachments and reference groups. Research in this area demonstrates that many people shift back and forth between sexual identities over the course of a lifetime. Reference group theories provide one framework for explaining these shifts, and they also provide a basis for understanding the potential conflict and stress related to certain behaviors: To the extent that we view certain behaviors from the perspective of conflicting reference groups (for example, "I'm a good Christian. How can I be gay?"), we are likely to be caught up in considerable personal turmoil. This kind of self-contradiction is explored more fully in Part IV.

How Do I Know What I'm Feeling? Naming Experience as a Process of Social Learning

In the early 1950s, during what has come to be known as the "beatnik era," Howard Becker, a young graduate student, spent his evenings playing jazz piano in Chicago-area nightclubs. Becker noticed that many patrons tried the drug marijuana, but only a few continued to use it. As a budding sociologist, Becker wondered why some people merely experimented and others became routine users. He was familiar with the "personality" and "physical" theories of his day, which suggested that those who continued to smoke marijuana were likely to have the sort of personality or physical makeup that inclined them to use drugs. But Becker wasn't satisfied with these theories. They didn't mesh with his observations.

Becker noted that those who continued to use marijuana described it as a pleasurable experience; they could rattle off lists of positive effects that they associated with marijuana, and when they introduced the drug to their friends they tended to pass on this information. He concluded that those who continued smoking marijuana had *learned* to define the experience and the effects as enjoyable. He wrote a paper titled "Becoming a Marihuana User," in which he suggested that people learn to *name* experiences and physical responses (see Reading 17). This naming process shapes a person's reactions to the event—in this case, the smoking of a drug and the corresponding physical reaction. He emphasized that people learn these names, or responses, through interaction with others. Regardless of how people might feel privately, they get cues from others about how they are expected to feel and behave publicly. They adjust their perceptions and behavior in response to these expectations. This profoundly social explanation for individual behavior—even in response to something as physically based as drug ingestion—helped alter the course of sociology and gained young Becker a reputation as a formidable social scientist.

Naming Physical Experience as a Social Act

In thinking about Becker's question—What does it take to become a marijuana user?—consider the possible range of responses from someone who ingests marijuana but doesn't know what it is. As a child, I once accidentally inhaled Clorox bleach. The physical sensation was similar to the one marijuana might produce when it is first inhaled: choking, followed by a burning sensation. When I inhaled the bleach, I thought I was going to die.

I was so convinced of my imminent demise that I wrote a note for my parents to find when they came across my body and didn't know how to explain my death. Clearly I did not seek to repeat the experience.

Becker asks a pertinent question when considering the relationship between physical stimuli and human response: Why would someone voluntarily seek out and continue to do something that, if evaluated simply as an undefined physical experience, is not likely to be considered immediately pleasant? Technically, when you first smoke marijuana, you are just as likely to feel as if you had inhaled bleach as you are to feel like you have inhaled something that might be a source of pleasure.

Becker illustrates the process of interaction and learning that helps us identify an experience with a particular meaning. One of the key points of his article is that getting high is something that must be *learned in interaction* with more experienced users. Becker points out, for example, that it is very common for novices not to feel high the first time they smoke marijuana and for an experienced user to smoke a placebo that smells like marijuana and report feeling high. In other words, smoking marijuana is not a simple physiological response to a psychoactive drug but a socially constructed experience that must be identified or named before people are able to recognize the intended effect. The fact that Becker's article is more than 50 years old is also important for the contemporary reader. It allows us to study a culture in its infancy, before the general public knew much about marijuana and its effects.

I live in Washington State, where recreational marijuana is now legal and available in multiple forms, including a wide array of "edibles." These marijuana chocolates, brownies, and cookies were wildly popular initially—the idea of pot delivered through tasty treats was very appealing. But soon people began to complain that they weren't getting high or that the high didn't feel the same and even made them sick in some cases. Recently, local sources have been educating people about the significant differences in absorbing marijuana through the stomach rather than the lungs. It's now common to overhear recreational marijuana users instructing one another about *how* to ingest edibles for the best possible high. In other words, even with wider cultural acceptance, the *physical experience* of marijuana use is still socially mediated.

Becker's article demonstrates that people do not respond directly to stimuli; rather, through interactions with others, we learn to assign meaning to a particular experience. Even in the case of physiological experiences, we have to learn to identify the effects and determine what is going on in a meaningful way before we know how to respond. Consider another example: How do you know when you are sick? In the course of your daily activities, you may notice aspects of your body or behavior that feel "off." As you become aware of these uncomfortable feelings, you attempt to make sense of them. In doing so, you likely rely not only on your observations of the specific symptoms—scratchy throat, upset stomach, aches and pains—but also on input from others.

Sociologist Bernice Pescosolido (1992) researched the process of deliberation people use to determine whether they should go to the doctor when something feels "off." Her research suggests that people rely on networks of friends and acquaintances to help them name the experience. People confer with an average of at least seven others before they decide to visit the doctor's office. Other people help us interpret the experience by drawing our attention to specific symptoms ("Do you have a fever? If you don't have a fever, you don't have the flu.") or reminding us of associations we may not have considered ("You've been partying every night for the past 2 weeks, so of course you feel run down."). Pescosolido's study reminds us that we must recognize and name even basic physiological experiences before we can make sense of and act on them, and this process is usually interactional and reflects socialization.

There is some very interesting research done by endocrinologists that shows that men experience regular hormonal fluctuations. Similar to the experiences of menstruating women, these fluctuations may be associated with mood change and related physiological effects such as a decrease or increase in appetite, sexual desire, and so forth. Although the fluctuations may have a pattern and be a source of mood shifts among men, it is unlikely that most men *recognize* the effects of these shifts. Culturally, men simply don't have a script for talking about, let alone recognizing, hormonal fluctuations in their bodies. In fact, the prevailing cultural belief is that most men have stable hormones and only women experience hormonal cycles. One conclusion that can be drawn from this research is that a significant physical process may be occurring in men's bodies, but without a name for it, it's not likely to be recognized or understood. Conversely, most women have considerable experience talking with others about bodily symptoms that they learn to associate with a menstrual cycle. Whether or not these symptoms are actually caused by the hormonal shifts that are presumed to be their source, most women talk with one another *as if* this were the case.

These examples illustrate that the ways we make sense of our experiences, even things as basic as bodily functions, are based on interactions with others. In these interactions, we learn how to define our experiences, we learn whether something is supposed to be pleasurable or painful, and we learn the attitudes and practices that are associated with the experience.

Naming Emotional Experience as a Social Act

Even if you don't know what your body is doing, you know your heart, right? One of the most commonly expected and widespread cultural ideals in U.S. society is that of romantic love. Finding "true love" is one of the top-rated goals most people list when asked to rank their life priorities. But where does love come from? How do you know when you are experiencing it? What are some of the symptoms of love? Ask some of your friends to generate a list of symptoms associated with falling in love. It's likely this list will include terms such as *distracted, nervous, anxious, giddy,* and similar words that convey a sense of being out of control. Does this sound like fun to you? In the absence of a culturally learned context, an anthropologist from Mars might conclude that the human experience of romantic attraction is similar to the experience of taking a dreaded exam.

Some excellent sociological research has been conducted on the ways in which young people learn about love and romance through their interactions with others. Similar to the process of learning to become a marijuana user, we *learn* how to be in love. In "The Development of Feeling Norms Underlying Romantic Love Among Adolescent Females,"

Robin Simon and colleagues describe the process whereby middle-school girls teach one another the socially expected feelings and attitudes regarding romantic love (Reading 18). Based on ethnographic research, Simon and colleagues provide detailed conversational accounts of young people explaining the rules of romance to one another. These rules include well-known adages such as "you should only be in love with one person at a time" and "you shouldn't take someone else's boyfriend." Also included is the admonition that "you must *always* be in love."

The experiences shared by the girls who were interviewed for Simon's research indicate that they use these "rules" as a source of self-evaluation. If they like someone else's boyfriend, they feel guilty. If someone tries to date more than one person, others feel justified in their indignation toward her. Significant cultural values are passed on in this process, some of which may actually be damaging to girls but are rarely questioned. For instance, young girls who are *not* attracted to anyone worry that there is something wrong with them. However, absent the social pressure to be in love, many adolescent girls have no interest in romance and would prefer to focus on developing interests such as sports, gaming, reading, and so on. But the pressure to fit in leaves many girls concerned that everyone else is caught up in the swirl of romance and that they are abnormal if they aren't. The idea that romance should take precedent over everything else (that we are consumed by it) perpetuates another damaging narrative common among adolescent girls: that a girl's worth is determined by her ability to attract boys.

Simon's article illustrates the significance of social learning, especially in the vulnerable formative years. Young people learn powerful lessons from one another about who they think they should be and how they are supposed to feel. The combination of the age vulnerability and the intensity of this socialization results in a deeply entrenched set of cultural attitudes and ideals that can be very difficult to alter. As these young women mature and encounter new ideas and experiences about love and romance, they may still find themselves evaluating their experiences through the socialization they acquired in their early teens.

CONCLUSIONS

These examples, and the readings in this section, demonstrate the significance of social learning as a process through which we not only learn culture attitudes, beliefs, and expectations, but also internalize them and incorporate them into a core understanding of who we are. In short, through the process of socialization, social norms become integrated into the individual as a perspective, or set of perspectives. These perspectives form the basis of self and social evaluation—we make sense of and judge our own feelings and behavior, as well as that of others, in accordance with these socially learned perspectives.

Socialization is essential to the coordination of social life. It is the basis of social order. One of the most fascinating aspects of social order is that, for the most part, we manage to pull off amazing feats of social coordination without really thinking about it. This production of social order through interaction routines is the subject of Part V. For now, the point to emphasize is that when we internalize social attitudes and expectations—when we gain the perspective of the generalized other—we are learning the social grammar that enables us to engage with others in routine and meaningful interactions.

Many people resist the idea of the "socialized" individual on the premise that socialization turns us into social robots or cultural conformists. This tension is revealed in the common notion of the *individual versus society*. However, consider for a moment what you've learned up to this point. We gain consciousness in the form of self-awareness through the acquisition of language. Language not only gives us the means to think and communicate with others, but also gives us the ability to *recognize* that we are thinking. As soon as we begin thinking and become aware of ourselves, we begin to take the social world into us in the form of organized attitudes, expectations, and perspectives of others. If we did not have this self-awareness, we wouldn't be conscious actors; we would simply be passive respondents. Furthermore, the inner witness that guides our behavior in accordance with the expectations of the generalized other is the basis for our social freedom. The key point here is the *ability* to observe and direct our own behavior. If we were not socialized, we would not have this awareness and we would therefore have no ability for self-engagement or self-control. Consider again the illustration from the beginning of this essay on the difference between the eccentric and the person who is "off." The former is in control of her behavior and therefore "free," whereas the latter can't even participate fully—he has no choice in the matter.

Through socialization, or the acquisition of social grammar, we become capable social players. We learn the social roles and scripts that enable us to coordinate our activities with others and to communicate meaningfully and successfully. Think for a moment about driving a car. If you wanted to drive in any direction and at any speed you desired in a large empty field, you could certainly do so, but chances are you want to drive in places where other people are also driving. Accordingly, you agree to follow the rules of the road. These rules are so mindless or automatic that you rarely think of them. With a few exceptions (e.g., the speed limit on certain occasions), you probably don't feel oppressed by the rules of the road. Rather, you recognize that by learning and participating in these shared rules, many people can coordinate a tremendously complex activity and share the road.

An understanding of the influential forces of socialization is key to self-understanding. When correctly understood, the processes of socialization reveal that we have the potential to be *both* overly conforming *and* liberated. The distinction is in our ability for *awareness* of the socialization process. An understanding of the social psychology of socialization and self-development (see Part IV) gives us the ability to scrutinize the sources of influence that form the basis of our core beliefs, expectations, and ideals. In other words, we can use this information to become more mindful of the social routines that we engage in. Recognizing that you are shaped by cultural forces does not take away from your individuality. In fact, students of social psychology often find that they have a better sense of themselves once they learn to identify the cultural influences that are shaping how they think and feel.

Social order exists, in part, because we are committed to our routines and we find meaning in the attitudes and beliefs we have learned through significant others and reference groups. This is simply a fact of socialization. The question we can usefully ask ourselves, if we want to be less conforming, is: To what extent are we *aware* of meaning and values underlying expected social scripts and norms? Are we engaging with these norms thoughtfully because they are effective (e.g., traffic rules) or meaningful (e.g., celebrating a special event), or are we participating out of habit or internalized guilt and other social pressures that take the form of a coercive inner conversation? Social order based on socialization is not the problem; it's actually an amazing human ability. The issue is not whether we are socialized (we are), but the extent to which we are awake to the socialization process and its consequences for who we think we can be and how we engage with others.

REFERENCES AND SUGGESTIONS FOR FURTHER READING

Berger, P., & Luckmann, T. (1966). *The social construction of reality.* New York, NY: Doubleday.

Denzin, N. (1966). The significant others of a college population. *Sociological Quarterly, 7,* 298–310.

Esterberg, K. (1997). *Lesbian and bisexual identities: Constructing communities, constructing selves.* Philadelphia, PA: Temple University Press.

Mead, G. H. (1962). *Mind, self, and society: From the standpoint of a social behaviorist.* Chicago, IL: University of Chicago Press.

Mills, C. W. (2000). *The sociological imagination* (40th anniv. ed.). New York, NY: Oxford University Press. (Original work published 1959)

Pescosolido, B. (1992). Beyond rational choice: The social dynamics of how people seek help. *American Journal of Sociology, 97,* 1096–1138.

SOCIALIZATION AND REFERENCE GROUPS

The readings in this section provide examples of socialization. Socialization is the process of internalizing the general ideas and expectations of our culture. As children become socialized, they are able to take the perspective of society or to imagine what it is that others think, feel, and expect. In this way, they are able to observe and direct their own behavior in harmony with others. Socialization is not a robotic operation whereby "society" is simply poured into the individual; rather, it is a dynamic process through which the developing individual learns to adopt the attitudes and behavior of significant others. This initial mimicking soon becomes a more complex set of willful behaviors and attitudes directed by a maturing internal conversation. This internal conversation reflects the perspectives and ideals of *reference groups*. Reference groups are the groups (real or fictional) that we refer to in our internal conversations when we are trying to make sense of things, to decide what actions to take and how to evaluate our feelings and behavior. For example, if you think of yourself as a leader, you probably have an idea of a general group of leaders whom you admire. When making decisions and judging your own actions, you reference this group in your mind. Or, if you are a devoted Christian, you may find yourself asking, "What would Jesus do?" and using this reference as a perspective for making decisions. Reference groups can be close and tangible, they can be abstract and distant, or they can even be fictitious. Regardless of the form they take, reference groups are a basic source of socialization and exert a strong influence on how we see the world and the choices that we make.

"The Self, the I, and the Me" is excerpted from the classic writings of George Herbert Mead. Mead discusses the process by which we come to see ourselves as objects and learn to describe our own actions. As this process develops, so does our ability to conceptualize our own actions as a separate, coherent self.

"The Internalization of Society" is a selection from a well-known book, *The Social Construction of Reality,* written by sociologists Peter Berger and Thomas Luckmann. In this short excerpt, Berger and Luckmann discuss the process by which society "gets into" the individual through interaction with significant others. The result is the individual's ability to take the perspective of others. They emphasize that this process includes a necessary emotional component: Our attachment to significant others motivates us to take their perspective and makes socialization a willing rather than a forced process.

"Reference Groups as Perspectives" is written by sociologist Tamotsu Shibutani. Shibutani expands on Mead's theory by introducing the idea that we are particularly concerned about the *reflected appraisals* of groups that are significant to us. According to Shibutani, we use our images of these groups as a reference point, or measuring rod, for defining and evaluating our own actions, beliefs, and values. When we internalize the beliefs and attitudes of specific groups, we have adopted the group's perspective and made it the basis of our own.

School environments provide significant sites for establishing peer reference groups. "Shades of White" is a selection from a book based on a study of two racially distinct high schools. Sociologist Pamela Perry was interested in the racial viewpoints that high school students develop based on the influence of their peers. In this article, Perry demonstrates that White students in a predominantly White school have very different racial perspectives from White students in a racially diverse school.

In "We Don't Sleep Around Like White Girls Do," Yen Espiritu explores the socialization of young immigrant Filipina/os whose immigrant families emphasize their own values and morality by contrasting it with what they perceive as the loose moral behavior of White Americans, especially daughters.

READING QUESTIONS

1. Make a list of your most cherished beliefs and values and also some of the expectations and goals you have for yourself. Identify the groups reflected in this list of ideals. Now trace the origins of your identification with these groups.

2. Consider an experience where you had to learn a new routine, new job, new school, or new culture. Who helped you and how? Do you recall a difference between feeling like an outsider and gradually becoming more at ease as an insider? Explain that difference in terms of socialization.

3. Consider the magazines that you read and the television shows that you watch frequently. For a few days, pay close attention to the types of images you see. What information do you get about who is attractive and popular? About who is successful? About who is a social problem? How are your personal age, gender, race, class, and sexuality most commonly portrayed?

4. Study the photos in your local newspaper for one week. Specifically, count the number of photos of men and of women. Do you notice anything about where pictures of women are likely to be posted in comparison with pictures of men? Count the number of pictures of members of minority groups that appear, and make a note of the context in which they are portrayed. Do you think these images send particular messages about what kind of person is most likely to be a political leader?

SOCIALIZATION AND REFERENCE GROUPS

12

The Self, the I, and the Me

George Herbert Mead

(1934)

We can distinguish very definitely between the self and the body. The body can be there and can operate in a very intelligent fashion without there being a self involved in the experience. The self has the characteristic that it is an object to itself, and that characteristic distinguishes it from other objects and from the body. It is perfectly true that the eye can see the foot, but it does not see the body as a whole. We cannot see our backs; we can feel certain portions of them, if we are agile, but we cannot get an experience of our whole body. There are, of course, experiences which are somewhat vague and difficult of location, but the bodily experiences are for us organized about a self. The foot and hand belong to the self. We can see our feet, especially if we look at them from the wrong end of an opera glass, as strange things which we have difficulty in recognizing as our own. The parts of the body are quite distinguishable from the self. We can lose parts of the body without any serious invasion of the self. The mere ability to experience different parts of the body is not different from the experience of a table. The table presents a different feel from what the hand does when one hand feels another, but it is an experience of something with which we come definitely into contact. The body does not experience itself as a whole, in the sense in which the self in some way enters into the experience of the self.

It is the characteristic of the self as an object to itself that I want to bring out. This characteristic is represented in the word "self," which is a reflexive, and indicates that which can be both subject and object. This type of object is essentially different from other objects, and in the past it has been distinguished as conscious, a term which indicates an experience with, an experience of, one's self. It was assumed that consciousness in some way carried this capacity of being an object to itself. In giving a behavioristic statement of consciousness we have to look for some sort of experience in which the physical organism can become an object to itself.

When one is running to get away from someone who is chasing him, he is entirely occupied in this action, and his experience may be swallowed up in the objects about him, so that he has, at the time being, no consciousness of self at all. We must be, of course, very completely occupied to have that take place, but we can, I think, recognize that sort of a possible experience in which the self does not enter. We can, perhaps, get some light on that situation through those experiences in which in very intense action there appears in the experience of the individual, back of this intense action, memories, and anticipations. Tolstoi as an officer in the war gives an account of having pictures of his past experience in the midst of his most intense action. There are also the pictures that flash into a person's mind when he is drowning. In such instances there is a contrast between an experience that is absolutely wound up in outside activity in which the self as an object does not enter, and an activity of memory and imagination in which the self is the principal object. The self is then entirely distinguishable from an organism that is surrounded by things and acts with reference to things, including parts of its own body. These latter may be objects like other objects, but they are just objects out there in the field, and they do not involve a self that is an object to the organism. This is, I think, frequently overlooked. It is that fact which makes our anthropomorphic reconstructions of animal life so fallacious. How can an individual get outside himself (experientially) in such a way as to become an object to himself? This is the essential psychological problem of selfhood or of self-consciousness; and its solution is to be found by referring to the process of social conduct or activity in which the given person or individual is implicated. The apparatus of reason would not be complete unless it swept itself into its own analysis of the field of experience; or unless the individual brought himself into the same experiential field as that of the other individual selves in relation to whom he acts in any given social situation. Reason cannot become impersonal unless it takes an objective, non-affective attitude toward itself; otherwise we have just consciousness, not *self*-consciousness. And it is necessary to rational conduct that the individual should thus take an objective, impersonal attitude toward himself, that he should become an object to himself. For the individual organism is obviously an essential and important fact or constituent element of the empirical situation in which it acts; and without taking objective account of itself as such, it cannot act intelligently, or rationally.

The individual experiences himself as such, not directly, but only indirectly, from the particular standpoints of other individual members of the same social group, or from the generalized standpoint of the social group as a whole to which he belongs. For he enters his own experience as a self or individual, not directly or immediately, not by becoming a subject to himself, but only insofar as he first becomes an object to himself just as other individuals are objects to him or in his experience; and he becomes an object to himself only by taking the attitudes of other individuals toward himself within a social environment or context of experience and behavior in which both he and they are involved.

The importance of what we term "communication" lies in the fact that it provides a form of behavior in which the organism or the individual may become an object to himself. It is that sort of communication which we have been discussing—not communication in the sense of the cluck of the hen to the chickens, or the bark of a wolf to the pack, or the lowing of a cow, but communication in the sense of significant symbols, communication which is directed not only to others but also to the individual himself. So far as that type of communication is a part of behavior it at least introduces a self. Of course, one may hear without listening; one may see things that he does not realize; do things that he is not really aware of. But it is where one does respond to that which he addresses to another and where that response of his own becomes a part of his conduct, where he not only hears himself but responds to himself, talks and replies to himself as truly as the other person replies to him, that we have behavior in which the individuals become objects to themselves.

Such a self is not, I would say, primarily the physiological organism. The physiological organism is essential to it, but we are at least able to think of a self without it. Persons who believe in immortality, or believe in ghosts, or in the possibility of the self leaving the body, assume a self which is quite distinguishable from the body. How successfully they can hold these conceptions is an open question, but we do, as a fact, separate the self and the organism. It is fair to say that the beginning of the self as an object, so far as we can see, is to be found in the experiences of people that lead to the conception of a "double." Primitive people assume that there is a double, located presumably in the diaphragm, that leaves the body temporarily in sleep and completely in death. It can be enticed out of the body of one's enemy and perhaps killed. It is represented in infancy by the imaginary playmates which children set up, and through which they come to control their experiences in their play.

The self, as that which can be an object to itself, is essentially a social structure, and it arises in social experience. After a self has arisen, it in a certain sense provides for itself its social experiences, and so we can conceive of an absolutely solitary self. But it is impossible to conceive of a self arising outside of social experience. When it has arisen we can think of a person in solitary confinement for the rest of his life, but who still has himself as a companion, and is able to think and to converse with himself as he had communicated with others. That process to which I have just referred, of responding to one's self as another responds to it, taking part in one's own conversation with others, being aware of what one is saying and using that awareness of what one is saying to determine what one is going to say thereafter—that is a process with which we are all familiar. We are continually following up our own address to other persons by an understanding of what we are saying, and using that understanding in the direction of our continued speech. We are finding out what we are going to say, what we are going to do, by saying and doing, and in the process we are continually controlling the process itself. In the conversation of gestures what we say calls out a certain response in another and that in turn changes our own action, so that we shift from what we started to do because of the reply the other makes. The conversation of gestures is the beginning of communication. The individual comes to carry on a conversation of gestures with himself. He says something, and that calls out a certain reply in himself which makes him change what he was going to say. One starts to say something, we will presume an unpleasant something, but when he starts to say it he realizes it is cruel. The effect on himself of what he is saying checks him; there is here a conversation of gestures between the individual and himself. We mean by significant speech that the action is one that affects the individual himself, and that the effect upon the individual himself is part of the intelligent carrying-out of the conversation with others. Now we, so to speak, amputate that social phase and dispense with it for the time being, so that one is talking to one's self as one would talk to another person.

This process of abstraction cannot be carried on indefinitely. One inevitably seeks an audience, has to pour himself out to somebody. In reflective intelligence one thinks to act, and to act solely so that this action remains a part of a social process. Thinking becomes preparatory to social action. The very process of thinking is, of course, simply an inner conversation that goes on, but it is a conversation of gestures which in its completion implies the expression of that which one thinks to an audience. One separates the significance of what he is saying to others from the actual speech and gets it ready before saying it. He thinks it out, and perhaps writes it in the form of a book; but it is still a part of social intercourse in which one is addressing other persons and at the same time addressing one's self, and in which one controls the address to other persons by the response made to one's own gesture. That the person should be responding to himself is necessary to the self, and it is this sort of social conduct which provides behavior within which that self appears. I know of no other form of behavior than the linguistic in which the individual is an object to himself, and, so far as I can see, the individual is not a self in the reflexive sense unless he is an object to himself. It is this fact that gives a critical importance to communication, since this is a type of behavior in which the individual does so respond to himself.

We realize in everyday conduct and experience that an individual does not mean a great deal of what he is doing and saying. We frequently say that such an individual is not himself. We come away from an interview with a realization that we have left out important things, that there are parts of the self that did not get into what was said. What determines the amount of the self that gets into communication is the social experience itself. Of course, a good deal of the self does not need to get expression. We carry on a whole series of different relationships to different people. We are one thing to one man and another thing to another. There are parts of the self which exist only for the self in relationship to itself. We divide ourselves up in all sorts of different selves with reference to our acquaintances. We discuss politics with one and religion with another. There are all sorts of different selves answering to all sorts of different social reactions. It is the social process itself that is responsible for the appearance of the self; it is not there as a self apart from this type of experience.

A multiple personality is in a certain sense normal, as I have just pointed out. There is usually an organization of the whole self with reference to the community to which we belong, and the situation in which we find ourselves. What the society is, whether we are living with people of the present, people of our own imaginations, people of the past, varies, of course, with different individuals. Normally, within the sort of community as a whole to which we belong, there is a unified self, but that may be broken up. To a person who is somewhat unstable nervously and in whom there is a line of cleavage, certain activities become impossible, and that set of activities may separate and evolve another self. Two separate "me's" and "I's," two different selves, result, and that is the condition under which there is a tendency to break up the personality. There is an account of a professor of education who disappeared, was lost to the community, and later turned up in a logging camp in the West. He freed himself of his occupation and turned to the woods where he felt, if you like, more at home. The pathological side of it was the forgetting, the leaving out of the rest of the self. This result involved getting rid of certain bodily memories which would identify the individual to himself. We often recognize the lines of cleavage that run through us. We would be glad to forget certain things, get rid of things the self is bound up with in past experiences. What we have here is a situation in which there can be different selves, and it is dependent upon the set of social reactions that is involved as to which self we are going to be. If we can forget everything involved in one set of activities, obviously we relinquish that part of the self. Take a person who is unstable, get him occupied by speech, and at the same time get his eye on something you are writing so that he is carrying on two separate lines of communication, and if you go about it in the right way you can get those two currents going so that they do not run into each other. You can get two entirely different sets of activities going on. You can bring about in that way the dissociation of a person's self. It is a process of setting up two sorts of communication which separate the behavior of the individual. For one individual it is this thing said and heard, and for the other individual there exists only that which he sees written. You must, of course, keep one experience out of the field of the other. Dissociations are apt to take place when an event leads to emotional upheavals. That which is separated goes on in its own way.

The unity and structure of the complete self reflects the unity and structure of the social process as a whole; and each of the elementary selves of which it is composed reflects the unity and structure of one of the various aspects of that process in which the individual is implicated. In other words, the various elementary selves which constitute, or are organized into, a complete self are the various aspects of the structure of that complete self answering to the various aspects of the structure of the social process as a whole; the structure of the complete self is thus a reflection of the complete social process. The organization and unification of a social group is identical with the organization and unification of any one of the selves arising within the social process in which that group is engaged, or which it is carrying on.

The phenomenon of dissociation of personality is caused by a breaking up of the complete, unitary self into the component selves of which it is composed, and which respectively correspond to different aspects of the social process in which the person is involved, and within which his complete or unitary self has arisen; these aspects being the different social groups to which he belongs within that process. . . .

Rational society, of course, is not limited to any specific set of individuals. Any person who is rational can become a part of it. The attitude of the community toward our own response is imported into ourselves in terms of the meaning of what we are doing. This occurs in its widest extent in universal discourse, in the reply which the rational world makes to our remark. The meaning is as universal as the community; it is necessarily involved in the rational character of that community; it is the response that the world made up out of rational beings inevitably makes to our own statement. We both get the object and ourselves into experience in terms of such a process; the other appears in our own experience insofar as we do take such an organized and generalized attitude.

If one meets a person on the street whom he fails to recognize, one's reaction toward him is that toward any other who is a member of the same community. He is the other, the organized, generalized other, if you like. One takes his attitude over against one's self. If he turns in one direction, one is to go in another direction. One has his response as an attitude within himself. It is having that attitude within himself that makes it possible for one to be a self. That involves something beyond the mere turning to the right, as we say, instinctively, without self-consciousness. To have self-consciousness one must have the attitude of the other in one's own organism as controlling the thing that he is going to do. What appears in the immediate experience of one's self in taking that attitude is what we term the "me." It is that self which is able to maintain itself in the community, that is recognized in the community insofar as it recognizes the others. Such is the phase of the self which I have referred to as that of the "me."

Over against the "me" is the "I." The individual not only has rights, but he has duties; he is not only a citizen, a member of the community, but he is one who reacts to this community and in his reaction to it, as we have seen in the conversation of gestures, changes it. The "I" is the response of the individual to the attitude of the community as this appears in his own experience. His response to that organized attitude in turn changes it. As we have pointed out, this is a change which is not present in his own experience until after it takes place. The "I" appears in our experience in memory. It is only after we have acted that we know what we have done; it is only after we have spoken that we know what we have said. The adjustment to that organized world which is present in our own nature is one that represents the "me" and is constantly there. But if the response to it is a response which is of the nature of the conversation of gestures, if it creates a situation which is in some sense novel, if one puts up his side of the case, asserts himself over against others and insists that they take a different attitude toward himself, then there is something important occurring that is not previously present in experience.

13

The Internalization of Society

Peter L. Berger and Thomas Luckmann

(1996)

Since society exists as both objective and subjective reality, any adequate theoretical understanding of it must [include] both these aspects. . . . [T]hese aspects receive their proper recognition if society is understood in terms of an ongoing dialectal process composed of the three moments of externalization, objectivation, and internalization. As far as the societal phenomenon is concerned, these moments ought *not* to be thought of as occurring in a temporal sequence. Rather society and each part of it are simultaneously characterized by these three moments, so that any analysis in terms of only one or two of them falls short. The same is true of the individual member of society, who simultaneously externalizes his own being into the social world and internalizes it as an objective reality. In other words, to be in society is to participate in its dialectic.

The individual, however, is not born a member of society. He is born with a predisposition toward sociality, and he becomes a member of society. In the life of every individual therefore, there *is* a temporal sequence, in the course of which he is inducted into participation in the societal dialectic. The beginning point of this process is internalization. . . .

Only when he has achieved this degree of internalization is an individual a member of society. The ontogenetic process by which this is brought about is socialization, which may thus be defined as the comprehensive and consistent induction of an individual into the objective world of a society or a sector of it. Primary socialization is the first socialization an individual undergoes in childhood through which he becomes a member of society. Secondary socialization is any subsequent process that inducts an already socialized individual into new sectors of the objective world of his society. . . .

It is at once evident that primary socialization is usually the most important one for an individual, and that the basic structure of all secondary socialization has to resemble that of primary socialization. Every individual is born into an objective social structure within which he encounters the significant others who are in charge of his socialization.[1] These significant others are imposed on him. Their definitions of his situation are posited for him as objective reality. He is thus born into not only an objective social structure but also an objective social world. The significant others who mediate this world to him modify it in the course of mediating it. They select aspects of it in accordance with their own location in the social structure, and also by virtue of their individual, biographically rooted idiosyncrasies. The social world is "filtered" to the individual through this double selectivity. Thus the lower-class child not only absorbs a lower-class perspective on the social world, he absorbs it in the idiosyncratic coloration given it by his parents (or whatever other individuals are in charge of his primary socialization). The same lower-class perspective may induce a mood of contentment, resignation, bitter resentment, or seething rebelliousness. Consequently, the lower-class child will not only come to inhabit a world greatly different from that of an upper-class child, but may do so in a manner quite different from the lower-class child next door.[2]

It should hardly be necessary to add that primary socialization involves more than purely cognitive learning. It takes place under circumstances that are highly charged emotionally. Indeed, there is good reason to believe that without such emotional attachment to significant others, the learning process would be difficult if not impossible.[3] The child identifies with the significant others in a variety of emotional ways. Whatever they may be, internalization occurs only as identification occurs. The child takes on the significant others' roles and attitudes, that is, internalizes them and makes them his own. And by this identification with significant others, the child becomes capable of identifying himself, of acquiring a subjectively coherent and plausible identity. In other words, the self is a reflected entity, reflecting the attitudes first taken by significant others toward it;[4] the individual becomes what he is addressed as by his significant others. This is not a one-sided, mechanistic process. It entails a dialectic between identification by others and self-identification, between objectively assigned and subjectively appropriated identity. . . .

What is most important for our considerations here is the fact that the individual not only takes on the roles and attitudes of others, but in the same process takes on their world. Indeed, identity is objectively defined as location in a certain world and can be subjectively appropriated only along with that world. Put differently, all identifications take place within horizons that imply a specific social world. The child learns that he is what he is called. Every name implies a nomenclature, which in turn implies a designated social location.[5] To be given an identity involves being assigned a specific place in the world. Because this identity is subjectively appropriated by the child ("I *am* John Smith"), so is the world to which this identity points. Subjective appropriation of identity and subjective appropriation of the social world are merely different aspects of the same process of internalization, mediated by the same significant others.

Primary socialization creates in the child's consciousness a progressive abstraction from the roles and attitudes of specific others to roles and attitudes in general. For example, in the internalization of norms, there is a progression from "Mummy is angry with me now" to "Mummy is angry with me whenever I spill the soup." As additional significant others (father, grandmother, older sister, and so on) support the mother's negative attitude toward soup-spilling, the generality of the norm is subjectively extended. The decisive step comes when the child recognizes that everybody is against soup-spilling, and the norm is generalized to "one does not spill soup"— "one" being himself as part of a generality that includes, in principle, all of society insofar as it is significant to the child. This abstraction from the roles and attitudes of concrete significant others is called the generalized other.[6] Its formation within consciousness means that the individual now identifies not only with concrete others but with a generality of others, that is, with a society. Only by virtue of this generalized identification does his own self-identification attain stability and continuity. He now has not only an identity vis-à-vis this or that significant other, but an identity in general, which is subjectively apprehended as remaining the same no matter what others, significant or not, are encountered. This newly coherent identity incorporates within itself all the various internalized roles and attitudes—including, among many other things, the self-identification as a non-spiller of soups.

The formation within consciousness of the generalized other marks a decisive phase in socialization. It implies the internalization of society as such and of the objective reality established therein, and, at the same time, the subjective establishment of a coherent and continuous identity. Society, identity, and reality are subjectively crystallized in the same process of internalization. This crystallization is concurrent with the internalization of language. Indeed, for reasons evident from the foregoing observations on language, language constitutes both the most important content and the most important instrument of socialization.

When the generalized other has been crystallized in consciousness, a symmetrical relationship is established between objective and subjective reality. What is real "outside" corresponds to what is real "within." Objective reality can readily be "translated" into subjective reality, and vice versa. Language, of course, is the principal vehicle of this ongoing translating process in both directions. It should, however, be stressed that the symmetry between objective and subjective reality cannot be complete. The two realities correspond to each other, but they are not coextensive. There is always more objective reality "available" than is actually internalized in any individual consciousness, simply because the contents of socialization are determined by the social distribution of knowledge. No individual internalizes the totality of what is objectivated as reality in his society, not even if the society and its world are relatively simple ones. On the other hand, there are always elements of subjective reality that have not originated in socialization, such as the awareness of one's own body prior to and apart from any socially learned apprehension of it. Subjective biography is not fully social. The individual apprehends himself

as being both inside and outside society.[7] This implies that the symmetry between objective and subjective reality is never a static, once-for-all state of affairs. It must always be produced and reproduced in actuality. In other words, the relationship between the individual and the objective social world is like an ongoing balancing act. . . .

In primary socialization, there is no *problem* of identification. There is no choice of significant others. Society presents the candidate for socialization with a predefined set of significant others, whom he must accept as such with no possibility of opting for another arrangement. *Hic Rhodus, hic salta.* One must make do with the parents that fate has regaled one with. This unfair disadvantage inherent in the situation of being a child has the obvious consequence that, although the child is not simply passive in the process of his socialization, it is the adults who set the rules of the game. The child can play the game with enthusiasm or with sullen resistance. But, alas, there is no other game around. This has an important corollary. Because the child has no choice in the selection of his significant others, his identification with them is quasi-automatic. For the same reason, his internalization of their particular reality is quasi-inevitable. The child does not internalize the world of his significant others as one of many possible worlds. He internalizes it as *the* world, the only existent and only conceivable world, the world *tout court*. It is for this reason that the world internalized in primary socialization is so much more firmly entrenched in consciousness than worlds internalized in secondary socializations. However much the original sense of inevitability may be weakened in subsequent disenchantments, the recollection of a never-to-be-repeated certainty—the certainty of the first dawn of reality—still adheres to the first world of childhood. Primary socialization thus accomplishes what (in hindsight, of course) may be seen as the most important confidence trick that society plays on the individual—to make appear as necessity what is in fact a bundle of contingencies, and thus to make meaningful the accident of his birth.

The specific contents that are internalized in primary socialization vary, of course, from society to society. Some are found everywhere. It is language that must be internalized above all. With language, and by means of it, various motivational and interpretative schemes are internalized as institutionally defined—wanting to act like a brave little boy, for instance, and assuming that little boys are naturally divided into the brave and the cowardly. These schemes provide the child with institutionalized programs for everyday life, some immediately applicable to him, others anticipating conduct socially defined for later biographical stages—the bravery that will allow him to get through a day beset with tests of will from one's peers and from all sorts of others, and also the bravery that will be required of one later—when one is initiated as a warrior, say, or when one might be called by the god. These programs, both the immediately applicable and the anticipatory, differentiate one's identity from that of others—such as girls, slave boys, or boys from another clan. Finally, there is internalization of at least the rudiments of the legitimating apparatus; the child learns "why" the programs are what they are. One must be brave because one wants to become a real man; one must perform the rituals because otherwise the gods will be angry; one must be loyal to the chief because only if one does will the gods support one in times of danger; and so on.

In primary socialization, then, the individual's first world is constructed. Its peculiar quality of firmness is to be accounted for, at least in part, by the inevitability of the individual's relationship to his very first significant others. . . .

Primary socialization ends when the concept of the generalized other (and all that goes with it) has been established in the consciousness of the individual. At this point, he is an effective member of society and in subjective possession of a self and a world. But this internalization of society, identity, and reality is not a matter of once and for all. Socialization is never total and never finished.

Notes

1. Our description here, of course, leans heavily on the Meadian theory of socialization.

2. The concept of "mediation" is derived from Sartre, who lacks, however, an adequate theory of socialization.

3. The affective dimension of early learning has been especially emphasized by Freudian child psychology, although there are various findings or behavioristic learning theories that would tend to confirm this. We do not imply acceptance of the theoretical presuppositions of either psychological school in our argument here.

4. Our conception of the reflected character of the self is derived from both Cooley and Mead. Its roots may be found in the analysis of the social self by William James (*The Principles of Psychology*, 1890).

5. On nomenclature, Claude Levi-Strauss, *La Pensée Sauvage* [1962], pp. 253 *ff.*

6. The concept of the "generalized other" is used here in a fully Meadian sense.

7. Compare Georg Simmel on the self-apprehension of man as both inside and outside society. Plessner's concept of "eccentricity" is again relevant here (*Die Stufen des Organischen und der Mensch*, 1928 and 1965).

14

Reference Groups as Perspectives

Tamotsu Shibutani

(1961)

Each person acts on the basis of his definition of the situation. He categorizes the transaction in which he is involved, locates himself within it, and thereby decides upon his obligations. The consistency with which he defines a succession of situations arises from the fact that he generally uses the same perspective, one that he shares with his associates. Once he has adopted a particular point of view it becomes his working conception of the world, and he brings this frame of reference to bear upon each situation he encounters, whether or not anyone else from the group is actually on the scene. Since people with diverse orientations are selectively responsive to different aspects of their natural environment, identical events may be seen in divergent ways. A prostitute and a social worker walking down the same street in a slum area often have remarkably contrasting experiences. The leering men they pass, the drunk sleeping on a doorstep, the drug addict purchasing a "fix"—all are seen differently. But their respective outlooks differ no more than those of a traffic officer and of a motorist stopped for excessive speeding. The offender is irked by the delay; much like a naughty child who has been caught misbehaving, he sulks. If the officer speaks curtly, the motorist is resentful of what he regards to be an unnecessary display of authority. It does not occur to him that only a half hour ago the same officer may have helped load the body of a dead child upon an ambulance, the victim of an accident involving two speeding automobiles. The diversity of interpretations often arises from the fact that key objects, though designated by the same symbols, assume different meanings for different people. It is not surprising, therefore, that immigrants and tourists almost invariably misinterpret much of what they see.

There have been a number of experimental studies demonstrating the manner in which the definition of identical situations varies with perspectives. Among them is one concerning the spectators of a crucial football game between Princeton and Dartmouth on November 23, 1951. It was a fiercely contested match in which a large number of penalties were called. In the second quarter a Princeton star who had been prominently mentioned for All-America honors had to leave the game with a broken nose and a concussion, and in the following period a Dartmouth player was carried off the field with a broken leg. Immediately after the contest there were charges in the press of "dirty" football. A week later undergraduate students in both universities were given a questionnaire concerning the game. All Princeton students described the game as "rough and dirty"; of the Dartmouth students a tenth thought it was "clean and fair," a third judged it as "rough and fair," and the remainder acknowledged that it was "rough and dirty." Of the Princeton spectators nine-tenths insisted that the Dartmouth players had started the foul tactics; but of the Dartmouth observers only a third held their own team guilty, and the rest blamed both sides. When the students were shown a motion picture of the game and asked to note and to evaluate infractions of the rules, the Princeton students detected twice as many violations and rated them as being more flagrant.[1] All of these students were either in the same stadium or were exposed to the same motion picture, but what they saw differed to a remarkable extent.

Divergent meanings can sometimes be reconciled by comparing assumptions, but misunderstandings become less amenable to clarification when differences exist over such fundamental categories as *time*. At first glance nothing appears as simple as the concept of time; it just passes on inexorably in increments like hours or days. But the passage of time is of different significance in different cultures. Precision in keeping time, for example, is relatively unimportant for a peasant, for he begins work soon after dawn and continues until sundown. He harvests his crops when they are ready and rests when weather conditions are such that he cannot work. In a peasant community that is becoming industrialized, however, keeping time takes on a new meaning, for men work by the clock. In some areas the owning of a wrist watch has become a status symbol among those desiring to be in line with the latest trends. At the other extreme are those who work for the railroads, among whom almost everything is measured in terms of accuracy in timing.[2] Such contrasts in the unstated premises about the passage of time sometimes lead people to conclude that others are indolent or unnecessarily aggressive.

Differences in the meaning of categories such as success can lead to serious misunderstandings, for the manner in which men organize their careers depends upon such conceptions. In the United States a high value is generally placed upon success. It is taken for granted that each individual will strive to improve his station in life, and those who do not succeed are often regarded as indigent. But there are many different conceptions of the kinds of goals that are regarded as worth pursuing. In some social worlds men in competitive situations are expected to exert themselves to the utmost to win; victory is all important, and considerations of decency and fair play are viewed as luxuries for "idealists." In intercollegiate athletics, for example, it has been reported that some athletes have been injected with amphetamine and similar stimulants by their coaches to make possible performances far beyond their normal capacity. Those who are familiar with the unreasonable pressures placed upon coaches and athletes view this practice with regret but with understanding. But many others are horrified, wondering what there could be about winning a contest that would justify risking the health of young men. Similarly, in some universities men doing research sacrifice themselves and their families, devoting themselves to their work 365 days a year; some of their colleagues wonder, however, whether anything such men may accomplish could really be worth the unbalanced lives they lead.[3] In some business circles the deception and exploitation of competitors and customers is regarded as perfectly natural; others wonder whether success built upon the misfortunes of other people can really be satisfying, and they condemn those who struggle so feverishly as being "power mad." Assumptions such as these provide the basis for deciding what goals are really worth seeking in life and the manner in which one is to go about pursuing his aspirations.

Many serious misunderstandings arise from differences in certain crucial values, especially in criteria of modesty, cleanliness, and sexual conduct. There are vast differences in standards of modesty. In some social worlds the exposure of the nude body, belching, and flatulence are simply accepted as a natural part of human life; in others such behavior is regarded as unforgivable and is concealed at all cost. The emphasis upon personal cleanliness ranges from high standards of sanitation to the retention of an outward appearance of neatness to a vague awareness of the problem. One person may be amused at those who are constantly washing themselves, while the latter wonder how their associate can possibly stand his own stench. There are norms in all groups concerning what constitutes proper sex conduct; this is true even in groups that are thought by outsiders to be without standards.[4] But there is remarkable variability in these norms, ranging from the open acceptance of sexual excitement as a part of human nature to the puritanical denial of sexuality. Practices that are condemned as sinful perversions in one circle are accepted as the normal part of life in another. Since each group takes it for granted that its own ways are right and natural, people are easily convinced that outsiders are either lewd or unduly inhibited. . . . Because understandings about sex are so deeply ingrained, people generally feel that there is something filthy or unnatural about the practices condemned in their group.

People with diverse cultural backgrounds often have different conceptions of human nature. In each universe of discourse explanations of the things men do are circumscribed by the available vocabulary of motives. There are a limited set of recognized intentions, approved and disapproved, which are thought to depict the natural inclinations of man. There are a limited number of words that are used to label these dispositions, and a motive that cannot be designated obviously cannot be imputed or avowed. Furthermore, in each social world there are shared assumptions as to the kinds of intentions that develop in each standardized context. In our

society it does little good for a murderer to insist that his hand had been guided by the spirit of an ancestor for whom he had been named; he is more likely to receive a sympathetic hearing by claiming that he was the victim of a mysterious "inner urge" that he could not understand.

As one compares the perspectives that are shared in diverse social worlds, it becomes apparent that what differs are the premises underlying action. Identical situations are perceived differently because those starting out with unlike assumptions project contrasting hypotheses and are selectively responsive to different sensory cues. What makes the clarification of these divergences so difficult is that the differences are about matters that are taken for granted, matters on which alternatives are not considered. Beliefs concerning the importance of punctuality, cleanliness, or success, convictions about the proper contact between the sexes, as well as assumptions about the nature of love—all these meanings are intertwined with thousands of others into an organized scheme. A successful challenge to any basic assumption can lead to searching questions about all the others. To challenge such fundamental beliefs is to challenge a man's orientation toward life. If he takes it seriously, he may be left dazed and bewildered, not knowing what is true and what is false. . . .

The contention that men think, feel, and see things from the standpoint peculiar to the group in which they participate is an old one which has been repeatedly emphasized by anthropologists and students of the sociology of knowledge. But what makes this hypothesis so important for the study of modern mass societies is the fact that people may assume the perspectives of groups in which they are *not* recognized members, sometimes of groups in which they have never participated directly, and sometimes of groups that do not exist at all. For example, those seeking to raise their status are more responsive to the opinions of people in the social set to which they aspire than to the views shared in the circle to which they belong. Members of ethnic minorities who are becoming assimilated examine themselves from the standpoint of the dominant group; they often develop strong feelings of inferiority and condemn others in the minority for failing to live up to these outside norms. Servants and slaves sometimes accept the standards of their masters, and adolescent boys in slum areas sometimes adopt the code of the underworld, as they learn of it from motion pictures. There are many people, then, who try to live up to the standards of social worlds of which they learn from vicarious participation—through observation or through the various media of mass communication.

Furthermore, in societies characterized by cultural pluralism each person may acquire several perspectives, for he can participate simultaneously in a number of social worlds. Because cultures are products of communication, a person develops a somewhat different perspective from each communication channel to which he is regularly exposed. Because of the ease with which one can gain access to a variety of channels, he leads a somewhat segmented life, engaging in turn in a succession of quite unrelated activities. Furthermore, the particular aggregate of social worlds of which one partakes differs from individual to individual; this is what led Simmel to declare that each person stands at that point at which the unique combination of social circles of which he is a part intersects.[5] This geometric analogy is a happy one, for it enables us to conceive of the almost endless permutations as well as the varying degrees of involvement in each circle. To understand any particular person, then, one must get a picture of his unique outlook. Since this is the product of his past experiences, real and vicarious, no two people are likely to have an identical outlook.

Since a given situation may be defined from so many different points of view, to understand what a man does, an observer must get at the assumptions with which he begins. One of the most important things to know about a person is what he takes for granted. To take his role and to anticipate what he is likely to do, it is necessary to identify the perspective he is using, the social world in which he is participating in a given act. The concept of *reference group* may be used to designate *that group, real or imaginary, whose standpoint is being used as the frame of reference by the actor.* This provides some notion of the meanings he is projecting upon the scene. Not only can different persons approach the same situation from diverse standpoints, but the same person in different transactions may utilize different perspectives. On a hockey field he has one orientation, and in a classroom he is participating in an entirely different social world. Each man acts, then, for some kind of *audience,* and it is important to know what this audience is and what kinds of expectations are imputed to it.

The reference group supports the values in terms of which a person estimates his own conduct; therefore, his line of activity depends upon the real or anticipated reactions of the other people for whom he is performing. There is a selective sensitivity to others; men are not equally responsive to the opinions of everyone present. Hardened criminals are well aware of the disapproval of most people but are not especially upset. Furthermore, the audience that counts need not consist of people whom one knows personally; frequently reference groups are quite large, and one can have direct contacts only with a few representatives. For example, those in ethnic minorities are usually highly responsive to the demands of others with whom they identify on the basis of common ancestry, but in most cases each knows on a personal basis only a small percentage of those who make up the category. In studying the behavior of human beings it is necessary to get "inside" the actor, to see the situation from his point of view, and the concept of the reference group is useful for this purpose.

There are as many reference groups for each person as there are communication channels in which he participates, and individuals differ considerably in their range of participation. Each lives in an environment of which he is the center, and the dimensions of his effective surroundings are defined by the direction and distance from which news comes to him. Each time a man enters a new communication channel—subscribes to a new periodical, joins a new circle of friends, purchases a television set, or begins to listen regularly to some radio program—he is introduced into a new social world. People who communicate develop an appreciation of one another's tastes, interests, and outlook upon life; and as one acquires new standards of conduct, he adds more people to his audience. Each man's outlook is both shaped and limited by the communication networks in which he becomes involved.

A reference group, then, is any identifiable group whose supposed perspective is used by the actor as a frame of reference in the organization of his perceptual field. Men are usually most responsive to the views imputed to those with whom they are in direct and constant association, but reference groups may also be imaginary, as in the case of artists who are "born ahead of their time," scientists who work for "humanity," or philanthropists who give for "posterity." Such persons estimate their endeavors from a postulated standpoint imputed to people who have not yet been born. They sometimes undergo incredible sacrifices in anticipation of being appreciated by some future audience that presumably would be more sensible than the people who are now living. They are not concerned with immediate rewards and work slavishly for people who may actually never come into existence. There are others who live for a distant past, idealizing some period in history, longing for the "good old days" and constantly criticizing current events from a standpoint imputed to people long since dead—as in the case of the Southerner pining for the days of the Confederacy. There are some people who create a paradise in the next world—Valhalla, Heaven, or the "happy hunting grounds"—and forego pleasures in their present life on the assumption that they will be rewarded after death. An interesting problem is that of ascertaining how perspectives imputed to such imaginary audiences are constructed. One can learn about the typical ways in which people in the "Greek world" presumably lived, acted, and thought by reading history and studying archaeology, but what of the audiences that will not be born for another thousand years? The fact that there is no material basis for such reference groups does not make them any less important.

There are some categories of people with which men occasionally identify which are so amorphous that they may almost be regarded as imaginary groups. Two examples of vaguely defined audiences that play an important part in our society are public opinion and social class. Politicians, administrators, labor leaders, advertising men, and even dictators are constantly concerned with what they call "public opinion." Sometimes even the man of the street may refrain from doing something on the ground that "people won't like it." But who are these "people"? How does one go about ascertaining what it is that the "people" want? Although surveys and polls give some indications, there is no way of knowing for certain until after mass reactions are aroused. Public opinion is the source of so much concern precisely because a miscalculation of what people will tolerate can lead to disastrous consequences—embarrassing demonstrations, the loss of an election, demands for changes that threaten those in privileged positions, or a spectacular drop in the sales of some product. But most of the time those who are concerned with public opinion can only guess, and their conjectures are usually based upon very limited contacts. The same is true of social class. In a study of social stratification in England, where class lines are more clearly drawn than they are in the United States, Bott found that people are class-conscious and do act in terms of their understanding of their class position. But their conception of class structure is often vague and develops from the ways in which the various individuals personally experience prestige and power in their daily lives. Most people are conscious of class differences, but their conception of the system varies with their experiences. Bott concluded that a social class is a constructed reference group—an audience to which people project their own respective expectations and of which they do not in fact possess accurate knowledge.[6]

Actually, men become acutely aware of the existence of divergent standpoints primarily when they are caught in situations in which conflicting demands are made upon them. While they avoid making difficult decisions whenever possible, these contradictions sometimes force one to choose between two social worlds. Such inner conflicts are essentially struggles between alternative ways of defining a given situation, the options arising from each of two or more perspectives that might be brought to bear upon it. Examples of such dilemmas were provided by William James: "As a man I pity you, but as an official I must show you no mercy; as a politician I regard him as an ally, but as a moralist I loathe him." In playing roles in different social worlds, contrasting expectations are imputed to competing audiences, and sometimes these differences cannot be compromised. The problem is that of selecting the standpoint from which the situation is to be defined. It is in contexts in which alternative definitions are demanded that problems of loyalty arise.

There are individual differences in the flexibility with which one shifts from one reference group to another. There are some people who have a dominant perspective and insist upon defining virtually all situations from this standpoint. Such persons are sometimes reluctant even to acknowledge the existence of other viewpoints and insist that everyone who disagrees with them is wrong. Most people have a limited number of perspectives and are aware of the existence of others, and though they may feel uncomfortable in the company of people whose views are too different, they can tolerate some diversity. Still others change with the wind so that even their close associates are not certain of where they stand. Some can compartmentalize their experiences into units; others apparently find it difficult to do so. . . .

NOTES

1. Albert H. Hastorf and Hadley Cantril, "They Saw a Game: A Case Study," *Journal of Abnormal and Social Psychology,* XLIX (1954), 129–34.

2. Cf. W. Fred Cottrell, *The Railroader* (Stanford: Stanford University Press, 1940); and Hallowell, op. cit., pp. 216–35.

3. Cf. Alvin W. Gouldner, "Cosmopolitans and Locals: Toward an Analysis of Latent Social Roles," *Administrative Science Quarterly,* II (1957–58), 281–306, 444–80.

4. William F. Whyte, "Slum Sex Code," *American Journal of Sociology,* XLIX (1943), 24–31.

5. Georg Simmel, *Conflict and the Web of Group-Affiliations,* trans. Kurt H. Wolff and Reinhard Bendix (Glencoe: The Free Press, 1955), pp. 127–95.

6. Elizabeth Bott, "The Concept of Class as a Reference Group," *Human Relations,* VII (1954), 259–85. Cf. Kurt Riezler, "What is Public Opinion?" *Social Research,* XI (1944), 397–427.

15

Shades of White

Pamela Perry

(2001)

"How would you describe white American culture?" I ask Laurie, a white, middle-class senior at Valley Groves High,* a predominantly white, suburban public school near the Pacific Coast of northern California. She pauses, her face looking visibly perplexed as if she did not understand the question or her mind was drawing a blank. Wondering if she heard me over the roar of the cappuccino machine in the background, I awkwardly reiterate, "Like, you know, what would you say white American culture is like?"

"I wouldn't be able to tell you. I don't know." She pauses again and laughs nervously. "When you think about it, it's like—[a longer pause]—*I don't know!*"

About twenty miles away from Valley Groves is the postindustrial city of Clavey. Clavey High School is composed of a brilliant mosaic of students from different ethnic and racial groups, about 12 percent of whom are white. In an interview with Murray, a white, Jewish, middle-class senior, he and I talked a great deal about the consequences of race in the United States and what privileges come with being a white person here. When I probed into his identification with being white or Jewish, he said,

[Cultural pride] doesn't make sense to me. To me it doesn't. I mean, what difference does it make what my great, great grandfather was or his whole generation. That's not affecting my life. . . . I'm still here now. I've got to make what's best for me in the future. I can't harp on what the past has brought.

Laurie and Murray express what the racial category "white" means to each of them. Although their responses differ markedly, they share something fundamental; they perceive white raciality as cultureless. For Laurie, whiteness is not culturally defined. She lives within it but cannot name it. It is taken for granted. For Murray, to be cultural means having emotional attachment to tradition and history. He eschews culture, in this regard, and lives in the present, looking forward.

I chose these two excerpts from qualitative research I carried out in 1994–97 at Valley Groves, a predominantly white, suburban high school, and Clavey, a multiracial, urban high school. The focus of this research was on what differences, if any, the two demographically distinct contexts made on the ways white youth reflected on and constructed white identities. I found that it made a large difference: white students at Valley Groves did not reflect on or

---

*All names of cities, schools, and individuals in this article are pseudonyms.

define white identity as a culture and social location to the extent that the white youth at Clavey did. Moreover, white identities at Clavey tended to be altogether more variable and contradictory than at Valley Groves. Elsewhere, I argue that these differences in white identities were conditioned by different experiences and structures of interracial association (Perry 1998).

I make a similar argument in this article but with a focus on the only similarity between the ways whites at both schools defined white identity. They defined white as cultureless. By that, I mean that white identity was understood to have no ties or allegiances to European ancestry and culture, no "traditions." To the white youth, only "ethnic" people had such ties to the past. The students would agree with George DeVos (1975) that a "feeling of continuity with the past" distinguishes an "ethnic" group from peoples with more "present-oriented" or "future-oriented" identities (p. 17)—such as whites.

However, although white students at Valley Groves and Clavey shared this perception of white identity, they did not arrive at it by the same processes. In what follows, I present and interpret ethnographic and interview data to argue that at Valley Groves, the tendency for youth to explicitly define themselves and other whites as people without culture came about through processes of *naturalization*—the embedding of historically constituted cultural practices in that which is taken for granted and seems "normal" and natural. At Clavey, culturelessness was achieved through processes of *rationalization*—the embedding of whiteness within a Western rational epistemology and value paradigm that marginalizes or subordinates all things "cultural."

Although there is some scholarly debate over whether there is such a thing as "white culture" (Ignatiev and Garvey 1996; Roediger 1994), my argument here is not so much about whether there is or is not a white culture but about the

power whites exercise when *claiming* they have no culture. Culturelessness can serve, even if unintentionally, as a measure of white racial superiority. It suggests that one is either "normal" and "simply human" (therefore, the standard to which others should strive) or beyond culture or "postcultural" (therefore, developmentally advanced).

This work seeks to advance on theories and research in critical white studies, the sociology of education, and racial-ethnic identity formation by vividly illustrating the social construction of white identities and culture in schooling and the ways that different social-structural contexts differently influence constructions of whiteness, including the construction of white as cultureless or the norm. . . .

METHOD AND REFLECTIONS

The vast wealth of excellent scholarship on the social construction of identities in schooling fundamentally shaped my research focus and methodology (Bourdieu and Passeron 1977; Davidson 1996; Eckert 1989; Fordham 1996; Fordham and Ogbu 1986; Kinney 1993; MacLeod 1987; Thorne 1993; Valenzuela 1999). The main focus of my work was what role, if any, close interracial association in school had on the racial consciousness and identities of white youth. Therefore, in choosing my research sites, I looked for two schools: one predominantly white and located in a predominantly white town or city; the other multiracial, minority white, and located in a minority white town or city. It also concerned me that the schools be in the same geographical region, of similar size and academic standing, and with student bodies of similar socioeconomic backgrounds to keep those factors as "constant" as possible. I studied census data and school statistics for different towns and cities across the United States before I decided on Valley Groves, which was 83 percent white, and Clavey, which was 12 percent white. Although Clavey was located in a city and Valley Groves a suburb, Clavey was very similar to Valley Groves in all respects besides racial composition, largely due to the fact that Clavey's catchment area encircled a largely middle- to upper-middle-class population. Particularly important for my research was that white students at Clavey were primarily middle class, which allowed me to focus on middle-class whites in both schools.

I spent two and a half years in the schools doing participant observation and in-depth interviewing. Daily practices included sitting in on classrooms with students, hanging out with them during breaks and lunch, attending school club meetings, and participating in student-administrator advisory committees, especially those concerned with race and cultural awareness on campus. I also observed or helped out with after-school programs and events, such as school plays, major rallies, games, and the junior and senior balls of each school. To familiarize myself with the music and leisure activities the students were involved in, after hours I listened to the local rap, R & B, punk, alternative, and classic rock radio stations; bought CD's of the most popular musical artists; went to live underground punk and alternative concerts; read fanzines and other youth magazines; watched MTV; studied music that students dubbed for me; and attended a large rave produced by some Clavey students.

Although I looked somewhat younger than my age (thirty-eight when the research began), I made concerted efforts to minimize the effects of age difference on how students related to me. I did not associate with other adults on campus. I dressed casually in attire that I was comfortable in, which happened to be similar to the attire students were comfortable in: blue jeans, sandals or athletic shoes, T-shirt or sweat-shirt, no jewelry except four tiny hoop earrings—one in one ear,

three in the other. I had students call me by my first name, and I did not talk down to them, judge them, or otherwise present myself as an authority figure. To the contrary, I saw the students as the authorities, and they seemed to appreciate that regard. Those efforts, on top of having developed some popular-cultural frames of reference with the students, contributed to my developing some very close relationships with several of the students and fairly wide access to different peer groups and cliques on campus. Having stood in the middle of secret hideouts, food fights, fist fights, tongue lashings, and over-the-top fits of goofiness, I can say that in most cases, I seemed to have little impact on students' behaviors.

My other most apparent traits—race, gender, and middle-class/intellectual appearance—had both positive and negative effects. I connected most readily and easily with girls. The results were that I have more narrative data and in-depth material from girls than boys. At Clavey, however, I did make a few close relationships with boys that I believe helped balance my findings at that school. Similarly, my class background made crossing class differences awkward at times for me and for some participants, particularly working-class males. However, since I was focusing on middle-class white students, my own middle-class whiteness seemed to work mostly on my behalf. With respect to students of color, of which I interviewed quite a few, my race limited my ability to hang out with them in groups at school. Because my focus was on white students, I do not feel this limitation seriously compromises my argument, but deeper perspectives from students of color would certainly have improved it.

I formally interviewed more than sixty students at Valley Groves and Clavey. They included, at Valley Groves, fourteen white youth, one Filipino female, and a group of ten African American students. At Clavey, I interviewed twenty-two white youth, ten African American youth, two Chinese American, one Filipino, and two Latino youth. A little more than half of my interviewees were female and the rest male. Most were middle class, but six were working class.

I did not randomly sample interview participants because I had very specific desires regarding to whom I wanted to speak: liberals and conservatives; whites, blacks, Asians, and Latinos; punks, hippies, homies, alternatives, rappers, and such; high achievers and low achievers; girls and boys; middle class and working class. So I sought out interviewees through multiple methods. Mostly, I directly approached students I observed in classrooms or in their cliques, but I also went to club meetings and asked for volunteers and, for the hard-to-find students, sought recommendations or introductions from youth.

Interviews took place on campus, in coffee shops, and in students' homes and generally lasted two hours. Students and their parents signed consent forms that explained that I was examining racial identities and race relations in the two demographically distinct contexts. In the interviews, I explored youth's experiences at school, their experiences of racial difference, how they thought of themselves racially, how they thought of racial-ethnic others, their cultural interests and other significant identities, and what types of meanings they gave to their interests and identities. Interviews and informal discussions were also a time for me to discuss with youth my interpretations of school practices, youth cultures, and other events around campus. Students spoke candidly and openly; they seemed eager to talk to an adult who would listen to and treat them respectfully.

The interviews were tape-recorded and transcribed. They and my field notes were manually coded and analyzed along the way to illuminate processes, practices, terms, and conceptions calling for deeper investigation or changes in focus. Along the way, also, I read widely, looking for existing studies and theories that might shed analytical light on my observations. My final coding and analysis were carried out without the aid of software—only colored markers, a Xerox machine, and lots of post-its.

IDENTITY NATURALIZATION AT VALLEY GROVES HIGH: PASSIVE CONSTRUCTION OF WHITE AS CULTURELESS

Valley Groves is a suburban city of roughly 115,000 people. Its residents are solidly white and middle to upper-middle class. In 1990, 83 percent of the population of Valley Groves was white, and the median household income was $42,095. Inside Valley Groves High School's catchment area is Mapleton, a small suburb of about 7,500 people. Ninety percent of Mapleton residents are white, and their median household income in 1989 was $70,000.

The racial and class demographics of Valley Groves and Mapleton cities were reflected in the composition of the Valley Groves High student body and staff. In the 1995–96 school year, white youth made up 83 percent of the school population, followed by Hispanics (7 percent), Asians (5 percent), Filipinos (2 percent), and African Americans (2 percent). The fifty-three teachers, five administrators, three campus supervisors, and fifty-odd service and administrative staff were 85 percent non-Hispanic white. There was only one African American among them.

Raymond Williams (1976) wrote,

Hegemony supposes the existence of something that is truly total . . . which is lived at such a depth, which saturates the society to such an extent, and which, as Gramsci put it, even constitutes the limit of commonsense for most people under its sway. (pp. 204–5)

At Valley Groves, whiteness "saturated" youths' lived experience. White youth and adults overwhelmed the demographic landscape. When I asked white students at Valley Groves how they would rate their experiences of people of color, most said "very little" or "none at all." In the school yard during lunch or break, students sauntered into the "quad," a large patio area in the center of the campus, to meet with friends and grab a bite to eat. At these times, the most open and public spaces were a sea of blonde- and brown-haired white girls and boys in blue jeans and T-shirts sporting logos of their favorite rock band or skateboard company. The popular and nondescript kids (usually called "normal") occupied the main quad, and the counterculture white students—druggies, skaters, hicks—claimed territory in outside areas adjoining the quad.

Some African American, Asian, or Latino students joined with white friends, and, when they did, they assumed the styles and demeanors of the crowd they were in, be it "popular," "skater," or merely "normal." Then, there were the students of color who clustered in groups of like-kind, racial ethnically. They wore their own styles; spoke in Tagalog, Spanish, or black English; and usually hung out in the cafeteria, classrooms, or distant corners of the campus, locations that kept them virtually invisible to the majority of students in and around the quad.

Similar spatial demographics, in which racial-ethnic difference was placed where it did not challenge the white norm, existed in the classroom structure (Fine 1989). The mainstream students—the popular kids, athletes, and college-bound youth—were in the honors and other high-tracked classes. The "regular" classes were made up of a hodge-podge of different types of youth—middle-class mainstream, working class, countercultural. With the exception of some of the high-tracked math classes, in which Asian American students were overrepresented, high- and regular-tracked courses were disproportionately white, with small

numbers of minority youth distributed equally among them. Just where the students of color were I am sorry to say I never learned the answer to, except that one day I saw a large (disproportionate) number of them in a remedial class.

Whiteness saturated Valley Groves's school life not only demographically but culturally as well. The dominant culture at Valley Groves—that which oriented the social organization of students, common styles and practices, and expected behaviors—was homologous with the dominant culture outside of the campus, namely, a white European American culture. By "white European American culture," I refer to two features of American culture, broadly. First, although the dominant culture in the United States is syncretic, that is, composed of the different cultures of the peoples that populate the United States, several of its core characteristics are of European origin. These include, as I have already suggested, the values and practices derived from the European Enlightenment, Anglican Protestantism, and Western colonialism, such as rationalism, individualism, personal responsibility, a strong work ethic, self-effacement, and mastery over nature. I include, also, carryover or "melted" material cultures of Western, Eastern, and Southern European peoples, such as hamburgers, spaghetti, cupcakes, parades, and line dancing. Second, by virtue of being numerically and politically dominant, whites tend to share certain dispositions, worldviews, and identities constituted by that, especially in predominantly white communities. Currently, a race-neutral or "color-blind" worldview and sense of oneself as normal are examples of that.

At Valley Groves, student cliques and social categories revolved around a norm-other dichotomy in which normal meant that one conformed to the dominant culture and expectations placed on them, and other meant one did not. For example, when I asked Billy how he would describe his group of friends he said,

"Normal. We don't smoke or drink or anything and [we] wear clothes we would call normal."

"And what is that?" I asked.

"Not oversized, baggy clothes like the skaters wear, or, obviously, we don't wear cowboy hats or boots."

The normal clothes Billy referred to were the styles one might find at mainstream department stores like The Gap: loose, not overly baggy blue jeans; cotton T-shirts and blouses; sundresses; khaki shorts. The kids who did not dress or act normal served to define the boundaries of what was and was not normal. For instance, skaters wore excessively baggy pants and overall filthy clothes; "hicks" wore ten-gallon cowboy hats, tooled-leather boots, and tight jeans with big brassy pants buckles; and druggies flagrantly carried and consumed illicit drugs. (*Flagrant* is the key word here since, as a popular girl told me, "Popular kids do drugs. They just don't want anyone to know it.") Carli, a white girl who considered herself "hippie," referred to the non-mainstream kids as "rebels." She said, "I call them rebels 'cause they know the system sucks."

This norm-other dichotomy was race neutral. Maria, a popular senior of Mexican American descent on her mother's side, told me that the "first cut of students starts with who is popular" and who fits in with the other cliques on campus. Anyone, regardless of racial-ethnic ascription, could be popular, a skater, a druggie—even a "homie," which, as groups went at Valley Groves, was the most nonwhite. Price of admission was conformity to the styles and demeanor of the group. Hence, black kids who were skaters were not "black skaters," nor were white kids who were homies "white homies"; they were simply "skaters" and "homies," respectively. A white skater I spoke to pointed to an African American boy in his crowd and said, "That doesn't matter. We all love to skate together, hang out together." And when I asked black students if the white kids who were homies were considered "wanna-be black," they looked flatly at me and said, "No." Ron, who was a homie himself, said, "One of the guys who hangs out with us is white. He's not a racist and we've known each other for years."

Students' measuring sticks for gauging normal styles, behaviors, and expectations were the common, everyday practices and the system of rewards at school. On any given day at Valley Groves High, students attended classes and romped into the Quad at break and lunch to purchase anything from fresh cinnamon rolls, cupcakes, rice crispy bars, and fudge for snacks to pizza, hamburgers, meat loaf, and spaghetti for something more substantial. On occasion, leadership students played rock music over the loudspeakers while students talked among themselves in their friendship groups. Circulating through the youth were members of the administrative staff, who would greet students by their first names and engage them in casual conversation, and the team of grounds supervisors, all of whom were greying, middle-aged women. One was affectionately referred to as "Grandma."

"These are all good kids," is what administrators, teachers, and ground supervisors would say to me nearly every time I spoke with them. As Bourdieu (1977) argues, the embodiment of practices and ideas into that which feels normal, natural, and "common sense" requires collective reinforcement and approval. Adult approval rating of the students was high, and they let students know that with their smiles and friendly banter. It was demonstrated also, I believe, through the grounds supervisors, who, by virtue of their title (as opposed to "security") and appearance, demonstrated an implicit trust the adults had that students would, for the most part, comply with expected behaviors. (At least, adults trusted that the white students would comply. Students of color, especially black boys who wore hip-hop styles, told me that they experienced considerable racial profiling by school administrators and the grounds supervisors. This explicitly racial treatment of students of color was either not witnessed by whites or rubbed out of their minds, which I believe played a role in maintaining the pretense of race neutrality on campus.)

At schoolwide rallies and events, collective consensus, reinforcement, and approval of white American norms came from an even wider span of individuals: school adults, other students, and the outside community. Such events seemed to secure a broad consensus of what is true, right, and white but always through nondiscursive practice, never by saying and, thus, never sayable. For example, homecoming—a high school tradition that celebrates the school football team—was a time to raise school spirit and, thus, excite the interest and imagination of the most students possible. It was, for me, an excellent time to observe shared assumptions and normative expectations of students and observe the rewards and sanctions applied to different types of behaviors.

One day during homecoming week, students held rallies in the gym for the entire student body. To the thunder of heavy-metal music, rivers of white students flowed into the gym and took seats in different quadrants of the auditorium reserved for different grade levels. Just before the official ceremony began, two big, husky white males (appearing to be seniors) dragged into the center of the auditorium a small boy (appearing to be a freshman) whose feet and legs were bound with silver duct tape. The crowd laughed and applauded. The two husky guys pumped their fists in the air to encourage the crowd then dragged the boy off center stage. After a brief greeting, members of the student leadership committee introduced the junior varsity and varsity football players. The players came out in succession and formed a line across the middle of the gym floor. The boys were all white except for three black players on the junior

varsity team and, on the varsity team, two boys with Hispanic surnames. As his name was called, each player stepped forward to acknowledge the applause. Most did so with an air of shyness or humility, their heads bowed, cheeks blushing, shoulders pulled up to their ears. Two boldly strutted out, trying to play up the roar of the crowd, but their efforts fell flat.

Then, the varsity cheerleaders bolted to center stage, leaping energetically before getting into formation for their choreographed performance. The girls were all thin, some overly so, and wore uniforms with close-fitted bodices that made them look all the smaller. But their body size betrayed their strength. Their routine, driven by the firm beat of a heavy-metal tune, was rigorously gymnastic, with lots of cartwheels, flips, and pyramid constructions that were punctuated by the top girls falling trustingly into the arms of their comrades. Long, silky blonde hair parachuted out with each acrobatic stunt. Through the performance, the audience remained silent and attentive, with an occasional collective gasp at the girls' athleticism, until the show was over. At that time, the cheerleaders received roaring, vocal applause.

On the day after the rally was the homecoming parade. The parade took off from the basketball field and wound its way onto a residential side street. Four adult males, two of whom appeared to be Mexican American, led the parade mounted on prancing horses and wearing Mexican serapes and sombreros. The front two carried large replicas of the California and American flags. Following the horsemen were two convertibles, one of which was a white Corvette carrying the (white) city mayor, who waved ceremoniously to the onlookers on the sidewalks.

The music of the marching band, which followed closely behind the mayor, announced the arrival of the parade along its path. A group of eight white and one African American female dancers led the band, tossing and spinning colored flags in sync with the beat of the band's percussion section. The fifty musicians in the band, most of whom appeared white with five or six exceptions, marched militarily in tight formation and played their instruments with competence and finesse. Following the band was a procession of American-built pickup trucks carrying, first, the varsity and junior varsity football players, then the "royalty"—the senior "king" and "queen" and underclass "princes" and "princesses"—and finally, an open-bed truck loaded with seniors, hooting and cheering as if their graduation day had already arrived.

The parade made its way through several blocks of residences before returning to the main street and slowly making its way back to the school. Proud parents were perched on the sidewalks with their thirty-five-millimeter and video cameras in hand. Community residents stepped onto their front landings to wave and cheer as the parade passed their homes. Others peered out through large pane windows with cats in arms and dogs at heel.

The homecoming rally and parade were, in my view, packed with assumptions, values, behaviors, and origin stories that privileged white European American perspectives as well as gender, sexuality, and class-based norms (all of which tend to coproduce one another). At the rally, for example, the display of the hog-tied freshman reinforced that white (male) dominance is sustained not only through the subordination of nonwhite others but of "other" whites as well (Hartigan 1997, 1999; Thandeka 1999; Wray and Newitz 1997). Second, the virtues of personal mastery and self-effacement were exemplified by the humble postures of the football players and reinforced by the slights the audience gave to those who presented themselves with more bravado. And, finally, the cheerleaders' thin, bounded physiques and gravity-defying athletic feats demonstrated that the girls had successfully learned to subjugate their bodies and overcome nature.

The homecoming parade, with its display of the national and state flags, American cars, marching band, and school royalty, was a stunning way to observe the coproduction of whiteness, Americanness, citizenship, and gendered codes of conduct. Included was even an origin story of white American colonial victory over Mexico. And, by virtue of who was there and who was not, the knitting together of the themes of mastery, domination, nationhood, and industry with whiteness was seamless. Other cultures in the school and community were not represented in the parade. There were no Filipino dancers, Asian martial artists, or African American rappers. The event was performed by whites and for whites and, thus, little contradicted the cultural and political assumptions at play.

In sum, at Valley Groves High, white people and white European American culture saturated school life. White youth had little to no association with people or cultures that would place whiteness in relief in such a way that students might reflect on it and consciously define it.

No Ties

Given this sociocultural milieu, white youth could say nothing when I asked them to describe white culture; they had no words to describe that which comes naturally. Laurie, whom I quoted at the beginning of this article, struggled to describe white culture and finally succumbed to "I don't know!" Billy, a popular white senior, had a similar response. I asked him what he thought was culturally specific about white American culture. After a long pause in which he said only, "hmmm," he asked, "Like, what's American culture?"

"Uh-huh," I replied.

"Hmmm. [Another long pause]—I don't really know, 'cause it's like [pause]—just [pause]—I'm not sure! I don't know!"

However, Valley Groves' white students were not always speechless about white identity. When my questions probed into the youths' social experiences and identities as whites and not their cultures, they could find something to say. Not too surprisingly, most told me that being white meant you had no cultural ties. Students I spoke to would explain that they had mixed European roots that held no significance to them; therefore they were "just white." For example, I asked Mara, a Valley Groves senior, what she would say if a census taker asked her, straight out without any prompting, "What are you?"

Mara: Like a race?

PGP: Could be a racial category.

Mara: I'd have to answer "Very white." I am, yeah. I am 100 percent white.

PGP: I noticed on your [consent form] you said you had a mix of European backgrounds, and you wrote, "Pretty much WHITE." Is that what "white" means to you, a European mix?

Mara: I just think that there's not much—I don't really think of myself as European. I think of myself as a white American girl. . . . I don't really go back to my roots, though I know I have family and where they come from but they're all white races.

PGP: You don't have any heartfelt devotion to your European past?

Mara: Not really. My family has lived here for generations, so I don't really draw on that.

Laurie had a similar response:

We're a bunch of everything. My great, great Grandmother is Cherokee. Whenever I fill out [questionnaires] about what's my ethnic background I write "white" because everything is so random. We have German, some family from Wales—but that means nothing to me. . . . I don't have ties to anything. I haven't heard about anything my parents have been through except for my grandparents in wars. It's all been about people, not culture.

Answers like Mara's and Laurie's, of which there were many, reflect that, although white youth at Valley Groves may not have thought about whiteness as a culture, they did think about it as a social category (Phoenix 1997), as a "group position" (Blumer 1958) with respect to other racial-ethnic groups. To Valley Groves' students, whites were a group because they did not have culture, and "minorities" did. Through mixed-European and other cultural amalgamation, whites were a new breed, a hybrid, removed from a past that was meaningless to them and for the loss of which they held no remorse.

Valley Groves' whites were speaking from the "postcultural" perspective that Rosaldo (1989) asserts is the perspective of all who are members of the dominant group of Western-style nation states. Naturalized whiteness complements and helps constitute this kind of postcultural identity because of the stability garnered from the fit between societal norms and the constructed identity of whites (powell 1997). The us-them construction revolves around "majority" (those who all look and act normal to one another) and the "minority" (those who do not look or act like the majority). Naturalized whiteness is securely grounded in and validated by the normal way of things in the present and therefore does not seek meaning in a cultural or past orientation.

CLAVEY HIGH SCHOOL: WHEN WHITE IS NOT THE NORM

Once a port of entry for African American, Mexican, and Asian immigration into northern California, Clavey City today has one of the most racially/ethnically diverse populations for its size in the United States. Of its 372,000 residents, 33 percent are white, 44 percent are black, 19 percent are of Hispanic origin, and 15 percent are of Asian origin. Median household income in 1989 was $27,095. More than 16 percent of families in Clavey City live below poverty.

Clavey High School stands like a fortress overlooking a dense urban landscape. The school's magnet academies draw in youth from all over the city, bringing in a mosaic of students from different racial and ethnic groups. At the time of my research, whites comprised 12 percent of the two thousand students at Clavey. African Americans were the majority, making up 54 percent of the school. They were followed in numbers by Asian Americans (23 percent), then Hispanics (8 percent), Filipinos (2 percent), and a few Pacific Islanders and Native Americans. At any given moment during lunch break, one could tour the campus and hear students speaking in standard English, black English ("ebonics"), Eritrean, Cantonese, Mandarin, Korean, Spanish, Spanglish, Tagalog, Samoan, Russian, and Vietnamese, among others.

The racial composition of the administrative and teaching staff at Clavey was also quite diverse. The principal of Clavey was a white male, but the other top administrators, two assistant principals and the dean, were African American. Of all the administrators and their staff, 50 percent were African American, 25 percent were Asian, and 25 percent were white. Clavey teachers were 53 percent white, 30 percent African American, 8 percent Asian American, 6 percent Hispanic, and 3 percent Pacific Islander.

Life at Clavey High was very different from that at Valley Groves. White youth at Clavey were in daily, up-close association with marked racial and cultural difference to whiteness, and race was the primary means of sorting out who was who and where one belonged in the social organization of the school. Clavey's tracking structure, which I say more about later, was racially segregated, with whites and Asians disproportionally represented in the high-tracked classes and African Americans and Latinos overrepresented in the low-tracked classes. As well, certain areas on the campus were "where the white kids hang out"; others were "where the black (or Asian American or Latino) kids hang out." And student cliques and subcultures were racially marked such that "straights" (who were like "normal" kids at Valley Groves), alternatives, hippies, and punks were all "white people's groups"; rappers, athletes, gangsters, and "fashion hounds" were "black people's groups"; housers, natives, newly arrived, and martial artists were "Asian people's groups"; and so forth. This meant that the styles, slangs, vernaculars, and demeanors that marked identification with a certain clique or subculture simultaneously inferred racial identification. In a word, peer group activities *racialized* youth.

Speaking to this fact and the sanctions that came with crossing racialized boundaries in styles or leisure activities, Gloria, an immigrant from El Salvador, said to me,

> For my race, if you start wearing a lot of gold, you're trying to be black. If you're trying to braid your hair, you'll be accused of trying to be black. I'm scared to do things 'cause they might say, "that's black!" Or if you're Latino and you listen to that, you know, Green Day—that [alternative rock] kinda thing. If you listen to that, then you wanna be white. . . . "Oh my god, why you listening to that music?" they'd say, . . . Aren't you proud of who you are?

Also different from Valley Groves was the dominant school culture. Overall at Clavey, African American youth claimed the majority of open, public spaces, and black popular cultural forms and practices shaped the normative culture of the school. By "black popular culture," I refer to the music, styles, and other meaningful practices that have risen out of black communities; are linked, if remotely, to diasporic traditions; and, most significantly, mark black identity and peoplehood (Gilroy 1991, 1993; Rose 1994; Wallace 1992). Hall (1992) defines three things that are distinctive of black diasporic culture: (1) *style* as the "subject of what is going on," (2) *music* as the "deep structure of [black] cultural life," and (3) the *body* as "canvases of representation" (p. 27). Gilroy (1991) adds that the body in black culture carries "potent meanings" (p. 226) because it rests at the core of historical efforts of blacks to assert their humanity.

Unlike at Valley Groves, where the dress code did not diverge much from white adult mainstream style, at Clavey, basic elements of black hip-hop style were generalized into the normative styles for all youth. One informant called it the "leveler" style because it made all who wore it "the same." This basic style included clean, oversized, and sagging denim pants or sweatpants; large and long untucked T-shirts or hooded sweatshirts; large, bulky parkas; and sparkling-clean athletic shoes. The look was particularly common for boys, but girls' styles were also influenced by it. Only if and when students wanted to mark a distinctive style and/or racial identification did they embellish on this basic, baggy theme. Duncan, a middle-class, white male skater and "raver" (someone who frequents rave parties) told me,

We all wear baggy pants, right? So parents think! But you find that ravers have cut-off bottoms to their [sagging] jeans, they wear bigger t-shirts they have hanging out of their pants, they carry packs that's full of crap that they take everywhere.

What Duncan specified as "raver" style, other students specified as "white," particularly the cut-off bottoms to large pants. Other markers of white kids' styles were Van shoes, instead of Nike or Fila brands (which marked black style), and macramé or silver-chain neck chokers.

Informal and formal activities on campus were also shaped by black popular culture. During breaks or at lunchtime, the ambient din of casual conversation was composed of the sounds, words, and inflections of black English and the most recent innovation in "street" slang. Lunchtime events, school rallies, and dances were enlivened with rap and R & B music, predominantly, with an occasional reggae tune or specially requested techno or alternative song. Often, students performed raps on the steps in front of the cafeteria or graced an audience with a spontaneous hip-hop dance performance.

Homecoming week at Clavey, like at Valley Groves, was a time to unite the school and raise the collective spirit. So, leadership students made attempts to appeal to the breadth of diverse interests and cultures of the school with "fashion shows" of traditional or native garments and a variety of games designed to mix students up. At lunch, they played a range of music, from R & B to techno and alternative rock, but songs by African American and Afro-Carribean artists were predominant. The main events—the rally and game—were attended by and played predominantly to a majority-black audience.

The rally took place during lunch on the day of the "big game." Students, of which all but a few were black, crammed into the auditorium to the heartbeat pulse of a rap song. The rally opened with a greeting from the student body president and a soulful a cappella song performed by three African American students. Then the cheerleaders, composed of one white and ten black girls, sprung out onto the gym floor. Their choreographed routine was fluid, rhythmic, and dancelike, with movements drawn from traditional and contemporary African and African American dance forms. To the infectious beat of an upbeat R & B song, the girls playfully flirted with their appreciative audience with beckoning hand and eye gestures. Several boys succumbed to the urge to dance in dialogue with the girls and leapt down to the floor to join them, but they were met by the arresting hands of campus security. Others, boys and girls alike, stood up and swayed or danced in place until the performance was over. Then, the varsity football players were called to line up in the center of the auditorium. The players were African American with the exception of two white boys and one Latino. When each name was announced, the football player leapt forward a few steps and embraced the cheers from the crowd. Each took his moment in the limelight proudly, with his fist in the air or maybe a little dance to augment the roar of his audience.

At Clavey, there was no homecoming parade that extended into the community, like at Valley Groves. At the game, a small procession of vehicles featuring the elected school "emperor" and "empress" circled the football field during half time. There was no marching band, either, but the award-winning school gospel choir sang several lively songs at halftime.

In short, school life at Clavey was heavily infused with styles, music, and activities that marked the identities and cultures of the majority black students. This had a few important implications for the experiences and identities of the white students. First, white was not the norm, either numerically or culturally. Barry, a middle-class, "straight" white male, told me, "School is like a foreign country to me. I come here to this foreign place, then go home where things are normal again." When I asked white students why they did not attend the rallies and dances, they said things like, "I don't enjoy the people," "They don't play my kind of music," and "I can't dance to that music." All in all, the message was that they could not relate to the dominant school culture.

Furthermore, whiteness was not entirely taken for granted. The racial organization of Clavey's social life, curricular structure, and schoolwide activities meant that white students were forced to grapple with their identities as whites and participate in active contestation over the meanings of white identity and culture. No white student I spoke to at Clavey was completely unable to describe something about white culture. All had reflected on it to some extent, even if only to ruminate on how difficult it was to define. And some youth could say a lot about white culture. One white, middle-class senior girl, Jessie, elaborated extensively on differences in attitudes toward food consumption that she noticed between her white, Filipino, and Chinese American friends, and she commented on how much more visible white culture is to her in places outside of California. She said, "Minnesota, Denver and . . . places like that. It seems like . . . you know, you've got the whole thing going on—beer bread, polka, parades, apple pie and things like that."

Most stunning to me about the white students at Clavey was not what they said explicitly about white culture but what they said implicitly. In our discussions about the types of music they liked and why, white students would tell me that they liked rock or punk or alternative music and not rap or R & B because "their" music spoke more to their "interests" or experiences as whites. For example, Kirsten and Cindi were good friends. They both were from middle-class homes, were juniors at the time, and liked alternative rock. Kirsten was white, European American, and Cindi was part white and part Chinese, although she admittedly "looked white" and hung out solely with other white youth. I asked them why they thought students tended to self-segregate on campus:

Cindi: I think there is . . . the factor that some people feel like they may not have very much in common with someone from a different race, which in some ways is true. Because you have, like, different music tastes, different styles of clothes. Also, like what your friends think.

Kirsten: Or like different things you do on weekends.

Cindi: Yeah, so I think that's something that separates the races.

Kirsten: It's kind of interesting because my musical interests have changed. . . . It seems like [in junior high school] everyone, regardless of if they were black or white or Asian, . . . listened to the [local rap and R & B station]. But then I think when you are little you don't really . . . have too much of an identity of yourself. As you get older and mature more you, like, discover what your "true being" is. So then people's musical tastes change. [Later in the conversation] I think punk is more of a "I don't get along with my parents" kind of music and rap is more of "let's go kill someone" music.

Cindi: Punk . . . expresses a simpler anger. It's just kind of like "Oh, I broke up with my girlfriend" . . . something like that. Usually rap has more to do with killing and gangs—stuff that doesn't really relate to me.

In this discussion, Kirsten and Cindi defined white identity and culture in terms of interests and tastes in leisure culture. This "discourse of taste" (Dolby 2000) was the language of choice among all groups of students for articulating racial-ethnic differences. Behind it was the belief that different life experiences accounted for different tastes. Sometimes, white youth named fairly explicit experiences they believed were most common to or defining of whites. Class experience, expressed by Kirsten and Cindi in terms of the type of neighborhood one lived in, was often evoked by youth. Other times, white youth spoke in terms of intangible but presumably race-based, emotional, aesthetic, and ethical sensibilities they felt when they listened to, say, punk or alternative music but not when they listened to rap.

ACTIVE CONSTRUCTION OF WHITE AS POSTCULTURAL

Ironically, even as Clavey whites demarcated white culture and identity boundaries through their popular-cultural tastes and leisure activities, they also imagined whiteness as cultureless, as postcultural. This was not as explicit as it was at Valley Groves. It would show its face when white students referred to people of color as people with "race" or "ethnicity," as though whites had neither. Tina, a working-class junior who had always been a racial minority in school and had many close black and Latino friends, told me that she "had a lot of ethnicity in [her] family . . . Hispanic, Korean. We all get along." By this she meant that white relatives had married "out" of whiteness and into culture, ethnicity.

Common also was the explicit and implicit definition of white as empty, meaningless, bland, and without tradition. This comment by Eric touches on all of those:

> I think it's more difficult [to define white culture] for Americans because the culture of America is more just consumption. In America, we buy stuff, and that's the basis of our culture. If you talk to people who want to come to America?—They want things. TV is a very American thing. We don't have lengthy traditions. . . . A lot has been

lost because of the good ol' melting pot. I heard a cool one about a salad bowl—that's what America is, and along comes the dressing and turns everything into dressing flavor. Vegetables all got that white American spin on it.

Note, too, that Eric equates "white" with "American" until his last line, when he specifies "white American." That is a faux pas that whites often fall into because of the dominant construction of white as the "unhyphenated" American standard.

Finally, several Clavey white students told me that they did not like to think about themselves as "white" but as "human." These students also expressed a more explicitly rationalist construction of whiteness that denied the significance of a past orientation and exalted a more individualistic and present- or future-oriented construction of the self. White, middle-class boys expressed this most boldly, which might be expected given that they are triply constructed as the most rational by race, class, and gender.

Murray, whom I quoted at the beginning of this article, best exemplifies this latter perspective. In Murray's comments, we can read several tenets of Western rational thought and a postcultural identity: the irrationality of past-oriented values, the future orientation of the self, and individual responsibility. Daniel was a white, middle-class, "straight" male with some Portuguese ancestry. He made comments similar to Murray's:

People have suggested I am a person of color or mixed. Then I decided, no, I'm European American. Ancestry doesn't matter. . . . People look back in the past and judge you for it, and I don't think that's right. Sure, people enslaved people. At one time every race had slaves. I think you need to move on and see what's going on now. History is important but you have to work on getting together now and don't use that as a divide.

A few scholars have observed a propensity among whites to deny the significance of the past, slavery particularly, in affecting the life chances of African Americans today. Some argue that this denial is a kind of defensive mechanism whites adopt to exonerate themselves from taking responsibility for the legacies of slavery and past discrimination against African Americans and other minorities (Gallagher 1995). I take a slightly different position and suggest that white identity and culture is constructed in such a way that the values of individuality, personal responsibility, and a future-oriented self create a cognitive inability to see things any other way (see also Alba 1990; Blauner 1989). A past orientation simply does not make sense to many whites from their cultural perspective.

In sum, at Clavey, white culture was not entirely naturalized and taken for granted; it was reflected on and even defined somewhat, particularly through the language of tastes and popular culture. To an extent, however, white students also considered themselves unmarked American, nonethnic, unmarked human, and/or present oriented. In a word, they saw themselves as cultureless. I might add that several students of color I spoke to also were quick to define white culture in terms of styles and tastes but not in terms of tradition. Johnetta, an African American senior, said, "It's hard to generalize [about white culture] because there's no ready answer to what is white culture."

Whereas I have proposed that the naturalization of whiteness greatly facilitated the passive construction of postcultural whiteness at Valley Groves, I suggest that at Clavey, different and more active social processes were in play. Namely, Western rational ways of knowing and making sense of social relations permeated Clavey school and social practices. As I have argued, Western rationalism exiles tradition and culture from the realms of truth and relevance and replaces them with reason. That which is reasonable or rational is separated from and raised above that which is not, like the elevation of mind over body, intellectual over emotional, and order above chaos. Whiteness benefits from those hierarchical dualities by being linked with the higher value of each—with orderliness, self-control, individualism, and rationality, which, not coincidentally, are recognized as standard or normal behaviors. Otherness is defined in terms of that which is passionate, chaotic, violent, lazy, irrational, and—since marginal to the norm—cultural.

Two school practices in particular stood out for me in terms of the ways they seemed to structure the meanings all youth gave to their experience through a Western rational value paradigm. The first and most obvious of those was the tracking structure. Scholars have long argued that racial segregation in tracking reproduces racial inequalities in the wider society, largely by preparing high-tracked students, who tend to be middle-class white and Asian, better than low-tracked students, who tend to be black, Latino, and poor white and Asian (Gamoran et al. 1995; Oakes 1985, 1994; Oakes and Guiton 1995). Tracking also reproduces racial inequalities by reinforcing, if not constituting, racial stereotypes. Jeannie Oakes (1994) has argued that "all but the most extraordinary schools have their stereotypes and prejudices reinforced by racially-identifiable high- and low-tracked classes" (pp. 86–87). She asserts that tracking "institutionalizes racist conceptions of intellectual capacity" (ibid.). I would add to her argument that tracking also institutionalizes the values of mind over body and self-control over lack of restraint and racializes those who are superior and inferior in those respects.

At Clavey, the high-tracked classes, those designed to prepare students for high-ranking colleges and universities, were 80 percent white and Asian, according to a school survey. Conversely, "preparatory" classes, which filled graduation requirements, were overwhelmingly black and Latino. Remedial classes were 100 percent black and Latino. Although, officially, youth were tracked according to their intellectual or achievement levels, the discourses that surrounded tracking at Clavey suggested that *behavior* (including expected behavior) was just as relevant.

Students in the high-tracked classes were generally understood to be "well-behaved," "good" students. In those classrooms, students acted in the utmost orderly fashion: always listening attentively and taking notes, speaking only when called on. They considered themselves hard working and sophisticated in their abilities to defer gratification, such as to study during lunch instead of hang out and have fun with their friends. They justified their privilege to be in the accelerated classes on these grounds and blamed underachievement on the behaviors of the underachieved. Linda, a white Jewish girl in accelerated classes, represented this viewpoint in the following comment:

> It's so sad because these kids could be pushed so far beyond what they are [doing]. Like, it's unbelievable. When I see a twelfth grader holding a geometry book, I cringe inside me. Because, *you can learn*, you can do it! People are so lazy, they don't care. They have no goals, no ambitions. It's frustrating! I don't get it!

The "lazy" and unambitious kids Linda referred to were black and Latino students in the preparatory classes. Other commonly used terms to describe those classes and the students in them were "bonehead," "rowdy," and "out of control." And, indeed, some of those classes had students who were inattentive or disruptive and who could, on occasion, set the whole class off into a blaze of rowdiness. But those students were aware that they had been assigned to the least valued and negatively stereotyped classes in the school. If they did not hear it through common discourse, they deduced it from the classes themselves. They were overcrowded and short of chairs, books, and other course materials. Sometimes, they did not even have full-time teachers. It is not a stretch to suggest that preparatory students behaved in "bonehead" ways that they thought were expected of them (Baron, Tom, and Cooper 1985; Eder 1981; Ferguson 1998; Lightfoot 1978; Steele and Aronson 1998).

In sum, tracking at Clavey asserted more than, simply, intellectual superiority but also the values of mind over body and self-control over lack of restraint. Furthermore, it marked standard, acceptable forms of behavior—standards within which middle-class whites and Asians were squarely located practically and symbolically.

"Multicultural" programs and discourses were other school practices that positioned whites as the school's most rational and postcultural. At Clavey, there were two main, formal multicultural events: the "cultural assemblies" and "multicultural week." Once every other month or so, an ethnic club—the African American Student Union, the Asian Student Union, Latino Student Union, or the Inter-Tribal Student Union—would put on a schoolwide assembly. A common assembly featured traditional ceremonial dances and rituals, music and song, poetry readings, historically informative slide shows, and clothing displays, all arranged and performed by the students.

Lunchtime activities during multicultural week were another opportunity for students to publicly display elements of their cultural heritage. Each day of the week was designed to feature a particular aspect of a culture—the music, dance, clothing, written texts, or narratives. For example, on a day featuring traditional or national clothing styles, youth held a fashion show in which African American youth in dashikis, Chinese American girls in brocade gowns, and Mexican American youth in ceremonial dance costumes paraded before youth gathered outside the cafeteria.

These events had their merits. They gave voice and visibility to the cultures and perspectives of people historically silenced by white colonialism. African American and Asian youth told me that they enjoyed having the opportunity to present their culture as well as learn about others. I propose, however, that multicultural events at Clavey coterminously reproduced white supremacist, rationalist tenets of white colonialism by making whiteness culturally invisible.

Rosaldo (1989) argues that, "as the Other becomes more culturally visible, the self becomes correspondingly less so" (p. 202). I believe this was true for many Clavey whites. When white students spoke about the assemblies, they usually expressed enthusiastic appreciation for "the chance to learn about so many cultures." But learning about other cultures merely gave them more references by which to define what they were not. As well, when they spoke in this way, it was as if "cultures" were like books—objective things that existed outside of the self but could be consumed to pleasure the self (Farley 1997). In a conversation with three middle-class white girls at Clavey, I asked them how they thought their experience at Clavey would influence their adulthood.

Ann:	I think it's going to be a very positive thing. [Melissa interjects: Yeah.] Because it teaches us how to deal with different kinds of people.
Sera:	Yeah, you learn more about others. . . . It's a positive experience.
Melissa:	Yeah, you gain street smarts. You gain stuff.

Greater knowledge of other cultures was something Ann, Sera, and Melissa appreciated because it gave them tools to enhance their sociability, but it did not make them reflect on their sociocultural location as whites. When other white students at Clavey spoke to me about the value of the multicultural events, they made very similar kinds of statements and inferences. Overall, multicultural events, as "add-on" school practices in which white students could pleasurably gaze on racial-ethnic others without putting themselves on the line, reinforced a sense of whiteness as center and standard (cultureless) and racial-ethnic others (by virtue of having culture to display) as different and marginal to that.

Furthermore, no white students I spoke to questioned why there was not a white-American cultural assembly. Granted, to most this was untenable, largely because it might be taken as a white-supremacist act. I talked to students about school clubs for whites only and they categorically dismissed the idea. One said, "There'd be a riot!" Another said, "It wouldn't be right. It would be taken all wrong." But it was also untenable because, as another student put it, "White is all around. It doesn't need special attention." The idea that white culture does not need special attention (read: white is the norm and standard) seemed to be another message multicultural events gave to white students. As if for the eyes of whites only, multiculturalism at Clavey gave white students new references to add to their mental cache of exotic others while further obscuring the invisible power of white culture.

CONCLUSION

For a while now, scholars of race and whiteness have understood that the construction of white culture as the invisible norm is one of the most, if not *the* most, pernicious constructions of whiteness in the post-civil rights era. However, very few have examined the everyday social processes by which white people come to think of themselves as normal and culturally empty (Frankenberg 1993; Kenny 2000a, 2000b; Twine

1997), and among those, no one has done a comparative study illuminating the ways that different social-structural institutional contexts influence different constructions of white identity as cultureless. My research suggests that, at Valley Groves, a predominantly white high school, white identity seemed cultureless because white cultural practices were taken for granted, naturalized, and, thus, not reflected on and defined. At Clavey, a multiracial school, white culture was not taken for granted—white youth thought about and defined it to an extent, particularly through their interests and tastes in popular culture. However, in part, whites also reflected on their sociocultural location through the lens of European American rational authority, which school structures and practices helped construct and reinforce. That lens refracted whiteness into all that was good, controlled, rational, and cultureless and otherness into all that was bad, out of control, irrational, and cultural. It may be that when naturalization processes are not possible because of close interracial association, then rationalization processes must come into play to preserve white hegemony.

This argument has theoretical and practical implications for critical white studies, the sociology of education, and general theories and research in racial-ethnic identity formation. Within critical white studies, there are two prevalent sets of assumptions about white culture that this research advances. The first is that white people experience themselves as culturally empty because whiteness is hegemonic and, therefore, undefined. To disrupt the insidious power of white culture, then, we must expose and define it. My study suggests that this is true but not everywhere the truth. The multiracial experiences of white youth at Clavey suggest that making white culture visible is not sufficient for challenging the construction of white as norm. What is also necessary are efforts to expose, challenge, and transform the rule of reason that frames white culture as rational and, therefore, *beyond* culture, postcultural or even anticultural.

Another assumption among some scholars of critical white studies, particularly "New Abolitionists," is that white culture is experienced as empty because, simply, there is no white culture. I am less concerned with the question of whether there really is a white culture than with what is reproduced through *denying* there is a white culture. The argument I have presented here proposes that the concept of culture denotes more than, simply, a way of life organized around sets of symbolic practices. It connotes a relationship of power between those who "have" culture (and are, thus, irrational and inferior) and those who claim not to (and are, thus, rational and superior). More research and thought needs to go into examining the ways postcultural whiteness is inculcated in daily practice and into the profits whites gain by denying that they have a culture.

This research also contributes to the growing scholarship on social and cultural reproduction in education. Although considerable research has examined the reproduction and subversion of societal norms in schools, including racial norms (for example, Carter 1999; Conchas 2000; Davidson 1996; Fine et al. 1997; Fordham 1996; Kenny 2000a; McCarthy and Crichlow 1993; Valenzuela 1999), more is still needed that closely examines the symbolic impact of certain school practices on how white students make sense of their own identities and the identities of people of color. This research only touched the surface of that and came on some disturbing and unexpected findings, namely, the active construction of postcultural whiteness. Research and evaluations of multicultural and other programs designed to redress racial inequalities have focused primarily on students of color. Important insights might be gained from more attention to white students and the meanings they assign to their experiences of those same programs.

Finally, this research embellishes on theories of racial-ethnic identity formation by vividly illuminating the socially constructed and contingent nature of race. Racial identities are made, not born, and they are made through the interaction of the specific social, structural, political, and cultural composition of a given context (Blumer 1958; Pinderhughes 1997). This means that racial identities are not fixed or uniform but variable and multiple. They may even be contradictory. These observances are often lost among scholars of whiteness and white racism who tend to represent whites and white identities as everywhere and always the same and contradictions as a form of "contemporary race prejudice" (Williams et al. 1999). My research affirms that the hegemonic construction of white as cultureless is stubbornly persistent but that even *it* is not the same across all contexts. To more effectively dismantle white domination, we need to be aware of and ready to work with its different manifestations and internal contradictions. Future research and antiracist scholarship may benefit from deeper exploration of the variability of white racial identities and the processes by which white racial domination is reproduced and subverted in distinct contexts.

REFERENCES

Alba, Richard. 1990. *Ethnic identity: The transformation of white America.* New Haven, CT: Yale University Press.

Allen, Theodore. 1994. *The invention of the white race, vol. 1: Racial oppression and social control.* London: Verso.

Almaguer, Tomas. 1994. *Racial fault lines: The historical origins of white supremacy in California.* Berkeley: University of California Press.

Apple, Michael W. 1995. *Education and power.* New York: Routledge.

Baron, Reuben, David Y. H. Tom, and Harris M. Cooper. 1985. Social class, race and teacher expectations. In *Teacher expectancies,* edited by Jerome B. Dusek. Hillsdale, NJ: Lawrence Erlbaum.

Blauner, Bob. 1989. *Black lives, white lives: Three decades of race relations in America.* Berkeley: University of California Press.

Blumer, Herbert. 1958. Race prejudice as a sense of group position. *Pacific Sociological Review* 1 (1): 3–7.

Bourdieu, Pierre. 1977. *Outline of a theory of practice.* Cambridge, UK: Cambridge University Press.

Bourdieu, Pierre, and J. C. Passeron. 1977. *Reproduction in education, society and culture.* Beverly Hills, CA: Sage.

Carter, Prudence L. 1999. Balancing acts: Issues of identity and cultural resistance in the social and educational behaviors of minority youth. Ph.D. diss., Columbia University, New York.

Conchas, Gilberto Q. 2000. Structuring failure and success: Understanding the variability in Latino school engagement. Working paper, Harvard Graduate School of Education.

Davidson, Ann Locke. 1996. *Making and molding identity in schools: Student narratives on race, gender, and academic engagement.* Albany: State University of New York Press.

De Vos, George. 1975. Ethnic pluralism: Conflict and accommodation. In *Ethnic identity: Cultural continuities and change,* edited by George De Vos and Lola Romanucci-Ross. Chicago: University of Chicago Press.

Dolby, Nadine. 2000. The shifting ground of race: The role of taste in youth's production of identities. *Race, Ethnicity, and Education 3* (1):7–23.

Dyer, Richard. 1997. *White.* New York: Routledge.

Eckert, Penelope. 1989. *Jocks and burnouts: Social categories and identity in high school.* New York: Teachers College Press.

Eder, Donna. 1981. Ability grouping as a self-fulfilling prophecy: A micro-analysis of teacher-student interaction. *Sociology of Education 54* (3): 151–62.

Essed, Philomena. 1996. *Diversity: Gender, color and culture.* Amherst: University of Massachusetts Press.

Farley, Anthony Paul. 1997. The black body as fetish object. *Oregon Law Review* 76 (3): 457–535.

Ferguson, Robert A. 1997. *The American Enlightenment, 1750–1820.* Cambridge, MA: Harvard University Press.

Ferguson, Ronald F. 1998. Teachers' perceptions and expectations and the black-white test score gap. In *The black-white test score gap,* edited by Christopher Jencks and Meredith Phillips, 318–74. Washington, DC: Brookings Institution.

Fine, Michelle. 1989. Silencing and nurturing voice in an improbable context: Urban adolescents in public school. In *Critical pedagogy, the state, and cultural struggle,* edited by Henry Giroux and Peter McLaren, 152–73. Albany: State University of New York Press.

Fine, Michelle, Lois Weis, Linda C. Powell, and L. Mun Wong, eds. 1997. *Off white: Readings on race, power and society.* New York: Routledge.

Fordham, Signithia. 1996. *Blacked out: Dilemmas of race, identity, and success at Capital High.* Chicago: University of Chicago Press.

Fordham, Signithia, and John Ogbu. 1986. Black students' school success: Coping with the "burden of 'acting white.'" *Urban Review 18* (3): 176–206.

Frankenberg, Ruth. 1993. *White women, race matters: The social construction of whiteness.* Minneapolis: University of Minnesota Press.

——. 1997. *Displacing whiteness: Essays in social and cultural criticism.* Durham, NC: Duke University Press.

Gallagher, Charles A. 1995. White reconstruction in the university. *Socialist Review 24* (1&2): 165–87.

——. 1997. White racial formation: Into the twenty-first century. In *Critical white studies: Looking behind the mirror,* edited by Richard Delgado and Jean Stefancic, 6–11. Philadelphia: Temple University Press.

Gamoran, Adam, Martin Nystrand, Mark Berends, and Paul C. LePore. 1995. An organizational analysis of the effects of ability grouping. *American Educational Research Journal 32* (4): 687–715.

Gilroy, Paul. 1991. *"There ain't no black in the Union Jack": The cultural politics of race and nation.* Chicago: University of Chicago Press.

——. 1993. *The black Atlantic: Modernity and double consciousness.* Cambridge, MA: Harvard University Press.

Giroux, Henry. 1996. *Fugitive cultures: Race, violence, and youth.* New York: Routledge.

_____. 1997. Rewriting the discourse of racial identity: Towards a pedagogy and politics of whiteness. *Harvard Educational Review* 67 (2): 285–320.

Goldberg, David Theo. 1993. *Racist culture: Philosophy and the politics of meaning.* Cambridge, UK: Blackwell.

Hall, Stuart. 1992. What is the "black" in black popular culture? In *Black popular culture,* edited by Gina Dent, 21–33. Seattle, WA: Bay.

_____. 1996. Introduction: Who needs identity? In *Questions of cultural identity,* edited by Stuart Hall and Paul du Gay, 1–17. London: Sage.

Haney Lopez, Ian F. 1996. *White by law: The legal construction of race.* New York: New York University Press.

Harris, Cheryl. 1993. Whiteness as property. *Harvard Law Review* 106:1707–91.

Hartigan, John, Jr. 1997. Locating white Detroit. In *Displacing whiteness: Essays in social and cultural criticism,* edited by Ruth Frankenberg, 180–213. Durham, NC: Duke University Press.

_____. 1999. *Racial situations: Class predicaments of whiteness in Detroit.* Princeton, NJ: Princeton University Press.

Hill, Mike, ed. 1997. *Whiteness: A critical reader.* New York: New York University Press.

hooks, bell. 1992. *Black looks: Race and representation.* Boston: South End.

Ignatiev, Noel. 1995. *How the Irish became white.* New York: Routledge.

Ignatiev, Noel, and John Garvey, eds. 1996. *Race traitor.* New York: Routledge.

Jacobson, Matthew Frye. 1998. *Whiteness of a different color: European immigrants and the alchemy of race.* Cambridge, MA: Harvard University Press.

Kenny, Lorraine Delia. 2000a. Doing my homework: The autoethnography of a white teenage girl. In *Racing research, researching race: Methodological dilemmas in critical race studies,* edited by France Winddance Twine and Jonathan Warren. New York: New York University Press.

_____. 2000b. *Daughters of suburbia: Growing up white, middle class, and female.* New Brunswick, NJ: Rutgers University Press.

Kinney, David A. 1993. From nerds to normals: The recovery of identity among adolescents from middle school to high school. *Sociology of Education* 66 (1):21–40.

Lightfoot, Sara Lawrence. 1978. *Worlds apart: Relationships between families and schools.* New York: Basic Books.

Lipsitz, George. 1995. The possessive investment in whiteness: Racialized social democracy and the "white" problem in American studies. *American Quarterly* 47 (3): 369–87.

Lott, Eric. 1993. *Love and theft: Blackface minstrelsy and the American working class.* New York: Oxford University Press.

MacLeod, Jay. 1987. *Ain't no makin' it.* Boulder, CO: Westview.

McCarthy, Cameron, and Warren Crichlow, eds. 1993. *Race, identity and representation in education.* New York: Routledge.

Morrison, Toni. 1993. *Playing in the dark: Whiteness in the literary imagination.* New York: Random House.

Oakes, Jeannie. 1985. *Keeping track: How schools structure inequality.* New Haven, CT: Yale University Press.

_____. 1994. More than a misapplied technology: A normative and political response to Hallinan on tracking. *Sociology of Education* 76 (2): 84–89.

Oakes, Jeannie, and Gretchen Guiton. 1995. Matchmaking: The dynamics of high school tracking decisions. *American Educational Research Journal* 32:3–33.

Perry, Pamela. 1998. Beginning to see the white: A comparative ethnography in two high schools of the racial consciousness and identities of white youth. Ph.D. diss., University of California, Berkeley.

Pfeil, Fred. 1995. *White guys: Studies in postmodern domination and difference.* New York: Verso.

Phoenix, Ann. 1997. "I'm white! So what?" The construction of whiteness for young Londoners. In *Off white: Readings on race and power in society,* edited by Michelle Fine, Linda C. Powell, Lois Weis, and L. Mun Wong, 187–97. New York: Routledge.

Pinderhughes, Howard. 1997. *Race in the hood: Conflict and violence among urban youth.* Minneapolis: Minnesota University Press.

powell, john a. 1997. Reflections on the self: Exploring between and beyond modernity and postmodernity, *Minnesota Law Review 81* (6): 1481–1520.

Roediger, David. 1991. *The wages of whiteness: Race and the making of the American working class.* New York: Verso.

———. 1994. *Towards the abolition of whiteness.* New York: Verso.

Rosaldo, Renato. 1989. *Culture and truth: The remaking of social analysis.* Boston: Beacon.

Rose, Tricia. 1994. *Black noise: Rap music and black culture in contemporary America.* Hanover, NH: Wesleyan University Press.

Saxton, Alexander. 1990. *The rise and fall of the white republic.* New York: Verso.

Segrest, Mab. 1994. *Memoirs of a race traitor.* Boston: South End.

Steele, Claude M., and Joshua Aronson. 1998. Stereotype threat and the test performance of academically successful African Americans. In *The black-white test score gap,* edited by Christopher Jencks and Meredith Phillips, 401–27. Washington, DC: Brookings Institution.

Thandeka. 1999. The cost of whiteness. *Tikkun 14* (3): 33–38.

Thorne, Barrie. 1993. *Gender play: Girls and boys in school.* New Brunswick, NJ: Rutgers University Press.

Twine, France Winddance. 1997. Brown-skinned white girls: Class, culture, and the construction of white identity in suburban communities. In *Displacing whiteness: Essays in social and cultural criticism,* edited by Ruth Frankenberg, 214–43. Durham, NC: Duke University Press.

Valenzuela, Angela. 1999. *Subtractive schooling: U.S.-Mexican youth and the politics of caring.* Albany: State University of New York Press.

Wallace, Michelle (a project of). 1992. *Black popular culture.* Edited by Gina Dent. Seattle, WA: Bay.

Ware, Vron. 1992. *Beyond the pale: White women, racism and history.* New York: Verso.

Wellman, David. 1977. *Portraits of white racism.* Cambridge, UK: Cambridge University Press.

Williams, David R., James S. Jackson, Tony N. Brown, Myriam Torres, Tyrone A. Forman, and Kendrick Brown. 1999. Traditional and contemporary prejudice and urban whites' support for affirmative action and government help. *Social Problems* 46 (4):503–27.

Williams, Raymond. 1976. Base and superstructure in Marxist cultural theory. In *Schooling and capitalism: A sociological reader,* edited by R. Dale, 202–10. London: Routledge and Kegan Paul.

Wray, Matt, and Annalee Newitz, eds. 1997. *White trash: Race and class in America.* New York: Routledge.

SOCIALIZATION AND REFERENCE GROUPS

16

"We Don't Sleep Around Like White Girls Do"

Yen Le Espiritu

(2005)

I want my daughters to be Filipino, especially on sex. I always emphasize to them that they should not participate in sex if they are not married. We are also Catholic. We are raised so that we don't engage in going out with men while we are not married. And I don't like it to happen to my daughters as if they have no values. I don't like them to grow up that way, like the American girls.

—Filipina immigrant mother

I found that a lot of the Asian American friends of mine, we don't date like White girls date. We don't sleep around like White girls do. Everyone is really mellow at dating because your parents were constraining and restrictive.

—Second-generation Filipina daughter

Gender is a key to immigrant identity and a vehicle for racialized immigrants to assert cultural superiority over the dominant group. For Filipino immigrants, who come from a homeland that was once a U.S. colony, cultural reconstruction has been especially critical in the assertion of their presence in the United States—a way to counter the cultural Americanization of the Philippines, to resist the assimilative and alienating demands of U.S. society, and to reaffirm to themselves their self-worth in the face of colonial, racial, class, and gendered subordination. Before World War II, Filipinos were barred from becoming U.S. citizens, owning property, and marrying Whites. They also encountered discriminatory housing policies, unfair labor practices, violent physical encounters, and racist as well as anti-immigrant discourse. While blatant legal discrimination against Filipino Americans is largely a matter of the past, Filipinos continue to encounter many barriers that prevent full participation in the economic, social, and political institutions of the United States. Drawing from my research on Filipino American families in San Diego, California, I explore in this essay the ways racialized

immigrants claim through gender the power denied them by racism.

My epigraphs, statements by a Filipina immigrant mother and a second-generation Filipina daughter, suggest that the virtuous Filipina daughter is partially constructed on the conceptualization of White women as sexually immoral. This juxtaposition underscores the fact that femininity is a relational category, one that is co-constructed with other racial and cultural categories. These narratives also reveal that women's sexuality and their enforced "morality" are fundamental to the structuring of social inequalities. Historically, the sexuality of racialized women has been systematically demonized and disparaged by dominant or oppressor groups to justify and bolster nationalist movements, colonialism, and/or racism. But as these narratives indicate, racialized groups also criticize the morality of White women as a strategy of resistance—a means of asserting a morally superior public face to the dominant society.

By exploring how Filipino immigrants characterize White families and White women, I hope to contribute to a neglected area of research: how the "margins" imagine and construct the "mainstream" in order to assert superiority over it. But this strategy is not without costs. The elevation of Filipina chastity (particularly that of young women) has the effect of reinforcing masculinist and patriarchal power in the name of a greater ideal of national/ethnic self-respect. Because the control of women is one of the principal means of asserting moral superiority, young women in immigrant families face numerous restrictions on their autonomy, mobility, and personal decision making. Although this essay addresses the experiences and attitudes of both parents and children, here I am more concerned with understanding the actions of immigrant parents than the reactions of their second-generation daughters.

"American" and Whiteness: "To Me, American Means White"

In U.S. racial discourse and practices, unless otherwise specified, "Americans" means "Whites." In the case of Asian Americans, U.S. exclusion acts, naturalization laws, and national culture have simultaneously marked Asians as the unassimilable aliens and Whites as the quintessential Americans. Excluded from the collective memory of who constitutes a "real" American, Asians in the United States, even as citizens, remain "foreigners-within" "non-Americans."

Cognizant of this racialized history, my Filipino respondents seldom identify themselves as American. As will be evident in the discussion below, they equate "American" with "White" and often use these two terms interchangeably. For example, a Filipina who is married to a White American refers to her husband as "American" but to her African American and Filipino American brothers-in-law as "Black" and "Filipino," respectively. Others speak about "American ways," "American culture," or "American lifestyle" when they really mean White American ways, culture, and lifestyle. A Filipino man who has lived in the United States for 30 years explains why he still does not identify himself as American: "I don't see myself just as an American because I cannot hide the fact that my skin is brown. To me, American means White." A second-generation Filipina recounted the following story when asked whether she defined herself as American:

> I went to an all-White school. I knew I was different. I wasn't American. See, you are not taught that you're American because you are not White. When I was in the tenth grade, our English teacher asked us what our nationality was, and she goes how many of you are Mexican, how

many of you are Filipino, and how many of you are Samoan and things like that. And when she asked how many of you are American, just the White people raised their hands.

Given the centrality of moral themes in popular discussions on racial differences, Michele Lamont (1997) has suggested that morality is a crucial site to study the cultural mechanisms of reproduction of racial inequality.

Family-Oriented Model Minorities: "White Women Will Leave You"

In his work on Italian immigrant parents and children in the 1930s, Robert Anthony Orsi (1985) reports that the parents invented a virtuous Italy (based on memories of their childhood) that they then used to castigate the morality of the United States and their U.S.-born or -raised children. In a similar way, many of my respondents constructed their "ethnic" culture as principled and "American" culture as deviant. Most often, this morality narrative revolves around family life and family relations. When asked what set Filipinos apart from other Americans, my respondents—of all ages and class backgrounds—repeatedly contrasted close-knit Filipino families to what they perceived to be the more impersonal quality of U.S. family relations. In the following narratives, "Americans" are characterized as lacking in strong family ties and collective identity, less willing to do the work of family and cultural maintenance, and less willing to abide by patriarchal norms in husband/wife relations:

> American society lacks caring. The American way of life is more individual rather than collective. The American way is to say I want to have my own way. (Filipina immigrant, 54 years old)

Our [Filipino] culture is different. We are more close-knit. We tend to help one another. Americans, ya know, they are all right, but they don't help each other that much. As a matter of fact, if the parents are old, they take them to a convalescent home and let them rot there. We would never do that in our culture. We would nurse them; we would help them until the very end. (Filipino immigrant, 60 years old)

Our [Filipino] culture is very communal. You know that your family will always be there, that you don't have to work when you turn eighteen, you don't have to pay rent when you are eighteen, which is the American way of thinking. You also know that if things don't work out in the outside world, you can always come home and mommy and daddy will always take you and your children in. (Second-generation Filipina, 33 years old)

Asian parents take care of their children. Americans have a different attitude. They leave their children to their own resources. They get babysitters to take care of their children or leave them in day care. That's why when they get old, their children don't even care about them. (Filipina immigrant, 46 years old)

Implicit in negative depictions of U.S. families as uncaring, selfish, and distant is the allegation that white women are not as dedicated to their families as Filipina women are to theirs. Several Filipino men who married white women recalled being warned by their parents and relatives that "White women will leave you." As one man related, "My mother said to me, 'Well, you know, don't marry a White person because they would take everything that you own and leave you.'" For some Filipino men, perceived differences in attitudes about women's roles between Filipina and non-Filipina women influenced their marital choice. A Filipino American navy man explained why he went back to the Philippines to look for a wife:

My goal was to marry a Filipina. I requested to be stationed in the Philippines to get married to a Filipina. I'd seen the women here and basically they are spoiled. They have a tendency of not going along together with their husband. They behave differently. They chase the male, instead of the male, the normal way of the traditional way is for the male to go after the female. They have sex without marrying. They want to do their own things. So my idea was to go back home and marry somebody who has never been here. I tell my son the same thing: if he does what I did and finds himself a good lady there, he will be in good hands.

Another man who had dated mostly White women in high school recounted that when it came time for him to marry, he "looked for the kind of women" he met while stationed in the Philippines: "I hate to sound chauvinistic about marriages, but Filipinas have a way of making you feel like you are a king. They also have that tenderness, that elegance. And we share the same values about family, education, religion, and raising children."

The claims of family closeness are not unique to Filipino immigrants. For example, when asked what makes their group distinctive, Italian Americans, Vietnamese Americans, South Asian Americans, and African Americans all point proudly to the close-knit character of their family life. Although it is difficult to know whether these claims are actual perceptions or favored self-legitimating answers, it is nevertheless important to note the gender implications of these claims. That is, while both men and women identify the family system as a tremendous source of cultural pride, it is women—through their unpaid housework and kin work—who shoulder the primary responsibility for maintaining family closeness. As the organizers of family rituals, transmitters of homeland folklores, and socializers of young children, women have been crucial for the maintenance of family ties and cultural traditions. In a study of kinship, class, and gender among California Italian Americans, di Leonardo argues that women's kin work, "the work of knitting households together into close, extended families," maintains the family networks that give ethnicity meaning (1984, p. 229).

Because the moral status of the community rests on women's labor, women, as wives and daughters, are expected to dedicate themselves to the family. Writing on the constructed image of ethnic family and gender, di Leonardo argues that "a large part of stressing ethnic identity amounts to burdening women with increased responsibilities for preparing special foods, planning rituals, and enforcing 'ethnic' socialization of children" (1984, p. 222). A 23-year-old Filipina spoke about the reproductive work that her mother performed and expected her to learn:

> In my family, I was the only girl, so my mom expected a lot from me. She wanted me to help her to take care of the household. I felt like there was a lot of pressure on me. It's very important to my mom to have the house in order: to wash the dishes, to keep the kitchen in order, vacuuming, and dusting and things like that. She wants me to be a perfect housewife. It's difficult. I have been married now for about four months and my mother asks me every now and then what have I cooked for my husband. My mom is also very strict about families getting together on holidays, and I would always help her to organize that. Each holiday, I would try to decorate the house for her, to make it more special.

The burden of unpaid reproductive and kin work is particularly stressful for women who work outside the home. In the following narrative, a Filipina wife and mother described the pulls of family and work that she experienced when she went back to school to pursue a doctoral degree in nursing:

> The Filipinos, we are very collective, very connected. Going through the doctoral program, sometimes I think it is better just to forget about my relatives and just concentrate on school. All that connectedness, it steals parts of myself because all of my energies are devoted to my family. And that is the reason why I think Americans are successful. The majority of the American people they can do what they want. They don't feel guilty because they only have a few people to relate to. For us Filipinos, it's like roots under the tree, you have all these connections. The Americans are more like the trunk. I am still trying to go up to the trunk of the tree, but it is too hard. I want to be more independent, more like the Americans. I want to be good to my family but what about me? And all the things that I am doing. It's hard. It's always a struggle.

It is important to note that this Filipina interprets her exclusion and added responsibilities as only racial when they are also gendered. For example, when she says, "the American people, they can do what they want," she ignores the differences in the lives of White men and White women—the fact that most White women experience similar competing pulls of family, education, and work.

RACIALIZED SEXUALITY AND (IM)MORALITY: "IN AMERICA . . . SEX IS NOTHING"

Sexuality, as a core aspect of social identity, is fundamental to the structuring of gender inequality. Sexuality is also a salient marker of otherness and has figured prominently in racist and imperialist ideologies. Historically, the sexuality of subordinate groups—particularly that of racialized women—has been systematically stereotyped by the dominant groups. At stake in these stereotypes is the construction of women of color as morally lacking in the areas of sexual restraint and traditional morality. Asian women—both in Asia and in the United States—have been racialized as sexually immoral, and the "Orient"—and its women—has long served as a site of European male-power fantasies, replete with lurid images of sexual license, gynecological aberrations, and general perversion.

Filipinas—both in the Philippines and in the United States—have been marked as desirable but dangerous "prostitutes" and/or submissive "mail-order brides."

Cognizant of the pervasive hypersexualization of Filipina women, my respondents, especially women who grew up near military bases, were quick to denounce prostitution, to condemn sex laborers, and to declare (unasked) that they themselves did not frequent "that part of town." As one Filipina immigrant said,

> Growing up [in the Philippines], I could never date an American because my dad's concept of a friendship with an American is with a GI. The only reason why my dad wouldn't let us date an American is that people will think that the only way you met was because of the base. I have never seen the inside of any of the bases because we were just forbidden to go there.

Many of my respondents also distanced themselves culturally from the Filipinas who serviced U.S. soldiers by branding them "more Americanized" and "more Westernized." In other words, these women were sexually promiscuous because they had assumed the sexual mores of White women. This characterization allows my respondents to symbolically disown the Filipina "bad girl" and, in so doing, to uphold the narrative of Filipina sexual virtuousness and White female sexual promiscuity. In the following narrative, a mother who came to the United States in her 30s contrasted the controlled sexuality of women in the Philippines with the perceived promiscuity of White women in the United States:

> In the Philippines, we always have chaperones when we go out. When we go to dances, we have our uncle,

our grandfather, and auntie all behind us to make sure that we behave in the dance hall. Nobody goes necking outside. You don't even let a man put his hand on your shoulders. When you were brought up in a conservative country, it is hard to come here and see that it is all freedom of speech and freedom of action. Sex was never mentioned in our generation. I was 30 already when I learned about sex. But to the young generation in America, sex is nothing.

Similarly, another immigrant woman criticized the way young American women are raised: "Americans are so liberated. They allow their children, their girls, to go out even when they are still so young." In contrast, she stated that, in "the Filipino way, it is very important, the value of the woman, that she is a virgin when she gets married."

The ideal "Filipina," then, is partially constructed on the community's conceptualization of White women. She is everything that they are not: she is sexually modest and dedicated to her family; they are sexually promiscuous and uncaring. Within the context of the dominant culture's pervasive hypersexualization of Filipinas, the construction of the "ideal" Filipina as family oriented and chaste can be read as an effort to reclaim the morality of the community.

In the next section, I detail the ways Filipino immigrant parents, under the rubric of "cultural preservation," police their daughters' behaviors in order to safeguard their sexual innocence and virginity. These attempts at policing generate hierarchies and tensions within immigrant families—between parents and children and between brothers and sisters.

THE CONSTRUCTION(S) OF THE "IDEAL" FILIPINA: "BOYS ARE BOYS AND GIRLS ARE DIFFERENT"

Although details vary, young women of various groups and across space and time—for example, second-generation Chinese women in San Francisco in the 1920s, U.S.-born Italian women in East Harlem in the 1930s, young Mexican women in the Southwest during the interwar years, and daughters of Caribbean and Asian Indian immigrants on the East Coast in the 1990s—have identified strict parental control on their activities and movements as the primary source of intergenerational conflict.

Although immigrant families have always been preoccupied with passing on their native culture, language, and traditions to both male and female children, it is daughters who have the primary burden of protecting and preserving the family. Because sons do not have to conform to the same image of an "ideal" ethnic subject as daughters do, they often receive special daily privileges denied to daughters. This is not to say that immigrant parents do not place undue expectations on their sons; rather, these expectations do not pivot around the sons' sexuality or dating choices. In contrast, parental control over the movement and action of daughters begins the moment they are perceived as young adults and sexually vulnerable. It regularly consists of monitoring their whereabouts and forbidding dating. For example, the immigrant parents I interviewed seldom allowed their daughters to date, to stay out late, to spend the night at a friend's house, or to take an out-of-town trip.

Many of the second-generation women I spoke to complained bitterly about these parental restrictions. They particularly resented what they saw as gender inequity in their families: the fact that their parents placed far more restrictions on their activities and movements than on those of their brothers. Some decried the fact that even their younger brothers had more freedom than they did: "It was really hard growing up because my parents would let my younger brothers do what they wanted but I didn't get to do what I wanted even though I was the oldest. I had a curfew and my brothers

didn't. I had to ask if I could go places and they didn't. My parents never even asked my brothers when they were coming home." As indicated in the following excerpt, many Filipino males are cognizant of this double standard in their families:

> My sister would always say to me, "It's not fair, just because you are a guy, you can go wherever you want." I think my parents do treat me and my sister differently. Like in high school, maybe 10:30 at night, which is pretty late on a school night, and I say I have to go pick up some notes at my friend's house, my parents wouldn't say anything. But if my sister were to do that, there would be no way. Even now when my sister is in college already, if she wants to leave at midnight to go to a friend's house, they would tell her that she shouldn't do it.

When questioned about this double standard, parents generally responded by explaining that "girls are different":

> I have that Filipino mentality that boys are boys and girls are different. Girls are supposed to be protected, to be clean. In the early years, my daughters have to have chaperones and curfews. And they know that they have to be virgins until they get married. The girls always say that is not fair. What is the difference between their brothers and them? And my answer always is, "In the Philippines, you know, we don't do that. The girls stay home. The boys go out." It was the way that I was raised. I still want to have part of that culture instilled in my children. And I want them to have that to pass on to their children.

Even among self-described Western-educated and "tolerant" parents many continue to ascribe to "the Filipino way" when it comes to raising daughters. As one college-educated father explains,

> Because of my Western education, I don't raise my children the way my parents raised me. I

tended to be a little more tolerant. But at times, especially in certain issues like dating, I find myself more towards the Filipino way in the sense that I have only one daughter so I tended to be a little bit stricter. So the double standard kind of operates: it's all right for the boys to explore the field but I tended to be overly protective of my daughter. My wife feels the same way because the boys will not lose anything, but the daughter will lose something, her virginity, losing face, that kind of thing.

Although many parents discourage or forbid dating for daughters, they still fully expect these young women to fulfill their traditional roles as women: to marry and have children. A young Filipina recounted the mixed messages she received from her parents:

This is the way it is supposed to work. Okay, you go to school. You go to college. You graduate. You find a job. *Then* you find your husband, and you have children. That's the whole time line. But my question is, if you are not allowed to date, how are you supposed to find your husband? They say "no" to the whole dating scene because that is secondary to your education, secondary to your family. They do push marriage, but at a later date. So basically my parents are telling me that I should get married and I should have children but that I should not date.

The above narratives suggest that the process of parenting is gendered in that immigrant parents tend to restrict the autonomy, mobility, and personal decision making of their daughters more than that of their sons. I argue that these parental restrictions are attempts to construct a model of Filipina womanhood that is chaste, modest, nurturing, and family oriented. Women are seen as responsible for holding the cultural line, maintaining racial boundaries, and marking cultural difference. This is not to say that parent-daughter conflicts exist in all Filipino immigrant families. Certainly, Filipino parents do not

respond in a uniform way to the challenges of being racial-ethnic minorities, and I met parents who have had to change some of their ideas and practices in response to their inability to control their children's movements and choices:

I have three girls and our boy. I used to think that I wouldn't allow my daughters to go dating and things like that, but there is no way I could do that. I can't stop it. It's the way of life here in America. Sometimes you kind of question yourself, if you are doing what is right. It is hard to accept but you got to accept it. That's the way they are here. (Professional Filipino immigrant father)

My children are born and raised here, so they do pretty much what they want. They think they know everything. I can only do so much as a parent. . . . When I try to teach my kids things, they tell me that I sound like an old record. They even talk back to me sometimes. . . . The first time my daughter brought her boyfriend to the house, she was eighteen years old. I almost passed away, knocked out. Lord, tell me what to do? (Working-class Filipina immigrant mother)

These narratives call attention to the shifts in the generational power caused by the migration process and to the possible gap between what parents say they want for their children and their ability to control the young. However, the interview data do suggest that intergenerational conflicts are socially recognized occurrences in Filipino communities. Even when respondents themselves had not experienced intergenerational tensions, they could always recall a cousin, a girlfriend, or a friend's daughter who had.

Sanctions and Reactions: "That Is Not What a Descent Filipino Girl Should Do"

I do not wish to suggest that immigrant communities are the only ones in which parents regulate their daughters' mobility and sexuality.

Immigrant families, though, have an additional strategy: they can discipline their daughters as racial/national subjects as well as gendered ones. That is, as self-appointed guardians of "authentic" cultural memory, immigrant parents can attempt to regulate their daughters' independent choices by linking them to cultural ignorance or betrayal. As both parents and children recounted, young women who disobeyed parental strictures were often branded "nonethnic," "untraditional," "radical," "selfish," and "not caring about the family." Female sexual choices were also linked to moral degeneracy, defined in relation to a narrative of a hegemonic White norm. Parents were quick to warn their daughter about "bad" Filipinas who had become pregnant outside marriage. As in the case of "bar girls" in the Philippines, Filipina Americans who veered from acceptable behaviors were deemed "Americanized"—as women who have adopted the sexual mores and practices of White women. As one Filipino immigrant father described "Americanized" Filipinas: "They are spoiled because they have seen the American way. They go out at night. Late at night. They go out on dates. Smoking. They have sex without marrying."

From the perspective of the second-generation daughters, these charges are stinging. The young women I interviewed were visibly pained—with many breaking down and crying—when they recounted their parents' charges. This deep pain, stemming in part from their desire to be validated as Filipina, existed even among the more "rebellious" daughters. One 24-year-old daughter explained:

> My mom is very traditional. She wants to follow Filipino customs, just really adhere to them, like what is proper for a girl, what she can and can't do and what other people are going to think of her if she doesn't follow that way. When I pushed these restrictions, when I rebelled and stayed out later than allowed, my mom would always say, "That is not what a decent Filipino girl should do. You should come home at a decent hour. What are people going to think of you?" And that would get me really upset, you know, because I think that my character is very much the way it should be for a Filipina. I wear my hair long, I wear decent makeup. I dress properly, conservative. I am family oriented. It hurts me that she doesn't see that I am decent, that I am proper, and that I am not going to bring shame to the family or anything like that.

This narrative suggests that even when parents are unable to control the behaviors of their children, their (dis)approval remains powerful in shaping the emotional lives of their daughters.

CONCLUSION

Mainstream American society defines White middle-class as the norm and whiteness as the unmarked marker of others' difference. In this essay, I have shown that many Filipino immigrants use the largely gendered discourse of morality as one strategy to decenter whiteness above the dominant group, demonizing it in the process. Like other immigrant groups, Filipinos praise the United States as a land of significant opportunity but simultaneously denounce it as a country inhabited by corrupted and individualistic people of questionable morals. In particular, they criticize American family life, American individualism, and American women. Enforced by distorting powers of memory and nostalgia, this rhetoric of moral superiority often leads to patriarchal calls for a cultural "authenticity" that locates family honor and national integrity in the group's female members.

Because the policing of women's bodies is one of the main means of asserting moral superiority, young women face numerous restrictions on their autonomy, mobility, and personal decision making. This practice of cultural (re)construction reveals how deeply the conduct of private life can be tied to larger social structures.

REFERENCES

Di Leonardo, Micaela. (1984). *The Varieties of Ethnic Experience: Kinship, Class, and Gender Among California Italian-Americans*. Ithaca, NY: Cornell University Press.

Orsi, Robert Anthony. (1985). *The Madonna of 115th Street: Faith and Community in Italian Harlem, 1880–1950*. New Haven, CT: Yale University Press.

NAMING FEELING AND EXPERIENCE

Just as we learn social attitudes and expectations from others, we also learn how to make sense of our experiences through interaction. People learn from one another what to think, feel, and expect from their experiences. Even when we experience something physical, such as illness, we talk with others about these symptoms to figure out what is really going on. People are sometimes surprised to learn that we don't just "know" how we are feeling. Socialization includes information for how we are expected to feel in various contexts; for example, we learn that grief is associated with death and funerals. Thus, when our emotions fit with our expectations of the situation, we are more easily able to identify and make sense of them—"My father died recently. That's why I'm feeling so sad." Oftentimes, however, we are not certain what we are feeling or why we feel a particular way that seems out of context for the situation. On these occasions, we usually talk with others (or internally to ourselves) in an effort to make sense of our experiences. It can be instructive to listen carefully to the way people help and coach one another when they are trying to define an experience. This doesn't necessarily imply that our feelings are "real." Rather, the implication is that our experiences, including feelings, make sense to us only when we are able to give them a name and categorize them.

Different groups and cultures place different emphasis on various feelings and experiences. For instance, if you are a member of a religious community, you learn to recognize and pay attention to your inner spiritual feelings. People trained in culinary arts have learned how to taste food and drink in more complex ways. There are cultures in which the dream experience is seen as central to social life, and people in these groups can remember and even participate lucidly in their dreams in ways that would astonish most Westerners. One of my students once did a presentation on the way in which funeral directors are trained, or socialized, in the art of guiding other people through the experience of grief while simultaneously helping them make practical decisions such as selecting a coffin and negotiating with insurance. Each of these examples illustrates that even taken-for-granted feelings have social origins and reflect cultural values and practices. We learn to focus on and attach meaning to certain experiences based on the values of our culture and reference groups.

"Becoming a Marihuana User" is a classic sociological article written by Howard Becker in 1953. Becker observed that people who use marijuana for pleasure have to learn how to smoke the drug, identify its effects, and consider the effects to be pleasant. If they don't learn these things, they won't continue smoking. It's an acquired taste—acquired through interaction with others who tell you what to do and feel. This article was a social research milestone in demonstrating that even physiological experiences have to be interpreted before we can understand them and "know" how to feel about them.

"The Development of Feeling Norms Underlying Romantic Love Among Adolescent Females" explores the socialization process of learning to be in love. Being in love is one of the most cherished experiences in Western culture. Yet, as Robin Simon and her colleagues

(Continued)

(Continued)

demonstrate in this article, even seemingly normal feelings such as love and attraction have to be learned. Based on interviews with adolescent girls in junior high, Simon and colleagues describe the social learning process through which young girls train one another to look for, recognize, and respond to feelings of attraction. This learning process includes a set of rules for acceptable and unacceptable feelings (e.g., you should only feel attraction for one person at a time and only for someone of the opposite sex).

READING QUESTIONS

1. Consider the expression "It's an acquired taste." Recall an experience in which you tried a food or activity that you didn't like at first, but now enjoy. What led you to try it again and eventually come to like it?

2. Recall an occasion when you were confused about something that happened to you or that you were feeling. With whom did you talk, and what can you remember about how that person defined the situation for you?

3. When children ask adults about sex, common first responses carry an emotional tone of shame and embarrassment. The child usually picks up the attitude that sex is a "big deal," but one that people don't talk about comfortably. Consider your own initial learning experience. When did you first become aware of sex (not your own sexuality, just the idea of sex)? What emotions or feelings do you associate with that experience? Were people helpful in their explanations, or did they seem embarrassed and abstract? Have subsequent experiences altered your first impressions, or do you still have the same initial feeling imprint based on your first questions?

4. Think about the last time you felt ill. How did you decide what was wrong with you?

5. Consider an occasion in which your feelings seemed inappropriate for the situation. Try to reconstruct the conversation you had with yourself about this experience and identify who or what made you feel your feelings were inappropriate.

17

Becoming a Marihuana User

Howard S. Becker

(1953)

The use of marihuana is and has been the focus of a good deal of attention on the part of both scientists and laymen. One of the major problems students of the practice have addressed themselves to has been the identification of those individual psychological traits which differentiate marihuana users from nonusers and which are assumed to account for the use of the drug. That approach, common in the study of behavior categorized as deviant, is based on the premise that the presence of a given kind of behavior in an individual can best be explained as the result of some trait which predisposes or motivates him to engage in the behavior.[1]

This study is likewise concerned with accounting for the presence or absence of marihuana use in an individual's behavior. It starts, however, from a different premise: that the presence of a given kind of behavior is the result of a sequence of social experiences during which the person acquires a conception of the meaning of the behavior, and perceptions and judgments of objects and situations, all of which make the activity possible and desirable. Thus, the motivation or disposition to engage in the activity is built up in the course of learning to engage in it

and does not antedate this learning process. For such a view it is not necessary to identify those "traits" which "cause" the behavior. Instead, the problem becomes one of describing the set of changes in the person's conception of the activity and of the experience it provides for him.[2]

This paper seeks to describe the sequence of changes in attitude and experience which led to *the use of marihuana for pleasure*. Marihuana does not produce addiction, as do alcohol and the opiate drugs; there is no withdrawal sickness and no ineradicable craving for the drug.[3] The most frequent pattern of use might be termed "recreational." The drug is used occasionally for the pleasure the user finds in it, a relatively casual kind of behavior in comparison with that connected with the use of addicting drugs. The term "use for pleasure" is meant to emphasize the noncompulsive and casual character of the behavior. It is also meant to eliminate from consideration here those few cases in which marihuana is used for its prestige value only, as a symbol that one is a certain kind of person, with no pleasure at all being derived from its use.

The analysis presented here is conceived of as demonstrating the greater explanatory usefulness of the kind of theory outlined above as

AUTHOR'S NOTE: This paper was read at the meetings of the Midwest Sociological Society in Omaha, Nebraska, April 25, 1953. The research on which this paper is based was done while I was a member of the staff of the Chicago Narcotics Survey, a study done by the Chicago Area Project, Inc., under a grant from the National Institute of Mental Health. My thanks to Solomon Kobrin, Harold Finestone, Henry McKay, and Anselm Strauss, who read and discussed with me earlier versions of this paper.

opposed to the predispositional theories now current. This may be seen in two ways: (1) predispositional theories cannot account for that group of users (whose existence is admitted)[4] who do not exhibit the trait or traits considered to cause the behavior and (2) such theories cannot account for the great variability over time of a given individual's behavior with reference to the drug. The same person will at one stage be unable to use the drug for pleasure, at a later stage be able and willing to do so, and still later, again be unable to use it in this way. These changes, difficult to explain from a predispositional or motivational theory, are readily understandable in terms of changes in the individual's conception of the drug as is the existence of "normal" users.

The study attempted to arrive at a general statement of the sequence of changes in individual attitude and experience which have always occurred when the individual has become willing and able to use marihuana for pleasure and which have not occurred or not been permanently maintained when this is not the case. This generalization is stated in universal terms in order that negative cases may be discovered and used to revise the explanatory hypothesis.[5]

Fifty interviews with marihuana users from a variety of social backgrounds and present positions in society constitute the data from which the generalization was constructed and against which it was tested.[6] The interviews focused on the history of the person's experience with the drug, seeking major changes in his attitude toward it and in his actual use of it, and the reasons for these changes. The final generalization is a statement of that sequence of changes in attitude which occurred in every case known to me in which the person came to use marihuana for pleasure. Until a negative case is found, it may be considered as an explanation of all cases of marihuana use for pleasure. In addition, changes from use to nonuse are shown to be related to similar changes in conception, and in

each case it is possible to explain variations in the individual's behavior in these terms.

This paper covers only a portion of the natural history of an individual's use of marihuana,[7] starting with the person having arrived at the point of willingness to try marihuana. He knows that others use it to "get high," but he does not know what this means in concrete terms. He is curious about the experience, ignorant of what it may turn out to be, and afraid that it may be more than he has bargained for. The steps outlined below, if he undergoes them all and maintains the attitudes developed in them, leave him willing and able to use the drug for pleasure when the opportunity presents itself.

I

The novice does not ordinarily get high the first time he smokes marihuana, and several attempts are usually necessary to induce this state. One explanation of this may be that the drug is not smoked "properly," that is, in a way that ensures sufficient dosage to produce real symptoms of intoxication. Most users agree that it cannot be smoked like tobacco if one is to get high:

> Take in a lot of air, you know, and . . . I don't know how to describe it, you don't smoke it like a cigarette, you draw in a lot of air and get it deep down in your system and then keep it there. Keep it there as long as you can.

Without the use of some such technique[8] the drug will produce no effects, and the user will be unable to get high:

> The trouble with people like that [who are not able to get high] is that they're just not smoking it right, that's all there is to it. Either they're not holding it down long enough, or they're getting too much air and not enough smoke, or the other way around or something like that. A lot of people

just don't smoke it right, so naturally nothing's gonna happen.

If nothing happens, it is manifestly impossible for the user to develop a conception of the drug as an object which can be used for pleasure, and use will therefore not continue. The first step in the sequence of events that must occur if the person is to become a user is that he must learn to use the proper smoking technique in order that his use of the drug will produce some effects in terms of which his conception of it can change.

Such a change is, as might be expected, a result of the individual's participation in groups in which marihuana is used. In them the individual learns the proper way to smoke the drug. This may occur through direct teaching:

> I was smoking like I did an ordinary cigarette. He said, "No, don't do it like that." He said, "Suck it, you know, draw in and hold it in your lungs till you . . . for a period of time."
>
> I said, "Is there any limit of time to hold it?"
>
> He said, "No, just till you feel that you want to let it out, let it out." So I did that three or four times.

Many new users are ashamed to admit ignorance and, pretending to know already, must learn through the more indirect means of observation and imitation:

> I came on like I had turned on [smoked marihuana] many times before, you know. I didn't want to seem like a punk to this cat. See, like I didn't know the first thing about it—how to smoke it, or what was going to happen, or what. I just watched him like a hawk—I didn't take my eyes off him for a second, because I wanted to do everything just as he did it. I watched how he held it, how he smoked it, and everything. Then when he gave it to me I just came on cool, as though I knew exactly what the score was. I held it like he did and took a poke just the way he did.

No person continued marihuana use for pleasure without learning a technique that supplied sufficient dosage for the effects of the drug to appear. Only when this was learned was it possible for a conception of the drug as an object which could be used for pleasure to emerge. Without such a conception marihuana use was considered meaningless and did not continue.

II

Even after he learns the proper smoking technique, the new user may not get high and thus not form a conception of the drug as something which can be used for pleasure. A remark made by a user suggested the reason for this difficulty in getting high and pointed to the next necessary step on the road to being a user:

> I was told during an interview, "As a matter of fact, I've seen a guy who was high out of his mind and didn't know it."
>
> I expressed disbelief: "How can that be, man?"
>
> The interviewee said, "Well, it's pretty strange, I'll grant you that, but I've seen it. This guy got on with me, claiming that he'd never got high, one of those guys, and he got completely stoned. And he kept insisting that he wasn't high. So I had to prove to him that he was."

What does this mean? It suggests that being high consists of two elements: the presence of symptoms caused by marihuana use and the recognition of these symptoms and their connection by the user with his use of the drug. It is not enough, that is, that the effects be present; they alone do not automatically provide the experience of being high. The user must be able to point them out to himself and consciously connect them with his having smoked marihuana before he can have this experience. Otherwise, regardless of the actual effects produced, he considers that the drug has had no effect on him:

"I figured it either had no effect on me or other people were exaggerating its effect on them, you know. I thought it was probably psychological, see." Such persons believe that the whole thing is an illusion and that the wish to be high leads the user to deceive himself into believing that something is happening when, in fact, nothing is. They do not continue marihuana use, feeling that "it does nothing" for them.

Typically, however, the novice has faith (developed from his observation of users who do get high) that the drug actually will produce some new experience and continues to experiment with it until it does. His failure to get high worries him, and he is likely to ask more experienced users or provoke comments from them about it. In such conversations he is made aware of specific details of his experience which he may not have noticed or may have noticed but failed to identify as symptoms of being high:

I didn't get high the first time . . . I don't think I held it in long enough. I probably let it out, you know, you're a little afraid. The second time I wasn't sure, and he [smoking companion] told me, like I asked him for some of the symptoms or something, how would I know, you know. . . . So he told me to sit on a stool. I sat on—I think I sat on a bar stool—and he said, "Let your feet hang," and then when I got down my feet were real cold, you know.

And I started feeling it, you know. That was the first time. And then about a week after that, sometime pretty close to it, I really got on. That was the first time I got on a big laughing kick, you know. Then I really knew I was on.

One symptom of being high is an intense hunger. In the next case the novice becomes aware of this and gets high for the first time:

They were just laughing the hell out of me because like I was eating so much. I just scoffed [ate] so much food, and they were just laughing at me, you

know. Sometimes I'd be looking at them, you know, wondering why they're laughing, you know, not knowing what I was doing. [Well, did they tell you why they were laughing eventually?] Yeah, yeah, I come back, "Hey, man, what's happening?" Like, you know, like I'd ask, "What's happening?" and all of a sudden I feel weird, you know. "Man, you're on you know. You're on pot [high on marihuana]." I said, "No, am I?" Like I don't know what's happening.

The learning may occur in more indirect ways:

I heard little remarks that were made by other people. Somebody said, "My legs are rubbery," and I can't remember all the remarks that were made because I was very attentively listening for all these cues for what I was supposed to feel like.

The novice, then, eager to have this feeling, picks up from other users some concrete referents of the term "high" and applies these notions to his own experience. The new concepts make it possible for him to locate these symptoms among his own sensations and to point out to himself a "something different" in his experience that he connects with drug use. It is only when he can do this that he is high. In the next case, the contrast between two successive experiences of a user makes clear the crucial importance of the awareness of the symptoms in being high and re-emphasizes the important role of interaction with other users in acquiring the concepts that make this awareness possible:

[Did you get high the first time you turned on?] Yeah, sure. Although, come to think of it, I guess I really didn't. I mean, like that first time it was more or less of a mild drunk. I was happy, I guess, you know what I mean. But I didn't really know I was high, you know what I mean. It was only after the second time I got high that I realized I was high the first time. Then I knew that something different was happening.

[How did you know that?] How did I know? If what happened to me that night would of happened to you, you would've known, believe me. We played the first tune for almost two hours—one tune! Imagine, man! We got on the stand and played this one tune, we started at nine o'clock. When we got finished I looked at my watch, it's a quarter to eleven. Almost two hours on one tune. And it didn't seem like anything. I mean, you know, it does that to you. It's like you have much more time or something. Anyway, when I saw that, man, it was too much. I knew I must really be high or something if anything like that could happen. See, and then they explained to me that that's what it did to you, you had a different sense of time and everything. So I realized that that's what it was. I knew then. Like the first time, I probably felt that way, you know, but I didn't know what's happening.

It is only when the novice becomes able to get high in this sense that he will continue to use marihuana for pleasure. In every case in which use continued, the user had acquired the necessary concepts with which to express to himself the fact that he was experiencing new sensations caused by the drug. That is, for use to continue, it is necessary not only to use the drug so as to produce effects but also to learn to perceive these effects when they occur. In this way marihuana acquires meaning for the user as an object which can be used for pleasure.

With increasing experience the user develops a greater appreciation of the drug's effects; he continues to learn to get high. He examines succeeding experiences closely, looking for new effects, making sure the old ones are still there. Out of this there grows a stable set of categories for experiencing the drug's effects whose presence enables the user to get high with ease.

The ability to perceive the drug's effects must be maintained if use is to continue; if it is lost, marihuana use ceases. Two kinds of evidence support this statement. First, people who become heavy users of alcohol, barbiturates, or opiates do not continue to smoke marihuana, largely because they lose the ability to distinguish between its effects and those of the other drugs.[9] They no longer know whether the marihuana gets them high. Second, in those few cases in which an individual uses marihuana in such quantities that he is always high, he is apt to get this same feeling that the drug has no effect on him, since the essential element of a noticeable difference between feeling high and feeling normal is missing. In such a situation, use is likely to be given up completely, but temporarily, in order that the user may once again be able to perceive the difference.

III

One more step is necessary if the user who has now learned to get high is to continue use. He must learn to enjoy the effects he has just learned to experience. Marihuana-produced sensations are not automatically or necessarily pleasurable. The taste for such experience is a socially acquired one, not different in kind from acquired tastes for oysters or dry martinis. The user feels dizzy, thirsty; his scalp tingles; he misjudges time and distances; and so on. Are these things pleasurable? He isn't sure. If he is to continue marihuana use, he must decide that they are. Otherwise, getting high, while a real enough experience, will be an unpleasant one he would rather avoid.

The effects of the drug, when first perceived, may be physically unpleasant or at least ambiguous:

It started taking effect, and I didn't know what was happening, you know, what it was, and I was very sick. I walked around the room, walking around the room trying to get off, you know; it just scared me at first, you know. I wasn't used to that kind of feeling.

In addition, the novice's naive interpretation of what is happening to him may further confuse and frighten him, particularly if he decides, as many do, that he is going insane:

> I felt I was insane, you know. Everything people done to me just wigged me. I couldn't hold a conversation, and my mind would be wandering, and I was always thinking, oh, I don't know, weird things, like hearing music different. . . . I get the feeling that I can't talk to anyone. I'll goof completely.

Given these typically frightening and unpleasant first experiences, the beginner will not continue use unless he learns to redefine the sensations as pleasurable:

> It was offered to me, and I tried it. I'll tell you one thing. I never did enjoy it at all. I mean it was just nothing that I could enjoy. [Well, did you get high when you turned on?] Oh, yeah, I got definite feelings from it. But I didn't enjoy them. I mean I got plenty of reactions, but they were mostly reactions of fear. [You were frightened?] Yes, I didn't enjoy it. I couldn't seem to relax with it, you know. If you can't relax with a thing, you can't enjoy it, I don't think.

In other cases the first experiences were also definitely unpleasant, but the person did become a marihuana user. This occurred, however, only after a later experience enabled him to redefine the sensations as pleasurable:

> [This man's first experience was extremely unpleasant, involving distortion of spatial relationships and sounds, violent thirst, and panic produced by these symptoms.] After the first time I didn't turn on for about, I'd say, ten months to a year. . . . It wasn't a moral thing; it was because I'd gotten so frightened, bein' so high. An' I didn't want to go through that again, I mean, my reaction was, "Well, if this is what they call bein' high, I don't dig [like] it." . . . So I didn't turn on for a year almost, accounta that. . . .

> Well, my friends started, an' consequently I started again. But I didn't have any more, I didn't have that same initial reaction, after I started turning on again.

> [In interaction with his friends he became able to find pleasure in the effects of the drug and eventually became a regular user.]

In no case will use continue without such a redefinition of the effects as enjoyable.

This redefinition occurs, typically, in interaction with more experienced users who, in a number of ways, teach the novice to find pleasure in this experience which is at first so frightening.[10] They may reassure him as to the temporary character of the unpleasant sensations and minimize their seriousness, at the same time calling attention to the more enjoyable aspects. An experienced user describes how he handles newcomers to marihuana use:

> Well, they get pretty high sometimes. The average person isn't ready for that, and it is a little frightening to them sometimes. I mean, they've been high on lush [alcohol], and they get higher that way than they've ever been before, and they don't know what's happening to them. Because they think they're going to keep going up, up, up till they lose their minds or begin doing weird things or something. You have to like reassure them, explain to them that they're not really flipping or anything, that they're gonna be all right. You have to just talk them out of being afraid. Keep talking to them, reassuring, telling them it's all right. And come on with your own story, you know: "The same thing happened to me. You'll get to like that after awhile." Keep coming on like that; pretty soon you talk them out of being scared. And besides they see you doing it and nothing horrible is happening to you, so that gives them more confidence.

The more experienced user may also teach the novice to regulate the amount he smokes more carefully, so as to avoid any severely uncomfortable symptoms while retaining the pleasant ones. Finally, he teaches the new user that he can "get to like it after awhile." He teaches him to regard those ambiguous experiences formerly defined as unpleasant as enjoyable. The older user in the following incident is a person whose tastes have shifted in this way, and his remarks have the effect of helping others to make a similar redefinition:

> A new user had her first experience of the effects of marihuana and became frightened and hysterical. She "felt like she was half in and half out of the room" and experienced a number of alarming physical symptoms. One of the more experienced users present said, "She's dragged because she's high like that. I'd give anything to get that high myself. I haven't been that high in years."

In short, what was once frightening and distasteful becomes, after a taste for it is built up, pleasant, desired, and sought after. Enjoyment is introduced by the favorable definition of the experience that one acquires from others. Without this, use will not continue, for marihuana will not be for the user an object he can use for pleasure.

In addition to being a necessary step in becoming a user, this represents an important condition for continued use. It is quite common for experienced users suddenly to have an unpleasant or frightening experience, which they cannot define as pleasurable, either because they have used a larger amount of marihuana than usual or because it turns out to be a higher-quality marihuana than they expected. The user has sensations which go beyond any conception he has of what being high is and is in much the same situation as the novice, uncomfortable and frightened. He may blame it on an overdose and simply be more careful in the future. But he may make this the occasion for a rethinking of his attitude toward the drug and decide that it no longer can give him pleasure. When this occurs

and is not followed by a redefinition of the drug as capable of producing pleasure, use will cease.

The likelihood of such a redefinition occurring depends on the degree of the individual's participation with other users. Where this participation is intensive, the individual is quickly talked out of his feeling against marihuana use. In the next case, on the other hand, the experience was very disturbing, and the aftermath of the incident cut the person's participation with other users to almost zero. Use stopped for three years and began again only when a combination of circumstances, important among which was a resumption of ties with users, made possible a redefinition of the nature of the drug:

> It was too much, like I only made about four pokes, and I couldn't even get it out of my mouth, I was so high, and I got real flipped. In the basement, you know, I just couldn't stay in there anymore. My heart was pounding real hard, you know, and I was going out of my mind; I thought I was losing my mind completely. So I cut out of this basement, and this other guy, he's out of his mind, told me, "Don't, don't leave me, man. Stay here." And I couldn't.
>
> I walked outside, and it was five below zero, and I thought I was dying, and I had my coat open; I was sweating. I was perspiring. My whole insides were all . . . , and I walked about two blocks away, and I fainted behind a bush. I don't know how long I laid there. I woke up, and I was feeling the worst, I can't describe it at all, so I made it to a bowling alley, man, and I was trying to act normal, I was trying to shoot pool, you know, trying to act real normal, and I couldn't lay and I couldn't stand up and I couldn't sit down, and I went up and laid down where some guys that spot pins lay down, and that didn't help me, and I went down to a doctor's office. I was going to go in there and tell the doctor to put me out of my misery . . . because my heart was pounding so hard, you know. . . . So then all weekend I started flipping, seeing things there and going through hell, you know, all kinds of abnormal things. . . . I just quit for a long time then.

[He went to a doctor who defined the symptoms for him as those of a nervous breakdown caused by "nerves" and "worries." Although he was no longer using marihuana, he had some recurrences of the symptoms which led him to suspect that "it was all his nerves."] So I just stopped worrying, you know; so it was about thirty-six months later I started making it again. I'd just take a few pokes, you know. [He first resumed use in the company of the same user-friend with whom he had been involved in the original incident.]

A person, then, cannot begin to use marihuana for pleasure, or continue its use for pleasure, unless he learns to define its effects as enjoyable, unless it becomes and remains an object which he conceived of as capable of producing pleasure.

IV

In summary, an individual will be able to use marihuana for pleasure only when he goes through a process of learning to conceive of it as an object which can be used in this way. No one becomes a user without (1) learning to smoke the drug in a way which will produce real effects; (2) learning to recognize the effects and connect them with drug use (learning, in other words, to get high); and (3) learning to enjoy the sensations he perceives. In the course of this process he develops a disposition or motivation to use marihuana which was not and could not have been present when he began use, for it involves and depends on conceptions of the drug which could only grow out of the kind of actual experience detailed above. On completion of this process he is willing and able to use marihuana for pleasure.

He has learned, in short, to answer "Yes" to the question: "Is it fun?" The direction his further use of the drug takes depends on his being able to continue to answer "Yes" to this question and, in addition, on his being able to answer "Yes" to other questions which arise as he becomes aware of the implications of the fact that the society as a whole disapproves of the practice: "Is it expedient?" "Is it moral?" Once he has acquired the ability to get enjoyment out of the drug, use will continue to be possible for him. Considerations of morality and expediency, occasioned by the reactions of society, may interfere and inhibit use, but use continues to be a possibility in terms of his conception of the drug. The act becomes impossible only when the ability to enjoy the experience of being high is lost, through a change in the user's conception of the drug occasioned by certain kinds of experience with it.

In comparing this theory with those which ascribe marihuana use to motives or predispositions rooted deep in individual behavior, the evidence makes it clear that marihuana use for pleasure can occur only when the process described above is undergone and cannot occur without it. This is apparently so without reference to the nature of the individual's personal makeup, or psychic problems. Such theories assume that people have stable modes of response which predetermine the way they will act in relation to any particular situation or object and that, when they come in contact with the given object or situation, they act in the way in which their makeup predisposes them.

This analysis of the genesis of marihuana use shows that the individuals who come in contact with a given object may respond to it at first in a great variety of ways. If a stable form of new behavior toward the object is to emerge, a transformation of meanings must occur, in which the person develops a new conception of the nature of the object.[11] This happens in a series of communicative acts in which others point out new aspects of his experience to him, present him with new interpretations of events, and help him achieve a new conceptual organization of his world, without which the new behavior is not possible. Persons who do not achieve the proper kind of conceptualization are unable to engage in the given behavior and turn off in the direction of some other relationship to the object or activity.

This suggests that behavior of any kind might fruitfully be studied developmentally, in terms of changes in meanings and concepts, their organization and reorganization, and the way they channel behavior, making some acts possible while excluding others.

NOTES

1. See, as examples of this approach, the following: E. Marcovitz & H. J. Meyers (1944, December), "The marihuana addict in the army," *War Medicine, 6,* 382–391; H. S. Gaskill (1945, September), "Marihuana, an intoxicant," *American Journal of Psychiatry, 102,* 202–204; S. Charen & L. Perelman (1946, March), "Personality studies of marihuana addicts," *American Journal of Psychiatry, 102,* 674–682.

2. This approach stems from George Herbert Mead's (1934) discussion of objects in *Mind, self, and society,* Chicago: University of Chicago Press, pp. 277–280.

3. Cf. R. Adams (1942, November), "Marihuana," *Bulletin of the New York Academy of Medicine, 18,* 705–730.

4. Cf. L. Kolb (1938, July), "Marihuana," *Federal Probation, 2,* 22–25; and W. Bromberg (1939, July 1), "Marihuana: A psychiatric study," *Journal of the American Medical Association, 113,* 11.

5. The method used is that described in A. R. Lindesmith (1947), *Opiate addiction,* Bloomington, IN: Principia, chap. i. I would like also to acknowledge the important role Lindesmith's work played in shaping my thinking about the genesis of marihuana use.

6. Most of the interviews were done by the author. I am grateful to Solomon Kobrin and Harold Finestone for allowing me to make use of interviews done by them.

7. I hope to discuss elsewhere other stages in this natural history.

8. A pharmacologist notes that this ritual is in fact an extremely efficient way of getting the drug into the blood stream. R. P. Walton (1938), *Marihuana: America's new drug problem,* Philadelphia: J. B. Lippincott, p. 48.

9. "Smokers have repeatedly stated that the consumption of whiskey while smoking negates the potency of the drug. They find it very difficult to get 'high' while drinking whiskey and because of that smokers will not drink while using the 'weed.'" Cf. New York City Mayor's Committee on Marihuana (1944), *The marihuana problem in the city of New York,* Lancaster, PA: Jacques Cattel, p. 13.

10. Charen & Perelman (1946), p. 679.

11. Cf. A. Strauss (1952, June), "The development and transformation of monetary meanings in the child," *American Sociological Review, 17,* 275–286.

NAMING FEELING AND EXPERIENCE

18

The Development of Feeling Norms
Underlying Romantic Love Among Adolescent Females

Robin W. Simon, Donna Eder, and Cathy Evans

(1992)

In American society, love is an important emotion (Cancian 1985, 1987; Cancian and Gordon 1988; Hochschild 1983a; Swidler 1980). Like other feelings, romantic love is a *social* sentiment, for which a cultural label and a set of ideological beliefs exist (Gordon 1981). Embodied in ideological beliefs about love are "feeling norms" which guide individuals' romantic feelings and behaviors* (Hochschild 1979, 1983a). Feeling norms that underlie romantic love not only influence whether we should or should not love (Hochschild 1983a), but also help us identify the appropriate object of romantic feelings. Yet in spite of the importance attached to love in American culture, we know little about the content of the feeling norms that govern romantic love and the ways in which cultural knowledge about love is acquired socially. . . .

In this paper we discuss the content of feeling and expression norms underlying romantic love as they emerge in adolescent girls' peer culture. We also discuss the various ways in which

feeling norms are communicated to group members. Although adolescent girls may obtain normative information about romantic feelings in other social relationships and in other social contexts—as well as through media such as romance novels, music, television, and films—the focus of this paper is limited to affective socialization processes among peers in school contexts because we do not have data on those other socialization agents. Peer groups, however, are an important source of emotional socialization because of the primacy of these groups to youths. In interaction with peers, young people draw on norms and beliefs that are available in the broader culture and make them meaningful by applying them to their everyday concerns and activities (Corsaro and Rizzo 1988; Mead 1934). By focusing on peer group socialization, we show that while adolescent girls are acquiring cultural knowledge about love, they also are creating and continuously negotiating feeling norms which pertain to the emergent concerns of their peer culture.

---

*Feeling norms are social norms that prescribe the appropriate intensity, duration, and target of emotions in social situations and relationships (Gordon 1981; Hochschild 1979).

DATA AND METHODS

We collected the data for this paper as part of an ethnographic study of adolescent socialization and peer interaction in a middle school. The school that was selected for the study was located in a medium-sized midwestern community. The school enrolls sixth-, seventh-, and eighth-grade students from a range of socioeconomic backgrounds, including youths from upper middle-class and lower working-class families. Most of the students were white, but a small number of black youths were enrolled at the school. The school was large, with approximately 250 students in each grade.

Data on peer interaction and relations were collected over a three-year period and involved a variety of methods, including participant observation, audio and audiovisual recording, and in-depth group interviews. Three female researchers observed a total of 10 female peer groups during lunch periods twice a week, over periods ranging from five to nine months. Three of these groups were studied for two years. . . .

At the beginning of the study, we told the students that we were interested in their lunchroom activities and conversations. Because we spent time with each group and avoided assuming any authority over the students, a high degree of rapport was established. Several weeks into the study, many students felt free to swear in front of us and often assured other students that we were "okay."

After observing groups for a minimum of three months, we made and transcribed audio and/or video recordings of conversations with eight of the groups. In addition, we conducted in-depth interviews on romance with the girls in two groups that had a strong interest in this topic. Field notes and transcriptions of naturally occurring conversations among these girls show that their views about romance were similar to those of girls in other groups that also had romantic interests. We coded each type of data for content relevant to the topic of romance. We conducted computer searches on the codes in order to identify all references to romance and feeling norms.

Data from interviews, recorded conversations, and field notes are employed in this paper. It is important to combine these various types of data to study thoroughly the development of feeling norms underlying romance. Data from in-depth interviews reveal the girls' current beliefs and norms about romantic love but fail to show how their knowledge is acquired through daily activities. For that purpose we turned to an examination of field notes and transcripts of naturally occurring conversations. These types of data are essential for identifying not only the content of feeling norms that underlie romantic love, but also the processes through which these norms are developed and conveyed in day-to-day interaction. Also, by examining daily speech activities we can examine how emotion norms and beliefs are reflected in actual discourse. Without this level of analysis, it is easy to assume greater conformity to emotion norms than actually exists. Finally, our analysis of field notes helps us identify certain feeling norms which are so taken for granted that they are no longer regarded as constraints.

Although data from all of the groups were analyzed for this paper, some groups of girls were more interested in romance and had more contact with boys than others. Among the girls who had romantic interests, relationships with boys varied considerably. In fact, at this school, the term "going together" was used widely by both girls and boys to refer to a variety of romantic relationships, ranging from those which lasted several months to those which lasted one or two days. In some cases, the girl and the boy spent their lunch period together; in others, the couple had minimal contact at school.* In most

---

*Often the best friend of the girl and of the boy arranged these relationships by contacting the interested parties over the telephone, so that the couple might not have had much direct contact either before or after they started "going together."

cases, the relationships were brief (less than two weeks) and were limited to some social contact at school, which sometimes included expressions of affection such as hand holding and kissing. . . .

FEELING NORMS
UNDERLYING ROMANTIC LOVE IN
ADOLESCENT FEMALE PEER CULTURE

We begin with the observation that romantic love was a frequent topic of conversation among the female students. By the seventh grade, most of the girls at the school had become concerned with romance and had begun to form relationships with boys. While the girls were obtaining normative information about romantic love, the feelings and behavior that group members considered appropriate were still in the process of negotiation. Some feeling norms were generally accepted; others were not shared by all group members. An examination of the girls' talk about romantic love revealed that they used a variety of discourse strategies to communicate normative information and clarify feeling norms.

Norm 1: Romantic relationships should be important, but not everything in life. Previous research shows that white adolescent females tend to embrace traditional feminine concerns of romance, marriage, and domesticity and to reject both academic and athletic values (Eder 1985; Griffin 1985; Kessler et al. 1985; Lever 1978; McRobbie 1978). Although romance was salient to most of the girls in this study, group members had mixed attitudes about the importance of relationships with boys in relation to their other interests and activities. Some girls thought "they could not live without boys"; others believed that "learning about themselves and their schoolwork" was primary (interview, eighth-grade group, March 30, 1983). Concerns about the relative importance of romantic love required the development of a feeling norm among adolescent females.

One such norm that had begun to emerge in some peer groups was that romantic relationships should be important, but not everything in life. Many seventh- and eighth-grade girls agreed that relationships with boys were important. Group members, however, also were becoming critical of friends who were perceived as "boy-crazy," a term used by adolescents to describe girls who made boys their primary interest and activity. As the following two examples illustrate, this norm still was being negotiated when the girls were in the eighth grade.

In the first example, one group of girls debates the relative importance of romantic relationships. This exchange was part of an in-depth group interview about romance novels, which many eighth-grade girls liked to read. Ellen, Hanna, Natalie, Peg, and Tricia* had been discussing why they liked reading romance novels when the researcher asked them how important romantic love was to them. Ellen began by expressing her view that boys are the most important thing in her life, a view that runs counter to the emerging feeling norm.

---

*All names are pseudonyms. The following notations are used in the examples from transcripts:

( )   refers to an uncertain or unclear utterance or speaker;

(( ))   refers to nonverbal behavior;

//   refers to the point at which the next speaker begins talking during someone else's turn;

/1/   first interruption; /2/ second interruption;

refers to a brief pause.

1. Ellen:	Boys [are] the most important thing in my life. That's what I	
2.	marked on my value chart today.	
3. Hanna:	Yes. I know.	
4. Researcher:	Why? Why are boys the most important / / thing?	
5. Hanna:	Boys, um (pleasure)	
6. Ellen:	You can't live without 'em!	
7. Natalie:	You can't live / / with 'em and you can't live without 'em!	
8. Peg:	You can't live with 'em.	
9. Ellen:	You can too.	
10. Tricia:	That's / / a matter of opinion.	
11. Ellen:	There is no way—there is no way a girl could live her	
12.	whole life without a boy.	
13. Tricia:	I can.	
14. Ellen:	You can live your whole life without a boy?	
15. Tricia:	Yeah. / / I'm not goin' to, though.	
16. Peg:	Uh uh!	
17. Ellen:	(be isolated) you never kissed one or nothin'.	
18. Natalie:	Lesbies can.	
19. Researcher:	That's true.	
20. Tricia:	You wouldn't know, Natalie. ((laughing)) (interview, eighth grade, March 30).	

In this example it is clear that group members had conflicting views about the relative importance of romance, and expressed their opinions openly. Yet even though the girls engaged in a normative debate, they expressed conflict in a playful, nonserious way. Rather than responding defensively to Ellen's question in Line 14, Tricia said teasingly that even though she could live without boys, she was not going to do so. In Line 18, Natalie's substitution of the word "lesbies" for lesbians contributes to the playfulness of this exchange.

Whereas normative debates often were carried out in a playful and joking manner, conflict exchanges over normative issues were sometimes quite serious. This was especially true when lighter disputes were unsuccessful at producing normative consensus, as in the next example. The following exchange was part of the same group interview. At this point Ellen not only had stated repeatedly that boys were her central interest, but also had been flirting with some boys at a nearby table.

1.	Researcher:	What about you, Tricia? How do you feel / / about it all?
2.	Peg:	Ellen, / / I'm only teasin', gosh! ((singsong voice))
3.	Tricia:	I feel the same way that Peg does. Especially now when
4.		we're just about to go into high school, our grades are more
5.		important than / / boys.
6.	Natalie:	See, we may be friends / / with them, but we're not sluts.
7.	Researcher:	Um hum, ((to Tricia))
8.	Hanna:	Will you repeat that, please? ((angry voice))
9.	Tricia:	No, /1/ you /2/ don't qualify.
10.	Natalie:	/1/ I know, but we're not sluts.
11.	Ellen:	/2/ ( ) fuck you (you guys))! ((Ellen stomps off, angry
12.		and upset)) (interview, eighth grade, March 30).

In both examples, the girls' openly expressed their conflicting views about the relative importance of romance and clarified this feeling norm to group members. In the second example, however, the conflict escalated and became more serious and more heated. Tricia and Peg became annoyed when the emerging norm was violated repeatedly, and engaged in confrontations when their friends' attitudes and behaviors did not match their expectations. In Lines 6 and 10, for example, Natalie accuses violators of this norm of being "sluts." Responses to norm violations are important ways in which group members develop and communicate knowledge about interpersonal and interactional norms (Eder and Sanford 1986; Mehan 1979). Although conflict was not resolved in either of these exchanges, the girls learned through these debates what their friends viewed as appropriate and inappropriate feeling and behavior with respect to this norm. Romantic love was a salient emotion for most of these girls, but several were concerned with setting some limits on its importance.

The Object of Romantic Feelings

According to Gordon (1981, p. 567), "sentiments," such as romantic love, are feelings that are "organized around a relationship to a social object, usually another person." While the girls were developing a norm about the relative importance of romance, they also were acquiring cultural knowledge about the object of romance. In fact, by the eighth grade, three norms concerning the object of romantic feelings had emerged.

Norm 2: One should have romantic feelings only for someone of the opposite sex. The most basic feeling norm concerning the object of romance was that one should have romantic feelings only for someone of the opposite sex. By the time they had become actively interested in romance, a norm of heterosexuality had developed in these groups of girls. In contrast to the previously discussed feeling norm, there was considerable consensus for this norm. In view of the general negative view of homosexuality at the school and the label attached to alleged norm violators, it is not surprising that this norm was widely accepted. We found that the girls used a variety of discourse strategies to clarify and reinforce the norm of heterosexuality to friends. The way in which this norm was communicated depended upon whether alleged norm violators were non-group or group members.

One way in which the norm of heterosexuality was communicated was through gossip about nongroup members' deviant affect and behavior. Girls who did not express romantic interest in boys or who had gender-atypical interests often were the targets of gossip. For example, Sandy and Paula were discussing Sandy's sister in the sixth grade, who did not share their romantic interest in boys and who was interested in sports and in becoming a mechanic.

Sandy said her sister is extremely different from her and has absolutely no interest in boys—she considers boys pests. Sandy referred to her sister as a tomboy. She said that since her sister is a tomboy, if she liked boys then she would be queer, but on the other hand, if she liked girls then she would really be queer. Then Paula added jokingly that if she didn't like anyone at all she would still be queer. I [researcher] said, "It sounds like she doesn't have a chance" (field notes, seventh grade, May 24).

This example shows that Sandy and Paula were reinforcing a feeling norm of which they had only limited understanding. Girls at this school were establishing violations of the norm of heterosexuality on the basis of gender-inappropriate behavior. Sandy's sister's outward disinterest in boys as well as her nontraditional interests and behaviors were considered by these group members to be deviant with regard to the norm of heterosexuality. Yet, by establishing violations of this norm on the basis of nonstereo-typical gender-role behavior, the girls were reinforcing and reproducing existing gender norms that ultimately constrain their own behavior.

In general, it was not uncommon for girls and boys who were not actively pursuing romantic relationships or who routinely engaged in gender-inappropriate behavior to be labeled homosexual. In fact, children at the school who were perceived to be deviant in other ways were the objects of these allegations as well (Evans and Eder 1989). Unpopular students who were viewed as unattractive and/or unintelligent also were singled out for group discussions in which they were accused indirectly of being homosexual.

Annie said, "I'm gonna beat that girl up someday," referring to twins and a little chubby girl in a green sweater who were sitting at the middle of the table pretty far down. So we all turned to look at her and Marsha agreed that she was really disgusting, that "they're gay" (field notes, seventh grade, February 3).

Rather than relying on the display of romantic feelings toward someone of the same sex as an indication of affective deviance, Annie and Marsha accused these girls of being "gay" solely on the basis of physical appearance.

A second way in which the norm of heterosexuality was communicated was by teasing group members. Humor often was used when the girls confronted their friends about norm violations. Group members frequently teased one another about behaviors that could be interpreted as homosexual, such as close physical contact between friends. Although many girls still viewed close physical contact between friends as acceptable, others were beginning to redefine such expressions of affection as inappropriate.

The little girl with glasses came over and actually sat on Andrea's lap. She's so tiny that she can do this easily, and Andrea laughed and said, "You're really not my type" (field notes, sixth grade, May 20).

Not only did the girls tease one another about overt expressions of affection, they also chided one another about their actual feelings.

Statements concerning both positive and negative affect for females were a frequent source of group humor.

> . . . they were talking about why would somebody like this particular girl. Debby said, "I wouldn't like her!" Melinda said, "Well, I should *hope* not" (field notes, eighth grade, April 20).

In addition to teasing one another about their feelings and behaviors, group members also chided each other about their best-friend relationships. In fact, adolescence is a period in which female friendships are faced with a dilemma. Even while intimate feelings between close friends usually deepen, girls routinely tease one another about the romantic implications of these relationships.

> Julie said something about how Bonnie and somebody were considered her best mates. Right away Mia said, "Ooooh . . ." as this sort of implied that they were gay. Hillary picked up on that and went "Ooooh!" (field notes, eighth grade, April 9).

The final way in which the norm of heterosexuality was communicated was through self-denial. Self-denials often were used to clarify the nature of intimate female friendships. Although many girls at the school continued to have strong positive feelings for their female friends, verbal and behavioral expressions of affection frequently were followed by a disclaimer. In light of the pressures for heterosexuality from peers and the seriousness of norm violations, it is not surprising that many girls at the school became quite concerned that their own feelings and behaviors toward their close friends might be perceived by others as homosexual.

> Sally was really talkative today, and it was interesting to see her being so talkative. She was going on and on about how somebody would sign her letters "love you queerly." She said, "I always sign my letters 'love you dearly, but not queerly.'" But

then she was joking, saying, "I didn't know what that meant," until Mary explained it to her. Then they were joking about how innocent she was and didn't even know what "queer" meant (field notes, seventh grade, March 3).

Whereas self-denials often were humorous, denials of affective deviance with respect to the norm of heterosexuality sometimes were quite serious. The girls were especially self-conscious about expressions of affection that were overt and therefore readily observable. They were concerned that nongroup members would misinterpret these visible signs of affection as romantic.

> Alice told me that she had taken a bunch of photographs recently. She said it was embarrassing because most of the pictures were taken when people happened to be hugging and kissing each other, and that she hoped she got hold of the pictures before her mother did when they got back from being developed. She said, for example, "Natalie and another girl were hugging each other in friendship" (which meant that she wanted me to know that that was differentiated from a romantic hug) (field notes, eighth grade, February 7).

Not only was Alice embarrassed by the hugging and kissing in the photographs, but she also was concerned that if her mother saw the pictures, she might interpret these actions as homosexual. By distinguishing between a "friendship" hug and a "romantic" hug, however, Alice clarified both to herself and to the researcher that this behavior was within the realm of acceptable conduct.

Overall the norm of heterosexuality was communicated among adolescent females through gossip, teasing, and self-denials. In these discussions, group members collectively explored what does and does not constitute homosexual feeling and behavior in order to develop an understanding of this feeling norm and of norm violations. Through these discussions, however, the girls not only expressed their own homophobic concerns but also supported and maintained the broader cultural norm of heterosexuality. Many girls at the school continued to value intimate relationships with females; nevertheless they upheld and reproduced what Rich (1980) called "the norm of compulsory heterosexuality."

Norm 3: One should not have romantic feelings for a boy who is already attached. Another feeling norm that had emerged in regard to the object of romance was that one should not have romantic feelings for a boy who is already attached. A corollary of this norm was that if one had such feelings, they should not be expressed. In most groups, the development of this norm was a direct response to changes in group members' romantic activities. The norm of exclusivity had only minimal relevance during an earlier phase, when the girls were first becoming interested in romance, but this norm had become highly salient by the time they began to form relationships with boys.

Early in the seventh grade, most of the girls talked about the boys they liked,* but often were shy about letting boys know their feelings. As long as romantic activities consisted of only talking about the objects of their affection, the norm of exclusivity had little significance. In fact, during this stage in the development of their romantic activities, it was not uncommon for many group members to like the same boy. Just as they might have other interests in common, sharing a romantic interest in a particular boy was considered to be acceptable, if not appropriate.

> Interestingly enough, Marsha and Josephine talked about how they both liked this guy Jack. They pointed him out to me and I [researcher] said, "Oh, oh, you both like the same guy?" They said, "Oh yeah, it's okay. We can do that. We always like the same people, but we don't get mad at each other" (field notes, seventh grade, March 30).

In an interview with another group of seventh-grade girls, it became clear that the distinction between *liking* and *going with* the same boy is important. The former is permissible; the latter is not.

Throughout this year, many girls began to pursue boys openly and to make their feelings more public, often through a friend who served as an intermediary. Once a group member had acted openly on her feelings and formed a relationship with a boy, it was no longer acceptable for other girls either to have or to express romantic feelings for him. At this point in the development of their romantic activities, the norm of exclusivity had become highly salient,

1.	Carrie:	They can like, like, like as much as they want, but they
2.		don't / / (go)
3.	Marla:	They don't two-time!
4.	Researcher:	But what?
5.	Carrie:	They can like a person as much as they want.
6.	Researcher:	Can two friends *go* together / / with the same boy?
7.	(Alice):	Oh, they don't have any choice / / (they)
8.	Carrie:	No.
9.	Bonnie:	No (interview, seventh grade, May 24).

*Although Zick Rubin's (1970, 1973) research shows that "liking" and "loving" are distinct emotional states, the girls in this study used these emotion words interchangeably, especially when referring to their romantic feelings for boys.

and violations began to be perceived as a serious threat. Most of the girls became concerned about violations; they were resentful and jealous of those who did not abide by the norm of exclusivity.

Gossip was one way in which the girls clarified and reinforced this norm. In the following example from a seventh-grade interview, Natalie is accusing Rhoda, an attractive group member, of flirting with her and Tricia's boyfriends.

1.	Natalie:	Rhoda, every time I get a boyfriend or Tricia gets a boyfriend
2.		# or we like somebody, she starts # y'know messing around
3.		with him and everything and # y'know—and everything, she
4.		shows her ass off and so, they start *likin'* her, right? And she
5.		did that, she was trying to do that to Sammy Jones #
6.		Tricia's boyfriend # ya know, the one that broke up with her
7.		after four months (interview, seventh grade, May 24).

Although gossip episodes such as this do not inform norm violators about the deviant nature of their behavior, they communicate normative information to other group members (Eder and Enke 1988; Fine 1986; Goodwin 1980).

The girls considered it inappropriate to have or express romantic feelings not only for a boy who was involved with someone else, but also for a boy whom a group member was in the process of pursuing. Group members sometimes engaged in confrontations with alleged norm violators in order to communicate their inappropriate behavior and affect. In the next exchange, several members of a seventh-grade group directly accuse Carol of flirting with Ted, a boy Betty is pursuing but not currently going with. Although Carol argues initially that she has not done anything wrong, later she agrees to be an intermediary for Betty in order to resolve the dispute.

1.	Mary:	Ted came up to Carol and said she—that he loved her.
2.	Linda:	Who?
3.	Betty:	*Carol!*
4.	Carol:	What?
5.	Betty:	I don't like you no more.
6.	Carol:	What'd I do?
7.	Linda:	Taking Betty's boyfriend.
8.	Carol:	I didn't either! ((pounds table as she half laughs))
9.	Mary:	It wasn't Carol's *fault*, though.
10.	Betty:	*Yes it was! She flirts!*

11.	Carol:	I was just walking there / / ( ).
12.	Betty:	You *flirt*. You *flirt*. Yes, you / /
13.	Carol:	I didn't even do nothing. ((laughter))
14.	Betty:	You *flirt*, Carol! You're mean! I don't like you no more.
15.	Carol:	You won't (mind me) after I get done talking # *if* you still
16.		want me to.
17.	Betty:	Huh?
18.	Carol:	If you—do you want me to still talk to him? / / ((Betty
19.		nods)) Alright, shut up. God.
20.	Nancy:	Hell, she called me up, she goes, "Nancy, call Ted and talk to
21.		him."
22.	Betty:	(I sank you) ((silly voice)) (taped conversation, seventh grade, May 5).

This example is interesting because it shows that these girls expect their friends to know not only with whom they are going, but also their *intentions* to become romantically involved with certain boys. Acceptable contact with these boys is limited to behavior that will promote their friends' romantic interests (e.g., serving as intermediaries), and excludes any friendly behavior that might encourage romantic feelings to develop. As shown in the previous example, such behavior makes a girl subject to the negative label "flirt."* It is also noteworthy that group members use confrontations such as this to sanction inappropriate behavior and affect. Because violations of the norm of exclusivity have serious consequences for group members, including the possibility of being in competition with friends over boys, it is not surprising that confrontations sometimes are used to clarify and reinforce this norm.

Although most group members increasingly saw the need for the norm of exclusivity to protect themselves from unpleasant feelings of jealousy, some girls were reluctant to give up the freedom to have or express romantic feelings whenever they desired. Because norm violations were viewed as serious, girls who continued to defy this norm occasionally engaged in playful modes of interaction whereby they could express their "deviant" feelings while acknowledging the norm of exclusivity.

---

*The label "flirt" has a double meaning among adolescent females. Whereas the term sometimes is used to describe girls who express romantic feelings toward a group member's boyfriend, it is also used to describe girls who express romantic feelings for more than one boy. In the previous example, the girls used it in the former sense. Like the labels "gay" and "slut," the girls also use the label "flirt" to refer to an emotional social type. Emotional social types are persons who routinely violate emotion norms and who serve as examples in correcting young people's feeling and/or expression. See Gordon (1989) for a discussion of the functions of the emotional social type in childhood emotional socialization.

For example, several seventh-grade girls were teasing Mary about "liking" Wally and dragged her over to the ball diamond, where Wally was playing softball. The teasing consisted of trying to get Mary to talk with him and telling Wally that Mary wanted to "go in the stairwell" with him. Mary refused to talk to Wally. This reaction led to some joking exchanges among the other group members, several of whom also had romantic feelings for Wally.

1.	Carol:	I'll take him if you don't.
2.	Elaine:	Whoo! You hear that one, Wally?
3.	Carol:	Well, I don't care.
4.	Elaine:	Wally, Wally, Wally, Wally. She says she'll take
5.		ya if Mary don't want ya. ((Unrelated talk for
6.		five turns.))
7.	Elaine:	She said she'd take ya if Mary don't want ya.
8.	Mary:	What'd you tell him Elaine? Elaine / / ( )
9.	Linda:	Hey you! If Mary don't want ya and Carol don't
10.		want ya, I'll take ya!
11.	Carol:	Uh uh, I will. I'll take him if Mary don't and
12.		then if I don't, you do (taped conversation, seventh grade, April 7).

Here the girls use playful teasing to inform Wally of their romantic feelings, while acknowledging at the same time that they will wait to act on these feelings until Mary no longer "wants" him. The joking nature of this exchange provides these girls with more freedom to express their feelings for Wally and thus to violate the norm of exclusivity.*

This finding suggests that feeling and expression norms do not determine adolescent girls' affect and behavior, but serve as an important cultural resource which is incorporated into their action. Through expressing their knowledge of this norm, in fact, these girls succeed in expressing their feelings for a boy who is being pursued by a friend. At the same time, their ability to transform cultural knowledge into a playful frame gives them an opportunity to violate the norm without negative sanctions.

In brief, when group members began to pursue boys and form romantic relationships, the girls developed the norm of exclusivity to deal with their new concerns. They communicated this norm through gossip and confrontations as well as in more playful modes of discourse. Yet even though norm violations were viewed negatively by most of the girls, several group members did not feel compelled to abide by this norm. Instead they responded with "resistance" by continuing to hold and express romantic feelings for boys who were already "taken." In some cases their resistance was communicated through playful teasing, which allowed them to express their normatively inappropriate feelings while simultaneously showing their awareness of the norm of exclusivity.

*Although an alternative interpretation of this exchange is that the girls actually are supporting Mary's romantic interest rather than violating the norm of exclusivity, ethnographic data on these girls show that several of them in fact had romantic feelings for Wally. Because Mary was somewhat overweight, the girls did not take her interest in him seriously.

Norm 4: One should have romantic feelings for only one boy at a time. The third feeling norm pertaining to the object of romance was that one should have romantic feelings for only one boy at a time. A corollary was that if one had romantic feelings for more than one boy, these feelings should not be expressed. In some groups, the development of the norm of monogamy reflected the girls' awareness of the societal norm of monogamy. In other groups, however, this norm was developed to deal with the problems created by having multiple boyfriends.

For example, when we asked one group of seventh-grade girls about the possibility of going with more than one person at a time, the reason they gave for avoiding this behavior was the likelihood of creating jealousy among boyfriends. Because jealousy and other forms of conflict among males were expressed frequently in physical fights, the consequences of creating jealousy were considered to be quite serious.

> I asked if you could only go with one person at a time and she said, "It depends on who you're talking about." She said that you should only go with one at a time but that some girls went with more than one. I asked why they shouldn't do that, and

she said because "then you get a couple of jealous boyfriends on your hands" and they might end up getting into a fight, and that it was best to avoid that (field notes, seventh grade, April 27).

Some girls continued to have multiple boyfriends, but were careful to become involved only with boys who were separated geographically. As long as a boy was unaware of his girlfriend's other romantic involvements, jealousy and its negative consequences could be avoided. For some of these girls, in fact, having multiple boyfriends was a source of status—something they bragged about to their female friends.

> Effie and Laura had a long conversation. Laura told Effie that she was going with two guys, one from Royalton and another from California. She said that they were both going to be coming down this summer and she didn't know what to do. She presented this as a dilemma, but she was laughing about it. She really wanted to show that she was popular with boys (field notes, eighth grade, April 6).

Although some groups developed the norm of monogamy to deal with the practical problems associated with having multiple boyfriends, in other groups the development of this norm

1.	Researcher:	How come two people can't go with the same boy at the same
2.		time? It seems like you could logi—
3.	Ellen:	Because you're only supposed to—when you go with a person
4.		like if you
5.	Natalie:	It's like a bigamist.
6.	Ellen:	Oh . . .
7.	Natalie:	You know, when you
8.	Ellen:	Like a what?
9.	Natalie:	A bigamist. Like when you go with somebody. Like it's, it's
10.	Ellen:	Two-timing.

(Continued)

(Continued)

11. Natalie:	When you go with each other the same—when you go with each
12.	other it's kinda like gettin' married or somethin', you
13.	know, and like if you're goin' with two people at the same
14.	time it's like a bigamist.
15. Ellen:	Like Natalie did!
16. Natalie:	Yeah, I did that once.
17. Ellen:	Yeah, with Steve and Robert.
18. Natalie:	I did it twice. ((Natalie and Ellen burst out laughing)) (interview, seventh grade, May 24).

reflected group members' knowledge of the cultural norm of monogamy. When we asked one group of seventh-grade girls whether two people could go with the same boy, their response turned to the inappropriateness of having multiple romantic partners.

This example illustrates that the girls are drawing on their knowledge of the societal norm of monogamy (which pertains to marriage) in order to develop a feeling norm regarding multiple partners which is relevant to their own romantic relationships. The exchange also shows that even though these girls agreed that it was inappropriate to have romantic feelings for more than one boy at a time, violations of this norm were not perceived as serious.

By the time these girls were in eighth grade, however, having romantic feelings for more than one boy was no longer viewed as acceptable. Moreover, they used different strategies to clarify this norm and to sanction deviant affect and behavior. In the following exchange, Ellen and Hanna are telling the other girls about what happened at church the night before. Because Ellen is already going with Craig, she is first accused and later reprimanded for going to church solely to meet other boys.

1. Ellen:	We were sittin' there starin' at guys at church last night,
2.	me and Hanna were, and—
3. Hanna:	And she saw one that looked just like Craig.
4. Natalie:	But # / / I was—
5. Ellen:	I wasn't starin' at him.
6. Hanna:	That was groaty.
7. (Natalie:)	You're going with Craig.
8. Ellen:	I know. I stared at Steve. ((laughs))
9. Hanna:	I know, but he looks like him in the face,
10. Natalie:	But, um, he just—
11. Peg:	You / / go to church for a different reason than that, Ellen!
12. Natalie:	I / / get stuck on one guy.
13. Peg:	Then you shouldn't of been there (interview, eighth grade, March 30).

Although Peg and Natalie considered this violation to be serious, Ellen continued to view it as humorous, laughing as she acknowledged that she "stared" at another boy. Given Ellen's reluctance to consider the seriousness of her violation, Peg and Natalie used more confrontive strategies to inform her about the inappropriateness of her affect and behavior with respect to this norm.

As girls begin to take this norm seriously, they need to become more aware of their romantic feelings. They may even begin to modify their emotions on certain occasions, changing romantic attractions to nonromantic feelings in order to avoid norm violations. Sometimes the girls explicitly discussed their feelings toward boys, thus showing their close monitoring of these feelings. Awareness of romantic feelings was especially important during times of transition from one boyfriend to another. Because "going together" arrangements typically lasted less than two weeks, these transitions were frequent.

> Gwen and Ellen went "cruising" with some boys over the weekend. The boy Gwen was with asked her to go with him but he broke up with her the next morning because another boy that Gwen went with last week threatened to beat him up. So then the other boy asked her back with him Monday morning and she's going with him again now. She said that "one thing I can say for certain is that I love (the boy she's going with), but I can also say for certain that I really like (the boy she went with on Saturday)" (field notes, eighth grade, March 30).

Through Gwen's claim that she "loves" the boy she is currently going with and "likes" the boy she went with on Saturday, her feelings appear to conform with the norm of monogamy. Although it is not clear whether her current feelings are the result of emotion (or expression) work, it is clear that she pays close attention to her feelings and can discuss them with "certainty."

Other girls expressed more confusion about their emotions. In some cases, their confusion stemmed from the discrepancy between their *actual* feelings and the feelings they thought they *ought* to have. Even though they knew that they *should* have romantic feelings for only one boy at a time, girls sometimes found themselves feeling multiple attractions.

> I heard Karla being teased when a specific boy walked by. Her friends were saying that she had a crush on him and once they yelled it at the boy. Karla acted rather embarrassed and angry about this. When they yelled at the boy, they asked Karla if it was true that she liked him. Karla said that she did like him "for a friend." They said that they had seen her walking with him in the halls. After a long pause Karla asked Laura rather indignantly, "How could I like him when I'm already going with somebody?" Effie said, "Two-timing." Karla was embarrassed and seemed rather mild in her denial (field notes, eighth grade, April 21).

Karla's feelings are creating some discomfort for her because they do not conform readily to this feeling norm. She claims that she likes the other boy only "for a friend," but she expresses embarrassment as well as anger toward her friends, who perceive it to be a stronger attraction. Although we do not know whether Karla subsequently modified her feelings and/or expressions toward this boy, emotion work might be necessary in situations such as this, if girls are to abide by the norm of monogamy.

Norm 5: One should always be in love. The final feeling norm that emerged was that one should always be in love. This norm differed from those discussed previously in that it was not devised to deal with group concerns, but was developed largely to deal with the concerns of individuals. Whereas violations of most feeling norms had consequences for other group members and peers (e.g., the norms of heterosexuality, exclusivity, and monogamy), violations of this final norm had consequences only for individual girls. Because such violations did not affect others, this norm was held even less widely than those discussed previously. For many girls at the school, however, this emotion norm was a basic part of their knowledge and understanding of romantic love.

For some girls, the onset of their first romantic attraction was the beginning of a continuous state of being in love, often with frequent changes in the object of their feelings. In fact, simply having romantic feelings may have been more important than the actual boys to whom these feelings were directed. For example, a researcher noticed that a girl had "I love" written on her hand and asked her about it. Although this girl's romantic feelings had no particular target, she explained that she was ready to add the name of a boy as soon as a suitable target was found.

The importance of always being in love became particularly evident when relationships with boys ended. For instance, when girls realized that a boy they had been going with now liked someone else, they often redirected their romantic feelings toward someone new.

> She said that she was just going to go up and ask him if he had any intention of going with her again, and if he didn't, she was just "going to have to find someone else." I don't think she has the concept in her mind that she could possibly not be involved with anyone (field notes, eighth grade, March 23).

The salience of this norm was related to the duration of adolescent romantic relationships. Although it might seem that "long-term" relationships would be preferred because girls would not continually have to seek out new boyfriends, some girls reported that being in a long-term relationship was a disadvantage because it took them out of circulation.

Apparently Alice's boyfriend broke up with her today and she was unhappy. She saw him walk by the media center and called to him several times, but he ignored her purposely. She said that the worst of it was that she had gone with him several months, and during that time had progressively cut herself off from contact with other boys so that she didn't even have any male friends left (field notes, eighth grade, March 4).

Within four days Alice had a new boyfriend, but her comments show that replacing her old boyfriend was an important concern.

During the early stage in the development of their romantic activities, when the girls were beginning to have romantic feelings but did not act on them, all group members could adhere easily to this norm. Once they started to form romantic relationships, however, only the girls who were popular with boys could continually attract new boyfriends. In fact, the status associated with being popular with boys contributed to the salience of this norm among the girls at this school. At the same time, group members also had a hand in reinforcing this feeling norm.

> When Nancy came up she asked, "Who do you like now, Carol?" a question which Nancy often asks Carol. Carol said, "Pete." Nancy said, "Oh yeah." Shortly after that Linda said, "Guess who Pete likes?" Betty said, "Carol." Nancy said, "God, you guys get everything you want" (field notes, seventh grade, April 14).

Even though less popular girls could not attract new boyfriends so easily, nevertheless they were able to abide by this norm. One strategy commonly used by these as well as by the more popular girls was to "recycle" the boys with whom they had had a previous relationship.

Natalie's comments suggest that her and her friends' feelings for former boyfriends sometimes are re-created for the purpose of conforming

1.	Ellen:	And then she went with George and then she went to likin' Tom
2.		again.
3.	Natalie:	Yeah. ((pause)) But sometimes it kinda switches on and off, like
4.		s— like you'll like one boy and then you'll get tired of 'im and
5.		you go with somebody else and then you'll like him again. Like
6.		with Bryan and Dale. I used to do that a lot (interview, seventh grade, May 24).

to this norm. Natalie's comments also imply that conformity is likely to result in emotion work on the part of these girls, who sometimes evoke romantic feelings for boys they were previously "tired of."

The advantages of conforming to this norm include appearing to be popular with boys as well as providing ongoing evidence of a heterosexual orientation; both are important concerns to girls at this age. At the same time, however, conformity carries several possible costs. One such cost is that emotion work may be necessary in order to always be in love. Although we can only speculate at this point, adolescent girls sometimes may create romantic feelings for boys to whom they are not attracted so they can conform to this norm. Hochschild (1983b) argued that when insincere feelings are created routinely, people lose touch with their actual feelings. Insofar as girls have insincere feelings, it is possible that eventually they will have difficulty in distinguishing between their "real" romantic feelings and their less authentic feelings, which they created in order to satisfy the requirements of this norm.

A second potential cost stems from the dilemma faced by adolescent females as a result of their adherence to this norm. On the one hand, girls consider being continuously in love as socially desirable because it is a way to reaffirm their popularity with boys and thus to increase their own status in relation to other females. On the other hand, group members who both attract too much attention from males and appear to be indiscriminate in their choice of romantic partners are often criticized by their friends for being "sluts," and ultimately are viewed in a negative manner.

Discussion

In this paper we argue that adolescence is a period during which females acquire cultural knowledge about romantic love, including the social norms that guide romantic feelings. In addition to obtaining normative information about romance, we found that the girls in this study had developed several feeling and expression no
rms to deal with their own concerns about romantic love. By the seventh and eighth grade, norms concerning the relative importance of romantic relationships as well as the appropriate object of romantic feelings had emerged in these groups of friends. Whereas some of these norms were highly developed and generally accepted (e.g., the norms of heterosexuality, exclusivity, and monogamy), others were not held by all group members and still were being negotiated (e.g., the norm concerning the relative importance of romantic relationships).

We also found that adolescent girls used a variety of discourse strategies to communicate normative information and to reinforce emotion norms to friends. In general, group members informed one another about feeling and expression norms through light and playful language activities, as well as through serious and confrontive modes of discourse. Language that involved humor was one of the more common discourse strategies used by these girls. Through joking and teasing remarks, group members could point out their friends' norm violations in an indirect, nonthreatening manner. Moreover, teasing and joking were ways in which the girls could show their awareness of feeling norms while simultaneously expressing their own normatively inappropriate emotions.

The girls also commonly used gossip and confrontations to clarify and reinforce feeling norms. Although gossip did not directly inform norm violators of their inappropriate affect and behavior, it provided normative information to other group members. Finally, confrontations sometimes were used when indirect strategies were ineffective at producing normative consensus and when norm violations had negative consequences for group members. In these exchanges, girls expressed social disapproval of affective deviance through accusations, insults, and reprimands. Not surprisingly, such exchanges often involved considerable conflict and tension. Overall, through these various language activities and modes of discourse, the girls conveyed what they viewed as appropriate and inappropriate in regard to the group's feeling and expression norms.

Even though girls obtain normative information about romantic love from friends, they do not always abide by emotion norms. Rather, our analysis of discourse revealed that group members sometimes responded with "resistance" and intentionally defied their group's feeling and expression norms. Therefore, feeling and expression norms underlying romantic love constrain but do not determine adolescent females' affect and behavior. Further research is necessary to determine the degree to which girls resist other emotion norms, as well as to identify the full range of emotion management processes used by adolescent females.

Romance is highly salient, however, because having a boyfriend enhances girls' popularity with peers at an age when being popular is important for their self-image. In fact, two norms that emerged in these peer groups reveal the salience of romance to girls during this period: the norms concerning the relative importance of romantic relationships and the importance of being in love continually. It is possible that even after romantic relationships become tied less closely to peer group status, females continue to feel that they always should be in a romantic relationship with a male in order to validate their attractiveness and worth to self and to others.

Although it was not our purpose to examine the actual emotional experiences of adolescent girls, our findings support the view that emotions are in part socially constructed and that feeling and expression are subject to normative influences. By focusing on romantic socialization in adolescent peer groups, we have shown how, in everyday interaction with friends, females obtain normative information about romantic feelings as well as maintaining, reproducing, and recreating one aspect of their society's emotion culture. . . .

REFERENCES

Berger, Peter L., and Thomas Luckman. 1967. *The Social Construction of Reality: A Treatise in the Sociology of Knowledge.* New York: Anchor.

Cancian, Francesca M. 1985. "Gender Politics: Love and Power in the Private and Public Spheres." Pp. 253–264 in *Gender and the Life Course,* edited by Alice S. Rossi. New York: Aldine.

———. 1987. *Love in America: Gender and Self Development.* Boston: Cambridge University Press.

Cancian, Francesca M., and Steven L. Gordon. 1988. "Changing Emotion Norms in Marriage: Love and Anger in U.S. Women's Magazines since 1900." *Gender and Society* 2(3):308–342.

Cantor, Muriel. 1987. "Popular Culture and the Portrayal of Women: Content and Control." Pp. 190–214 in *Analyzing Gender,* edited by Beth Hess and Myra Marx Ferree. New York: Sage.

Clark, Candice. 1987. "Sympathy Biography and Sympathy Margin." *American Journal of Sociology* 93:290–321.

Corsaro, William A., and Thomas A. Rizzo. 1988. "Discussione and Friendship: Socialization Processes in the Peer Culture of Italian Nursery School Children." *American Sociological Review* 53:879–894.

Eder, Donna. 1985. "The Cycle of Popularity: Interpersonal Relations Among Female Adolescents." *Sociology of Education* 58:154–165.

———. 1988. "Teasing Activities among Adolescent Females." Paper presented at conference "Gender Roles through the Life Span," Ball State University, Muncie, IN.

Eder, Donna, and Janet Enke. 1988. "Gossip as a Means of Strengthening Social Bonds." Paper presented at the annual meeting of the American Sociological Association, Atlanta.

Eder, Donna, and Stephanie Sanford. 1986. "The Development and Maintenance of Interactional Norms among Early Adolescents." *Sociological Studies of Child Development* 1:283–300.

Evans, Cathy, and Donna Eder. 1989. "'No Exit': Processes of Social Isolation in the Middle School." Paper presented at the annual meeting of the American Sociological Association, San Francisco.

Fine, Gary Alan. 1986. "The Social Organization of Adolescent Gossip: The Rhetoric of Moral Evaluation." Pp. 405–423 in *Children's Worlds and Children's Language,* edited by Jenny Cook-Gumperz, William Corsaro, and Jurgen Streeck. Berlin: Moulin.

Goodwin, Marjorie H. 1980. "He-Said-She-Said: Formal Cultural Procedures for the Construction of a Gossip Dispute Activity." *American Ethnologist* 7:674–695.

Gordon, Steven L. 1981. "The Sociology of Sentiments and Emotion." Pp. 562–592 in *Social Psychology: Sociological Perspectives,* edited by Morris Rosenberg and Ralph H. Turner. New York: Basic Books.

———. 1989. "The Socialization of Children's Emotions: Emotional Culture, Competence, and Exposure." Pp. 319–349 in *Children's Understanding of Emotion,* edited by Carolyn Saarni and Paul Harris. New York: Cambridge University Press.

Griffin, Christine. 1985. *Typical Girls?: Young Women from School to Job Market.* London: Routledge and Kegan Paul.

Harris, Paul, and Tjeert Olthof. 1982. "The Child's Concept of Emotion." Pp. 188–209 in *Social Cognition: Studies of the Development of Understanding,* edited by George Butterworth and Paul Light. Chicago: University of Chicago Press.

Hochschild, Arlie R. 1979. "Emotion Work, Feeling Rules, and Social Structure." *American Journal of Sociology* 85(3):551–575.

———. 1983a. "Attending to, Codifying and Managing Feelings: Sex Differences in Love." Pp. 250–262 in *Feminist Frontiers: Rethinking Sex, Gender, and Society,* edited by Laurel Richardson and Verta Taylor. New York: Addison-Wesley.

———. 1983b. *The Managed Heart: Commercialization of Human Feeling.* Berkeley: University of California Press.

Holland, Dorothy, and Margaret Eisenhart. 1990. *Educated in Romance: Women, Achievement, and College Culture.* Chicago: University of Chicago Press.

Kessler, S., D. Ashenden, R. Connell, and G. Dowsett. 1985. "Gender Relations in Secondary Schooling." *Sociology of Education* 58:34–47.

Lees, Sue. 1986. *Sexuality and Adolescent Girls.* London: Hutchinson.

Lever, Janet. 1978. "Sex Differences in the Complexity of Children's Play and Games." *American Sociological Review* 43:471–483.

Lofland, Lyn H. 1985. "The Social Shaping of Emotion: Grief in Historical Perspective." *Symbolic Interaction* 8:171–190.

McRobbie, Angela. 1978. "Working Class Girls and the Culture of Femininity." Pp. 96–108 in *Women Take Issue,* edited by The Women's Study Group, Centre for Contemporary Cultural Studies. London: Hutchinson.

Mead, George Herbert. 1934. *Mind, Self, and Society.* Chicago: University of Chicago Press.

Mehan, Hugh. 1979. *Learning Lessons: Social Organization in the Classroom.* Cambridge, MA: Harvard University Press.

Rich, Adrienne. 1980. "Compulsory Heterosexuality and Lesbian Existence." *Signs: Journal of Women in Culture and Society* 5:631–660.

Rosenberg, Florence, and Roberta Simmons. 1975. "Sex Differences in the Self-Concept in Adolescence." *Sex Roles* 1:147–159.

Rubin, Lillian B. 1977. *Worlds of Pain: Life in the Working-Class Family.* New York: Basic Books.

Rubin, Zick. 1970. "Measurement of Romantic Love." *Journal of Personality and Social Psychology* 16: 265–273.

_____. 1973. *Liking and Loving: An Invitation to Social Psychology.* New York: Holt, Rinehart and Winston.

Saarni, Carolyn. 1979. "Children's Understanding of Display Rules for Expressive Behavior." *Developmental Psychology* 15(4):424–429.

Schofield, Janet. 1982. *Black and White in School.* New York: Praeger.

Stearns, Carol Z., and Peter N. Stearns. 1986. *Anger: The Struggle for Emotional Control in America's History.* Chicago: University of Chicago Press.

Swidler, Ann. 1980. "Love and Adulthood in American Culture." Pp. 120–147 in *Themes of Work and Love in Adulthood,* edited by Neil J. Smelser and Erik H. Erickson. Cambridge, MA: Harvard University Press.

Thoits, Peggy A. 1989. "The Sociology of Emotions." *Annual Review of Sociology* 15:317–342.

Waller, Willard. 1937. "The Rating and Dating Complex." *American Sociological Review* 2:727–734.

Wulff, Helena. 1988. *Twenty Girls: Growing Up, Ethnicity and Excitement in a South London Microculture.* Stockholm: University of Stockholm Press.

Youniss, James, and Jacqueline Smollar. 1985. *Parents and Peers in Social Development: A Sullivan-Piaget Perspective.* Chicago: University of Chicago Press.

PART IV

PRODUCING SOCIAL SELVES

We come into this world as individuals, achieve character, and become persons.

—Robert Park (1952), *Human Communities*

We talk, therefore I am.

—Anna Quindlen (1989), *Living Out Loud*

Tell me who you love and I'll tell you who you are.

—Creole Proverb

WHO AM I? DEVELOPING CHARACTER

Jodi O'Brien

Who am I? This is one of the most common and persistent questions that we ask ourselves. The question implies that we really don't know who or what we are. We are constantly searching for answers to this question. And our answers change over the course of a lifetime. Despite this fluctuation in self-understanding, we tend to think of our self as something that is knowable and stable. Self-understanding is a central topic in social psychology. Social psychologists consider the self to be an aspect of social interaction. The self—an organized, stable sense of who you are—develops through social interaction with other people. The emphasis in this essay and in the reading material that follows is on the *social self.*

There are certainly aspects of who you are that cannot be explained entirely by the theories that follow. For instance, your physiology and aspects of your spirituality can be usefully understood in terms of biology and theology, respectively. However, after reading this material it's likely that you will find theories of the social self to be extraordinarily useful in helping you understand why you think about yourself in certain ways and how these perceptions shape your sense of who you can be, what you can do, and how you feel. This section of the book introduces the basic social psychological theories of self development.

Try this exercise: Write down 20 personal responses to the question "Who am I?" Take a look at your list and see if you notice anything about it. In 1954, social psychologists Kuhn and McPartland published what they called the "Twenty Statements Test." They asked people to give 20 responses to the question "Who am I?" Most people can do this quickly, without too much thought. What Kuhn and McPartland noted was that people's answers fall into two categories: social roles (e.g., mother, son, sister, boyfriend, student, dentist, conservative, activist) and personality expressions (e.g., funny, happy, generous, friendly, shy, helpful, trustworthy). What's interesting about this is that people see themselves in reference to others, either as a role (e.g., when you think of yourself as a father, you are thinking of yourself in reference to your child) or as a relational characteristic (e.g., I am hardworking in the eyes of my employer). This observation led Kuhn and

McPartland to conclude that self-image is shaped largely in reference to social roles and other people's impressions of us. This conclusion is consistent with social psychological theories of the self. Our sense of self is formed in terms of social positions and our ideas about what other people think of us.

Self-Awareness and Agency

Part III explored the way in which children develop self-awareness. As they learn language, they learn to recognize their own behavior and to attribute meaning to it (and shortly thereafter to judge it). When very young children first become aware that they are agents in the world, they are fascinated with their ability to control things in their environment. For example, a toddler will spend many contented hours opening and shutting a door or flipping a switch to an electronic device. This repetitive and seemingly boring action is actually quite exciting for infants who are suddenly aware that they can make things happen. This becomes even more exciting when children learn that they can "control" others in their environment. When the child repeatedly throws a toy and an adult picks it up and returns it, the child learns that she can engage in actions that bring about expected responses from others. This initial awareness is the beginning of what Mead refers to as the child's ability to comprehend the self as an object—like other objects in the environment, the child realizes that she is an object herself, but, simultaneously, she also realizes that she has agency; she can maneuver both herself and other objects. This is a profound awareness.

Many parents might suggest that this internal sense of self becomes most pronounced as the child learns the concept of "mine!" Indeed, as the self-concept develops, the child begins to take on a more internal and organized sense of ownership for his feelings and actions. In this process, the child internalizes the names and categories that others have used to describe his object-self and begins to self-identify with them. Accordingly, a child moves from expressions such as "Alex is a nice boy" to "*I* am a nice boy." At this point in self-development, Alex understands (1) the meaning of *nice*, (2) that this characteristic is being attributed to him as a unique being in the world, and (3) that he can cause people to make this attribution by acting or behaving in a certain way. This is an amazing and complex learning process. Child development experts say that we learn more in the first 5 years of life than over the rest of our entire lifetime. During this time, children not only develop the idea or concept of a self, but also begin to acquire information that forms the basis of their particular sense of what their self-concept is—in other words, the general script for their answer to the question "Who am I?"

This process involves differentiating between people and contexts. Consider a child who is learning to play with an object called a "ball." She learns that a certain activity associated with the ball, such as hurling it across space, meets with particular responses from those around her. She also learns that these responses are either positive or negative and come in the form of reactions toward herself. Thus, she learns that she is the source of the activity that generates the response. She also learns that in certain situations—for example, indoors—people react more negatively when she hurls the ball than they do when she is outside.

The child also learns to distinguish between the responses of differently named persons in her environment. "Mom" may praise her "athletic ability" when she hurls the ball. "Dad" may attempt to "settle her down." By observing the reactions of significant others, the child learns to form complex associations among persons, things, and situations. Most importantly, the child learns what stance to adopt in a given setting in relation to specific categories of people and objects. This process of learning names and the associated rewards and punishments is both the foundation of human socialization and the basis of the social self. The process of identifying or naming behaviors that we come to see as an aspect of self involves an internal conversation with the generalized other (see Part III) and people or groups that are important to us. Accordingly, the self is a *social construction* that takes shape through interaction—interaction outwardly with others and, most importantly, internally through the conversations we have with ourselves about those interactions.

The Looking-Glass Self

In much the same way that we each learn to define the meaning of things in our environment, we learn about who we are through observing the responses of others to us as objects. Mead was interested in the relationship between mind and self, and the relationship of both to language acquisition and subsequent social engagement. His contemporary, Charles Horton Cooley (Reading 19), was interested in *how* people acquire the information that they use to form a self-image. Cooley proposed that this process is like a mirror, or looking glass. When we encounter others, we look to see how they are responding to us, similar to looking into a mirror to see how we look. If we perceive the other person to be responding positively, then we feel good about ourselves "pride" in Cooley's terms). If we perceive a negative reaction, then we feel mortification. According to Cooley, we form ideas about who we are and how to feel about ourselves based on what we think others think of us. Cooley called this the *looking-glass self.* Both Mead and Cooley emphasize social interaction as a central element in self-development. When we interact with others, we are alert to their responses and engage in self-evaluation in accordance to these responses.

The looking-glass self consists of an internal image we generate about our self when we are trying to figure out what others think of us. We gain information about ourselves by casting ourselves in the role of an observer, *imagining* how our actions appear to that person, and then attaching some reaction (such as pride or mortification) to that perception. In short, we imagine what we think someone else thinks of us, and then we judge ourselves accordingly. Cooley refers to these self-assessments based on perceived reactions from others as *reflected appraisals.*

According to Mead, Cooley, and most contemporary social psychologists, other people have a great deal of potential to shape our possible selves because we use perceived assessments (reflected appraisals) of others to shape our own self-assessment. In other words, we name our own behavior (including how we feel about it) based on what *we think* others think about us. For example, a teacher whom you admire a great deal may appear to think very highly of your writing. This reflected appraisal may lead you to focus more intently on your writing; in time, your writing may become quite good, and you may begin to see yourself as a "writer." If you have a difficult decision to make regarding whether to take a high-paying job or attend a graduate writing program, you are likely to ask yourself what this teacher would think of your decision. In this process, you literally conjure an image of yourself and hold it in front of your ideal of your teacher and develop a self-assessment accordingly. You may find yourself thinking, "This teacher will be so disappointed in me if I don't pursue my writing." (Notice that the teacher is not actually present in this self-conversation; rather you are imagining the response yourself. This is an important distinction that we will return to later. Typically we assess ourselves according to what we think other people are thinking of us, but unless we ask them directly, we often don't really know what they're thinking.)

Combining the theories of Mead and Cooley yields a theory of self-development that suggests that our sense of who we are and our self-evaluations are formed in interaction with others—that is, the self is a *social* process. We develop self-awareness in the process of learning language. During this same process, we derive self-meaning in the form of names and characteristics directed at us from significant others in our environment. These names or characteristics coalesce into an organized self-concept and, eventually, become a basis from which we learn to see ourselves (from the inside out) and determine the meaning and value of our actions.

Significant Others

According to the theories of Mead and Cooley, we are constantly engaged in internal self-evaluation based on our ideas about what we think others expect of us. However, Cooley made an important distinction in this process: We are not equally sensitive or persuaded by the views of everyone we encounter. We are much more likely to pay attention to and be influenced by the reactions of someone who is significant to us. Long before the term became a popular way of referring to an intimate partner, Cooley (1902/1983) used the term *significant others* to refer to those people whose opinions and influence are particularly important in an individual's self-assessment. Cooley used the concept of significant other to explain this process. We pay more attention to the gestures and responses of those who are important to us. As we observe the reactions of those we are close to, we continuously evaluate and reevaluate our own behavior. For instance, consider a young man who identifies strongly with his grandfather as someone who is courageous and honest. While hanging out with a group of friends who decide to shoplift, this particular young man may find himself thinking about how his grandfather would react if he were to observe his grandson engaged in theft. Consequently, he might decide not to join his friends; he would rather appear noble in the imagined eye of his grandfather.

Young children form their initial self-image in the presence of adults who feed, shelter, and nurture them. These adults (usually parents) are therefore likely to be a child's first significant others and, as such, will have a strong influence on the child's early self-image. As the children mature and come into contact with others, they develop additional relationships that will exert significant influence on self-image. The beliefs, tastes, and habits of significant others are also an important source of cultural input that we use in trying on and discarding various social identities. Consider some of your own preferences for types of food, clothing, and music. Is there a type of food or music that you thought you didn't like, but you reconsidered because someone you were attracted to liked it? In such instances, you are putting yourself into the position of the other and willing yourself to simulate the other person's experiences. You are motivated to do so because you like the person, and in trying on new attitudes and behaviors, you are stretching the boundaries of your own self.

In Reading 20, sociologist Thomas Scheff notes that because language acquisition is so complex, all children are geniuses when it comes to language. This view is shared by linguists who claim that the ease with which children learn language is evidence that the ability is innate. Scheff agrees, but argues that this is only part of the equation. He asks, "Why does genius appear in everyone in language but so rarely in other areas?" His answer is that the method of instruction, especially as delivered through significant others, differs markedly. Certainly there is considerable mirroring or mimicking involved in the early learning stages but, as Scheff notes, parents tend to reward success rather than punish error. Every utterance a child makes is seen as a miracle and lavishly praised. Parents are also competent in language themselves, and much of what is passed on is not in the form of conscious instruction. This is a very different learning process than most children experience in other areas such as music or mathematics, where the focus is typically on a learning method and error. Scheff is especially interested in the role of shame and creativity in self-development. Genius, he suggests, emerges from the opportunity to play with and practice certain activities free of constraining methods and shame. (He notes, for example, that Mozart came from a family of highly talented musicians, including his father, who was considered a master violin teacher.) Scheff also links shame to self-esteem and discusses how chronic shaming from significant others cuts down a child's enthusiasm for experimenting with social relations, thereby limiting opportunities to practice being a competent social actor.

THE SOCIAL MEDIA–MEDIATED SELF

In a world of Facebook, Instagram, and Twitter, who is the audience in your head when you're posting? The ideas of the looking-glass self and significant others take on additional meaning when applied to the social self and social media. Consider this short essay from a former student:

WHO'S THE AUDIENCE IN MY HEAD?

Facebook posting is always filled with uncertainty for me. As in any social situation, my internal conversation begins with trying to figure out or identify the specific audience. How should I adapt myself to this social situation? What parts of myself should I hide? What kinds of jokes will go well? I feel this uncertainty with Facebook because it is impossible to figure out who the audience is. . . . This is part of the danger of social media, and the source of warnings from your mom like: "You don't know who might see that picture of you in your bikini!"

Yes, there are ways to filter and even hand pick your Facebook audience. You can "block" or "unfriend" someone and thus remove them from your audience. But that's not really the point. I don't know if the Facebook audience that really exists in your head changes at all when you have the ability to physically alter and construct it. Perhaps it aids in the ability to think confidently, when posting a picture of yourself in your bikini you can say to yourself: "It's fine, only my friends will see it. I unfriended my high school teacher."

When I think about my Facebook audience, there is a sea of random people I've met at some point and don't really care much about. And then there are my sister and my elementary/middle school teacher: Ms. Golden. My sister and Ms. Golden are my two significant others that exist in the blurry mass of my Facebook audience. When I post a picture or write a status, these are the two people I think about, they are at the center of my internal conversation, especially Ms. Golden. "I probably shouldn't post this picture, I look kinda drunk . . . would Ms. Golden judge me? She might. It might upset her. Yea. I won't post the picture." Often my Facebook statuses are extremely impulsive. . . . It's finals week so my status reads: "OMG FFF SCHOOL I JUST WANT TO DRINK TEQUILA!!!!!!" But since becoming Facebook friends with Ms. Golden I would never in a million years post this status.

The contradiction I experience via Facebook is intrinsically connected with my internal audience. . . . Social media is (ideally) supposed to be this place where you can represent who you are, you can sit at your computer alone at home and think: "Yea, this picture with this witty quote as its caption really sums me up as a person. People will get an idea of who I am when they see this." But the contradiction with all social media is that those "people" are just as constructed as the self you are presenting to them. The "internalized voices of significant groups" (aka your constructed Facebook audience) occurs while you're sitting at your computer deciding whether or not to press "post."

—Elena Kazanjian

From Social Positions and Identities to Selves: The Process of "Becoming"

Students of social psychology often point out that we play different social roles in different situations, but we are not equally invested in each of these roles. For example, you may work part-time as a clerk at the local convenience store. Although you spend several hours a week in this position, it's probably not on your "Who am I?" list. Why do some of our social identities and behaviors take on the significance of an aspect of self while others do not? For instance, some people like to play golf but do not necessarily think of themselves as golfers, while others include this as an important part of who they are. Not everyone who regularly attends church considers "religious" to be part of their self-concept. Why is this the case for some and not others? Or what is the difference between someone who says funny things (a behavior) and someone who thinks of "funny" as an aspect of her or his self-concept?

Under the right circumstances, we begin to think of everyday behaviors as identities and then, perhaps, to incorporate these identities into an organized sense of self. This is likely to occur when people whose opinions we value continually reinforce a specific behavior or identity ("I think you have a great sense of fashion," "I think you are a remarkable person," and so forth). The identity becomes solidified into an aspect of self as we incorporate it into our internal dialogue (internalization) and hold it up as a reflection of a personal, ideal sense of being. Consider the implications of this process as you reread your "Who am I?" list. Can you describe the social relations or social processes that occurred over time to give you a sense that you are these identities and possess these characteristics?

My own list includes the identity "teacher." How did I come to see myself this way? When I entered graduate school, like most graduate students, I was required to be a teaching assistant as part of my training. Most of us had been undergraduate students ourselves only a few years earlier and we were quite nervous about playing the role of teacher. One exercise we engaged in was to try to remember favorite teachers and consider the traits that made them great teachers. With these images in mind, we would then perform the role of teacher in our own classes. All of us had to teach, but only a few of us began to eventually think of teaching as a central aspect of who we were. What made the difference? In my case, I received *role support* from several sources. My family thought that my teaching was a wonderful thing to be doing. When I talked with them about my studies, we talked mostly about my teaching. (No one else in my family had gone to graduate school and they didn't really understand my graduate research, but teaching was something they could relate to.) I was also invited by the chair of the department to participate in a pilot seminar that was part of a national project aimed at making scholars into better teachers. (Most graduate students receive little or no training in teaching.) This seminar became an important social group for me. It became one of my main reference points, and the instructors and fellow participants were significant people to me. Through this seminar, which included a lot of videotaping of our teaching, I began to think constantly about teaching: how to do it, what made it special, and so forth. My new seminar buddies and I talked together about these things as well. Within a few years, I was giving seminars to other graduate students on how to teach. I even wrote articles about teaching. I woke up one day and realized that over the course of several years and through engagement with a specific significant group, I was not just a scholar who also taught classes; I was a *teacher*.

Role support from those who are significant is a central factor in the development of aspects of self that we consider to be core components of who we are. However, significant others can sometimes be a source of conflicting information. In addition to the teaching support I received in graduate school, I also had faculty mentors who considered my teaching activities a waste of time. These professors wanted me to focus on scholarly writing and to get a job at a top research school. They worried that I had become too identified with faculty at teaching schools and that I would "throw away" a good research career. These conflicts can be painful and difficult to reconcile, but at the same time, the conflicts are also a form of internal conversation that reveals our deepest values and commitments. I valued *both* primary groups—researchers and teachers—and I had significant relationships with mentors in both areas. The depth of my own conflict reflected these social relationships and commitments.

Ultimately, I was able to reconcile my conflict by engaging in an alternative conversation with myself: I didn't have to be one or the other—I could be both. I became aware of this *possible self* (see below) in a conversation with a retired faculty member who was very famous for his scholarly work on social research methods. This famous scholar would visit me in my graduate student cubicle and ask how my teaching was going. He was the one who told me I could do both. He introduced a new possibility into my existing (and limited) classification of the situation—he reframed it. In so doing, he probably changed the course of my life.

To the extent that I have a current vocation for teaching, I can trace it to the interactional effects of groups who provided me with a vocabulary for thinking about and performing the teaching role, and significant others who provided role support in the form of encouragement. Even those who were discouraging had an impact in making my commitment to teaching even stronger.

Ossification of Cultural Roles

Philip Blumstein was one of my mentors in the field of social psychology. He developed a theory to explain how specific social roles and behaviors can evolve into coherent, consistent aspects of self-concept through the process of interaction with significant others. Blumstein (1991) was particularly interested in the ways in which evolving selves reflect pre-established cultural ideals—ideals that we may, in theory, not agree with, but that have a tendency to become incorporated into our sense of self when reinforced by significant others. Thus, we are often surprised to wake up and discover that we have "become" something or someone that we could never have imagined.

Blumstein's thesis is that significant others, particularly intimate partners, are important contributors to our sense of self because we value their reflected appraisals so highly.

For example, in the process of coordinating activities, a couple may name particular behaviors as identities, such as "provider" or "homemaker." The partners may become attached to, or grow into, these identities through *routinization* and the reflected appraisals of each other. This is especially likely to be the case when we perform contextual social roles or identities that correspond with highly idealized cultural expectations. For instance, a heterosexual couple who insists, early in their marriage, that they will not conform to gendered expectations about marital roles may find themselves surprised at the extent to which they have fallen into these roles anyway. If they trace it back, they may recognize many small but cumulatively significant moments when parents, friends, and others have focused on these behaviors and, in order to maintain the social harmony, the married couple may have played the expected social identity. Friends and relatives who constantly comment on a man's "earning power" are singling out this behavior as an important characteristic of a "successful" married man. Each of these interactions reinforces a social expectation that the man should be the breadwinner. In time, even though he may not think he believes in this expectation, the newly married man may find himself shifting his behavior more and more to fit the expectations of "the married man." For instance, he might be more inclined to pursue a job that, earlier in his life, he would have seen as "selling out." Blumstein refers to this process as *ossification*, meaning that identities have the potential to harden, like bone, into selves.

I ask my students to engage in the following exercise as a way to illuminate the specific interactional steps that occur in the process of moving from a series of identities or behaviors to internalized self-ideals, especially roles and ideals we may think we are opposed or immune to. Begin a paper with the phrase "I never thought I would become _____." Then fill in the blank with something that you could never imagine yourself doing (joining a religious cult, becoming a particular type of politician, "selling out" in your choice of employment). Now consider the ways in which persons who are significant in your life could actually change your ideals, beliefs, and sense of who you are.

In your understanding of your self take some time to ponder your internal conversations; ask yourself who or what you're in conversation with, especially when you experience strong motivation to do something that makes you feel uneasy or conflicted. This internal *witnessing* can help you become more awake to the processes whereby you incorporate the reflected appraisals of others into your concept of self and then judge and evaluate your behavior accordingly. Recall the lesson on mindlessness from Part II: To what extent do mindless categories of behavioral expectations shape your internal conversation about who you think you *should* be and what you think you *should* do?

"Anchors Against Drift"

Blumstein was also interested in the ways in which significant others keep us from experimenting too much with new aspects of self. One of the implications of our sense of a core stable self is that others expect us to behave consistently as that self. If you are considered the easygoing one and you suddenly snap at your friends, they will wonder what's going on and you might feel compelled to offer an explanation. You will have an internal conversation and try to make sense of what feels like behavior that is contradictory to your core self. You may feel badly about your behavior, even if, upon examination, it was entirely justified in the moment. Whereas, if you are typically churlish, no one will notice a grumpy comment and you won't be likely to give it a second thought yourself.

Behavioral consistency is reinforced by our sense that others expect us to behave in certain ways, especially significant others. Blumstein calls this *anchors against drift*. Significant others expect us to behave in ways that align with how they see us; we know this and adjust our behavior accordingly. In other words, behavioral consistency is the result of *interactional expectations*. Our sense of *stable social relations* is based on behavioral consistency, and this consistency is achieved, in large part, by our concern with the judgment (reflected appraisals) of others if we deviate from expected behavioral patterns. When we contemplate straying from what we think of as our core self, we imagine the startled (often negative) responses of significant others and bring our behavior back into line with their expectations. The significant others transform our perceived rebellious behavior into a revenant. If we do deviate, we feel that we must have a good excuse, an excuse that provides a contextual explanation for inconsistent behavior and preferably indicates that the deviant behavior is temporary. For instance, if you have never been religiously inclined and you suddenly decide to start praying regularly, you would likely feel that you should hide it from your friends and family or that you should have an acceptable explanation. Perhaps you have a big decision to make and "prayer can't hurt, right?" This explanation indicates a temporary, contextual shift in your behavior but doesn't threaten what others see as an aspect of your core self, in this case, being non-religious.

We organize and evaluate our behavior and feelings around the interactional expectations of significant others. This consistency gives us a sense of belonging and familiarity, but at the same time, when we are in very new situations and away from significant others, we may notice (often with curiosity and sometimes alarm) sides of ourselves that are less familiar. We may find ourselves being more gregarious, more daring, or expressing novel opinions. Self-awareness through relational stability can be a good thing; without it we would be all over the behavioral map, so to speak. However, it's worth keeping track of the ways in which we may restrain or eclipse some of our feelings and tendencies because of the interactional pressure to be a consistent self.

Along these lines, the social status of significant others also has an impact on self experience. Some observers have commented that our friends and lovers are as more or less accessories to the self we are trying to be—we seek the company of those who enhance our sense of self and avoid those who disrupt it. This may be a glib observation, but when a close friend or family member undergoes a significant change, it impacts us as well.

For instance, in a study of working-class mothers who were some of the first activists in the toxic waste movement, sociologist Celene Krauss (1998) found that as these stay-at-home moms became more active in public political life, their husbands felt threatened in their position as head of household and asked their wives to cease their activism. But the women were undeterred. Political activism and public recognition changed the way they experienced themselves. They were no longer content to let their husbands handle "worldly affairs," and they were fighting for their children's health (their initial motivation was the alarming rate of unexplained deaths, especially among children, in their rural communities). They had changed. In some cases, the husbands were able to shift themselves into new alignment with their wives, but in other cases, couples divorced as a result of a major shift in who they could be to one another.

Cameron Whitley (Reading 21) explores a similar phenomenon among the family members of transgender people. As Whitley notes, there is considerable literature on the personal transgender experiences, but less emphasis on the experience of family members and close acquaintances. A gender change is one of the most significant shifts a person can make, and it has a considerable impact on relationships with others. In the afterword to Jennifer Finney Boylan's (2003) memoir, *She's Not There,* novelist Richard Russo writes about his best friend's transition in middle age from Jim to Jenny. In this passage, Russo is sharing the news with his wife:

> Barbara said, "Oh, this is just insane. There *has* to be something else going on. We *know* this man." She was looking over at me as if I too, at any moment, might be revealed to her as a stranger. I understood all too well what this was doing to her. What she knew—what she *knew* she knew—was being challenged. The ground beneath her feet had shifted, was no longer stable. . . . We were flying down the pitch black interstate, peering out the windshield at a newly unfamiliar world. It occurred to me that what I'd told my wife—that none of this was about us—wasn't true. It *was* about us. (p. 285)

This passage conveys the experiences that Whitley chronicles through interviews with "trans-kin." Family members experience the gender transition as an unraveling of what they think they know about the world (expectations of gender immutability) and the person (I related to this person primarily as a specific gender). More generally, this material invites us to consider the ways in which our own sense of self is interconnected with our expectations of significant others—who we think they can be and what we think they can do. When a significant other undergoes a major change, we also must adjust. Our ability to do so with grace and creativity will depend on how tightly caught up we are in the cultural scripts that organize our understanding of self and others. How do we stretch our self/other scripts when significant others reveal aspects of themselves that don't fit our expectations for who they are supposed to be (religious, political, economic status, gender, and sexuality)? Because selves are interactional, it's not just about them, it's also about us.

Social Context

The preceding examples illustrate that our ideas about who we can be and what we can do come largely from social sources, including significant others and reference groups. The scripts that we get from these sources reflect specific social historical contexts. In other words, *what* we learn and *how* we learn varies across time and place, and this has tremendous impact on what we think we can do and be.

For instance, sociologists Jiannbin Lee Shiao and Mia H. Tuan are interested in the development of ethnic identity among Korean adoptees (Reading 22). How do people born in one distinct ethnic culture and raised in another view themselves? Korean adoptees raised in White American families have varying investments in their Korean heritage. Some adult adoptees are highly motivated to develop their Korean identities while others expressly distance themselves. Shiao and Tuan find that this difference is based in social context, specifically when the adoptees were born and what schools they attended. Those born in the 1960s and 1970s were less likely to be exposed to other Korean adoptees and less likely to have college experiences that included ethnic literacy. At best, they might have taken "heritage" trips to Korea, but, for the most part, their primary reference groups consisted of White-American cultural groups. Those born later, and especially those who attended college, were much more inclined to pursue knowledge of their ethnic background and to seek contact with others like them. Since the publication of Shiao and Tuan's article (2008), the social context around Korean adoption has shifted in light of information that indicates that babies might have been forcibly taken from their Korean mothers. This news has led to anti-adoption social movements and increased encouragement for Korean adoptees to critique their U.S. upbringing and embrace their Korean ethnicity. As the socio-historical context shifts, Korean adoptees are exposed to new ways of thinking about themselves.

Dana Rosenfeld explores the socio-historical context for gay men and lesbians who are now in their 70s and 80s (Reading 23). The scripts for how to be gay were very different in the 1950s and 1960s. The general portrayal was of a pervert or deviant, and one was expected to be ashamed and to hide these tendencies. This surface social script fostered a thriving underground culture, largely hidden from the public eye. In a time of no Internet, how would you gain access to this world and its promise of alternative identities? Without any knowledge of this world, what would you do if you felt these "deviant" desires yourself? A recent survey of 3,600 "sexually non-conforming" individuals indicates significant generational shift. For instance, persons older than 40 tend to prefer terms such as *gay* or *lesbian* when referring to themselves, and they are less accepting of bisexuals, while younger persons typically prefer queer and many increasingly self-identify as bisexual or fluid. The difference reflects shifts in the social context and especially the rise of social media and Internet-based information that provides vastly expanded portrayals of same-gender attraction. In only a few decades, homosexuality has gone from being seen generally as a sickness and perversion to an increasingly acknowledged social status. This doesn't mean that homophobia is less rampant in some groups, only that cultural awareness is greater and that, as a result, many young adults now think that sexual identity is something they should consider about themselves in their own self-development. As Rosenfeld chronicles, older gays and lesbians have had very different identity trajectories across their life-span due to significantly shifting social contexts.

Possible Selves

Hazel Markus and Paula Nurius (1986) are known for their studies on how people develop ideas about who and what they think they can be. So far, this text has emphasized the idea that we learn cultural expectations from others. These expectations include categories and scripts that provide details about appropriate behavior (identities) for various situations. Markus and Nurius are interested in the specific sources of information that individuals have for who they think they can be. They are also interested in how this information varies for different people in different walks of life. For instance, your economic background, your racial or ethnic background, and your gender are some of the significant differences that shape ideas about who you think you can be.

Markus and Nurius are particularly keen on studying the details of how we imagine possible selves. According to their research, individuals who can "see" themselves in a particular social position are more likely to eventually achieve this position. However, it's not enough to have a general idea of the social position that you would like to occupy; rather, you need to be able to imagine the actual *process* of getting into that position. They propose that people who have access to the information, or stories, that provide specific details of how to become a certain self will be more able to *imagine* themselves going through these steps and, in turn, will be better able to organize their lives so that they achieve their desired positions.

One example of their work focuses on the different expectations of fourth graders who are from either wealthy or low-income families. When asked what they want to be when they grow up, the children from higher-income families usually name a profession such as lawyer, doctor, software designer, and so on. What is noteworthy for Markus and Nurius is the children's ability to describe, in very specific detail, the paths to achieving these professional roles. The children have a well-mapped route, which includes an understanding that they will have to go to college (a good one), graduate school, and so forth. They also understand the detailed steps of how to get there—for example, they know they need to score well on college entrance exams such as the SAT and they are aware of the resources (such as tutors and study manuals) to help them achieve high scores.

In contrast, children from low-income families often have highly unrealistic desires—they most frequently want to be music stars or star athletes. When asked how this might come about for them, they have very little idea about what they might have to do to realize these desired selves. According to Markus and Nurius (1986), the difference is in the type of information children receive about the actual processes of becoming specific social roles. If the information is specific and well charted, the children develop a highly articulated sense of a *possible self.* They can hold this image in their minds and rehearse what it will be like to go through each stage of development toward the imagined end. Children who have no immediate role models and no information about the path also have ideals, but they have no real sense of how to accomplish the phases that lead to these ideals.

Related research on athletic performance demonstrates that athletes who *imagine* themselves going through specific maneuvers actually perform better. These athletes take themselves through a mental workout that enables them to create a mental path through anticipated performance routines. This mental or imaginative process was the basis of an extremely popular book by Timothy Gallwey, *The Inner Game of Tennis,* published originally in 1974. The book was subtitled *The Classic Guide to the Mental Side of Peak Performance.* Several related books, such as *Inner Skiing* (1977), *The Inner Game of Golf* (1981), and even *The Inner Game of Music* (1986), followed soon after. In these books, Gallwey instructed his readers in the usefulness of tuning into the mental or inner dialogue and imagery in order to better manage physical performance. A later book by Gallwey, *The Inner Game of Work* (2001), extends this concept to activities such as the job interview, illustrating that people can mentally prepare for this experience by rehearsing their peak performance. This imaginative process includes engaging in inner dialogues about potential nervousness, feelings of inadequacy, and so forth, and learning to beat these *mental opponents*.

Markus and Nurius, along with many other educational researchers, observe that children in low-income schools receive very different information from those in high-income schools. Higher-income children are not only tracked for professional-level jobs, but also exposed to many successful role models and to considerable information about the specific steps required to progress toward these professions. For example, teachers and administrators in these schools routinely talk with parents and students about services that provide instruction and sample testing for college entrance exams. These conversations point students toward valuable services, and they also enable the students to imagine themselves in potential roles and to conceive the specific routes for getting there.

CONCLUSIONS

One implication of these theories on the *social* self is that the company you keep and the ideas that you cultivate *do* matter. Before parents the world over start jumping for joy and saying, "See, I told you so, that person/group *will* be a bad influence," we should remember that these effects are (1) a process and (2) the result of complex conversations we have with ourselves in which we reference multiple perspectives and consider many different significant others. We are not social robots; the attitudes of others are not simply poured into our heads, causing us to behave heedlessly. Nor are we "Stepford" people who can be easily programmed to fulfill an ideal social role (such as husband or wife). As Mead has stated, the self is an *ongoing conversation*. Significant others are a part of our internal conversations, but just as we do not allow people to act as dictators over our external lives, so we do not allow the imagined voices of significant others to dictate our internal lives. We also adopt different reference group perspectives when we evaluate our behavior and make decisions. We conjure these different perspectives as a way to enable us to see our possibilities from different points of view. Thus, the company you keep will certainly have an impact on your internal conversations and deliberations, but the form this influence takes will be (1) to allow new voices into your conversation—in the form of significant others, and (2) to cultivate new and alternative perspectives from which to make sense of and guide your own behavior.

Far from being robotic influences, a richly cultivated set of reference perspectives can actually make us freer. The processes described in this essay can be used as a guide to becoming more observant or mindful of the kind of conversation we are having with ourselves about who and what we can be. Other people and their ideas usually do not have a direct effect on our behavior, but they have an influence to the extent that the *expectations* of significant others make us feel more or less free to make certain choices and to behave in certain ways. One thing to keep in mind is that a broad range of possible selves and a care-fully considered set of diverse reference groups will result in self-conversations that provide many different perspectives on how to see and direct your own behavior. This expansion of imagined possibilities provides you with a basis for bringing more individuality to various social roles. For instance, there are many different ways to be a minister or a teacher or a student or a spouse. The specific ways in which you grow into social identities, and eventu-ally make them your own as part of your organized self-concept, will depend on the models you have for how you can play these roles. The broader your range of possibilities, the more variations you will be able to imagine, and the more individuality you will cultivate.

A final thing to keep in mind as we leave this topic is that significant others and reference groups can operate "oppositionally" as well as directionally. Most of us can recall occasions, at some time or another, when we have been focused primarily on *not* being something or on formulating a point of view that is in *opposition* to a significant other or reference group that feels problematic in our lives. Oppositional self-conversations can be very powerful in leading us to behave in emotionally charged ways. Thus, parents who are inclined to protect their children from "undesirable" external influences might consider whether their ways of doing so are teaching their children healthy ways of trying on various identities and refer-ence perspectives so that they can judge for themselves or, rather, whether their methods are hindering their children from gathering the variety of perspectives that enable healthy self-engagement and development. In the case of the latter, one of the first strong opposi-tional perspectives the child might develop will be against the parent. In so doing, the child might be less selective about various identities he tries on and less inclined to assess the fit of these identities in terms of a thoughtful self process. Instead, in the eagerness to take on perspectives that challenge or oppose the parent, the child may actually eclipse or ignore other significant internal voices that are telling him that this identity is not a good fit.

In short, trying on various identities under conditions of support and wisdom leads to the cultivation of a rich and healthy internal conversation whereby we learn the skill of mindful self-assessment and feel able to develop a variety of responses that we can feel good about in difficult situations. Conversely, external attempts to limit the opportunities for *identity play* may lead to less mindful rebellion aimed in opposition to single perspec-tives. The study of the self as a social process opens up the avenues to greater self-awareness and, consequently, to more nuanced ideas about who we think we can be and what we think we can do.

References and Suggestions for Further Reading

Blumstein, P. (1991). The production of selves in personal relationships. In J. Howard & P. Callero (Eds.), *The self–society dynamic* (pp. 305–322). Cambridge, UK: University of Cambridge Press.

Boylan, J. F. (2003). *She's not there: A life in two genders.* New York, NY: Broadway Books.

Cooley, C. H. (1983). Looking-glass self. In *Human nature and the social order* (pp. 182–185). New York: Transaction. (Original work published 1902)

Denzin, N. (1966). The significant others of a college population. *Sociological Quarterly, 7,* 298–310.

Gallwey, T. (1974). *The inner game of tennis: The classic guide to the mental side of peak performance.* New York, NY: Random House.

Gallwey, T. (1977). *Inner skiing.* New York, NY: Random House.

Gallwey, T. (1981). *The inner game of golf.* New York, NY: Random House.

Gallwey, T. (1986). *The inner game of music.* New York, NY: Random House.

Gallwey, T. (2001). *The inner game of work.* New York, NY: Random House.

Krauss, C. (1998). Challenging power. In N. Naples (ed.), *Community activism and feminist politics* (pp. 129–150). New York, NY: Routledge.

Kuhn, M. H., & McPartland, T. S. (1954). An empirical investigation of self-attitudes. *American Sociological Review, 19,* 68–76.

Markus, H., & Nurius, P. (1986). Possible selves. *American Psychologist, 41,* 954–969.

Mead, G. H. (1962). *Mind, self, and society: From the standpoint of a social behaviorist.* Chicago, IL: University of Chicago Press.

Park, R. E. (1952). *Human communities.* Glencoe, IL: Free Press.

Quindlen, A. (1989). *Living out loud.* New York, NY: Random House.

Sandstrom, K. L., Martin, D. D., & Fine, G. A. (2003). *Symbols, selves, and social reality.* Los Angeles, CA: Roxbury. (See especially Chapters 3–5)

Snyder, M. (1987). *Public appearances/private realities: The psychology of self-monitoring.* New York, NY: W. H. Freeman.

SELF AS A PROCESS OF CONTRADICTIONS AND CONFLICT

Jodi O'Brien

George Herbert Mead's theory of the self (Reading 12) is grounded in the notion of an ongoing internal conversation regarding a struggle between the experiences and desires of the *I* and the moral boundaries drawn by the *me*. The self is not one or the other; rather, it is a manifestation of the conversation between the socialized *me* and conflicting desires and ideals that occur through ongoing social encounters. In Mead's words,

> The "I" is the response of the individual to the attitude of the community as it appears in his own experience. . . . [I]f one puts up his side of the case, asserts himself over against others and insists that they take a different attitude toward himself, then there is something important occurring that is not previously present in experience. (p. 156)

In other words, we are in constant conversation with ourselves about the expectations of significant others, reference groups, and the generalized other as we understand it. What we think of as self is actually this conversation. The self develops and evolves as we grapple with our own responses to social expectations, many of which involve tension and conflict. In this section I suggest that it is the *process of conversing with ourselves about these tensions and contradictions* that reveals and shapes who we are; the self is a process of wrestling contradiction.

Consider this passage from *Living With Contradictions: A Married Feminist*, written by Angela Barron McBride in 1973:

> I am a married feminist. What does that mean? Am I part of a new breed of women, or someone about to burst because of the contradictions in my person? There are weeks and months when I'm not sure which description best fits me, but such tensions are the essence of being a married feminist.
>
> I am a woman who feels pulled in two directions—between traditional values and conventions on one hand, and a commitment to feminist ideology on the other. A woman who finds custom appealing and comforting, yet despises the patriarchal patterns that make women

second-class citizens. I am a woman who wants a loving, long-term relationship with a man, but bitterly resents being considered only someone's other *half*. A woman who values family life, but deplores the sterile, functional view of man as the head of the family and woman as its heart. A wife who wants to belong to one man, yet not be his private property.

The apparent contradictions felt by a married feminist are legion. I've listened to fashion plates sing the hedonistic pleasures of not being a mother, and felt like putting them over my knees and spanking them for their selfishness. I've heard gingham types say all they ever wanted out of life was to be a wife and a mother, and felt choked by their smugness. I bristle when people spit out the word "feminist" as if it were a communicable disease. I protest when others sneer at marriage as if it were an outdated misery. Press the button and I can feel guilty about anything. I feel guilty that I never seem to have the time to make an assortment of Christmas cookies from scratch, *and* I feel guilty about feeling guilty about that. (pp. 1–3, emphasis in original)

Note the teeter-totter between two roles, two selves—each is significant relative to specific groups, but both are defined in opposition to each other. McBride's conversation with herself is a veritable ricochet from one wall to another. In searching for her own sense of self, she wrestles with her generalized notions of what these possible selves represent. For middle-class White women in the 1960s and 1970s, the cacophony of voices about who and what they should be was loud and, in many ways, contentious.

Consider the content of these generalized voices today. Are people still inclined to represent the extremes in women's identities as "gingham types" and "radical feminists"? To some extent, these contradictions have been bridged, and the boundaries are now less sharply etched into the consciousness of young women (and men). This result stems from the attempts by the women of McBride's generation to establish some balance on the teeter-totter.

The search for new names for one's self is often prompted by the attempt to reconcile contradictions. The process can be much more complex than simply choosing one option or the other. Often the individual does not have a choice. Although contradiction and conflict may lead to change, the form of the change is always informed by the existing social expectations and boundaries.

Terminology and Social Positions

In recent decades, many scholars have focused their attention on understanding the ways in which social position affects persons differently. It's obvious, for instance, that a wealthy person has a different perspective on her options when she is shopping than someone with a low-paying hourly job. But do these economic differences affect the self-image of each person, and if so, how? Certainly, both persons have the potential to have high self-esteem and a positive self-image, but it is also true that each is likely to have vastly different day-to-day experiences. These experiences combine to become the focus of the internal dialogue that makes up a sense of self. In this way, social position can have profound effects on self development.

Regardless of what one thinks of oneself, certain features or characteristics denoting social status "mark" the interactional milieu in predictable ways. These marked interactions can affect one's sense of self.

To continue the example, someone who is wealthy is likely to be treated with respect whenever she shops. Overall, a day of shopping is likely to be a positive experience for her, and the appraisals she receives from others will likely reflect her own sense of high self-worth. Conversely, there is a tendency among store clerks to treat persons who look poor as potential thieves. Thus, regardless of her own sense of personal integrity, a person marked as poor frequently encounters rude stares and attitudes of suspicion when she is shopping. Whereas the wealthy person takes her high self-worth for granted and has her self-impression reaffirmed through interaction, the poor person may know that she must manage interactions in which she is treated as if she may not be honest despite her self-knowledge that she is a decent and valuable human being.

Many concepts have been developed to describe this process of differentiation in interaction. A few of these terms are reviewed here with the aim of providing a working vocabulary. Then we turn our focus to the ways in which these processes of interactional differentiation influence self-image.

Hegemonies

Some of the terms you may have encountered to refer to a person's social position are *hegemonic position, hierarchical status, center/margin, subject/object,* and *marked/ unmarked.* Here is one way to make sense of this terminology: Although there are many different, often competing, stories and perspectives that make up a culture, there are usually some stories or perspectives that are more acceptable and dominant than others. The dominant perspective is referred to as the *hegemonic* position. Whether they agree with it or not, most persons are aware of the hegemonic position, and its legitimacy is usually taken for granted. It is the position that is seen as "most normal" and "most desirable." In the contemporary United States, some of the hegemonic positions include rational, heterosexual, middle-class, Protestant, male, and White.

Some scholars refer to this hegemonic cluster as *the center.* Recall the discussion of default assumptions in Part II, and you will recognize the center as the default categorical perspective. From this default perspective, people who do not have these centrist characteristics (for example, those who are not White) are considered "other" or "marginal." Some scholars study various hegemonies and look at the consequences for persons who are in marginal positions in the hegemony. Another way of saying this is that persons who are low in a particular social hierarchy are defined in terms relative to the hegemonic position. For instance, it can be said that economic status is a significant or hegemonic status marker in this society. There is a social hierarchy that exists according to economic status. "Middle-class" is the dominant or taken-for-granted position in this hierarchy (not necessarily the best position, but the one that is assumed to be normal). Persons who are poor are seen as low in the hierarchy and marginal.

Marked Positions

For the purpose of understanding how these positions operate in interaction, the terms *marked/unmarked* are useful. When a person has characteristics that are consistent with the default position in a social hierarchy, then the status of the person is said to be unmarked. The default position is unmarked because, cognitively, it is what people expect to see, all else being equal. A person's status is said to be marked if it is distinct from the expected norm. Thus, as was noted in Part II, when we refer to a basketball player, we are inclined to think of a male basketball player. If we are talking about a basketball player who is female, we tend to mark this by saying "the woman basketball player." Similarly, when White people mention someone who is not White, race is one of the first character-istics mentioned ("I was just talking to that Black guy over there"). Alternately, when ref-erencing a White person, mention is seldom made of race ("I was just talking to that guy over there"). The latter sentence is racially unmarked and thus reflects a cultural hege-mony wherein white is considered normal.

We turn now to a discussion of some of the ways in which marked/unmarked statuses shape perception, interaction, and self-image. Keep in mind that the significant analytical point is the varying degrees to which persons in interaction have *control* over the roles and images they are able to present to others. We will look at just a few manifestations of this process: privilege and entitlement, marked positions and social awareness, subjective freedom, stigmatized identities, interactional mirrors, and authenticity. Each of these processes reflects tensions and contradictions that occur as persons attempt to *realize* themselves in interaction with others.

Privilege and Entitlement

A noteworthy feature of hegemonic or unmarked positions is that people with these social statuses are often unaware of their own relative freedom in interaction. They are more likely to pass through their everyday interactions without much friction. Their actions usually go unchallenged or don't need to be accounted for. They are generally given more space to express themselves, and their definition of the situation is likely to be accepted as the basis for the working consensus. For such people, the relationship between who they would like to be, who they think they are, and who they think they should be is likely to be more or less in sync and noncontradictory. This unified and clearly delineated self-image is reflected back to them and reaffirmed in myriad small ways, especially through the ease with which they conduct their everyday interactions. This is not to say that such persons may not occupy contradictory roles—they simply have more control to make sure that these identities don't come crashing together.

Consider a small example: It is sometimes incorrectly assumed by middle-class people who live in suburbs that working-class people living in urban areas are more likely to engage in extramarital sex. In fact, the rates of extramarital sexual encounters may be the same across both classes, but middle-class people often have more resources for compart-mentalizing their contradictory activities. Single-family homes ensure more privacy than do apartments with shared entries and thin walls. If you have money and credit cards, you can lead a duplicitous life farther away from prying eyes than if you do not have these resources. In short, it may be easier for a person with material wealth to move between one reality and another without experiencing too much social contradiction.

In *Carte Blanche,* a painting by René Magritte, a group of horseback riders is engaged in a fox hunt. In the foreground is a woman in fine riding clothes atop a handsome stallion. She sits astride her horse with ease and grace looking as if she hasn't a care in the world. In the background are several riders, less well clad, who are hunched low in the saddle, earnestly navigating their way around the trees of the forest through which they are riding. The woman, who represents privilege, is unaware of the trees because her horse is simply passing through them. The obstacles that exist for others don't exist for her. This is carte blanche. The implication is that her life is like a blank check—relatively speaking, she can do as she pleases, because her social position eclipses obstacles that others must navigate.

One interactional consequence of this privilege is a sense of social entitlement. In a powerful essay about growing up as "poor white trash," author Dorothy Allison (1994) writes,

> [My people] were the *they* everyone talks about . . . the ones who are destroyed or dismissed to make the "real" people, the important people, feel safer. . . . Why are you so afraid? my lovers and friends have asked me the many times I suddenly seemed a stranger, someone who would not speak to them, would not do the things they believed I should do, simple things like applying for a job, or a grant, or some award they were sure I could acquire easily. Entitlement, I have told them, is a matter of feeling like we rather than they. You think you have a right to things, a place in the world, and it is so intrinsically a part of you that you cannot imagine people like me, people who seem to live in your world, who don't have it. I have explained what I know over and over, in every way that I can, but I have never been able to make clear the degree of my fear, the extent to which I feel myself denied . . . [that] I was born poor into a world that despises the poor. (p. 14, emphasis in original)

Entitlement in this sense can be defined as a taken-for-granted expectation that one has a *right* to pursue certain goals and to participate in various interactions. The person who feels entitled does not worry about being seen as an imposter or about being rejected or dismissed. Consider what sorts of internal conversations we are likely to have if we feel entitled to participate in most realms of social life versus those who would like to participate but are not sure if they have a right to do so. To what extent does this sense of entitlement provide someone with a script for pursuing such things as asking advice from professors, asking for letters of recommendation for graduate school, and so forth? A sense of entitlement is enhanced through repeated interactions in which we are affirmed for our efforts. The more affirmed we feel, the more we will pursue new and risky opportunities that may lead to even greater social advantages. Also, people who feel entitled to certain things are more likely to get upset if things don't go as they planned. Relatively speaking, those with a strong sense of entitlement are more likely to expect that situations will unfold according to their plans.

Marked Positions and Social Awareness

For those who occupy marginal, marked statuses, the simplest interaction may pose a contradiction between how they would like to see themselves and how others see them. A lack of role support combined with the necessity of pushing harder to project a definition of the situation can have profound effects on someone's sense of self. Social psychologists have studied the relationship between self-esteem and people's tendency to attribute successes and failures to external or internal factors. For instance, if you perform well on an exam and attribute this outcome to your own intelligence and the fact that you studied, you have made an *internal attribution*—the result is a consequence of something you did. If, on the other hand, you perform poorly and say that it was because the exam was unfair, you have made an *external attribution*—the outcome is due to factors beyond yourself.

A second attributional dimension is the extent to which you perceive the cause to be stable and within your control. For instance, if you perform poorly on an exam but attribute your performance to lack of study, you have made an internal attribution and concluded that the circumstances are potentially within your control: "I could pass that exam. I just need to study harder." If, however, you attribute your grade to the instructor's dislike of you, you have concluded that your evaluation is based on external factors beyond your control. Social psychologists are inclined to agree that external attributions lead to feelings of helplessness—the individual feels that nothing he or she can do will alter the outcome.

In a class exercise, I asked students to write a description of an occasion when they were uncertain about whether some outcome in their lives was due to personal (internal) factors or social (external) factors. Most of the students were middle class, but some interesting differences in their responses did appear. When students read their responses, several of the women told of instances in which they had not gotten jobs or had not been allowed to participate in certain activities. They were unsure whether the outcome was because they were female or because they didn't have the right skills. Students of color had thought of similar instances. One Chinese American student told of winning an essay contest in his first year of college. Subsequently, he was invited to a national forum to read the essay. When he arrived, he noted that all the other winners were also students of color. He was uncertain whether he had won because he wrote a terrific essay or because of his ethnicity. Many of the Latin American and Asian American students related similar experiences. All of them were familiar with the day-to-day uncertainty about whether to attribute events in their lives to personal or social factors. For them, everyday self-awareness includes an ongoing internal conversation about whether their experiences result from ethnic, racial, or gendered processes or from personal skill and talent. One consequence of this ongoing deliberation is a feeling of walking along volatile boundary lines and never being certain if one is inside or outside.

The White men, meanwhile, looked increasingly ill at ease during this classroom activity. One by one, they read papers that began, "I'm not sure what the question is" or "I'm not sure what you're getting at here." In subsequent reflective essays, however, many of these young men noted that they had gained a much greater recognition of how complicated self-awareness and self-evaluation are for people who cannot be certain whether an outcome in their lives is because of something within their control or because they are marked as particular objects. The White male students also began to take note of the many additional boundaries, such as social class and society's expectations for them (for instance, financial productivity, heterosexuality, masculinity) that shape who and what they think they can be.

Whatever a person's status, greater self-awareness occurs as a result of recognizing the complex interplay among the positions that constitute social boundaries. Like other social routines that become ossified, and even naturalized over time, these positions are likely to be taken for granted by some and not by others. The less able a person is to take them for granted, the more likely he or she is to be aware of the boundaries—and the conflicts and contradictions—within all social systems. One outcome of dealing with contradiction is an ability to comprehend more social complexity.

Subjective Freedom

Subject refers to the person who is in an active role; *object* refers to the person upon whom the subject is acting. This is probably the definition you were taught in English grammar. In the vocabulary of symbolic interaction, persons are *subjects* to the extent that they are able to actively project their own contextual sense of self into the interactional dynamics. Someone is an *object* if he or she is seen by others only in terms of some marked social characteristic. The paradox of subject/object is that to some extent we are always objectifying others when we interact with them. As you have learned by now, we put others into categorical boxes (label them) to locate their identity, and our own, in the interaction. A problem arises, however, when we interact with someone only in terms of stereotypical categories—when we do not give them the opportunity to project their own subjectivity. *Persons who are identified by marginal, marked statuses are more likely to be treated as objects and less likely to be perceived as subjects.* A way to think about this is to ask yourself how free you are to write your own narrative in a given interaction. As we have seen, power determines who can do and say what in many interactions. To what extent does a highly marked status give you even less power in an interaction? Or, conversely, when do you find yourself treating someone else in terms of a social category (as an object) rather than as a subject?

Subjective freedom can be described as how much freedom one has to successfully convey a definition of the situation. If others in the interactional setting see the person only in terms of a particular stereotypical status—as an object—then the person cannot expect to be seen on her or his own terms. For instance, in education research, it has been demonstrated that college students respond very differently to the same material depending on whether it is taught by a White man or a woman of color. The White man, who occupies the unmarked or expected position for the role of a college professor, is usually seen as "in control," "apolitical," "fair," and "informative" when he teaches material such as the ideas being discussed in this essay. A woman of color teaching exactly the same thing is often evaluated by students as being "too political," "too biased," "lacking authority," and "uninformed." Not only do perceptions differ dramatically, but in this case the man has more subjective freedom than the woman. A woman who is aware of these stereotypical reactions among students can develop strategies to counter this tendency, but in doing so, she has to shape the interaction in response to stereotypical perceptions. She is not as free to be herself in the same way that the man is. In presenting her subjective position (in this case as a teacher), she must navigate around the ways in which others mark her only as an object of her race and gender.

Persons who occupy significantly marked positions are usually aware of the contradictions between how they see themselves and how others see them. The dilemma is complicated further by the fact that these marked positions are also a part of someone's subjectivity. A professor who is also Black does not necessarily want to be treated as if she were White. This "color-blind" attitude reinforces the hegemony that White is the default and desired position. The challenge in developing *multicultural consciousness* is to overcome mindless stereotypes so that persons do not have to navigate their way out of boxes that objectify them in order to present their own subjectivity.

Ironically, dismantling stereotypes requires a *more* discriminating attitude. This does not mean discrimination in the sense of stereotyping, but discrimination as a form of discernment and awareness. We have to train ourselves to *pay more attention* to details that otherwise go unnoticed because they may not fit the stereotype. An employer who is mindfully discerning, for instance, will force herself to get over the fact that the job interviewee is in a wheelchair and focus instead on features such as the person's seemingly high intelligence and expert experience. At the same time, she will be aware that the person is in fact in a wheelchair and that this is obviously of some consequence for him. The ways in which it is of consequence should be the subject's own story to tell, however. The more he perceives that he is being treated genuinely as a subject within the situation—in this case, as a potential employee—rather than as a "handicapped" object, the freer he will be to present his own subjective rendering of himself.

Stigmatized Identities

Some statuses are not only highly marked, but marked in ways that are stigmatizing for the individual and for those associated with the individual. This stigmatization can have significant consequences for interaction and self-image. Consider a person who responds with the following profile to the "Who Am I?" question (see Part III):

daughter	computer geek
granddaughter	cat lover
graduate student	religious
White feminist	music lover
from Indiana	

Are you formulating an image of this person? Can you tell something about the important things and people in her life from this list (for example, parents, grandparents, cats, school)? This is her own subjective rendering of herself. All of these self-referential characteristics are features that she would probably be able to bring up in conversation with others and not expect conflict to occur (except maybe in terms of types of computers or favorite bands, but this would only reaffirm her commitment to these aspects of self). In other words, there doesn't appear to be a lot of role conflict in this initial list. Suppose, however, that she added "queer" to the list. Is this something that she can tell her grandmother about? Obviously, that depends on the grandmother and the relationship between the two of them. Regardless, we can assume that this particular aspect of self may exist in conflict with some of the other relationships that she may value. Even if her parents are accepting of her queer status in their interactions with their daughter, they may find themselves in conflict when they encounter old friends who ask if their daughter is married yet. Do they "come out" as the parents of a lesbian or deflect the question in a way that will preserve their own unmarked (that is, heterosexual) status?

For many people, once they are aware of this particular status, all other aspects of the person fade to the background. A stigmatized identity has a tendency to become a *master identity*. Everything else about the person takes a back seat to, or is evaluated in terms of, the master identity. Stigmatized master identities also reflect archetypal social beliefs, such as the belief that someone can be gay or religious but not both simultaneously. These sorts of ideas reflect entrenched social expectations about which social roles go together and which do not. There is a tendency to assume that a person with a stigmatized role is nothing other than that particular role.

A person who engages in activities that are considered stigmatized has to do a great deal of interactional work to manage information. This example illustrates a highly marked, problematic aspect of self (*stigma*) that has consequences in interaction with others. It also illustrates the fact that all of us have multiple, contradictory, shifting selves. We are many things both to ourselves and to one another. We enact various selves contextually. We may push out one aspect of self in one setting (spiritual) and another in another setting (participation in a seminar on LGBTQ experiences). We may keep certain features hidden (queer) to preserve a valued relationship (with a grandmother). Stigma is an interactional feature. An aspect of self is stigmatized only to the extent that persons define it as beyond the boundaries of expected or acceptable practices. Yet stigma can have very real consequences in shaping how persons make sense of the contradictions they perceive in their own self-image and how they grapple with these contradictions in interaction with others.

Many stigmatized identities exist in the form of highly marked stereotypes (handicapped, homeless, ex-convict, hooker, drug addict, mental patient, welfare recipient, "illegal" immigrant, and so on). But any aspect of self about which someone feels extreme shame or embarrassment has the potential to operate as a stigmatized identity. If you are struggling with being gay, lesbian, or transgender, or being from a working-class background, or being a single parent, or because of your religious background, and so forth, then you may feel compelled to hide this aspect of yourself from others. Many social psychologists suggest that shame about an aspect of self-identity develops when a person internalizes social scripts that convey certain statuses as marked and undesirable.

The person's own internal gaze or mirror is a reflection of social images whereby the identity is defined as loathsome. As a consequence of looking at this internal image, the person develops a sense of self-loathing. Persons who engage in behaviors that are stigmatized may or may not feel shame or embarrassment themselves. The extent to which they are able to deflect the shame directed at them by others depends on what sort of larger repertoire of self-understanding they have, their history of interactions with significant others, and their position in various social hierarchies.

For instance, when I am traveling in certain areas, I can expect to be called names or even spat at by persons who perceive me to be a lesbian. At times I feel unsafe in some places. However, for the most part I have the freedom to avoid these situations, and to the extent that I do have to deal with bigotry, I have a well-developed set of responses. My self-image as a lesbian (a nonstigmatized identity for me) is shaped by the fact that I am a tenured professor in a respectable university. I am aware that one part of who I am—my sexual identity—is socially stigmatized, but I view that part as normal and unremarkable. In interaction, I project a definition that invites others to treat me accordingly. And for the most part, they do. Students and colleagues may privately dislike me for this part of who I am, but I don't provide any opportunity for them to project this definition onto my interaction. My ability to achieve this interactional de-stigmatization is based on much critical reflection about how I want to incorporate this aspect of myself into my everyday interactions, many positive experiences in which my own self-view has been affirmed by people who matter to me, and, perhaps most important, the fact that I have a great deal of power in the particular context in which I spend most of my time—a college campus.

Accordingly, in most of my interactions I am able to engage in ways that reflect and reaffirm what I think of as my core self: a leader, thoughtful, fair, easy-going. However, recently I chaired a high-level university committee and one of the members was openly critical of my position: He did not like lesbians and did not think I should be chairing an important committee. He actively spoke out against me during the meetings and the result was a tense situation for everyone. Externally, the situation was challenging because, technically, I was in charge and people were looking to me to manage the situation, but they also felt embarrassed for me. Internally, the situation forced me to have some difficult conversations with myself. I was very angry with this man and his behavior also confused and unsettled me. My first impulse was to tell him what a prejudiced idiot he was, but I countered this impulse with my internalized expectations that this is not how a "good leader" would behave. I had to have several conversations with friends and colleagues before I was able to come up with a way of handling the situation that reconciled my sense of injustice and dignity with my ideas of what good leaders would do. In short, the situation introduced a scratchiness or tension that forced me into deeper awareness and conversation with myself.

All of us experience some degree of tension and contradiction (such as shame and guilt) in the various behaviors that we consider to be aspects of our core self. The way in which we work through these contradictions shapes our developing sense of self. Our resources for wrestling with these contradictions reflect personal interactional history and the repertoire of stories we have for ourselves as well as our own relative power in situations.

Interactional Mirrors

One of the features of a hegemonic or central position is that persons who occupy these positions can be relatively certain of encountering others like them wherever they go. One outcome of this is that the person's reality is likely to be reflected back by others and thereby continually reaffirmed. In contrast, persons who occupy marginal positions and who interact primarily with persons who hold mainstream positions may often feel isolated and conflicted about how to interpret their own experiences. In the words of poet Adrienne Rich (1984/1994),

> When those who have the power to name and to socially construct reality choose not to see you or hear you . . . when someone with the authority of a teacher, say, describes the world and you are not in it, there is a moment of psychic disequilibrium, as if you looked in the mirror and saw nothing. It takes some strength of soul—and not just individual strength, but collective understanding—to resist this void, this non-being, into which you are thrust, and to stand up, demanding to be seen and heard. (p. 199)

Being able to interact with others whose experiences and struggles match your own is not simply a privilege; it is an occasion to (re)affirm the reality of your own impressions and feelings. Many of us transgress boundaries every day because we are "outsiders." The vertigo of these experiences can be overcome, to some extent, if we are able to interact with others who share our conflicting circumstances and contradictory experiences. Conversations with those who share our experiences provide us with new names and meanings that help us bridge the contradictions. This opportunity to associate and redefine reality is one of the reasons why special interest groups and clubs are important for people who share marginalized, marked, or stigmatized statuses. These groups provide interactional mirrors that reflect the complexities of crossing through contradictory states of being. In encounters with others who experience similar contradictions and tensions, people broaden their repertoire, learn new scripts for acting, and have an opportunity to express more subjective freedom.

In the United States, suicide is the leading cause of death among gay, lesbian, and transgender youths aged 15 to 24 (Suicide Prevention Resource Center, 2008). Despite rapidly changing cultural norms, these young people often experience their sexual or gender feelings as being completely outside the boundaries of the self-images expected by significant others, such as parents, family, friends, teachers, and church and community leaders. Without positive imagery and role models for how to incorporate their differences into the rest of their self-image, these young people suffer the contradictions deeply. Irreconcilable feelings of helplessness can lead to extreme despair. The opportunity to encounter people whose self-image reconciles the identities of "homosexual" and "productive, accepted member of society" can turn these young people away from the brink of suicide.

Similarly, female students and students of color benefit from programs designed specifically for them to interact with others who share similar points of view. For these alternative perspectives to be interactionally supported and to gain the stature of commonly understood realities, they must sometimes be enacted separately from mainstream culture. Renato Rosaldo (1993), an anthropologist who has participated actively in the development of such programs at Stanford University, calls the programs "safe houses":

> Why do institutions need safe houses? Safe houses can foster self-esteem and promote a sense of belonging in often alien institutions. Safe houses are places where diverse groups—under the banners of ethnic studies, feminist studies, or gay and lesbian studies—talk together and become more articulate about their intellectual projects. When they enter the mainstream seminars such students speak with clarity and force about their distinctive projects, concerns, and perspectives. The class is richer and more complex, if perhaps less comfortable, for its broadened range of perspectives. (p. xi)

Rosaldo is delineating the interactional steps whereby persons have an opportunity to express their subjectivity without having to navigate the imposition of stereotypes and prejudices. In the kind of interactional setting that he describes, persons develop a clearer and more articulate sense of who they are *in all their complexity.* When they bring this complexity into mainstream interactions, it can have the effect of altering the stereotypical routine.

It is important to note that status as an insider or an outsider is situational and may change with circumstance. In *Falling From Grace,* Katherine Newman (1988) describes the experiences of men in middle and upper managerial positions who have lost their jobs. For most of these men, selfhood pivots around their ability, as holders of privileged positions, to move with ease through a world in which they wield considerable control. When they lose their jobs, they lose access to a tremendous amount of interactional privilege (such as control over space and conversation) that was their basis for maintaining a positive self-image. Many of these men are unaccustomed to contradictory self-images and, as a result, are ill prepared for the quick downward spiral that they experience when they fall outside the lines of their primary reference group. Lacking alternative points of reference and feeling ashamed of having been "downsized," these men are at high risk for suicide. Support groups for these men do not simply provide a way to get through the hard times—they are interactional situations in which the men learn to project and juggle a new self-image, one that is quite different from the self they have been accustomed to being.

Authenticity

The preceding discussion reveals a picture of the social self as multiple, shifting, and contradictory. How we see ourselves and the selves we present to others shifts from context to context and can be contradictory within a given situation. We are more committed to some aspects of self than others. We may be inclined to hide or deflect certain significant identities in some situations. These observations lead to the question "Who are you really?" The question of authenticity is something that concerns many scholars as well as individuals. One answer to the question comes in the form of a paradox: We all live contradictory lives, but we tend to act as if our lives were not filled with ambiguity and contradiction. One cultural expectation that many of us share is the *norm of consistency.* Is consistency the same thing as authenticity? For many people, it is. We tend to believe people are authentic when we observe them behaving consistently across different settings and circumstances ("She must be genuinely kind, because she is kind even when someone is mean to her"). It is possible that persons strive to make their behavior consistent because others expect them to behave consistently. Over the course of time, with repeated interactions and affirmation, we may develop self-routines that are so consistent that we believe them to be authentic expressions of self. Furthermore, to the extent that others strive to show us consistency and to hide the inconsistencies, we may come to believe that people are, indeed, consistent or authentic.

In a related way, we may strive to hide aspects of self that might strike others as contradictory according to preexisting social scripts about what sorts of behaviors go together ("He can't possibly be gay and also be a football player"). In doing so, we reaffirm these social scripts and fail to express the fact that selves are indeed multiple and contradictory.

From the perspective of symbolic interactionists who recognize the existence of multiple, shifting, contradicting self-expressions, one answer to the question "Who are you really?" is this: We are really the *way* in which we work through the contradictions that characterize our day-to-day interactions. We are the *process of wrestling contradiction*. This process is reflected in internal conversation and external expression. Two people can have a similar profile of self-referential identities and characteristics but very different self-images and interactional responses. Consider again the woman described in the "Who am I?" question above. She might keep her more stigmatized statuses (lesbian, religious) closeted from others whom she suspects will not be able to handle the contradictions these statuses imply, or she might reveal all and express an attitude of "I have a right to be *all* these various selves, even if it confuses you." How she views her own selves and how she chooses to portray them to others—in all their complexity and ambiguity— reveals the process of who she really is. In this way, it can be concluded that *selves are always in a state of becoming*. This becoming is shaped through the processes of interaction and revealed through the internal dialogues in which we observe, comment on, feel, and try to make sense of our own complexity.

Recall some of the general principles that have been formulated throughout this book. All humans use language-based systems to create conceptual meaning. This process creates definitional boundaries. All people compartmentalize. Different individuals encounter these boundaries differently. The process of self-understanding is a continual interplay between personal experience and attempts to fit experience into existing conceptual categories and representations. All of us struggle to make sense of ourselves, to find ways of self-expression, and to be heard and understood. The self undergoes constant revision as it encounters friction, contradiction, and conflict among the various boundaries that give the self meaning.

Conclusions

One of the paradoxes of human social life is that cultural practices both constrain us and make our lives meaningful. Another writer and activist, Gloria Anzaldúa, who passed away in 2004, left a powerful legacy regarding cultural complexity. In one of her essays, "*La Conciencia de la Mestiza*/Toward a New Consciousness" (1987), she describes the experiences of those who walk the boundaries and live the contradictions of being outsiders in terms of class, gender, race, religion, sexuality, immigration status, and so on. According to Anzaldúa, such people develop a multiple, or *mestiza,* consciousness that makes them more aware of both the advantages and limitations of entrenched cultural practices. The *mestiza* is "a product of the transfer of the cultural and spiritual values of one group to another" (p. 78). This cultural transfer or border navigation can be tremendously difficult. Anzaldúa describes the clash this way:

> The clash of voices results in mental and emotional states of perplexity. Internal strife results in insecurity and indecisiveness. The mestiza's dual or multiple personality is plagued by psychic restlessness. . . . These numerous possibilities leave *la mestiza* floundering in uncharted seas. In perceiving conflicting information and points of view she is subjected to a swamping of her psychological borders. (p. 78)

How does *la mestiza* cope?

> The new *mestiza* copes by developing a tolerance for contradictions, a tolerance for ambiguity. She learns to be an Indian in Mexican culture, to be a Mexican from an Anglo point of view. She learns to juggle cultures. She has a plural personality, she operates in pluralistic mode. . . . Not only does she sustain contradictions, she turns the ambivalence into something else. (p. 79)

One of the implications of *la mestiza,* or multiple consciousness, is cultural awareness. Those who cannot take their social positions for granted, who cannot assume that their definition of the situation will be shared by others, are likely to have a more expansive awareness of the situation and its possibilities. This is what Anzaldúa refers to as the "consciousness of the borderlands." Borderland consciousness, and the struggle it involves, is a central aspect of change. Anzaldúa concludes,

> The struggle is inner. The struggle has always been inner, and is played out in the outer terrains. Awareness of our situation must come before inner changes, which in turn come before changes in society. Nothing happens in the "real" world unless it happens first in the images in our heads. (p. 87)

Although Anzaldúa is writing specifically about the borders that divide the consciousness of Chicana/os who are also Indians and also trying to live in Anglo worlds, her words resonate with many people who traverse multiple social borders. Contradiction is not necessarily a bad thing, especially when struggle leads to awareness. To the extent that each of us recognizes and learns to wrestle with the contradictions that are an inevitable part of social existence, we expand the definitions of who and what we imagine we can be. We increase our social muscle and enrich our repertoire of possibilities.

A similar process occurs at the societal level. As groups engage in boundary skirmishes regarding respective definitions of morality, entitlement, and the power to define cultural institutions such as politics, law, religion, and family, there is the possibility of increased awareness. This potential is shaped, in large part, by a group's power to participate in cultural definitions of what is "real" and "acceptable." If you live in the United States, consider what it means to live in a country that promotes the ideal of "freedom and justice" for all. Cultural pluralism is the bedrock of this freedom. For the ideal to become real, it is necessary to foster a national *mestiza* consciousness and all the struggle and debate that go along with it.

REFERENCES AND SUGGESTIONS FOR FURTHER READING

Allison, D. (1994). *Skin: Talking about sex, class and literature.* Ithaca, NY: Firebrand Books.

Anzaldúa, G. (1987). *Borderlands/La Frontera: The new mestiza.* San Francisco, CA: Aunt Lute Books.

Barthes, R. (2000). *Mythologies* (A. Lavers, Trans.). London, UK: Vintage. (Original work published 1957)

Lorde, A. (1984). *Sister/outsider: Essays and speeches by Audre Lorde.* Berkeley, CA: Crossing Press.

McBride, A. B. (1973). *Living with contradictions: A married feminist.* New York, NY: HarperCollins.

McIntosh, P. (1992). White privilege and male privilege. In M. L. Anderson & P. H. Collins (Eds.), *Race, class, and gender: An anthology* (pp. 70–81). Belmont, CA: Wadsworth.

Newman, K. (1988). *Falling from grace.* New York, NY: Free Press.

Rich, A. (1994). Invisibility in academe. In *Blood, bread, and poetry: Selected prose (1979–1985).* New York, NY: W. W. Norton. (Original work published 1984)

Rosaldo, R. (1993). *Culture and truth: The remaking of social analysis.* Boston, MA: Beacon Press.

Suicide Prevention Resource Center. (2008). *Suicide risk and prevention for lesbian, gay, bisexual, and transgender youth.* Newton, MA: Education Development Center.

SIGNIFICANT OTHERS AND SELF-DEVELOPMENT

Who am I really? This is a question we often ask ourselves. The psychologist William James once remarked that our selves are as numerous as the number of people with whom we interact. Most people believe that the self is a fixed and immutable set of *core personality traits*—something that we are born with. This section introduces the concept of the self as a social process. Sociologists George Herbert Mead and Charles Horton Cooley were contemporaries of James, writing in the United States in the 1930s. They introduced the idea that people develop a sense of themselves in the same way that they develop an understanding of other social objects and events: We learn to name ourselves and our actions. This naming process occurs through interaction, especially with those who are significant to us. We learn how to think and feel about ourselves based on the impressions and names others have for us. The readings in this section provide the theoretical basis for understanding the social self.

In his classic article "Looking-Glass Self" Cooley proposed that we learn what to think and feel about ourselves by watching how others react to us. Much like looking into a mirror, if we perceive someone as viewing our actions with admiration, then we feel pride. If we perceive them as viewing us with disdain, we feel mortification. Through these *reflected appraisals*, we gain information from others about ourselves and our actions.

In his article "A Theory of Genius," sociologist Thomas Scheff uses these theories as a framework for explaining the development of genius. Scheff proposes that significant others exert a powerful influence on self-development through the process of *shaming*. According to his theory, "genius" is more likely to occur among those who are able to escape the interactional shaming processes that lead us to conform to the status quo.

When a significant other undergoes a major change, we also must adjust. In "Trans-Kin," Cameron Whitley chronicles the experiences of people who have transgender family members. This material is a reminder that when someone undergoes a major change, those close to them are also affected in significant ways.

READING QUESTIONS

1. Make a list of 20 responses to the question "Who am I?" How many of the characteristics on your list are social roles—that is, aspects of yourself that exist only in reference to others (for example, daughter)?

2. If you listed behavioral characteristics (for example, friendly, funny), try to recall how you came to think of yourself this way. Do you have significant others who notice, expect, and reinforce these self-images? How do you feel when you don't behave in ways that are consistent with these expected characteristics?

(Continued)

(Continued)

3. According to Cooley, we rely on the impressions of others in forming our own self-assessments. If we are watching others' perceptions of us, how do we know whether our read of their reaction to us is accurate or not? Does it matter?

4. For a day, practice paying attention to how you are imagining others are thinking of you. What evidence are you using to confirm your impressions of their judgments of you?

5. Discuss the idea of shame as a process that preserves the status quo. How does this process work interactionally? How does it work internally?

6. Consider experiences in which you have felt shame. Do you avoid certain behaviors or situations because you *imagine* you might experience shame? When you imagine this shame, who or what is the audience in your head?

7. Consider a major change someone close to you has made. How did it affect your interactions with that person?

8. Have you ever hesitated about making a major change in your life because of your concerns about how a significant other might respond?

19

Looking-Glass Self

Charles Horton Cooley

(1983)

The social origin of [self] comes by the pathway of intercourse with other persons. There is no sense of "I" . . . without its correlative sense of you, or he, or they. . . . In a very large and interesting class of cases the social reference takes the form of a somewhat definite imagination of how one's self—that is any idea he appropriates—appears in a particular mind, and the kind of self-feeling one has is determined by the attitude . . . attributed to that other mind. A social self of this sort might be called the reflected or looking-glass self:

> Each to each a looking-glass
>
> Reflects the other that doth pass.

As we see our face, figure, and dress in the glass, and are interested in them because they are ours, and pleased or otherwise with them according as they do or do not answer to what we should like them to be; so in imagination we perceive in another's mind some thought of our appearance, manners, aims, deeds, character, friends, and so on, and are variously affected by it.

A self-idea of this sort seems to have three principal elements: the imagination of our appearance to the other person; the imagination of his judgment of that appearance, and some sort of self-feeling, such as pride or mortification. The comparison with a looking-glass hardly suggests the second element, the imagined judgment, which is quite essential. The thing that moves us to pride or shame is not the mere mechanical reflection of ourselves, but an imputed sentiment, the imagined effect of this reflection upon another's mind. This is evident from the fact that the character and weight of that other, in whose mind we see ourselves, makes all the difference with our feeling. We are ashamed to seem evasive in the presence of a straightforward man, cowardly in the presence of a brave one, gross in the eyes of a refined one, and so on. We always imagine, and in imagining share, the judgments of the other mind. A man will boast to one person of an action—say some sharp transaction in trade—which he would be ashamed to own to another.

The process by which self-feeling of the looking-glass sort develops in children may be followed without much difficulty. Studying the movements of others as closely as they do, they soon see a connection between their own acts and changes in those movements; that is, they perceive their own influence or power over persons. The child appropriates the visible actions of his parent or nurse, over which he finds he has some control, in quite the same way as he appropriates one of his own members or a plaything, and he will try to do things with this new possession, just as he will with his hand or his rattle. A girl six months old will attempt in the most evident and deliberate manner to attract attention to herself, to set going by her actions some of those movements of other persons that she has appropriated. She has tasted the joy of being a cause, of exerting social power, and wishes more of it. She will tug at her mother's skirts, wriggle, gurgle, stretch out her arms, etc., all the time watching for the hoped-for effect. These performances often give the child, even at this age, an appearance of what is called affectation, that is, she seems to be unduly preoccupied with what other people think of her. Affectation, at any age, exists when the passion to influence others seems to overbalance the established character and give it an obvious twist or pose. It is instructive to find that even Darwin was, in his childhood, capable of departing from truth for the sake of making an impression. "For instance," he says in his autobiography, "I once gathered much valuable fruit from my father's trees and hid it in the shrubbery and then ran in breathless haste to spread the news that I had discovered a hoard of stolen fruit."[1]

The young performer soon learns to be different things to different people, showing that he begins to apprehend personality and to foresee its operation. If the mother or nurse is more tender than just, she will almost certainly be "worked" by systematic weeping. It is a matter of common observation that children often behave worse with their mother than with other and less sympathetic people. Of the new persons that a child sees, it is evident that some make a strong impression and awaken a desire to interest and please them, while others are indifferent or repugnant. Sometimes the reason can be perceived or guessed, sometimes not; but the fact of selective interest, admiration, prestige, is obvious before the end of the second year. By that time a child already cares much for the reflection of himself upon one personality and little for that upon another. Moreover he soon claims intimate and tractable persons as *mine,* classes them among his other possessions, and

maintains his ownership against all comers. M., at three years of age, vigorously resented R.'s claim upon their mother. The latter was "*my* mamma," whenever the point was raised.

Strong joy and grief depend upon the treatment this rudimentary social self receives. In the case of M. I noticed as early as the fourth month a "hurt" way of crying which seemed to indicate a sense of personal slight. It was quite different from the cry of pain or that of anger, but seemed about the same as the cry of fright. The slightest tone of reproof would produce it. On the other hand, if people took notice and laughed and encouraged, she was hilarious. At about fifteen months old she had become "a perfect little actress," seeming to live largely in imaginations of her effect upon other people. She constantly and obviously laid traps for attention, and looked abashed or wept at any signs of disapproval or indifference. At times it would seem as if she could not get over these repulses, but would cry long in a grieved way, refusing to be comforted. If she hit upon any little trick that made people laugh she would be sure to repeat it, laughing loudly and affectedly in imitation. She had quite a repertory of these small performances, which she would display to a sympathetic audience, or even try upon strangers. I have seen her at sixteen months, when R. refused to give her the scissors, sit down and make-believe cry, putting up her under lip and snuffling, meanwhile looking up now and then to see what effect she was producing.

In such phenomena we have plainly enough, it seems to me, the germ of personal ambition of every sort. Imagination cooperating with instinctive self-feeling has already created a social "I," and this has become a principal object of interest and endeavor.

Progress from this point is chiefly in the way of a greater definiteness, fullness, and inwardness in the imagination of the other's state of mind. A little child thinks of and tries to elicit certain visible or audible phenomena, and does not go back of them; but what a grown-up person desires to produce in others is an internal, invisible condition which his own richer experience enables him to imagine, and of which expression is only the sign. Even adults, however, make no separation between what other people think and the visible expression of that thought. They imagine the whole thing at once, and their idea differs from that of a child chiefly in the comparative richness and complexity of the elements that accompany and interpret the visible or audible sign. There is also a progress from the naive to the subtle in socially self-assertive action. A child obviously and simply, at first, does things for effect. Later there is an endeavor to suppress the appearance of doing so; affection, indifference, contempt, etc., are simulated to hide the real wish to affect the self-image. It is perceived that an obvious seeking after good opinion is weak and disagreeable.

NOTE

1. Darwin, F. (1959). *Life and letters of Charles Darwin.* New York: Basic Books, p. 27.

SIGNIFICANT OTHERS AND SELF-DEVELOPMENT

20

A Theory of Genius

Thomas Scheff

(1990)

The explanation of genius that is most common is that it is a product of inherited genes. Galton (1869) sought to demonstrate this point by studying the family lines of artists, scientists, and statesmen. Cox (1926) conducted a similar but more extensive study. Both show a strong relationship between genius in a certain field, for example, music, and a family background of talent in that field. Bach and Puccini, for example, were both descended from five generations of musicians. Although these two examples are extreme, the relationship is general; most of the great musicians came from families in which there was already musical talent.

This article is aimed not at dismissing the genetic argument but offers an alternative model of explanation which could either complement or replace it, depending on the findings of future research. As has been pointed out many times, family inheritance has both a biological and a social character. In the study of genius it is difficult to disentangle the two since we deal with a small number of cases. Since I propose only a necessary cause, not a sufficient one, there is no need to evaluate the validity of the genetic argument.

The theory proposed concerns two processes of development—one of *talent,* the other of *self-esteem.* I argue that both processes are necessary. The development of talent will be discussed first.

Modern linguistics has (unintentionally) contributed to the issue by the discovery that all humans have genius in language. Since this contention is not obvious, I first review the contribution that linguists have made: the competent use of language is an achievement of such staggering complexity that it seems a miracle.

There is a large literature on the complexity of even the simplest utterances. The attempt to program computers for automatic translation is one of the bases of the new appreciation of the immense intelligence required to use language. There is no way to program a computer to solve a relatively simple problem of competent language use: choosing from among fixed, multiple meanings of a word. This can be demonstrated by . . . the simple statement . . . , "The box is in the pen." Is pen to be construed as a writing instrument or an enclosure? To answer this question, the program would have to have access to an encyclopedia, not merely a dictionary, and would have to have the resources to know how to comb the encyclopedic reference for its relevance to the context in the sentence.

Compared with creating a metaphoric expression or even merely understanding one, words with two or more meanings are very simple problems indeed. There is the story of the computer program which translated the expression "The spirit is willing, but the flesh is weak" into Russian as "The whiskey is good, but the meat is bad," and "Out of sight, out of mind" as "First blind, then insane." These illustrations are apocryphal, but they make the point: using language correctly is a creative process beyond the power of even the most sophisticated computer program, or of living creatures other than humans, for that matter.

It will be helpful here to define what I mean by creative intelligence, the basis of genius. For my purposes, it is the ability to find a new solution to a new problem. In the living world outside humans, creatures that have even a modicum of this ability are very rare. The psychologist Köhler showed that a few of the most intelligent in the most intelligent of the primates, the chimpanzees, had a limited amount of creative intelligence. A representative problem was to reach fruit on a shed that was too high to climb. The ingredients of the solution, jointed sticks and packing crates, were scattered around the yard. Only a few chimpanzees solved the problem: stacking the crates near the shed, carrying the jointed sticks to the top, joining them, using the pole created to get the fruit. This simple problem would confound almost all the nonhuman living world.

At the other end of the scale of complexity was the problem facing physicists at the turn of the century . . . when it was becoming apparent that classical physics was inadequate for dealing with the accumulating evidence on the nature of the physical universe. Hilbert (cited in Feuer 1982) raised the question of why it was that Einstein solved the problem rather than any one of a group of men, all of whom seemed to be so much better prepared than he: Lorentz, Hilbert himself, Poincaré, Mach, and Minkowski. His question can be used to illustrate my conception of creative intelligence. The others were all more erudite than Einstein, but their very erudition led them to keep applying the old solutions that were no longer appropriate. Only Einstein saw that it was the very successes of classical physics that were standing in the way of a solution. What was needed was not merely modifying the old solutions but discarding them entirely and starting over with new ones.

The physicist Boltzmann (1899) described the problem in general terms. He noted that when a new method yields "beautiful results," many become unconsciously wedded to it; they come "to believe that the development of science to the end of all time would consist in the systematic and unremitting application of it." . . .

Even among humans, many kinds of creative activity are rare: only a few solve an artistic or scientific problem in their lifetimes; that is, they do not create a new solution to a new problem.

However, as already suggested, in one field, language, virtually every human by the age of five is a creative genius. Most five-year-olds can understand and even create a correct sentence that they have never heard before. Not infrequently, at a somewhat later age, a child can create a correct sentence that no one has ever heard before. In one field, language, almost everyone is creative, spontaneously creating new solutions to new problems as they arise in everyday life.

How do linguists account for the immense human creativity they have discovered? Chomsky (1957, 1965, 1969) offers what turns out to be a conventional genetic explanation. He suggests that linguistic competence is based on "deep structures," genetically programmed sequences, which would have been called instincts if that term had not been discredited. In his view, all humans are linguistically creative because that creativity has been genetically inherited.

I wish to broaden the linguists' question so that the issue includes all creative genius, not just language use. The question becomes: *Why is it that almost everyone is a genius at language, but only a few rare individuals are geniuses in all other spheres of activity?* As already suggested, Chomsky's answer to this question is genetic; he would assume that language creativity is genetically inherited by everyone and that genius in other areas belongs to only a few individuals with the right genetic inheritance, as Galton and Cox both tried to show.

My alternative explanation does not exclude genetics but opens several new areas of investigation. First, assume that the capacity for creative genius in all spheres of activity, not just in language, is genetically inherited by all human beings. Apparently the human brain is more complex and powerful than the largest and most sophisticated computer. Von Neumann estimated that it is capable of processing 140 million bits of information per second. The philosopher Emerson (whose conception of human nature

will figure prominently in this essay) did not know this, of course, but he seemed to sense it: "We lie in the lap of immense intelligence" (1837).

If humans have the capacity for genius in all areas, not just in language, why does genius appear in everyone in language but almost never in other areas? Suppose we assume that the disparity is caused by differences not in genetics but in systems of instruction. That is, it is possible that the system of instruction which leads children to learn language is enormously effective, while the systems of instruction which lead children to learn other activities, such as musical composition or mathematics, are relatively ineffective. These two suppositions raise what seems to me to be a new question. *How is the system of instruction of children in language different from other systems of instruction?*

A careful answer to this question might require considerable investigation. In this paper I will attempt only a provisional answer in order to formulate a rudimentary theory of the origins of genius. I will describe only some of the most obvious characteristics which differentiate language instruction from all other types of instruction.[1]

1. Exposure to language begins at the moment of birth and goes on almost constantly throughout infancy and childhood, and indeed for the whole of the individual's life. In terms of sheer quantity, for most individuals, exposure to language is probably vastly greater than any other type of instruction.

2. Language instruction is supremely interactive. Only very early in infancy is the child merely passively exposed to language. Long before any speech is acquired, parents and others speak directly to the infant, usually seeking a response, any response, to their utterances. The immediate rewarding of the infant's responses, often with boundless

enthusiasm, is the beginning of a process of interaction between the infant and competent speakers which instructs the child in correct usage.

3. Virtually all of an infant's prelanguage and language tutoring is with tutors who are, as has already been pointed out above, extraordinarily competent in the subject they are imparting. This characteristic of language instruction surely differentiates it from instruction in other subjects. With subjects other than language, the instructors are often only routinely competent, if that. As will be illustrated below for the case of musical creativity, most of the children who go on to become creative geniuses had been instructed by a teacher, usually a parent or other close relative, of much more than routine competence.

4. Language instruction is built upon the infant's own spontaneous gestures and utterances. Virtually all other systems of instruction require the learner to conform to the conventions of the subject to be learned. With a baby, however, one instructs by responding to its cooing, crying, or babbling with language, thereby gradually but relentlessly shaping native impulses. This characteristic may profoundly influence the results of instruction. It also serves to tie together the two parts of the present argument. Since language instruction appears to be so integral with the infant's spontaneous impulses and gestures, it would probably serve to affirm the infant's sense of self, resulting in small but cumulating additions to the level of self-esteem. By contrast, most other systems of instruction, which require the learner to adapt to an alien system of conventions, may cause small but cumulating deficits of self-esteem.

It is conceivable that a system of instruction for music or mathematics or other subjects could be constructed, as language is, out of the learner's spontaneous activities. In music, for example, the instructor could begin by responding to the infant's pitch and rhythms as if they were musical notes and shaping them as one does with language. Similarly a system of mathematical instruction could be built upon the learner's spontaneous counting activities.

The intention to build upon the learner's spontaneous actions appears to lie at the core of the Montessori method of teaching. Children are allowed to play with instructional toys which usually give rise to spontaneous mathematical, musical, and other types of activity. The teacher is trained to base his or her teaching on these spontaneous activities. Although this is an excellent idea, it is not able to capture many of the characteristics of language instruction in the family setting. It takes place only at certain hours of the day and only when the child has reached school age. The instructor may be at least routinely competent in the Montessori method but only routinely competent, if that, in the special area of music, mathematics, and so on. Finally, the teacher is a stranger, at least at the beginning of instruction, rather than being someone, like a parent or other relative, to whom the learner is already strongly attached.

The ideal teacher for a budding genius would be a close relative who is gifted in the area of instruction, always available because of living in the same abode, who uses the learner's spontaneous acts as the basis for instruction. Also ideal would be the presence in the home of one or more back-up teachers, so that at least one teacher would be always available.

If we look at the families of the greatest composers, these conditions were usually met. Of course there is no way of knowing in detail their methods of instruction. Most of the greatest composers had at least one close relative who was a gifted musician: Bach, Beethoven, Bizet, Brahms, Chopin, Dvorak, Gounod, Grieg, Ives, Liszt, Mendelssohn, Mozart, Puccini, Rossini, Scarlatti, Schubert, Stravinsky, and Vivaldi. It would appear from their biographies that these composers had access to instruction from at least one gifted musician during infancy and early childhood. However, there are three composers who appear to be exceptions: Tchaikovsky, Verdi, and Wagner. I could find no obvious indication that there was a gifted musician available to them from the time of their births. Judging from these three exceptions, it would appear that although access to a gifted teacher from birth is strongly correlated with the appearance of genius, it is not a necessary condition. I will return to this issue after the discussion of self-esteem, below.

One last comment on musical instruction must be made with respect to Mozart, one of the most prodigiously gifted of the great composers. Like most of them, in his earliest years he had access to more than one competent musician. His father, Leopold, was a performer, composer, and teacher of music; and his older sister, Nannerl, a gifted performer. Of great interest for my argument, there is evidence that his father may have been extraordinarily gifted as a teacher of music. His manual of instruction for the violin, now almost two-hundred-years old, is still the standard text for that instrument. The vitality of his written teaching at least suggests that he may have also been a supremely competent teacher for his son.

The fifth characteristic which may differentiate instruction in language from instruction in other fields is the nature of the response to the learner's progress or lack of progress. In language acquisition in infancy, at least, the instructors seem to concentrate on rewarding correct speech rather than punishing error. Many parents seem to regard each new word as a miracle, often completely disregarding errors. One does not expect infants to know how to speak. We feel no contempt for their errors. (This is in contrast to our native reaction to the difficulties foreign adults have with our language.) At least in the earliest years of instruction, the young learner is not ridiculed for making errors. Perhaps this is one of the reasons for the remarkable effectiveness of learning in language and the ineffectiveness of most other kinds of instruction: early language use may be almost completely free of shame.

In this section I have suggested that the methods that lead to language acquisition are vastly richer than other kinds of instruction. They begin at birth and are virtually continuous during the child's waking hours. They are carried on by a close relative who is extraordinarily gifted in the use of language. One or more back-up teachers are also usually available to ensure continuous training even in the absence of the primary teacher. Language instruction in infancy and early childhood is also intensely interactive, with the learner getting virtually instant feedback on her or his fluency. I have also suggested that language instruction in the family is built upon the shaping of the learner's native impulses rather than the acquiring of new ones. This method may lead to high levels of self-esteem. A fifth characteristic may also build self-esteem: the overwhelming prevalence of positive, rather than negative, feedback in the early years of language acquisition. There seems to be a moratorium on criticism in the initial response of adults to children's early efforts at language.

The Real and the False Self

I introduce the topic of self-esteem and its relation to genius by referring again to Emerson's thought. He believed that self-reliance was the basic virtue because, he argued, at the core of every human is a self of unbelievable brilliance (1837, 18):

What is the aboriginal Self, on which a universal reliance may be grounded? What is the nature and power of that science-baffling star, without parallax, without calculable elements, which shoots a ray of beauty even into trivial and impure actions, if the least mark of independence appear? The inquiry leads us to that source, at once the essence of genius, of virtue, and of life, which we call Spontaneity or Instinct. We denote this primary wisdom as Intuition, whilst all later teachings are tuitions. This aboriginal self is the origin of intuition, and therefore of inspiration, of effortless genius.

Emerson points out that one aspect of genius, the completely accurate perception of reality, is totally involuntary:

Every man discriminates between the voluntary acts of his mind and his involuntary perceptions, and knows that to his involuntary perceptions a perfect faith is due. He may err in the expression of them, but he knows that these things are so, like day and night, not to be disputed. My willful actions and acquisitions are but roving; the idlest reverie, the faintest native emotion, command my curiosity and respect. Thoughtless people contradict as readily the statement of perceptions as of opinions, or rather much more readily; for they do not distinguish between perception and notion. They fancy that I choose to see this or that thing. But perception is not whimsical, but fatal. If I see a trait, my children will see it after me, and in the course of time all mankind—although it may chance that no one has seen it before me. For my perception of it is as much a fact as the sun.

If all humans have access to boundless intuition and perception, according to Emerson, why is not everyone a genius? The answer he gives is that with few exceptions, everyone is terrified by the specter of being deviants from the collective vision of reality that is held in the community. We conform out of shame.

A man must consider what a blindman's bluff is this game of conformity. . . . most men have bound their eyes with one or another handkerchief, and attached themselves to some one of these communities of opinion. This conformity makes them not false in a few particulars, authors of a few lies, but false in all particulars. Their every truth is not quite true. Their two is not the real two, their four not the real four; so that every word they say chagrins us and we know not where to begin to set them right.

Conformity to the popularly held version of what is real and what is possible blinds most individuals to their own inner visions. *Only that person whose self-esteem is so high that he can withstand social rejection will be able to propose new solutions to new problems.* Emerson's formulation of this issue is so lengthy that I have separated and enumerated the main components (emphasis added).

[1]   To believe your own thought, to believe that what is true for you in your private heart is true for all men—that is genius. Speak your latent conviction, and it shall be the universal sense; for the inmost in due time becomes the outmost, and our *first thought* is rendered back to us by the trumpets of the Last Judgment.

[2]   A man should learn to *detect and watch that gleam of light which flashes across his mind from within,* more than the lustre of the firmament of bards and sages.

[3]   Yet he dismisses without notice his thought, because it is his. In every work of genius we recognize our own *rejected thoughts;* they come back to us with a certain alienated majesty.

[4]   Great works of art have no more affecting lesson for us than this. They teach us to abide by our spontaneous

impression with good-humored inflexibility than most when the whole cry of voices is on the other side. Else tomorrow a stranger will say with masterly good sense precisely what we have thought and felt all the time, and we shall be forced to take with *shame* our own opinion from another.

There are several important ideas in this passage, but they are not developed by Emerson, only mentioned casually in passing. Perhaps the most fundamental basis of his thought is found in (2): "A man should learn to detect and watch that gleam of light which flashes across his mind from within, more than the lustre of the firmament of bards and sages." The key word is "flashes." In the context of the sentence, he seems to be suggesting that the flashes are extremely fast, so fast, perhaps, that unless one trains one's self, it is almost impossible even to become aware of them, much less try them out.

This sentence may serve to clarify what is otherwise a confusing issue in the advice that Emerson gives us. He tells us to trust ourselves but, aside from this sentence, does not give us any further guidance about what self it is that we are to trust. In the passage quoted earlier he calls it the "aboriginal self" and identifies it with intuition and spontaneity. But we have many different types of spontaneous impulses and thoughts, some of which are notoriously unreliable. We need a more specific description of the type of spontaneous intuitive thought.

In the sentence about the gleam of light, Emerson may have provided an important clue to what he meant. He seems to have anticipated Freud's discovery of the unconscious, the "aboriginal self" as Emerson calls it. In order to teach his patients "to learn to detect and watch" the gleam of light, Freud developed the method of free association. He devised a practical workaday technique for giving his patients access to

their "aboriginal" selves. Once the patient discovered this access, therapy usually advanced more rapidly.

In systematically applying the method of free association, Freud made a discovery that went beyond Emerson. He found that most of his patients actively resisted acquaintance with their aboriginal selves (the repressed parts of their experiences). . . .

The patient's resistance, Freud later found, was due to unresolved painful emotion that was often also a part of the aboriginal self. I will return to the issue of unresolved emotion below, in the section on shame and guilt. . . .

Emerson's idea and Freud's later work teach that intuitive thought is unsolicited and nonverbal, an "involuntary perception," to use Emerson's term; second, it appears and disappears so rapidly as to seem instantaneous; and finally, it is always the *first* thought, rather than the second, third, or later thought, that is unedited and uncensored and therefore uncompromised by bias. The unsolicited first thought appears always, "invariably" to use Freud's word, to be the most inclusive, complex, and original of our thoughts. (But this is not necessarily true; Emerson was careful to state that intuitive ideas always need to be tested in reality.)

Einstein, when he sought to explain the origins of his creative ideas, often hinted at these characteristics. He usually explained that ideas did not come to him in words but in "images." The greatest of the chess masters also explain their deliberation in a similar way, not in words or moves but in fluid images that come to them involuntarily. Like Einstein, they struggle in their descriptions because they are attempting to describe a nonverbal process in words. . . .

If we return to Emerson's passage, a second idea is suggested in (1), "To believe your own thought, to believe that what is true for you in your private heart is true for all men—that is genius." This statement makes a connection between self-esteem and genius. It evokes the idea, in the strongest possible terms, that what differentiates the genius most strongly from other, ordinary persons is not talent—no mention is made of that—but self-esteem. Emerson seems to suggest that for the genius, his or her unique vision does not lead to a feeling of alienation from others, of being "different," that is, a freak, as is usually the case, but of feeling connected with others in that what is true for you is also true of all others. In the discussion of the relationship between self-esteem and shame below, I suggest how such an extraordinary high level of self-esteem might come about.

One last thought in the original passage, (4), is in need of elaboration. I refer to the last part of this sentence, about the "whole cry of voices" being on the other side. The implication is that the person who expresses his or her unique vision will be persecuted for it. This sentence again implies a connection between genius and self-esteem. In this case it is implied that one will need a high level of self-esteem in order to withstand the cry of voices. The case of Galileo affords a familiar example. The tragic lives of the mathematician Georg Cantor and the physicist Boltzmann are less familiar. Relentless criticism of their work, which was far advanced over that of their contemporaries, drove Boltzmann to suicide and Cantor to the insane asylum. Emerson's paragraph appears to comprehend, in a single glance, the whole situation of the genius—his inner turmoil and his place in society. . . .

Self-Esteem: Coping with Shame and Guilt

One last reference to Emerson evokes another aspect of genius—single-minded dedication to one's work: "I shun father and mother and wife and brother, when my genius calls me." Once again the image which Emerson evokes refers to a high level of self-esteem, in this case, the absence of guilt. I suggest that self-esteem rests upon a very specific process, the management of shame and guilt, and that this process, in conjunction with the development of talent, gives rise to genius.

I have been using the term "self-esteem" as if its meaning were self-explanatory. Actually, there is no agreed-upon definition of this idea. The nearest thing to be found in the literature is the idea that level of self-esteem concerns the degree to which one has positive feelings about oneself. Although this idea is a good place to start, since it concerns feelings rather than thoughts or images, it is much too vague. It does not tell what kind of positive feeling: joy, love, pride, interest, thrill, and so on. In order to proceed further with the theory of genius, I discuss one particular feeling: shame. I define self-esteem as freedom from chronic shame.

Even a child who has no wish to express a unique vision, who wishes merely to be conventional in every possible way, must run a gauntlet of potentially shaming situations. The problem that the child faces is of almost inexpressible magnitude: in order to become an acceptable member of a community, she must learn a myriad of conventions and execute them in virtually perfect manner, as if each were second nature. There is a further characteristic of the job at hand. The child must learn to suppress her understanding that most of these conventions are completely arbitrary. The question "Why do we kiss on the lips rather than rub noses?" or a similar question is tolerated from a three-year-old, but in an older child it already is taken as intimating frivolousness or worse. These conventions "go without saying"; that is, they are sacred. Even to notice the arbitrariness of conventions, much less make an issue of them, invites ridicule and ostracism.

Rapid learning of a large mass of conventions makes errors inevitable. Mispronouncing a word is as much a part of learning as pronouncing it correctly, yet each error invites scorn or ridicule. (In a family I know, one of the members is still being teased about the time she thought that a friend of the parents named Dennis was a dentist.) A repeating error, such as lisping, stammering, or stuttering, creates a nightmare of ridicule. Language errors are particularly rife. There are millions of details of pronunciation, inflection, grammar, syntax, and nonverbal gesture that must be performed, letter perfect.

There is a further twist to language that must seem almost diabolical to the learner. On the one hand, the correct use of language requires creativity. As already indicated, one often needs to invent new linguistic solutions for new situations. A vexing problem faced by children, however, is that some of their inventions are accepted but others are ridiculed. . . .

THE SHAME CONSTRUCT

. . . A useful place to start is to compare shame with a much less complex and much more prestigious affect: guilt. In most cases, the feeling of guilt is evoked by a specific and quite delimited act or failure to act, for example, to forget one's spouse's birthday or to scream at one's helpless infant. The thread which seems to be common to the actions or inactions which produce guilt is that they all involve the possibility of injuring another. Whether one person steals another's purse or curses or berates him in public, the victim has been injured.

When a child misunderstands a word like "Dennis," however, or invents a motive for soccer players, no injury has occurred. Harmless errors of these kinds do not produce guilt in the perpetrator but a different emotion: shame. The possibility that one could injure another assumes a potent, powerful, *capable* self. Making a gross error raises a question about the *adequacy* of the self, its basic worth: If you could make an error like that, are you really a person like me, or are you some kind of freak that need not be taken into consideration?

When one feels guilt, one's self feels *intact*. In feeling shame, one experiences what must be the most vertiginous of all feelings, the *disintegration of the self*, or its potential for disintegration. It is for this reason that guilt is infinitely more prestigious than shame. Guilty persons may even feel pride (the reverse of shame) that they are feeling guilt: it shows that they are basically moral persons; that is, they have intact, capable selves.

A vast ocean of errors is built into the child's existence. These errors, for the most part, are unavoidable, as is the normal shame that is the result of making errors. What may be avoidable, however, is to have innumerable experiences lead to *chronic* shame.

Shame is probably the most intensely painful of all feelings. Each person has spent what feels like an eternity of time and effort in constructing a competent, valuable self. The threat of losing that self may be more painful than the threat of losing one's life. In all cultures and historical eras, personal disgrace usually leads to extreme measures, even suicide.

There are two further premises about shame which need to be discussed before I return to self-esteem and genius. Many readers might agree that shame is a profoundly painful emotion but will assume that it seldom occurs and, when it does, one is fully aware of it. I am assuming, on the contrary, that shame is ubiquitous, not only in the lives of children but also in adult life, and virtually invisible. How can one be consumed with shame and still not be aware of it? To understand this issue, I will again review the concept of "unacknowledged shame" and the two forms this type of shame takes: "*bypassed* shame" and "*overt,* undifferentiated shame" (Lewis 1971).

According to Lewis, there are two opposite paths that one can take in order to avoid noticing the feeling of shame: one can bypass the feeling, swallow it, so to speak, so that one does not feel the pain at all (except for one extremely brief instant, when the shame is initially evoked). Although by following this path, one manages to decrease substantially the *intensity* of pain, at the same time the *duration* is increased. The shame is experienced as obsessive ideation or speech. During episodes of compulsive thinking or speaking, one experiences little feeling. On the contrary, one may be aware of an absence of feeling, of blankness or emptiness. Bypassed shame takes the form of too much ideation and too little feeling.

The other form, unacknowledged shame, the overt, undifferentiated type, leads to the opposite experience, too much feeling and too little ideation. One is so flustered by the threat of incompetence (paralysis, disintegration) that one is unable to observe and analyze what is happening. "I feel like a perfect idiot" is one rendering. "Embarrassment," "humiliation," and "mortification" are examples of words used to describe overt shame; "bashfulness," "shyness," "modesty," and "discomfiture" are less-intense but longer-lasting variants.

Many of the commonly used references to undifferentiated painful feelings appear to be shame experiences, or mixtures of shame with another emotion, such as anger: awkward, uncomfortable, foolish, silly, strange, and "in a stew" are examples. In adolescent terminology, one is "bummed," "freaked," or "weirded out." These words appear to be substitutes or euphemisms for shame, just as there are many euphemisms for sexual and "toilet" terms. Shame, like these other functions, appears to be subject to taboo (Scheff 1984).

The discussion so far has focused on shame as a *response,* a stereotyped biopsychological response which is virtually omnipresent in human communities. To describe shame further, it is necessary to shift to the *stimulus* that is common to all situations in which shame arises. This stimulus seems to be social in character: shame appears to be the stereotyped emotional response to a threat of loss of connection to another person or persons. This element is fairly obvious in most cases of overt, undifferentiated shame. One becomes painfully embarrassed and flustered when one "loses face" in public: caught in a lie, a gross error, or caught unawares by an obvious trick (we feel humiliated that we "swallowed it hook, line, and sinker" without a trace of redeeming suspicion).

In bypassed shame, the social source is less obvious since this experience often arises when one is alone. Here is a characteristic moment described by a male college student:

> I am on campus, walking to class. On the way, I am remembering an earlier conversation with a great deal of pleasure. I believe I made a good impression on this woman that I am interested in. But then I remember a remark I made about her ex-boyfriend. At the time I felt witty saying it, but suddenly I saw it from her point of view. I felt like a turd. I kept re-playing that scene, even when I was sitting in class, thinking what I might have said instead.

The obsessive replaying of the scene suggests that this experience involved bypassed shame. It occurred when the student shifted from his point of view to that of the woman. This shift exposes the social nature of the stimulus to bypassed shame. It occurred not in social interaction in the real world, as overt, undifferentiated shame usually does, but in imagined social interaction in the "internal theater," the interior dialogue that goes on in our minds.

The stricken feeling of shame indicated by the phrase "I just felt like an idiot" may occur in actual social interaction. Just as likely, it can occur in solitude, when one is reenacting a transaction from memory or inventing a meeting with another which has never taken place, and may never take place—imagining a conversation with "the man on the street" or with Shakespeare.

In interior dialogue, we are very often engaged with some other person, whose image we create for an inner enactment or reenactment: one's spouse, son, or daughter, boss or subordinate, or even one's self in some other guise, older or younger, in one or another of one's many hats or disguises. This internal theater often results in emotional responses. When we imagine the other as approving or accepting ourselves, we bask in the glow of self-generated pride. When we imagine the other as critical, contemptuous, or scornful, we roast in the hell of self-generated shame or guilt.

EMOTION AND CREATIVITY

The last step in describing the relationship of genius and self-esteem concerns feeling traps (Lewis 1971). Normal emotions—fear, anger, grief, and shame—are usually quite short-lived, a few seconds perhaps. They ordinarily are crisis responses. Referring to anxiety, Freud suggested that it has a "signal function"; it is an interior warning that something is wrong. If normal emotions are short-lived, how is it possible that one may be constantly angry, frightened, and, especially for our purposes here, ashamed? Chronic shame states are significant because they are probably the basis of what is called low self-esteem: one is usually not proud of one's self but ashamed.

The concept of the feeling trap may explain what otherwise might seem to be a paradox: emotional states which are virtually life long. Feeling traps occur when one has an emotional reaction to one's emotional reaction, and another reaction to that reaction, and another and

another, and so on, ad infinitum. Panic seems to be one outcome of a fear spiral: of being frightened that one is so afraid. In fear panics, people may stampede like animals, inadvertently killing each other, or, as in the case of voodoo death, die of anoxia. Being ashamed of being ashamed is another spiral that has runaway possibilities: "What an idiot I am (how shameful it is) that I should get so upset (ashamed) over something so trivial." One outcome of this spiral, stage fright, can reach such proportions that the victim is paralyzed in mind and body.

In interpersonal relations, the lethal feeling trap seems to be the shame-rage spiral, of being ashamed that you are angry ("How could I be so angry at someone who loves me? What a monster I am.") and angry at self or at the other that you are shamed: "You asshole. Don't stand around moping over your ego. Get your ass in gear." The anger may be directed at the other rather than one's self: "It's all your fault. You made me feel bad." This particular spiral may be experienced as humiliated fury (e.g., the "wronged woman")—anger bound by shame. This state may not be represented in consciousness, however. Frequently it is not experienced at all since it has been going on so long as a virtually automatic response. Another possibility is that it is experienced as the absence of any feeling at all, as blankness or emptiness.

Another of the isotopic representations of shame-rage is intermittent but lengthy bouts of resentment, jealousy, or guilt. These are all molecules of the same two atoms, but with the anger pointing in different directions. . . . In chronic jealousy, the anger may be pointed at the putative rival or at the love object or at both. In guilt, the anger seems to be pointed back at the self. One is enraged at the self for injuring another and, at the same time, ashamed both of one's actions and of being so enraged ("out of control").

Is there any possibility of escaping from a feeling trap, once caught up? The most common gambit used in daily life seems to be the attempt to talk one's self out of it, which seldom works. Telling one's self "You should be ashamed of being so upset at something so trivial" only sinks one deeper in the trap. In psychotherapy, a frequently used technique is to try to get the victim to express or discharge his anger. This seldom works either because it ignores the shame component of the trap. A common reaction is to become embarrassed (shamed) by the "artificiality" of showing anger when you are "not really mad," which is another variant of feeling that one's anger is not adequately justified, or feeling guilty about being loud or "selfish."

One method which almost always dispels shame is laughter, good-humored or affectionate laughter. This idea is very much in accord with popular belief that laughter relieves embarrassment. Lewis (1983) has shown that it is also supported by Freud's analysis of wit and laughter, although he does not make the idea explicit. Retzinger (1985, 1987) has shown that it is also implied by McDougall's analysis of laughter, although, like Freud, he does not make the sequence explicit.

If one laughs good-naturedly when shame is evoked, it will be quickly dispelled. If one does not laugh, one is often faced with unpleasant after effects. Usually the shamed person will blush or attempt to hide (cover face with hand, look away, try to leave the scene, or at least imagine he has left) or begin to talk or think obsessively. This is the setting for entry into a feeling trap. A common sequence is to become angry or hostile toward the other who is perceived as shaming one, then to feel guilty that one is angry, then to feel ashamed that one is so upset, and so on.

Good-natured laughter, if it occurs immediately when shame is evoked, avoids entry into the spiral. If it occurs when the spiral is in operation, it ends the cycle. Apparently when one laughs during a shame-rage spiral, the dispelling of the shame, which was binding the anger, allows the anger to discharge also. In her video studies of resentment, Retzinger (1985, 1987) has investigated the effects of laughter on anger. In the episodes where laughter occurred during the recalling of a resentment-laden memory, facial flushing and body heat, which are the markers of anger discharge (Scheff 1984), occurred simultaneously with the laughter. Retzinger showed that the frequency, intensity, and duration of verbal and facial anger expressions decreased dramatically after laughter.

THE LAUGHING GENIUS

Having reviewed the concepts of unacknowledged shame and the shame-rage feeling trap; I return to genius and its relationship to self-esteem. I have argued that for genius to appear, the bearer must have extraordinarily high self-esteem, be able to catch his or her first thoughts in flight, and have the confidence to develop and express these thoughts. There are probably two paths which lead to this level of self-esteem. The first path concerns humane treatment: the budding genius may have undergone less humiliation than others and therefore spent less time in shame-rage spirals than the less gifted. . . .

It seems likely, however, that the development of ways of managing shame would be far more important in the development of self-esteem than the extent to which one was treated with respect or contempt. Shame seems to be an unavoidable aspect of the human condition, even for those who are fortunate enough to have been treated well in most of their relationships. The gamut of errors through which children must pass in learning their culture, and the shame which results, has already been mentioned. A second universal source of shame is that love is always ambivalent. Intimate relationships are invariably a source of frustration, and therefore of anger, as well as fulfillment, and a source of shame as well as pride. That is, intimacy inevitably leads to a situation in which one is rejected or feels rejected, a basic source of shame.

If, as has been argued here, shame is unavoidable, then self-esteem must rest on effective ways of dispelling shame. The most effective way of dispelling shame, I have suggested, is through laughter. If this is the case, the great geniuses should have been laughers. . . .

Although it is difficult to test the laughing-genius hypothesis with written biographies, it might be possible in interviews with living artists and scientists. I think that the laughing hypothesis probably is much more relevant to a certain type of creator, which I have termed the "easy" creator. These creators work very rapidly and with little revision. Goethe wrote *Werther* in 24 days; Nietzsche . . . wrote *Zarathustra* in 30 days. I suspect that creativity is extraordinarily rapid with this type because there is freedom from self-censure and therefore access to the aboriginal self. Schubert and Mozart were certainly composers of this type, and also the mathematician John von Neumann (the person most responsible for the invention of the computer). By investigating the nature of the emotional lives of these creators, and particularly the amount and quality of their laughter, it might be possible to clarify some of the issues that have been discussed here.

CONCLUSION

This paper has outlined a rudimentary theory of genius. Creative intelligence may arise out of two interrelated processes, the development of extraordinary talent and the growth of extremely high levels of self-esteem. Extraordinary talent, whether or not it also involves genetic inheritance of talent, also requires a system of highly effective instruction. The model for this system of instruction may be the kind of language instruction children receive for the first five or six years. The formulation of this model raises what may be an important question for investigation: In what ways is early language instruction different from all other types of instruction, and do these differences account for the creativity that occurs in the correct use of natural language?

The second process in the growth of creative intelligence may be the development of high levels of self-esteem. I argue that self-esteem is essentially freedom from chronic shame. This type of shame is usually unacknowledged. It is virtually invisible because it appears in multiform guises. The basic mechanism of chronic shame, it is argued, is the feeling trap, which may convert emotions, normally brief, into life-long states. Finally it is suggested that chronic shame is most effectively dispelled by good-humored laughter. If this is the case, we should expect to find the genius, especially the easily creative genius, to be a laugher.

One final question: Is there any reason to believe that one or the other of these two processes, the one involving talent, the other, self-esteem, is in any way more important than the other in the appearance of genius? No doubt they are equally important in the lives of most geniuses. However, it seems possible, for theoretical reasons, that the development of self-esteem may be more important. It is possible that the early growth of high levels of self-esteem may allow the potential genius to find the effective instruction needed to develop extraordinary talent. This is one way of interpreting the three deviant cases—Tchaikovsky, Verdi, and Wagner—who do not appear to have had early access to a musically talented teacher. This possibility, like the others suggested here, awaits future research for clarification. . . .

NOTE

1. Howard Becker called to my attention a comparison of schooling and language acquisition which parallels mine, in Paul Goodman, "Education of the Young" (1969).

REFERENCES

Boltzmann, Ludwig. 1899. "The Recent Development of Method in Theoretical Physics." *Monist* 11:229–30.

Chomsky, Noam. 1957. *Systematic Structures.* The Hague: Mouton.

_____. 1965. *Aspects of a Theory of Syntax.* Cambridge, Mass.: MIT Press.

_____. 1969. *The Acquisition of Syntax in Children from 5 to 10.* Cambridge, Mass.: MIT Press.

Cox, Catherine M. 1926, *The Early Mental Traits of 300 Geniuses.* Stanford, Calif.: Stanford University Press.

Emerson, R. W. 1837/1983. *Essays and Lectures.* New York: Library of America.

Feuer, Lewis S. 1982. *Einstein and the Generations of Science.* New Brunswick, NJ: Transaction.

Galton, Francis. 1869. *Heredity Genius.* Cleveland: Meridian.

Goodman, Paul. 1969. *New Reformation.* New York: Vintage.

Lewis, H. B. 1971. *Shame and Guilt in Neurosis.* New York: International Universities Press.

_____. 1976. *Psychic War in Men and Women.* New York: New York University Press.

_____. 1983. *Freud and Modern Psychology.* 2 vols. New York: Plenum.

Retzinger, Suzanne. 1985. "The Resentment Process: Videotape Studies." *Psychoanalytic Psychology* 2: 129–51

_____. 1987. "Marital Conflict: Case Study of an Escalating Quarrel." Typescript.

_____. 1987a. "Resentment and Laughter: Video Studies of the Shame-Rage Spiral." In Helen B. Lewis, ed., *The Role of Shame in Symptom Formation.* Hillsdale, NJ: Erlbaum.

Scheff, T. J. 1966. *Being Mentally Ill.* Chicago: Aldine (2d ed., 1984).

_____. 1984. "The Taboo on Coarse Emotions." *Review of Personality and Social Psychology* 5: 156–169.

SIGNIFICANT OTHERS AND SELF-DEVELOPMENT

21

Trans-Kin Undoing and Re-Doing Gender: Negotiating Relational Identity Among Friends and Family of Transgender Persons

Cameron T. Whitley

(2013)

While campaigning, on October 30, 2012, Vice President Joe Biden declared that transgender issues would be the "civil rights issue of our time" (Bendery 2012), a historic and controversial statement establishing a place for transgender equality in American politics. This statement marks a decade where transgender individuals saw expanding social and political recognition that was amplified by the disclosures of celebrities like Chaz Bono (Cher's son), Stephen Beatty (Warren Beatty's son), and Miss Universe Canada's contestant Jenna Talackova.

Existing scholarly work has focused directly on the transgender community, which is important, but it has largely ignored significant others, family members, friends, and allies (SOFFA) who must also contend with stigma and bias directed at the transgender community, as well as the emotional challenges associated with the transition of a loved one. They must do this with few resources and virtually no language to describe their experiences.

IDENTITY THEORY AND DOING RELATIONAL IDENTITY PERFORMANCE

While theoretical and empirical scholarship addressing the experiences of significant others, family members, friends, and allies is limited, there is a wealth of sociological research that provides the theoretical basis for this study. Specifically, I ground SOFFA relational identity formation in concepts from the symbolic interaction tradition. Mead (1934), Cooley (1902; 1983), and Blumer (1937; 1998) laid a foundation for understanding identity formation, development, and self-presentation through social interaction. Identity theory, which grew out of this tradition, maintains that the individual self and society is constructed and reinforced through social interaction (Blumer 1980; Stryker 2002). Because this theory asserts that identity is formed and reinforced through social exchange, performance, or "doing" in the context of gender, this is the ideal framework to situate a discussion of how SOFFAs deconstruct and reform their relational identities in relationship with a transgender loved one.

Since social environments dictate our relations with others, when the perceived sex of a loved one changes, or we are asked to acknowledge the transgender status of a loved one through social cues such as language, the familiar social script changes as well and we must negotiate and manage a new possibly unfamiliar role and set of displays, which may create role conflict.

REFLECTED APPRAISALS AND STIGMA AS MEDIATORS IN RELATIONAL IDENTITY DEVELOPMENT

Cooley's (1902) concept of the "looking-glass self," or what Mead (1934) termed the "reflexive self," plays an important role in SOFFAs' relational identity development, where both reflected appraisals and stigma mediate how effective a SOFFA will be in "undoing" and "redoing" gender as a means to negotiate a changing relational identity. Reflected appraisals, what we think others think about us, are not always positive. While these perceptions may impact our behavior and ultimately alter some of our identities, other identities may be slow to change or may even be immutable (due to power or resources). One identity that may be impossible to alter without ending a relationship is the relational identity a SOFFA has with a transgender person. In this instance, the SOFFA must consider how his or her identity is based on the connection with their transgender loved one. This involves a careful and calculated assessment of past interactions as a means of intentional undoing and redoing of gender in future interactions. For instance, the SOFFA may need to adjust to a pronoun shift and name change when addressing the transgender person, as well as changes to the loved one's outward presentation and reception in society. This adjustment is mediated by the feedback and stigma the SOFFA endures during this process.

Since transgender individuals have been stigmatized across most cultures, with society by and large identifying "transgender" as an undesirable trait, individuals in relationships with transgender persons are likely to experience stigma as well. However, stigma across relational identities (SOFFAs) is expected to be unique, so that the mother of a transgender child experiences stigma differently than a significant other, though there may be parallel themes. Additionally, it is likely that the closer the SOFFA is to the transgender person, the greater the effect stigma will have on the SOFFA's identity. While SOFFAs do not experience the same level of stigma that transgender people face and cannot internalize this stigma as transphobia, stigma can increase the likelihood of self-deprecation or hatred in all individuals and may be associated with internalized homophobia if a significant other's sexual orientation is challenged. The internalization of stigma could also manifest in restricted self-disclosure or problems with coming to terms with the transgender status of a loved one, the inability to "undo" and "redo" gender.

To bring these theoretical concepts together, imagine a mother of a transgender child who has chosen to disclose her child's transgender status—and as a result display her identity—to a group of friends. In the dramaturgical tradition, this outward disclosure would be considered a "front stage" performance designed to publicly deconstruct former gender perceptions of her child (undoing), while simultaneously reconstructing perceptions of her child's new gender (redoing). Over time, as the mother discloses to various audiences, she will receive social cues about the disclosure (her performance) and the acceptability of the undoing and redoing gender process; based on these cues, she will imagine how people perceive her, her role, and the associative display of that role. As the "front stage" performance ends, the mother will assess her perception of her audiences' responses. This assessment period is considered a "back stage" activity where the mother reflects on her disclosure, performance, and audience feedback.

If she believes her performance was positively received, she will be more likely to repeat it, perhaps with greater confidence, meaning she will be more likely to continue to become more comfortable with her child's transition. If, on the other hand, she perceives a negative reaction from her audience, she will be more likely to question her role and associated display. In this example, reflected appraisals and social stigma mediate the mother's ability to process through "undoing" and "redoing" gender in the construction of her relational identity, which ultimately impacts her acceptance of her child. Complicating this dynamic is how connected the mother feels to the group to which she performs her identity. If there is a strong connection and this connection informs other components of her identity, then she will be more likely to internalize the positive or negative appraisals and incorporate them into her sense of self. For instance, if the mother is involved in a religious community that does not accept transgender people, then she will be more likely to internalize these negative perceptions. This may result in the rejection of her child's transgender status and ultimately rejecting her relationship with her child.

Although SOFFAs I interviewed shared uniquely personal stories, three primary relational identity themes surfaced in the analysis: sexual orientation, social role, and religion. Much like the coming out of lesbian, gay, bisexual, and transgender individuals, the potential loss of family, friends, religious communities, and so forth weighed heavily on SOFFAs as they decided to remain in or end their relationship with a transgender person.

SIGNIFICANT OTHERS

Changing one's sex when in an intimate relationship alters the social perceptions and expected gender norms of the relationship, forcing the nontransitioning partner to engage in a relational identity change in order to stay in the relationship or to make a decision to reject the relationship. Reflected appraisals and social stigma are integral components in how significant others negotiate challenges to their identities and how these challenges manifest in the acceptance or rejection of a transgender loved one. More importantly, while significant others may "undo gender" by resisting normative gender constructions in order to accept their transgender partner and confront challenges to their existing sexual orientation, they also may use inventive measures to reconfigure normative gender dynamics "redoing gender" within their relationships. Significant other interviewees fell into two distinct categories: those who entered into a relationship before their partner identified as transgender, and those who entered into a relationship after their partner identified as transgender.

Those who entered into a relationship with a transgender person prior to their partner coming out and decided to remain in the relationship after their partner had started to transition often experienced intense internal and external struggles with their sexual orientation. For example, Lisa, who was married to a newly out transgender woman, reported:

> I'm not gay. I have gay friends, but I wouldn't consider myself to be gay. When he transitioned things changed. It was really hard for me. I don't want to be gay, but he used to be my husband and now he wants to be my wife. . . . How does one deal with that? . . . I try not to think about it too much because I love him. . . . Initially it was just the cross-dressing and you can hide that, but you can't hide your husband changing his sex.

A key issue in Lisa's relationship was how to support her partner's transition while also validating her own identity. In relation to this, she mentioned the need for social recognition of her identity and not just the recognition of her partner's transgender status. In other words, she did not want her identity to be based solely on her partner's transition, but she felt that because she wanted to stay in her marriage people often assumed she was "secretly" gay. Her family and friends also struggled with her decision to remain in her relationship; in fact, many encouraged her to reconsider this choice. She talked about this external pressure making her feel "confused," "frustrated," and "overwhelmed" about her sexual orientation. Additionally, she worried about being able to validate her partner's identity, while not identifying as "gay." As an act of "undoing gender" Lisa was intentionally engaged in the deconstruction and reconstruction of her perception of, and relational interactions with, her partner while also trying to resist traditional definitions of her changing relationship, an act of "undoing" and "redoing" gender that could be considered both "normative resistance" and "inventive pragmatism" (see, e.g., Pfeffer 2012).

Similarly, significant others who identified as lesbian, gay, or bisexual prior to learning about their partner's transgender status also experienced challenges to their sexual orientation and sought ways to "undo" and "redo" gender. Most often these individuals mentioned a fear of community rejection. Lara, who identified herself as a "transsensual femme," reported:

> I had fought so hard to be seen as a high femme lesbian. . . . Femmes are already invisible in the lesbian community and I felt like I would be even more invisible if she transitioned to he. I came across the term transsensual femme. I couldn't really call myself a lesbian anymore, because the people I was most attracted to were trans guys, but I wasn't straight either.

Because of language flexibility within some queer spaces, Lara was able to validate her identity through the use of a newly constructed term. Lisa noted that she received validation of this term from friends and from her partner. Specifically, she shared that her partner felt validated in his identity because her identity honored his process. This is an ideal example of the "undoing" and "redoing" of gender as an act of dual validity to deconstruct normative gender dimensions and reconstruct them into something that validates both partners.

Significant others who met their partners after they transitioned and/or came out faced unique identity challenges as well. Although all reported sexual orientation as an identity factor, sexual orientation in this context was often related to a couple's desire to be out or open about a partner's transgender status versus remaining "stealth" or not disclosing. Additionally, other identities and roles were made more prominent over sexual orientation concerns. An example of this conflict is found in Brianna's story.

Brianna, who identified as heterosexual, chose not to disclose her partner's transgender status to her family. "I wouldn't tell them [my family]. My family is Catholic and Mexican and they wouldn't understand. . . . They might even think I was a lesbian." Brianna went on to discuss how her partner was welcomed into the family and that disclosing his status would have "tarnished that relationship." For Brianna, and others who entered into a relationship with a transgender partner after coming out, other identities were made prominent.

As Brianna hinted to in the narrative above, religion became a key factor in assessing how her community would accept or reject her transgender partner. In another example, Marcy, who was married to a cross-dresser, was "displeased" with her husband's transgender "revelation." She could not rationalize her husband's desire to occasionally wear women's clothing and her own deeply held religious beliefs. Although she expressed love for her husband, she felt that she had no choice but to leave him after 11 years of marriage. She explained, "For me it is about

religion. . . . I don't think God is ok with it and I know my church is not ok with it." Marcy's choice to end her relationship was marked by an assessment of how her religious community would view her situation, adopting these reflected appraisals as part of her own understanding, and then using them to develop an understanding of the self. For some, as was the case with Marcy, the external pressure could not be reconciled with the desire to remain in a relationship with a transgender loved one, so the relationship ended. This is a prime example of how reflected appraisals and stigma mediated Marcy's ability to "undo" and "redo" gender in the context of her relational identity. An added dimension is the prominence of religion that served as a forefront identity, on which all other identities were based.

Common among significant others was the recognition that their perceived sexual orientation was relationally connected to their partner's transgender status. This meant that, regardless of how a significant other identified, when their partner chose to transition, their sexual orientation was put into question. This relational identity made significant others hyperaware of how others perceived them, and reflected appraisals and social stigma facilitated how, and if, they were able to negotiate and make meaning out of their partner's transition. While some were able to construct new terms for their identities, engaging in "undoing" and "redoing" gender, many felt marginalized by their partner's transgender status and concerned with how they would find their voice in their partner's transitional journey. Concerns over sexual orientation were present for both gay and straight individuals, while experiencing a challenge to one's religious identity was only mentioned by a handful of people who identified as straight and who were involved in congregations that did not accept lesbian, gay, bisexual, or transgender individuals.

FAMILY MEMBERS

Although family members did not mention their sexual orientation being compromised or "challenged" when coming to terms with the transgender status of a loved one, they did mention sexual orientation as it related to their transgender loved one. A common theme among parents was to note that as their child transitioned, their child's sexual orientation also changed. While most admitted that their child's sexual orientation did not directly change, as they were still attracted to the same sex or gender of individuals they had always been attracted to, their changing sex or gender meant that their perceived sexual orientation had changed. Michelle, the mother of a transgender male child, noted: "Alicia was a lesbian. . . . Before Alicia came out I dreamed about her wedding . . . buying her a big dress and all. Now my son, Mike, is getting married to a woman. . . . He went from being gay to straight." Michelle reported a recognition that Mike's attractions had not changed, but that she had to adjust to a new set of social expectations influenced by his sexual orientation and transgender status. She continued: "Raising a son is just different. There are different things you want for a son compared to a daughter. . . . I had to change my expectations." This relational identity was a central theme for family members, where identity as a parent, sibling, etc. is directly related to the sex of the transgender individual and dictates how family members relate, socialize, and raise that child.

For instance, Elizabeth, who was informally interviewed, reported: "At birth she was a girl, for 20 years she has been a girl, thinking of her as a boy is really hard. . . . People know I had a little girl. How do you 'come out' as a parent of a transsexual child?" When probed about her pronoun use, Elizabeth reported that she is still adjusting to the shift in pronouns and that it is often easier to refer to her child with female pronouns while talking to others, but she intentionally uses, or tries to use, male pronouns when directly addressing her child. When friends ask about her child, she still often uses female pronouns, as she reported that she does not know how to "come out" in ordinary conversation to acquaintances. Additionally, Elizabeth noted that when considering whether to reveal her child's trans status, she looks for cues that her audience will be accepting. Similarly, Halley, a mother of two gender-variant children, explained: "I had a boy and a girl, now I have two boys. It's different and it's hard to explain."

Repeatedly parents shared their awareness that transness was an undesirable trait in society and that transgender persons face social stigma. Because of this recognition, parents were concerned with both how others perceived their parenting skills and how their transgender children would be treated. All nine parents interviewed reported that they feared being blamed for their child's transgender status, and that they had encountered stigma as a parent of a transgender child. However, they also experienced guilt when they chose not to explain their child's transgender status to friends and family members who asked about their child. The awareness and overall concern with the perceptions from others mediated how parents engaged their child's transgender status. Those who received social support were better able to "undo" past gender perceptions and "redo" their associations, while those who received little support struggled with self-blame and social stigma.

One of the clearest representations of this is found in Mark's discussion of his relationship with his transgender sibling:

> She was always my sister. Now she is my brother. How do you tell your friends that you don't have a sister anymore? I don't like to deal with their questions. . . . Why should I have to be the one to talk about this? I think I will always think of her as my sister. . . . She gets mad when we use the wrong

name, but it's hard to call your sister a girl's name for your whole life and then use a male name. She doesn't even look like a guy.

The second most common relational identity theme, mentioned by ten out of thirteen family members interviewed, was religious identity. Similar to significant others, family members struggled with how they would maintain their religious identity or affiliation while also being supportive of their transgender loved one. James, the father of a transgender child who was informally interviewed, reported that he and his wife had severed their relationship with the Catholic Church when their son came out as a transgender woman. They knew their congregation would not understand, and after years of searching and coming to terms with their son's decision to transition, they reported that "we chose our child over the church." At first they did not attend a church at all, but they eventually found a home in an open and affirming congregation, though they no longer identify as Catholic. Some of the words James used to describe this transition included "hurtful," "frustrating," "painful," "exhausting," and "depressing." While not identifying as Catholic, James asserted that his family still follows some Catholic traditions like not eating meat on Fridays during lent. James described this simple act as "grounding" his family in their cultural faith, while also seeking to find a supportive community with which to worship. The need for positive affirmation and religious group acceptance was so important for James, and he and his family joined a church that would support them.

Friends

Of the friends who were interviewed, twelve out of thirteen had been friends with a transgender individual prior to transition. Like family members, friends were not overtly concerned with their sexual orientation; however, interviewees did report being concerned with how the transition of a friend might change their relationship with that friend, should romantic feelings develop. As Jessica noted, "When Mark became a guy, I was worried because you know, guys and girls can't be friends, not without romantic feelings on one side." Jessica explained that once Mark started to transition the process was gradual and that she and their relationship had time to adjust, but that her current boyfriend, who does not know about Mark's transgender status, is often suspicious of their relationship.

When discussing how their identity had changed in relation to a transgender loved one, friends mentioned the need to assess their relationship in terms of social roles. For instance, Josh reported that when his friend told him that he would be transitioning to she, he wondered if she would still be interested in sports. He recounts, "I don't have girlfriends. When he told me, I was shocked. . . . We played hockey together and [other] sports. . . . I don't like girl stuff and I didn't think he did." What this quote emphasizes is how Josh thought men and women should be in the world. For Josh, men occupy a certain role, which involves an interest in sports; women occupy a role as well, but not the same role as men. Josh went on to explain that at first it was hard to come to terms with, but over time he learned that his friend had not changed much. "He [She] was still the same, he [she] still likes sports and girls." The end of this statement is interesting; although he was not concerned with his own attractions changing, Josh did not want his friend's sexual preference to change either, even though without a preference change, society would classify his friend as a lesbian. When pressed about it, he stated: "I didn't want him to be gay." When asked why this would concern him, Josh stated: "He [She] might check me out and that would be weird, but he's [she's] not gay."

After a few minutes, he said: "She's kind of gay, like a lesbian or something." In this last statement, Josh had changed pronouns for his transgender friend, acknowledging that she was interested in women and also identified as a woman. When asked about the use of various pronouns, Josh asserted that "it's like thinking about two different people. When I talk about him before, he was just a guy and when I think about my friend now, he's a girl." He expressed that he does not know what pronoun to use or how to talk about his friend's transition to others, but that he often worries about being offensive. Josh, in his process to come to terms with his friend's transition, is actively engaged in "undoing" his perceptions of his friend as male, while also "redoing" the gender script so that it he perceives and interacts with his friend as female.

Though most of the friends interviewees maintained their relationships, a select few felt betrayed in their friendship. While some reported that this feeling had abated with time, others continued to have negative feelings about the transition. Religious identity served as the primary mediating factor for those who continued to struggle over the transgender status of a loved one. Jamie, a self-described "lifelong friend" of a transgender person, who was informally interviewed, agreed to share some of her online postings from her personal blog, which were made six months prior to our interview. She posted that her friend was not meant to be a guy and that she loved her friend, but their relationship had been a lie. She also noted that she believed her friend needed to make peace with God and rely on God to resolve her identity confusion. When asked about her relationship with her transgender friend, she reported that they were still in communication, but that she still could not reconcile her friend's decision to transition with her own religious beliefs. Eight out of twelve friends mentioned religious identity during their interview. For most, religious identity was

something they came to terms with, making statements like "God told us to love everyone" or "It is not my place to judge." Still, the coming out of a transgender loved one pushed many friends to evaluate how their friend's transgender status fit into their understanding of religion. This negotiation process was often managed through social interaction. Sylvia, who identified as a friend and ally, reported: "I talked to my pastor about it [her friend's transgender status]. I think God wants us to love all people." Sylvia reported that what was difficult for her to reconcile was the idea that God made a mistake. Yet after careful consideration, lots of prayer, and discussion with others in her religious community, she was able to reconcile her own faith with the knowledge of her friend's transgender status. What assisted in this process was her membership in a congregation that was open and affirming and the positive affirmations she received from others who supported her and her transgender friend.

Conclusion

SOFFAs actively engage in the act of "undoing" and "redoing" gender as they negotiate their own relational identities when coming to terms with the transgender status of a loved one.

A common theme among family members and friends was concern over social roles and expectations as they relate to their transgender loved one. Parents alluded to this in regard to the gender socialization they imparted on their children, with a key concern being how to relate to a transitioning child. Friends reported that they experienced and had concerns about the social roles and expectations connected to sex and gender in their friendships, suggesting that what it means to be in a same-sex or -gender friendship is different than what it means to be in a mixed-sex or -gender friendship. Both parents and friends were concerned that their relationship with a transgender loved one would change as their loved one transitioned. Many of these concerns stemmed from worries that the likes and dislikes of the transgender person would change or that the transgender person's sexual orientation would change, posing relationship challenges. Religion was only a concern when the SOFFA's religious identity or affiliation posed a barrier to accepting a loved one's transgender status.

All interviewees reported a dialectical process, where they communicated with others to make meaning out of their changing relational identities. Similar to other marginalized communities, SOFFAs used their "front stage" performance to gauge acceptance. The information they received from their audience when presenting their SOFFA status along with social stigma mediated their ability to "undo" and "redo" gender in the context of their relational identity. Given that transsexuality is generally viewed as an undesired trait in society, SOFFAs reported that stigma from external sources (family, friends, community members, and religious affiliations) hindered their ability to make meaning out of their own identities and to come to terms with the transgender status of a loved one (Whitman, Cormier, & Boyd, 2000). For example, parents described the difficulty in articulating their child's transgender status to friends and family members in their communities. This became especially difficult when reconnecting with lost friends, as inevitably the friend would ask about their son or daughter, forcing the parents to consider disclosing their child's transgender status. SOFFAs' ability to negotiate one or all of their relational identities mediated the process of acceptance of the transgender loved one's status and the SOFFA's acceptance of their own shifting relational identity.

The process SOFFAs take to come to terms with the transgender status of a loved one, mediated by reflected appraisals and social stigma, has far-reaching consequences for how they will be able to negotiate their own identities and make decisions regarding their relationship with a transgender individual. We know that support networks are extremely important for transgender persons, so understanding how SOFFAs are impacted by the transition of a loved one can assist in the development of educational resources and support networks for SOFFAs and transgender persons more broadly.

REFERENCES

Blumer, Herbert. 1937. "Social Psychology." Pp. 144–98 in *Man and Society: A Substantive Introduction to the Social Sciences,* edited by E. P. Schmidt. New York: Prentice-Hall.

———. 1980. "Mead and Blumer: The Convergent Methodological Perspectives of Social Behaviorism and Symbolic Interactionism." *American Sociological Review* 45(1):409–19.

———. 1998. *Symbolic Interactionism: Perspective and Method.* Berkeley: University of California Press.

Cooley, Charles H. 1902. *Human Nature and the Social Order.* New York: Scribner's Press.

———. 1983. *Human Nature and the Social Order.* Piscataway, NJ: Transaction Publishers.

Mead, George H. 1934. *Mind, Self, and Society: From the Standpoint of a Social Behaviorist.* Chicago: The University of Chicago Press.

Pfeffer, Carla A. 2010. "Women's Work? Women Partners of Transgender Men Doing Housework and Emotion Work." *Journal of Marriage and Family* 72(1):165–83.

———. 2012. "Normative Resistance and Inventive Pragmatism: Negotiating Structure and Agency in Transgender Families." *Gender & Society* 26(14):574–602.

Stryker, Sheldon. 2002. *Symbolic Interactionism: A Social Structural Version.* Caldwell, NJ: The Blackburn Press.

West, Candace, and Don H. Zimmerman. 1987. "Doing Gender." *Gender & Society* 1:125–51.

SELF AND SOCIAL CONTEXT

"Korean Adoptees and the Social Context of Ethnic Exploration" looks at the experiences of Korean children adopted into White families. The authors find that some of these adoptees identify strongly with Korean culture and others do not. The difference depends on the time period in which they were adopted and whether they had educations that emphasized ethnic literacy.

"Identity Careers of Older Gay Men and Lesbians" invites us to take a step back a few years and look at the historical context of people who identify as gay and lesbian. Sociologist Dana Rosenfeld uses a life-course interview method to learn about the distinct historical conditions that influenced the experiences and self-understanding of older gay men and lesbians. In this article, the interviewees share their recollections of some of the significant events of the days when they were coming of age. Through their stories, Rosenfeld demonstrates the profound effects of social context on the direction and development of a "deviant" identity.

READING QUESTIONS

1. Consider the various ways in which family members are similar or different to one another in terms of social connections such as religion, political commitments, sexuality, and even ethnicity. How do these differences come into play across the lifetime and how might they affect family relationships?

2. Interview some of the elders in your life and ask them to describe the events and experiences that had the greatest impact on their beliefs, ideals, and commitments. Do their stories reflect a social context that might be shared by others who had similar experiences?

SELF AND SOCIAL CONTEXT

22

Korean Adoptees and the Social Context of Ethnic Exploration

Jiannbin Lee Shiao and Mia H. Tuan

(2008)

INTRODUCTION

Raised by white parents in a predominantly white town, I considered myself to be white. Others saw me differently, though people stared at me as if I were an alien, and children asked if I could see through my "Chinese, slant eyes." The worst episodes were when teenage boys surrounded me on the school bus and yelled obscenities and racial slurs at me. My race shouldn't have mattered, I thought, because it didn't matter to my friends and family. In college, new worlds of thought opened to me. Amid a boiling student struggle to create an Asian American studies program at Northwestern University, I began to see myself as an Asian American and to see my race in positive ways. That year, my sister and I decided to write to our birth mother.

The opening passage by Crystal Lee Hyun Joo Chappell (1997, p. 126), a 23-year-old Korean adoptee journalist, illustrates the salience of race and the role of personal exploration in ethnic identity development. In her narrative, Chappell contrasts a childhood of confronting mixed social acceptance with an early adulthood of exploring her ethnicity and developing racial self-esteem. Ethnic exploration is the personal examination of one's ethnic ancestry and its relevance for one's life. In more sociological terms, ethnic exploration marks a shift in attitude about one's ancestry from descriptive category toward a meaningful sense of membership.

In this article, we focus on early adulthood as a crucial life stage for the ethnic explorations of Korean transracial adoptees. The legal, social, and geographic separation from family that characterizes early adulthood (Rosenfeld and Kim 2005) distances Korean adoptees from their white families, potentially rendering them more visible as racial minorities and increasing the salience of their ethnic ancestry, while also granting them greater discretion over their personal involvement in ethnic activities. Even more than adolescence, this life stage initiates a higher level of exposure to ethnic status, racial stereotypes, personal independence, and opportunities for both experimentation and maturity.

Using the case of Korean adoptees, we illustrate how the social environment for this stage mediates ethnic exploration and its relationships to racial inequality and ethnic renewal.

Korean adoptees are a compelling case for studying the social implications of ethnic identity development because their ethnic explorations indicate how much the status of being nonwhite remains a barrier even when nonwhites are highly acculturated to majority-group culture.

In addition to indicating the salience of race, the ethnic explorations of Korean adoptees also provide a unique window into the social processes that sustain ethnicity because their socialization in white families gives them an exceptionally intimate familiarity with majority culture. They exemplify the transracial adoption paradox: "Adoptees are racial/ethnic minorities in society, but they are perceived and treated by others, and sometimes themselves, as if they are members of the majority culture (i.e., racially white and ethnically European)" (Lee 2003, p. 711). When adoptees leave home in early adulthood, they also leave an important anchor of their status as honorary whites, while their status as nonwhites remains unchanged and may increase in salience. We anticipate historical variations in both the motivations and effects of explorations, including especially a greater availability of opportunities and a wider range of options for more recent cohorts.

DATA AND METHODS

We employed data from life-history interviews with 58 adult Korean adoptees recruited from a gender-stratified random sample of international adoption placement records. We restricted the range of placement years in order to interview subjects who were 25 years of age or older at the time of the interview in 2000 and could reflect with sufficient distance upon their childhood and its salience for their adult lives.

We also sorted our subjects into three categories of early adulthood cohort by the decade in which they spent their first five years after high school: 1970s, 1980s, and 1990s. Had they been traditional college students, the subjects ages 40–51 would have started college no earlier than 1968 and finished no later than 1983. Similarly, the subjects age 30–39 would have matriculated starting in 1980 and graduated by 1993, and those age 25–29 would have entered starting in 1990 and left by 1998. By these approximate criteria, 26 adoptees spent their early adulthoods during the 1970s, 11 during the 1980s, and 21 during the 1990s.

CONDITIONS FOR ETHNIC EXPLORATION

The Necessity of Opportunity

Among the 16 nonexplorers without opportunities for exploration, we found three mutually exclusive groups: *(a)* three adoptees who had been traditional students during the earlier decades, two during the 1970s and one during the early 1980s; *(b)* eight adoptees who found employment in racially homogeneous workplaces and communities with few other Asians; and *(c)* five adoptees who came into substantial family or life responsibilities relatively early in their adult lives.

Traditional students during earlier decades. Marianne Townsend, a 45-year-old accountant, reported having had a long-standing interest in what it meant for her to be Asian, preceding even her years as a traditional college student. However, her first act of exploration did not occur until her thirties, on a Holt-sponsored trip to Korea. Her situation suggests the relative lack of opportunities for ethnic exploration confronting adoptees who attended college during the 1970s. Even by the 1980s, Jenine Peterson, a 38-year-old elementary schoolteacher, found that her small, homogeneously white Christian college in the Midwest had developed only modestly greater opportunities. In this setting, the only diversity programming she recalled was a small debate on interracial dating that solidified her suspicion that, unlike most of her follow students, she would not be finding a spouse during her college years. "This is the way I saw it. I don't know . . . if any of them at that school would have married me 'cause I wasn't the same race. They might date me, . . . but I don't know if they would have married me. . . . Like even now, I don't think I would be able to meet or marry someone in the Midwest, because I really believe that they're still more close-minded about that kind of thing."

Racially homogeneous workplaces and communities. Outside of higher education, other adoptees spent their early adulthoods in similarly homogeneous settings, demographically and culturally dominated in most cases by whites. For example, Jim Moreau's social and work contacts have remained as homogeneous as the small white town in which his parents raised him. When we asked Jim what he did after high school, he replied:

Jim: [I] pretty much worked. And I moved out with a bunch of friends and worked at different jobs. I did construction for a little bit. And then went and started painting. And I ended up, my brother got me a job working for this guy who was doing [body work at a] shop, . . . and then I ended up doing that. I have other friends, when we left high school pretty much everybody was doing one thing or the other as far as where they [all] ended up now. I have a couple friends, they're plumbers. And they did that in high school. And they ended up doing it as far as their businesses now.

Interviewer: This group of friends, are they all white?

Jim: Yeah.

Interviewer: So you're the only minority among all of them?

Jim: Yeah. Pretty much, yeah. . . . Most of us that went to high school are still around. I mean it's pretty much your usual. You get out of high school and you get people who graduate and go to college

and go their way, and some people usually stay.

Interviewer: During all this time how much interest did you have in exploring your racial or ethnic identity?

Jim: Not really that much [*laughs*].

Especially for working-class adoptees like Jim, an automotive painter, their social networks did not change much from the predominantly white communities in which they grew up. As a result, there was almost no language for ethnic identity because there were few resources to stimulate its development.

Substantial family and life responsibilities. For somewhat different reasons, the adoptees who started bearing significant life responsibilities during early adulthood also reported having very few contacts with other Asian Americans. These nonexplorers simply had no free time between school, work, marriage, and parenthood. Instead, meeting and marrying their significant others and finding full-time employment were far more crucial events in their early adulthood than ethnic exploration. Although Thomas Ryan, a 26-year-old probation officer, began as a traditional college student, he got married and after college went straight to work as a corrections officer.

Thomas: I went to . . . a small school, I didn't want to [go] to some place big. While I was going there I enlisted in the Marine Corps reserves for six years so we went to boot camp. And then I transferred down to community college so I could go for free. Got my associate degree in art, and then I went to State [college] and graduated in '97. I met my wife there at State. Our child was born in '97, so I was married my last year in college, so that made life a little more interesting. . . . Fortunately for me I was able to get a job straight out of college.

Interviewer: Some folks say that college is a time for exploring their racial or ethnic identity. Was that the case for you?

Thomas: Oh, not really. I think I was pretty much determined to get my degree. . . . I was kind of focusing on my major and things like that.

Interviewer: And then your getting married.

Thomas: Actually we got pregnant before we got married, so pretty much I had to hurry up and get my life on track.

Ultimately he finished his bachelor's degree, through a level of perseverance that precluded much consideration of his ethnic background.

The Relative Salience of Race and Ethnicity

Among the 10 nonexplorers who reported exposure to opportunities for exploration, we found two separate groups: (*a*) for five adoptees, race and ethnicity were not salient enough to warrant more than a casual curiosity, whereas (*b*) the other five adoptees did not explore their ethnicity because they were averse to other Asians and Asian Americans. In their minds, Asians were "the other," associated with negative characteristics and to be avoided when encountered. Revealingly, the nonexplorers who voiced this kind of sentiment were all in their forties and had experienced their early adulthoods in the 1970s.

Insufficient salience of race and ethnicity. Among those with a genuine lack of interest, two adoptees reported more important life commitments that overrode any interest in exploration. In brief, they were "on a mission" and could not be dissuaded. Jennifer Welch, a 41-year-old corporate manager, asserted that she was far more conscious of her relatively lower social class background while attending her elite East Coast institution:

Interviewer: So [college] was a vehicle really to move to the next stage.

Jennifer: Yeah. It was definitely not a social outing for me. It had a part in my future that I was serious about and didn't want to mess up on. I remember being told, "You know, you should have more fun while you're in college. It's your college years, for God's sake. Pretty soon you'll be in the working world." And I said, "You know, I don't care," you know? [laughs] "I'm here to do what I need to do." So I took challenging classes and I worked really hard that I'd not goof around at all in college.

Jennifer stayed at her elite East Coast institution and hewed to a strict academic path, with no room for ethnic exploration, with the result that she has no lasting friendships from this time in her life.

Others had less an alternative mission than a secure sense of community among whites. For Sherwin Wright, a 44-year-old finance manager, college brought him into contact with non-adopted Asian Americans whose affinity for coethnics surprised him.

Interviewer: How much contact did you have with other Asians in college?

Sherwin: Well, that was funny. In college I started having more contact with others and kind of started becoming aware. So I guess I always thought of myself as a white guy, more or less. . . . Then I got new friends, and they would even, you know, they would say stuff to me like, "Oh yeah, so what are you? Are you Japanese?" And stuff like that. So I became much more aware of my cultural background. . . . And I got to know some more Asian people and saw how they actually were kind of, you know, drawn to me just 'cause I was Asian. I just never experienced that in my life. That somebody was drawn to me or that I was somebody's soulmate because I was not a white guy [*laughs*] or something, you know? And that kind of surprised me.

However, neither this discovery nor his realization of not actually being white threatened his sense of self. In fact, he confidently tolerated being the target of ethnic teasing, albeit of a gentle variety, without feeling compelled to participate in order to distance himself from other Asians.

Yeah, I remember . . . a discussion, a bunch of us sitting around and, you know, all of the bull sessions in college. And the discussion was, "Do you think Sherwin is a white guy or what?" [*laughs*] I'm not kidding, and some of them said, "You know, I never really thought of him as . . . " or "Yeah, to me, he's like my little Asian friend" [*laughs*]. I mean a couple of them said that. It was kind of interesting to me. It was like five of us and a couple of them go, "You know, I didn't even think of it" [*laughs*].

Nonexplorers like Sherwin found an exceptional level of acceptance in a predominantly white community that simply made ethnic

exploration unnecessary. Although he experienced racial visibility, it was not a salient distinction in his early adulthood.

Aversion to Asians and Asian Americans. By contrast, the other half of the nonexplorers actively distanced themselves from ethnic exploration. Judy Hudson, a 42-year-old surgical dental assistant, provides a relatively mild example of this attitude in the form of her distaste for race-based association.

Interviewer: Okay, in college then, that's when you then encountered these Korean students. . . . Were they other Korean Americans, or were they international students?

Judy: I don't know. I mean they could have been Vietnamese, they could have been you know, Laotian, I don't know. I felt like a lot of them want to bond because of their race. [Whereas] to me when race is pointed out, it makes me feel separate. That's just me. I don't know why. But I think that if I were to pray about that, that God would tell me that we're all His kids, you know, no matter what our race is. That's how I come to terms with it.

While not entirely averse to contact with other Asians, she glosses the ethnic distinctions between Chinese, Japanese, Koreans, Vietnamese, and Laotians and prefers Asian Americans who aspire to greater acculturation or, more specifically, those who do not emphasize their being Asian. Indeed, her de facto white networks suggest that her disinterest in racial solidarity was more accurately an anxiety about being separated from whites, whom she regarded as making friendships in a more appropriate manner.

More strongly, Ross Green avoided associating with any Asians. The 42-year-old construction foreman reflected on his avoidance in early adulthood as the result of childhood experiences with racism and the inadequacy of his mother's response to them.

Interviewer:	And did you have any interest in exploring your ethnic or racial identity during that time?
Ross:	No. I was, you know, ashamed to be Asian at that point.
Interviewer:	Did you avoid Asians during that time? After high school?
Ross:	You know, probably if I saw them I probably would steer away from them.
Interviewer:	Did you have any particular feelings about seeing other Asians around?
Ross:	Yeah. It probably made me uncomfortable.

Ironically, his aversion coincided with his entry into military service, which he describes as more welcoming or at least more tolerant of Asians than his childhood geography. Although he had less reason to dissociate.

CONTEXT AND CONTENT OF ETHNIC EXPLORATION

The experiences of our 32 ethnic explorers suggest how social context shapes the level and form of ethnic exploration in early adulthood.

Nominal and Personal Exploration

Our analysis of how four of our adoptees became nominal explorers and personal explorers suggests the distal effects of historical period and institutional setting, respectively. Although the activities of our two nominal explorers resembled exploration, they had actually grown up with Asian American friends and simply continued their social involvements into their college years. Not surprisingly, they were young adults during the 1990s, when the Asian American population, especially its second generation, was larger than in earlier decades. One of these was Karen Granger, a 26-year-old bookkeeper, who had had Asian American friends since high school. During her interview, she laughed at our inventory of formal ethnic explorations as unnecessary activities.

Interviewer:	[It sounds as if] you've been in a number of different Asian American social groups, but not organizations.
Karen:	No, no.
Interviewer:	Have you ever attended a special program on adoptees since graduating from high school?
Karen:	What programs?
Interviewer:	Like, I mean even things like a motherland tour, or . . .
Karen:	Oh no, no, no, no.
Interviewer:	A conference, symposium.
Karen:	No.
Interviewer:	Have you ever attended a special program or event on ethnic or minority issues?
Karen:	No. [*laughs*]
Interviewer:	Have you ever been to Korea?
Karen:	No. [*laughs*]
Interviewer:	[But] you've obviously been in predominantly Asian American places before. Have you been to Koreatown?

Karen:	Oh yeah.
Interviewer:	What was it like to be in a place that was predominantly [your ethnic group]?
Karen:	I liked it. Yeah. You can just do whatever you want, and it's . . . I don't know, I just liked it. I like the environment. I like everything, you know?

Karen's affection for Asian American environments and the sense of freedom they afforded her are notable because she specifically refers to Korean-centered situations dominated by adult immigrants whose cultural expectations typically make many adoptees uncomfortable. Her experiences cast in relief the narratives of most other explorers who pursued formally organized ethnic exploration precisely because the opportunities for informal exploration were absent from their childhood geographies.

Our two personal explorers reported taking a college course not centrally focused on Asians or Asian Americans but with the opportunity to focus an assignment on the Asian adoptee experience. Their activities resembled ethnic exploration but actually focused on their adoption alone or primarily. Gabrielle Anderson, a 43-year-old notary public, used an assignment to examine her personal documents. "In college, in my speech class I did a paper on my passport. What it meant to me. And it kind of made me dig up feelings and everything. It's like, it kind of proved to me that that's who I am. It kind of reaffirmed that I was adopted, I guess."

Pursuing Social Exposure in College, Unequal Interactions, and Employment

Of the 19 who pursued any social exposure, seven adoptees stopped at a modest level, while 12 adoptees continued to a more substantial

level. Our data suggest that their institutional setting shaped their opportunities for intensifying their ethnic explorations. Of our 13 explorers who found their opportunities in college, nine became substantial explorers, while only four stayed modest explorers.

The modest explorers pursued some combination of taking a single course in Asian American studies, writing a paper on a Korean adoptee–related topic in a non-Asian-specific course, and participating in student networks that were unusually diverse but not predominantly Asian. Carrie Bennett, a 31-year-old therapist, had thoughtful personal reasons for taking an Asian American history class, which, however, did not lead to Asian American networks or further exploration as such classes did for the substantial explorers.

Interviewer:	What was your motivation for taking that class [on Asian American history]?
Carrie:	It almost seemed like, part of me really wants to know, and part of me, even now. . . . I feel like I need to understand, historically, how Koreans have been treated, or what's happened to them in this country . . . and other Asian groups. And at the same time, I feel like, I don't know [if] any of my ancestors . . . went through that.

Despite not having immigrant parents, much less Korean ancestors in the United States, Carrie felt drawn to learning about how the United States had treated Korean Americans and other Asian Americans. However, her perceived connection with other Asians had limits. Like other modest explorers, she experienced ambivalence about interacting with other Asians, especially within the context of the ethnic organizations on campus. Although Carrie found a greater comfort in the higher representation of Asian Americans around her, she saw joining the available Asian student organization as an entirely different step. In brief, the modest explorers appreciated their new proximity to nonadopted Asian Americans, but also kept them at a friendly distance. By contrast, the substantial explorers moved past an initial sense of discomfort and even bonded with other Asians over common experiences with racial issues.

When adoptees pursued deeper connections with other Asian Americans, they continued course work in Asian American studies, added course work in Asian studies, participated in predominantly Asian American social networks, and even joined Asian American student organizations. While sharing their explorations, they often reported shifts in self-perception involving the redefinition of American identity and a greater recognition of its racialization. Natalie Johnson, a 41-year-old business executive turned homemaker, recalls her opportunities for exploration during college as transformative. Despite an early curiosity about her Korean roots, by adolescence, she felt ashamed of looking so different from others. Her attitude changed immensely, however, after she entered college, where she met nonadopted Koreans and other Asian Americans. "So when I went to college, I studied Korean. I mean, I really got into it. . . . My freshman year, I studied Korean. Sophomore year I lived with two Koreans. . . . Yeah, I really got into it freshman and sophomore year. . . . I had a Korean boyfriend. I met a lot of Asian Americans, in my classes and stuff. And it's funny—it happened in almost every class—Asian Americans would just sort of gravitate together. It wasn't so much Korean to Korean, but, you know, a lot of the friends I made were Asians in college." As with other substantial explorers, a critical event for Natalie was taking courses that were related to her ethnicity or had a critical mass of Asian American students

because they connected her with ethnic social networks. Her white friends and family, however, became concerned about her exploration and excitement over something that was unfamiliar and foreign to them.

> And I remember my high school friends, who were all white. . . . They really didn't understand what I was going through, and they thought it was kind of weird. . . . Because to them, you know, I was just one of them. And they didn't understand why I was gravitating towards the Asians. And I got really into this Asian thing. There was a group—I forget what they're called—[maybe] Asian Student Union. . . . I joined. . . . and I even did this march against the Charlie Chan movie. It's the only protest march I've ever been in. I remember, then, my dad kind of scared me from it, saying, "Oh, they may be members of the ACLU or something. You might not want to . . . ." That kind of freaked me out. . . . But I was really in the exploring mood, and. . . . you know, what it was [was] just being around other Asian Americans.

Her father's caution reflects a parent's fear that his child was getting in over her head—in particular, with charismatic radicals who, at minimum, did not have her best interests at heart. Rather than seeing herself as being led astray, Natalie reflects on this period as a counterweight to earlier negative experiences that she once accepted as normal.

Interviewer: What do you think [was] the spark behind that [exploration]?

Natalie: [College] was a tremendous influence on me. . . . I took Asian American studies and. . . . I think that's where I really developed pride in being Asian. . . . It's partly in numbers, you know, there's strength in numbers. And meeting so many people who were, you know, they were never ashamed of it, and I don't know if they were teased or not, but it just gave me a lot of pride.

For Susette Morgan, a 29-year-old homemaker and administrative assistant, the child in question was her own son, who began asking questions about his father's mixed Peruvian and Chinese parentage. However, she set the same ground rules that her adoptive parents set on her childhood curiosity.

Interviewer: Since high school, have you. . . . started to explore your ethnic heritage . . . ? Or your adoptee identity?

Susette: I [explained] to Tim, my son, about his background. And he has some interest. Especially with the Chinese side. Because he has three different cultural, you know, he has the Peruvian, he has the Chinese and he has the Korean. And the Chinese is more what he wants to do. And the same thing as my parents said for me, or explained to me that, you know, you do what you want to do. But . . . if you really want something, *then you have to go get it yourself* [emphasis added].

This message suggests a peculiarly American mix of freedom and responsibility that conveniently defines parents' orientations to ethnic exploration (Waters 1990). They also resemble a cultural socialization strategy that Lee (2003) terms "child choice," which keeps lines of communication open within the family but also places the burden of exploration on the child. Like Susette in childhood, Tim was free to raise questions, but he would have to find any deeper answers for himself.

By contrast, peer interactions were pervasive in the opportunities that the substantial explorers found through employment at Asian-themed and Asian American–owned businesses (a Korean hotel, a Chinese restaurant, and a pan-Asian supermarket), where their employers and/or co-workers took them "under their wing." That none of these explorers were members of the oldest cohort suggests that historical change was a distal cause for the availability of these opportunities. For Melissa Garvey, a 29-year-old chiropractic assistant and office manager, becoming a waitress at a large Chinese restaurant opened the door to a new social world.

Melissa: I was very [receptive] to new stuff when it came to working there. Because I was like part of the family. At lunch time when we had our break—you know, most of the waitresses there are white, so they would just ask for . . . the American Chinese food . . . [whereas] the people in the back, the cooks, they actually made authentic Chinese food. They went all out, and I would always eat with them. . . . They made me eat with chopsticks. I cannot eat with chopsticks. So they would teach me how to do that. And, just eating the food, they wouldn't tell me what it was. They go, "No [just eat]." And that's when I started going over to Seattle with friends.

Interviewer: Just to hang out and stuff?

Melissa: Yeah. Hanging out, going over there. We would stay with their family or, you know, always just hang out in Chinatown, and. . . . hang out with only Asians. And so that was, it was just the first time doing that. And I was just slowly getting more comfortable. And just really liking it. Because they were great people to me. I mean, to this day I could call one up, and they would be there for me. I can't say that for some of my friends from high school.

In brief, Melissa became friends with her Chinese co-workers and followed them off the job into their social world.

Kerry Nowitsky, a 25-year-old computer support technician and student, spent his early adulthood first playing professional baseball in Japan before returning to the United States, where working at a pan-Asian supermarket connected him to the local Korean community. His experience abroad raised his consciousness of not "blending in" in the United States, where he was accustomed to being singled out for racial visibility; however, it was not until he returned to the United States and started working at the supermarket that he encountered Korean Americans.

Kerry: I met a couple of Korean kids out there, and just one day they were like, "Hey, why don't you come with us to X," and [this city is] not a very big town, you know, so the Korean community is pretty tight-knit. And I was so surprised in how accepting they were. . . . I wasn't really expecting that. I was kind of thinking, you know, they'll just be like any other people that I've ever met before, but any time I've run into a Korean person in this town they're always like, "Hey are you Korean? Come on in my house."

Interviewer: Do you mention that you're adopted?

Kerry: Sometimes, yeah. And they're always like, "Do you speak Korean?" And I tell them, "No." And they're like, "Why don't you come by, and I'll teach you." . . . Everyone's always trying to teach me Korean.

In their early adulthoods, Melissa and Kerry found themselves employed at workplaces with significant numbers of Asian co-workers. Their interactions provided them with opportunities to explore their ethnic identities by expanding their social networks. Like their counterparts in college, they remember their explorations as positive experiences that resulted in an appreciation and affection for a coethnic and/or panethnic community.

Exploring Cultural Heritage in College, Study Abroad, and Military Service

Of the 12 who explored their cultural heritage, only one stopped at a modest level, while 11 continued to a more substantial level, including three who also pursued social exposure. As with the pursuit of social exposure, our data suggest that both institutional setting and historical period shaped their opportunities for exploring their cultural heritage. The sole modest explorer and eight substantial explorers found their opportunities in college across all cohorts, but especially in the 1990s. Lisa Packard, a 26-year-old interior designer for a housing development firm, halted her explorations in early adulthood after a single Asian studies class, which she took primarily to fulfill a graduation requirement. Like the nominal explorers and unlike the remaining cultural heritage explorers, she had grown up surrounded by Asian Americans and felt little need to continue exploring her ethnicity.

By contrast, the substantial explorers continued their studies of Asian languages and/or the history of Asian nations and participated in other internationally oriented college programs, which in turn led most to travel to Asia, typically through study-abroad programs.

When adoptees traveled to Asia, they experienced a combination of culture shock, self-reflection on their identity as well as their adopted nation, and a welcome sense of "blending in" for the first time in their lives, in addition to confronting new perspectives on adoption.

Brandon Luebke, a 27-year-old rafting-trip guide, discovered Japan through language studies and international studies course work that ultimately led to a second major in international business. Despite extensive preparation, he experienced a shock that was not only cultural but also racial. In fact, his advance studies had encouraged a confidence that proved quite mistaken. Upon returning, his primary community did not shift to an Asian or Asian American network; however, he began to introduce his racial experience abroad into discussions within the international studies community. Brandon's new experience of invisibility abroad ultimately prompted a realization of difference at home. He became conscious of how race had multiple social meanings: one's appearance and its categorization; one's relative fit with a mental prototype of the category—that is, a stereotype; the demographic prevalence of his and other categories; and their relative association with the surrounding nation. In brief, his racial visibility became more salient as a result of his international experiences.

Exploring Asia but not Korea. Notwithstanding the salience of race, Brandon's study abroad in Japan raises the question of why he and other Korean adoptees pursued non-Korean explorations in Asia. One reason was simply that Korean language study and study abroad in South Korea were not options at many colleges, whereas studying Japanese was more popular, given Japan's stature as the leading Asian economy at the end of the 20th century. The ironic consequence of these historical geopolitics was a greater familiarity with Japan than with Korea among many of our adoptees. When we asked Brandon whether he felt more comfortable in Korea or Japan, his response initially hinged on his greater academic exposure to Japan.

Another, more personal reason was that Korea was not merely the nation of his birth, as it is for most Korean immigrants, but also the place that had "given him up" and made him an orphan.

> Yeah, when I went [to Korea during] my first time to Japan, I was living in Tokyo, and my parents, toward the very end of my stay there, flew out and we traveled around Japan for a little while and then flew to Korea. And we actually did go to the Holt agency in Seoul and looked at our files and everything and went to the adoption center that's right next to the agency there. So we were in Seoul for maybe three days, which was a very, very interesting experience because I'm Korean, and I look Korean, but I don't speak any Korean, and I don't know anything about Korean culture . . . to this day. *And even back then it was just as bad, if not worse. I didn't know anything* [emphasis added]. I knew Japanese, but all these people, they'd come up to me on the street, and they'd start talking to me and my sister as well. I don't know if it affected my sister as much as me, but I was weirded out by it, I was like, I can't speak anything in this country. I don't know anything, but I look—and I'm from "here," but I don't know anything about it. So it never forced me to want to say, "Oh, I'm going to learn a whole bunch about it," but in fact I think it kind of had the opposite effect, a little bit, as it kind of freaked me out enough where I was just kind of like, "Whoa, get [me] out of here!" [*laughs*]

Brandon wanted to return to Korea after achieving sufficient emotional distance because in the moment of his first visit, he felt only fear and dislocation. By contrast, Japan also provided cultural exploration and racial immersion, yet without personal significance and thus without demanding even deeper reflection about its implications.

Even so, upon arrival in Japan, Brandon found that his adoptive history remained unavoidable because his ability to blend into the crowd depended not only on his appearance but also his performance of its associated cultural expectations. His obvious lack of linguistic fluency prompted questions from locals, which typically led to his explanation of his adoption. We learned of this routine experience when we asked him about his relative consciousness of being Korean versus being Asian.

Brandon: That's a good question. I've never really thought of that before. Like do I consider myself Asian sometimes and then Korean at different times?

Interviewer: Right. . . . Does that differ, or is it basically just one thing for you?

Brandon: Growing up it was definitely just one thing. But . . . when I went over [to Japan], they thought I was Japanese. And then I opened my mouth, and they knew that I wasn't Japanese, and I'd say I was from America, and they were like, "No, you're not from America" [*laughs*]. I'm like, "No, I am, really" [*laughs*]. And they're like, "Well, so what's your story, like your parents aren't from America," and I'm like, "Well actually I am because I'm adopted." And they don't understand the concept of adoption at all. And so, like every time I met somebody new, I'd have to go into this, like, 10-minute

elaborate story of question and answer on what my background was. And then I always considered myself just Asian. It didn't really matter to me. You know, I was always considered, or I always considered myself just kind of one big lump along with my Vietnamese and Chinese friends. But when I went to Japan I was labeled Korean more often than I was American, right, so I thought of myself as being Korean for the first time in my life. Which has very big ramifications once you consider the bitter hatred between those two countries and whatnot.

In brief, his identity became more complex in an environment that did not casually lump Koreans with Japanese and where adoption by non-relatives remained an unusual occurrence.

Blending in. In their experiences abroad, other adoptees reported similar themes, above all the surprising privilege of racially "blending in." Diane Genovese, the 31-year-old director of an international visitor program, went to Japan to teach English immediately after graduation. Her two years there were spent in the popular Japan Exchange and Teaching (JET) program, which she remembers fondly.

Yeah. I went to Japan. I lived there from '95 to '97. Lived in a tiny town, 7,000 people in the entire village, and I was the English teacher. I taught kids from age 1 to 15, plus an adult class. And that was great, so interesting really. *And interestingly, I felt more at home in Japan than I've had just about anywhere else* [emphasis added]. And part of that, I think, is sort of the novelty of being in a place where people looked basically like me, which I've never really had. When I traveled, yes, but not to actually live. And it was sometimes a mixed experience because people would forget that I wasn't

Japanese and would expect me to know things that I didn't. Or expect my language to be better than it was. And things like that. But all and all, it was great, [and] I think that being Asian really [helped].

Whereas female adoptees encountered gendered expectations that they experienced as constraining, Christopher Hurley, a 51-year-old train engineer, encountered a flattering form of attention when he traveled through Asia.

Christopher: The very first time I went to Asia, I was like 24 years old, it's like prime of my age, I was really big and stocky. Everywhere I went, I drew a lot of attention. You know. When I went to Hong Kong, they just stare at you. And then when I went to like, one of the guys I met at the college there, I was using their weight room, he said, "You know what? You're the biggest Chinese I've seen." I said, "Well I'm not Chinese. I'm Korean." He said, "Oh wow." And then, when I went to Tokyo, and these cops, they saw me walking, they stopped and they asked me some questions. And I said, "Oh I'm trying to go here." And so they gave me a ride. They say, "You're a big Japanese." "I'm not Japanese. I'm Korean," Then when I go to Korea, these guys I met, they all want to arm-wrestle me and everything, you know?

Interviewer: Was it emotional for you to visit Korea?

Christopher: Yeah. You know what? When I saw the people, they all look like me. It felt kind of good.

Because his distinctiveness made him more masculine rather than less feminine, more a celebrity than an outcast, the attention actually accented his feeling of belonging.

Confronting cultural censure. However, not all of our adoptees' experiences abroad were positive. The experience of Stephanie Muller, a 27-year-old working in corporate finance, reveals the variation in adoptee experiences abroad. Unlike Brandon, she chose to visit Korea instead of Japan. Whereas he found the revelation of his adoption to be a repetitive but not unpleasant occasion for explanation and cultural translation, Stephanie was frustrated by the additional attention she received. Her narrative recalls the experience of cultural censure reported by nonadopted Asian American returnees: being questioned, challenged, and even denigrated for their weak or nonexistent linguistic abilities and general lack of cultural competence. In particular, her experiences are consistent with the observation that cultural censure tends to be more intense and negative in Korea than in other Asian nations (Kibria 2002b; Kim 2007). In addition, our adoptees sometimes encountered intense reactions to their adoptive status: expectations that they were seeking their birth mothers, negative judgments about their mothers' social background and moral character, and nationalistic feelings involving both shame and outrage. In response, Stephanie idealized the United States as more generous and egalitarian with respect to both adoption and gender roles.

Interviewer: So you go there, and it's total culture shock.

Stephanie: Absolute total cultural shock. . . . I ran into a lot of cultural differences like, I ran into, "You were adopted, therefore your mother must have been bad because she gave you up." So you are like less than dirt, they can be very hierarchical. . . . I spoke to some Koreans at school, and the concept of being abandoned . . . because I was female—I had no idea. I was just like, "Oh," and then I felt really insulted [*laughs*]. [Or] being abandoned because the mother's poor, or she was a teenage mom is more acceptable because I was a girl! And that's because of how I was raised. My mother raised me to be a very independent woman. You know, I can do anything I want. I could fly if I wanted to. . . . In America, "You're an adoptee from Korea, that's so wonderful." And it seems like, you know, I come from this family, we were all special because we were adopted. And then I go to Korea and like, "You're just dirt, your family must have been bad" [*laughs*]. When I came home. . . . I felt very lucky to be. . . . to have been adopted, and to be taken out of that environment where I would have been treated so poorly. [In the United States] if you are a girl or boy in our family, you're a part of our family. If you are adopted or not adopted, you're a part of the family.

Challenged to negotiate a status that would preserve her dignity, Stephanie characterized herself as the best of both Koreans and Americans, endowed with a genetic drive for excellence and raised with cultural independence and rationality.

I can see how [genetics] play such a . . . much bigger role than I previously thought. . . . These people have these traits and these attributes. . . . but I could see how my environment had changed that. . . . And being raised to be so independent, because they're very conformist. They're like sheep. And it used to drive me crazy, but you know, that's just the way they are. You can never change the way anybody thinks, but for a whole culture to be like that, I just thought it was real funny. I could see how my environment has changed me to be this free-spirited and independent and . . . not to be held back by any social norms, and feel that kind of pressure. But at the same time I can see where my drive comes from. Where I had to get straight As, where I had to be smart. Because everybody . . . I mean everybody there's literate. They're very intelligent people. They just are afraid to be different. So I started to see a lot of these things where genetically that's the only place it could have come from.

In light of the South Korean attitudes she faced, we suggest that Stephanie's claims about Korean culture and genetics were rhetorical efforts to use Western stereotypes of the East to counter the Korean association of adoption with low status and degradation.

Although her narrative bears similarities to those of nonadopted returnees in the literature, her adoptive status was uniquely salient to her experience and response. While nonadopted returnees face cultural censure, their reaction tends to be less extreme; instead they reject only parts of their homeland's culture, such as what they perceive to be a greater preoccupation with status distinctions, and they evaluate their immigrant family culture as a positive hybrid and develop affection for an ethnic American identity. By contrast, Stephanie repudiated Korean culture in toto in favor of American culture while finding ethnic pride in the one thing that South Korean prejudices did not denigrate—their shared genetic ancestry.

Despite their exploration of cultural heritage, most adoptees limited their cultural fluency to language acquisition and persisted in seeing Asians as the "other" (Said 1979). To some extent, this standpoint was conditioned by their peer context for exploration. Kirsten Young, a 29-year-old homemaker and nonprofit staffer, described a common milieu for international explorations—among adventurous white students interested in meeting the racially and culturally different other, rather than Asian American students seeking their familial or ethnic roots.

Interviewer:	Who were your closest friends . . . in college?
Kirsten:	Most of my closer friends were Caucasian. . . . They're the ones that introduced me to the international student organization. And that's how I became an international student advisor. And then I met a lot of Asians, a lot of people from Russia, Czech . . . mostly foreign. I had taken Spanish in college at the same time I was taking Chinese. When I was in my Chinese class, I think most of them were Caucasian. I think there might have been one Japanese girl in our Chinese class. And then in my Spanish class, they were all mostly Caucasian. . . . Most of [the minorities] were just exchange students.

Among the adoptees exploring their cultural heritage, Brandon Luebke was an exception for his reflections on the domestic implications of his experiences abroad. While all of his counterparts enjoyed the racial comfort of being in the majority for once, most responded by occupying themselves with the cultural differences that set them apart from other Asians and the commonalties that strengthened their sense of belonging with the Americans who populated their families and social networks.

Our three cultural heritage explorers who found their opportunities outside of college were not only substantial explorers but also on active military duty during the 1970s and 1980s. Service with the U.S. Air Force, Marines, and Navy in or near South Korea provided these adoptees with experiences highly similar to those reported by adoptees who studied abroad. Samantha "Sam" Cawthorne, a 41-year-old air traffic controller, narrated an account that echoed the above themes of "blending in" racially, standing out linguistically and culturally, and negotiating social acceptance.

Interviewer:	So you were stationed in Korea.
Sam:	Yeah. Right. I was stationed in the air force.
Interviewer:	What was that like, living in Korea for a year?
Sam:	Oh, well, for the first six months, it was kind of hard. But the last six months was a blast [*laughs*]. But the first six months it felt kind of weird, because the Koreans didn't really accept me . . . because I couldn't speak Korean. And that really made them mad.
Interviewer:	So people tried to speak to you.
Sam:	Yeah . . . they'd see me, and then they'd speak, and I couldn't answer them back. And then they would get really mad, and I tried to explain to them that I was

adopted . . . and it was like, uhh. It was really horrible. But then, . . . as they got to know me, . . . they realized that I was a GI [*laughs*] . . . and I had lots of stripes, and that I must be smart, because . . . I had lots of stripes [*laughs*]. That's what they said. And then they began to like me. And then, gosh, I was [*laughs*], five times I was offered to be, they wanted to marry me. Five different guys. Isn't that funny? [*laughs*] But my time there was a blast. I mean, it was great to see, I'd go downtown or go to the open market, and they all had black hair. And I'd go on the bus, and they all had black hair. I mean, that was . . .

Interviewer: You blended in.

Sam: Yeah. It was amazing. I'd go to the school rallies, and if I didn't open my mouth, . . . I didn't get stared at [*laughs*].

Interviewer: Whereas that wasn't the case in the U.S.

Sam: Oh! Oh! Of course not [*laughs*].

Despite similarities with the study-abroad participants, adoptees in the military like Sam also experienced Asia through the distinct lens of their institutional membership. Sam's military rank gave South Korean locals a reason to take pride in her despite the stigma attached to her adoption. While South Koreans may not have associated every adoptee with the U.S. military, the latter's visibility was a reminder of the Korean War and the subsequent inability of Korea to take care of its orphans without sending them abroad. In other words, while the U.S. military directly

shaped the exposure of adoptee officers and servicemen, its continuing presence also influenced the reception of adoptees who visited South Korea as participants of study-abroad programs.

Institutional Contexts for Ethnic Exploration

In combination with the results of the above section on the absence of opportunities for ethnic exploration in homogeneous workplaces, our analysis here suggests that higher education has been a critical context for adoptees to experience opportunities for ethnic exploration. Although our adoptees reported explorations in both college and noncollege settings, those in primarily nonschool settings had to work harder to pursue substantial exploration to the point of social or cultural immersion.

With respect to social exposure, student adoptees could take Asian- or Asian American-themed classes or join ethnic organizations and in the process gain social networks where they "blended in" visually or at least were not the only Asian individuals. To gain a similar level of access to ethnic networks, nonschool adoptees had to find employment in an Asian business, an opportunity that our adoptees did not report before the 1980s, or they had to have grown up in, or moved to, places with high concentrations of Asian Americans. If adoptees were not comfortable with social immersion, those in college could still participate in purely academic explorations, whereas nonschool adoptees had interactions with primarily small children who by nature were limited sources of information.

Relative to our adoptees in primarily school contexts, their counterparts who spent their early adulthoods in primarily nonschool contexts faced social environments with scarcer and arguably less approachable resources for exploration. If opportunities for exploration were available and they were not distracted by the challenges of starting their own families, they still confronted the dramatic choice of remaining within the same predominantly white milieu familiar to them from childhood or plunging into unknown situations either steeped in ethnicity or half a world away. In brief, this choice suggests the degree to which Asian people and culture were absent from their normal contexts and perhaps also the extent to which whites and white culture were dominant.

REFERENCES

Alba, Richard, and Victor Nee. 2003. *Remaking the American Mainstream: Assimilation and Contemporary Immigration.* Cambridge, Mass.: Harvard University Press.

Altstein, Howard, and Rita James Simon, eds. 1991. *Intercountry Adoption: A Multinational Perspective.* New York: Praeger.

Anderson, Stacey J., and Joel T. Johnson. 2003. "The Who and When of 'Gender-Blind' Attitudes: Predictors of Gender-Role Egalitarianism in Two Different Domains." *Sex Roles: A Journal of Research* 49:527–32.

Bloom, Allan David. 1987. *The Closing of the American Mind.* New York: Simon & Schuster.

Bobo, Lawrence, James R. Kluegel, and Ryan Smith. 1997. "Laissez-Faire Racism: The Crystallization of a Kinder, Gentler, Antiblack Ideology." Pp. 15–41 in *Racial Attitudes in the 1990s: Continuity and Change,* edited by Steven Tuch and Jack Martin. Westport, Conn.: Praeger.

Bobo, Lawrence, and Camille L. Zubrinsky. 1996. "Attitudes on Residential Integration: Perceived Status Differences, Mere In-Group Preference, or Racial Prejudice?" *Social Forces* 74:883–909.

Bonilla-Silva, Eduardo. 2003. *Racism without Racists: Color-Blind Racism and the Persistence of Racial Inequality in the United States.* Lanham, Md.: Rowman & Littlefield.

Brady, Henry E., and David Collier. 2004. *Rethinking Social Inquiry: Diverse Tools, Shared Standards.* Lanham, Md.: Rowman & Littlefield.

Chappell, Crystal Lee Hyun Joo. 1997. "Now I'm Found." In *Seeds From a Silent Tree: An Anthology,* edited by Tonya Bishoff and Jo Rankin. Glendale, Calif.: Pandal.

Charmaz, Kathy. 2006. *Constructing Grounded Theory: A Practical Guide through Qualitative Analysis.* London: Sage.

Choy, Catherine Ceniza. 2007. "Institutionalizing International Adoption: The Historical Origins of Korean Adoption in the United States." Pp. 25–42 in *International Korean Adoption: A Fifty-Year History of Policy and Practice,* edited by Kathleen Bergquist, M. Elizabeth Vonk, Dong Soo Kim, and Marvin D. Feit. New York: Haworth.

Clark-Ibanez, Marisol, and Diane Felmlee. 2004. "Interethnic Relationships: The Role of Social Network Diversity." *Journal of Marriage and Family* 66:293–305.

Cross, William E. 1978. "The Thomas and Cross Models of Psychological Nigrescence: A Review." *Journal of Black Psychology* 5:13–31.

Demarest, Jack, and Rita Allen. 2000. "Body Image: Gender, Ethnic, and Age Differences." *Journal of Social Psychology* 140:465–72.

Dhingra, Pawan. 2003. "Second-Generation Asian American Professionals' Racial Identities." *Journal of Asian American Studies* 6:117–47.

D'Souza, Dinesh. 1991. *Illiberal Education: The Politics of Race and Sex on Campus.* New York: Free Press.

Duster, Troy. 1991. "The Diversity Project: Final Report," University of California, Berkeley, Institute for the Study of Social Change.

Edles, Laura Desfor. 2004. "Rethinking Institute for the Study of Social Change, 'Race,' 'Ethnicity,' and 'Culture': Is Hawai'i the 'Model Minority' State?" *Ethnic and Racial Studies* 27:37–68.

Feigelman, William. 2000. "Adjustments of Transracially and Inracially Adopted Young Adults." *Child and Adolescent Social Work Journal* 17 (3): 165–83.

Feigelman, William, and Arnold R. Silverman. 1983. *Chosen Children: New Patterns of Adoptive Relationships.* New York: Praeger.

Gim Chung, Ruth H. 2001. "Gender, Ethnicity, and Acculturation in Intergenerational Conflict of Asian American College Students." *Cultural Diversity and Ethnic Minority Psychology* 7:376–86.

Glaser, Barney G., and Anselm L. Strauss. 1967. *The Discovery of Grounded Theory: Strategies for Qualitative Research*. Chicago: Aldine.

Glazer, Nathan. 1997. *We Are All Multiculturalists Now*. Cambridge, Mass.: Harvard University Press.

Goossens, Luc, and Jean S. Phinney. 1996. "Commentary: Identity, Context, and Development." *Journal of Adolescence* 19:491–96.

Gordon, Milton Myron. 1964. *Assimilation in American life: The Role of Race, Religion, and National Origins*. New York: Oxford University Press.

Grow, Lucille J., Deborah Shapiro, and CWLA (Child Welfare League of America).

Kibria, Nazli. 1999. "College and Notions of 'Asian American': Second-Generation Chinese and Korean Americans Negotiate Race and Identity." *Amerasia Journal* 49:29-51.

—. 2002a. *Becoming Asian American: Second-Generation Chinese and Korean American Identities*. Baltimore: Johns Hopkins University Press.

—.2002b. "Of Blood, Belonging, and Homeland Trips: Transnationalism and Identity among Second Generation Chinese and Korean Americans." pp. 295–311 in *The Changing Face of Home: The Transnational Lives of the Second Generation*, edited by Peggy Levitt and Mary Waters. New York: Russell Sage.

Kim, Nadia. 2007. "Finding Our Way Home: Korean Americans, 'Homelands' Trips, and Cultural Foreignness." Paper presented at the annual meeting of the American Sociological Association, New York, August 11–14.

Lee, Stacey J. 1996. *Unraveling the "Model Minority" Stereotype: Listening to Asian American Youth*. New York: Teachers College Press.

Lee, Richard. 2003. "The Transracial Adoption Paradox." *Counseling Psychologies,* 31:711–44

Portes, Alejandro, and Rubén G. Rumbaut. 1996. *Immigrant America: A Portrait*. Berkeley and Los Angeles: University of California Press.

Rosenfeld, Michael J., and Byung-Soo Kim. 2005. "The Independence of Young Adults and the Rise of Interracial and Same-Sex Unions." *Americans Sociological Review* 70:541–62.

Said, Edward. 1979. *Orientalism*. New York: Vintage Books.

Waters, Mary C. 1990. *Ethnic Options: Choosing Identities in America*. Berkeley and Los Angeles: University of California Press.

SELF AND SOCIAL CONTEXT

23

Identity Careers of Older Gay Men and Lesbians

Dana Rosenfeld

(2003)

C. Wright Mills (1959) once argued that biographical narratives are not just accounts of lifelong experience, but are significantly shaped both in form and in content by the ideas and values of the historical period in which they are embedded. How people experience their later years, for example, is strongly influenced by the historical context in which they came of age. This bears especially on their sense later in life of who and what they were and have become—their *identity careers*.

The ways in which identities are shaped by their historical context were strikingly impressed upon me during a recent study I conducted to explore the lives and experiences of older gay men and women (see Rosenfeld 1999). In 1995, I conducted open-ended, in-depth interviews with 50 self-identified gay men and lesbians of various class and ethnic backgrounds, who were aged 64 to 89 years. I identified subjects in the greater Los Angeles area by means of "snowball" sampling and conducted interviews in subjects' homes. I tape-recorded these interviews, collecting demographic information and life histories, which included accounts of current and future concerns, friendship and family networks, religious beliefs and practices, and feelings about the organized lesbian and gay communities.

As I started analyzing the transcripts from these interviews, I immediately noted how the emergence of gay liberation in the late 1960s and 1970s—which divided subjects' lives into an era in which homosexuality was exclusively constructed as a shameful stigma and a new period in which being gay was increasingly viewed as a positive identity—affected their recollections of sexual experiences and the identity issues that flowed from them. A central theme resonated throughout the interviews: These subjects were members of a cohort who formed sexual identities at a time of tremendous change, and they were now constructing narratives of life experiences that reflected just how much their identity careers were still being shaped by these events, even later in life.

GAY LIFE AND HISTORICAL CHANGE

Consider the climate for homosexuals who were coming of age or first considering their sexual identities in the early to mid-twentieth century. Throughout my subjects' youth and middle age, homosexuality was defined and treated as a medical, legal, and moral aberration. The medical establishment considered homosexuality to be a disease until 1973, when the nascent gay movement's lobbying efforts resulted in the American Psychiatric Association's vote to rescind this definition. Homosexuality was widely viewed as an unnatural existence devoid of healthy social, familial, or emotive ties. Indeed, throughout the 1950s and 1960s, medical and psychiatric constructions of homosexuality increasingly informed the popular depiction of gay men and women as isolated, immature, ashamed, and incapable of achieving either personal satisfaction or social integration. These images dominated the limited press coverage of homosexual life, and censorship of gay-positive texts and films kept homosexuals dependent upon a medical and popular literature that stigmatized them (Faderman 1991). These depictions were invoked and elaborated by the federal government during the McCarthy era (Nardi and Sanders 1994: 11), when homosexuals were constructed as security risks by the State Department and other federal agencies (D'Emilio 1983: 43–44). Federal policy toward homosexuality found a natural ally in state and local police, who had a long history of harassing gays and lesbians.

The construction of homosexuality as a pathological condition provided gay men and women with both an identity category in which to place their often-secretive feelings and a language with which to discuss and describe themselves and their position in society. This language, of course, was negative and stigmatizing. As a result, while some homosexuals embraced the stigmatized roles made available by the gay underground (Chauncey 1994), others saw their sexual desires as a condition to be suppressed, remaining single and celibate or adopting heterosexual marriage patterns. Yet others engaged in sexual, social, and emotional relations with other gay men or lesbians, understanding their homosexuality to be an aberrant condition which, while capable of being satisfied, nonetheless required them to pass as heterosexual. While the severe stigmatization of homosexuality was seen by these individuals as merited, they saw their persecution as avoidable through their own attempts at normalization. They condemned both the underground homosexual life that exploded in the post-war years and those immersed in it as unnecessarily legitimating stereotypes of gay men and women, which they figured invited the persecution of all homosexuals.

The civil rights and the New Left movements of the 1960s informed an emergent oppositional stance within the homosexual subculture, which began to formulate homosexuality as a valid identity to be openly embraced and enacted, rather than a stigmatizing condition to be hidden. Both the gay liberation and the lesbian feminist movements (Weitz 1984; Faderman 1991) of the early 1970s called for all homosexuals to condemn both the stigmatized understanding of homosexuality as well as those who continued to embrace this view, and to come "out of the closets and into the streets" (Young 1972) to live openly as gay men and lesbians. This position is the dominant ideology of lesbian and gay communities today.

(Homo)Sexual Identity Careers

My subjects were born between 1906 and 1931 and were aged 39 to 64 when gay liberation began to systematically challenge both the dominant stigmatization of homosexuality and homosexuals' adaptation to it. While most had identified as homosexual according to the stigmatized formulation of homosexuality, living relatively secret lives by passing as heterosexual in public, some had not then identified as homosexual at all, although many had had same-sex desires and relationships. The latter group encountered gay liberation and lesbian

feminism at a time in their lives when they were aware of their attraction to members of their own sex, but did not yet view themselves as gay or lesbian. The emerging formulation of homosexuality provided them with a new way of understanding and enacting these feelings, and they adopted the new homosexual identity that was now available.

When recounting their identity careers, these subjects often described "always knowing" that they were different. They spoke of being attracted to members of their own sex during their early years, often in childhood. When speaking of these early desires, many echoed 77-year-old respondent Manny's (pseudonyms are used throughout) statement that "I knew something was wrong with me all my life." Recognizing and evaluating inchoate desires were, for these subjects, coterminous aspects of the same project: to understand the nature of their desires and their implications for self. They described feeling bewildered about both the meaning of these desires (and, often, their own fulfillment of them) and their implications for identity and value. Brian, aged 74, for example, "kept thinking, 'Well, that's quite different. Is it something you outgrow?' I remember having that in my mind."

Some did not act on this awareness for years, as there was little in the air at the time that encouraged them to develop related identities. Susan, aged 75, reported that when she "was in high school, I was aware of certain girls. And I found myself attracted or interested. But I didn't do anything about it. I just, I was conscious of it. It was one of those things. I lived with it." Similarly, 72-year-old Tex's belief that a man could be attracted to him was "a phase [he] was going through" prevailed well into his marriage. As he explains, he

> was attracted to men, the more I fought it, the more I dreamed about it. I thought it was a phase that I would get over, but I didn't. I never tried to

put a name for it. I thought I was different. I didn't think anybody else felt like that except me.

Most, however, pursued these desires, still failing to understand their meaning for self. Many experienced their associations and relations as relatively unproblematic. While they "knew" that these were best enacted in certain contexts and not in others, pursuing same-sex relations while unaware of their severely stigmatizing "nature" allowed them to experience these connections as "natural." Jan, aged 68, noted, for example, that she

didn't label it because I didn't know there was such a thing as a lesbian, it was just the most natural thing in the world. I don't suppose I knew what a homosexual was. If someone had asked me: "I don't have a clue." As I told you I started dating a neighbor kid, even before I got involved with this woman. And I always assumed that I would marry and you know do all this stuff because that was what people did where I grew up.

Most subjects spoke of searching for accounts of these differences in textual and cultural representations and in others' remarks. For example, Rodney, aged 81, wrote to the editor and publisher of a homoerotic "muscle" magazine for advice to "determine where I stood in life." Jeannine, aged 66, and her female lover searched the dictionary for female versions of the word "faggot." Others described pondering their interactions and characterizations to uncover the nature and consequences of their desires. Without exception, the accounts formulated same-sex desires as a pathological yet curable condition. This discourse "explained" subjects' experiences to them in stigmatizing terms, and thus supplied a much-needed identity category. The interpenetration of these messages and responses can be seen in 66-year-old Sharon's account of

reading medical journals on how to deal with the brain because I thought I was crazy because of

being gay. I thought I was insane because it was not normal. Probably by the age of ten or twelve I was getting books at the library on Havelock Ellis and Kraft-Ebbing because I would look up the term homosexual—don't ask me how I found that word—but I would look up the term homosexual and would refer to notes. And it told about all the horrible things that the insane people did, so I thought that's what gay people did.

The stigmatizing discourse of the times provoked the challenge of making the self intelligible and, at the same time, preserving its value in the face of a devalued identity. Subjects described feeling caught between a need to understand and pursue their desires on the one hand and to avoid the negative implications of a stigmatized identity on the other. Recognizing and fulfilling sexual desires served to discredit them, making them subject to ridicule and rejection.

Distancing

Many found the implications of a stigmatized identity so severe that they worked to avoid interpreting their desires in its terms, managing the tension between their desires and the consequences of enacting them by distancing themselves from one, the other, or both. "Distancing" refers to the variety of ways in which subjects modified, weakened, or resisted the applicability of the term "homosexual" to themselves; these consisted of "putting it on the back burner," pursuing heterosexual relations, and cultivating a heterosexual identity.

Those who "put it on the back burner" made same-sex desire a background concern of significantly less importance to them than other interests, needs, and obligations, which, according to them, provided greater rewards. Ryan, aged 81, "would see men that I thought I liked, you know at a distance, and I would like to get better acquainted with them, but I didn't dare go any further than that, and I just let it go at that."

Similarly, Marge, aged 81, recalled "staying away from it."

> There was a female that everybody called "old dyke" because she was out and she had a girlfriend. She was almost like an outcast. [Also] conversation would come up with the kids that I would associate with and other people and they would speak of people like this, not only women but men, too, that were feminine. I knew I was connected with it, but I wanted to stay away from it because I did not want to be ridiculed. I didn't do anything about it. I went out with guys, you know.

For many, distancing included pursuing heterosexual relations. For example, Patricia, aged 77, "had boyfriends," Kate, aged 76, "occasionally would accept a date, usually fixed up by anxious family or anxious friends," and 81-year-old Ryan saw heterosexual relations as "the lesser of two evils." According to Ryan, in his teen years, he was

> semi-interested in girls. It was the lesser of two evils, let's put it that way. We would be going to parties or to dances and things like that, I enjoyed dancing in those days, and we enjoyed dinners and bake-outs.

Subjects said they had expected that the frustration of unmet needs and desires would be precluded or offset by replacing those needs with others which were more easily met and which presented no negative implications for self. After her psychoanalysis failed to "cure" her lesbianism, Kate sought to fulfill herself through her job. "I was also deeply involved in my school and my teaching, which was very satisfactory, very all-consuming. And the other stuff I put on the back burner."

For many, however, distancing techniques caused them to see themselves as without value or definition. Dan, aged 70, spoke of defining himself as "active neuter. No sex, nothing" while engaged in distancing. Deborah, aged 74,

explained that "I wasn't defining myself at all," and Kate considered herself "a mess, sexually, practically without identity." This distress led some to actively pursue a heterosexual identity, which they saw as providing a fulfilling family life on the one hand and protection from the harassment and ridicule homosexuals faced on the other.

They did this in one of two ways. Some entered conventional heterosexual marriages, less as a means of "hiding" their homosexuality than as a way to achieve a heterosexual identity that provided positive rewards. A few had married, only to have their homosexual desires emerge and coalesce during their marriages. Luke, aged 69, for example, accounts for his heterosexual marriage by stating that when he "met her I was trying to get away from gay life. I was trying to get out of being gay. I was trying to get out and raise a family and everything. I don't know. I just wanted a family." Mark, aged 71, married when he realized that the man he was in love with

> was more interested in what I had to give. Then along came June, my ex-wife. I decided that I was going to give up being gay. I figured that [there] just wasn't any future in it for me. We went to a dance, came home, I took her underneath the porch, I had sex with her. And then four months later, she says, "I'm pregnant." So I says, "Well, better get married." We got married and I gave up Joe. I was 28, 29.

Others constructed a kind of liminal heterosexuality by embracing the medicalized formulation of homosexuality as curable through therapy, which provided a positive and rewarded role and promised a future heterosexual identity. Rather than see themselves as permanently diseased, these subjects embraced the medicalized discourse's most positive version of "pervert"—s/he who is committed to a cure. Although immanently homosexual and thus stigmatized, this constructed them at the same time as adequately oriented to the medical establishment's norms and goals and committed them to achieving a normal life. Seventy-two-year-old Leonard, for example, sought therapy after being fired from the State Department for being homosexual.

> So I went to New York at that time, mainly because they had suggested that, you know, therapy in New York was the place. I was gonna get cured. I was in pretty bad shape. I went to therapy with this general idea in mind.

Embracing a New Identity

Several subjects who had had same-sex desires but who did not know how to interpret them described their first sexual or erotic contacts as clarifying these desires, learning how to fulfill them on the one hand and providing insight into "what they were" on the other. Dan, aged 70, for example, reported that he "still wasn't aware of anything" when, in his mid-twenties, he

> wanted to get rid of my glasses, so I went for eye exercises, and the guy giving [them] was gay. So, he started massaging my eyes and things and I was very attracted to him, and then finally he kissed me. And then I was in heaven, you know. And that's when I became aware, when he kissed me in New York.

Meeting and associating with other homosexuals either alone or in groups was key to subjects' interpreting their desires in a new light. At the very least, it showed them that they were not "the only ones in the world" and that there were venues for associating with others like themselves. Many searched for and patronized lesbian and gay bars to determine if they had anything in common with the other patrons. They spoke of feeling as though they belonged "there" ("there" being a subcultural homosexual world). Abby, aged 70, described this happening

> the first time that I went to a bar . . . I was 25. I think it was Bleecker Street, and it was the Swing Rendezvous was the name of the place. It was primarily women. As soon as I walked in there, I don't think it took me very long to realize that this is exactly where I belong. And that was my first introduction.

Subjects also explained how changing relational contexts inspired a reformulation of homosexuality and its relation to self. Many spoke of the emergence of emotional needs that could only be fulfilled through erotic or romantic relationships with same-sex partners. While they had initially limited their same-sex connections to sexual ones that did not, for them, implicate a homosexual identity, these new desires caused them to reexamine their sexual selves. While 75-year-old George, for example, "did homosexual things before," he didn't "realize" he was gay until

> that night that I told Jack. We were sitting in my car, holding hands. This is when I had this wave of emotion, and I turned and looked out the window and I said, "I want to tell you something." And he said, "Don't worry about it, so am I." He was also at the same point where I was. In coming out we were discovering ourselves. I knew that I wanted him; he knew that he wanted me.

The breakup of Mark's marriage provided a new context through which to reassess his sexuality and his future. Having given up "being gay" (see above), he "found out that the straight life wasn't what it's kicked up to be" when he found his wife in bed with his brother. He then "went back to Joe, said 'let's get the hell out of Syracuse.' And Joe and I moved to California. We were lovers for three years after that."

For 66-year-old Mary, her husband's request for an "open marriage" provided the opportunity for experimenting sexually, allowing her to look "at women differently." Her first lesbian affair, "other problems in the marriage," and pressure from her female lover created a need "to make a decision."

I started going around with a girlfriend of mine who had always played around. And all the men that we ran into, everybody was telling me how good-looking I was and what they could do for me, and I thought, "Oh no." So I don't know, somewhere along the line. . . . And I had always had gay and lesbian friends, and all at once I realized I was looking at women differently than I had before. So, I got myself involved in an affair, and told my husband about it. There were some other problems in the marriage. I finally decided that I needed to make a decision. I didn't like living that way. And of course by this time the other lady had decided that I wasn't ever gonna leave my husband, and so I asked my husband to move.

As a result, she added, "I made a conscious choice to my way of thinking to become a lesbian when I was about forty-three."

For these individuals, who were still engaged in distancing practices when gay and lesbian liberation emerged, the movement provided both a very broad social context through which to form new relationships with gay men and lesbians and a new symbolic framework through which to assess their desires and actions. This granted the opportunity to reformulate oneself not from a non-homosexual to a stigmatized homosexual, but from a non-homosexual self to a liberated gay or lesbian person. Marilyn, aged 66, who encountered lesbian-feminism and the possibilities for a new identity at a meeting of the National Organization for Women in the early 1970s, referred directly to the link between changing times and changing selves.

It was a gradual process. What really kicked it off for me was reading an article by a woman in the National Organization for Women, and I said, "Hey, that's me." It was just a revelation. I went to the National Organization for Women. I met other women who identified themselves as lesbian. It was the first time that I had lesbians around me, identifiable lesbians. I became involved, we had a march in West Los Angeles and had speakers for

hours. It was a *fantastic* time for feminism and gays and lesbians and a lot of energy; it was a great time.

Coming Out to Family Members

For those who identified as homosexual before gay liberation, close relations with family hinged on avoiding discussion of their homosexuality. Those who came out by way of gay liberation, in contrast, were committed to broaching the issue with family members at various times and places.

Members of the first group saw their homosexuality as a private matter that should not be raised as a topic by any members of the family, including themselves. They explained that doing so was unnecessary and could create tensions and even distress for their loved ones. For example, Brian, aged 74, "kept that separate from the family." Even his nephew, to whom he is extremely close, has

no idea. We're so separated geographically that there's never been any reason to tell [the family], you know, or for them to think anything of it. All they know is, "Oh, he was married once and he's divorced." So it doesn't enter their mind, you see. I haven't felt that there's any reason to talk to them about it; it'd just shock them.

These subjects felt this way even though several felt that their families "already knew." As 77-year-old Manny put it, "I don't tell anybody that I'm gay, but everybody knows. But nobody says anything. It's taken for granted." Declining to discuss their sexuality was not necessarily a matter of passing as heterosexual, but was rather understood as respecting the family's perceived feelings of discomfort and shame were the topic to be raised. Patricia, aged 77, stated that she

never mentioned it. They all know that I am. My sisters know I am but we've never talked about it. I'm sure my dad and mother [knew but] we never discussed it. They knew when I went to live with Deborah, especially my mother, but never discussed it. It was just something that [they] didn't want to have to go through [or] live with. My sisters are very good friends and I talk to them but we don't discuss anything like this. We discuss everyday life. Things that are going on.

Similarly, Jan, aged 68, describes herself as "still very, very *guarded* in terms of being open with most of the people that I know," explaining that "I guess I came up in the wrong era," expressly tying her biography to history. She feels that

> there are no illusions, everybody who knows me I'm sure knows that I'm a lesbian, I'm sure they do, but it's never discussed. It's not something I would particularly bring up, but I wouldn't *avoid*.

Indeed, these same subjects were upset and insulted when other members of their families disclosed their homosexuality to them. Seventy-seven-year-old Manny described a nephew's including him in the process of coming out to his family as an unwelcome intrusion into the appropriate distance he had established with his relatives. In his view, this was ultimately irrelevant to him and his position in the family.

> I have a nephew that's gay, in Montreal. He's a college kid. And he came out to his mother and father when he was in college. And of course, I went home, and this is part of the family that I don't like. So the mother said, "Manny, call Josh. Manny, call Josh." I said, "Okay, I'll call Josh." So I'm leaving Montreal and I didn't call Josh. So Josh calls me, "Uncle Manny? You're leaving—I'm gay." So I said, "What do you want *me* to do?" You know?

Given the commitment of this set of subjects to keeping their homosexuality private, it is not surprising that the rare instances when they were expected to disclose their homosexuality to others were met with outrage. Sixty-nine-year-old Lillian, for one, felt that her cousin's anger at her failure to come out to him was unwarranted, and his expectation that she come out to him unreasonable. As she explained, his desire that she disclose her lesbianism to him displaced his responsibility for raising the topic onto her shoulders. Since he was the one who saw her sexuality as relevant to their relationship, it was his obligation to ask her about it. To expect her to raise the issue was to expect her to "make an announcement," to gratuitously make her sexuality evident and obtrusive.

> My cousin Louie did something I didn't like and he got very mad at me because I never told him I was gay. I said I never heard of something like that. First of all, I'm not one to wear a sign on my back, and like I told him if he were that curious to know what my lifestyle was, why didn't you ask? If you would have asked me I would have told you, but I'm not about to come to you and say, "Hey, Louie, I'm gay," you know. I just don't want to deal with that, you know what I'm saying? I mean he's 72 years old. I said, "You're a grown man, if you were that curious, why didn't you ask me? I would have told you. But I'm not about to make an announcement."

Subjects who identified as gay or lesbian by way of gay liberation, however, viewed the discussion of their homosexuality as essential to close relations with family members. Marilyn, aged 66, made this explicit when discussing her relationship to a niece, equating being close with being out (clearly, she was not close to the niece she discusses below).

> If you're asking me close, I'm not out to her. I don't tell her my personal problems. I tell her about, you know, problems with the apartment and other things. But she's not somebody I would go to with relationship problems.

This equation is even clearer when we consider Marilyn's relationship to her cousin, who is "almost like a sister to me" and to whom she did, in fact, come out.

Kate, aged 76, spoke in similar terms of her

cousin in Chicago to whom I'm out. In an odd sort of way, I'm fond of her. She came the closest to being a sister, simply because for a while, in Texas, we lived near each other and our mothers were not only sisters but very, very fond of each other, and we had a lot of contact as children.

In stark contrast to Manny's account above, these subjects welcomed younger gay people into their lives, offering support and guidance, even help in handling their homosexuality in the context of the family. Seventy-year-old Abby, for example, suspects that

one of my great-nieces is going to turn around some day and say something to me, and if she does, then I will tell her flat out, and I will tell her where to go and what to [do], and steer her away from any of the pitfalls that I possibly can. And if I have to run interference for the rest of her family and mine, I will.

Similarly, Susan, aged 75, described how she looked forward to a visit from her granddaughter and her gay friend:

My whole family's fully aware of who I am and that's what's important to me. . . . My granddaughter's supposedly coming to visit here. She's bringing a couple of friends with her and it so happens, she tells me, one of her friends is gay, a young girl. She said, "I told her about you, Grandma. She'd love to talk to you." I said, "Sure, fine." So they think I'm gonna be an advisor to this young kid. Anyway, it'll be interesting to talk to her. But I think it's kind of cute, that she's gonna take her friend to visit her grandmother who's gay.

While Manny fumed when his nephew told him of his own homosexuality, 66-year-old Sharon was incensed that her brother has not come out to her, interpreting his reticence as an affront to the closeness they'd felt while growing up.

My brother is not married. He has never said anything to me about being gay. *Ever*. Can you believe it? And he and I were just *this close*. We grew up like twins, there was a year difference. We were very close, he and I were raised very close. Yet he will not tell me he's gay.

BEING OLD AND GAY

Clearly, there are many ways to experience being old and gay. In discussing the impact that homosexuality had on their lives and on growing older, gay men and lesbians often related to family issues in contradictory terms. Many expressed regret that they lacked the "support system" that the traditional family offers. For example, Ryan, aged 81, noted that, for homosexuals, growing older was "much more difficult. I don't think I have the support system, I don't have the family support system that I would otherwise have. I guess that's the main thing." Sixty-six-year-old Ricardo felt that "because we grow old normally separated from families" and heterosexuals "grow old *within* the families," gay aging

is by definition a little different. You just can't define [yourself] isolated without any relationship to family or society. So in this case you have to project yourself to your family. I don't have any family, possibly because I wouldn't feel comfortable in the heterosexual world. So growing older, it makes a little difference.

At the same time, many also claimed that the absence of traditional family ties made for a better life in old age. For example, Jeannine, aged

66, while recognizing the importance of children as caregivers to older people, saw the family as a potential obstacle to happiness in old age, as the following interview exchange suggests.

Jeannine: They don't have the family support that straights would. They don't have a daughter that's dutifully going to—usually—take care of Mom. Or a son who's going to be an advocate. So, in that sense, they're a little more isolated, they don't have the broad family thing. But it may be a blessing, too. 'Cause I've seen the vultures circle too, with straights.

DR: You mean waiting for Grandma to die so that they can have the Porsche?

Jeannine: Yeah. Or jostling to be nice to her before she dies so that they can have the Porsche.

Several subjects felt that the absence of conventional family relations freed them from constraints and concerns that took their toll on individuals' freedom, appearance, and health. These respondents linked the absence of a conventional family to what they perceived as the relative vitality and youthfulness of the gay and lesbian elderly. For 68-year-old Jan, childlessness is said to free older homosexuals from children's constant reminder of their relatively advanced age, resulting in subjective feelings of youthfulness.

> I don't think of myself as old, elderly, or even aging. And I think if I were in the regular mode—a husband and kids, grandchildren—I'd have grandchildren at this point, and a constant *reminder* from all these years that have crept up and having all these generations younger than myself I would tend to feel much older I think than perhaps I do now. [Heterosexuals] usually do age faster.

Others explained that the relative vitality of older homosexuals was due to their freedom from the worries over family, from which heterosexuals suffered. Brian, aged 74, compared his gay friends to his heterosexual friends from his days in the Navy, claiming that the latter's marital and parental roles bring with them "worries" that cause "feebleness":

> Maybe gays aren't quite as feeble as straights now. Because I think that these friends I see just don't seem as old as the straight friends that are the same age. They haven't had kids and all this and that. I'm sure that [straight] people have kids, and they're with spouses. It's just maybe a little more worries or something.

Still others, such as Luke, aged 69, described the traditional family as threatening the autonomy and freedom of the elderly. According to Luke, older homosexuals are free from these impositions and hence relatively carefree in their youthfulness. He saw older heterosexuals, in contrast, as vulnerable to institutionalization by their children, which makes them "lonelier."

> Their sons and their daughters take them and make them lonelier by putting them in convalescent homes and getting rid of them. When you're gay, no one can do that to you, you have to do it to yourself. So you go on by yourself until you don't have any more strength to go on. And that's why I'm 68 and I still feel like I'm 55.

Some saw their homosexuality as irrelevant to their old age, resisting the narrative linkage of sexual nonconformity, social stigmatization, and their impact on the later years typical of many others. As William, aged 76, put it, "Some people, both gay and heterosexual, age gracefully and some don't. And I don't know that being gay has anything specifically to do with it." Mary, aged 66, felt that "getting old is just getting old, as far as I can tell." To 75-year-old Susan, "You're a person first, aren't you? Gay people get ill, gay people have the same problems that straight people do." For Kate, aged 76, the circumstances under which people age center on social support, which she felt is independent of sexuality. As she explained, the isolation of older persons depends upon

> whether they were ever married or had children, what kind of families they have. A straight woman who never married, if she has a loving niece, you know, great. If she doesn't, too damned bad. I think it's a matter of old age *per se* and the kind of friends and the kind of family you have. It's a question of you're single, you damned well better have a support system and/or some sort of family. You know most people that are my age and single do have nieces and nephews, you see. Having been a single child I don't have that. I think that cuts across the whole society in terms of old age. That has nothing to do with the gay/lesbian part. We join the mainstream in old age.

FUTURE COHORTS

In considering future ways of aging among gays and lesbians, we need to avoid a full reliance on the heterosexual/homosexual divide. History has shown that this divide is now not as clear as it was for the older subjects under consideration. Just as the historical era in which my subjects identified as homosexual affected their identity careers, so will the historical era in which future cohorts of lesbians and gays age affect their identities and their views of the later years. Future cohorts of homosexual elderly will have moved through life in the context of concerns and opportunities related to sexuality almost unimaginable a generation ago.

The shape of lesbian and gay families (see Weston 1991), if not legally binding, is nonetheless now part of the discourse and practice of lesbian and gay life. The emergence of same-sex partner benefits, while by no means universal, allows gay men and women to cement their relationships financially and legally, and to move to and from jobs as families, with massive implications for security in old age. This also allows gay men and women to be "out" at work, an almost mind-boggling change from the 1950s, when homosexuality was grounds for immediate dismissal from a job. Indeed, the homosexual "baby boom" of the 1980s and 1990s will undoubtedly have immense consequences for the quality of gay life in old age later in the century. The emergence of gay voting blocs and of gay lobbying will provide a new arena for the political engagement with, and enactment of, diverse homosexual identities and policies in the public sphere. These rapidly developing historical changes will undoubtedly provide new biographical opportunities for future generations of homosexual elders.

Accompanying this is the explosion of venues for the discussion and contesting of homosexual identity in the mass media, which suggests that future cohorts of older gay men and lesbians will have devoted a shorter period of their lives to identity issues surrounding their sexuality. It is doubtful that today's teenagers experiencing same-sex desires will spend as much time plowing through a discourse of difference to interpret their desires. Indeed, the now classic coming out story may become less dramatic and less painful than it has been, one which seems to have been a narrative watershed for the older subjects of the generation under consideration.

Gay liberation, lesbian-feminism, and queer politics have complicated a field of sexual discussion that had, in my subjects' earlier years, been dominated by an identity landscape almost wholly reliant upon the condemnation of homosexuality. Imagining the future impact of these changes on the identity careers of homosexuals further highlights the importance of the link between biography and history as it relates to ways of aging.

References

Chauncey, George. 1994. *Gay New York: Gender, Urban Culture, and the Making of the Gay Male World, 1890–1940*. New York: Basic Books.

D'Emilio, John. 1983. *Sexual Politics, Sexual Communities: The Making of a Homosexual Minority in the United States*. Chicago: University of Chicago Press.

Faderman, Lillian, 1991. *Odd Girls and Twilight Lovers: A History of Lesbian Life in Twentieth-Century America*. Middlesex, UK: Plume.

Mills, C. Wright. 1959. *The Sociological Imagination*. New York: Oxford University Press.

Nardi, Peter M. and Sanders, David. 1994. *Growing Up Before Stonewall: Life Stories of Some Gay Men*. London: Routledge.

Rosenfeld, Dana. 1999. "Identity Work Among Lesbian and Gay Elderly." *Journal of Aging Studies,* 13(2):121–44.

Weitz, R. 1984. "From Accommodation to Rebellion: The Politicization of Lesbianism." In T. Darry and S. Potter (eds.), *Women-Identified Women*. Palo Alto, CA: Mayfield, pp. 233–48.

Weston, Kath. 1991. *Families We Choose: Lesbians, Gays, Kinship*. New York: Columbia University Press.

Young, A. 1972. "Out of the Closets, Into the Streets." In Karla Jay and Allen Young (eds.), *Out of the Closets: Voices of Gay Liberation*. New York: Pyramid Books, pp. 6–30.

CONTRADICTIONS AND CONFLICT IN SELF-PRODUCTION

The previous sections (Parts III and IV) suggest an explanation for the development of a social self through interaction. This section explores the more complicated process that occurs when our self-expectations and self-images are in conflict. People often identify with conflicting reference groups, for example. Similarly, we may receive ambiguous and confusing messages from various sources about who and what we should be. The articles in this section explore how people make sense of these contradictions. They also illustrate a powerful theme in the social psychology of the self: People have an amazing capacity to construct some kind of coherency out of the most extreme contradictions. This observation suggests that we are infinitely creative in constructing our own life stories.

"Double Consciousness and the Veil" is an excerpt from the writings of a famous sociologist, W. E. B. DuBois. DuBois was a highly influential thinker during the period known as the Harlem Renaissance in the 1920s. His ideas were instrumental in the advancement and politics of the "New Negro." Although his ideas were criticized by the next generation of black artists and intellectuals as being too bourgeois and too assimilationist in reference to a White middle class, DuBois is widely regarded as one of the great intellectuals of his time. This selection is an early essay in which he considers the experience of being "other" and of cultivating a "Negro" self in a White world.

How do openly gay Christians make sense of the contradictions between Christian doctrine and being homosexual? I explore this question in "Wrestling the Angel of Contradiction: Queer Christian Identities." This study traces the ways in which openly gay and lesbian Christians define the contradictions they experience and the ways in which they reconcile these contradictions. This process of reconciling contradictions may have some surprising effects on mainstream Christian congregations.

In "Life as the Maid's Daughter," sociologist Mary Romero describes a research interview with a young Chicana regarding her recollections of growing up as the daughter of a live-in maid for a White, upper-class family living in Los Angeles. Romero describes the many ways in which this girl learns to move between different social settings, adapt to different expectations, and occupy different social positions. This girl must constantly negotiate the boundaries of inclusion and exclusion, as she struggles between the socializing influence of her own ethnic group and that of the White, upper-class employers she and her mother live with. Through this juggling, she illustrates the ways in which we manage the different, often contradictory, identities that we take on in different situations.

READING QUESTIONS

1. Return to your list of responses to the question "Who am I?" (Part III). Are there any items on this list that you would be embarrassed or ashamed to have someone close to you know about? If not, imagine what kinds of items might be on the lists of others that could be potentially conflicting.

(Continued)

(Continued)

2. Self-concept emerges from a person's unique intersection of social positions such as class, gender, race, religion, sexuality, age, and so forth. Review the concepts in the essay "Self as a Process of Contradictions and Conflict" for this section and consider which aspects of your social position are more or less central and more or less marginal. What impact might your specific position have had on your interactions and experiences?

3. Discuss the proposition that social power is the extent to which you can author your own position. What are some interactional factors that enable people to be more or less in control of how others define them?

4. Consider some experiences of self-ambiguity or self-conflict in your own life. Trace the specific reference groups or significant others that are the source of this conflict.

5. The material in this section offers both a theory of self-stability and a theory of self-change. Explain.

CONTRADICTIONS AND CONFLICT IN SELF-PRODUCTION

24

Double Consciousness and the Veil

W. E. B. DuBois

(1903)

O water, voice of my heart, crying in the sand,
All night long crying with a mournful cry,
As I lie and listen, and cannot understand
The voice of my heart in my side or the voice of the sea,
O water, crying for rest, is it I, is it I?
All night long the water is crying to me.

Unresting water, there shall never be rest
Till the last moon droop and the last tide fail,
And the fire of the end begin to burn in the west;
And the heart shall be weary and wonder and cry like the sea,
All life long crying without avail,
As the water all night long is crying to me.

—Arthur Symons

Between me and the other world there is ever an unasked question: unasked by some through feelings of delicacy; by others through the difficulty of rightly framing it. All, nevertheless, flutter round it. They approach me in a half-hesitant sort of way, eye me curiously or compassionately, and then, instead of saying directly, How does it feel to be a problem? they say, I know an excellent colored man in my town; or, I fought at Mechanicsville; or, Do not these Southern outrages make your blood boil? At these I smile, or am interested, or reduce the boiling to a simmer, as the occasion may require. To the real question, How does it feel to be a problem? I answer seldom a word.

And yet, being a problem is a strange experience—peculiar even for one who has never been anything else, save perhaps in babyhood and in Europe. It is in the early days of rollicking boyhood that the revelation first bursts upon one, all in a day, as it were. I remember well when the shadow swept across me. I was a little thing, away up in the hills of New England, where the dark Housatonic winds between Hoosac and Taghkanic to the sea. In a wee wooden schoolhouse, something put it into the boys' and girls' heads to buy gorgeous visiting-cards—ten cents a package—and exchange. The exchange was merry, till one girl, a tall new-comer, refused my card—refused it peremptorily, with a glance. Then it dawned upon me with a certain suddenness that I was different from the others; or like, mayhap, in heart and life and longing, but shut out from their world by a vast veil. I had thereafter no desire to tear down that veil, to creep through; I held all beyond it in common contempt, and lived above it in a region of blue sky and great wandering shadows. That sky was bluest when I could beat my mates at examination-time, or beat them at a foot-race, or even beat their stringy heads.

Alas, with the years all this fine contempt began to fade, for the words I longed for, and all their dazzling opportunities, were theirs, not mine. But they should not keep these prizes, I said; some, all, I would wrest from them. Just how I would do it I could never decide: by reading law, by healing the sick, by telling the wonderful tales that swam in my head—some way. With other black boys the strife was not so fiercely sunny: their youth shrunk into tasteless sycophancy, or into silent hatred of the pale world about them and mocking distrust of everything white; or wasted itself in a bitter cry: Why did God make me an outcast and a stranger in mine own house? The shades of the prison-house closed round about us all: walls strait and stubborn to the whitest, but relentlessly narrow, tall, and unscalable to sons of night who must plod darkly on in resignation, or beat unavailing palms against the stone, or steadily, half hopelessly, watch the streak of blue above.

After the Egyptian and Indian, the Greek and Roman, the Teuton and Mongolian, the Negro is a sort of seventh son, born with a veil, and gifted with second-sight in this American world—a world which yields him no true self-consciousness, but only lets him see himself through the revelation of the other world. It is a peculiar sensation, this double-consciousness, this sense of always looking at one's self through the eyes of others, of measuring one's soul by the tape of a world that looks on in amused contempt and pity. One ever feels his twoness—an American, a Negro; two souls, two thoughts, two unreconciled strivings; two warring ideals in one dark body, whose dogged strength alone keeps it from being torn asunder.

The history of the American Negro is the history of this strife—this longing to attain self-conscious manhood, to merge his double self into a better and truer self. In this merging he wishes neither of the older selves to be lost.

He would not Africanize America, for America has too much to teach the world and Africa. He would not bleach his Negro soul in a flood of white Americanism, for he knows that Negro blood has a message for the world. He simply wishes to make it possible for a man to be both a Negro and an American, without being cursed and spit upon by his fellows, without having the doors of Opportunity closed roughly in his face.

This, then, is the end of his striving: to be a co-worker in the kingdom of culture, to escape both death and isolation, to husband and use his best powers and his latent genius. These powers of body and mind have in the past been strangely wasted, dispersed, or forgotten. The shadow of a mighty Negro past flits through the tale of Ethiopia the Shadowy and of Egypt the Sphinx. Through history, the powers of single black men flash here and there like falling stars, and die sometimes before the world has rightly gauged their brightness. Here in America, in the few days since Emancipation, the black man's turning hither and thither in hesitant and doubtful striving has often made his very strength to lose effectiveness, to seem like absence of power, like weakness. And yet it is not weakness—it is the contradiction of double aims. The double-aimed struggle of the black artisan—on the one hand to escape white contempt for a nation of mere hewers of wood and drawers of water, and on the other hand to plough and nail and dig for a poverty-stricken horde—could only result in making him a poor craftsman, for he had but half a heart in either cause. By the poverty and ignorance of his people, the Negro minister or doctor was tempted toward quackery and demagogy; and by the criticism of the other world, toward ideals that made him ashamed of his lowly tasks. The would-be black *savant* was confronted by the paradox that the knowledge his people needed was a twice-told tale to his white neighbors, while the knowledge which would teach the white world was Greek to his own flesh and blood. The innate love of harmony and beauty that set the ruder souls of his people a-dancing and a-singing raised but confusion and doubt in the soul of the black artist; for the beauty revealed to him was the soul-beauty of a race which his larger audience despised, and he could not articulate the message of another people. This waste of double aims, this seeking to satisfy two unreconciled ideals, has wrought sad havoc with the courage and faith and deeds of ten thousand people—has sent them often wooing false gods and invoking false means of salvation, and at times has even seemed about to make them ashamed of themselves.

Away back in the days of bondage they thought to see in one divine event the end of all doubt and disappointment; few men ever worshipped Freedom with half such unquestioning faith as did the American Negro for two centuries. To him, so far as he thought and dreamed, slavery was indeed the sum of all villainies, the cause of all sorrow, the root of all prejudice; Emancipation was the key to a promised land of sweeter beauty than ever stretched before the eyes of wearied Israelites. In song and exhortation swelled one refrain—Liberty; in his tears and curses the God he implored had Freedom in his right hand. At last it came—suddenly, fearfully, like a dream. With one wild carnival of blood and passion came the message in his own plaintive cadences—

Shout, O children!

Shout, you're free!

For God has bought your liberty!

Years have passed away since then—ten, twenty, forty; forty years of national life, forty years of renewal and development, and yet the swarthy spectre sits in its accustomed seat at the Nation's feast. In vain do we cry to this our vastest social problem—

Take any shape but that, and my firm nerves

Shall never tremble!

The Nation has not yet found peace from its sins; the freedman has not yet found in freedom his promised land. Whatever of good may have come in these years of change, the shadow of a deep disappointment rests upon the Negro people—a disappointment all the more bitter because the unattained ideal was unbounded save by the simple ignorance of a lowly people.

The first decade was merely a prolongation of the vain search for freedom, the boon that seemed ever barely to elude their grasp—like a tantalizing will-o'-the-wisp, maddening and misleading the headless host. The holocaust of war, the terrors of the Ku-Klux Klan, the lies of carpetbaggers, the disorganization of industry, and the contradictory advice of friends and foes, left the bewildered serf with no new watchword beyond the old cry for freedom. As the time flew, however, he began to grasp a new idea. The ideal of liberty demanded for its attainment powerful means, and these the Fifteenth Amendment gave him. The ballot, which before he had looked upon as a visible sign of freedom, he now regarded as the chief means of gaining and perfecting the liberty with which war had partially endowed him. And why not? Had not votes made war and emancipated millions? Had not votes enfranchised the freedmen? Was anything impossible to a power that had done all this? A million black men started with renewed zeal to vote themselves into the kingdom. So the decade flew away, the revolution of 1876 came, and left the half-free serf weary, wondering, but still inspired. Slowly but steadily, in the following years, a new vision began gradually to replace the dream of political power—a powerful movement, the rise of another ideal to guide the unguided, another pillar of fire by night after a clouded day. It was the ideal of "book-learning";

the curiosity, born of compulsory ignorance, to know and test the power of the cabalistic letters of the white man, the longing to know. Here at last seemed to have been discovered the mountain path to Canaan; longer than the highway of Emancipation and law, steep and rugged, but straight, leading to heights high enough to overlook life.

Up the new path the advance guard toiled, slowly, heavily, doggedly; only those who have watched and guided the faltering feet, the misty minds, the dull understandings, of the dark pupils of these schools know how faithfully, how piteously, this people strove to learn. It was weary work. The cold statistician wrote down the inches of progress here and there, noted also where here and there a foot had slipped or someone had fallen. To the tired climbers, the horizon was ever dark, the mists were often cold, the Canaan was always dim and far away. If, however, the vistas disclosed as yet no goal, no resting-place, little but flattery and criticism, the journey at least gave leisure for reflection and self-examination; it changed the child of Emancipation to the youth with dawning self-consciousness, self-realization, self-respect. In those sombre forests of his striving his own soul rose before him, and he saw himself—darkly as through a veil; and yet he saw in himself some faint revelation of his power, of his mission. He began to have a dim feeling that, to attain his place in the world, he must be himself, and not another. For the first time he sought to analyze the burden he bore upon his back, that deadweight of social degradation partially masked behind a half-named Negro problem. He felt his poverty; without a cent, without a home, without land, tools, or savings, he had entered into competition with rich, landed, skilled neighbors. To be a poor man is hard, but to be a poor race in a land of dollars is the very bottom of hardships. He felt the weight of his ignorance—not simply of letters, but of life, of business, of the humani-

ties; the accumulated sloth and shirking and awkwardness of decades and centuries shackled his hands and feet. Nor was his burden all poverty and ignorance. The red stain of bastardy, which two centuries of systematic legal defilement of Negro women had stamped upon his race, meant not only the loss of ancient African chastity, but also the hereditary weight of a mass of corruption from white adulterers, threatening almost the obliteration of the Negro home.

A people thus handicapped ought not to be asked to race with the world, but rather allowed to give all its time and thought to its own social problems. But alas! while sociologists gleefully count his bastards and his prostitutes, the very soul of the toiling, sweating black man is darkened by the shadow of a vast despair. Men call the shadow prejudice, and learnedly explain it as the natural defence of culture against barbarism, learning against ignorance, purity against crime, the "higher" against the "lower" races. To which the Negro cries Amen! and swears that to so much of this strange prejudice as is founded on just homage to civilization, culture, righteousness, and progress, he humbly bows and meekly does obeisance. But before that nameless prejudice that leaps beyond all this he stands helpless, dismayed, and well-nigh speechless; before that personal disrespect and mockery, the ridicule and systematic humiliation, the distortion of fact and wanton license of fancy, the cynical ignoring of the better and the boisterous welcoming of the worse, the all-pervading desire to inculcate disdain for everything black, from Toussaint to the devil—before this there rises a sickening despair that would disarm and discourage any nation save that black host to whom "discouragement" is an unwritten word.

But the facing of so vast a prejudice could not but bring the inevitable self-questioning, self-disparagment, and lowering of ideals which ever accompany repression and breed in an atmosphere of contempt and hate. Whisperings and portents came borne upon the four winds:

Lo! we are diseased and dying, cried the dark hosts; we cannot write, our voting is vain; what need of education, since we must always cook and serve? And the Nation echoed and enforced this self-criticism, saying: Be content to be servants, and nothing more; what need of higher culture for half-men? Away with the black man's ballot, by force or fraud—and behold the suicide of a race! Nevertheless, out of the evil came something of good—the more careful adjustment of education to real life, the clearer perception of the Negroes' social responsibilities, and the sobering realization of the meaning of progress.

So dawned the time of *Sturm und Drang:* storm and stress today rocks our little boat on the mad waters of the world-sea; there is within and without the sound of conflict, the burning of body and rending of soul; inspiration strives with doubt, and faith with vain questionings. The bright ideals of the past—physical freedom, political power, the training of brains and the training of hands—all these in turn have waxed and waned, until even the last grows dim and overcast. Are they all wrong—all false? No, not that, but each alone was oversimple and incomplete—the dreams of a credulous race-childhood, or the fond imaginings of the other world which does not know and does not want to know our power. To be really true, all these ideals must be melted and welded into one. The training of the schools we need today more than ever—the training of deft hands, quick eyes and ears, and above all the broader, deeper, higher culture of gifted minds and pure hearts. The power of the ballot we need in sheer self-defense—else what shall save us from a second slavery? Freedom, too, the long-sought, we still seek—the freedom of life and limb, the freedom to work and think, the freedom to love and aspire. Work, culture, liberty—all these we need, not singly but together, not successively but together, each growing and aiding each, and all striving toward that vaster ideal that swims before the Negro people, the ideal of human brotherhood, gained through the unifying ideal of Race; the ideal of fostering and developing the traits and talents of the Negro, not in opposition to or contempt for other races, but rather in large conformity to the greater ideals of the American Republic, in order that some day on American soil two world-races may give each to each those characteristics both so sadly lack. We the darker ones come even now not altogether empty-handed: There are today no truer exponents of the pure human spirit of the Declaration of Independence than the American Negroes; there is no true American music but the wild sweet melodies of the Negro slave; the American fairy tales and folklore are Indian and African; and, all in all, we black men seem the sole oasis of simple faith and reverence in a dusty desert of dollars and smartness. Will America be poorer if she replaces her brutal dyspeptic blundering with light-hearted but determined Negro humility? or her coarse and cruel wit with loving jovial good-humor? or her vulgar music with the soul of the Sorrow Songs?

Merely a concrete test of the underlying principles of the great republic is the Negro Problem, and the spiritual striving of the freedmen's sons is the travail of souls whose burden is almost beyond the measure of their strength, but who bear it in the name of an historic race, in the name of this the land of their fathers' fathers, and in the name of human opportunity.

CONTRADICTIONS AND CONFLICT IN SELF-PRODUCTION

25

Wrestling the Angel of Contradiction: Queer Christian Identities

Jodi O'Brien

(2004)

I wanted gays to be in the vanguard, battling against racial and economic injustice and religious and political oppression. I never thought I would see the day when gays would be begging to be let back into the Christian Church, which is clearly our enemy.

(Edmund White, author)

Seven reasons why you should absolutely, positively stay away from church . . . [reason number four]. The way some churches can get God to fit into those little boxes.

(Posted flyer, Spirit of the Sound: Gay and Lesbian Followers of Jesus)

I had to go to a non-Christian church for four years before I understood what it means to be a good Christian. A good Christian has a very big god.

(Larry, gay male and practicing Catholic)

INTRODUCTION

Several years ago I attended Gay Pride Parades in three different cities during the same month (San Francisco, Chicago, and Seattle). . . . Each parade felt distinct to me. The differences were not surprising. In many ways, they reflect the mosaic of responses to the proliferation of lesbian and gay presence and politics in recent decades. Perhaps this is why I was so surprised at one notable similarity that occurred at all three parades. Among the marchers in each parade were groups representing friends and supporters of lesbians and gays: PFLAG, AT&T

Queer Allies, US Bank LGBT Employee Support, and so forth. In each case, the crowd responded enthusiastically to this display of support and acceptance. People clapped and cheered and whistled in appreciation. The marchers glowed in acknowledgment. This is not what surprised me. Rather, it was the contrast in the crowd's response to another group of marchers: lesbian and gay Christians and, specifically, Mormons (who march under the banner of Affirmation) and Catholics (who call their association Dignity). In these three very distinct US cities I wandered up and down the streets during each parade, watching as merry crowds fell silent at the appearance of these marchers. Everywhere the response was the same: silence, broken only by an occasional boo. I was stunned. These otherwise very "normal" looking but openly queer men and women (some of whom really did look like the stereotypical Mormon missionary) were being booed at their own Pride Parades. . . .

It is likely that many parade bystanders were genuinely confused at what must have seemed an obvious contradiction: openly queer, openly religious. For some parade-goers, the presence of these lesbian and gay Christians might even have been a form of betrayal given the active anti-homosexual preaching of both the Vatican and Mormon leaders. In any case, my curiosity was aroused. What compelled someone to want to parade both statuses? My initial impression was that lesbian and gay Christians must experience a form of "double stigma." . . . What seemed to confuse and unsettle the crowd was the open expression of such an apparent contradiction. Why would any self-respecting queer want also to embrace Christianity with its seemingly inevitable denouncement and exclusion? And why, especially, would they want to announce this involvement to fellow queers, knowing the disdain and rejection that this was likely to incur?

Compelled by these questions I began to research what I called "double stigma." Specifically, I was interested in lesbians and gays who are openly queer and openly Christian. How did they make sense of and manage this "double stigma" I wondered? The concept of "double stigma" was sociologically rigorous enough to garner me research support for the project. Armed with this idea, the financial blessing of the American Sociological Association, and a solid track record of ethnographic experience, I set off in search of answers. Five open-ended interviews into the project, I knew the concept of "double-stigma" was completely off the mark. I was missing the main point. When I raised the idea of "double-stigma"—How do you deal with

it? Why do you deal with it?—the first round of interviewees all looked at me with similar confusion. Yes, they understood the question. Yes, they could understand how others would see it that way. But it did not resonate for them. Each of these five people, none of whom knew one another, said the same thing. This was not about stigma. It was about "living a contradiction that defines who I am."

Forty-two interviews and many hours of congregational participation later I was still hearing the same thing: the contradiction of being Christian and being queer is who I am. When I gave talks describing the research project I noticed the vigorous head-nodding among self-described queer Christians at the mention of the phrase, "living the contradiction." My orienting perspective at the launch of this project reflected my penchant for sociological abstraction and personal experiences that disincline me toward participation in mainstream religions (I am a former Mormon with a typical "flight from religion" experience through the process of becoming a lesbian). Through sustained contact and participatory experience with self-described "queer Christians" and the congregations that welcome them, I developed an understanding of the deeply complex process of living the contradiction of being queer and Christian. In fact, over time, I have come to have considerable appreciation for this process.

RESEARCH SETTING AND METHODOLOGY

This article is based on a more comprehensive project in which I develop the thesis that the contradictions between Christianity and homosexuality are the driving tensions in the formulation of a historically specific expression of queer religiosity. These expressions are manifested in individual identities and practices, in community practices (i.e., Christian congregations), and in ideological discourses (i.e., theological and doctrinal discourses). The transformative processes occurring at each of these levels are mutually constitutive. In this article I focus specifically on the processes whereby lesbian and gay Christians[1] forge an integration of Christian doctrine, spirituality, and sexuality.[2] My central interpretive claim in this paper is that this integrative struggle is experienced by lesbian and gay Christians as a raison d'être. Wrestling this contradiction has given rise to a particular expression of queer Christian identity. Among the many implications of these expressions of queer Christian identity is their impact on mainstream Christian congregations and Christian ideologies and practices. I describe these implications briefly in the conclusions.

As I have noted in the introduction, my original intent was to understand the motivations and experiences of lesbian and gay Catholics and Mormons who wished to be recognized explicitly for both their religiosity and sexuality. I began the project by talking with several such individuals, including my hairstylist, a self-described "flaming queen with a flair for building miniature houses" who is also active in his local Catholic parish. Larry's openly gay behavior was considered outrageous even by the standards of the gay-friendly hair salon that he worked in. Quite frankly, I could not imagine what his fellow parishioners made of his queerness. Yet Larry seemed to have found quite a home there. He spoke often and enthusiastically about his involvement with the parish. He invited me to attend services and, eventually, several meetings of the lay ministry, to experience for myself what his "contradictory" world was like. Another point of entry came through a colleague who had granted me a formal interview and then invited me to attend services at Seattle's First Baptist where he was an active participant. Later his congregation invited me to

participate as a speaker in their ongoing "Adult Education" series—a version of Sunday School. They wanted to explore the theme of sexuality and asked if I would kick-off the topic. Jim, my colleague and interview subject, was instrumental in organizing the series and in setting me up with subsequent interviews.

Through participation in these congregational activities I was introduced to more lesbian and gay Christians who granted me interviews and put me in contact with other friends and colleagues throughout the western United States and British Columbia. I also learned first-hand of the tensions taking place within the congregations that were supportive of lesbian and gay members.[3] The late 1990s was a time of ferment within Christian congregations regarding the presence and affirmation of lesbian and gay members. In this respect, the timing of my research was serendipitous. In recognition of these community and organizational tensions, I expanded my interviews to include heterosexual congregants and clergy members. I also expanded my participation to several regional congregations representing Episcopalian, Methodist, Unitarian, and Presbyterian denominations, in addition to my initial participation with Baptist, Catholic, and Mormon groups. My formal research process included 63 open-ended interviews and sustained contact with five congregations and two lesbian/gay Christian groups (Affirmation and Dignity) for a period of three years.

During this time I came to recognize what I term a "field of relations," which includes lesbian and gay Christians, the congregations in which they have found a "spiritual community," the general membership of these congregations, the congregational ministries, and the relationships between these congregations and their denominational organizations. There is awareness among these congregations that they are part of a historical moment that is fraught with considerable tension and debate regarding the very definition of Christianity. In this regard, I think it accurate to talk in terms of a social movement that is taking place within the pews (with a distinctly different genesis and process from LGBT political movements as they are typically presented in the social movements literature).

My research methods are consistent with ethnographic interpretive methodologies in which the intent is to articulate fields of relations and the intrapersonal and interpersonal relations that occur within these fields. My approach is especially informed by feminist methodologies, according to which my intent is to ascertain what persons within the field of inquiry have to say for themselves while remaining cognizant of my own relationship with these persons and my influence with the field of relations. At the same time, my work is strongly influenced by sociological theories that orient me toward ascertaining patterned discourses regarding how people make sense of themselves—what stories they tell themselves about who they are and what they can do—especially regarding conflict and contradiction (O'Brien 2001a; Plummer 1995). My observations and conclusions are interpretations that reflect my sociological orientation. Throughout the research process I presented myself as a sociologist with special interests in religion and sexuality. Early in the research process people became aware of my project and approached me about being interviewed and/or having me visit their congregations. This awareness and interest confirms my observation that a self-aware field of relations regarding queer Christian identities exists. My interpretations are limited to the specific context of this research project. However, my aim with this in-depth inquiry is to provide empirical insight and grounding for the conceptual frameworks through which scholars attempt to understand the integration of religion and sexuality generally.[4]

The "Gay Predicament": An Irreconcilable Contradiction

Homosexuality is intrinsically disordered.

(Catechism of the Catholic Church 1994, 566)

The "question of homosexuality" has been a central focus of discussion in Catholic and Protestant denominations since the 1960s. Historically, homosexuality is forbidden in most Christian doctrines. In these texts the homosexual has been variously defined as "disordered," "evil," and "sinful" (Conrad and Schneider 1980; O'Brien 2001b). In many texts homosexuality is rendered as absolutely irreconcilable with the basic tenets of Christianity. Recent revisions of a few doctrines offer a slightly more forgiving interpretation wherein homosexual behavior is separated from homosexual identity.[5] The new Catechism, for instance, defines homosexual inclinations (identity) as a "condition" that is not chosen and is experienced as a "trial" (Catechism of the Catholic Church 1994, 566). Grappling with this affliction can be a lifetime struggle and those who are "successful" in taming the beast of homosexuality can expect the same joys and blessings as other good Catholics.[6] In this rendering the act is the sin, while desire is an affliction. In an accompanying passage, the text admonishes all Catholics to treat persons who suffer the condition of homosexuality with "respect, compassion and sensitivity" (1994, 566). Progressive Catholics see this doctrine as at least an acknowledgement that homosexuality exists. The separation of act and identity is considered by some to be a statement of acceptance. Still, even in this supposedly progressive statement, the "homosexual" is rendered as someone (something) lacking, someone whose desires are a potential source of shame and exile.

Doctrines that condemn homosexuality constitute the ideological backdrop against which

Christians initially experience their homosexuality. At worst, they are irredeemable sinners: at best, they suffer from problems or afflictions. Given this discourse of rejection, non-Christians might assume that the simplest path would be the renunciation of religion. For many Christians struggling with feelings of homosexuality the path is not so simple.

Psychologists of religion offer a holistic explanation for sustained Christian participation, even when the participation involves conflict. According to this thesis, Christianity is a well-established and deeply meaningful cosmology that weaves together spirit, intellect, body, and community (Fortunato 1982). Christianity offers answers to big questions such as the meaning of life and death. Religious participation is also a means of transcending the oppressions and banalities of everyday living. For many Christians, the traditional ceremonies of religious expression are both evocative and comforting. Thus, motivation for participation is not so much the puzzle. In fact, to frame the question this way, as many studies of religion and homosexuality (including my own initial research proposal) do, is arguably to impose a secular perspective on a religious question.[7] Rather, the puzzle becomes: How does the homosexual make sense of the fact that, by definition, he/she is considered an exile who is beyond the promised redemption of Christian theology? Christian therapist John Fortunato refers to this as the "gay predicament." The "gay predicament," simply put, is that one cannot be a good Christian and also be queer.

The intensity of this contradiction can only be fully understood within a framework of Christian experience. Within a heteronormative culture, lesbians and gays are (often painfully) aware that they are social cast-offs. Within Christianity, active homosexuals are also aware that, in addition to their being social cast-offs, their souls have been cast off as well. This predicament poses a tremendous existential crisis. To experience homosexual desires, and certainly to pursue fulfillment of these desires, will result in being cast out from the cosmology through which one makes sense of one's life. One obvious solution is to cast off Christian theology in favor of the homosexual identity. This is easier said than done, however. Bending the rules is one thing, but shedding an entire structure of meaning may leave one cast adrift in a sea of meaninglessness—which may be even less tolerable than the knowledge that one is potentially damned. This is a defining predicament for lesbian and gay Christians. It is also a profound set of contradictions. Abandoning Christianity may mean losing a sense of meaning and purpose, yet keeping this particular religion means facing the prospect of damnation.

Queer Secularism

In addition to the predicament of exile, lesbian and gay Christians who are open about their religiosity face rejection from other queers. Lesbian and gay political activists, scholars, and writers tend to be critical and dismissive of Christianity. The following remark from gay author John Preston (known especially for his anthologies of gay male short stories) is indicative of the discourse of disdain prevalent among lesbian and gay activists and artists. Preston was invited by Brian Bouldrey to write a chapter for his anthology, *Wrestling with the Angel: Religion in the Lives of Gay Men*. This is his response:

> I'd have nothing to say in your anthology. As an atheist I have no angels with which to wrestle, and, to be honest, I think adults who worry about such a decrepit institution as organized religion should drink plenty of fluids, pop an aspirin, and take a nap, in hopes that the malady will pass. (Quoted in Bouldrey 1995, xi).

Thus, lesbian or gay Christians who seek comfort and insight among fellow queers may be setting themselves up for further disdain and rejection because of their religious affiliation. The queer Christian is doubly damned: according to Christian doctrine, homosexuality is an affliction; among fellow (non-Christian) lesbians and gays, religious affiliation may be the affliction. Not only can one not be a good Christian and be queer, apparently one cannot be a good queer and be religious. Or, as Elizabeth Stuart, author of a guide for LGBT Christians, so aptly phrases it, "queer Christians find themselves caught as it were between the devil and the rainbow, aliens in both lands" (1997, 13).[8]

Persons who have been "spun off from their galaxy of meaning" (Fortunato 1982)—in this case, heteronormative acceptance and Christian systems of meaning and purpose—seek reintegration into new systems of meaning. For instance, heterosexual persons who are inclined, for whatever reasons, to denounce their religious roots usually construct new systems of meaning within secular frameworks. Persons who find themselves spun off from heterosexual culture often find meaning in queer groups that have articulated anti-straight philosophies and practices. . . .

Responses to the Gay Predicament[9]

Anecdotal and experiential information suggests three general sorts of responses to the gay predicament: denunciation and flight, acceptance of the doctrine of shame, and articulation of an alternative (queer) religiosity. The first, denunciation and flight, is a well-known story among many lesbians and gay men. Many "coming out" stories involve a process of renouncing religious roots. These stories can be interpreted as a statement of renunciation and opposition against a system of meaning in which lesbians and gays find no place for themselves. These expressions involve a process of reshaping one's sense of self and identity in opposition to religious teachings and practices. For many

individuals, this is a painful and alienating process that involves not only casting off an entire system of meaning and belonging, but forging a new (non-Christian) ideology. As one former Mormon missionary-turned-lesbian put it:

> Non-Mormons don't get that Mormonism answers your questions about everything. Now I have to wonder about every little thing. Do I still believe in monogamy? Or is that something I should throw out along with Mormonism? Do I still believe in life-after-death? Marriage? Commitment? What do I believe in? It's all a big gaping hole for me now. (Lori)[10]

For many the struggle is about how to (re)integrate with society more generally. This is often done through alignment with other queer groups and the articulation of a discourse whereby the religious community, not the individual, is seen as the problem. In this instance, throwing off the cloak of religious shame is seen as an act of liberation:

> Healthy living means finding ways to throw off the guilt. It's not just the guilt of feeling like you've betrayed your family and friends and their expectations for you. It's the guilt that comes from messages all around you that you don't belong. That you're an aberration. Until one day you start to get it and say, hey, I'm here. I'm doing okay. I must belong. When you figure that out you have the courage to walk away from the [church] and realize the problem is them. They're not big enough to let you belong. (Brian)

This group of "recovering Christians" may be the least tolerant of lesbians and gays who attempt to find a place for themselves within Christianity.

Another familiar, and similarly complex, response is to learn to accept Christian teachings that render homosexuality an affliction. In such instances, the struggle to be a good Christian (and a good person generally as defined through adherence to Christian principles) revolves around the struggle to sustain celibacy. Homosexual reintegration into Christianity involves accepting the definition of an afflicted self, donning a cloak of shame regarding one's homosexuality (or, minimally, a cloak of sickness), and embarking upon the struggle indicated by this affliction. The literature on ex-gay therapies and ministries, most of which consists of personal narratives and "undercover" participant observation, indicates that those who seek out these "therapies" are likely to come from strong Christian backgrounds. Often they are referred to the therapies by a Church leader in whom they have confided (see, for instance, Harryman 1991). In these cases, the homosexual Christian who is not "cured" is encouraged to remain "closeted" if he/she wishes to maintain a position in the religious community.

My focus is on those individuals who endeavor to maintain both a strong Christian identity and an open and "proud" lesbian or gay identity. These people recognize their distinct position with respect to those who renounce Christianity and those who accept Christian definitions of affliction. A defining feature of this group is the desire to (re)integrate within a Christian system of meaning while maintaining a queer identity and, ideally, to integrate both identities within a common community. Given this, especially viewed within the framework of the other paths of response, it is possible to assert that lesbian and gay Christians are a distinct group who have at least some awareness that they are forging a unique response to their predicament. It must be noted, however, that, at least initially the responses to this predicament are local and individual. In this regard, the convergence of responses into similar themes is sociologically noteworthy.

In this paper, I am particularly interested in the content of themes that lesbian and gay Christians have articulated. As I note in the

concluding section, it is the expression of these themes and the performance of a queer Christianity within congregations that creates a critical mass, or groundswell, that can be interpreted as a particular form of queer Christian religious movement. In other words, none of the individuals in this project started out with an inclination to reform religion or to make a sociopolitical statement. Rather, each was primarily interested in the question of (re)integrating within a Christian community. Given this context, meaningful research questions include: how do lesbian and gay Christians make sense of and manage their predicament? What motivates their involvement in a system of meaning from which they have been spun off, socially and spiritually? What (if any) source of (re)integration do they articulate for themselves?

RAISON D'ÊTRE

Despite the threats of damnation and rejection among other queers, lesbian and gay Christians remain undaunted in their commitment to both a queer identity and Christian religiosity. Each of the 42 lesbian and gay Christians that I interviewed described having a sense of deep spirituality. Many of them offered details of what they felt to be an "early sense of vocation." As one interviewee phrased it, "religion has always been a natural and necessary part of existence for me."

At the same time, lesbian and gay Christians recognize that these proclamations of Christian spirituality put them at odds with other queers. Detailed statements about religious conviction are usually accompanied by accounts of having to defend this spirituality as a "thoughtful, meaningful enterprise and not some sort of brain-numbing self-denial" (Sean). He continues, "When I see it through the eyes of other gays, I often wonder if my religiosity is a character flaw."

Each of the interviewees articulated an awareness of a secular hegemony in this culture ("educated professional people in general are often embarrassed about their spiritual leanings"). To be religious in a secular society is a struggle. To be religious and queer is to expect ongoing struggle. The theme of struggle is constant throughout my own interviews, in my ethnographic participation in various congregations and in related writings.

The theme of struggle is also familiar and persistent throughout Christian doctrine and teachings. For example, in the Catechism, persons are instructed that appropriate sexual behavior (chastity) is an "apprenticeship in self-mastery which is a training in human freedom" (Catechism of the Catholic Church 1994, 562). This mastery (which culminates in sexual expression contained within a marriage blessed by the Church) will bring happiness and fulfillment. Failure to achieve it will lead to enslavement by the passions. "Struggle" may be a definitive trope of Christianity itself. Certainly one of the religion's most enduring themes is that persons will confront challenges and afflictions. The implied lesson is that the way they handle these struggles shapes their character. In this regard, lesbian and gay Christians can be seen as playing out a variation on an old theme: the contradiction of spirituality and sexuality is their particular struggle; the manner in which they engage the struggle defines their character. Struggle is paramount in each of the three responses to the "gay predicament"—struggle to reinterpret or renounce a dominant system of meaning; struggle to suppress and hide homosexual desire. A common distinction among the lesbian and gay Christians in this study is the extent to which struggle with a contradiction is a definitive aspect of self-understanding and identification (cf. White and White 2004). Two themes in particular emerged from my interviews and observations. First, wrestling the contradiction of spirituality and sexuality defines that self-proclaimed lesbian or gay Christian. Second is the sense among them that they are better Christians—indeed, better persons—as a consequence of this struggle. In other words, the struggle is the crucible in which their character is forged.

Articulating the Self as a Process of Contradiction

There is a version of social psychology that suggests the "articulated self" develops through the process of managing tensions and contradictions in aspects of life that the person considers most meaningful. In my own work I make the claim that the "self" can be usefully defined in terms of this process. In other words, the ways in which we make sense of and manage these contradictions are the definitive features of the social self (O'Brien 2001a). One common experience among the persons I interviewed was an early awakening of both spirituality and homosexuality.[11] Several participants indicated that their awareness of both their spirituality and their homosexuality was simultaneous. For each of them this was a profound realization, and one that was followed almost immediately by a sense of dread and panic:

> I was about 14 or so. I had this heightened sense that I was very special. Very spiritual. God has something special in mind for me. At the same time I had this sense of myself as sexual and that felt so good and so right. And then it occurred to me that these two feelings didn't fit and were going to get me into big trouble. That's when I started trying to figure out what God wanted with me. What was this struggle supposed to teach me? I was really a mess about it for a long time. I think I have some answers now. But I still struggle with it every day. (Jim)

Fortunato remarks that it is "no surprise that gay people ask an inordinate number of spiritual questions." For those who fit comfortably within an accepted system of meaning such as Christianity, the extent to which they think about their spirituality is probably in terms of some benign Sunday school lesson, or perhaps something that is mildly comforting in times of need.[12] Christians who have acknowledged their homosexuality do not have the luxury of semiconscious spirituality. The discovery that one's sexuality is so deeply contradictory "requires awakening levels of consciousness far beyond those necessary for straight people" (Fortunato 1982, 39). Thus, lesbian and gay Christians may have a more articulated sense of what it means to be a Christian precisely because they have to make ongoing sense of deeply felt contradictions.

For the most part this struggle for articulation is seen as positive and definitive. Every interviewee remarked in some way or another that her/his core sense of being was shaped significantly by the struggle to reconcile homosexuality and religiosity. Comments such as "I wouldn't be me if I didn't have this struggle" were typical.

> This is what has forged me, my defining battle. I'd probably be a very conservative evangelical Christian if I wasn't gay—everything is different as a result, especially my spirituality. Wrestling this marginality has become the thing that shapes me more than anything else. (Jim)

For these individuals, self-understanding comes through the process of engaging with persistent contradiction. The experience of contradiction is ongoing, both in conversations with oneself and in interactions with others. Lesbian and gay Christians constantly find themselves in situations in which they must explain (and often defend) their seemingly contradictory statuses to others. This experience is seen both as an occasion that can be tiresome and also as an occasion for growth and self-articulation. As one lesbian Baptist put it:

> You can never take yourself for granted. If I go to an event with lesbians and somehow it comes up that I'm an assistant pastor, I have to listen to this barrage of criticism about the history of Christianity and what it's done to us. I get soooo tired of that. What's amazing is that it never seems to occur to them that maybe I've thought about this. Maybe I have complicated reasons for being who I am. But they don't ask. As tiresome as it can be, it's still a good experience for me. I tend to go home and ask myself, why are you doing this? And I find that I understand my own answers better and better. Does that make any sense? (Carol)

Or this comment from a gay Methodist:

> It's like coming out over and over again. Every time someone new joins [the congregation] we're going to go through the same ol' dance about how the Sunday School coordinator is this gay guy. Thankfully, I'm so well-known now that the other members warn the newcomers. But there's always someone who wants to bait you, y'know, corner you at a social or something and quiz you on doctrine. Like they know doctrine!. . . I wanted to be able to scoff at their ignorance. The funny thing is, now that I know what I do, it turns out I want to educate them instead of show them up. I guess this whole thing has made me much more conscious of being a good Christian. (Mark)

This comment is from a student of Theology and Ministry:

> It seems like everyday, everywhere I go I'm a problem for somebody. It's a problem for white America that I'm black. It's a problem for gay America that I'm in the ministry. It's a problem for the ministry—a big, big problem—that I'm gay. Always a problem. Weird thing is, and you might think this is funny, but being a problem has made me really strong. I mean, as a person. I'm always having to think about who I am and not let it get to me. That makes you strong in yourself. You really know who you are. (Everett)

Another common feature in these narratives is the prevalence of contradiction.

These experiences are similar in tone and expression to some of the narrative reflections on multiple consciousness (for example, Anzaldua 1987). Persons who occupy contradictory social positions find themselves traversing the boundaries, or borders of multiple worlds. In so doing they develop a consciousness that reflects their marginal position. Persons in such positions usually have a heightened awareness of their own marginality; they are also more likely to be critically aware of expressions and practices that less marginalized persons take for granted. Most individuals perceive this heightened awareness as an advantage. At the very least, as noted in the illustrative quotes, contradictory positions are an occasion for reflection and articulation.

A significant outcome of these reflections among lesbian and gay Christians is the articulation of contradiction itself as useful and worthwhile in the shaping of a Christian identity. Not only is contradiction a catalyst for self-reflection, but ultimately it is a source of challenge for Christian congregations. Lesbians and gays who denounce Christianity and leave often make sense of their departure by recognizing that their religion is "too small" to accept "the likes of me." This (re)conception of the church and/or God as being too small to accommodate difference is a common basis for renouncing religious affiliation among lesbians and gays. Among those who remain (or become) active participants in their religious communities, there is a slightly different and highly significant twist to this discourse. The strands of this twist include the articulation of the theme that "my gay presence in this too small church is an opportunity for members to stretch their own limits of love and acceptance" and the even more radical notion, "homosexuality is a gift from God." The articulation and convergence of this uniquely queer response to Christianity is the subject of the next section.

ARTICULATING A QUEER CHRISTIAN IDENTITY

Biography and faith traditions intersect to produce discursive strategies toward religion.

(Wade Clark Roof)

Homosexuality is a gift from God.

(John McNeill,
formerly of the Society of Jesus)

In the foregoing comments I have suggested that lesbian and gay Christians are aware that they occupy a unique, marginal, and contradictory position with regard to fellow (heterosexual or closeted) Christians and to (former-Christian or non-Christian) lesbians and gays. This contradiction is experienced as a source of insight and as an occasion for articulating a self that these individuals perceive as stronger, more purposeful and, in many cases, indicative of the true meaning of Christianity. In other words, I suggest that rather than attempt to resolve the apparent contradiction of being queer and Christian, these individuals see "living the contradiction" as a purpose in itself, a raison d'être.

One additional theme that emerged from my conversations with lesbian and gay Christians is this: "my contradictory presence is good for the Church." This revision of the discourse on homosexuality (from problem to useful challenge) serves to reintegrate the homosexual into Christianity (at least in terms of her/his personal articulation of the religion). Further, it renders the homosexual a sort of modern-day crucible with which Christianity must grapple. In doing so, mainline Christian denominations must revisit and redefine the message of love and redemption. In this regard, lesbian and gay Christians redefine "affliction" as an ability; the ability to embrace contradiction and ambiguity is articulated as a manifestation of Christian goodness and character.

This articulation can be interpreted in terms of Roof's thesis of religious individualism (Roof 1999). Individuals enter into a "creative dialogue with tradition" and articulate discursive strategies that enable them to retain significant (often contradictory) aspects of self while maintaining religious commitments.[13] In this instance, the homosexual biography intersects with familiar aspects of Christianity—faith in God's divine wisdom, acceptance of challenge, struggle, oppression, awakening, and rebirth—to produce a particularly queer discursive response toward religion. The lesbian and gay Christians who took part in my research, as well as those interviewed by Wilcox (2000), are a unique group in that they have not rejected religion altogether, nor have they accepted the terms of a "divinely ordered closet" (i.e., donning the cloak of shame and silence in order to maintain Christian commitments and status). Instead, they have articulated a position that can be interpreted as a unique queer Christian identity. This identity merges elements of essentialist reasoning, Christian doctrines of love and acceptance, Christian histories of oppression, and collective struggle to attain godly virtues. The emergence of a common discourse among individuals who are, for the most part, engaged in solitary struggle, is noteworthy. I attribute this emergent queer Christian discourse, in its initial phases, to the common threads in Christianity generally. In articulating a queer Christianity, lesbians and gays take up similar threads regarding the formation of identity and their position within their congregations.

The most common theme I heard among both the lesbian and gay Christians I came to know and the congregants who fully accepted them was that we are "all God's children." A point of reconciliation with one's homosexuality and Christianity seems to be the acknowledgment

that "God created me; He must have created me this way for a reason." This "realization" is marked by many lesbian and gay Christians as a turning point: "All of a sudden it hit me, I believe in God, I believe He is perfect and has created a perfect world. Why would I have these desires if they weren't part of a perfect plan?" Or as one lesbian pastor phrased it, "Yes I've been reborn through my faith in God's love. Turns out I was born queer."[14]

Coupled with the theme of struggle, this discourse becomes a narrative whereby homosexuality is "both a gift and my cross to bear." In this regard, homosexuality becomes a personal crucible for forging character. This discourse is buttressed by the Christian belief that God creates everything for a purpose. The good Christian's task is to nurture faith in God and to live out the purpose evident in her/his own creation—in this case, the creation of homosexuality. Queer Christians find doctrinal support for their homosexuality in the principle, "God is love." A loving God loves and accepts all Her/His creations; a Church founded on these principles must make room for all that God has created and loves. From this thread comes the idea that a Church is only as big as its god, and its god is only as big as the extent of her/his love. Thus, a truly Christian church is a church that is big enough to love and accept homosexual members.

The third and most critical thread in this discourse combines with the others to weave the theme whereby the homosexual is a necessary and useful challenge for contemporary Christianity. In the words of former Jesuit and self-declared gay liberation theologian John McNeill, "God is calling us to play an historical role" (1996, p. 192). This role is to extend to Christian congregations and denominations the challenge of stretching to accept all who enter and wish to belong—in short, to become as big as God's love, which is infinite. This discourse reclaims the proverbial phrase, "love the sinner but hate the sin," but it reframes sin as failure to love and accept all God's creations. In this conceptualization, God and Christianity *per se* are not the problem; rather, the problem is the institution through which God's intent is interpreted. In the words of a gay Methodist minister, "I never had any doubts about my relationship with God. It's the church that's been a problem for me." Thus, the institution of Christianity becomes the problem and lesbian and gay Christians become the chosen few whose special calling it is to redeem institutional Christianity by liberating its narrowly defined god.

Articulating a queer Christian identity involves transforming a discourse of shame and silence (with the promise of exile) into a narrative of pride and expression. For lesbian and gay Christians, pride is based on a belief that homosexuality has a place in God's plan. The particular place at this particular moment in history is to foment Christian renewal and reformation. In this way, lesbian and gay Christians manage their original predicament by renaming themselves and their positions within their congregations in terms of a gay Christian activism. This discursive strategy is consistent with both lesbian and gay social movements and a Christian tradition of faith-based struggle and martyrdom. It elevates the homosexual from a position of "irredeemable problem" to one of "path to redemption." In this particular instance, it is institutional Christianity that is in need of redemption. Just as the individual must struggle in order to grow and to achieve character and, ultimately, exaltation, so too must the institution of Christianity struggle. The "latter-day homosexual" is the occasion for this institutional metamorphosis. Within this discourse, lesbian and gay Christians become both modern-day Christian soldiers and sacrificial lambs. . . .

Implications: Theology

What are the ideological consequences of a gay and lesbian presence in mainstream Christianity? I have suggested that lesbian and gay Christians are authoring a historically specific queer religiosity to make sense of their predicament of exclusion. This queer Christianity is likely to have transformative effects at the individual, community, and organizational levels—all of which are mutually constitutive. Similarly, there are implications for Christian ideologies as well. I offer the following as preliminary observations. Whether one is in agreement with it or not, the articulation of a queer Christian theology, especially as it has emerged within the ranks of individuals trying to make sense of their own contradiction, has implications.

Queer Christian theologies resituate and redefine the parameters for discussions of sexuality and morality. Regardless of one's views, the conversation is different as a consequence of acknowledging homosexuality. Another significant implication is the authoring of a "gay liberation theology" whereby homosexuality is identified as a gift from God. Again, regardless of whether one agrees, this particular discourse is already leading to a re-examination in many denominations of what it means to say that theology should be a "living guide" that reflects its times.

In my own assessment, one of the most noteworthy ideological considerations is the implication of focusing on "unconditional love" as a discursive strategy for accepting and affirming a homosexual presence. Concerning the case of homosexuality, the belief that "god is love" sits in tension with the notion of a patriarchal god who, like the unchallenged parent, sets down rules that are not to be questioned. An ideology of unconditional love implies a love that is growing and stretching; a love that is manifest among members of a community who interpret for themselves the extent and expression of this love. This is a long-standing tension in Christian theology. Deliberations regarding homosexuality that are framed in terms of "god's unconditional love" tip the equation one degree further toward a rendering of a Christian god who is not an anthropomorphic figure handing down his particular rules. Rather, this god is an expression of agreement and affirmation among a collective body united in spirit and intent. In short, "god" becomes the extent of the community's expression of love. The larger the reach of the group's love, the bigger their god.

A Final Note Regarding "Oppositional Consciousness"

In an attempt to explain lesbian and gay involvement in Christian organizations, some lesbian and gay political activists have suggested that religion is one of the "last citadels" of gay oppression (see Hartman 1996 for a review). These observers see the struggle for inclusion in mainstream religions as a final step toward attaining cultural and political acceptance. In this literature, lesbian and gay Christian involvement is interpreted as a form of political expression whereby queers are taking on traditional homophobia by acting from within. This thesis presumes an "oppositional consciousness" (Mansbridge 2001) that conflates outcomes (religious reform) with motivation and presumes a motivation (desire to reform religion) that is not necessarily reflective of the actual experiences of lesbian and gay Christians. My research suggests that there are several stages in self-awareness and articulation that occur before any form of "oppositional consciousness" develops among lesbian and gay Christians. To the extent that such a consciousness is developing, I suggest that it is historically unique and should be understood within the context in which it is developing. Specifically, the motivation should be understood in terms of the homosexual Christian's desire for self-understanding in Christian terms and reintegration into a system of meaning from which he/she has been cast off.

Sociological theses such as Mansbridge's "oppositional consciousness" or Roof's "creative dialogue" are useful in providing a general framework of analysis, but they miss the mark in interpreting motivations and commitments. Roof's thesis is intended to explain what he views as a "shopping" mentality regarding contemporary religion, in which the individual shops around in search of a congregation or denomination that fits personal needs. Queer Christian identities appear to be motivated more by the desire for (re)integration within Christian traditions, at which point the individual may begin to "shop" for a welcoming congregation. Similarly, while it is certainly possible to view the growing lesbian and gay visibility within Christian organizations as a manifestation of "oppositional consciousness," I think it would be inaccurate and misleading to assume a political motivation for this involvement. An intended contribution of this study is to make clear that lesbian and gay Christian participation (and related activism) must be understood on its own terms, in its own context, and in terms of the particular historical moment.

NOTES

1. In this paper I use the phrase "lesbian and gay" because it is the most accurate description of the group about which I am writing. The term "lesbian/gay/bisexual/transgender" (LGBT) is politically strategic and meaningful, but often not descriptively accurate in specific case studies.

2. Several colleagues and interviewees have indicated that the experiences of Jewish lesbians and gays are similar. In this project, I have maintained a focus on mainstream Christian denominations because of my familiarity with Christian theology. For studies in Jewish queer experience, see Schneer and Aviv (2002) and Balka and Rose (1991).

3. During the course of my formal research, Seattle First Baptist was one of a handful of recent Baptist denominations in the United States that were threatened with revocation of their charter for affirming lesbian and gay membership. Other congregations that were the spiritual homes to several of my interviewees struggled with similar tensions within their denominational organizations, especially congregations attempting to appoint lesbian and gay ministers and those that supported standing ministers who had recently "come out" to the congregation.

4. This ethnography is limited, especially in what it suggests regarding variations of gender, race, and geography on the articulation of and circumstances surrounding a queer Christian identity. I expect that there are significant variations in terms of the dimensions of gender and race, and I suspect these interact differently in different geographical regions. This study highlights one variation on the theme of individual reconciliation of homosexuality and Christianity. It should be read in terms of what it can suggest for further research regarding different variations on this theme.

5. There is a notable historical correlation between gay political movements, Christian denominations' heightened discussion of the "homosexual question"—including the revision of the Catechism—and the removal of "homosexuality" as a category of pathology in the 1974 *Diagnostic and Statistical Manual* used by the American Psychiatric Association to identify and diagnose psychological disorders.

6. Article Six, section 2359: "Homosexual persons are called to chastity. By the virtues of self-mastery that teach them inner freedom, at times by the support of disinterested friendship, by prayer and sacramental grace, they can and should gradually and resolutely approach Christian perfection" (Catechism of the Catholic Church 1994, 566).

7. This explanation is consistent with a social psychological literature demonstrating that dominant belief systems are usually not rejected in the face of contradiction. Rather, individuals attempt to make sense of the contradictions through "secondary elaborations" (Mehan and Wood 1975, 197). The motivation for continued engagement in the belief system is the desire to maintain a coherent system of meaning regarding the meaning and purpose of one's life. Even problematic positions within the system of meaning can be less threatening than having no sense of meaning or basis for self-understanding. This literature can be used to explain seemingly incomprehensible behavior such as attendance at one's own "degradation ceremony" (e.g., the Mormon who participates in her/his own excommunication process).

8. Stuart also points out the similarities with other Christians, such as Christian feminists or Christian ecologists, who must also explain and justify their religious commitments.

9. I am not implying that these responses are mutually exclusive or fixed. Rather, it is probable that during the course of a queer Christian career individuals try on aspects of each of these responses. It is beyond the scope of this paper to develop an explanation for primary self-expression through one response or another—a settling in to a particular expression of identity. I assume that various reference groups play a part in this process and that, over time, the proliferation of an articulated queer Christianity will in itself serve as one such point of reference for a new generation of queer youth. I offer some suggestions toward such an explanation in the conclusions.

10. All quotes from subjects used in this article are intended to be illustrative (rather than analytically definitive). For this reason I do not give detailed subject descriptions. These descriptions are available on request. All of the interviewees in this study elected to use their real names. For reasons of "voice" this is my preferred ethnographical practice.

11. Although nothing conclusive can be ascertained from my few interviews, this phenomenon of simultaneous awakening of homosexuality and spiritual vocation may be more prevalent among young men. Nineteen of the 25 men I interviewed spoke of this experience. Only two of the women mentioned a similar feeling. In fact, the women tended to develop a strong sense of spirituality and desire for religious involvement sometime after coming to terms with their homosexuality. Two of the men offered an explanation of their early sense of vocation as being a means of making them feel better about their homosexuality. As one put it, "God wouldn't have made me this way if

he didn't have something special in mind for my life." Another noted that he considered his experience somewhat normal "for someone who was meant to be a priest . . . after all, aren't all priests supposed to be gay? I figured that my attraction to men, including one of the teachers at my [Catholic] school, was just God's way of making it clear that I was meant to be a priest."

12. Evangelicalism is another domain of Christianity whose members experience struggle and are likely to view this struggle as a definitive aspect of themselves and their religious commitment. (Smith, C. 1998. *American Evangelicalism: Embattled and Thriving.* Chicago: University of Chicago Press.)

13. For another interesting example, see Gloria Gonzalez-Lopez's (2004) study of Catholic Mexican immigrant women and their sex lives.

14. In the past two decades, many lesbian and gay Christians embraced the hypothesis that homosexuality is genetic rather than socially determined. This essentialist position was consistent with the idea that if homosexuality exists, God must have intended it. Catholicism has accepted the essentialist proposition of biological determinism explicitly without accepting the corollary that homosexuality is a positive characteristic. The latter is the queer twist on the essentialist proposition. But belonging to a denomination that accepted the initial proposition made it easier to make the case for the possible goodness and purpose of homosexuality. Other denominations, notably Mormonism, state explicitly that homosexuality is a "lifestyle choice" that a person should resist by every possible means, no matter how strong the inclination. For a discussion of the intersection of essentialist and constructionist reasoning within Christian considerations of sexuality, see Boswell (1997).

REFERENCES

Anzaldua, G. 1987. *Borderlands/La Frontera: The new Mestiza.* San Francisco: Aunt Lute Books.

Balka, C., and Rose, A., ed. 1991. *Twice blessed: On being lesbian, gay and Jewish.* Boston, MA: Beacon.

Boswell, J. 1997. Concepts, experience, and sexuality. In *Que(e)rying religion: A critical anthology,* ed. G. D. Comstock and S. E. Henking. New York: Continuum.

Bouldrey, B., ed. 1995. *Wrestling with the angel: Faith and religion in the lives of gay men.* New York: Riverhead Books.

Catechism of the Catholic Church. 1994. United States Catholic Conference, *Libreria Editrice Vaticana.* Mahwah, NJ: Paulist Press.

Comstock, G. D. 1997. *Que(e)rying Religion: A Critical Anthology.* New York: Continuum.

Conrad, P., and Schneider, J. 1980. Homosexuality: From sin to sickness to lifestyle. In *Deviance and medicalization: From badness to sickness,* ed. P. Conrad and J. Schneider. Philadelphia: Temple University Press.

Cornell-Drury, P. 2000. Seattle First Christian Church unanimously becomes "open & affirming" letter to the congregation, 6 November, Seattle, WA.

Fortunato, J. 1982. *Embracing the exile: Healing journeys of gay Christians.* San Francisco: Harper Collins.

Gill, S., ed. 1998. *The lesbian and gay Christian movement: Campaigning for justice, truth, and love.* London: Cassell.

Gluckman, A., and Reed, B., ed. 1997. *Homo Economics.* New York: Routledge.

Gonzalez-Lopez, G. 2004. *Beyond the bed sheets, beyond the borders: Mexican immigrant women and their sex lives.* Berkeley: University of California Press.

Harryman, Don D. 1991. With all thy getting, get understanding. In *Peculiar people: Mormons and same-sex orientation,* ed. R. Schow, W. Schow and M. Raynes. Salt Lake City: Signature Books.

Hartman, K. 1996. *Congregations in conflict: The battle over homosexuality.* New Brunswick, NJ: Rutgers University Press.

Mansbridge, J. 2001. The making of oppositional consciousness. In *Oppositional consciousness: The subjective roots of social protest,* ed. J. Mansbridge and A. Morris. Chicago: University of Chicago Press.

McNeill, J. 1996. *Taking a chance on god: Liberating theology for gays, lesbians, and their lovers, families, and friends.* Boston, MA: Beacon.

Mehan, H., and Wood, H. 1975. Five features of reality. In *Reality of ethnomethodology,* ed. H. Mehan and H. Wood. New York: Wiley.

Nestle, J. 2002. How a "liberationist" fem understands being a Jew. In *Queer Jews*, ed. D. Schneer and C. Aviv. New York: Routledge.

O'Brien, J. 2001a. Boundaries and contradictions in self articulation. In *The production of reality*, ed. J. O'Brien and P. Kollock. Newbury Park, CA: Pine Forge Press.

O'Brien, J. 2001b. Homophobia and heterosexism. In *International encyclopedia of the social and behavioral sciences*. London: Elsevier Science.

Plummer, K. 1995. *Telling sexual stories: Power, change, and social worlds*. London: Routledge.

Roof, W. C. 1999. *Spiritual marketplace: Baby boomers and the remaking of American Religion*. Princeton, NJ: Rutgers University Press.

Schneer, P. and Aviv, C. 2002. *Queer Jews*. New York: Routledge.

Smith, R. L. 1994. *AIDS, gays and the American Catholic church*. Cleveland, OH: Pilgrim Press.

Stuart, E. 1997. *Religion is a queer thing: A guide to the Christian faith for lesbian, gay, bisexual and transgendered people*. Cleveland, OH: Pilgrim Press.

Tigert, L. M. 1997. *Coming out while staying in: Struggles and celebrations of lesbians and gays in the church*. Cleveland, OH: United Church Press.

White, D. and White, O. K. 2004. Queer Christian confessions: Spiritual autobiographies of gay Christians. *Culture and Religion* 5 (2).

Wilcox, M. 2000. Two roads converged: Religion and identity among lesbian, gay, bisexual and transgender Christians. Doctoral Dissertation, University of California, Santa Barbara.

CONTRADICTIONS AND CONFLICT IN SELF-PRODUCTION

26

Life as the Maid's Daughter

Mary Romero

(1995)

INTRODUCTION

. . . My current research attempts to expand the sociological understanding of the dynamics of race, class, and gender in the everyday routines of family life and reproductive labor. . . . I am lured to the unique setting presented by domestic service . . . and I turn to the realities experienced by the children of private household workers. This focus is not entirely voluntary. While presenting my research on Chicana private household workers, I was approached repeatedly by Latina/os and African Americans who wanted to share their knowledge about domestic service—knowledge they obtained as the daughters and sons of household workers. Listening to their accounts about their mothers' employment presents another reality to understanding paid and unpaid reproductive labor and the way in which persons of color are socialized into a class-based, gendered, racist social structure. The following discussion explores issues of stratification in everyday life by analyzing the life story of a maid's daughter. This life story illustrates the potential of the standpoint of the maid's daughter for generating knowledge about race, class, and gender. . . .

SOCIAL BOUNDARIES PRESENTED IN THE LIFE STORY

The first interview with Teresa,[1] the daughter of a live-in maid, eventually led to a life history project. I am intrigued by Teresa's experiences with her mother's white, upper-middle-class employers while maintaining close ties to her relatives in Juarez, Mexico, and Mexican friends in Los Angeles. While some may view Teresa's life as a freak accident, living a life of "rags to riches," and certainly not a common Chicana/o experience, her story represents a microcosm of power relationships in the larger society. Life as the maid's daughter in an upper-middle-class neighborhood exemplifies many aspects of the Chicano/Mexicano experience as "racial ethnics" in the United States, whereby the boundaries of inclusion and exclusion are constantly changing as we move from one social setting and one social role to another.

Teresa's narrative contains descriptive accounts of negotiating boundaries in the employers' homes and in their community. As the maid's daughter, the old adage "Just like one of the family" is a reality, and Teresa has to learn when she must act like the employer's child and when she must assume the appropriate behavior as the maid's daughter. She has to recognize all the social cues and interpret social settings correctly—when to expect the same rights and privileges as the employer's children and when to fulfill the expectations and obligations as the maid's daughter. Unlike the employers' families, Teresa and her mother rely on different ways of obtaining knowledge. The taken-for-granted reality of the employers' families do not contain conscious experiences of negotiating race and class status, particularly not in the intimate setting of the home. Teresa's status is constantly changing in response to the wide range of social settings she encounters—from employers' dinner parties with movie stars and corporate executives to Sunday dinners with Mexican garment workers in Los Angeles and factory workers in El Paso. Since Teresa remains bilingual and bicultural throughout her life, her story reflects the constant struggle and resistance to maintain her Mexican identity, claiming a reality that is neither rewarded nor acknowledged as valid.

Teresa's account of her life as the maid's daughter is symbolic of the way that racial ethnics participate in the United States; sometimes we are included and other times excluded or ignored. Teresa's story captures the reality of social stratification in the United States, that is, a racist, sexist, and class-structured society upheld by an ideology of equality. I will analyze the experiences of the maid's daughter in an upper-middle-class neighborhood in Los Angeles to investigate the ways that boundaries of race, class, and gender are maintained or diffused in everyday life. I have selected various excerpts from the transcripts that illustrate how knowledge about a class-based and gendered, racist social order is learned, the type of information that is conveyed, and how the boundaries between systems of domination impact everyday life. I begin with a brief history of Teresa and her mother, Carmen.

LEARNING SOCIAL BOUNDARIES: BACKGROUND

Teresa's mother was born in Piedras Negras, a small town in Aguas Calientes in Mexico. After her father was seriously injured in a railroad accident, the family moved to a small town outside Ciudad Juarez. . . . By the time she was fifteen she moved to Juarez and took a job as a domestic, making about eight dollars a week. She soon crossed the border and began working for Anglo families in the country club area in El Paso. Like other domestics in El Paso, Teresa's mother returned to Mexico on weekends and helped support her mother and sisters. In her late twenties she joined several of her friends in their search for better-paying jobs in Los Angeles. The women immediately found jobs in the garment industry. Yet, after six months in the sweatshops, Teresa's mother went to an agency in search of domestic work. She was placed in a very exclusive Los Angeles neighborhood. Several years later Teresa was born. Her friends took care of the baby while Carmen continued working; childcare became a burden, however, and she eventually returned to Mexico. At the age of thirty-six Teresa's mother returned to Mexico with her newborn baby. Leaving Teresa with her grandmother and aunts, her mother sought work in the country club area. Three years later Teresa and her mother returned to Los Angeles.

Over the next fifteen years Teresa lived with her mother in the employer's (Smith) home, usually the two sharing the maid's room located off the kitchen. From the age of three until Teresa started school, she accompanied her mother to work. She continued to live in the Smiths' home until she left for college. All of Teresa's live-in years were spent in one employer's household. The Smiths were unable to afford a full-time maid, however, so Teresa's mother began doing day work throughout the neighborhood. After school Teresa went to whatever house her mother was cleaning and waited until her mother finished working, around 4 or 6 P.M., and then returned to the Smiths' home with her mother. Many prominent families in the neighborhood knew Teresa as the maid's daughter and treated her accordingly. While Teresa wanted the relationship with the employers to cease when she

went to college and left the neighborhood, her mother continued to work as a live-in maid with no residence other than the room in the employer's home; consequently, Teresa's social status as the maid's daughter continued. . . .

ONE OF THE FAMILY

As Teresa got older, the boundaries between insider and outsider became more complicated, as employers referred to her and Carmen as "one of the family." Entering into an employer's world as the maid's daughter, Teresa was not only subjected to the rules of an outsider but also had to recognize when the rules changed, making her momentarily an insider. While the boundaries dictating Carmen's work became blurred between the obligations of an employee and that of a friend or family member, Teresa was forced into situations in which she was expected to be just like one of the employer's children, and yet she remained the maid's daughter. . . .

Living under conditions established by the employers made Teresa and her mother's efforts to maintain a distinction between their family life and an employer's family very difficult. Analyzing incidents in which the boundaries between the worker's family and employer's family were blurred highlights the issues that complicate the mother-daughter relationship. Teresa's account of her mother's hospitalization was the first of numerous conflicts between the two that stemmed from the live-in situation and their relationships with the employer's family. The following excerpt demonstrates the difficulty in interacting as a family unit and the degree of influence and power employers exerted over their daily lives:

> When I was about ten my mother got real sick. That summer, instead of sleeping downstairs in my mother's room when my mother wasn't there, one of the kids was gone away to college, so it was

just Rosalyn, David and myself that were home. The other two were gone, so I was gonna sleep upstairs in one of the rooms. I was around eight or nine, ten I guess. I lived in the back room. It was a really neat room because Rosalyn was allowed to paint it. She got her friend who was real good, painted a big tree and clouds and all this stuff on the walls. So I really loved it and I had my own room. I was with the Smiths all the time, as my parents, for about two months. My mother was in the hospital for about a month. Then when she came home, she really couldn't do anything. We would all have dinner, the Smiths were really, really supportive. I went to summer school and I took math and English and stuff like that. I was in this drama class and I did drama and I got to do the leading role. Everybody really liked me and Ms. Smith would come and see my play. So things started to change when I got a lot closer to them and I was with them alone. I would go see my mother every day, and my cousin was there. I think that my cousin kind of resented all the time that the Smiths spent with me. I think my mother was really afraid that now that she wasn't there that they were going to steal me from her. I went to see her, but I could only stay a couple of hours and it was really weird. I didn't like seeing my mother in pain and she was in a lot of pain. I remember before she came home the Smiths said that they thought it would be a really good idea if I stayed upstairs and I had my own room now that my mother was going to be sick and I couldn't sleep in the same bed 'cause I might hurt her. It was important for my mother to be alone. And how did I feel about that? I was really excited about that [having her own room]—you know. They said, "Your mom she is probably not going to like it and she might get upset about it, but I think that we can convince her that it is ok." When my mom came home, she understood that she couldn't be touched and that she had to be really careful, but she wanted it [having her own room] to be temporary. Then my mother was really upset. She got into it with them and said, "No, I don't want it that way." She would tell me, "No, I want you to be down here. ¿Qué crees que eres hija de ellos? You're gonna be

with me all the time, you can't do that." So I would tell Ms. Smith. She would ask me when we would go to the market together, "How does your mom seem, what does she feel, what does she say?" She would get me to relay that. I would say, "I think my mom is really upset about me moving upstairs. She doesn't like it and she just says no." I wouldn't tell her everything. They would talk to her and finally they convinced her, but my mom really, really resented it and was really angry about it. She was just generally afraid. All these times that my mother wasn't there, things happened and they would take me places with them, go out to dinner with them and their friends. So that was a real big change, in that I slept upstairs and had different rules. Everything changed. I was more independent. I did my own homework; they would open the back door and yell that dinner was ready—you know. Things were just real different.

The account illustrates how assuming the role of insider was an illusion because neither the worker's daughter nor the worker ever became a member of the white, middle-class family. Teresa was only allowed to move out of the maid's quarter, where she shared a bed with her mother, when two of the employer's children were leaving home, vacating two bedrooms. . . .

Teresa and Carmen did not experience the boundaries of insider and outsider in the same way. Teresa was in a position to assume a more active family role when employers made certain requests. Unlike her mother, she was not an employee and was not expected to clean and serve the employer. Carmen's responsibility for the housework never ceased, however, regardless of the emotional ties existing between employee and employers. She and her employers understood that, whatever family activity she might be participating in, if the situation called for someone to clean, pick up, or serve, that was Carmen's job. When the Smiths requested Teresa to sit at the dinner table with the family, they placed Teresa in a different class position than her mother, who was now expected to serve her daughter alongside her employer. Moving Teresa upstairs in a bedroom alongside the employer and their children was bound to drive a wedge between Teresa and Carmen. There is a long history of spatial deference in domestic service, including separate entrances, staircases, and eating and sleeping arrangements. Carmen's room reflected her position in the household. As the maid's quarter, the room was separated from the rest of the bedrooms and was located near the maid's central work area, the kitchen. The room was obviously not large enough for two beds because Carmen and Teresa shared a bed. Once Teresa was moved upstairs, she no longer shared the same social space in the employer's home as her mother. Weakening the bonds between the maid and her daughter permitted the employers to broaden their range of relationships and interaction with Teresa.

Carmen's feelings of betrayal and loss underline how threatening the employers' actions were. She understood that the employers were in a position to buy her child's love. They had already attempted to socialize Teresa into Euro-American ideals by planning Teresa's education and deciding what courses she would take. Guided by the importance they place on European culture, the employers defined the Mexican Spanish spoken by Teresa and her mother as inadequate and classified Castillan Spanish as "proper" Spanish. As a Mexican immigrant woman working as a live-in maid, Carmen was able to experience certain middle-class privileges, but her only access to these privileges was through her relationship with employers. Therefore, without the employers' assistance, she did not have the necessary connections to enroll Teresa in private schools or provide her with upper-middle-class experiences to help her develop the skills needed to survive in elite schools. Carmen only gained these privileges for her daughter at a price; she

relinquished many of her parental rights to her employers. To a large degree the Smiths determined Carmen's role as a parent, and the other employers restricted the time she had to attend school functions and the amount of energy left at the end of the day to mother her own child.

Carmen pointed to the myth of "being like one of the family" in her comment, "¿Qué crees que eres hija de ellos? You're gonna be with me all the time, you can't do that." The statement underlines the fact that the bond between mother and daughter is for life, whereas the pseudofamily relationship with employers is temporary and conditional. Carmen wanted her daughter to understand that taking on the role of being one of the employer's family did not relinquish her from the responsibility of fulfilling her "real" family obligations. The resentment Teresa felt from her cousin who was keeping vigil at his aunt's hospital bed indicated that she had not been a dutiful daughter. The outside pressure from an employer did not remove her own family obligations and responsibilities. Teresa's relatives expected a daughter to be at her mother's side providing any assistance possible as a caretaker, even if it was limited to companionship. The employer determined Teresa's activity, however, and shaped her behavior into that of a middle-class child; consequently, she was kept away from the hospital and protected from the realities of her mother's illness. Furthermore, she was submerged into the employer's world, dining at the country club and interacting with their friends.

Her mother's accusation that Teresa wanted to be the Smiths' daughter signifies the feelings of betrayal or loss and the degree to which Carmen was threatened by the employer's power and authority. Yet Teresa also felt betrayal and loss and viewed herself in competition with the employers for her mother's time, attention, and love. In this excerpt Teresa accuses her mother of wanting to be part of employers' families and community:

> I couldn't understand it—you know—until I was about eighteen and then I said, "It is your fault. If I treat the Smiths differently, it is your fault. You chose to have me live in this situation. It was your decision to let me have two parents, and for me to balance things off, so you can't tell me that I said this. You are the one who wanted this." When I was about eighteen we got into a huge fight on Christmas. I hated the holidays because I hated spending them with the Smiths. My mother always worked. She worked on every holiday. She loved to work on the holidays! She would look forward to working. My mother just worked all the time! I think that part of it was that she wanted to have power and control over this community, and she wanted the network, and she wanted to go to different people's houses.

As employers, Mr. and Mrs. Smith were able to exert an enormous amount of power over the relationship between Teresa and her mother. Carmen was employed in an occupation in which the way to improve working conditions, pay, and benefits was through the manipulation of personal relationships with employers. Carmen obviously tried to take advantage of her relationship with the Smiths in order to provide the best for her daughter. The more intimate and interpersonal the relationship, the more likely employers were to give gifts, do favors, and provide financial assistance. Although speaking in anger and filled with hurt, Teresa accused her mother of choosing to be with employers and their families rather than with her own daughter. Underneath Teresa's accusation was the understanding that the only influence and status her mother had as a domestic was gained through her personal relationships with employers. Although her mother had limited power in rejecting the Smiths' demands, Teresa held her responsible for giving them too much control.

Teresa argued that the positive relationship with the Smiths was done out of obedience to her mother and denied any familial feelings toward the employers. The web between employee and employers' families affected both mother and daughter, who were unable to separate the boundaries of work and family.

MAINTAINING CULTURAL IDENTITY

A major theme in Teresa's narrative was her struggle to retain her Mexican culture and her political commitment to social justice. Rather than internalizing meaning attached to Euro-American practices and redefining Mexican culture and bilingualism as negative social traits, Teresa learned to be a competent social actor in both white, upper-middle-class environments and in working- and middle-class Chicano and Mexicano environments. To survive as a stranger in so many social settings, Teresa developed an acute skill for assessing the rules governing a particular social setting and acting accordingly. Her ability to be competent in diverse social settings was only possible, however, because of her life with the employers' children. Teresa and her mother maintained another life—one that was guarded and protected against any employer intrusion. Their other life was Mexican, not white, was Spanish speaking, not English speaking, was female dominated rather than male dominated, and was poor and working-class, not upper-middle-class. During the week Teresa and her mother visited the other Mexican maids in the neighborhoods, on weekends they occasionally took a bus into the Mexican barrio in Los Angeles to have dinner with friends, and every summer they spent a month in Ciudad Juarez with their family. . . .

Teresa's description of evening activity with the Mexican maids in the neighborhood provides insight into her daily socialization and explains how she learned to live in the employer's home without internalizing all their negative attitudes toward Mexican and working-class culture. Within the white, upper-class neighborhood in which they worked, the Mexican maids got together on a regular basis and cooked Mexican food, listened to Mexican music, and gossiped in Spanish about their employers. Treated as invisible or as confidants, the maids were frequently exposed to the intimate details of their employers' marriages and family life. The Mexican maids voiced their disapproval of the lenient child-rearing practices and parental decisions, particularly surrounding drug usage and the importance of material possessions:

> Raquel was the only one [maid] in the neighborhood who had her own room and own TV set. So everybody would go over to Raquel's. . . . This was my mother's support system. After hours, they would go to different people's [maid's] rooms depending on what their rooms had. Some of them had kitchens and they would go and cook all together, or do things like play cards and talk all the time. I remember that in those situations they would sit, and my mother would talk about the Smiths, what they were like. When they were going to negotiate for raises, when they didn't like certain things, I would listen and hear all the different discussions about what was going on in different houses. And they would talk, also, about the family relationships. The way they interacted, the kids did this and that. At the time some of the kids were smoking pot and they would talk about who was smoking marijuana. How weird it was that the parents didn't care. They would talk about what they saw as being wrong. The marriage relationship, or how weird it was they would go off to the beauty shop and spend all this money, go shopping and do all these weird things and the effect that it had on the kids.

The interaction among the maids points to the existence of another culture operating invisibly within a Euro-American and male-dominated community. The workers' support system did not include employers and addressed their concerns as mothers, immigrants, workers, and women. They created a Mexican-dominated domain for themselves. Here they ate Mexican food, spoke Spanish, listened to the Spanish radio station, and watched novellas on TV. Here Teresa was not a cultural artifact but, instead, a member of the Mexican community.

In exchanging gossip and voicing their opinions about the employers' lifestyles, the maids rejected many of the employers' priorities in life. Sharing stories about the employers' families allowed the Mexican immigrant women to be critical of white, upper-middle-class families and to affirm and enhance their own cultural practices and beliefs. The regular evening sessions with other working-class Mexican immigrant women were essential in preserving Teresa and her mother's cultural values and were an important agency of socialization for Teresa. For instance, the maids had a much higher regard for their duties and responsibilities as mothers than as wives or lovers. In comparison to their mistresses, they were not financially dependent on men, nor did they engage in the expensive and time-consuming activity of being an ideal wife, such as dieting, exercising, and maintaining a certain standard of beauty in their dress, makeup, and hairdos. Unlike the employers' daughters, who attended cotillions and were socialized to acquire success through marriage, Teresa was constantly pushed to succeed academically in order to pursue a career. The gender identity cultivated among the maids did not include dependence on men or the learned helplessness that was enforced in the employers' homes but, rather, promoted self-sufficiency. However, both white women employers and Mexican women employees were expected to be nurturing and caring. These traits were further reinforced when employers asked Teresa to babysit for their children or to provide them with companionship during their husbands' absences.

So, while Teresa observed her mother adapting to the employers' standards in her interaction with their children, she learned that her mother did not approve of their lifestyle and understood that she had another set of expectations to adhere to. Teresa attended the same schools as employers' children, wore similar clothes, and conducted most of her social life within the same socioeconomic class, but she remained the maid's daughter—and learned the limitations of that position. Teresa watched her mother uphold higher standards for her and apply a different set of standards to the employers' children; most of the time, however, it appeared to Teresa as if they had no rules at all.

Sharing stories about the Smiths and other employers in a female, Mexican, and worker-dominated social setting provided Teresa with a clear image of the people she lived with as employers rather than as family members. Seeing the employers through the eyes of the employees forced Teresa to question their kindness and benevolence and to recognize their use of manipulation to obtain additional physical and emotional labor from the employees. She became aware of the workers' struggles and the long list of grievances, including no annual raises, no paid vacations, no social security or health benefits, little if any privacy, and sexual harassment. Teresa was also exposed to the price that working-class immigrant women employed as live-in maids paid in maintaining white, middle-class, patriarchal communities. Employers' careers and lifestyles, particularly the everyday rituals affirming male privilege, were made possible through the labor women provided for men's physical, social, and emotional needs. Female employers depended on the maid's labor to assist in the reproduction of their gendered class status. Household labor was expanded in order to accommodate the male members of the employers' families and to preserve their privilege. Additional work was created by rearranging meals around men's work and recreation schedules and by waiting on them and serving them. Teresa's mother was frequently called upon to provide emotional labor for the wife, husband, mother, and father within an employer's family, thus freeing members to work or increase their leisure time.

DISCUSSION

Teresa's account offers insight into the ways racial ethnic women gain knowledge about the social order and use the knowledge to develop survival strategies. As the college-educated daughter of an immigrant Mexican woman employed as a live-in maid, Teresa's experiences in the employers' homes, neighborhood, and school and her experiences in the homes of working-class Mexicano families and barrios provided her with the skills to cross the class and cultural boundaries separating the two worlds. The process of negotiating social boundaries involved an evaluation of Euro-American culture and its belief system in light of an intimate knowledge of white, middle-class families. Being in the position to compare and contrast behavior within different communities, Teresa debunked notions of "American family values" and resisted efforts toward assimilation. Learning to function in the employers' world was accomplished without internalizing its belief system, which defined ethnic culture as inferior. Unlike the employers' families, Teresa was not able to assume the taken-for-granted reality of her mother's employers because her experiences provided a different kind of knowledge about the social order.

While the employers' children were surrounded by positive images of their race and class status, Teresa faced negative sanctions against her culture and powerless images of her race. Among employers' families she quickly learned that her "mother tongue" was not valued and that her culture was denied. All the Mexican adults in the neighborhood were in subordinate positions to the white adults and were responsible for caring for and nurturing white children. Most of the female employers were full-time homemakers who enjoyed the financial security provided by their husbands, whereas the Mexican immigrant women in the neighborhood all worked as maids and were financially independent; in many cases they were supporting children, husbands, and other family members. By directly observing her mother serve, pick up after, and nurture employers and their families, Teresa learned about white, middle-class privileges. Her experiences with other working-class Mexicans were dominated by women's responsibility for their children and extended families. Here the major responsibility of mothering was financial; caring and nurturing were secondary and were provided by the extended family or children did without. Confronted with a working mother who was too tired to spend time with her, Teresa learned about the racial, class, and gender parameters of parenthood, including its privileges, rights, responsibilities, and obligations. She also learned that the role of a daughter included helping her mother with everyday household tasks and, eventually, with the financial needs of the extended family. Unlike her uncles and male cousins, Teresa was not exempt from cooking and housework, regardless of her financial contributions. Within the extended family Teresa was subjected to standards of beauty strongly weighted by male definitions of women as modest beings, many times restricted in her dress and physical movements. Her social worlds became clearly marked by race, ethnic, class, and gender differences.

Successfully negotiating movement from a white, male, and middle-class setting to one dominated by working-class, immigrant, Mexican women involved a socialization process that provided Teresa with the skills to be bicultural. Since neither setting was bicultural, Teresa had to become that in order to be a competent social actor in each. Being bicultural included having the ability to assess the rules governing each setting and to understand her ethnic, class, and gender position. Her early socialization in the employers' households was not guided by principles of creativity, independence, and leadership but, rather, was based on conformity and accommodation. Teresa's experiences in two different cultural groups allowed her to separate each and to fulfill the employers' expectations without necessarily internalizing the meaning attached to the act. Therefore, she was able to learn English without internalizing the idea that English is superior to Spanish or that monolingualism is normal. The existence of a Mexican community within the employers' neighborhood provided Teresa with a collective experience of class-based racism, and the maids' support system affirmed and enhanced their own belief system and culture. As Philomena Essed (1991, 294) points out, "The problem is not only how knowledge of racism is acquired but also what kind of knowledge is being transmitted."

Teresa's life story lends itself to a complex set of analyses because the pressures to assimilate were challenged by the positive interactions she experienced within her ethnic community. Like other bilingual persons in the United States, Teresa's linguistic abilities were shaped by the linguistic practices of the social settings she had access to. Teresa learned the appropriate behavior for each social setting, each marked by different class and cultural dynamics and in which women's economic roles and relationships to men were distinct. An overview of Teresa's socialization illustrates the process of biculturalism—a process that included different sets of standards and rules governing her actions as a woman, as a Chicana, and as the maid's daughter. . . .

NOTES

This essay was originally presented as a paper at the University of Michigan, "Feminist Scholarship: Thinking through the Disciplines," 30 January 1992. I want to thank Abigail J. Stewart and Donna Stanton for their insightful comments and suggestions.

1. The names are pseudonyms.

REFERENCE

Essed, Philomena. 1991. *Understanding Everyday Racism*. Newbury Park, Calif.: Sage Publications.

THINKING ABOUT THE READING

Teresa's childhood is unique in that she and her mother lived in the household of her mother's employer, requiring them to conform to the expectations of the employers even when her mother was "not at work." Her childhood was shaped by the need to read signals from others to determine her position in various social settings. What were some of the different influences in Teresa's early socialization? Did she accept people's attempts to mold her, or did she resist? How did she react to her mother's employers' referring to her as "one of the family"? Teresa came from a poor family, but she spent her childhood in affluent households. With respect to socialization, what advantages do you think these experiences provided her? What were the disadvantages? How do you think these experiences would have changed if she was a *son* of a live-in maid, rather than a daughter? If she was a poor *white* girl rather than Latina?

PART V

PRODUCING SOCIAL LIFE THROUGH INTERACTION

All the world's a stage,

And all the men and women merely players:

They have their exits and their entrances;

And one man in his time plays many parts.

—William Shakespeare, *As You Like It*

We are told on good authority, Callicles, that heaven and earth and their respective inhabitants are held together by the bonds of society and love and order and discipline and righteousness, and that is why the universe is an ordered whole or cosmos and not a state of disorder and license.

—Plato, *Gorgias*

MEANING IS NEGOTIATED THROUGH INTERACTION

Jodi O'Brien

Imagine you are staying in a hotel and return to your room one evening to find a stranger undressed and sitting in the bed. What do you do? A likely first response would be to check your key and the door number to see if you have the wrong room. How the stranger reacts will also give you important cues about the situation. If the person immediately begins to scream, you will likely conclude that you definitely have the wrong room or some other mistake has been made. However, what if the person were to wink at you and say, "Hi there, I've been waiting for you." This comment would likely generate an entirely different scenario playing out in your head. As we discussed in earlier sections of the book, your response will depend on how you interpret the situation; in an ambiguous situation you look for clues from the other person to figure out what is going on. Once you have decided what is going on, you will have a better idea of how to respond. Another way of looking at this is that once you know the scene, you'll have an idea of the social identities that are expected for that scene.

WHAT'S GOING ON?
PROJECTING A DEFINITION OF THE SITUATION

For the socialized actor, most situations are not this ambiguous. When we enter a situation, we immediately name it; we *define the situation*. Some sociologists call this *framing*. Once we know the definition of the situation or the frame, we know the scene and what is likely to be expected of us and others. In other words, frames set into motion a series of related categories in our minds that include the appropriate scripts for feeling and acting. Part III described the process by which we learn these social scripts and identities. In this section, the focus is on the ways in which people signal to another and *negotiate* the definition of the situation. Most social interaction goes so smoothly that we are not aware of the underlying work we are doing as social actors to create a meaningful situation.

This interaction work is obvious in the imaginary play of children who spend a great deal of time defining the situation and negotiating the appropriate roles. "Pretend you are a pirate and this tree is your ship," one child might say. "I am the good guy and this table is my ship and you try to get onboard and we'll have a sword fight with these sticks. OK?" This scene setting will continue throughout the game, which requires continuous active announcements about what each prop stands for, who each player is, and so forth. Scuffles break out when one child wants to be something that is "not appropriate" for the scene. "I'll be a cowboy who comes and ropes the pirate," another child might announce. "There *are no* cowboys in pirates," the other children will explain in exasperation.

As Mead discussed in his theory of self-development through play (see Part III, Reading 12), children initially take on different roles and play them without concern for the interactional context: A cowboy, a pirate, and a nurse can all play happily together. In this case, each child is simply practicing the characteristics associated with the respective character. However, as the child becomes more sophisticated and socialized, she begins to associate different characters with specific scenes or frames and becomes more vigilant about populating the play with characters that are appropriate to the scene as she has learned it. For Mead, this form of interactional play is key to becoming fully socialized. One learns to adopt social identities that are specific to the definition of the situation.

Children work actively at establishing the definition of the situation, but for most of us, social life involves a series of moving from one encounter to another in which the situation is more or less defined by cues such as location (church, classroom, grocery store) and event (date, exam, funeral). Through the socialization process, we learn to associate specific social identities—and corresponding behavior and feelings—with specific locations and events. In other words, we have a series of *event schemas* and *place schemas* that trigger associative responses that seem and feel automatic. These schemas include grand events such as a wedding or moments as trivial as an encounter with an old acquaintance while walking down the street. In each case, we define the situation (mostly automatically and mindlessly) and respond accordingly. This seemingly automatic behavior masks the extent to which these patterns are socially learned and *interactionally maintained.*

Erving Goffman is a sociologist who devoted most of his career to describing and explaining the ways in which we continuously create and recreate social experience through our interactions with one another. Goffman (Reading 27) invites us to slow down each frame of interaction and to explore the systematic ways in which, much like children at play, we are constantly making social reality. What seems orderly and routine on the surface is actually the result of *interaction work.* The appearance of order comes from the fact that, as socialized beings, we share similar scripts or expectations of various situations and we work together to *realize*—make real—our own scripts or expectations. Thus, according to Goffman, social life can be usefully analyzed as a form of theater in which social actors, knowing the script, do their best to enact the appropriate identities for the situation. Goffman also notes that because humans are prone to error, we are always making performance mistakes. But just as the audience waits in suspended animation for an actor to remember her or his line, we help each other smooth over the mistakes so that the performance can continue. These actions include *tact, giving accounts,* and practicing the *nothing unusual bias.* Let's look more closely at some of Goffman's ideas.

LIFE AS THEATER

"Life as theater" uses the metaphor of *performance* to explain interaction routines. Like any metaphor, it is not a complete description of social reality, but in many ways, our interactions with others do seem to resemble a theatrical performance.

The theater metaphor can be seen in the origins of the word *person,* which comes from the Latin *persona,* meaning "a mask worn by actors." We behave differently (play different roles) in front of different people (audiences). We pick out clothing (a costume) that is consistent with the image we wish to project. We enlist the help of friends, caterers, and decorators (fellow actors and stage crew) to help us successfully "stage" a dinner for a friend, a birthday party for a relative, or a gala for a fundraiser. And if we need to adjust our clothing or wish to say something unflattering about one of our guests, we are careful to do so out of sight from others (backstage).

The presentation of ourselves to others is known as *dramaturgy,* and the use of the theatrical metaphor for analyzing human interaction is known as the *dramaturgical perspective.* Goffman is one of the most noted writers on this subject. In 1959, he published *The Presentation of Self in Everyday Life.* In this classic book, Goffman analyzes everyday "performances." He details the care people take in preparing and presenting their performances—that is, the manner in which people *manage* the impressions others form of them.

Why do people spend so much time and energy thinking about what they should say and how they should look? Some would say that we should simply "be ourselves" and that only those who are deceitful need to worry about managing their image. They would say that con artists and the insincere have to be concerned about these issues, but what about good, decent people? In fact, however, even saints are concerned with the presentation of self. To tell us to simply be ourselves implies that who we are is easily, quickly, and accurately perceived by those with whom we interact. But if we have just met someone or will be interacting with someone for only a short length of time (for example, in a job interview), we certainly can't count on the person to see us as we see ourselves. Dramaturgy can be an issue even when we interact with people who have known us for some time. Who we are may not be obvious to others—most of us do not wear our personal characteristics and convictions tattooed onto our foreheads.

Private Minds, Public Identities: Impression Management

A simple but profound truth about human interaction is that minds are private. Our thoughts, desires, beliefs, and character cannot be directly perceived and evaluated by others. We are not a species of mind readers, and so we must depend on signs and gestures to comprehend one another. Recall the example of the border guard from the essay in

Part II. The guard sizes people up and treats them according to their appearance. Therefore, it is in people's best interest to appear in a way that gets them treated as they wish. In this case, they want to appear "law-abiding."

The fact that minds are private doesn't mean that people are obligated to accurately display their thoughts and desires to others, but it does mean that even the most honest people must be concerned about how they come across to others. In Goffman's (1959) words,

> Whether an honest performer wishes to convey the truth or whether a dishonest performer wishes to convey a falsehood, both must take care to enliven their performances with appropriate expressions, exclude from their performances expressions that might discredit the impression being fostered, and take care lest the audience impute unintended meanings. (p. 66)

Impression management is something everyone does in everyday activities. To one degree or another, we all manage others' impressions of us in interactions. We have to "perform" or "project" our intentions and desires, because people can't read our minds.

Because minds are private, people typically behave so as to highlight important facts about themselves that might otherwise go unnoticed. Goffman calls this activity *dramatic realization*. For example, when you are in a job interview, you might describe in great detail a position of responsibility you held in the past. Or if you are in traffic court, you might point out the absence of any past traffic violations to the judge. This feature may be true about you, but you probably wouldn't bring it up as a way to impress a potential date. Instead, you might focus on highlighting your favorite music or activities. Dramatic realization is an attempt to make traits and characteristics "real" and noticeable that might otherwise go unnoticed. If these traits are not noticed, they don't exist as "real" aspects of the performance. It is up to the individual to bring them into play.

Goffman also makes the point that we often try to present ourselves in a favorable light, a process he calls *idealization*. We might simply accent those aspects about ourselves that are positive (for example, mentioning that you are on the varsity team but not mentioning that you have just lost your job), or we might engage in outright deception (saying you are on the varsity team when you are not).

People also have a general tendency to convey the impression that the role they are currently engaged in is their most important role. For example, when an individual walks into a store to buy an expensive suit, she will be interacting with a salesperson. The salesperson may also be a parent, spouse, community volunteer, jogger, gardener, and so forth, but if that salesperson is good at the job, he will take part in the interaction as if serving customers is the most important role in his life at that moment.

Before an interaction can proceed successfully, two actors must agree about the sort of situation they are in and the role each is to play. Is it a friendly chat between acquaintances, a seduction between lovers, or a coaching session between subordinate and supervisor? This process is referred to as *identity negotiation*. People in an interaction each project an identity, and their responses to each other indicate whether they accept the projected identity. For example, if you ask your boss how old she is and she doesn't acknowledge the question, she has chosen not to grant you the identity of "familiar acquaintance." When two people agree on the identities they are both going to play in an interaction, they have arrived at what Goffman refers to as a *working consensus.*

Public agreement on identities does not necessarily reflect the actor's *private* beliefs. People often have pleasant chats with coworkers they dislike. There are many possible reasons for doing this—to be polite, to prevent an awkward scene, to ensure good relations in the workplace, or perhaps to stay in the good graces of a person who controls resources that might be needed sometime. Whatever the private reality might be, it is the public, socially agreed upon definition of the situation that will guide the interaction.

Once a public agreement has been reached (whether implicitly or explicitly), it carries the weight of a contract. The working consensus has a moral character to it. Each actor feels as if he or she has the right to be treated in a particular way by other actors. The actors also feel as if they have an obligation to behave in ways that are consistent with the presented identity. For example, in an interaction between a teacher and a student, the person who is in the role of the teacher expects certain behavior from the person who is the student; these behaviors include being treated respectfully, being treated as a status superior, being treated as an expert on the subject, and so on. At the same time, the person who has claimed the identity of teacher has numerous obligations or duties, such as competently carrying out the teacher's role, being respectful of students, knowing a great deal about the subject, and being able to convey that knowledge to students. The rights and duties associated with an identity that has been publicly accepted must be respected if the expected social order of the interaction is to continue. If a math teacher is unable to solve a problem in front of the class or if a student treats the teacher like a younger sibling, the interaction grinds to an uncomfortable halt.

In sum, interaction has two key elements: publicly defining (and presenting) a personal identity and defining what sort of situation the individual is in with others. There are many possible answers to the questions "Who am I?" "Who are you?" "What's going on?" For successful interaction to occur, these definitions must be projected and negotiated by the participants. The participants jockey to claim identities and to define the situation in ways that will help them accomplish their personal goals. Once identities are established, they must be actively maintained.

Who Are We and What Are We Doing Here?

When an individual enters the presence of others, they commonly seek to acquire information about him or to bring into play information already possessed. They will be interested in his general socio-economic status, his conception of self, his attitude toward them, his competence, his trustworthiness, etc. (Goffman, 1959, p. 1)

When they come together, people must actively strive to present a definition of the roles they wish to play in the interactional moment and the definition of the situation as they see it. Failure to do so may lead to misunderstandings, embarrassment, and the breakdown of the interaction. In a study of gym trainers and their clients, sociologist Linda Van Leuven

(2001) describes the different definitions that client and trainer may bring to the interaction. Clients sometimes define the situation as a personal friendship or even a romantic encounter. Accordingly, they may enter the situation prepared to act out the identity of "engaging flirt." Trainers, who are aware of this propensity in some clients, develop strategies designed to let the client know immediately what they can expect of the situation—a workout and not an occasion to visit or to flirt. For instance, a trainer may grill potential clients about their commitment in advance. During the sessions, the trainer might carefully avoid eye contact so as to discourage conversation. These interactional strategies help to establish a frame around the situation and to signal to participants what the boundaries and expectations are.

Goffman notes that many skills are required to bring off a reasonable interactional performance. Because interaction requires the ongoing cooperation of participants, it is vulnerable and can break down. A situation might be defined in an inappropriate way. Or the identities the participants claim might somehow be discredited (as when a math teacher cannot solve a problem in front of the class). In that case, the result is embarrassment.

From a dramaturgical perspective, embarrassment can be defined as a breakdown in a projected identity. It is striking to note how uncomfortable we are with embarrassment and how hard we work to avoid it. Indeed, embarrassment makes us so uncomfortable that we usually cooperate to prevent or smooth over other people's embarrassing actions, even if they are strangers. We might look away when someone stumbles clumsily, pretend not to hear the fight a couple is having at a nearby table, or readily and eagerly accept other people's explanations for their unacceptable behavior. Engaging in cooperative support of each other's identities to avoid or repair embarrassment is called *tact*. The presence and prevalence of tact is an extraordinary thing. Humans apparently have a very deep commitment to support each other's identities, even the identities of strangers.

True, there are times when someone might react to an embarrassing moment without tact (or even have engineered the moment, if it involves a rival), but these instances stand out because they are exceptions. Practical jokes that make someone look foolish (that is, those that discredit someone's "face") would not be funny if they were not a deviation from the usual norm of tact.

The mutual obligation to avoid "scenes" and to be who we claim to be means that whenever a situation or identity is threatened, someone must repair the interaction. When the audience helps in the repair work, they are being *tactful*—but, of course, the person whose identity is threatened can also work to repair the interaction. When someone behaves in ways that threaten an identity or disrupt the expected routine, that person typically offers an explanation or gives an *account* of the actions.

Offering accounts after an inappropriate act does not guarantee that others will accept (honor) the account. Not every explanation is acceptable. "I had car trouble" might be a reasonable excuse for not getting to class on time, but "Voices told me to come late today" is not considered reasonable. And some explanations are acceptable in some situations but not in others. Burning the stew because "I was distracted by a phone call" is acceptable, but the same excuse would certainly not be honored as an explanation for why someone failed to show up for a court date. What is judged to be an acceptable account varies from situation to situation. It can also vary tremendously from one culture to another.

Goffman emphasizes just how fragile and potentially disruptable interaction routines really are. His intent is not so much to present people as cynical and calculating as to draw our attention to the tricky interpersonal gymnastics required of social actors. What is remarkable—and Goffman's respectful awe is apparent in his voluminous writings—is that people somehow do manage to project mutually understood definitions of self and situation, despite all the things that could go wrong.

It's important to note that people *learn* acceptable definitions of identity and situation. Some of these learning processes are very explicit. For instance, business schools frequently hold "mock cocktail parties" to teach students how to network with clients. Informal social networking is an important factor in successful business encounters. For this reason, business schools provide students with an opportunity to "try on" and practice performing social networking identities. Students learn tips such as "don't have both hands full with drink and food, because you won't be able to shake someone else's hand" and "you have to appear eager but not like you're a 'social climber.'"

Whether we intend to project an identity of competent instructor, capable businesswoman, earnest priest, or intimidating thug, we all have to engage in impression management; we have to signal to others our definition of the situation and our intended position.

Negotiating a Working Consensus

The generative quality of social structure is observable in these face-to-face encounters. Individuals bring different ideas, goals, and expectations to social encounters. As they strive to achieve a working definition of what is going on, they translate their private definitions, as well as their immediate feelings, into a form that they think others will understand and accept. In other words, people manage, despite many differences, to engage in meaningful, sustainable discourses. We all do this through continual negotiation.

The theatrical form most indicative of the generative, negotiated quality of interaction is improvisation. "Theater sports" is a form of entertainment in which the audience calls out a frame or setting—usually one involving some sort of controversy or misunderstanding—and the actors then improvise their roles within the parameters of the setting. The actors and audience share a general understanding of what the scene or setting consists of, but how it is played out is largely determined by each actor's performance repertoire (that is, each actor's familiarity with how people might react in this situation) and how the other performers respond. If you have participated in theater sports, you know that the fun is in seeing how the actors play off one another when they don't know what the others are likely to do. In Reading 28, sociologist Mark Cohan uses his experience as a participant in the fantasy world of "steampunk" to illustrate how the scene is established in live-action role-play. This adult fantasy world consists of players who adopt historical characters and, together, act out action scenes. As he notes, establishing the historical scene and the boundaries between real and fantasy requires tremendous collective activity.

Everyday interaction is an ongoing series of such moments, even if we aren't typically aware of it. The ability to negotiate working understandings of different situations is the genius of human sociability. The fact that everyday encounters feel more or less like comfortable routines—rather than a madcap scramble of miscues, misunderstandings, and maladies—is a testament to the existence of shared social scripts. The negotiation process becomes apparent in situations that are less familiar and routine. On those occasions, people are likely to be more aware of the potential gap between the private and projected definitions of various participants. These situations are often precarious.

In a study of interaction between patients and staff in gynecological exams, sociologist Joan Emerson (1970) illustrates the impression management that must take place when participants have strongly competing definitions of the situation. The patient is likely to feel that the examination is a violation of her body and her dignity, whereas the medical staff wants to establish an atmosphere of professional detachment. The doctors and nurses performing this medical procedure must take care to ensure that the situation continues to be defined as a medical examination, because the exam includes many sensitive behaviors that could threaten this definition. In other words, there are *competing definitions of the situation*. The medical staff wants to establish distance and sterility—this is just a procedure—while the patient may find the situation deeply invasive. The situation is additionally precarious because the patient is not always a reliable co-performer. She *is* being invaded and may be inclined to resist the technical approach of the medical staff and their insistence that this is all very ordinary.

Another example that requires careful scene setting is the funeral. In a classic reading taken from the annals of symbolic interactionism, Ronny Turner and Charles Edgley write about "death as theater" (Reading 29). They describe the precarious situation of funeral directors who must manage the bereaved with care and respect and set up a ceremony that presents the deceased in the most positive light while also underplaying the profit motive of the typical mortuary service.

Although most interactions are not as precarious as this situation, any interaction can end up being redefined in a negative light. Thus, the concerns and dramaturgical activity that are brought out so clearly in the gynecological examination or modern mortuaries are relevant to many settings. Kari Lerum examines similar processes of setting the scene and maintaining the definition of the situation in a strip club (Reading 30). Contrary to the popular notion that sex is always in the air, Lerum demonstrates that establishing an erotic atmosphere requires careful staging. There are many possible disruptions to the established mood as patrons move in and out of the scene.

EMOTIONAL LABOR, STIGMA, AND RESISTANCE

One aspect of interaction routines that has been the subject of considerable study is *emotional labor*. Because interaction routines require us to adjust our behavior to public expectations, we can reasonably ask: What about the underlying private feelings? What happens when these don't mesh well with public expectations? Most of us have been in situations in which we had to engage in public behavior that required us to "put on a happy face" when we weren't feeling up to it. The ability to engage in appropriate social performance even when you're experiencing inner turmoil or tragedy is sometimes seen as a form of grace or maturity. What about situations in which the happy face is required as part of the job—that is, part of the idealized or ideal type expectations for a particular social identity? Sociologist Arlie Hochschild was one of the first to explore that aspect of performance, and she called it *emotional labor*. Most interaction routines require some degree of emotional labor (i.e., we are often publicly pushing out what is expected of us). People who are in positions of less power or those who suffer from social stigma are likely to be more aware of disparities between how they feel privately and what is expected of them publicly. People who have power are usually able to define the situation according to their desires and thus are more likely to feel satisfied with the interaction and less aware of the emotional labor.

Hochschild is interested in the emotional labor that is required as part of paid employment. In a classic sociological study (*The Managed Heart*, 1983), she looked at the emotional labor that is a required aspect of the performances of flight attendants. In Reading 33, Hochschild reports on the ways in which flight attendants are socialized to put on a happy face no matter how rude, drunk, or inappropriate the passengers are. This type of performance requires what Hochschild calls *deep acting*. She asks: What are the costs of this deeply acted emotional labor? How does it affect the flight attendants' ability to accurately gauge how they really feel?

Goffman was particularly interested in stigma and its consequences for interaction. According to him, stigmas are an aspect of social interaction and reflect particular social statuses and ideals. For instance, certain professions or ethnicities may be stigmatized in some contexts or cultures and not others. Goffman was interested in the way in which people manage stigmatized identities. Panhandling is usually considered a stigmatized or problematic activity in contemporary society. Often associated with identity, we think of panhandlers as stigmatized people rather than people who happen to panhandle. Stephen Lankenau (Reading 34) describes aspects of panhandling as a form of interaction routine in which the person is actively engaged in a performance intended to get the "audience" to treat him as a person. The typical script when someone encounters a person panhandling is to act as if nothing unusual is going on and to ignore the person panhandling. Lankenau notes that some people who panhandle are active and creative in performing routines to disrupt the stigma or *nonperson* identity.

Interactional routines lead people to reproduce taken-for-granted cultural patterns. Because minds are private, we all must dramatize (in other words, signal) the identities we wish to claim and our definition of the situation. To be effective in interactions, we select symbolic representations that we know to be reliable signals of our intentions. This selection of culturally typical or expected symbols is a process of *idealization*. You may not like business attire, for instance, but you will put one on for a job interview because you believe it to be the appropriate costume for presenting the identity of an eager and professional potential employee. When you present yourself with the appropriate costume, props, and mannerisms, you effectively reproduce a set of cultural expectations or *ideals*—one of them being that business people wear suits. In other words, you will be presenting a symbolic *ideal type*, and through your self-presentation, you will be affirming the ideal type.

The implications of idealization for perpetuating social stereotypes and expectations are significant. In some cases, people knowingly resist the taken-for-granted routine; they are disrupting idealized expectations. In his ethnographic study of gang life, Victor Rios examines the motives behind stealing a bag of potato chips and other small acts of defiance (Reading 35). He suggests that these actions reflect a *resistance identity* that develops among young men who feel excluded from networks of positive credential, education, and employment. They have been cast as criminals by local police and neighborhood shopkeepers. Paradoxically, breaking the rules through small acts of criminality is one of the only ways they can exercise agency. The acts may get them into trouble, but within a context in which they are perpetually criminalized, the resistance also conveys a sense of dignity.

CONCLUSION:
PERFORMING INTERACTION RITUALS

Goffman opens *The Presentation of Self in Everyday Life* (1959) with the following lines from the philosopher George Santayana:

> Masks are arrested expressions and admirable echoes of feelings, at once faithful, discreet, and superlative. Living things in contact with the air acquire a cuticle, and it is not urged against cuticles that they are not hearts; yet some philosophers seem to be angry with images for not being things, and with words for not being feelings. Words and images are like shells, no less integral parts of nature than are the substances they cover, but better addressed to the eye and more open to observation. (p. vi)

Through this quotation, Goffman anticipates readers' reactions to his theory that we "perform" ourselves, our ideals, and our beliefs rather than somehow simply exuding them naturally. Some people are inclined to associate "performance" with fakery or trickery. They assume that, behind the stage, there is something "more real."

Goffman and sociologists of his persuasion do not disavow the existence of a physiology, a psyche, and perhaps even a soul that may be independent of social forces, but their theoretical and analytical focus is on *social* relations. Reality is in the expression of social meaning achieved through interaction. We are, first and foremost, *expressive* creatures. To express ourselves, we must transform individual urges, amorphous images, and fuzzy ideas into communicable form. We do so through interactional speech and gesture. Thus, reality consists of shared forms of expression that, as we have noted, take on patterns. Goffman calls these patterns *interaction rituals.*

Producing a shared reality requires give and take, concession, and acknowledgment of others. Interaction rituals are enactments of ceremony that reinforce cultural symbols and expectations. The rituals range from simple greeting exchanges (in which people acknowledge the presence of other people) to elaborate ceremonies (such as weddings and funerals). And these interaction rituals have a conservative aspect: Through ritual presentations of the ideal, people conserve or maintain the status quo.

For Goffman (1959), everyday ceremonies, or rituals, give meaning to our collective existence:

> To the degree that a performance highlights the common official values of the society in which it occurs, we may look upon it as a ceremony—as an expressive rejuvenation and reaffirmation of the moral values of the community. . . . To stay in one's room away from the place where the party is being given . . . is to stay away from where reality is being performed. The world, in truth, is a wedding. (pp. 35–36)

REFERENCES AND SUGGESTIONS FOR FURTHER READING

Charon, J. (1989). *Symbolic interactionism* (3rd ed.). Englewood Cliffs, NJ: Prentice Hall.

Emerson, J. (1970). Behavior in private places: Sustaining definitions of reality in gynecological examinations. In H. P. Dreitzel (Ed.), *Recent sociology No. 2* (pp. 74–97). London, UK: Macmillan.

Goffman, E. (1959). *The presentation of self in everyday life.* Garden City, NY: Doubleday.

Hochschild, A. R. (1983). *The managed heart.* Berkeley: University of California Press. (See also 20th Anniversary edition, 2003)

Kuhn, M. H., & McPartland, T. S. (1954). An empirical investigation of self-attitudes. *American Sociological Review, 19,* 68–76.

Turner, R. (1976). The real self: From institution to impulse. *American Journal of Sociology, 81,* 989–1016.

Twain, M. (1946). *The adventures of Tom Sawyer.* New York, NY: Grosset & Dunlap. (Original work published 1875)

Van Leuven, L. (2001). What does this service include? In J. O'Brien & P. Kollock (Eds.), *The production of reality* (3rd ed., pp. 254–264). Thousand Oaks, CA: Pine Forge Press.

PROJECTING THE DEFINITION OF THE SITUATION

One of the simplest but most profound aspects of social interaction is that we are not mind readers. Because of this, much of social interaction is a *signaling process* that involves letting each other know what's going on. Our gestures, cues, and conversation are attempts to communicate a definition of the situation. This process includes signaling what kind of moment or event we think we're in: What's the script? Is this a casual conversation at the store, an argument, or a celebration? Through our gestures and remarks, we let people know what our expectations of the situation are and what social role we are trying to play in the moment (flirtatious potential date, hassled shopper, betrayed spouse, etc.). Although most day-to-day behavior seems routine and automatic, we're actually working together all the time to signal to one another. The signaling may be as simple as "I see and acknowledge you as a comrade" or as complex as trying to get a raise from a boss you disrespect. Much human social interaction can be analyzed in terms of the kinds of signaling of expectations that people are doing with one another. When people encounter one another, whether they are strangers or close friends, they have to define their expectations. Social expectations are often taken for granted, and people play out the routines with enough ease that it seems "natural." However, whether we are aware of it or not, we are constantly negotiating a definition of the situation. Hurt feelings, anger, and frustration are often the results of differing expectations that cannot be reconciled.

Erving Goffman is a name that appears repeatedly throughout this book. The reading included here is excerpted from his book *The Presentation of Self in Everyday Life.* In this now-classic book, Goffman uses the metaphor of the theater to describe everyday encounters. According to Goffman, much of our behavior is an attempt to project social identities to others. Regardless of whether we are trying to manipulate someone, persuade them, or just get their attention, we must perform a social role to let them know what script we are trying to enact and what our expectations are.

In "Establishing the Scene in Steampunk Live-Action Role Play" (Reading 28) and "Death as Theater: A Dramaturgical Analysis of the American Funeral" (Reading 29) the authors describe the backstage work that actors engage in to create a specific atmosphere or impression. Steampunk role-players follow carefully scripted rules in producing their fictional reality and funeral directors employ carefully crafted methods to create the appropriate atmosphere.

Kari Lerum explores the processes of defining the situation in a strip club in "'Precarious Situations' in a Strip Club." In this particular case, the club owners want to convey a "high-class" impression. They use several strategies to balance the impression that the situation is both respectable and erotic.

READING QUESTIONS

1. Based on Goffman's article, why do people often behave politely in encounters with someone they privately dislike?

(Continued)

(Continued)

2. Recall an occasion in which you mentally practiced an interaction before going into the situation. What impression were you hoping to convey? What resistance, if any, did you anticipate? Are you more likely to consciously practice a performance if the situation is new or if it's routine?

3. Recall a situation in which you were embarrassed. Was the embarrassment due to playing the wrong role for the situation or misplaying the expected role for the situation? What's the difference?

4. Use the concepts of interaction routines, idealization, definition of the situation, and negotiating a working consensus to explain why people become so upset when things go wrong at special events such as weddings.

5. Why are children not allowed at certain events? Who else might be considered "socially incompetent" in certain settings?

6. Consider other events that involve precarious or competing definitions of the situation. In these events, do participants have to be more or less strategic in their performances? Why?

7. Consider other events or situations that require scene-setting work similar to funerals or role play. What precarious or competing definitions of the situation might arise? In these events, do participants have to be more or less strategic in their performances? Why?

8. Think about someone you know who is just a little bit "off" (for example, the aunt who talks too loudly about sex, the uncle who drinks too much, the classmate who never "gets it"). How is it that you and others know this person is "off"? What unspoken interaction rules do you hold in common that the "off" person seems not to get? How do you and others respond to this person? Do the responses preserve the definition of the situation (that is, do you accommodate the person), or do you respond in ways that give the person information that he or she is "off"?

27

The Presentation of Self in Everyday Life: Selections

Erving Goffman

(1959)

INTRODUCTION

When an individual enters the presence of others, they commonly seek to acquire information about him or to bring into play information about him already possessed. They will be interested in his general socio-economic status, his conception of self, his attitude toward them, his competence, his trustworthiness, etc. Although some of this information seems to be sought almost as an end in itself, there are usually quite practical reasons for acquiring it. Information about the individual helps to define the situation, enabling others to know in advance what he will expect of them and what they may expect of him. Informed in these ways, the others will know how best to act in order to call forth a desired response from him.

For those present, many sources of information become accessible and many carriers (or "sign-vehicles") become available for conveying this information. If unacquainted with the individual, observers can glean clues from his conduct and appearance which allow them to apply their previous experience with individuals roughly similar to the one before them or, more important, to apply untested stereotypes to him. They can also assume from past experience that only individuals of a particular kind are likely to be found in a given social setting. They can rely on what the individual says about himself or on

documentary evidence he provides as to who and what he is. If they know, or know of, the individual by virtue of experience prior to the interaction, they can rely on assumptions as to the persistence and generality of psychological traits as a means of predicting his present and future behavior. . . .

The expressiveness of the individual (and therefore his capacity to give impressions) appears to involve two radically different kinds of sign activity: the expression that he *gives,* and the expression that he *gives off.* The first involves verbal symbols or their substitutes which he uses admittedly and solely to convey the information that he and the others are known to attach to these symbols. This is communication in the traditional and narrow sense. The second involves a wide range of action that others can treat as symptomatic of the actor, the expectation being that the action was performed for reasons other than the information conveyed in this way. As we shall have to see, this distinction has only an initial validity. The individual does of course intentionally convey misinformation by means of both of these types of communication, the first involving deceit, the second feigning.

Taking communication in both its narrow and broad sense, one finds that when the individual is in the immediate presence of others, his activity will have a promissory character.

The others are likely to find that they must accept the individual on faith, offering him a just return while he is present before them in exchange for something whose true value will not be established until after he has left their presence. (Of course, the others also live by inference in their dealings with the physical world, but it is only in the world of social inter-action that the objects about which they make inferences will purposely facilitate and hinder this inferential process.) The security that they justifiably feel in making inferences about the individual will vary, of course, depending on such factors as the amount of information they already possess about him, but no amount of such past evidence can entirely obviate the necessity of acting on the basis of inferences. As William I. Thomas suggested:

> It is also highly important for us to realize that we do not as a matter of fact lead our lives, make our decisions, and reach our goals in everyday life either statistically or scientifically. We live by infer-ence. I am, let us say, your guest. You do not know, you cannot determine scientifically, that I will not steal your money or your spoons. But inferentially I will not and inferentially you have me as a guest.[1]

Let us now turn from the others to the point of view of the individual who presents himself before them. He may wish them to think highly of him, or to think that he thinks highly of them, or to perceive how in fact he feels toward them, or to obtain no clear-cut impression; he may wish to ensure sufficient harmony so that the interaction can be sustained, or to defraud, get rid of, confuse, mislead, antagonize, or insult them. Regardless of the particular objective which the individual has in mind and of his motive for having this objective, it will be in his interests to control the conduct of the others, especially their responsive treatment of him.[2] This control is achieved largely by influencing the definition of the situation which the others

come to formulate, and he can influence this definition by expressing himself in such a way as to give them the kind of impression that will lead them to act voluntarily in accordance with his own plan. Thus, when an individual appears in the presence of others, there will usually be some reason for him to mobilize his activity so that it will convey an impression to others which it is in his interests to convey. . . .

I have said that when an individual appears before others his actions will influence the defi-nition of the situation which they come to have. Sometimes the individual will act in a thor-oughly calculating manner, expressing himself in a given way solely in order to give the kind of impression to others that is likely to evoke from them a specific response he is concerned to obtain. Sometimes the individual will be calcu-lating in his activity but be relatively unaware that this is the case. Sometimes he will inten-tionally and consciously express himself in a particular way, but chiefly because the tradition of his group or social status require this kind of expression and not because of any particular response (other than vague acceptance or approval) that is likely to be evoked from those impressed by the expression. Sometimes the traditions of an individual's role will lead him to give a well-designed impression of a particular kind and yet he may be neither consciously nor unconsciously disposed to create such an impres-sion. The others, in their turn, may be suitably impressed by the individual's efforts to convey something, or may misunderstand the situation and come to conclusions that are warranted nei-ther by the individual's intent nor by the facts. In any case, insofar as the others act *as if* the indi-vidual had conveyed a particular impression, we may take a functional or pragmatic view and say that the individual has "effectively" projected a given definition of the situation and "effectively" fostered the understanding that a given state of affairs obtains. . . .

When we allow that the individual projects a definition of the situation when he appears before others, we must also see that the others, however passive their role may seem to be, will themselves effectively project a definition of the situation by virtue of their response to the individual and by virtue of any lines of action they initiate to him. Ordinarily the definitions of the situation projected by the several different participants are sufficiently attuned to one another so that open contradiction will not occur. I do not mean that there will be the kind of consensus that arises when each individual present candidly expresses what he really feels and honestly agrees with the expressed feelings of the others present. This kind of harmony is an optimistic ideal and in any case not necessary for the smooth working of society. Rather, each participant is expected to suppress his immediate heartfelt feelings, conveying a view of the situation which he feels the others will be able to find at least temporarily acceptable. The maintenance of this surface of agreement, this veneer of consensus, is facilitated by each participant concealing his own wants behind statements which assert values to which everyone present feels obliged to give lip service. Further, there is usually a kind of division of definitional labor. Each participant is allowed to establish the tentative official ruling regarding matters which are vital to him but not immediately important to others, e.g., the rationalizations and justifications by which he accounts for his past activity. In exchange for this courtesy he remains silent or noncommittal on matters important to others but not immediately important to him. We have then a kind of interactional *modus vivendi.* Together the participants contribute to a single overall definition of the situation which involves not so much a real agreement as to what exists but rather a real agreement as to whose claims concerning what issues will be temporarily honored. Real agreement will also exist concerning

the desirability of avoiding an open conflict of definitions of the situation.[3] I will refer to this level of agreement as a "working consensus." It is to be understood that the working consensus established in one interaction setting will be quite different in content from the working consensus established in a different type of setting. Thus, between two friends at lunch, a reciprocal show of affection, respect, and concern for the other is maintained. In service occupations, on the other hand, the specialist often maintains an image of disinterested involvement in the problem of the client, while the client responds with a show of respect for the competence and integrity of the specialist. Regardless of such differences in content, however, the general form of these working arrangements is the same. . . .

. . . Given the fact that the individual effectively projects a definition of the situation when he enters the presence of others, we can assume that events may occur within the interaction which contradict, discredit, or otherwise throw doubt upon this projection. When these disruptive events occur, the interaction itself may come to a confused and embarrassed halt. Some of the assumptions upon which the responses of the participants had been predicated become untenable, and the participants find themselves lodged in an interaction for which the situation has been wrongly defined and is now no longer defined. At such moments the individual whose presentation has been discredited may feel ashamed while the others present may feel hostile, and all the participants may come to feel ill at ease, nonplussed, out of countenance, embarrassed, experiencing the kind of anomy that is generated when the minute social system of face-to-face interaction breaks down. . . .

We find that preventive practices are constantly employed to avoid these embarrassments and that corrective practices are constantly employed to compensate for discrediting occurrences that have not been successfully avoided.

When the individual employs these strategies and tactics to protect his own projections, we may refer to them as "defensive practices"; when a participant employs them to save the definition of the situation projected by another, we speak of "protective practices" or "tact." Together, defensive and protective practices comprise the techniques employed to safe-guard the impression fostered by an individual during his presence before others. It should be added that while we may be ready to see that no fostered impression would survive if defensive practices were not employed, we are less ready perhaps to see that few impressions could survive if those who received the impression did not exert tact in their reception of it.

In addition to the fact that precautions are taken to prevent disruption of projected definitions, we may also note that an intense interest in these disruptions comes to play a significant role in the social life of the group. Practical jokes and social games are played in which embarrassments which are to be taken unseriously are purposely engineered.[4] Fantasies are created in which devastating exposures occur. Anecdotes from the past—real, embroidered, or fictitious—are told and retold, detailing disruptions which occurred, almost occurred, or occurred and were admirably resolved. There seems to be no grouping which does not have a ready supply of these games, reveries, and cautionary tales, to be used as a source of humor, a catharsis for anxieties, and a sanction for inducing individuals to be modest in their claims and reasonable in their projected expectations. The individual may tell himself through dreams of getting into impossible positions. Families tell of the time a guest got his dates mixed and arrived when neither the house nor anyone in it was ready for him. Journalists tell of times when an all-too-meaningful misprint occurred, and the paper's assumption of objectivity or decorum was humorously discredited. Public servants tell of times a client ridiculously misunderstood form instructions, giving answers which implied an unanticipated and bizarre definition of the situation.[5] Seamen, whose home away from home is rigorously he-man, tell stories of coming back home and inadvertently asking mother to "pass the fucking butter."[6] Diplomats tell of the time a near-sighted queen asked a republican ambassador about the health of his king.[7]

To summarize, then, I assume that when an individual appears before others he will have many motives for trying to control the impression they receive of the situation. This report is concerned with some of the common techniques that persons employ to sustain such impressions and with some of the common contingencies associated with the employment of these techniques. It will be convenient to end this introduction with some definitions. . . . For the purpose of this report, interaction (that is, face-to-face interaction) may be roughly defined as the reciprocal influence of individuals upon one another's actions when in one another's immediate physical presence. An interaction may be defined as all the interaction which occurs throughout any one occasion when a given set of individuals are in one another's continuous presence; the term "an encounter" would do as well. A "performance" may be defined as all the activity of a given participant on a given occasion which serves to influence in any way any of the other participants. Taking a particular participant and his performance as a basic point of reference, we may refer to those who contribute the other performances as the audience, observers, or co-participants. The pre-established pattern of action which is unfolded during a performance and which may be presented or played through on other occasions may be called a "part" or "routine."[8] These situational terms can easily be related to conventional structural ones. When an individual or performer plays the same part to the same audience on different occasions, a social relationship is likely to arise. Defining social role as the enactment of rights and duties attached to a given status, we can say that a social role will involve one or more parts and that each of these different parts may be presented by the performer on a series of occasions to the same kinds of audience or to an audience of the same persons. . . .

PERFORMANCES

Front

I [use] the term "performance" to refer to all the activity of an individual which occurs during a period marked by his continuous presence before a particular set of observers and which has some influence on the observers. It will be convenient to label as "front" that part of the individual's performance which regularly functions in a general and fixed fashion to define the situation for those who observe the performance. Front, then, is the expressive equipment of a standard kind intentionally or unwittingly employed by the individual during his performance. For preliminary purposes, it will be convenient to distinguish and label what seem to be the standard parts of front.

First, there is the "setting," involving furniture, décor, physical layout, and other background items which supply the scenery and stage props for the spate of human action played out before, within, or upon it. A setting tends to stay put, geographically speaking, so that those who would use a particular setting as part of their performance cannot begin their act until they have brought themselves to the appropriate place and must terminate their performance when they leave it. It is only in exceptional circumstances that the setting follows along with the performers; we see this in the funeral cortège, the civic parade, and the dreamlike processions that kings and queens are made of. In the

main, these exceptions seem to offer some kind of extra protection for performers who are, or who have momentarily become, highly sacred. . . .

It is sometimes convenient to divide the stimuli which make up personal front into "appearance" and "manner," according to the function performed by the information that these stimuli convey. "Appearance" may be taken to refer to those stimuli which function at the time to tell us of the performer's social statuses. These stimuli also tell us of the individual's temporary ritual state, that is, whether he is engaging in formal social activity, work, or informal recreation, whether or not he is celebrating a new phase in the season cycle or in his life-cycle. "Manner" may be taken to refer to those stimuli which function at the time to warn us of the interaction role the performer will expect to play in the oncoming situation. Thus a haughty, aggressive manner may give the impression that the performer expects to be the one who will initiate the verbal interaction and direct its course. A meek, apologetic manner may give the impression that the performer expects to follow the lead of others, or at least that he can be led to do so. . . .

Dramatic Realization

While in the presence of others, the individual typically infuses his activity with signs which dramatically highlight and portray confirmatory facts that might otherwise remain unapparent or obscure. For if the individual's activity is to become significant to others, he must mobilize his activity so that it will express *during the interaction* what he wishes to convey. In fact, the performer may be required not only to express his claimed capacities during the interaction but also to do so during a split second in the interaction. Thus, if a baseball umpire is to give the impression that he is sure of his judgment, he must forgo the moment of thought which might make him sure of his judgment; he must give an instantaneous decision so that the audience will be sure that he is sure of his judgment.[9] . . .

Similarly, the proprietor of a service establishment may find it difficult to dramatize what is actually being done for clients because the clients cannot "see" the overhead costs of the service rendered them. Undertakers must therefore charge a great deal for their highly visible product—a coffin that has been transformed into a casket—because many of the other costs of conducting a funeral are ones that cannot be readily dramatized.[10] Merchants, too, find that they must charge high prices for things that look intrinsically inexpensive in order to compensate the establishment for expensive things like insurance, slack periods, etc., that never appear before the customers' eyes. . . .

Idealization

. . . I want to consider here another important aspect of this socialization process—the tendency for performers to offer their observers an impression that is idealized in several different ways.

The notion that a performance presents an idealized view of the situation is, of course, quite common. Cooley's view may be taken as an illustration:

> If we never tried to seem a little better than we are, how could we improve or "train ourselves from the outside inward"? And the same impulse to show the world a better or idealized aspect of ourselves finds an organized expression in the various professions and classes, each of which has to some extent a cant or pose, which its members assume unconsciously, for the most part, but which has the effect of a conspiracy to work upon the credulity of the rest of the world. There is a cant not only of theology and of philanthropy, but also of law, medicine, teaching, even of science— perhaps especially of science, just now, since the

more a particular kind of merit is recognized and admired, the more it is likely to be assumed by the unworthy.[11]

Thus, when the individual presents himself before others, his performance will tend to incorporate and exemplify the officially accredited values of the society, more so, in fact, than does his behavior as a whole.

To the degree that a performance highlights the common official values of the society in which it occurs, we may look upon it, in the manner of Durkheim and Radcliffe-Brown, as a ceremony—as an expressive rejuvenation and reaffirmation of the moral values of the community. Furthermore, insofar as the expressive bias of performances comes to be accepted as reality, then that which is accepted at the moment as reality will have some of the characteristics of a celebration. To stay in one's room away from the place where the party is given, or away from where the practitioner attends his client, is to stay away from where reality is being performed. The world, in truth, is a wedding.

One of the richest sources of data on the presentation of idealized performances is the literature on social mobility. In most societies there seems to be a major or general system of stratification, and in most stratified societies there is an idealization of the higher strata and some aspiration on the part of those in low places to move to higher ones. (One must be careful to appreciate that this involves not merely a desire for a prestigeful place but also a desire for a place close to the sacred center of the common values of the society.) Commonly we find that upward mobility involves the presentation of proper performances and that efforts to move upward and efforts to keep from moving downward are expressed in terms of sacrifices made for the maintenance of front. Once the proper sign-equipment has been obtained and familiarity gained in the management of it, then this equipment can be used to embellish and illumine one's daily performances with a favorable social style.

Perhaps the most important piece of sign-equipment associated with social class consists of the status symbols through which material wealth is expressed. American society is similar to others in this regard but seems to have been singled out as an extreme example of wealth-oriented class structure—perhaps because in America the license to employ symbols of wealth and financial capacity to do so are so widely distributed. . . .

Reality and Contrivance

. . . Some performances are carried off successfully with complete dishonesty, others with complete honesty; but for performances in general neither of these extremes is essential and neither, perhaps, is dramaturgically advisable.

The implication here is that an honest, sincere, serious performance is less firmly connected with the solid world than one might first assume. And this implication will be strengthened if we look again at the distance usually placed between quite honest performances and quite contrived ones. In this connection take, for example, the remarkable phenomenon of stage acting. It does take deep skill, long training, and psychological capacity to become a good stage actor. But this fact should not blind us to another one: that almost anyone can quickly learn a script well enough to give a charitable audience some sense of realness in what is being contrived before them. And it seems this is so because ordinary social intercourse is itself put together as a scene is put together, by the exchange of dramatically inflated actions, counteractions, and terminating replies. Scripts even in the hands of unpracticed players can come to life because life itself is a dramatically enacted thing. All the world is

not, of course, a stage, but the crucial ways in which it isn't are not easy to specify. . . .

When the individual does move into a new position in society and obtains a new part to perform, he is not likely to be told in full detail how to conduct himself, nor will the facts of his new situation press sufficiently on him from the start to determine his conduct without his further giving thought to it. Ordinarily he will be given only a few cues, hints, and stage directions, and it will be assumed that he already has in his repertoire a large number of bits and pieces of performances that will be required in the new setting. The individual will already have a fair idea of what modesty, deference, or righteous indignation looks like, and can make a pass at playing these bits when necessary. He may even be able to play out the part of a hypnotic subject[12] or commit a "compulsive" crime[13] on the basis of models for these activities that he is already familiar with.

A theatrical performance or a staged confidence game requires a thorough scripting of the spoken content of the routine; but the vast part involving "expression given off" is often determined by meager stage directions. It is expected that the performer of illusions will already know a good deal about how to manage his voice, his face, and his body, although he—as well as any person who directs him—may find it difficult indeed to provide a detailed verbal statement of this kind of knowledge. And in this, of course, we approach the situation of the straightforward man in the street. Socialization may not so much involve a learning of the many specific details of a single concrete part—often there could not be enough time or energy for this. What does seem to be required of the individual is that he learn enough pieces of expression to be able to "fill in" and manage, more or less, any part that he is likely to be given. The legitimate performances of everyday life are not "acted" or "put on" in the sense that the performer knows in advance just what he is going to do, and does this solely because of the effect it is likely to have. The expressions it is felt he is giving off will be especially "inaccessible" to him.[14] But as in the case of less legitimate performers, the incapacity of the ordinary individual to formulate in advance the movements of his eyes and body does not mean that he will not express himself through these devices in a way that is dramatized and performed in his repertoire of actions. In short, we all act better than we know how.

When we watch a television wrestler gouge, foul, and snarl at his opponent we are quite ready to see that, in spite of the dust, he is, and knows he is, merely playing at being the "heavy," and that in another match he may be given the other role, that of clean-cut wrestler, and perform this with equal verve and proficiency. We seem less ready to see, however, that while such details as the number and character of the falls may be fixed beforehand, the details of the expressions and movements used do not come from a script but from command of an idiom, a command that is exercised from moment to moment with little calculation or forethought. . . .

Personality-Interaction-Society

In recent years there have been elaborate attempts to bring into one framework the concepts and findings derived from three different areas of inquiry: the individual personality, social interaction, and society. I would like to suggest here a simple addition to these interdisciplinary attempts.

When an individual appears before others, he knowingly and unwittingly projects a definition of the situation, of which a conception of himself is an important part. When an event occurs which is expressively incompatible with this fostered impression, significant consequences are simultaneously felt in three levels of social reality, each of which involves a different point of reference and a different order of fact.

First, the social interaction, treated here as a dialogue between two teams, may come to an embarrassed and confused halt; the situation may cease to be defined. Previous positions may become no longer tenable, and participants may find themselves without a charted course of action. The participants typically sense a false note in the situation and come to feel awkward, flustered, and, literally, out of countenance. In other words, the minute social system created and sustained by orderly social interaction becomes disorganized. These are the consequences that the disruption has from the point of view of social interaction.

Secondly, in addition to these disorganizing consequences for action at the moment, performance disruptions may have consequences of a more far-reaching kind. Audiences tend to accept the self projected by the individual performer during any current performance as a responsible representative of his colleague-grouping, of his team, and of his social establishment. Audiences also accept the individual's particular performance as evidence of his capacity to perform the routine and even as evidence of his capacity to perform any routine. In a sense these larger social units—teams, establishments, etc.—become committed every time the individual performs his routine; with each performance the legitimacy of these units will tend to be tested anew and their permanent reputation put at stake. This kind of commitment is especially strong during some performances. Thus, when a surgeon and his nurse both turn from the operating table and the anesthetized patient accidentally rolls off the table to his death, not only is the operation disrupted in an embarrassing way, but the reputation of the doctor, as a doctor and as a man, and also the reputation of the hospital may be weakened. These are the consequences that disruptions may have from the point of view of social structure.

Finally, we often find that the individual may deeply involve his ego in his identification with a particular part, establishment, and group, and in his self-conception as someone who does not disrupt social interaction or let down the social units which depend upon that interaction. When a disruption occurs, then, we may find that the self-conceptions around which his personality has been built may become discredited. These are consequences that disruptions may have from the point of view of individual personality.

Performance disruptions, then, have consequences at three levels of abstraction: personality, interaction, and social structure. While the likelihood of disruption will vary widely from interaction to interaction, and while the social importance of likely disruptions will vary from interaction to interaction, still it seems that there is no interaction in which the participants do not take an appreciable chance of being slightly embarrassed or a slight chance of being deeply humiliated. Life may not be much of a gamble, but interaction is. Further, insofar as individuals make efforts to avoid disruptions or to correct for ones not avoided, these efforts, too, will have simultaneous consequences at the three levels. Here, then, we have one simple way of articulating three levels of abstraction and three perspectives from which social life has been studied.

Staging and the Self

The general notion that we make a presentation of ourselves to others is hardly novel; what ought to be stressed in conclusion is that the very structure of the self can be seen in terms of how we arrange for such performances in our Anglo-American society. . . .

The self, then, as a performed character, is not an organic thing that has a specific location, whose fundamental fate is to be born, to mature, and to die; it is a dramatic effect arising diffusely from a scene that is presented, and the characteristic issue, the crucial concern, is whether it will be credited or discredited.

In analyzing the self then we are drawn from its possessor, from the person who will profit or lose most by it, for he and his body merely provide the peg on which something of collaborative manufacture will be hung for a time. And the means for producing and maintaining selves do not reside inside the peg; in fact these means are often bolted down in social establishments. There will be a back region with its tools for shaping the body, and a front region with its fixed props. There will be a team of persons whose activity on stage in conjunction with available props will constitute the scene from which the performed character's self will emerge, and another team, the audience, whose interpretive activity will be necessary for this emergence. The self is a product of all of these arrangements, and in all of its parts bears the marks of this genesis.

The whole machinery of self-production is cumbersome, of course, and sometimes breaks down, exposing its separate components: back region control; team collusion; audience tact; and so forth. But, well oiled, impressions will flow from it fast enough to put us in the grips of one of our types of reality—the performance will come off and the firm self accorded each performed character will appear to emanate intrinsically from its performer.

Let us turn now from the individual as character performed to the individual as performer. He has a capacity to learn, this being exercised in the task of training for a part. He is given to having fantasies and dreams, some that pleasurably unfold a triumphant performance, others full of anxiety and dread that nervously deal with vital discreditings in a public front region. He often manifests a gregarious desire for teammates and audiences, a tactful considerateness for their concerns; and he has a capacity for deeply felt shame, leading him to minimize the chances he takes of exposure.

These attributes of the individual *qua* performer are not merely a depicted effect of particular performances; they are psychobiological in nature, and yet they seem to arise out of intimate interaction with the contingencies of staging performances.

And now a final comment. In developing the conceptual framework employed in this report, some language of the stage was used. I spoke of performers and audiences; of routines and parts; of performances coming off or falling flat; of cues, stage settings, and backstage; of dramaturgical needs, dramaturgical skills, and dramaturgical strategies. Now it should be admitted that this attempt to press a mere analogy so far was in part a rhetoric and a maneuver. . . .

And so here the language and mask of the stage will be dropped. Scaffolds, after all, are to build other things with, and should be erected with an eye to taking them down.

This report is not concerned with aspects of theater that creep into everyday life. It is concerned with the structure of social encounters—the structure of those entities in social life that come into being whenever persons enter one another's immediate physical presence. The key factor in this structure is the maintenance of a single definition of the situation, this definition having to be expressed, and this expression sustained in the face of a multitude of potential disruptions.

A character staged in a theater is not in some ways real, nor does it have the same kind of real consequences as does the thoroughly contrived character performed by a confidence man; but the *successful* staging of either of these types of false figures involves use of *real* techniques—the same techniques by which everyday persons sustain their real social situations. Those who conduct face to face interaction on a theater's stage must meet the key requirement of real situations; they must expressively sustain a definition of the situation: but this they do in circumstances that have facilitated their developing an apt terminology for the interactional tasks that all of us share.

NOTES

1. Quoted in E. H. Volkart, editor, *Social Behavior and Personality,* Contributions of W. I. Thomas to Theory and Social Research (New York: Social Science Research Council, 1951), p. 9.

2. Here I owe much to an unpublished paper by Tom Burns of the University of Edinburgh. He presents the argument that in all interaction a basic underlying theme is the desire of each participant to guide and control the responses made by the others present. A similar argument has been advanced by Jay Haley in a recent unpublished paper, but in regard to a special kind of control, that having to do with defining the nature of the relationship of those involved in the interaction.

3. An interaction can be purposely set up as a time and place for voicing differences in opinion. But in such cases participants *must* be careful to agree not to disagree on the proper tone of voice, vocabulary, and degree of seriousness in which all arguments are to be phrased, and upon the mutual respect which disagreeing participants must carefully continue to express toward one another. This debaters' or academic definition of the situation may also be invoked suddenly and judiciously as a way of translating a serious conflict of views into one that can be handled within a framework acceptable to all present.

4. Goffman, *op. cit.,* pp. 319–27.

5. Peter Blau, "Dynamics of Bureaucracy" (Ph.D. dissertation, Department of Sociology, Columbia University, forthcoming, University of Chicago Press), pp. 127–29.

6. Walter M. Beattie, Jr., "The Merchant Seaman" (unpublished M.A. report, Department of Sociology, University of Chicago, 1950), p. 35.

7. Sir Frederick Ponsonby, *Recollections of Three Reigns* (New York: Dutton, 1952), p. 46.

8. For comments on the importance of distinguishing between a routine of interaction and any particular instance when this routine is played through, see John van Neumann and Oskar

Morgenstern, *The Theory of Games and Economic Behaviour* (2nd ed.) (Princeton: Princeton University Press, 1947), p. 49.

9. See Babe Pinelli, as told to Joe King, *Mr. Ump* (Philadelphia: Westminster Press, 1953), p. 75.

10. Material on the burial business used throughout this report is taken from Robert W. Habenstein, "The American Funeral Director" (unpublished Ph.D. dissertation, Department of Sociology, University of Chicago, 1954). I owe much to Mr. Habenstein's analysis of a funeral as a performance.

11. Charles H. Cooley, *Human Nature and the Social Order* (New York: Scribner's, 1922), pp. 352–53.

12. This view of hypnosis is neatly presented by T. R. Sarbin, "Contributions to Role-Taking Theory. I: Hypnotic Behavior," *Psychological Review*, 57, pp. 255–70.

13. See D. R. Cressey, "The Differential Association Theory and Compulsive Crimes," *Journal of Criminal Law, Criminology and Police Science*, 45, pp. 29–40.

14. This concept derives from T. R. Sarbin, "Role Theory," in Gardner Lindzey, *Handbook of Social Psychology* (Cambridge: Addison-Wesley, 1954), Vol. 1, pp. 235–36.

PROJECTING THE DEFINITION OF THE SITUATION

28

Establishing the Scene in Steampunk Live-Action Role Play

Mark Cohan

(2015)

*I*n 1862, a mysterious toxic, electric cloud known as the Æster advanced from both poles of the earth to engulf the world, leaving only a small band between the Tropics of Cancer and Capricorn unaffected, and forever changing the course of human history. The story of humanity from that point forward has been one of ecological disaster, political alliances shifted by the demands of survival, and human adaption and technological achievement in the face of an uncertain future. The United States rejoined the British Empire as British America (a maneuver necessitated by the fact that no American lands were sufficiently free of the Ester to sustain ample food production). California and Texas seceded from America, one becoming an independent republic (California), the other a separate dominion (Texas). As a result

of rising ocean levels, the Mississippi River was transformed into the Great Mississippi Bay. Native Americans reclaimed large swaths of North America, particularly in the Black Hills and traditional Cherokee lands. Scientists, like Nikolas Tesla, spearheaded the development of technology, such as building materials and clothing, that shields humans from the harsh effects of the Æster. These advances have allowed for air travel and the development of Cities of Light in areas previously rendered uninhabitable by the Æster.

Now it is 88 PÆ (post-Æster), and I am in the single grungy bar that serves a remote mining town at the base of a mountain. I've come here with a disparate hodge-podge of people corralled by the Royal Geographic Society. We are scientists, naturalists, engineers, businesspeople, military *officers, and security personnel, each with some stake in our expedition to explore the mountain and its surrounding environs. Now that the Great War between British America and the Ottoman Empire is over, the Society wants to help humankind turn the page. They want to reintroduce the thrill of discovery and the promise of better living that comes with advanced knowledge of the world as it has been remade by the Æster. But I am just a lowly civil servant, a demographer by training, who, for the sake of earning some publications and the good graces of the Royal Geographic Society, must brave this trip among people I am not sure I can trust to places I know I cannot be kept safe. In the not-too-distant future, I may freeze to death somewhere in the snow on that mountain, be killed by some opportunistic member of the expedition, or be eaten by a moose that, due to exposure to the Æster, weighs several tons. But my immediate future is being decided here, at this table in this bar. A local—a small, dark-haired woman—is offering me and three of my fellow travelers information on a shortcut up the mountain, for a price. Should we trust this stranger, surrender some of our limited wealth, and follow the directions she gives us? Or will we be paying for the privilege of finding a quick and painful way to die . . . ?*

What if you were dissatisfied with the world you lived in day-to-day? You weren't depressed about it or angry with it, it just wasn't enough. For you, it was too bland and restrictive. It wasn't pretty or creepy or silly or magical or daring enough. What would you do? Could you make another world? The answer is yes, you could, but you'd need the help of a lot of other people. How do I know? Because I've seen it done. I've spent time in the retrofuturistic dream world, the elastic imaginary known as steampunk.

Steampunk is a leisure scene in which members play with time and history. Driven by a love of Victorian science fiction, active imaginations, and unceasing creativity, steampunks look back

to the 19th century—its technology, materials, geopolitical alignments, fashion, décor, music, dance, social arrangements—and imagine new, fantastic destinies for humankind with roots in that time. Then, collectively, they *perform* these fantasies into reality. According to skills and inclinations, they each draw, write, sew, paint, work leather, forge metal, or compose songs to bring to life a particular vision of a world where the Mechanical Age, with its steam power, clockworks, automatons, and airships, never gave way to the Digital Age. This (often idealized) past is now the future. Some of what they imagine is dystopian, such as a world in which a miasmic cloud has settled over an entire city, forcing its denizens underground or high above in massive dirigibles. Some is optimistic, such as a place where mechanical precision can bring inanimate metal to life. Whatever their particular vision, steampunks are united in this one fact: They have each made a hobby out of bringing to life a future that likely never will be because it emerges from a past that never was.

LIVE-ACTION ROLE PLAY

You have probably already guessed that none of what I described before about the Æster and the mining town is real in the conventional sense. But it is a very real manifestation of how some steampunks play. Some scratch their steampunk itch by dressing up in fantastic, Victorian-inspired costumes and taking a ride on a steamboat or gathering for tea. Some write, paint, sculpt, make jewelry, or play mad scientist.[1] Some write songs about the adventures of airship pirates or make music using only old-timey instruments. Some are gamers. And, finally, some of those gamers, like those on this imaginary expedition with me in the post-Æster world, are into live-action role play; they are LARPers.

Live-action role play is pretty much exactly what it sounds like. People get together, assume different fictional characters—often ones they have designed themselves—and they act out those characters in a pre-established context. Think of it as adventure improv, rather than comedy improv. If you know the early paper-based role-playing games, like *Dungeons and Dragons*, or role-playing video game adventures, like *Gauntlet*, you can think of LARPing as these games brought to life.

The steampunk live-action role playing game that gave rise to the scene in the mining-town bar is called Rise of Æster.[2] As my description suggests, that minor scene, like all scenes in the game, emerge from an elaborate backstory. That backstory is *so* elaborate, in fact, that it takes up five chapters in the 500+-page book, *Rise of Æster World Guide and Rulebook* (2011), that birthed the game and teaches players how to play. Take moment to appreciate that: A game—something people do for fun and play—has a guidebook that is 500 pages long![3]

Why does Rise of Æster need a 500-page guidebook? Because although we typically think of "play" as the most liberating, unstructured activity people can engage in, all play has boundaries. Simple games only need simple boundaries. The game of hopscotch only needs a series of boxes drawn on the ground in a particular order and players who agree that they are "out" if they put both feet down in a single box or hop on a line. The creation of a world, through live-action role play, takes a lot more boundaries, both to define the "space" of play and to make the interactions between players in that space meaningful. Some of these constructed boundaries are mental, some are material, and some are interactional; all depend on the people involved believing in these boundaries as thoroughly as football fans believe that an offensive player crossing the goal line results in a "touchdown," and a touchdown counts for six points.

MENTAL BOUNDARIES

If you are a participant in the episode of the Rise of Æster game, you look around and see a hive of activity in this mining-town bar, as scientists on the expedition try to get information from locals and locals try to trade with the explorers for coffee or tobacco. If you are not a gamer and you wander into the room accidentally, you look around and see about 40 oddly-dressed people milling around a drafty church basement, focusing their activity around two rickety banquet-length folding tables encircled by folding chairs. Unlike a casual onlooker, the gamer holds within her mind some knowledge of the Rise of Æster world. This world exists, fictional though it is, because the creators mentally crossed a boundary of time (i.e., thought back to America in 1862), imagined an environmental disaster (i.e., the rise of Æster clouds), and painstakingly documented how that disaster would redraw societal, morphological, zoological, agricultural, historical, geographic, and geopolitical boundaries. As a result, when our player, with the help of others, crosses from the real world into the Æster fantasy world, she sees herself, others, and the environment differently. She is mapping the fictional world of the Æster onto ordinary places and objects. The rickety folding table is, for all intents and purposes, a massive, worn, and weathered oak table that has been host to decades of drinking and debauchery. The man sitting across from her who has a stiff white beard, wears a heavy leather vest, speaks in a vaguely Scottish accent, and swills golden liquid (apple juice) from a tankard is an intimidating, inebriated local from the mining town. And all of this makes sense because she is not who she was when she walked in the door. She came in as a twenty-something technology professional. But she put on a modest, high-collared lace top, accented it with a broach, added glasses, gloves, and a simple feathered hat, and now she is the demure but determined spokesperson of the Royal Geographic Society. When it comes down to it, of course, how she sees herself, the others, this room and the objects in it is all in her head. But it is in all of the heads of the people who occupy the space with her, and that's why it works.

Shared meaning explains *why* it works; all the players accept the existence (and basic nature) of a fictional Æster-afflicted world. But familiarity with the *Rise of Æster World Guide and Rulebook* does not, in itself, make a LARP happen. To understand *how* it works—that is, how 40 people can, with a minimum of conflict and confusion, move in and out of a fictional play space—we have to examine some other, more specific mental boundaries. One of the most basic of these is when the game is "on." The LARPers use a combination of command structure and ritual to signal to one another when the drafty basement has become a specific location in the Rise of Æster world and when they go from being adults in costumes to characters in an unfolding drama.

For this day's game, the Lead Navigator is Marcus. A Navigator is like a Dungeon Master in *Dungeons & Dragons*. He or she sets the scene for players, guides them in determining the consequences as they act on the environment and players around them, and decides any disputes about or outside of the established rules. Since this game involves so many people, Marcus has several associates who will also serve as Navigators during game play, but he is the ultimate authority for organizing and managing the enterprise.

Our first sign that we are moving toward "game on" comes when Marcus, flanked by two associates, stands on the largest piece of permanent furniture in the otherwise barren room—a wooden platform, the size of a small stage, which is raised about four feet from the floor and covered in dingy white carpet. He asks us all to gather, breaking up groups of people who are plotting collective action in the upcoming scene, groups that have been working on final details for the game, like distributing money (in the form of fake British pounds, shillings, and pence), other groups who are simply socializing, and individuals who are milling aimlessly. Without really trying, we arrange ourselves in a large semicircle in front of the "stage." Marcus welcomes us all, introduces his fellow Navigators, describes the new serial (series of storylines that will be played out over multiple days of game play) we are beginning today, and makes sure those who have played before understand that things will be different with this new story arc. Then he initiates a ritual that is pivotal to moving us across the threshold into a fantasy realm. Beginning on my right and going around the semicircle, he asks every person to introduce themselves with their real name, followed by the name and role of the character they will be playing in the game. This is the first time we each acknowledge publicly that who we are is not who we will be shortly.

When introductions are complete, we are herded toward a hallway that inclines like a ramp out of the main room. As we move in that direction, Marcus shouts above the murmuring of the group, "When you get into the hallway, you will be in character. Please stay in character from that point until our first break." He then stands before us at the bottom of the ramp, just inside the main room and reiterates the description he provided of the first scene we are about to play out:

> British America has just emerged a lengthy, bruising war with Ottoman Empire, and the Royal Geographic Society has organized this scientific expedition in an effort to rekindle people's faith in humanity and excitement about discovery. The expedition participants are now meeting—many for the first time—in a conference room at the

Society's offices. The task for all involved is to get to know participants with compatible interests and to agree on some mechanism through which decisions will be made as the expedition proceeds.

With a slight bow and grand, arcing wave of his hand, he steps to the side, players move from the ramp into the vast main room, and the game is on.

INTERACTIONAL BOUNDARIES: PEOPLE

With the game started, new boundaries—interactional boundaries—spring into life. The existence of these boundaries means that, once the game is on, no one can interact with anyone else the way they did just moments before; they must interact in terms of the game, not in terms of "real life." Most prominent among the interactional boundaries are those created by the different types of participants in the game, and the social boundaries that divide characters in the fictional milieu of the game.

Player characters, non-player characters, and Navigators

The differences in types of participants mean that some individuals are assigned different reality statuses than others. The bulk of the gamers are playing characters they have created and that they plan to inhabit and develop from scene to scene and episode to episode over multiple days of gaming. These **player characters**[4] are the most permanently real in the game. In the final analysis, the game is *for* them.

Kat is a player character *par excellence*. She is a member of the Glass Knives tribe of Nightmen. Like all Nightmen, she is determined to eek [*sic*] out an existence in the rural areas of Æster darkness, refusing to settle in the Cities of Light. Her affiliation with the Glass Knives means her survival strategy is to use her skills as a shrewd trader and get the best of trading partners in the

St. Louis City of Light and the Junction City Outpost. It also means that she is prepared to use physical violence to achieve her goals.

But Kat is so much more than a reflection of her social position. She has been a staple of this monthly Rise of Æster game for *years*, and in that time her creator (the person who plays her), Eliza, has built Kat into a character with an elaborate backstory and a multidimensional personality. In an interview in 2011, Eliza proudly told me that one of Kat's survival strategies is to be different things to different people. Sometimes she comes off as a complete ditz; sometimes she explodes in anger. But in the final analysis, she *really* is an incredibly smart and fierce competitor who uses her multiple personas to manipulate people to her own ends. Over the years, Kat has also developed complex and evolving relationships with other player characters. Kat's brief period as Grant's lover, for instance, started as a joke between them but, Eliza says, things took on a life of their own. In addition, Kat has a hate-filled rivalry with Gwendolyn, a character who happens to be played by Eliza's best friend, and she has come to see Vladimir as a kind of "big brother," despite the fact that he comes from a competing (and particularly savage) tribe. These relationships Kat has developed have no parallel with Eliza's relationships with the individuals who play these characters. Eliza has never had so much as a flirtation with the young man who plays Grant. But it is these long-term, deep relationships, which seem to evolve of their own accord during the course of game play, that make Kat so real within the game and so real for Eliza. So much so, in fact, that Eliza admits that if Kat were ever killed off in the game, she would almost certainly cry.

Other individuals act as **non-player characters.** Their reality status is temporary. They appear in particular scenes as sort of interactive props that the player characters can engage with, learn from, and sometimes clash with in ways that move the story along. In the first scene at the Society's offices, while playing the role of aspiring demographer, Gerard Ichabod Whistlebottom, I met Lady Gwendolyn Spivey, a petite woman in her early 20s with curly blonde hair and piercing blue eyes. She wore the most professional attire, presented herself with a sophisticated air, and carried a small bound journal, into which she continually jotted notes. She spoke eagerly about soliciting my services on behalf of the Royal Geographic Society and, before the scene ended, she had me under contract. Lady Spivey was a compelling figure in this first scene, but I soon learned that she was a non-player character (NPC). She had been brought to life by Karen, a veteran of the Rise of Æster LARP, to serve as an engine for the storyline involving the Royal Geographic Society, and she would cease to exist, unless or until the demands of the evolving story called for her again. This freed up Karen to be someone completely different in the following scene.

And so, when I and my fellow explorers arrived at the mining town bar, Lady Spivey was nowhere to be seen. But sitting at one of the massive oaken tables (rickety folding tables, to the uninitiated) was a woman with curly blonde hair and piercing blue eyes. She called herself Mary, spoke with a bright Scottish accent, and her image was anything but professional. She wore a dingy blue shirt, and most of her hair was covered by a simple bandana. She seemed to be getting more inebriated by the minute, and it wasn't long before she was aggressively promoting herself and her male companion—a heavily bearded fellow—to me and my fellow travelers as capable guides for our trip up the mountain.

The last participant type is the **Navigator.**[5] Navigators are critical to the proceedings, but they occupy a liminal state in relation to them. Before the game, they are essential organizers, helping players with last minute details, and secretly preparing the final elements of the story

that is about to unfold. During this pre-game period, I chatted easily with Ruby, one of the longest-tenured R of Æ players, as she helped me understand the new character I would be playing. But once the game began, she, like the other Navigators, remained in the room, monitoring the proceedings, but existing outside the reality of the game, unseen and unacknowledged.

Unseen, that is, until one of the players—a young woman with glasses and her dark hair in a bun, carrying a black, antique medical bag—raised one of her hands up with her fingers crossed. Ruby had noticed the woman trying to catch her eye and was by her side by the time the woman made the gesture. Moments earlier, this woman—the medic of our expedition—had been speaking loudly and confidently in a British accent, but as Ruby arrived, her voice dropped in volume and the accent disappeared. She spoke in a quiet, conspiratorial tone with Ruby, as if the two of them were engaging in a private aside, and, in fact, that is precisely what they were doing. The "fingers crossed" gesture is recognized in LARPing circles—or in this LARPing community, at least—to designate that an actor is stepping out of character temporarily. It allows individuals or small groups of players to move across the boundary from fantasy back to ordinary reality, without significantly disrupting the illusion for others. (It is not unusual to see a solitary player rushing hurriedly around the edges of the room toward the hall that leads to the restroom, hand raised and fingers crossed.) In this case, the young woman wanted Ruby, in her capacity as a Navigator, to clarify how much familiarity her character was presumed to have with the others on the expedition. Ruby answered, then walked away, fading back into non-person status in the eyes of the players. The young woman uncrossed her fingers, turned back to the characters around her, and our medic was back.

Social divisions

One of the complexities of R of Æ world, like that of other LARPs, is the unique social arrangements that exist within it. In this elaborate fiction, human relations, not just the physical environment, are radically transformed by the Æster. Entirely new social statuses emerge as the populace learns to cope with the Æster and its consequences.

Interwoven with these social commitments is the heightened concern for propriety and knowing "one's place" that characterized the Victorian Era. While gender boundaries are typically not maintained in the Victorian way, class boundaries are acknowledged, even if they are not kept as rigidly as they were historically. For instance, as I, Gerard Ichabod Whistlebottom, milled about the Society's offices in the first scene, I came upon a young woman with dark hair whose clothes and carriage indicated sophistication and high social standing. She had on a dazzling blue evening dress, with a fur stole wrapped around her shoulders. She was engaged in conversation with others, so I introduced myself to the woman next to her, who seemed affiliated with her in some way. This woman had short hair and a round, pleasant face, but her appearance provided a stark contrast to the lady. She seemed plainer and more masculine in her dark pants and unadorned white shirt. She said her name was Pauline, and she was Lady Preston's handmaiden. I asked, "What is your interest in the expedition?" And she replied, "I have no interest of my own. My only concern is attending to my Lady's needs throughout the trip." I asked a few additional questions, but she was clearly uncomfortable talking about herself. And it seemed she was unsure how or if she should interact with me, given that she suspected that, as a scholar, I ranked above her socially. In this and a multitude of other situations, the fictional world redrew the boundaries of social interaction, such that friends and acquaintances who otherwise saw themselves as equals (like myself and these two women) related to one another as rivals, as the servant and the served, or as the noble and the commoner.

INTERACTIONAL BOUNDARIES: CHALLENGES

After the initial gathering in the Society offices, our expedition set out for Mount Blackcombe in a group of six all-terrain vehicles. During this travel phase, the entire expedition, some 30 people strong, was packed tightly onto the ramp and hallway that lead from the main room to the building exits, physical spacing that reflected our cramped mode of transport. As we traveled, we broke into small groups, trying to come to agreement about how decisions should be made for the expedition.

The vehicles were making good progress, until Marcus, the Lead Navigator, informed us that a massive boulder now blocked the path. Four members of the expedition, including our security officer and an engineer, had training with explosives, and the group decided these four should try to blow a hole through the boulder big enough for the vehicles to pass through. They moved to the front of the throng of players, while others murmured their concern about the obstacle and the sophisticated Lady Preston lamented that she didn't think she could tolerate these rough conditions much longer. The explosives experts met Marcus at the bottom of the ramp, where it met the entrance to the main room. I was a little ways back, pressed against the wall as two men—one black-haired and one brown-haired—spoke in Russian accents and aggressively asserted that they were far more qualified to lead the expedition than "scientists," a word they practically spit out of their mouths. Even from my vantage, however, I could see the four explosive experts standing in front of

Marcus. I heard him count, "One, two, three," and on "three" all of them, including Marcus, brought out one hand with some fingers raised. It was as if they were playing a game within the game, something akin to "rock, paper, scissors." Marcus added the total number of fingers displayed by himself and each of the explosive experts, consulted his notes, and declared that the team had been successful in creating a large enough hole in the boulder. The expedition was able to resume its progress toward Mount Blackcombe.

This ritual within the game is called a challenge. It occurs whenever a player or group of players wishes to act upon or is acted upon by other players, non-player characters, or the environment. Trying to climb a frail-looking rope ladder, defending yourself when another player attacks you with a rapier, shooting your crossbow in hopes of taking down an Æster moose for food—the outcome of all of these efforts would be determined by a challenge. The contestants in the challenge—one of which may be a Navigator, representing the environment—throw out fingers, and the success or failure of the challenge is determined by a formula that relates an odd or even result to the (previously-determined) strengths and weaknesses of the character.

Challenges are unique instances because they require that the boundary between what is and isn't part of the game be managed with particular nuance. If you watched an explosives team set charges around the base of a bridge, then each team member stepped back and purposively thrust one hand in the air with some fingers extended, this would strike you as exceedingly odd. Live-action role play games need a means of introducing and managing chance, otherwise what's happening is less a game and more a play following a script. But resolving challenges requires that everyone involved put their actions in a kind of parenthesis—a bracket that straddles the border between the real and fantasy worlds. The throwing of fingers is not seen by the characters in the unfolding story—these actions are implicitly understood to be part of the "real world"—but the *results* of challenges are. Players work to minimize the disruption to the fantasy world by resolving challenges quickly and dramatizing the results. This dramatization can be as simple as our medic hobbling around after she had difficulty scaling a rocky incline and twisted her ankle, or as elaborate as a character falling heavily to the floor and writhing in agony after receiving a knife wound in a fight.

MATERIAL BOUNDARIES

The first time I participated in a steampunk LARP, years before the game involving the expedition to Mount Blackcombe, one of the first things I saw was a large man with grey hair and a thick grey beard—a sweet, grandfatherly fellow—working intently with a mop head he had just taken out of the package. He used fabric scissors to snip away the strands from one continuous section that covered about one quarter of the whole head. Then he put down the scissors, shook out the head so that the remaining strands fell down evenly, stood upright, and, with a flourish, plopped the mop top on his head. He arranged his new "tresses" about his back and shoulders and peered out, smiling, from the area he had cut away. Len—who was about to play a judge in a murder trial taking place in one of British America's most influential cities, East St. Louis—now had a very convincing barrister's wig.

Instances of creativity of this sort involving costuming, sets, and props abound in LARPing and steampunk as a whole. At first blush, this may not seem to involve boundaries; it's just decoration, right? Wrong. Effectively transforming objects so that they are recognized by others as something else, something that belongs in an alternate reality, is not as easy as it seems. When it is not done effectively, as when a military officer on our expedition to Mount Blackcombe carried a toy gun of white and orange plastic that she had not painted to look aged, dark, and metallic, it stands out. The object is physically there, in the collectively-constructed fantasy world, but it has not itself crossed the barrier to that world. It screams 21st century.

Here's another example. During one R of Æ episode from years back, I was one of a band of four pirates plotting to attack a steamship. We decided we could more easily coerce the passengers' cooperation by bringing a bomb on board. In the discarded items around the edges of the main room, we found a small, empty helium canister that looked vaguely like a bomb. We could have simply boarded the ship with it and declared we had a bomb, but then the canister would have been as distant from the Rise of Æster world as the unmodified plastic gun. Instead, one of our team set to work attaching a series of little yellow lights to the body of the tank, just below the handle, and then added one red light on the handle to suggest that the "bomb" was armed. Where the original lettering on the tank said, "balloon," we used black electrical tape to edit it so it read, "Boom." When we finished, we had something much more than a helium canister. We had a recognizable instrument of terror that was both a little bit believable and a little bit cartoonish.

The Serious Work of Play

What steampunk LARPing demonstrates in grand fashion is that reality is incredibly elastic. If we are dedicated to making something new and novel, it is possible to engage our imagination and surround ourselves with others who will accept the meanings we have made and make new ones with us. Together, we cross the boundaries, and the world is transformed. When the Rise of Æster LARPers do it, it's called play. But this play is taken very seriously and involves considerable time and cooperation among the performers. In similar fashion, though typically less notably so, we cross boundaries and create new worlds of interactional meaning all throughout our days simply as we move from situation to situation. LARPer creative enactments throw this collective reality-making process into relief; through the collaborative production of fantasy their activity shows us something about the production of reality.

Works Cited

Hunter, Marshal. 2011. *Rise of Æster Steampunk Live Action Role Playing Game: World Guide and Rulebook.* Seattle: Æsterlight Steampunk Studios.

Notes

1. Examples of "mad scientist" projects include experimenting with electrolytic etching or recreating Benjamin Franklin's original musical instrument, the glass harmonica.

2. I have created pseudonyms for all of the participants and characters in the game, but the game itself is, in fact, called Rise of Æster. The name and storylines are used with permission.

3. To be clear, it's not just fun and play for the creators of Rise of Æster. They hope to profit from all of their effort, through sales of the game book and supplements offering additional story lines. They are even working to produce a series of Rise of Æster feature films.

And, to be fair, the creators and dedicated players of R of Æ will tell you that you don't need to study the rule book—you don't have to have any prior knowledge, in fact—to jump in and play the game. That's true, to a point. When I played for the first time in 2011, I would have only been able to tell you that the game took place in a fictional past where toxic clouds filled the skies. The players welcomed me with open arms, but I was fairly lost. You don't have to be familiar with the world to play in it, but I can assure you will never be a full participant in that case. You will always be a bit player, fulfilling some small role that is handed to you, without understanding how it fits into the larger picture. You will always be a tourist, never a native.

4. The Rise of Æster guidebook makes specific use of the terms "player," "character," and "actor," so

that participants can distinguish between the individual outside and inside the game ("player" vs "character") and between the qualities of the made-up person and the actions of that person ("character" vs "actor"). While these distinctions are important for the game, I have decided not to adhere to them here, as I think they would introduce technicalities irrelevant to my purpose.

5. Some player types are not mutually exclusive. It is common for Navigators to also take on roles as non-player characters.

PROJECTING THE DEFINITION OF THE SITUATION

29

Death as Theater: A Dramaturgical Analysis of the American Funeral

Ronny E. Turner and Charles Edgley

(1976)

THE PERFORMATIVE NATURE OF FUNERAL DIRECTING

Funeral directors and allied members of their team may be seen as actors whose job it is to stage a performance in such a way so that the audience to it (the bereaved family and friends) will impute competence, sincerity, dignity, respect, and concern to their actions. Given the one-shot nature of the funeral service, and the impossibility of doing it over in the event of mistakes, the funeral director must necessarily be concerned with those performative aspects of his business which will lead the audience to be impressed favorably by his effective staging of the show. As in any other performance, the concern is likely to be with whether the show comes off

or falls flat, and consequently, to use Goffman's phrase, the expressions given off must be arranged in such a way so that the images and impressions formed are favorable ones.

From the standpoint of the sociology of work, the funeral director is in a unique business. He draws his living from a relatively fixed resource, the death rate in a community. He cannot increase the amount of business available to him by increasing the number of deaths in the community, and he must be very careful of how he advertises lest someone gain the impression that he wants more people to die. (One does not, for example, see funeral homes sponsoring such risky events as the Indianapolis 500.) His choices for increasing the flow of money, then, are limited and center basically around two options: (1) Getting more than his share of the business from deaths that do occur in the community; and (2) merchandizing up, so that the average cost of funerals rises. In short, his opportunities to make money stem from his performative ability to stage dramas which are meaningful to his audience, and will leave them with a favorable enough impression to contribute to the all-important "reputation" which funeral homes find is in many respects their most marketable, if not tangible quality.

Role-Distance:
The Sacred and the Profane

The performative necessities of his works are, however, made more difficult by another aspect of the relationship between the funeral director and his audience which has been pointed out repeatedly by various studies: the amount of social distance that exists both between him and his clients and between the object of his work (death), and the public he undertakes to perform before. He deals with objects which are both sacred and profane; simultaneously loved and loathed. As a result, the funeral director often attempts to separate the body work from the directive work, thereby putting distance between himself and his traditionally assigned role. Sometimes this is accomplished in the same routine as when he dresses out differently for embalming and for directing; at other times role-distance is accomplished by simply hiring separate functionaries to do the body work so that he can concentrate on staging the show without being seen as someone who has been contaminated by contact with the dead. What is separated here by the funeral director is not so much himself from his role, but rather himself from a loathsomeness ordinarily attributed to certain aspects of that role by his audience.

As in other occupations (the medical profession being the most salient example), some emotional detachment from the objects one is manipulating is desirable. Funeral directors and their staff, therefore, tend to separate their own personal identity from the task of embalming bodies. The language and nonverbal conduct in the preparation room, then, demonstrate a type of role-distance which effectively communicates detachment and sometimes even disdainful alienation from the role one is performing.

Backstage Regions:
Preparation and Rehearsal

A successful funeral is a sequence of activities performed by the funeral director and his staff that are later seen by the bereaved as a respectful, appropriate tribute to the life and memory of the deceased. It requires an extensive series of preparations backstage, or behind the scene and the enclosed performance. A backregion or backstage is simply the space and the enclosed activities strategically hidden from the audience. It is ordinarily a place, but it may also be constituted simply by the shielding and masking of information in an interpersonal situation so that the audience does not realize certain things that would conflict with the performance as staged. A backstage region, whether a place, or an interpersonal strategy is "bounded to some degree by barriers to perception."

The necessity of backregions is due, obviously, to the fact that preparations for performances, if seen, may contradict, alter, qualify, or destroy the impressions fostered frontstage. Because people seem to have a limited capacity for seeing ritual as ritual, and since funerals, like any other drama, are prepared for, the viewing of the preparations may undercut the impressions fostered frontstage. Similarly, those who have worked in the backregions of a restaurant, in the kitchen or afterhours, and have participated in the preparation of food, the classification of customers by the staff, and so forth, may have difficulty seeing the frontstage performances in the same manner again.

In the backstage, equipment and props used to produce the performance are stored, the behavior within the area is considered "private," and the scenes that go on are protected from public observance by various territorial imperatives socially constructed and enforced: doors, curtains, locks, and "employees only" signs.

The Backstage Setting

What we have said about backstage regions are [sic] generally applicable with few qualifications to the dramas of the American funeral. The preparation room, referred to by some morticians as a "medical laboratory," is spatially segregated from the funeral chapel, visitation rooms, viewing rooms, offices, and other regions the public frequents. It may be noted that the awesome and sacrosanct qualities of such places may be heightened by successfully identifying them with medicine, a line of endeavor which seems to establish particularly esoteric meanings for the bulk of Americans.

The social and physical boundaries that separate the preparation room from other parts of the home are essential to the ceremonial performances that will be given later. Here the corpse is washed, shaved, sprayed with disinfectant, sliced, pierced, creamed, powdered, waxed, stitched, painted, manicured, dressed, and positioned in a casket. Embalming involves the draining of blood *via* the major arteries while simultaneously refilling them through an injection point in the neck or armpit with fluid. Through the use of other chemicals the flesh is softened, stretched, shrunk, restored, colored, and even replaced.

Obviously, these procedures would be likely to shock "nonprofessionals" such as the friends and family of the deceased. But more than that,

such viewing would tend to present the audience with an impression that would contradict that being fostered frontstage. As Goffman notes, "if the bereaved are to be given the impression that the loved one is really in a deep and tranquil sleep, they will have to be kept away from the area where the corpse is drained, stuffed, and painted for its final performance." In the presence of family and friends the casketed body is never touched by mortuary personnel; they honor a distance of two to three feet from the body. However, the preparation room is characterized by handling of the body (a naked body in some procedures) in ways that would appear disrespectful and even inhuman, even if one were unaware of the identity of the deceased. One might respond to all of these by asking just how it is possible to talk about inhumanity when the object is a corpse, and yet it is precisely this "human identity" conception of the enterprise that supports the funeral profession, and indeed, becomes the basic polarity between which the mortician must balance his act. At any rate, the embalming, restoration, and other preparatory procedures requiring manual labor might appear to the layman as morbidly intimate, repulsive, and a violation of dignity, even to the dead. Virtually all of the amenities persons accord to each other in everyday life are violated by the attendants who prepare a corpse for the service.

In order to maintain the historically hard-won image as a legitimate professional and counselor rather than an "undertaker," with all of its attendant morbid stereotypes, a funeral director must seclude the backstage by utilizing rhetoric less suggestive of what transpires behind closed doors. Here we come to the interpersonal shielding we discussed earlier that is at least as important as the barriers formed by physical space. It should be noted that backstage regions are protected not only by the funeral director, but also by others; most people, except some curious sociologists of everyday life, voluntarily avoid areas where they are uninvited. They exercise the sort of tact regarding settings that constitutes "discretion." In this sense, the audience actively, rather than passively, participates in the distinctions we have drawn. They want to be put on by the show as much as the producers of it, and they seem to recognize that part of the meaning of any performance will be diluted with disenchantment if one knows too much.

Even though the specifics of the preparation room are a mystery, most people know enough to choose acceptable ignorance and avoid trespassing into the region. Once again, the audience is a party to the stage production, avoiding asking questions about embalming procedures, and generally managing their behavior in such a way as to suggest they know nothing of such preparations, and want to keep it that way.

The Rhetoric of Backstage Regions

Both the technical and the informal nomenclature which mark the universe of discourse of backstage regions serve a number of functions, but they are sufficiently different from the language characterizing the frontstage that they must be segregated from clients who seek funeral services. There exists quite clearly in the funeral business a backstage language and other rubric entirely for those occasions in which the performance that has been so laboriously prepared as being staged. A superb example of frontstage rhetoric is a sign on the door of the embalming room at one of the establishments we studied:

REMEMBER
_____

This preparation room becomes sacred when a family entrusts us with one of its most precious possessions. Keep faith with *them* by conducting *yourself* as though the family were present. The body is dear to them . . . Treat it reverently.

Backstage, however, morticians develop a very different set of behaviors toward their activities. Rather than being a person, the body becomes an object upon which one performs restorative art. And while the deceased is a dearly beloved, Mr. Doe, a father, loved one, etc., during frontstage encounters with the bereaved family, backstage references are to various types of bodies such as "floaters" (one who has drowned and was not recovered until the body floated to the surface), "Mr. Crispy" (one who burned to death in an airplane crash), a "fresh" or "warm" one (a body received shortly after death), a "cold" one (a frozen body) are encountered in the conversations of the backstage crew. References to restorative art in the information materials given the public may in fact be referred to in the preparation room as "pickling" or "curing a ham." The use of "bod" instead of "body," especially with younger female corpses, is not uncommon. Joking, singing, the discussion of political issues, and (infrequently) open sexual remarks, racial slurs, complaints about the size of some bodies, profanity, and other rhetoric inconsistent with the frontstage regions are employed as ways of distancing the embalmer from the role he is performing.

Similarly, frontstage references to the burial containers such as casket, gift to the deceased, home, place of rest, and so on, are referred backstage as coffins, stuffing boxes, tin cans, containers, stove pipes (a cheap metal over wood casket), or brand names given to caskets by manufacturers.

Such role-distance behavior may manifest alienation from the role "but the opposite can well be true: in some cases only those who feel secure in their attachment may be able to chance the expression of distance." Expression of distance may serve also to relax those attending the task and/or convey an atmosphere of "just another job" in what otherwise would be a situation permeated by anxiety and tension. As in other occupations, role-distance behavior can be noted in the many instances where the actor does "two things at once," singing, joking, and using the aforementioned backstage rhetoric while preparing the body.

The preparation room is a scene constructed in such a way as to establish the impression of a sterile medical atmosphere. Even though the backstage crew may humorously refer to themselves as a "bod squad," they more often refer to themselves and their behavior in medical rhetoric, thereby borrowing credence and legitimacy from that professional most esteemed in American society: the medical doctor. The medical atmosphere and terminology is also a part of ongoing role-distance; the white surgical garb, the white walls, and the operating table help the practitioner to see and present himself as at least a quasi-medical professional rather than simply a handler of corpses.

Just as theaters have their makeup rooms, the preparation room serves as a setting for the cosmetology that will turn the corpse into the star of the show. As makeup-artists, morticians are unsurpassed, and have elevated their skill to a high art. Given the various causes of death and subsequent kinds of bodily disfigurement, "restorative art" is designed to make the deceased look natural and, in a sense, "alive." Cosmetics in the hands of a skilled mortician can cover a multitude of wounds, bruises, ravages of long-term disease and discoloration, and even major forms of disfigurement. (One funeral director told us with pride of a suicide he had reconstructed, even though the man had succeeded in blowing the top of his head off.) When successful, an unblemished star is born for a magnificent final performance.

As with other performers, the actor is not supposed to appear "made up," but rather the makeup is applied to convey "natural" impressions rather than the artificiality the makeup room as a backstate region implies. (One is reminded of the cosmetic company that advertises that women can achieve the "natural look"

only by using their new line of cosmetics.) Funeral directors take as a compliment remarks that the deceased looked natural, at peace, younger than before, asleep, etc., apparently because his art is being validated by the very audience at which it is directed. What might seem as "art-for-art's sake" is justified by funeral directors as a vital element in what has come to be known as "grief therapy," a vocabulary of motives which most practitioners in the industry now espouse. Such a set of rationales hold that the viewing of the body by the bereaved is a necessary step in the acceptance of death. It is of interest to note that an economic vocabulary of motives might also apply (open-casket funerals usually generate a larger expenditure of money because the interior designations of the casket become significant to the buyer.

FRONTSTAGE PERFORMANCES: BRINGING OFF THE SHOW

The change of titles from "undertaker" to "funeral director" has been perhaps the largest single clue to the dramaturgical functions the industry now sees itself as performing. He is indeed a "director," controlling a dramatic production. The staged performance is supported by elaborate backstage preparations of the body, equipment, and props, and the immediate family is rehearsed as to the schedule of events and protocol. In order to preclude any miscues in the performance, the rehearsal covers entrance cues, exit, places to sit, and timing of events; special requests by the family can also be included in the script and program.

The funeral director and his crew continue backstage activities during the funeral service: automobile drivers, pallbearers, ministers, and musicians must all be orchestrated in a smooth and uninterrupted performance. As a skilled director, the mortician is available but largely unnoticed, particularly by the audience of friends and acquaintances who come to pay their respects. He is often acutely sensitive to matters of "promptness, overall courtesy, ushering, and other tasks involving a sizable number of people" (Raether, 1971:121). His demeanor, of course, establishes a model of appropriate behavior in a funeral setting:

> The funeral director should not strut, nor should he appear to be mousey. His demeanor should show dignity, concern, and confidence . . . [he] should not talk loud, nor should he whisper secretly. He should speak in a subdued voice . . . should not walk around unnecessarily . . . should not snap his fingers or hiss to get attention. (Raether, 1971:121)

In addition, he constantly checks the floral pieces for placement, fallen petals, water leakage, and all such tidying is made prior to the family's arrival.

Controlling the Situation: The Cast of Characters

The funeral as a staged performance features a marquee listing a well-respected director affiliated with National Funeral Directors Association; a star, the deceased, whose life and attributes comprise the plot; a supporting cast of the bereaved (one of whom usually takes charge of managing details); supporters of the bereaved; ministers; musicians; and pallbearers; and, of course, the audience of friends and acquaintances. The bereaved are themselves supporting actors and actresses, for they too are part of the performance. They are "on-stage" in that their behavior is reviewed and judged by others whose comments on how well the family "held up" at the funeral will later be taken into account. Observations of funerals and especially postfuneral gatherings show that such evaluations comprise much of the conversation, and the bereaved who shows too little emotion for the audience's

conception of their relationship to the deceased, or those who show too much when it is known that the relationship did not warrant it, are likely to be judged negatively. Mourners are aware of this, and may construct their performances accordingly. Sometimes, in fact, part of the directing task is coaching mourners on how to act.

Cast members must also be controlled: one of the most potentially troublesome of these is the minister. As such, he may, if not carefully managed, act in such a way as to construct a counter-reality which can cast doubt on the entire show. Historically, the undertaker was a minor functionary whose role was under the direct supervision of the minister. However, with the emergence of the professional "funeral director" the minister has been increasingly shunted to the background, and now it may be properly said that *he* is the minor functionary. The counter-reality that the minister may establish is the idea that all of this funeral business is really nonsense because the body is a shell and the "soul" has departed. In addition, he may feel that there is too much emphasis on rituals involving the body, and that these smack of paganism and status seeking, as well as being a waste of money. The minister may have long years of close association with the family, and if allowed to operate unmanaged, can be a significantly moderating influence on the family's choice. Consequently, trade journals devote occasional space to giving helpful advice on how to control this potentially truculent member of the cast. *Mortuary Management*, for example, suggest the following when a minister comes with the family to make arrangements:

> We tell the family to go ahead and look over the caskets in the display room, and that the minister . . . will join them later. We tell the minister that we have something we would like to talk to him about privately, and we've found that if we have some questions to ask him, he seems to be flattered that his advice is being sought, and we

can keep him in the private office until the family has actually made its selection.

The Funeral Home as Theater and Stage

Seldom are funeral homes space-age in architectural design; rather they present themselves with traditional white columns. Colonial style, or even proudly as older structures. They are usually decorated profusely with flowers, the walkways are carefully landscaped, the grass must be sprayed green during the winter months and, of course, the interiors are meticulously decorated. Such appearances are ways of establishing other meanings besides the usual ones of death and morbidity. Brightly colored drapes, curtains, and fixtures seem to breathe life; black hues are out, for they conspicuously portray the image of "undertaker." Even the traditional black limousine is no longer fashionable among more modern funeral homes; colors such as grey, white, and blue are now seen as more appropriate to death-free imagery.

The stage itself, the funeral chapel, is a model of theatrical perfection; many chapels would make a Broadway star envious. The chapel is usually arranged with ample entrances and exits, and may be served by back doors, halls, tunnels, and passageways that lead from the preparation room without ever trespassing frontstage areas. Equipment and props such as flower holders, religious symbols, and decorative roping are used to set the stage for the performance. In addition, the basic stage area is often neutral so that appropriate props can be used to establish the correct symbols for the various religious types of funerals common in our society.

If all of this background is successfully arranged, the funeral director—like other persons responsible for the direction of performances in our society—is in a position to control the kind of definitions that arise in the situation. Having had little opportunity to rehearse for such rituals, the majority of mourners face a highly problematic, tense, and relatively undefined situation. Consequently, monitoring the director's cues become a way of apprehending what the situation calls for.

Establishing the Mood

A crucial, and therefore precarious, feature of virtually all human affairs is mood. And it is important to remember that actions establish mood. The putting on of certain conduct will lead the reviewer to feel this way or that; and, as we have already shown, the review of the funeral director's show is in many ways the most tangible product he sells.

Probably the single most effective way of establishing the right mood for a funeral is the judicious use of music. Emanating usually from a veiled location, "appropriate" organ music (as opposed to "inappropriate" music such as amplified guitar) is the vital medium through which the atmosphere of the funeral is created. In counsel with the family, the musical selections are planned to set the mood for serenity, beauty, respect, or whatever values are desired. Many mortuaries offer lists of musicians upon which the family can call, and who will perform for a fee; other establishments have their own musicians available for hire. As in other shows, the selection, volume, tone, and timing of the music provide cues for the series of events or acts that are presented. With the aid of a printed program, music cues the audience in sequence: be respectfully quiet; the service is beginning; the choir is about to sing; a prayer is forthcoming; a minister is about to speak; the eulogy is being delivered; it is time for the processional view of the deceased; the service is over—you may leave. Mood management, then, is a major means by which the director controls the situation.

Frontstage Rhetoric and the Denial of Death

Although one of the consensually stated objectives of funerals is the acceptance of death by the family, the rhetoric of the frontstage as well as the social and physical setting of the funeral service itself tends to contradict such claims. Despite the many criticisms and subsequent industry denials and changes in procedure, the metaphors used in the American funeral continue to be those of sleep, transition to other worlds, and eternal life, rather than death. Much of this denial, of course, stems from religious traditions which tend to treat death as a kind of minor nuisance on the way to glory. And there is little in the funeral to contradict such ideas. "Mr. Jones" reposes in a "slumber room" in a casket whose mattress rivals the posturepedics designed for those of us still alive but suffering from back trouble. The titles and words of songs frequently sung at a funeral ("Death is only a Dream," "Asleep in Jesus," "It is not Death to Die") pointedly do not say "death has occurred, I am sorry" but rather "he or she is still with us."

In addition to this socially established denial of death, funerals serve as morality plays which weave social commentary into the rituals. Eulogies to the deceased will ordinarily contain references to his community service, character, righteousness, and approved identities. Certain behaviors are validated as noble, while others are by implication denounced. The audience is thereby advised to take note, for they too will someday be reviewed in such a public ceremony. One comforting aspect of such eulogizing, however, is that the deceased is usually given the benefit of the doubt; the eulogizer selectivity, of course, makes for considerable juggling of the available facts of a person's life, especially when dealing with those whose lives have been less than sterling.

CONCLUSION

The dramaturgical metaphor we have employed in this chapter offers an alternative way of viewing the interactions and relationships comprising the American funeral. Death and dying obviously involve ritual and ceremony; without these much of what we take for granted among the living such as respect, character, and substance would likely vanish.

We also wish to enter a *caveat* regarding our use of a metaphorical argument. To say that funerals may be seen as performances does not suggest that they *are* performances. Rather, the dramaturgical metaphor offers an interpretive framework that serves to illuminate what is often obscured by those perspectives that center on either the structural apparatus of the society in which death occurs or on the alleged psychological characteristics and states of the participants. Dramas can, of course, be viewed as expressions of either psychological or social determinants, but what we have suggested here is that there may be value in viewing them as fundamental realities in their own right. For no matter how standard the ritual expression becomes, each drama must still be brought off on its own with all the attendant opportunities for error. It is this possibility that makes our dramas at once precarious and satisfying.

30

"Precarious Situations" in a Strip Club

Exotic Dancers and the Problem of Reality Maintenance

Kari Lerum

(2001)

In her classic article, "Behavior in Private Places: Sustaining Definitions of Reality in Gynecological Examinations" (1970), Joan Emerson uses the example of a gynecological exam to demonstrate how social order can prevail even when a social situation is rife with contradictions. In this article, I use Emerson's work as a reference point for another contradictory social situation: a contemporary strip club. The point of this comparison is to examine some similarities and differences in how "reality" is created, threatened, and maintained in each setting, and to gain insight into how specific social conditions impact the process of reality maintenance.

DEFINING REALITY
IN A PRECARIOUS SITUATION

Emerson explains that the process of undergoing a gynecological exam can bring about two diametrically opposed messages: (1) the gynecological exam is *sexual and/or intimate* because it involves the (female) patient's genitals being touched by a (male) physician, and (2) the gynecological exam is merely a *routine, scientific procedure;* therefore the exam is completely free of sexual or emotional meaning. Such contradictory messages create what Emerson calls "the

problem of reality maintenance"; a problem that is particularly acute for the people most invested in maintaining a certain understanding of reality. In Emerson's case, those people are the gynecologists—since they (as well as most medical experts) base their professional legitimacy upon behaving in a scientific, professional manner, they have tremendous incentive to project an objective, detached image, while extinguishing any threats to this image.

For gynecologists, a contradictory image takes root when their client considers the following question: "Is this *truly* just a professional routine, or is it a sexual and/or intimate act?" Interestingly, in my research of the commercial sex industry, including field work as a waitress in a strip club,[1] I have seen the reverse question arise among clients of sex workers; that is, "Is this *truly* a sexual and/or intimate act, or is it just a professional routine?" In both cases these questions cast doubt on the definition of reality projected by the worker, thus jeopardizing their control over clients.

It is within these questioning moments, suspended between contradictory definitions of what is "really" going on, that Emerson sees a "precarious situation." The situation is precarious because the pendulum of meaning could easily swing either way; if it swings in favor of the worker's definition, the worker succeeds in performing her or his transaction with professional and personal integrity intact. If, however, the pendulum swings in favor of any contradictory definition, the routine is disrupted and the worker's grip on the situation is loosened.

To some extent, this problem is embedded everywhere; all social situations contain symbols or messages that people may interpret in numerous ways. However, this only becomes a problem when new perceptions of reality conflict with institutionalized ones. If people perceive an institution to have meaning contradictory to its "purpose," people are left with no established pattern, or guide, for behavior. Lacking any clear definition of what is "really" going on, the situation becomes one of confusion; people may get nervous and perplexed, and their behavior becomes unpredictable.

This is an unsettling possibility for anyone engaged in an activity requiring the full cooperation of others such as performing a gynecological exam or performing a private "lap dance"[2] at a strip club. While at first glance these two actions may seem to have little in common—the first being an unpleasant but necessary medical procedure performed on a woman for "her own good"; the second being an unnecessary act performed primarily on men simply because it "feels good"—workers in both situations face strikingly similar problems of reality maintenance.

In both cases, the medical worker and the sex worker perform actions that their clients may interpret in contradictory ways. Due to the precarious situation that this brings, a considerable amount of effort on the part of workers is needed to ensure client cooperation. Initially, the desired definitions of reality appear as opposites—medical workers want their actions understood as *standardized* and *non-intimate* while sex workers want their

actions understood as *intimate* and *non-standardized*. However, in both cases workers also occasionally find it useful to intentionally project contradictory messages, or counterthemes. For example, the gynecologist occasionally includes a few personal (non-standardized) touches to keep the patient from feeling humiliated and de-humanized; the sex worker occasionally reminds the customer of his customer (standardized) role as a way to squelch any expectations that their relationship will carry on outside of work boundaries. As a result, skillful workers in both fields alternate between themes of standardized professionalism and personalized intimacy as it suits their immediate needs.

The point of these maneuvers is to get clients to succumb to the worker's definition of reality, thus allowing the worker to complete a successful transaction. However, since both transactions involve objects or behaviors with deeply symbolic meanings (for the gynecological exam, exposure to genitals = sexual intimacy; for the lap dance, sexual intimacy = a "real" relationship), convincing people to think otherwise is not an easy task. Reality maintenance in these circumstances requires considerable skill and collective effort; it is a process that works best when it is invisible to the client. As Emerson (1970) writes, successful reality maintenance creates the feeling that "reality seems to be out there before we arrive on the scene."

Due to the symbolic and contradictory meanings found in both gynecological exams and lap dancing, many of the ways that the medical worker's definition of reality is maintained in a gynecological exam also work toward maintaining the sex worker's definition of reality in a strip club. However, a number of structural and interactional factors make the process of reality maintenance in the strip club more precarious.

FACTORS THAT EXACERBATE PRECARIOUS SITUATIONS

Perhaps the most important factor that impacts the management of a precarious situation is that of institutional legitimacy. Unlike the gynecological business, whose legitimacy is protected by massive institutions like the American Medical Association and the U.S. government, the social and legal legitimacy of exotic dancing is far shakier and subject to regional, state, and local variation.

This lack of institutional legitimacy in many strip club settings leads to a number of related problems, including the likelihood of intrusive troublemakers. Namely, a strip club's projection of reality is subject to constant and serious threat from troublemakers such as police officers, jealous lovers, and misguided customers (imagine a jealous husband or a police officer busting up a gynecological exam). All of these intrusions interfere with normal business, sometimes requiring workers to halt operations.

In addition to serious troublemakers, clients in strip clubs are generally less predictable and cooperative than clients in gynecological exams. In part, this lack of customer predictability is due to the nature of the business: One-on-one interactions with customers require the worker to individually tailor her approach. However, workers who provide other intimate, individually tailored services (such as hair styling, massage, counseling, or even gynecological exams) do not generally face uncooperative customers, so it is clear that the problem again stems from a lack of social legitimacy. In other words, customers might simply not see the worker as "legitimate"; thus an internalized sense of respect for the worker is lacking.

Additionally, the stigmatized work of selling and performing exotic dances may pose unique emotional requirements. As opposed to working within an arena built on emotional detachment (such as medicine), sex work requires the simultaneous *encouragement* of and *containment* of highly charged emotions. This, in addition to managing the stigma of sex work, may require more emotional labor for the sex practitioner in both managing her own and her customers' emotions. This in turn may make the process of reality maintenance more precarious.

Finally, the gendered, service-oriented nature of female erotic dancing might give customers the idea that control and power is in their hands rather than in the workers'. Since the broader culture still deems men more legitimately powerful than women, women in many occupations face problems of establishing interactional legitimacy. This combined with a culture of customer service (where the customer is allegedly "always right"), makes for a situation where worker control is not guaranteed.

In sum, with a lack of institutional, social, and interactional legitimacy, erotic dancers (and sex workers in general) cannot take their control for granted. Not only is their work itself often precarious legally, but on an interactional level, control over the definition of the situation must be continuously negotiated. Thus, in these settings, workers are more challenged in maintaining their definition of the situation.

MAINTAINING REALITY IN A STRIP CLUB

Despite differences in legitimacy, in both the gynecological examining room and the strip club, a successful reality maintenance campaign involves a practiced performance using several techniques. These techniques fall into two steps of reality maintenance: (1) *setting the mood* (setting and maintaining an overall message or atmosphere), and (2) *enforcing the rules* (enacting and enforcing that message with individual clients). When both levels of reality maintenance are employed, the likelihood of client cooperation increases.

Setting the Mood

The creation of an overall "mood" or atmosphere is accomplished through the use of several techniques, images, and props, all of which work in concert. In gynecological exams, an atmosphere of *objectivity, rationality,* and *standardization* is projected by normalizing and routinizing the exam, donning medical uniforms, and downplaying any emotional content. In the strip club where I worked (referred to here as "Club X"), an atmosphere of *excitement, intrigue,* and *exclusivity* was accomplished by heightening clients' emotions, making them believe that the experience was fun, sexy, exclusive, and slightly taboo, although also legitimate and professional. In both settings, workers intentionally influence the content and tone of clients' emotions. In one setting, the worker maintains control by making sure the client does not blush; in another setting, the worker maintains control by making sure the client *does*.

At Club X, the goal of making clients both emotionally "charged up" *and* compliant to workers' wishes was first accomplished by routinizing and standardizing the club's "mood." This was achieved by manipulating the appearance, language, and behavior of staff members, the images projected, the music and lighting, and the DJ's announcements.

On a typical night at Club X, the DJ had the greatest immediate influence over the mood; thus this person's routine was key for reality maintenance. The DJ was responsible for controlling the television channel (linked to five TV monitors in the club), as well as the light level of the club and, of course, the music. Each DJ had their unique style (one favored loud music, another kept the light level low), but all DJs had to ultimately comply with the company CEO's standards—the club could not be "too" dark, "too" loud, and the music had to stay fairly upbeat.

The DJ was also the official "voice" of the club; his or her words and tone influenced the mood and acted as a vocal tour guide for customers, encouraging them to see the experience from the club's point of view. One such viewpoint was that the experience was exciting and fun, similar to a sporting event. This message was made most explicit once an hour, when the DJ announced that it was time for the "Texas Teaser." All the dancers (sometimes numbering over thirty) gathered on the front stage, smiling, posing, and flirting with the customers on the floor, while the DJ goaded the crowd:

> Just *look* at all those gorgeous ladies! Guys, what do you say?! Take your hands out of your pockets and show some appreciation! On the count of three I want you to all shout as loud as you can, and the guy who makes the most noise will get a *free pass* to the club!! One . . . Two . . . Threeeee!!!! [The crowd goes wild, some young men standing on their seats, yelling, and pumping their arms in the air.]

These exuberant displays of concentrated emotion might have resulted in a loss of control for the workers, but interestingly, it rarely did. Rather, customers seemed to clearly understand that this game was not serious and that the workers controlled the rules. This understanding was reinforced immediately after the contest—the dancers would descend from the stage, flood the floor, and choose a customer for a "free" dance (while the DJ explained that they must buy a second dance). Since not every customer could get chosen for this free dance, and since the choosing process was up to the dancer, in a matter of moments the customers' demeanor shifted from noisy swaggering to humble anticipation (or dread). If a customer was overlooked this would sometimes turn to embarrassment; as one young man said to me, laughing and pointing to his friend, "Look at him, he was sitting there waiting on the couch, but no one wanted to give him a dance!"

In addition to the vulnerability that comes with waiting to be chosen, customers were also put in their place by the DJ, who routinely teased them by questioning both their heterosexual virility ("What are ya, a bunch of wussies?! What's wrong with you, don't ya like naked chicks?!") and their manners ("Didn't your mother teach you any manners?! Show some appreciation and buy a dance. And buy that lady a drink while you're at it.").

During all this excitement and teasing, an implicit message of professionalism and customer service was also projected by workers. One way this was demonstrated was in the standardized dress of staff members. Just as medical professionals and staff wear specific and unique clothing to both distinguish themselves from their patients and to project a certain (detached) message, the dancers and staff of Club X also used clothing as a method of intentional reality maintenance. One obvious use of this method was found in the rule that all staff members—including waitresses, doormen, bartenders, DJs, floor managers, and the parking lot attendant—wear the same uniform: a white tuxedo shirt, black slacks, and black shoes. The one variation in this uniform was that male staff members (essentially, everyone except the waitresses) were additionally required to wear a bow tie. As a fellow waitress explained to me, this dress code was established because "some of the waitresses were wearing really short skirts . . . but they [the management] wanted us to look classier."

This "professional" and sexually de-emphasized dress code for staff members also created a distinct contrast to the dancers—all of whom wore costumes meant to symbolize and create a sexually alluring image. None of the dancers wore identical outfits, and these outfits often changed by the night (and sometimes two or three times on the same night), but most of them fell within a narrow range of variability, ranging from short tight dresses to lingerie and g-string

panties. These differences between the dancers' and staff members' costumes are not unlike the costume differences found within medical staff ranks where each variation symbolizes a difference in the person's status and role. However, in the strip club setting, costume variety between dancers and staff members also served to simultaneously portray a seemingly contradictory mixture of messages.

Another mood-shaping tool in Club X were the TV monitors. When I first began working at this club, every night brought a variety of soundless video images. Many of these images were of male sporting events, but sometimes the DJ would decide to watch the news, cartoons, or the Nature channel. Scrolling across these images were club advertisements such as "Welcome to Club X!," "$5 table dances; $12 couch dances, and $20 VIP dances!" and "If you've been overcharged, contact a manager." While these messages seemed congruent with images of football, race cars, and wrestling, the image of Dan Rather discussing Middle East politics made for a comically ironic fit. Eventually, these contradictory video messages stirred higher management to create new rules about acceptable video images. At one employee meeting, the general manager of Club X was particularly upset about the showing of cartoons, inspiring him to instigate a "no cartoon" rule.

> Absolutely no cartoons! That drives me crazy! No more cartoons! You wanna know why? Cuz cartoons make you think of kids. When I see cartoons, I think of my kids. It makes me miss my kids, I wish I could see them more often. So if you've got some pervert in here, spending three, four hundred dollars, and he sees cartoons up on the TV, he's going to think of his kids, feel like shit, and he's going to leave. So no more cartoons!

In other words, the point of these televised images was to encourage a specific mood as well as to sustain customers' attention by keeping them entranced and undistracted by their external emotional ties.[3]

The language of the staff also shaped the club's mood. Just as the use of clinical terms in a gynecological office creates an atmosphere of emotional and sexual detachment, the language at Club X was used to create an atmosphere that was sexually exciting as well as professional and polite. The DJ would routinely describe a dancer as a "beautiful showgirl" or a "hottie," but the language in this club was generally not sexually explicit. Rather, body parts were euphemized or avoided altogether. As a result, the club could be distinguished as a "gentlemen's club" rather than as "pornographic" or "raunchy."

The language of waitresses and doormen also served to create an atmosphere of exclusivity and politeness to both customers and dancers. Club X advertised that it gave *every* customer "VIP" treatment, and staff members were instructed to treat dancers with old-fashioned respect (at least in front of customers). For instance, when a dancer was found sitting with a customer, waitresses were trained to formally ask the customer, "Would you like to buy the lady a drink?" As Emerson puts it, such scripted language serves to "embody intentional themes." In other words, by routinizing worker behavior, specific messages can be reliably portrayed to customers. Thus, by consistently referring to dancers as "ladies," the message was sent that— although this was a place where one could get rowdy and receive good service—this was a place where one had to be polite to dancers.

In both the gynecological examining room and in the strip club, the work routine also includes similar specialized work areas—a table in the examining room; a couch in the strip club. Both also have "chaperones" (either a floor manager or a nurse) whose presence serves to discourage deviations from the intended reality.

Although the DJ was a heavyweight in creating the initial "mood," Club X's reality relied on the cooperation of all employees. Management was aware of this need for cooperation, judging by the messages staff members received such as a sign in the break-room which read: "T.E.A.M.— together everyone achieves more." Here the point of working together was to create a reality that was "respectable," service-oriented, and profitable. This emphasis on professional customer service is evident from the following quote from the general manager of Club X:

> Our competitors turned up the music, turned down the lights, and let the hand jobs fly . . . but that's not the kind of operation I'm running here . . . we need to stress service and entertainment. . . . When people go to a restaurant, they don't go there for the service, but it is what brings them back. So when customers come in, take care of them . . . be friendly, say, "Hey how's it going? If you see a girl you'd like, just let me know, and I'll get her for you." You know, take care of them.

From the worker's point of view, the ideal result of all these images, routines, and props is to prevent situations from becoming precarious—to barrage the client with consistent implicit (and sometimes explicit) messages, asserting that "this is how it's done here," and hoping for client cooperation.

Enforcing the Rules

Once the mood is set, a secondary process of enforcement is sometimes necessary. In both Emerson's observations of the gynecological exam and my own at Club X, rule enforcement was typically accomplished by simply instructing uninitiated clients (as well as co-workers) about their expected roles. In both settings, workers expect obedience and passivity from clients. And just as the physician guides the patient through the precarious scene by taking the initiative, controlling the encounter, and carefully monitoring the patient's reactions, so does the exotic dancer.

At Club X, once a dancer got a customer to agree to a dance, she was responsible for guiding the client into his or her proper role. While some role expectations were basic and mandatory (e.g., "no touching" and "keep your hands by your sides"), other role expectations were subtler—requiring the dancer to strategically combine her messages.

For instance, when an ambivalent customer conceded to a dance, dancers often found it useful to interact with the customer in a way that made him (or her) feel special and "really" cared for, yet also aware that the feeling came with a price. After getting paid, a dancer sometimes gave her customer a friendly hug and kiss on the cheek, reinforcing the message that she really did care about him. With younger male customers (who were notoriously "cheap" and who might have been embarrassed about paying for a temporary girlfriend), dancers would frequently walk with them hand-in-hand, leading them to the cash machine, but looking like high school kids going steady. With such shy, young, "cheap," emotionally sensitive, or uninitiated customers, subtle emotional management was often required.

For the hostile or uncooperative customer, rule enforcement relied upon the threat of physical force from male employee "chaperones." The primary chaperone at Club X was the floor manager, but all employees (especially male employees) were expected to jump in if trouble started. This club also had an informal enforcement team, composed of a few men who were allegedly not employees, but who were frequent visitors and known as "friends of the club." As one veteran waitress explained to me, these "friends" "watch out for the girls and pitch in if they're needed."

Fortunately, the majority of customers accepted the reality of Club X and played along with the expected rules: that is, they applauded the dancers on stage, stood up and yelled when the DJ told them to do so, accepted all "free" dances, sat passively while a private dance was performed on them, and then graciously paid the previously negotiated price (mostly ranging from ten to forty dollars, with the average being twenty dollars a dance). However, some customers remained mystified or shy observers, some were arrogantly skeptical of the rules, and others became aggressive or hostile.

In one case, Nicki[4] had just finished two lap dances and had successfully collected her fee, but as she turned to leave the customer reached his hand up inside of her underwear and squeezed her buttock. Nicki became very upset and immediately told Aaron, who was working as the doorman. As Aaron later told me the story, he "told the guy to get the fuck out of here" before he "beat the shit out of him." The threat worked, and the deviant customer departed.

Other, perhaps even more troublesome intruders were jealous lovers of dancers, delusional customers who refused to accept that they could not have a "real" relationship with their favorite dancer, as well as customers who were simply belligerent and looking for a fight. Due to the highly explosive nature of these situations, staff members had to stay alert and immediately call for help if needed—even if this involved asking for help from another set of troublesome intruders, the police.

Despite their role as potential protectors, the most precarious situations often arose with the entrance of the police. Since this club was in a suburban area where strip clubs were a highly contentious political issue, police officers occasionally stopped by to make their presence known and to monitor the club's activities. When this happened, Club X's reality was severely interrupted. Word would quickly spread throughout the club that the police were there. If there was enough lead time, special red lights would flash behind the bar to warn workers that the police were coming. The manager would then put on a friendly face, greet the officers at the door, and give them a tour of the facility.

While business appeared to continue, with waitresses serving drinks, the music continuing, and the DJ introducing each dancer as she appeared on stage, the money exchange would essentially halt; dancers would quit performing lap dances and sit quietly next to their customers or with each other. Sometimes, if a dancer was not notified quickly enough of the threat, she would get caught in the middle of an illegal lap dance[5] and be ticketed. The heart of the entire business (lap dances) would not resume until the departure of the police.

Although far less frequent, precarious situations also rose from the actions of dancers. Often coming from dancers who had previously worked in more sexually lenient clubs, their deviations came in the form of intimacy transgressions—in other words, they went "too far" with their customers. In my six months of work at Club X, there were several cases of dancers who were chastised and sanctioned by other dancers for such transgressions.

For example, Tasha, a dancer at Club X who routinely grabbed at men's genitals through their trousers, was overwhelmingly disliked by the other dancers and staff. As one waitress told me, "You know who I really don't like? Tasha. She's really not classy; that's when I hate working here, when it feels like a whorehouse." It probably was no coincidence that Tasha did not last long as a Club X dancer; without the respect of the other dancers and staff members, negotiation of precarious situations becomes far more difficult.

In some cases, the initiation of a new dancer or the sanctioning of an established dancer simply involved a cold shoulder. But many times the punishment of inappropriate behavior was more direct. In one case, Janessa—a dancer with experience at several other clubs around the United States—was surrounded by several dancers in the dressing room and scolded for putting her crotch in a customer's face. Janessa left her shift early, crying.

In another case, a veteran Club X dancer lashed out at a newer dancer who she felt had gone "too far." The verbal explosion (below) was witnessed by several other dancers and staff:

> I'm fucking old school! Remember how much shit you gave me when I started working here?! [directed at another veteran dancer, who nods her head.] That Regina girl's letting people grab her and shit and only charging twelve dollars! If she wants to do that she should put her ass on the street!! I'm fucking old school. She needs to be taught.

The newer dancer also took a verbal shot or two, but the veteran had publicly and definitively made her point. The manager then quickly intervened, taking both dancers into her office for a private "consultation."

If a manager directly witnessed an intimacy transgression, the dancer would risk harsher penalties. Officially, each dancer was allowed two warnings about such behavior, and on the third offense they would get "termed" (i.e., their independent business contract with the club would be terminated). In one case, a new dancer, Cyndi, performed stage shows that were more sexually graphic than the norm (which other dancers described as "gross"). She was also observed on a number of occasions physically groping the genitals of her customers (through their clothing)—which is against both the club's rules and the state's laws. In her short time at the club, Cyndi had already received two warnings. I observed Cyndi's third offense: She was on a female customer's lap, fondling her breast, and kissing her on the lips. It was the kissing more than anything that shocked the rest of the dancers and staff, since kissing in these circumstances was seen as outrageously intimate. The floor manager was notified and Cyndi was immediately terminated.

In all of these examples, it is clear that when a dancer heightened her sexual intimacy with customers, the club's (as well as the dancers') definition of reality was threatened. These actions made the club more at risk of legal sanctions, increased customers' expectations (which subsequently created more competition between dancers), and threatened the "high class" aim of Club X. In an atmosphere where workers were greatly invested in distancing themselves from prostitutes, most dancers and staff members were personally offended by such behavior.

Conclusions

Comparing Emerson's observations on gynecological exams with my own observations of Club X leads to a number of insights about reality maintenance. One is simply that the process of creating and maintaining reality in both situations is strikingly similar. However, by examining the contrasting points of each case, one also finds that different settings create the need for different techniques. The most relevant contrasts are the *level of institutionalized legitimacy* and the *required amount of client management*. It seems that the higher the social legitimacy of an industry, and the lower the need to constantly monitor and manage one's customers, the lower the threat of a precarious situation. In such a situation, the worker's power is assured and automatic client compliance is likely. In contrast, lower social legitimacy combined with a "high maintenance" customer results in a more precarious situation that needs constant monitoring, manipulation, and rule enforcement.

While rule enforcement at Club X occasionally required the threat of physical force, the vast majority of this enforcement was enacted through the skillful manipulation of messages. Emerson claims that if one pays better attention to the interplay between implicit and explicit messages, then a richer understanding of reality maintenance will emerge. Unlike gynecological exams, contradictory *explicit* messages are the key to reality maintenance at Club X. In other words, in

order for the sex workers in this context to "pull it off," a simultaneous explicit expression of both professionalism and intimacy was not only possible, but necessary to maintain control.

In sum, strip clubs and gynecological exam rooms are both infused with contradictory messages, which can result in precarious definitions of the situation. In a sense, both are getting away with highly "intimate" acts in a commercial setting. However, Club X is doing so with a lack of social and legal legitimacy, making it more dependent on the efforts of individual workers to create a reality where business can be done.

Notes

1. As part of my dissertation research, during 1998–1999 I spent six months working as a strip club waitress.

2. In contrast to a stage dance, where dancers perform for the entire audience and sometimes collect tips, lap dances are performed for the enjoyment of one customer and must be individually paid for. For most exotic dancers, the lap dance is the primary source of income.

3. Interestingly, pornography was rarely shown at Club X. During my six months of work, I only saw it shown twice. On both occasions, dancers complained loudly, calling these images lewd and disgusting.

4. All names have been changed.

5. Strip clubs within this police jurisdiction are subject to a "four-foot" rule; that is, erotic dances performed closer than four feet away from the patron are against the law. The problem is, it is virtually impossible for a dancer to make any money unless she dances closer than four feet.

Reference

Emerson, J. P. (1970). "Behavior in Private Places: Sustaining Definitions of Reality in Gynecological Examinations." In P. Dreitsel (ed.), *Recent Sociology* (pp. 74–97). New York: Macmillan.

SELF-PRESENTATION AND IDENTITY WORK

As Goffman points out, we must all engage in impression management in order to project a definition of the situation and to signal our intentions to others. This identity work is often simple and unnoticed, such as when you acknowledge a friend on the street with, "Hi, how's it going," or engage with a store clerk, or enter a familiar and well-established scene, such as a classroom or church. However, some identities are precarious or likely to be contested. For instance, the cheating spouse who claims, "but I really *do* love you" will have to work very hard to convey a believable impression. Other identities may carry a stigma that requires the person to engage in stigma-countering impression management in order to be treated with dignity and respect. "The Practice of Headscarf Adoption Among American College Girls" (Reading 31) is about the ways in which headscarf adoption has become a source of identity management for Muslim women in U.S. colleges and universities. The authors present information from several interviews in which these women talk about what wearing hijab means for them and the identities they hope to project. "In Pursuit of the 'Real Deal' . . . " the authors describe how transgender inmates in California prisons for men accomplish gender identities as women. This setting is especially risky and requires significant identity work.

READING QUESTIONS

1. What are some of the stigmas that Muslim women encounter in the U.S.?

2. The authors describe hijab wearing as an aspect of both personal identity reinforcement and a reproduction of community identity. Explain.

3. What are "situated gender practices" and what are some examples from transgender inmates in men's prisons?

4. 4. Consider other situations where stigmatized identities may conflict with characteristics the person wants to project (e.g., the former inmate trying to get a job).

SELF-PRESENTATION AND IDENTITY WORK

31

The Practice of Headscarf Adoption Among American College Girls

Mustafa E. Gurbuz and Gulsum Gurbuz-Kucuksari

(2009)

Inspired by Goffman's work on stigma management strategies, we found that Muslim girls as stigmatized individuals consciously present their headscarf adoption practice as liberating. Second, unlike some Muslim majority countries where the practice becomes a social norm, headscarf adoption provides a powerful source for identity (re)construction in a minority situation in a secular environment. Thus, we argue that the headscarf phenomenon in the American secular college environment provides a rich venue to study Muslim girls' uneasiness and resistance in everyday life. Torn in between dominant secular norms in the society and values of Islamic faith, most American Muslim college girls see their headscarf practice as "liberating" and "empowering". Our analysis shows how headscarf adoption practice suggests a wide-ranging repertoire for multiple identity constructions of American Muslim college girls, including primarily religious, feminine, moral, and communal identities.

METHODOLOGY

The data presented in this work is derived from our personal observations in three American colleges in New England and lengthy semi-structured interviews with sixteen American-born Muslim girls who are adopters of the headscarf practice. All of the interviewees are foreign descendants, specifically speaking from Egyptian, Pakistani, Bengali, or Arab families.

The process of capitalism has enabled two contradicting demands: (1) eliminating the traditional forms of culture by stigmatizing them as "backward" and (2) inciting need for the identity re-construction by traditional means as well as modern ones. In terms of the headscarf practice, then, we might claim that capitalist secularization process and the consumer culture of the modern society has both (1) stigmatized the headscarf adoption as backward and (2) enabled the headscarf to become a symbol of identity re-construction.

Erving Goffman's conceptualization of "stigma" is very useful to consider here:

> (When a stranger) is present before us, evidence can arise of his possessing an attribute that makes him different from others. . . . He is thus reduced in our minds from a whole and usual person to a tainted, discounted one. Such an attribute is a stigma.

According to Goffman, stigma constitutes a special discrepancy between "virtual" and "actual" social identity. In a secular consumer society, Muslim girls who practice *hijab* believe that a particular discrepancy between virtual and actual identity exists in the eyes of people around them. The discrepancy further leads these women to assert their identity with the veiling practice: "I cannot imagine myself without headscarf. . . . I am more than my scarf, of course, I am not just a headscarf; but, my headscarf is a part of me." Therefore, as explicitly stressed in the interviewee's statement, there is a direct and close relationship between stigma management and identity construction.

Codes of dress can reveal social norms and define boundaries that alert people to make them realize what deviance is. In his thought-provoking work, *The Fashioned Self*, Finkelstein argues that reading and classifying people by reference to their body, dress, and overall appearance is one of the significant legacies of modernity, which is still relevant today.

In such a consumer society the practice of headscarf is seen as a sign of oppression. Specifically, religious dress codes have been condemned as being an instrument for the social control of the body. This mode of understanding leads people to see headscarf adopters as unmodernized, backward, not open-minded, radically religious, and non-free. The story of a college student articulates how the stigma works on Muslim women's identities and their choices of scarf adoption:

My parents never objected to my wearing the *hijab*. They thought that I needed to do what seemed right to me. However, I was still a teenager and there was a lot of pressure coming from classmates in high school. I was discriminated against, people pointed their fingers at me. I felt like people discriminated against me, because I made them feel uncomfortable by wearing the *hijab*. I was strong for two years and then I just decided to unveil. That was very difficult as well. The only excuse I have is that I was very young, and I wasn't strong enough to deal with self-esteem issues, adults and my own classmates attacking me verbally among other things. As always, I got a lot of support from my parents who once again reminded me that

I was free to make my own decisions, and that nobody else mattered as long as I was doing the right thing. Then, I decided to wear *hijab* again.

Here, as we see in the story above, the stigma spoils the girl's identity. Torn in between, the girl feels that she performs a social role rather than an individual act. This feeling is understandable for the headscarf adopters because religious obligation specifies the situations for Muslim women to practice *hijab*; that is, one should wear the headscarf when she is before men who are not close relatives to the woman. Hence, the headscarf practice defined by Islam is meaningful in a particular social context because it addresses a social relation. In this sense, the headscarf can be considered as a "social performance".

The stigma on Muslim girls empowers identity re-construction in two ways: reinforcement of personal identity and reproduction of a communal identity. First, the adopters of the headscarf practice internalize their value symbol as part of their personal identities and attach a positive powerful meaning to it. The attachment of positive meaning to the headscarf seems very interrelated with the negative attitudes and stigma in American society that labels the practice as a symbol of oppression. For example, almost all of the respondents reported that they see headscarf as a symbol of liberation. This common stance is not a coincidence; instead, this type of meaning of the practice is intentionally reproduced by adopters to overcome hardships that their "spoiled identity" suffers from.

Second, the headscarf adoption is generally viewed by many Muslims and non-Muslims as a symbolic expression of Muslim-ness as one collective group. In other words, people have a tendency to see the headscarf adopters as representative of Islam. This tendency produces either much positive feedback or much negative reaction toward the adopters. Moreover, social expectations either from Muslims or non-Muslims have a remarkable influence on the women with headscarves. In our research, a considerable number of individuals expressed that they feel that they represent Islam when they wear headscarf.

IMPACT ON PERSONAL IDENTITY

By internalizing and personalizing the headscarf practice, people actively become a "Muslim" identity not because of their parents' appreciation of Islam but their own enthusiastic embracement of that identity. This process can be seen as a transformation from ascribed status of Muslim identity to an achieved Muslim-ness. Sanaa, a 19-year-old Egyptian American, described her own experience as follows:

> I wore the hijab beginning 10th grade. As a kid, it was always something my mother did that I looked up to. I had always intended to start, but pressure from my father actually initiated wearing it full time. After a few months, I grew into it. I have changed my opinion, sometimes drastically, about it. Anxiety about my identity, Muslim and foreigner, in a possibly hostile country to both facets of my identity made me stop wearing it in the beginning at college. Personal lack of strength intertwined with a changing mindset made it continue. Over the years, I have changed views from it being cultural context specific, to "obligation" only in terms of male chauvinistic views, to "no, it's liberating".

As Sanaa struggles with the stigma, the meaning of the headscarf practice gradually changes in her mind and becomes a "liberating" symbol. The interviewees expressed the different dimensions of the practice; some insisted upon its religious meanings, some pointed out a gender component, and some others mentioned moral aspects. In their diverse accounts, however, almost all of them referred to the one similar point: the liberating and empowering force of the practice.

Hijab as a Performance of Religious Identity

Headscarf is first and foremost a religious symbol for its adopters. Almost all interviewees, in one way or another, stated that they wear *hijab* because of their desire to actively appreciate their religious identities. As Fatimah, a 19-year-old Bengali girl, asserted:

> I am covering myself for protection and as a duty to God. I am not, however, hiding myself from the world. . . . Through *hijab*, I find I have grown for the better as a Muslim and as I am a full-time Muslim, I think it appropriate for the rest of my practices as a Muslim to be full-time as well.

As a performance of religious identity, the practice of headscarf reinforces the religiosity. Another respondent's answer clearly shows her strength in her belief:

> I do not simply think that the veil is a religious obligation; instead I am absolutely certain that it is. The evidence for this is in the *Qur'an* and *Sunnah* and all of the traditional Islamic literature. As a Muslim woman who considers herself to be "practicing" the religion, these sources are what bring me to this belief. . . . Hijab doesn't just mean a head covering for women, it is a modest dress code for all Muslims. My view has been influenced by one line in the Quran that instructs the believing women to cover their hair and guard their modesty.

In this regard, Muslim women's practice of headscarf cannot be totally separated from their practice of explaining Islamic modesty to people around them. Under the pressures of implicit secular norms and due to the stigma attached to scarves, the performer of religious identity usually starts to explain reasoning of the hijab to others. Some authors called Muslim women's strategy to explain her beliefs in a deliberate pedagogical form as "educational accounting" in which the account giver combats stigma by correcting stereotypes. Giving informational substance to the audience, the Muslim women engage in what Goffman calls "normalization" after the stigmatization process.

The educational accounting further reinforces one's own religious identity. As Aisha, a Pakistani American girl, expressed:

> I think wearing *hijab* has definitely worked for the better for me. I became more assured of myself. Through having to defend my reasons for wearing it, I have acquired more knowledge of Islam.

Thus, by defending their beliefs, Muslim girls transform their ascribed Islamic identity into an achieved status. The feeling to acquire an Islamic identity as a personal choice seems very attractive to young Muslim girls since it reflects their "American" side. Since Muslim girls have hyphenated identities such as Bengali-Muslim-American or Muslim-American-Bengali, what being "American" means is often obscure in their minds. In most cases, however, they feel that their American identity means being free individuals and having independent choices. Therefore, their choice to wear headscarf makes them better Americans as well as better Muslims. As Haddad and her colleagues noted, many immigrant American Muslims affirm that their dual orientation as being both Muslim and American are mutually supportive rather than exclusive.

Hijab as a "Performance" of Gender Identity

Adopters of the *hijab* practice see headscarf as a "shield" and "protection" from the American secular lifestyle. The metaphor of shield leads to a new definition of feminine identity as Abida, a 21-year-old Arab American, put it straightforwardly:

> Wearing hijab has made me a stronger woman; I feel that I have a stronger sense of self, since people listen to me rather than look at my body. . . . Many people critique *hijab* as a force to oppress women

and curtail a woman's freedom. However, I severely question these critiques, in order to be liberated must a woman be judged for external beauty rather than internal beauty and intellect? My life is more focused on matters that are important to me, rather than finding the nicest hair style that will attract attention, or even dress in order to deter unwanted gazes and comments.

What we see in Abida's account is not an emphasis on religious obligation but, instead, her dissent against definitions of liberation in terms of external beauty. Abida, rather, gives her own definition of being empowered in a bold fashion:

> It is easy to forget the "oppression" that women are confronted with daily via mass media who display images of the "ideal woman". The unrealistic goal of obtaining the ideal body to flaunt steals our time that we could dedicate to helping others, learning, educating, or any number of things. When we are free from the constraints of the society we are truly liberated, and I feel anything but oppressed when I walk outside on a warm sunny day with pastel chiffon *hijab* covering something that I, my religion, and most importantly God considers to be a treasure.

Here, we see that the concepts of freedom, self-respect, important values, and liberation are redefined in terms of new identity. The practice of hijab is intertwined with true liberation. Being a slave of God is emphasized in a liberating manner: obey God in order to be free from social pressures. The adopters' emphases on liberation go together with a new characterization of femininity. Nadeema, a third year college student, asserted that her attractiveness of personality should be more important than her sexual attractiveness:

> I don't need to worry about men checking me out, or talking to me for sexual reasons. . . . I find it

more impressive to have a male attracted to my personality, sense of modesty, values, internal beauty, and obviously so much more than only he can see and enjoy.

Nadeema added that she avoids going to certain places such as entertainment clubs because her adoption of the headscarf becomes a constant reminder of her identity. For her, the headscarf symbolizes not oppression but rather "a shield against the danger of getting dirty looks from perverted guys, verbal and sexual harassment, provocative fashions and, most of all, being viewed as a piece of meat".

Thus, contrary to the Western idea that the practice of *hijab* is a controlling mechanism over women's bodies, American Muslim college girls would rather believe that their *hijab* provides a greater physical mobility in public space since they feel free from the male gaze.

The headscarf as "shield" and "protection" works as a reminder for both self and others. It regulates self performances as well as responses to the self in a social context. However, this self attempt of shaping the desired response from others does not always bring success for the adopters of the headscarf who are stigmatized. The headscarf adopters as stigmatized individuals usually are getting either much positive reactions or much negative ones. As one interviewee described it:

From strangers, the reaction is usually mixed. Some are outright rude or presumptuous, glaring at me in the subway, making comments, or teasing. Others have sincere curiosity and are extremely friendly. At times they are too friendly.

Having extreme reactions in either way, the headscarf adopter becomes more assured of her connection with other headscarf adopters. In fact, this point is particularly related to the collective identity reproduction, which we shall elucidate in the following section.

Hijab as a "Performance" of Moral and Cultural Identities

Unlike the other respondents, Husna does not only refer to religious concerns but also mentions how she finds the practice as a symbol of modesty:

I don't think the veil is a religious obligation, but rather is symbolic of modesty, not only what you wear, but also in your thoughts and actions. . . . Needless to say I think the entire objective here is for us to be modest and I do consider that very important.

Husna's headscarf adoption exemplifies a performance of a moral identity, in which acquisition of symbolic modesty becomes more prevalent than seeking active religious duty. Husna's story also reveals some Muslim immigrant girls' search for conformity with their indigenous culture. As some scholars pointed out, modesty is also seen as a feature of being Arab, or Indonesian, or Nigerian among the Muslim immigrant communities as being the minority group in the United States, and therefore Islamic identity is simply considered as an ingredient in that particular national identity. Thus, in this vein, the donning of the headscarf reinforces the cultural identities as well.

Moreover, as discussed in previous sections, the American cultural and social environment generally remains as "foreign" in the eyes of immigrants due to the threat of assimilation in the melting pot of the United States. Tabassum Ruby's study among immigrant Muslim families in Canada, for instance, indicated that adopters of veiling practice in the host land are stricter in the use of their *hijab* than are those "back home". We might argue that people become more loyal to their traditions and identity symbols if their group identities are threatened by the larger society.

Confirming Ruby's findings in the Canadian context, a number of informants emphasized their enthusiasm to keep their own cultural identities in a racist environment. For darker-skin immigrant females, their social interactions with white males do not turn out to be a threat to their own self-confidence:

> Wearing *hijab* gives me a great freedom of not being afraid to express myself and that has worked well with my interactions with others. I believe, my outgoing nature has been influenced partly by my observing *hijab*. (Husna)

The practice, thus, allows Muslim immigrant girls to have a greater confidence and social mobility in the public sphere.

(Re)Production of a Collective Identity as Liberating Endeavor

People's definitions of the headscarf adopters' roles have a significant impact on the performers' communal identities as well. This dimension of the identity re-production is not only related with stigmatization of Muslim women in negative ways; but also, the high level expectations the larger Muslim community has of the headscarf adopters.

Headscarf adopters are often likely to encounter positive encouragement or negative frustration from their social environment because they are seen as representatives of a group rather than simple individuals. Twenty-year-old Amina's account succinctly describes the situation:

> Many people assume that a woman who wears a veil is better than other Muslim women and that she is much more religious than a woman who doesn't wear one. That she is very strict in her beliefs and is not flexible. I think that this is all wrong. When Muslims say these things they are making Muslims the "other" and the ostracized just as much as a non-Muslim who puts barriers between "us" and "them". That is discrimination and misconception from within which is by far worse. A Muslim woman who wears a veil is not better than another Muslim woman who doesn't because she may be lacking in an area that the unveiled sister is strong in. They can learn from each other. There is only one Judge, God. He is the only one that sees the level of belief and sincerity in a person's heart. For me as a veiled woman to say I am more religious than my sister who does not, is inconceivable and reprehensible because how could I dare to put myself at a level at which only my Creator has. All of the patronizing myths aside, I am a flexible person—and that comes from Islam as well, the middle path—because an extreme in any direction is not what God loves.

What is interesting in Amina's account is that the communal identity reproduction usually comes with an idea of individual strengthening and self-development. We can catch the similar feelings of being more *free* and *independent* in other girls' accounts as well. One interviewee, Faheema, an 18-year-old Pakistani girl, stated her appreciation of the communal identity as the following:

> I feel that wearing the veil has enabled me to express my identity as a Muslim woman more openly. Additionally, it has made me conscious that since it identifies me as a Muslim woman, I have to make sure that my actions and behavior are in accordance with Islam. Wearing the *hijab* makes me a representative of Islam, and therefore, I am required to project it in a positive light so that others will not see Islam with negativity. Similarly, I have become more conscious of behaving in a way that conforms with the hijab when interacting with other people, so that they get the correct message of Islam.

Thus, even the communal identity of Muslimness is perceived by Muslim college girls as a "great freedom" and a liberating practice in nature.

SELF-PRESENTATION AND IDENTITY WORK

32

In Pursuit of the "Real Deal": Accomplishing Gender Among Transgender Inmates in Prisons for Men

Valerie Jenness and Sarah Fenstermaker

(2014)

Gender scholars are turning to the experiences of transgender people to re-interrogate the workings of gender in social life (e.g., Gagne, Tewksbury, and McGaughey 1997; Halberstam 2005). These treatments underscore the situated character of gender, resist the impositions of the binary, and raise possibilities for structural disruption and social change. As Susan Stryker explained with regard to transgender studies writ large, a focus on transgender people and their experiences in specific institutional contexts brings to the fore "myriad specific subcultural expressions of gender atypicality" (Stryker 2006, 3). More recently, Raewyn Connell directs analytic attention to how a changed embodied position in gender relations grounds new practices. She reminds us that " . . . a transsexual woman must generate a practice" and asks, "What is to be done?" (Connell 2012, 868). Taking this call seriously, we turn to the unique experience of transgender prisoners to unearth gender practices occurring within the dual realities of incarceration and contradictory embodiment.

In prison, transgender women reside in a setting where "everyone knows" they are biologically male, but where they nevertheless are motivated to seek continuous affirmation of their "natural" female and womanly characters. Under the sometimes brutal, and always difficult, conditions of the prison, transgender prisoners engage in a competitive pursuit of a femininity that does not constitute "passing" but does involve accountability to a normative standard and a "ladylike" ideal. Such practices require an intense preoccupation with bodily adornment and appearance as well as a deferent demeanor and a studied comportment. The result is the achievement of a *recognition* from others that one is close enough to a "real girl" to be deserving of a kind of privilege.

The unique and often predatory environment of the prison is defined by deprivation, including both loss of freedom and markers of individuality typically used on the outside. In this context, transgender prisoners are distinct from their counterparts on the outside who seek to pass, and often do pass, as women. Precisely because transgender prisoners' lives are so radically unconventional, we use this article as an occasion to give voice to the pursuit of femininity in a men's prison and to reaffirm the value of a theoretical and empirical focus on the actual practices that constitute our gendered lives.

RESEARCH METHODS AND DATA

California, home to one of the largest correctional systems in the Western world (Petersilia

2008), is an ideal site for collecting data on transgender prisoners. When data collection began in 2008, approximately 160,000 adult prisoners were incarcerated in California's 33 prisons. Well over 90 percent of California state prisoners are housed in 30 prisons for adult men. Among these prisoners, there are over 300 transgender inmates in prisons for men (Jenness, Sexton, and Sumner 2011). Assuming Brown and McDuffie's (2009) estimate that there are approximately 750 transgender prisoners in the U.S. is correct, California is home to nearly half of all transgender prisoners in the U.S.

Recognizing that distinct types of gender-variant people may or may not identify as transgender, for this work transgender prisoners were identified by deploying four specific criteria. A transgender inmate is a prisoner in a men's prison who: (a) self-identifies as transgender (or something comparable); (b) presents as female, transgender, or feminine in prison or outside of prison; (c) receives any kind of medical treatment (physical or mental) for something related to how she presents herself or thinks about herself in terms of gender, including taking hormones to initiate and sustain the development of secondary sex characteristics to enhance femininity; or (d) participates in groups for transgender inmates. Meeting any one of these criteria qualified an inmate for inclusion in the larger study from which this article derives (Jenness 2010; Jenness, Sexton, and Sumner 2011).

Inmates in California prisons who met the eligibility criteria described were invited to participate in the study. The field data collection process began in late April 2008 and ended in late June 2008. During this time, a trained interview team of eight interviewers traveled to 27 California prisons for adult men, met face-to-face with over 500 inmates identified by the California Department of Corrections and Rehabilitation (CDCR) as potentially transgender, and completed interviews with 315 transgender inmates.

TRANSGENDER PRISONERS IN CALIFORNIA

The transgender population in California prisons for men is paradoxically visible and invisible (Jenness 2014; Tewksbury and Potter 2005). Prison officials and prisoners alike distinguish transgender prisoners as a special population of inmates in prisons for men. Transgender inmates constitute a highly visible population because their gender displays—for example, the shape of their eyebrows—often mark them as a distinct type of prisoner in an alpha male environment. Because transgender prisoners do not conform to the dictates of an extremely heteronormative and masculinist environment, corrections officials perceive transgender prisoners as a potential source of in-prison disorder and attendant management problems. Corrections officials and prisoners alike share an understanding of transgender prisoners as prisoners failing to "man-up" in prisons for men (Jenness 2010, 2011).

Distinguished from the prison population and reporting a diverse repertoire of identities, sensibilities, and desires, transgender prisoners bring a plethora of understandings that are manifested in their daily embodied gender practices; their bodies are, quite literally, locked up. In this institutional context, transgender prisoners face very different interactional challenges from those faced by their counterparts on the outside. These challenges reveal a great deal about the situated character of gender as well as how gender practices unfold in the context of contradictory embodiment.

PURSUIT OF THE "REAL DEAL"

One of the basic underlying assumptions of prison operations is that there are two types of people—males and females—and that fact looms large. Until the latter part of the 20th century, sex segregation in prison was arguably the least contested prison policy/practice across geographical region, local government, prison level, and inmate population. In short, the institutional manifestation of the prison culture's sex/gender binary is taken for granted and defines prison existence in virtually every aspect.

It is within this context that we focus on the pursuit of the "real deal" to refer to the complicated dynamic whereby transgender prisoners claim and assert their femininity in prison—a hegemonically defined hypermasculine and heteronormative environment with an abundance of alpha males, sexism, and violence. By their own account, transgender prisoners assert themselves with well-understood motivations, patterned manifestations, and an understanding of very real consequences for themselves and others. To quote them, they are "the girls among men." For these inmates, their very presence in a men's prison establishes their sex categorization as male; subsequent and ongoing interaction, however, offers the chance to vie for an "authentic" femininity.

We use the term "gender authenticity" to refer to the pursuit of full recognition, or what some transgender prisoners refer to as the "real deal," or being a "real girl." This pursuit begins with an orientation to, and acknowledgment of, the self as male (at least in the first instance) and an awareness of the fact that, as prisoners in a men's prison, transgender prisoners are immediately understood as male in a prison for men. The manifest desire to be taken as feminine, and thus female, prompts and sustains a commitment to "act like a lady." The commitment to, and everyday practice of, acting like a lady sets the stage for a playful *and* serious competition among transgender prisoners for the attention and affection of "real men" in prison. The attention and adoration of "real men," in turn, is taken to be an important measure of gender status among transgender prisoners. These features of the competitive

pursuit of gender authenticity are crucial to the social organization of gender in prison. The effort to be recognized as "a lady" is not something one finally achieves, but pursues as an ongoing proposition. The status of lady—as authentically female—is a provisional one deployed in a context in which transgender prisoners are "clocked," a subject to which we now turn.

Being Known as Male: "I'm in Here and I'm Already Clocked"

Transgender prisoners often used the word "clocked" as a way of indicating that their ability to pass as women is effectively denied in a prison built for and inhabited exclusively by males. The institutional context in which they reside determines which side of the sex categorical binary system they are thought to belong. Being clocked, therefore, is not about attempting to pass and being "discovered" so that some are privy to the "truth" and others are not. A sex-segregated prison for men is a unique environment where there is no other truth possible: Every prisoner is male, no matter how they look or act. It is here where the institutionalization of sex category membership interacts so critically with gender practice. Being clocked sets the terms and conditions for doing gender in prison precisely because it precludes passing as it is conventionally understood.

A white transgender prisoner in her mid-twenties reported taking hormones when she was 15 and coming to prison when she was 18 for "an armed robbery and carjacking I did with my boyfriend." She explained, "I was stupid, just stupid. But, I've learned the hard way. Twenty-four years of my life! That's the hard way." Comparing her life outside prison to her life in prison, she said, "I lived as a girl in high school, passed on the streets. Now [in prison], everyone knows, so who cares?" She explained that now that she is in prison there is no passing "because

I'm in here and I'm already clocked." Elaborating, she described how outside prison she didn't wear shorts because she has "manly legs," but contrasted this to life in prison with "now I'll wear shorts, too, even though I have manly legs." She went on to say "my legs are not manly in a good way—not like Tina Turner's." In this case, even as "clocking" makes one vulnerable to certain dangers, it can also be liberating to be relieved of the need to pass.

Likewise, an African American transgender prisoner in her mid-thirties who identified herself as a "pre-op transsexual" with "some facial surgery (chin, cheeks, and nose)" reported, "I've never been clocked on the streets." However, later in the interview she explained that, while in prison, she is treated by CDCR personnel and other inmates alike as male. When asked how correctional officers treat her, she reported being harassed routinely: "Most of the time, actually. Just today an officer said, 'Your jaw is wired shut, you're out of service.' C'mon, how rude is that? They also call me 'sissy boy.' That gets old." Later in the interview she made it clear how correctional officers and other prisoners reveal that "they think I'm gay or a gay boy."

Other transgender prisoners made explicit connections between being clocked and the many challenges they face being transgender in prison, including the ongoing management of the threat and reality of violence. A biracial transgender prisoner serving time for fraud reported that she came to California from a state in the Midwest because she assumed California would be more tolerant of alternative lifestyles. She described the nature of being transgender in a men's prison this way: "Everyone in prison knows I'm transgender. But outside they don't." Later in the interview, she lamented, "Yes, but most people don't know. They think, 'You like men, you're gay.' Most people don't get it—that I'm transgender, not gay." An African American transgender prisoner, who lived as a woman on the streets in Los Angeles and worked as a prostitute for over 20 years, proclaimed, "I know I'm not a girl; I was born a boy. But I have tendencies as a girl."

Regardless of whether one believes one is inherently female, the biologic remains a crucial reference point, as transgender prisoners expressed enthusiasm for being as close to the real deal as possible. An Hispanic transgender prisoner with a long history of engaging in sex work, struggling with drug addiction, and enduring imprisonment explained, "They [respect me because they] see that I'm all the way out—that I'm the real deal. I'm going all the way. I'm hoping to have surgery. I'm not a transgender, I'm a woman. I have my breasts from hormones. I'm the real deal. I want Marcy Bowers to do the surgery." Expressions such as these are often accompanied by self-assessments regarding how close to the goal—the real deal—one is, and is becoming.

What we might call the "problem of approximation" is an ever-present normative benchmark to separate the biologic from both the real woman and the failed pretender, even when intentions to seek sex reassignment surgery are in play. Therefore, extant theories of passing as a sociological process are inapplicable, and accountability to membership in one's sex category is no longer at issue. However, orienting accountability to a locally defined authenticity puts a premium on the process of pursuing a convincingly feminine appearance and demeanor. The context renders sensible and recognizable the ongoing effort (and its consequence) that seeks to move beyond the (known) biological truth to approach the real deal, even if it is inevitably a "Memorex." Accordingly, passing is less about biological and anatomical secrets to be managed and more about making gender commitments visible.

The prison environment sets the stage for embodiment to be understood as unforgiving

("Everyone knows") *and* eminently *deniable* ("Who cares?"). Through the pursuit of the real deal, however, gender expectations remain and demand that the transgender prisoner's behavior reflects an inherent femininity—"*as if*" one were really and truly female. To do this requires participation in an additional dynamic—acting like a lady in prison—which, as we describe in the next section, reveals the distinct ways in which gender is embedded in individual selves, cultural rules, social interaction, and organizational and institutional arrangements (Lorber 1994).

The Importance of Acting Like a Lady: "It's Being Proper"

To enhance one's feminine appearance and approach the real deal, transgender prisoners emphasized the importance of "acting like a lady." As they did so, particular constructs of classed normative understandings were employed to establish a valued femininity as a route to respect, as revealed in the following exchange:

Interviewer: How do transgender inmates get respect?

Prisoner: Act like a lady.

Interviewer: Why does acting like a lady in a men's prison get you respect?

Prisoner: If a man is a gentleman and they see a queen act that way, it's important for him to trust you because you're showing self-confidence in an environment that is crazy. That's why queens don't get hurt. You being a lady is like a gold credit card.

The dynamic nexus between being transgender in a sex-segregated environment and the centrality of earning respect as a lady is anchored in the embrace of a feminine ideal akin to the iconic Victorian era normative construct first described by Barbara Welter in "The Cult of True Womanhood, 1820–1860" (Welter 1966).

When asked "What does a 'lady' act like?," transgender prisoners provided illuminating answers. A Mexican transgender prisoner explained that acting like a lady entailed "staying in the women's spot. Don't talk bad. Don't make comments about things that don't concern you. Being a woman is about staying in line." Another transgender prisoner, who attributed many of her problems throughout her adult life to methamphetamine use that led to prostitution, went further:

Interviewer: What does a lady act like?

Prisoner: No sleeping with everyone. No going out on the yard with just a sports bra on. C'mon, you know what a lady acts like. It's being proper.

Many transgender prisoners were quick to talk about other transgender prisoners as "skanks," a clear reference to sexual promiscuity with connotations of disapproval in a context in which the values of social and sexual restraint are privileged. Jennifer Sumner explained the transgender code of conduct: "Transgender inmates who are seen to be 'messing' with another's man or 'messing' with too many men are labeled as 'slutty' and considered to be 'whores' or 'skanks'" (Sumner 2009, 190).

For transgender prisoners in men's prisons, a commitment to acting like a lady often was revealed in response to questions designed to solicit respondents' sense of what gets them—and other transgender prisoners—respect in prison. When asked "Does appearing more feminine get you respect from other (nontransgender) inmates?," the majority of the respondents (64.3 percent) said "Yes." When asked "Why?," a transgender prisoner in her mid-thirties serving her third term explained the benefits of acting like a lady in prison this way:

Prisoner: They [other prisoners] give me a different pardon. If I'm going in line to chow, it's likely someone will let me go first.

Interviewer: What exactly is a different pardon?

Prisoner: A pardon is a special consideration. That's what makes me feel respected. It's tasteful, especially if it comes from a regular guy. That's him telling me that I'm carrying myself like a lady. It's about being treated like a lady and made to feel like a lady. That's a special pardon. The more you get special pardons, the more you are being treated like a lady.

In a more dramatic illustration, a middle-aged African American transgender prisoner who introduced herself by using a famous model's name and later in the interview called herself a "crack whore" invited the interviewer to see the poster above the toilet in her cell and said, "I act like a lady and I have a poster that says so above the toilet in my cell." She explained that she sits when she pees, and because cells are shared and visible to other prisoners in the cell block, everyone can see that she sits when she pees. For her, this is a sign that indicates she is acting like a lady, and for all to see that she pees accordingly.

Life for transgender prisoners is nothing if not variable and a set of contradictions, and here is where the multiplicities of gender are evident. Transgender prisoners reported circumstances in which the luxury of "acting like a lady" necessarily gave way to expressions of violence. Almost half (44.7 percent) of the transgender prisoners in this study reported being involved in violence while living in their current housing

unit, and, on average, they have been in their current housing unit only about a year. Moreover, well over half (89.2 percent) of the transgender prisoners in this study reported being involved in violence while incarcerated in a California prison, with an average sentence in California prisons of 10.9 years.

For some, engagement in physical violence was not at odds with acting like a lady insofar as any woman in a situation that requires violence would behave similarly. A middle-aged African American transgender prisoner convicted of a second strike for "great bodily injury" explained how she initiated a violent confrontation with a group of four men on the yard after they refused to cease making pejorative comments about her husband (who was also her cellmate for over three years) because he was openly involved with her. She approached the men on the yard, confronted them about their harassment, asked them if there was a problem, told them to "cut the comments," and advised them that if the comments continued she would have to "get busy" with them:

Interviewer: What do you mean by "get busy"?

Prisoner: You know, put the cheese on the crackers and make it happen.

Interviewer: And what does that—"put the cheese on the crackers"—mean?

Prisoner: Fight.

In response to being asked "Does fighting feel at odds with being a woman?," she said:

Oh, girl, you just don't understand. Let's review. Take a transgender. Take any female. A Black woman. A Latina woman. A Asian woman. *Any* woman. There is no way a woman with a strong will and self-respect is going to let themselves be mistreated. You'd be surprised what women can do. Women will cut you. Women will stab you. Violence is violence. There's no such thing as transgender violence and other women's violence. It's all the same. People do what they have to do to take care of themselves. The difference with us is, well, violence is ugly. We don't want to be violent. We want to be beautiful. We're on hormones, girl. But hit me or disrespect me and I'll knock you out. I will. You would knock someone out, too. You'd be surprised what you would do if you had to; you just haven't had to—have you?

Others described situations in which they had to "man up," "put on my shoes," and "put down my purse and fight." In many cases, transgender prisoners reported taking a "time out" or a "stop pattern" to acting like a lady, and engaging in physical altercations with other prisoners as a way to protect or marshal respect. An older white transgender prisoner explained:

> If you don't respect yourself, no one will. You don't have to be tough. I can fight and lose and get respect. I can run from a fight and get no respect. I'd be a coward. So, it's not about being tough, it's about standing your ground.

In more dramatic terms, when asked if there are situations in prison in which violence between inmates is necessary, an HIV-positive transgender prisoner said:

> Yes. Gang bangers come in here and say something—like, "Hey, half dead!" [to HIVs] or "You're dying anyway." With me, if it becomes too much I put my purse down and fight. I'll let that part of me come out.

Interviewer: What part is that?

Prisoner: The non-ladylike. The ugly side of me.

Here the dual status of clocked as male and feminine like a lady exist in close social proximity. The situatedness of gender in this context allows us to see this dynamic as far more than a choice between absolutes— *either* femininity *or* masculinity. The violence engaged in may draw its content from forms of expression typically understood as masculine, but such forms are undertaken in the context of a *suspended* ladylike "ideal" or an extension of what a woman has to do to demand, secure, and demonstrate respect. In other words, violence represents an "ugly side" of a lady, and not the lady herself. As a consequence, the accomplishment of gender to invoke a normative *feminine* standard rests next to the accomplishment of gender to invoke a normative *masculine* standard. In the context of a prison, there is perhaps no better example of the situated character of gender than when one pees "like a lady" in one moment and "stands her ground" in the next.

For transgender prisoners, however, violence can carry consequences for the successful pursuit of the real deal. Being clocked as male means that any deployment of the "ugly side" constitutes a counter affirmation of a "natural" status as male. Thus, transgender prisoners are motivated to find ways to avoid physical violence. A white transgender prisoner with long flowing hair who has been doing time—off and on—since the late 1980s and is now in her mid-forties explained this dilemma:

Prisoner: I am a man, but I choose to look like a woman and I want to be treated like a woman. That's what makes me transgender. I recently had an argument with my cellie and he told me to put my shoes on, which means to fight. I wouldn't put them on. I wouldn't fight.

Interviewer: So women don't fight?

Prisoner: Right.

Interviewer: What else makes you feel treated like a woman?

Prisoner: All the courtesies a man would afford a woman, like my trays are cleared by my cellie—he takes my tray in chow line.

Whether transgender women actually fight or not—and the data suggest they do—is not the point; it is the fact that they render fighting sensible through a gendered lens.

Competition Among the Ladies: "Fun, Dangerous, and Real"

Ample self-report evidence reveals friendly competition among ladies. For example, when asked "Would you prefer more transgender inmates in your housing unit," quite often transgender prisoners expressed ambivalence born of wanting more "girls" in their living environments in the hopes of importing understanding and support, but at the same time expressed reluctance at the prospect of increased competition for social status in the prison order. An African American transgender prisoner said, "It's hard. I want the company of men, but I feel safe around the transgenders, I like women friends." When asked the same question, a Hispanic transgender prisoner replied:

> We call them [other transgender inmates] bitches, but with affection. Because the straights will try to hit on them as much. It's odd. You want friends, but you don't want the hassle, the drama that comes with them. I'm torn. I want them around, but I don't want them around. It's good and bad.

Similarly, an HIV-positive transgender prisoner who reported recently breaking up with her cellmate/institutional husband and having "a gentleman on the street who is waiting for me" described her relationship with other transgender prisoners:

> Yes, they flirt, but it's not pressure. That's just play. They know what kind of person I am—monogamous. I don't behave like a slut. Most of the other girls do, but I don't. I respect myself too much. [I] don't want to live with other transgenders—it's like too many women in the kitchen. It sounds so selfish, but less transgender inmates is better; like I said, too many women in the kitchen. Too much promiscuity. I want a relationship that is monogamous. Some of the girls, I don't respect. They are more promiscuous. They are nasty. Skanky. They are. I'm not like that.

When asked "Does appearing more feminine get you respect from other transgender inmates?," a white transgender prisoner living among many other transgender prisoners explained, "It tends to get negative. They get jealous. Because I look and act like a woman; they have to try harder [than I do]. They feel threatened by how natural it is for me." Similarly, a white transgender prisoner who has served almost 20 years of a life sentence in more than ten different prisons said, "I'm not sure. Sometimes it's jealousy, competition. If people compete with me that means they respect me enough to treat me as a girl—and they do compete." An older, more subdued white transgender inmate who explained "I didn't become transgender until I hit [current housing unit] at [current prison]," and "My morals have come a long way [since being in prison]" also commented on the complexities of femininity and respect:

> Some respect you a lot; some are angered because you do better than they—you look better; some are angry because you're not normal. Lots goes on when you're trying to be fem. It's fun, dangerous, and it's real. All girls learn from other girls. Transgenders learn from other transgenders. It's a way of learning to do things better, to be better women.

Finally, a young Hispanic transgender inmate said, "No, they're jealous. It's like a beauty pageant. You're all here and seemingly getting along. But not really. Really, it's a competition. They smile to your face, but not sincerely. There's only one winner and maybe runner-up."

This "pageant" requires other prisoners—the men—to be judges socially positioned to bestow status on transgender prisoners. The accomplishment of gender by transgender prisoners must draw crucial meaning from their primary audience. In various ways, transgender prisoners reported the centrality of securing attention from men (i.e., non-transgender prisoners). An older white transgender prisoner playfully described:

> I was going into chow and a couple of other inmates grabbed my ass and told me how sweet it is. They are males who are here and want sex. It's like a guy who goes to the strip club. I'm the entertainment and the meat. I wasn't offended. Those kinds of comments and gropes—I find it complimentary at my age. I'm [over 50]. I'm glad I can still draw the attention.

Moving beyond stories of (seemingly) superficial pleasure, transgender prisoners told touching stories of caretaking from other non-transgender prisoners with whom they formed intimate relationships. In an emotional interview, a very ill transgender prisoner who reported struggling with addiction most of her adult life, living on the streets before coming to prison, engaging in prostitution for many years, and being HIV-positive explained how important her prison husband is to her ability to manage in prison:

Prisoner: We [my husband in prison and I] clicked and we have a lot in common. He's very supportive of me. Because I'm on an HIV regime he does nice things for me.

Interviewer: Like what?

Prisoner: Well, like hold my hair when I vomit in the cell and not get mad at me.

This simple consideration took on significant meaning to her because it came at the hands of a man (and a husband, no less) and is easily seen by her as an affirmation of her status as female (i.e., a woman worthy of being cared for and taken care of like a wife). Throughout the interviews, transgender prisoners expressed appreciation for caring interactions with real men that served to recognize them as women. These simple, but much desired, interactions included being walked across the yard, given cuts in the chow line, and having an umbrella held over your head in the rain.

From the point of view of many transgender prisoners, the non-transgender prisoners are seen as protectors as well as providers. When asked "What is the best way for transgender inmates to avoid being victimized?," a white transgender prisoner who worked as a marketing researcher before coming to prison described a familiar gendered reciprocity: "Get someone to protect you. He'll take you under his wing. He'll become protective of you—like men do with women." She went on to explain her own relationship situation:

> We're involved, but it's not sexual yet. It's been a month. It's good for us to be in a marriage. We can and we can't fend for ourselves. He's our protector—just like on the streets. If someone did something to you, he would take care of them. If someone were to put his hands on me or degrade me, he would go and tell him, "Don't disrespect her. If you're disrespecting her, you're disrespecting me." See, I can get some respect through him.

She paused and added, "One of the things I have to do as a transgender is to deal with men who always want sex. So, I've found that the best thing to do is to make them give me something. I make them give me things—like take me to the mini canteen. It's like going on a date." She then described the similarities in terms of "give and take" in which "I give them a little flirt—it doesn't take much," concluding, "It's like petting a dog, only the dog pays you. I've found that men need women to be vulnerable. They want to take care of you—almost like a pet. I like it."

When asked about the best way to avoid victimization in prison, another transgender prisoner said, "I've been lucky to have guys who look at me as female and then they want to take care of me. They have that natural instinct—to protect me as a woman—from other men. That's how men are." Here, the bargain that results in a borrowing of respect depends on acceptance of the accomplishment of gender as indicative of a "natural" state, whether a male instinct to protect a woman, or the essential female qualities exhibited by transgender prisoners. According to transgender prisoners, non-transgender prisoners may be moved to chivalry, solicitous or protective behavior toward them as "ladies," calling forth a "natural" response from men. For some, respect is the precursor to love. An African American transgender prisoner said, "It just means getting to be nice, getting to be taken care of, and getting to be, you know, understood and loved."

The pursuit of femininity within this particular context illuminates the body's uncanny ability to override the biological convictions that are being imposed on it through institutional conditions. The absence of biologics within the men's prison system does not undermine gender, nor does the obvious lack of the real deal suspend the pursuit of femininity inside this alpha male space. In the context of prisons for men (and only men), it is not the commitment to biological differences that dictate the gender dynamics among members, but the *commitment of bodies* to act like, and be received as, "ladies" and "men." Though biological considerations are readily available, they are systematically rendered incompatible with the business of upholding categorical distinctions between women and men. The dynamics reported in this analysis

reveal that transgender women in men's prisons are simultaneously positioned as a source of cultural affirmation, intervention, and critique.

Discussion and Conclusion

The empirical analysis we present in this article suggests that, under the harsh conditions of the prison, transgender prisoners engage in a set of activities that together constitute what we refer to as a pursuit of gender authenticity, or what they call the real deal. These activities begin with an orientation to sex category through an acknowledgment that prisoners are institutionally understood as male. Transgender prisoners in men's prisons express a desire to secure standing as a "real girl" or the "best girl" possible in a men's prison. This desire translates into expressions of situated gendered practices that embrace male dominance, heteronormativity, classed and raced gender ideals, and a daily acceptance of inequality. To succeed in being "close enough" to the real deal requires a particular type of participation in a male-dominated system that can, under the right conditions, dole out a modicum of privilege and respect.

The playful yet serious competition among transgender prisoners for the attention and affection of "real men" allows the community of prisoners—transgender and non-transgender alike—to participate in a gendered existence that orders everyday expectations and behaviors, as well as the allocation of resources, symbolic and material. The experiences of transgender inmates illustrate that whatever femininity is undertaken, in whatever way, and for whatever ends, it is not done to pass—to mask a secret that, if revealed, could be discrediting. In prison the pursuit of femininity involves accountability to a set of normative standards, informed by cultural constructions of a "ladylike" ideal, even when sometimes transgender prisoners engage in a "stop pattern" and allow the "ugly side" to be revealed. What is sought is accountability to a putative sex category: If, through the accomplishment of gender in this setting, one can appear to embody the imagined biologic real deal, then one is close enough—and good enough—to be deserving of some privilege and respect.

In her recent article, Raewyn Connell writes eloquently of the "multiple narratives of embodiment" (Connell 2012, 867), such that we cannot speak meaningfully of *the* transgender or *the* transsexual experience. This should come as no surprise to gender theorists, which is likely why Connell calls for greater empirical and analytic attention to the multiplicities of transsexual lives. Those social scientists who study gender are less likely to be seduced by a unitary construction of transgender or a new binary comprised of "us" and "transgender." Attention to both the complexities of transgender and its situated character reveals the myriad ways in which social change is—and is not—made. Transgender women in prison for men are, to borrow the words of Connell one last time, "neither enemies of change nor heralds of a new world" (Connell 2012, 872).

Transgender inmates exemplify a will to present and live one's "real" self, even under impossible—and sometimes impossibly dangerous—conditions. Future research that includes not only the "real girls" but also the "real men" would be able to contribute to the picture we paint here of how masculinity and femininity are accomplished by transgender prisoners. What are, after all, "real girls" *without* "real men" and vice versa?

Transgender inmates do not hide and they cannot deceive. Their gendered behavior in prison can be understood as part of an ongoing, cooperative collusion where the search for the real deal is fundamentally a pursuit of recognition, respect, and belonging.

REFERENCES

Brown, George R., and Everett McDuffie. 2009. Health care policies addressing transgender inmates in prison systems in the United States. *Journal of Correctional Health Care* 15: 280–91.

Connell, Raewyn. 2012. Transsexual women and feminist thought. *Signs* 37: 857–81.

Fenstermaker, Sarah, and Joan Budesa. 2013. Contradictory embodiment. Unpublished manuscript.

Gagne, Patricia, Richard Tewksbury, and Deanna McGaughey. 1997. Coming out and crossing over. *Gender & Society* 11: 478–508.

Halberstam, Judith. 2005. *In a queer time and place*. New York: New York University Press.

Jenness, Valerie. 2010. From policy to prisoners to people. *Journal of Contemporary Ethnography* 39: 517–53.

Jenness, Valerie. 2011. Getting to know "the girls" in an "alpha-male community." In *Sociologists backstage*, edited by Sarah Fenstermaker and Nikki Jones. New York: Routledge Press.

Jenness, Valerie, Cheryl L. Maxson, Jennifer Macy Sumner, and Kristy N. Matsuda. 2010. Accomplishing the difficult, but not impossible. *Criminal Justice Policy Review* 21: 3–30.

Jenness, Valerie, Lori Sexton, and Jennifer Sumner. 2011. Transgender inmates in California prisons. Report to the California Department of Corrections and Rehabilitation. Irvine, CA: University of California, Irvine.

Lorber, Judith. 1994. *Paradoxes of gender*. New Haven, CT: Yale University Press.

Miller, Jody. 2008. *Getting played*. New York: New York University Press.

Petersilia, Joan. 2008. California correctional paradox of excess and deprivation. In *Crime and justice*, edited by Michael Tonry. Chicago: University of Chicago Press.

Stryker, Susan. 2006. (De)Subjugated knowledges. In *The transgender studies reader*, edited by Susan Stryker and Stephen Whittle. New York: Routledge.

Sumner, Jennifer. 2009. Keeping house. Ph.D. diss., University of California-Irvine, Irvine, CA.

Tewksbury, Richard, and Roberto H. Potter. 2005. Transgender prisoners—a forgotten group. In *Managing special populations in jails and prisons*, edited by Stan Stojkovic. New York: Civic Research Institute.

Welter, Barbara. 1966. The cult of true womanhood, 1820–1860. *American Quarterly* 18: 151–74.

EMOTIONAL LABOR, STIGMA, AND RESISTANCE

The previous sections deal with the interactional processes of *impression management* and *identity work*. Similar to acting in the theater, this social performativity is intended to induce particular understandings and responses in others, or the "audience." There are many occasions when portraying an identity that is consistent with the expected definition of the situation can be a lot of work for the person. For instance, if you do not like your spouse's parents but feel you must make a good impression to "keep the peace," you may find yourself working hard to maintain a smiling, friendly demeanor when you're actually feeling irritated and resentful. This kind of emotion work is not uncommon in everyday interaction and illustrates the distinction between private experiences and public performance (and the ability to be aware of both). *Emotional labor* refers to the ways in which we regulate our private feelings and bring them into line with social expectations. In particular, the concept refers to situations in which people are required to perform certain emotions as part of their job. Depending on the job and the circumstances, emotional labor can be very challenging and personally costly.

Emotional labor as an aspect of impression management has been a subject of extensive study in recent years. *Emotional capital* is a relatively new concept that refers to the process whereby certain impression management situations provide us with greater self-insight and a wide repertoire of emotions to use in subsequent interactions. For example, the boss who learns that employees respond better to criticism when she makes an attempt to engage with them on friendly terms has expanded her emotional capital. In other words, there is more than one way to manage impressions in a given situation. The person with the greater emotional capital is more likely to approach the situation creatively and effectively.

Sociologist Arlie Russell Hochschild was one of the first sociologists to discuss emotion management and emotional labor. The selection here is from her book *The Managed Heart*. This excerpt is based on a study of flight attendants and their interactions with the public. One of the services airlines try to provide in a highly competitive industry is a friendly experience. Flight attendants must present a friendly face despite the fact that the situation is often tense and passengers may be frightened, rude, and sometimes drunk. What do flight attendants do to signal a friendly situation, and how does this *emotion work* affect them personally? These are some of the questions Hochschild addresses in this reading.

Stephen E. Lankenau conducted interviews and engaged in many hours of observation for his research on impression management among panhandlers. In "Panhandling Repertoires and Routines for Overcoming the Nonperson Treatment," he describes various strategies that panhandlers engage in to manage their stigmatized identities and simply get people to engage in the most fundamental of interaction routines: acknowledging the existence of the other.

Victor Rios examines the motives behind stealing a bag of potato chips and other small acts of defiance. He suggests that these actions reflect a *resistance identity* that develops among young men who feel excluded from networks of positive credential, education, and

(Continued)

(Continued)

employment. Paradoxically, breaking the rules through small acts of criminality is one of the only ways they can exercise agency. The acts may get them into trouble, but in a context in which they are perpetually criminalized, the resistance also conveys a sense of dignity.

READING QUESTIONS

1. Make a list of jobs that require *emotional labor*. What are some of the activities that constitute emotional labor in specific jobs?

2. When does emotional communication feel like work, and when does it feel like authentic self-expression? What's the difference?

3. Recall an experience in which you learned some new skills for emotion management. Describe this emotional capital and how it has been of benefit to you.

4. One of the consequences of emotional labor is disassociation—the inability to have authentic emotional engagement. Consider the circumstances through which this might occur.

5. Think of other social identities that are often stigmatized. How do you react in the presence of these people? In what sort of interactions have you felt stigmatized?

6. Consider the relationship between skillful creativity and successful management of stigmatized identities. Think of examples of stigmatized people you know who are able to put others at ease. How do they do this?

33

The Managed Heart: Commercialization of Human Feeling

Arlie Russell Hochschild

(1983)

BEHIND THE SUPPLY OF ACTING: SELECTION

. . . Even before an applicant for a flight attendant's job is interviewed, she is introduced to the rules of the game. Success will depend in part on whether she has a knack for perceiving the rules and taking them seriously. Applicants are urged to read a preinterview pamphlet before coming in. In the 1979–1980 *Airline Guide to Stewardess and Steward Careers,* there is a section called "The Interview." Under the subheading "Appearance," the manual suggests that facial expressions should be "sincere" and "unaffected." One should have a "modest but friendly smile" and be "generally alert, attentive, not overly aggressive, but not reticent either." Under "Mannerisms," subheading "Friendliness," it is suggested that a successful candidate must be "outgoing but not effusive," "enthusiastic with calm and poise," and "vivacious but not effervescent." As the manual continues: "Maintaining eye contact with the interviewer demonstrates sincerity and confidence, but don't overdo it. Avoid cold or continuous staring." Training, it seems, begins even before recruitment.

Like company manuals, recruiters sometimes offer advice on how to appear. Usually they presume that an applicant is planning to put on a front; the question is which one. In offering tips for success, recruiters often talked in a matter-of-fact way about acting, as though assuming that it is permissible if not quite honorable to feign. As one recruiter put it, "I had to advise a lot of people who were looking for jobs, and not just at Pan Am. . . . And I'd tell them the secret to getting a job is to imagine the kind of person the company wants to hire and then become that person during the interview. The hell with your theories of what you believe in, and what your integrity is, and all that other stuff. You can project all that when you've got the job." . . .

The trainees, it seemed to me, were also chosen for their ability to take stage directions about how to "project" an image. They were selected for being able to act well—that is, without showing the effort involved. They had to be able to appear at home on stage.

* * *

TRAINING

The training at Delta was arduous, to a degree that surprised the trainees and inspired their respect. Most days they sat at desks from 8:30 to 4:30 listening to lectures. They studied for daily exams in the evenings and went on practice flights on weekends. There were also morning speakers to be heard before classes began. One morning at 7:45 I was with 123 trainees in the Delta Stewardess Training Center to hear a talk from the Employee Representative, a flight attendant whose regular job was to communicate rank-and-file grievances to management and report back. Her role in the training process was different, however, and her talk concerned responsibilities to the company:

> Delta does not believe in meddling in the flight attendant's personal life. But it does want the flight attendant to uphold certain Delta standards of conduct. It asks of you first that you keep your finances in order. Don't let your checks bounce. Don't spend more than you have. Second, don't drink while in uniform or enter a bar. No drinking twenty-four hours before flight time. [If you break this rule] appropriate disciplinary action, up to and including dismissal, will be taken. While on line we don't want you to engage in personal pastimes such as knitting, reading, or sleeping. Do not accept gifts. Smoking is allowed if it is done while you are seated.

The speaker paused and an expectant hush fell across the room. Then, as if in reply to it, she concluded, looking around, "That's all." There was a general ripple of relieved laughter from the trainees: so that was *all* the company was going to say about their private lives.

Of course, it was by no means all the company was going to say. The training would soon stake out a series of company claims on private territories of self. First, however, the training prepared the trainees to accept these claims. It established their vulnerability to being fired and their dependence on the company. Recruits were reminded day after day that eager competitors could easily replace them. I heard trainers refer to their "someone-else-can-fill-your-seat" talk. As one trainee put it, "They stress that there are 5,000 girls out there wanting *your* job. If you don't measure up, you're out."

Adding to the sense of dispensability was a sense of fragile placement vis-à-vis the outside world. Recruits were housed at the airport, and

during the four-week training period they were not allowed to go home or to sleep anywhere but in the dormitory. At the same time they were asked to adjust to the fact that for them, home was an idea without an immediate referent. Where would the recruit be living during the next months and years? Houston? Dallas? New Orleans? Chicago? New York? As one pilot advised: "Don't put down roots. You may be moved and then moved again until your seniority is established. Make sure you get along with your roommates in your apartment."

Somewhat humbled and displaced, the worker was now prepared to identify with Delta. . . . Training seemed to foster the sense that it was safe to feel dependent on the company. Temporarily rootless, the worker was encouraged to believe that this company of 36,000 employees operated as a "family." The head of the training center, a gentle, wise, authoritative figure in her fifties, appeared each morning in the auditorium; she was "mommy," the real authority on day-to-day problems. Her company superior, a slightly younger man, seemed to be "daddy." Other supervisors were introduced as concerned extensions of these initial training parents. (The vast majority of trainees were between nineteen and twenty-two years old.) As one speaker told the recruits: "Your supervisor is your friend. You can go to her and talk about anything, and I mean *anything*." The trainees were divided up into small groups; one class of 123 students (which included three males and nine blacks) was divided into four subgroups, each yielding the more intimate ties of solidarity that were to be the prototype of later bonds at work.

* * *

The company claim to emotion work was mainly insinuated by example. As living illustrations of the right kind of spirit for the job, trainers maintained a steady level of enthusiasm despite the long hours and arduous schedule. On Halloween, some teachers drew laughs by parading through the classroom dressed as pregnant, greedy, and drunk passengers. All the trainers were well liked. Through their continuous cheer they kept up a high morale for those whose job it would soon be to do the same for passengers. It worked all the better for seeming to be genuine.

Trainees must learn literally hundreds of regulations, memorize the location of safety equipment on four different airplanes, and receive instruction on passenger handling. In all their courses, they were constantly reminded that their own job security and the company's profit rode on a smiling face. A seat in a plane, they were told, "is our most perishable product—we have to keep winning our passengers back." How you do it is as important as what you do. There were many direct appeals to smile: "Really work on your smiles." "Your smile is your biggest asset—use it." In demonstrating how to deal with insistent smokers, with persons boarding the wrong plane, and with passengers who are sick or flirtatious or otherwise troublesome, a trainer held up a card that said "Relax and smile." By standing aside and laughing at the "relax and smile" training, trainers parried student resistance to it. They said, in effect, "It's incredible how much we have to smile, but there it is. We know that, but we're still doing it, and you should too."

HOME IN THE SKY

Beyond this, there were actual appeals to modify feeling states. The deepest appeal in the Delta training program was to the trainee's capacity to act as if the airplane cabin (where she works) were her home (where she doesn't work). Trainees were asked to think of a passenger *as if* he were a "personal guest in your living room."

The workers' emotional memories of offering personal hospitality were called up and put to use. . . . As one recent graduate put it:

> You think how the new person resembles someone you know. *You see your sister's eyes in someone sitting at that seat.* That makes you want to put out for them. I like to think of the cabin as the living room of my own home. When someone drops in [at home], you may not know them, but you get something for them. You put that on a grand scale—thirty-six passengers per flight attendant—but *it's the same feeling.*

On the face of it, the analogy between home and airplane cabin unites different kinds of experiences and obscures what is different about them. It can unite the empathy of friend for friend with the empathy of worker for customer, because it assumes that empathy is the *same sort of feeling* in either case. Trainees wrote in their notebooks, "Adopt the passenger's point of view," and the understanding was that this could be done in the same way one adopts a friend's point of view. The analogy between home and cabin also joins the worker to her company; just as she naturally protects members of her own family, she will naturally defend the company. Impersonal relations are to be seen *as if* they were personal. Relations based on getting and giving money are to be seen *as if* they were relations free of money. The company brilliantly extends and uses its workers' basic human empathy, all the while maintaining that it is not interfering in their "personal" lives.

* * *

By the same token, the injunction to act "as if it were my home" obscured crucial differences between home and airplane cabin. Home is safe. Home does not crash. It is the flight attendant's task to convey a sense of relaxed, homey coziness while at the same time, at takeoff and landing, mentally rehearsing the emergency announcement, "Cigarettes out! Grab ankles! Heads down!" in the appropriate languages. Before takeoff, safety equipment is checked. At boarding, each attendant secretly picks out a passenger she can call on for help in an emergency evacuation. Yet in order to sustain the *if,* the flight attendant must shield guests from this unhomelike feature of the party. As one flight attendant mused:

> . . . If we were going down, if we were going to make a ditching in water, the chances of our surviving are slim, even though we [the flight attendants] know exactly what to do. *But I think I would probably*—and I think I can say this for most of my fellow flight attendants—*be able to keep them from being too worried about it.* I mean my voice might quiver a little during the announcements, but somehow I feel we could get them to believe . . . the best.

Her brave defense of the "safe homey atmosphere" of the plane might keep order, but at the price of concealing the facts from passengers who might feel it their right to know what was coming.

Many flight attendants spoke of enjoying "work with people" and adopted the living room analogy as an aid in being as friendly as they wanted to be. . . . Others spoke of being frustrated when the analogy broke down, sometimes as the result of passenger impassivity. One flight attendant described a category of unresponsive passengers who kill the analogy unwittingly. She called them "teenage execs." . . .

> Teenage execs are in their early to middle thirties. Up and coming people in large companies, computer people. They are very dehumanizing to flight attendants. You'll get to their row. You'll have a full cart of food. They will look up and then look down and keep on talking, so you have to interrupt them. They are demeaning . . . you could be R2-D2 [the robot in the film *Star Wars*]. They would like that better. . . .

It is when the going gets rough—when flights are crowded and planes are late, when babies bawl and smokers bicker noisily with nonsmokers, when the meals run out and the air conditioning fails—that maintaining the analogy to home, amid the Muzak and the drinks, becomes truly a monument to our human capacity to suppress feeling.

Under such conditions some passengers exercise the privilege of not suppressing their irritation; they become "irates." When that happens, back-up analogies are brought into service. In training, the recruit was told: "Basically, the passengers are just like children. They need attention. Sometimes first-time riders are real nervous. And some of the troublemakers really just want your attention." The passenger-as-child analogy was extended to cover sibling rivalry: "You can't play cards with just one passenger because the other passengers will get jealous." To think of unruly passengers as "just like children" is to widen tolerance of them. If their needs are like those of a child, those needs are supposed to come first. The worker's right to anger is correspondingly reduced; as an adult he must work to inhibit and suppress anger at children.

Should the analogy to children fail to induce the necessary deep-acting, surface-acting strategies for handling the "irate" can be brought into play. Attendants were urged to "work" the passenger's name, as in "Yes, Mr. Jones, it's true the flight is delayed." This reminds the passenger that he is not anonymous, that there is at least some pretension to a personal relation and that some emotion management is owed. Again, workers were told to use terms of empathy. As one flight attendant, a veteran of fifteen years with United, recalled from her training: "Whatever happens, you're supposed to say, I know just how you feel. Lost your luggage? I know just how you feel. Late for a connection? I know just how you feel. Didn't get that steak you were counting on? I know just how you feel."

Flight attendants report that such expressions of empathy are useful in convincing passengers that they have misplaced the blame and misaimed their anger. . . .

* * *

RESPONSES TO THE CONTRADICTION

The slowdown is a venerable tactic in the wars between industrial labor and management. Those whose work is to offer "personalized service" may also stage a slowdown, but in a necessarily different way. Since their job is to act upon a commercial stage, under managerial directors, their protest may take the form of rebelling against the costumes, the script, and the general choreography. . . .

For a decade now, flight attendants have quietly lodged a counter-claim to control over their own bodily appearance. Some crews, for example, staged "shoe-ins." ("Five of us at American just walked on the job in Famolares [low-heeled shoes] and the supervisor didn't say anything. After that we kept wearing them.") Others, individually or in groups, came to work wearing an extra piece of jewelry, a beard a trifle shaggier, a new permanent, or lighter makeup. . . . Sometimes, as in the case of body-weight regulations, the issue was taken to court. . . .

Workers have also—in varying degrees—reclaimed control of their own smiles, and their facial expressions in general. According to Webster's Dictionary, "to smile" is "to have or take on a facial expression showing pleasure, amusement, affection, friendliness, irony, derision, etc., and characterized by an upward curving of the corners of the mouth and a sparkling of the eyes." But in the flight attendant's work, smiling is separated from its usual function, which is to express a personal feeling, and attached to another one—expressing a company

feeling. The company exhorts them to smile more, and "more sincerely," at an increasing number of passengers. The workers respond to the speed-up with a slowdown: they smile less broadly, with a quick release and no sparkle in the eyes, thus dimming the company's message to the people. It is a war of smiles.

* * *

The smile war has its veterans and its lore. I was told repeatedly, and with great relish, the story of one smile-fighter's victory, which goes like this. A young businessman said to a flight attendant, "Why aren't you smiling?" She put her tray back on the food cart, looked him in the eye, and said, "I'll tell you what. You smile first, then I'll smile." The businessman smiled at her. "Good," she replied. "Now freeze, and hold that for fifteen hours." Then she walked away. In one stroke, the heroine not only asserted a personal right to her facial expressions but also reversed the roles in the company script by placing the mask on a member of the audience. She challenged the company's right to imply, in its advertising, that passengers have a right to her smile. This passenger, of course, got more: an expression of her genuine feeling.

The slowdown has met resistance from all quarters and not least from passengers who "misunderstand." Because nonstop smiling had become customary before the speed-up occurred, the absence of a smile is now cause for concern. Some passengers simply feel cheated and consider unsmiling workers facial "loafers." Other passengers interpret the absence of a smile to indicate anger. As one worker put it: "When I don't smile, passengers assume I'm angry. But I'm not angry when I don't smile. I'm just not smiling." . . .

What is distinctive in the airline industry slowdown is the manner of protest and its locus. If a stage company were to protest against the director, the costume designer, and the author of a play, the protest would almost certainly take the form of a strike—a total refusal to act. In the airline industry the play goes on, but the costumes are gradually altered, the script is shortened little by little, and the style of acting itself is changed—at the edge of the lips, in the cheek muscles, and in the mental activities that regulate what a smile means.

The general effect of the speed-up on workers is stress. As one base manager at Delta frankly explained: "The job is getting harder, there's no question about it. We see more sick forms. We see more cases of situational depression. We see more alcoholism and drugs, more trouble sleeping and relaxing." The San Francisco base manager for United Airlines commented:

I'd say it's since 1978, when we got the Greyhound passengers, that we've had more problems with drug and alcohol abuse, more absenteeism, more complaints generally.

It's mainly our junior flight attendants and those on reserve—who never know when they will be called up—who have the most problems. The senior flight attendants can arrange to work with a friend in first class and avoid the Friendship Express altogether.

There are many specific sources of stress—notably, long shifts, disturbance in bodily rhythms, exposure to ozone, and continual social contact with a fairly high element of predictability. But there is also a general source of stress, a thread woven through the whole work experience: the task of managing an estrangement between self and feeling and between self and display.

EMOTIONAL LABOR, STIGMA, AND RESISTANCE

34

Panhandling Repertoires and Routines for Overcoming the Nonperson Treatment

Stephen E. Lankenau

(1999)

Some of the people just walk by and don't say nothin'. I call them zombies [laughs]. You ask them for change and they don't say "yes," "no," or "maybe I be back." They just walk by you like they don't even see you—it's like I'm not even sitting there. They could say "I ain't got none" or "no" or something. They just walk by.

—Alice, a homeless panhandler*

---

*All quotations in this article are by persons who gave their informed consent to participate in this research. All names in this study are pseudonyms, and certain biographical details have been deleted or altered to protect anonymity.

We use a variety of ploys to avoid the gaze or overtures extended by panhandlers—we avert our eyes, quicken our pace, increase the volume on our headphones. Some panhandlers manage to capture our attention, less frequently our money, using humor, offering services, telling stories, or by using other dramatic devices. A close examination of the exchanges between panhandler and passersby reveals that these interactions occur within a multilayered, theatrical context; dramas are enacted at the face-to-face level yet display the larger social relations among the poor and nonpoor.

Goffman's (1959) dramaturgical perspective presents social life as a play in which persons or actors conduct themselves before various audiences according to scripted roles. Compared with the exchanges among everyday persons, however, interactions between panhandler and pedestrian more closely resemble the basic structural features of a play. The panhandler, who is the main actor, is like an improvisational performer who uses a repertoire of pieces or routines to accomplish the act of panhandling. I refer to a panhandler's collection of these actions as his or her panhandling repertoire. Similarly, in reaction to the performer, pedestrians serve as the audience and respond to the panhandling routine by selecting from a menu of responses, like engaging or ignoring the panhandler. Being ignored by a passerby, which Goffman (1963) referred to as the "nonperson treatment," is a primary problem confronted by panhandlers, but one that is directly addressed through a repertoire of panhandling routines. The fact that I am categorizing panhandlers according to various routines, however, does not necessarily imply that certain individuals are acting or feigning need and distress. Rather, panhandling repertoires are one way of describing the public drama between panhandler and passersby.

A PRIMARY PROBLEM FACING PANHANDLERS—THE NONPERSON TREATMENT

Negative stereotypes of homeless persons, such as being dangerous, dirty, diseased, and mentally ill, are often connected to panhandlers, which then fuels a fearful desire to maintain a certain physical distance from panhandlers (Liebow 1993; Wagner 1993). Similarly, owing to the common associations between poverty and crime in the minds of middle-class persons (Reiman 1970), panhandlers are often merged into the "dangerous class." Additionally, race and gender differences also add strangeness as the great majority of panhandlers in this study are Black and male, whereas the pedestrian population in contact with the panhandling population is much more racially diverse and gender balanced.

These attitudes and perspectives among passersby typically prompt a particular response toward panhandlers and their overtures for money or food—the nonperson treatment. A person withholding glances or close scrutiny of another and effectively treating the other as though he or she did not exist characterizes the nonperson treatment.

In general, the nonperson treatment is one type of interaction occurring among unfamiliar persons in public places. When approaching a stranger in public, one typically ignores the other completely; provides the other with a subtle, noninvasive form of acknowledgment; or explicitly engages the other in some fashion. Goffman (1963) referred to these three types of interactions, respectively, as the nonperson treatment, civil inattention, and encounter or face engagement.

As suggested earlier by Alice, passersby commonly direct the nonperson treatment toward panhandlers. Pedestrians accomplish the nonperson treatment by effectively using props to pretend that the panhandler is neither seen nor heard or by simply looking down or straight ahead as though the panhandler were an inanimate object, like a tree or statue. From a panhandler's perspective, passersby using these variations of the nonperson treatment appear then as "zombies." Such explicit attempts to avoid and ignore reveal that the nonperson treatment is sometimes a conscious form of interaction rather than a passive or default disposition.

I propose that panhandlers devise a repertoire of panhandling routines to break out of the role of stranger or to awaken pedestrians from the blasé state; these dramaturgical actions then minimize the nonperson treatment and pave the way for encounters. Framing panhandling as a theatrical exchange between two classes of actors with dissimilar material resources, different interactional objectives, and contrasting viewpoints, however, is a critical factor toward understanding the repertoire of routines enacted by panhandlers. Despite these inequalities, this analysis shows that panhandling repertoires lead to exchanges between the zombie and the stranger and thereby foster greater understanding among both classes of actors.

PANHANDLING REPERTOIRES

Panhandlers overcome the nonperson treatment by initiating encounters through the use of dramaturgical techniques, routines, acts, pieces, or routines, which I collectively call panhandling repertoires. Often enacted in a performancelike manner, repertoires capture the attention and interest of passersby by appealing to a range of emotional qualities, such as amusement, sympathy, and fear.

On the basis of ethnographic research conducted on the streets of Washington, D.C., I have conceptualized five primary panhandling routines: the entertainer, the greeter, the servicer, the storyteller, and the aggressor, along with strategies within certain routines. The entertainer offers music or humor, the greeter provides cordiality and deference, the servicer supplies a kind of service, the storyteller presents a sad or sympathetic tale, and the aggressor deals in fear and intimidation. Generally, the entertainer and greeter attempt to produce enjoyment or good feelings, whereas the storyteller and aggressor elicit more serious or hostile moods. The servicer, who occupies a more neutral position, is focused on providing some sort of utility. Fundamentally, the moods or impressions created by the routines are largely attempts to attenuate strangeness or awaken pedestrians from their blasé condition, which then paves the way for an encounter and possible contributions.

Storyteller

Of all the panhandling routines, the storyteller approach most clearly conveys the dramaturgical nature of panhandling. The storyteller routine is based on using stories to evoke understanding, pity, or guilt from pedestrians. The primary message is need in virtually all cases. Stories consist of various signs, appearances, lines, or narratives that focus on shaking pedestrians from their blasé state. The storyteller routine is then accomplished by means of one or more specific subroutines: the silent storyteller, the sign storyteller, the line storyteller, and the hard luck storyteller. Here, Duane, a long-time homeless panhandler, points to the tactics or arts of capturing the sympathy of passersby with a good story:

What makes my panhandlin' successful and any other panhandlin' successful is the emotions. Now if you were reared in a good moral background and I come up to you [he pulls his face close—about six inches away], "Excuse me sir, I'm really tired. I just moved in and I've got five kids. Me and my wife—we can't get jobs." Now when you say the word *kids*—"Forget me—I've got babies I'm tryin' to feed." Or sickness—"I'm dyin'" or "my wife, my mother." More than just I'm givin' them money to get something to eat. These things are tactics. They'll be touched. [Duane gets up and demonstrates by calling out onto the sidewalk.] "Ma'am, my wife only has one hour to live! I'm tryin' to raise money. Please, someone help!" [He returns to the table] Now, did you catch some of the arts? There's an appeal to your emotions. And you got those regulars who are sittin' down, "Hey, I'm homeless. Can you spare some change sir?" And you see the same jerk on the same corner every day. And then you get into a habit, "Well here's a dollar." But the real money comes from the emotions.

In addition to narratives, stories are conveyed symbolically through down-and-out facial expressions, as Ray indicates:

> People look at me—the way I talk—and you know, feel sorry for me. They know I'm homeless by the way I'm lookin'! And I give them a sad little look.

Clothing, appearances, and presentation of self may also be manipulated or used to tell the desired story. In fact, becoming a successful storyteller is contingent on developing a look that works, as Fox suggests:

> When I first started panhandling I couldn't understand why people weren't giving me money—I looked too clean. So I grew this ratty beard and figured so that's the trick of the trade. As long as I was looking presentable like I was doing a 9-to-5 job—say working as a computer specialist—I wasn't getting a dime [laughs].

Hence, storytellers may have to consciously manage their appearance more than others to foster the impression of need. On buying or receiving new or secondhand clothes and shoes, for instance, storytellers find themselves in the difficult position of negotiating those symbols that do not suggest need, as compared with other routines that rely less on a sympathetic or pitiful appearance or story. I now discuss the four storyteller subroutines in greater detail.

The silent storyteller relies primarily on symbolic communication rather than verbal exchanges to gain the attention of passersby. The silent storyteller uses attire, expressions, movements, and other props to advertise his or her situation and needs. Movements might entail limping down the street or shivering unprotected in the rain and cold. Props may include crutches, a wheelchair, or other symbols of disability; bags of belongings; or children. Generally, silent storytellers, who often sit with their cup on the sidewalk and refrain from unnecessary interactions, are the most passive of all panhandlers. Harlan, a panhandler for the past six years, explains his silent approach:

> Over the years I've looked at all the guys' styles and when I first started some of the guys used signs and some of the guys talked, some the guys sing, some of the guys danced, some of the guys do everything—I mean I can do all that too. I don't like to ask people for money so when I first started I used to say "Excuse me sir, can you spare some change?" Then I started to develop my own thing—something told me not to say anything. In other words, I let my cup do the talking. People used to tell me a long time ago, if anyone wants you to have anything they'll give it to you. You know, you don't have to ask. I'm not gonna ask everybody that comes up and down the street to give me a nickel [laughs]. I've tried it, I've done it. You know, I just let my cup do the talking.

Like the silent storyteller, the sign storyteller typically waits passively for a pedestrian to initiate an encounter. A sign is a tool that effectively creates interest and concern within passersby with minimal effort exerted by the panhandler. A sign, as compared with a verbal exchange, reduces the likelihood of being subjected to a negative or humiliating interaction, as explained by Walt:

> I let the sign do the talking. I don't speak unless I'm spoken to or unless to say "good morning" or something like that or "good afternoon." I just hold a sign and if people want to give me money they give me money and if they don't they walk by and nothing is ever said. There's no dirty looks, no nothin' because you can't look nasty to everyone that doesn't give you money because you'd be looking nasty to 90 percent of the world [chuckles].

Lou also uses a cardboard sign that reads, "Homeless and Hungry. Please Help. Thank you. God Bless All." He includes his name in the lower right corner of the sign. Lou sits on the sidewalk with his back against a building, his belongings on either side, and his sign and cup positioned in front of him. For Lou, the sign removes the uncomfortable process of verbally soliciting money and minimizes negative exchanges:

> I don't like asking people for money straight out—that's why I use my sign. And incidentally, I don't feel as bad because I'm not asking people. A lot of people are afraid of me if I ask. With the sign they have the option of walking by or not walking by.

Thus, sign storytellers view the sign as an unobtrusive, non-threatening device but one that still conveys a message of need. Generally, signs protect panhandlers from degrading interactions by allowing agreeable donors to initiate an exchange without compulsion or intimidation.

The line storyteller is the most common among all storytellers and possibly the most ubiquitous routine in the panhandling repertoire. The line storyteller typically remains stationary and simply presents a line to pedestrians as they pass. Almost all lines focus on money in one form or another. The most basic, unadorned money line is "Can you spare some change?" but

specific higher amounts, such as a quarter or a dollar are often inserted in place of *change*. Another variation on the money line is to ask for very little money, such as "Can you help me out? Pennies will do" or an odd amount of money, such as "Can you spare 27 cents?"

Other lines may refer to "help" rather than money while specifying how the help would be put to good use. In these instances, food is a typical theme, such as "Can you help me get something to eat?" or "Can you spare some change to get a burrito?" In addition to food, transportation needs are another common theme used by line storytellers, such as "Can you spare two or three dollars for bus fare?" Lines invoking transportation may also include a destination and purpose, like returning to the shelter for the evening, buying medication at a hospital, or going to a job interview. Lines also focus on the return from unintended destinations, such as a hospital or jail, which may involve displaying evidence of a stay, like an institutionally marked identification wristband. Beyond money, food, transportation, and destinations, line storytellers focus on innumerable topics, but lines typically center on subjects that a homeless or poor person might realistically need.

The hard luck storyteller uses a more direct approach than the teller of a line story and offers an in-depth narrative focusing on difficult or unusual circumstances. On gaining the person's attention, the hard luck storyteller then presents an extended narrative to elicit sympathy and a contribution. Often, hard luck storytellers elaborate and combine themes used by line and sign storytellers. Here is an example of a hard luck story told to me one afternoon:

> I know this is a little unusual but I need you to save me. God told me to approach the man with the pink shirt. [I was wearing a pink shirt.] I almost just committed suicide by jumping off the bridge. You need to help me and my two daughters.

We're trying to get a bus ticket to Philadelphia. I've been in prison for the past five years and I've been out a month and I'm broke. When I was in prison my wife was raped and murdered. I need $15—Travelers Aid is going to pay the rest of the ticket. [I gave him a dollar from my wallet.] Can you help me get something to eat from Roy Rogers then? I'll put that dollar towards the bus but I need some money for food as well.

In sum, storytellers attempt to negate the blasé state by emphasizing the apparent disparities between themselves and pedestrians. These differences then create feelings of sympathy or pity within passersby and often lead to encounters and contributions. The storyteller's dramatized tales or physical appearance, however, may actually exacerbate the level of strangeness between panhandler and pedestrian—a result that is in contrast to more positive routines that neutralize strangeness, such as the entertainer, greeter, and servicer routines. Aggravating strangeness through stories or appearances, though, places storytellers in the "sick role" (Parsons 1951) or a position of alienated dependency, which then paves the way for sympathy and contributions.

Aggressor

The aggressor technique is premised on evoking guilt and fear in pedestrians by using either real or feigned aggression. Compared with the storyteller, the aggressor captures the attention of a pedestrian in a more pointed and dramatic fashion. Like the storyteller routine, however, the aggressor increases feelings of strangeness by highlighting disparities and differences. Primarily, the aggressor obtains food, money, and other items through intimidation, persistence, and shame.

Intimidation is accomplished through sarcastic and abusive comments, or fearful movements, like walking alongside, grabbing hold of the pedestrian, or silently using intimidating looks or stares. For instance, I encountered an unidentified panhandler using a kind of physical intimidation by standing in front of an ATM machine and then darting and lunging at pedestrians as they passed. Finally, a woman who initially refused his overtures gave him some money after completing her transaction at the ATM machine.

Persistence entails doggedly pursuing a contribution after it has been refused or seeking more money after an initial donation. Rita, for example, displayed this kind of persistence, though politely, during our hour-long encounter. After meeting her in front of McDonald's and buying her lunch, she then requested the change from lunch, asked for additional money to help her pay rent, and then asked for any old articles of clothing. During our meeting, Rita clearly displayed need especially after describing how she had been partially disabled by a stroke. Her method of asking, however, conveyed this element of aggressiveness and persistence.

Shame is evoked by making the donor feel that his or her quarter or dollar donation is insufficient and cheap given the vast material discrepancies between donor and panhandler. For example, my first encounter with Mel incorporated a sad tale with a shameful admonishment. After meeting him on the street, he lifted his shirt with his left hand revealing a long scar extending from his sternum to his belly button. The scar was folded over like it had recently been sewn up. "See this," he said, pointing to the scar with his right hand, "I need to eat right now. It's also about time for me to take my insulin. I'm a diabetic." I responded by giving him a dollar. "Can you tell me what I can get with that?" he returned somewhat indignantly.

Any of these prior examples may have constituted a form of aggressive panhandling under the District of Columbia's Panhandling Control Act, enacted in 1993. This act prohibits panhandling in an aggressive manner, which includes "approaching, speaking to, or following a person in a manner as would cause a reasonable person to fear bodily harm" and "continuously asking, begging, or soliciting alms from a person after the person has made a negative response."

Most panhandlers are well aware of this law and the prohibitions surrounding aggressive panhandling. Consequently, panhandlers often distinguish themselves from other panhandlers who act in an aggressive fashion, as Lou suggests:

> You have people out there with the cup going right up to people and saying "Help me out." That's what they call aggressive panhandling. That makes a bad name for me because I use a sign. And I mean that says it all. I'm not in people's face. I'm just off on the side. That's how I do it.

Up until now, I have described the aggressor routine as one that is consciously initiated by the panhandler. However, it also is clear that due to the many negative comments and interactions panhandlers report receiving from passersby, at least some of the time behaving aggressively is a reaction rather than a role, as suggested by Vern:

> I have no problem [with] people askin' for change because you can always say no. Some people have attitudes but you got to keep a good mind because I've been through it with people: "You got some spare change?" "Get the hell out of my face." You can't lose your spot over that because as soon as you get aggressive [makes police siren noise]. Don't let one dollar mess you up from a hundred dollars. They [fellow panhandlers] tell me that four or five times a night.

Hence, panhandlers generally understand the economic and legal imperatives behind remaining silent when publicly humiliated. Although easier said than done, managing one's emotions in the face of rejection or abusive comments is part of the job, as suggested by Ray:

> I don't do aggressive panhandling. I don't harass nobody. If you have a problem with me I have nothin' to say to you—I'm a panhandler. If people have something to say I just let it go—words are words.

Whereas the aggressor routine is often good at stirring pedestrians from their blasé condition, such action runs the risk of furthering strangeness and alienating potential donors. Particularly among panhandlers who are tempted to react aggressively to humiliating interactions with passersby or police, the job of panhandling is akin to service occupations that require emotional labor (Hochschild 1983) or publicly managing one's feelings.

Servicer

In contrast to all other routines, the servicer provides specific services to stimulate social interaction and exchange. Using various dramaturgical techniques, the servicer transforms the exchange into something different than merely giving money to a panhandler. The servicer dispels the blasé attitude by ostensibly offering a service while lessening the sense of strangeness by converting the interaction into a kind of business transaction. In other words, giving money to a stranger in public is an unfamiliar practice, whereas being engaged by a salesperson offering a service is a familiar ritual. Regardless of whether a service is desired or not, however, providing a service dampens strangeness by establishing a sense of obligation and reciprocity between panhandler and pedestrian. Although this rapport may be contrived in some cases and more akin to "counterfeit intimacy" (Enck and Preston 1988), that is, interaction supporting the illusion that a legitimate service is being performed when both parties know this to be false.

The servicer repertoire consists of a formal, proactive component and an informal, reactive aspect. The formal servicer consciously seeks out situations to provide a service in exchange for a tip, much like a bellhop or bathroom attendant. Roaming the streets in search of an opportunity is a particular characteristic of the formal servicer; in contrast, the informal servicer is more typically sought out by virtue of possessing something desirable, such as information. Additionally, the informal servicer can be viewed as a secondary type of routine that emerges owing to the failure of a primary one or arises when a panhandler is in the right place at the right time.

Car parking, that is, pointing out parking spaces to drivers in exchange for a tip, is the most prevalent type of formal service. This practice, however, is illegal under the Panhandling Control Act. The maximum penalties for violating the statute are a $300 fine and 90 days in jail. Despite its illegality and potential costs, parking cars remains a booming business in certain neighborhoods.

I gained a sense of the car-parking routine one evening by observing Spike, who is one of among a half-dozen car parkers that work a certain neighborhood. As we spoke alongside a busy street, Spike motioned to an approaching luxury sedan that a spot would be vacant. As the vehicle backed diagonally into the space, Spike stood behind and yelled out directions: "Turn your wheel to the left. You're OK. Come on." The driver—a tall, professionally dressed man—took several minutes to emerge. Spike noted the car's Georgia license plate and asked the man as he opened his door what part of Georgia he was from. "I'm from Atlanta," the car owner said. "Oh yeah, I'm from Statesboro," Spike responded. The man then gave Spike some change. During this exchange, Spike's friendly demeanor also demonstrates how car parkers often integrate the greeter rap into their parking routine.

In terms of earnings, car parking appears to be the most lucrative of all the panhandling routines. [Because] most car parkers panhandle in addition to parking cars, it is difficult to gain an accurate understanding of the payoffs of car parking alone. In any case, regular car parkers report a minimum of $40 of total earnings on a good evening compared with the median level of $35 among all panhandlers. However, earnings reportedly can exceed $100 if a car parker encounters extra generous drivers who give $10 or $20 at a time.

The increased earnings netted by car parkers may stem from any one of numerous factors, including drivers giving out of fear, generosity, appreciation, a desire to impress friends or dates, or inebriation. However, Mel, a long-time car parker, offers his own explanation for why car parkers earn such relative high earnings:

> It's free money out there. I don't ask for nothing. I just direct cars into parking spaces and people give me money—some change, one dollar, five dollars, ten dollars, twenty dollars. Sometimes they're so happy to give me money even though they could've paid for an actual space in a parking lot for less. If you ever get hard up for money, go over there and try it. It's almost like they're trained. They expect it when they come into the neighborhood.

In contrast to the formal servicer, such as the car parker, the informal servicer provides services to pedestrians, vendors, storeowners, and the police. These services, which result from a panhandler's propensity for being in the right place at the right time, include offering an umbrella to a soaked pedestrian; giving directions to specific street addresses; escorting unchaperoned, sometimes inebriated persons to their final destinations; or hailing a taxi for the less streetwise or infirm. These exchanges convert the panhandler into an informal service provider.

Beyond informally offering everyday information and help, panhandlers occasionally encounter more significant and valued news. Owing to their near omnipresence on the streets, panhandlers are frequently knowledgeable of many important happenings. Information absorbed by panhandlers, particularly facts about persons relating to crimes, are sought after by storeowners and police, as explained by Vance:

> We provide services to some of the storeowners. If there's a break-in or vandalism, we usually know who did it within a 24–48 hour period, whereas it might take the police several days to a week to find out the same information.

However, not all panhandlers capitalize on the opportunity to provide information to the powers that seek it. Each panhandler may have personal reasons for not offering up important information, such as fear of retaliation, a code of silence among street people, not knowing the desired facts, or not trusting the police. Hence, a witness who fails to cooperate with the police when the stakes are high may feel the stick rather than being handed a carrot, as Mel explains:

> I went to jail because I wouldn't open my mouth. So they said I was in contempt of court. I was the witness of a murder and they all pointed their fingers at me man—I'm telling you Joe—"He saw it. He was there." I was just walking past. I didn't see who was blowing who away. I be everywhere. I see a whole lot of things—and that be my business. I hear the gunshot goin' off, but do you think I looked around to see what time it was? I keep with my straight steady walk—outta there—caught a cab.

In sum, the servicer captures a pedestrian's attention by creating the impression that he or she has some valuable utility to offer in exchange for payment, much like the relationship between salesclerk and patron. Although intimacy or familiarity may increase the likelihood of a pedestrian giving money to a servicer, the quality of strangeness is attenuated by the panhandler's ability to turn the interaction into a kind of neutral business exchange. Because of their presence on the streets, overcoming the nonperson treatment is occasionally a moot point as panhandlers are sometimes actively approached for information or assistance. As indicated, however, panhandlers must intermittently use other dramaturgical routines to avoid encounters (and thereby foster strangeness) with more powerful persons, such as the police, who seek to develop exchanges that may be disadvantageous or detrimental to their existence on the streets.

Greeter

The greeter offers friendliness, respect, flattery, and deference to passersby in exchange for contributions and cordial responses. This routine largely revolves around polite behavior, such as greeting pedestrians with a "hello" or "good morning," quite like department store employees who welcome customers at store entrances. Like these service occupations, the greeter routine is firmly rooted in dramaturgically managing emotions. Additionally, the routine is enhanced when a panhandler becomes familiar with a panhandling locale and then remembers faces, names, and biographical facts about contributors. Hence, a command of these more intimate details about passersby allows the greeter to personalize each greeting and devise a more comprehensive panhandling repertoire.

Sanford personifies the greeter routine. During numerous observations and encounters, Sanford always offered a pleasant greeting and a distinctive, friendly smile. Sanford typically stands at the top of the Metro (subway) or along a busy side street greeting passersby during their commute or afternoon stroll. As he explains,

> I greet people in the morning—say "good morning" to them—say "hello." I try to make people

happy and everything. I generally get a good response—a happy greeting in a happy way especially with a smile. They always like my smile. Everybody has their own different style. My style is my smile. That's how a lot of people remember me you know.

Whereas Sanford capitalizes on his friendly smile and good nature, Lonnie, a 40-year-old native of the West Indies, appeals to pedestrians through his pleasing Caribbean accent and interactional flair:

I just talk to people because I'm gifted. I know that I'm gifted, ok. It doesn't matter what you have on as long as you are a gentle person and your mind is proper. As long as you have a pleasant personality it doesn't matter [exclaimed] what you have on—how stinky you feel or whatever. If you are nice to people, people will give.

Although some panhandlers possess specific attributes that facilitate the greeter routine, such as a friendly smile or a courteous manner, a certain amount of on-the-job learning is usually involved. Wally implicitly describes his evolution from the aggressor to the greeter, which required emotion management skills:

I always say "good morning" to the people. It makes them feel real good. And most of the time I'm good at it but I was a nasty motherfucker when I came here. But now I've learned my lesson—I've learned from my mistakes. Now that I'm so nice to the people I can get anything I want. When I was nasty and dirty I used the "f" word. Now I think things have changed. Now I just like being friendly with my cup in hand—"Hey, how are you doin'!"

Just as a panhandler's repertoire may undergo an evolution, city commuters often require a breaking-in period before moving from the nonperson treatment toward being open to encounters with panhandlers new to their daily schedule. As Sanford explains, pedestrians were generally skeptical of him and his routine until he developed a presence in the neighborhood:

When I first came up here [to this neighborhood] people didn't really know me or nothin' and I didn't get no friendly greetin'. I got a couple right. But then they saw what kind of guy I was, right. There's a lot of stereotypes—guys who are homeless panhandlin'—cussin' people out bein' disrespectful to people and everything. Or they feel a lot of them are alcoholics or crack addicts or whatever. So you know, they saw that it wasn't like that with me so as soon as they got to know me I got a better greetin'. Cause I couldn't even get a dollar when I first got here [laughs].

Once a panhandler is known in a certain area and rapport is established with a group of regular contributors, the greeter may be emboldened to mix compliments, such as "You're looking good today," with more conservative salutations, like "good morning." Alternatively, a more confidant, forward greeter may deal largely in compliments.

In sum, the greeter deploys pleasantries to maintain friendships with regular contributors or displays politeness and deference to newcomers. Given its versatility, it is a routine used by nearly all panhandlers. Although some use it as a primary part of their repertoire when dealing with large processions of anonymous crowds, storytellers and others typically use it as a secondary routine on encountering persons who give regularly.

Entertainer

The entertainer provides humor and enjoyment and encompasses two more specific routines: the joker and the musician. Both typically awaken pedestrians from their blasé state through a benign or positive offering, such as a joke or a song. Strangeness is then reduced by creating rapport or intimacy by performing a familiar tune or by developing an ongoing presence in a particular neighborhood. Generally, the entertainer routine most clearly resembles an actor staging a performance before an audience.

The joker entertains by telling funny stories, making irreverent comments, or offering bizarre appearances. Minimally, the joker's goal is to make an unsuspecting pedestrian smile or laugh. Once the pedestrian is loosened up, it is hoped that a contribution will follow.

For instance, Yancy demonstrates the joker by presenting a strange appearance in conjunction with humorous lines. One evening, I observed Yancy walking along a crowded sidewalk with the collar of his blue shirt pulled over his forehead, exposing only his face and a green leaf drooping over his left eye and cheek. Donning this clownish look and occasionally saying, "Can you help me out? I'm trying to get on the Internet," he moved about holding out an upturned baseball cap. During an interview, Yancy explained how confronting a weary afternoon commuter with a humorous scenario, like the incongruity between a homeless panhandler and the Internet, is a good antidote for the nonperson treatment:

> A certain line can make their day or a little bit of laughter. If a person may have his briefcase or purse and whatnot and they may have two bags of groceries from Sutton Place Gourmet and a bottle of beaujolais nouveau. They want to go home and smoke a cigarette and watch cable and you're telling them that you're panhandling and trying to get on the Internet.

Humor sometimes emerges spontaneously, seemingly without any instrumental intentions. For instance, while standing outside the Metro late one quiet evening, Ralph called out to a Metro system repairman riding up the escalator: "Hey, I caught my foot in the escalator last week." While walking away, the repairman sarcastically replied, "Sue Metro." Ralph then excitedly responded, "But you're the Metro man!" And then to the cadence of the Village People's song "Macho Man," Ralph sang "Metro, Metro man, I'd like to be a Metro man." No money was exchanged, but all parties within earshot appeared amused.

The musician is another variation on the entertainer routine and covers a range of musical acts from polished saxophonist to struggling crooner. Often, musicians play familiar and fun tunes to maximize appeal. Likewise, singers frequently enhance their act by interspersing humorous lines or jokes into songs.

For instance, a companion and I were abruptly accosted one evening by a man standing five-and-a-half-feet tall with long sideburns and cowboy boots who introduced himself as "Blelvis"—Black Elvis. Blelvis announced that he could sing over 1,000 Elvis songs and could relate any word to an Elvis song. As we continued walking toward our destination, I mentioned the word *cat* and Blelvis began singing a tuneful Elvis melody containing the word *cat*. Eventually, Blelvis asked for $1.50 for his performance.

This encounter with Blelvis, though largely promoted as a musical/comedy act, also contained elements of the aggressor technique. After initiating the encounter, Blelvis followed close behind and offered us little choice but to engage him. When my companion produced only $0.50 in response to his solicitation, Blelvis deftly grabbed a bottle of beer from the bag I was carrying.

Because many street performers are less aggressive than Blelvis or lack genuine musical talent, contributions may be more linked to sympathy and respect than to performing abilities. For example, late one afternoon, Alvin sat on a milk crate and played a Miles Davis tune, "Solar," on his worn clarinet. Several moments after Alvin ceased his playing, which was inspired but not exceptional, a group of young men walked past, and one dropped a handful of coins into Alvin's green canvas bag. Alvin responded to the contributions by pulling the bag next to his side and reasserting his identity as a musician: "Sometimes people hear me when I'm playing good but give me money when I'm playing bad or just warming up. They might give me money now or later. But I don't want anyone to think I'm a panhandler."

Hence, some ambiguous performers, like Alvin, occasionally struggle to prevent one routine, such as the musician, from being misinterpreted for another act that may be more degrading to the self, like the storyteller.

In sum, entertainers awaken pedestrians from their blasé state through benign or positive offerings, such as a song or a joke. Strangeness is reduced by performing familiar tunes or developing a welcoming presence in a particular neighborhood. Many panhandlers devise a coherent repertoire based largely on the entertainer and greeter routines, given the affinity between these two routines.

CONCLUSION

I have shown that dramaturgical routines are a useful way of describing and theorizing about the interactions and exchanges that constitute panhandling. From this symbolic interactionist perspective, sidewalks serve as stages on which panhandlers confront and overcome the nonperson treatment. Given the numerous contingencies facing panhandlers, the most successful panhandlers devise a repertoire of several routines to stir the blasé attitude, to minimize strangeness, and to maximize contributions.

Fundamentally, however, panhandling and panhandling routines are a response to economic and social marginality. After years of homelessness, joblessness, or health problems,

few panhandlers possess the resources or skills necessary to gain stable jobs in the formal economy. Rather than relying exclusively on programs designed for the poor and homeless, such as food stamps, soup kitchens, or shelters (which many view as controlling, humiliating institutions), the individuals described here support themselves by creatively, sometimes desperately, engaging the consciences of passersby. Surviving in this manner is an accomplishment given that the majority of Americans do not believe the homeless should be allowed to panhandle publicly (Link et al. 1995).

In a broader sense, panhandling routines represent general strategies that any person might use to get what he or she wants from reluctant others. For instance, the salesperson who humors her clients to facilitate sales is being the entertainer, whereas the minister who dramatizes the church's financial status to increase contributions is playing the storyteller. Viewed in this manner, panhandler routines perform the same function as those deployed by the salesperson or the minister. When enacted by a panhandler, however, the entertainer, the storyteller, and the other routines appear in their boldest terms; that is, the performing and staging are done in the most unadorned settings and without the protection of position or prestige. In light of such difficulties, panhandlers who devise routines to overcome the nonperson treatment demonstrate a certain resiliency and fortitude, qualities that, were it not for their position as a poor panhandler, might have earned them raises and promotions rather than leftovers and spare change.

REFERENCES

Enck, Graves E. and James D. Preston. 1988. "Counterfeit Intimacy: A Dramaturgical Analysis of an Erotic Performance." *Deviant Behavior* 9:369–81.

Goffman, Erving. 1959. *The Presentation of Self in Everyday Life*. New York: Anchor/Doubleday.

_____. 1963. *Behavior in Public Places*. New York: Free Press.

_____. 1974. *Frame Analysis: An Essay on the Organization of Experience*. New York: Harper & Row Colophon.

Liebow, Elliot. 1993. *Tell Them Who I Am: The Lives of Homeless Women*. New York: Free Press.

Link, Bruce G., Sharon Schwartz, Robert Moore, Jo Phelan, Elmer Struening, Ann Stueve, and Mary

Ellen Colten. 1995. "Public Knowledge, Attitudes, and Beliefs About Homeless People: Evidence for Compassion Fatigue." *American Journal of Community Psychology* 23(4): 533–55.

Parsons, Talcott. 1951. *The Social System*. New York: Free Press.

Reiman, Jeffrey. 1970. *The Rich Get Richer and the Poor Get Prison*. New York: Simon & Schuster.

Wagner, David. 1993. *Checkerboard Square: Culture and Resistance in a Homeless Community*. Boulder, CO: Westview Press.

EMOTIONAL LABOR, STIGMA, AND RESISTANCE

35

Stealing a Bag of Potato Chips and Other Crimes of Resistance

Victor Rios

(2012)

Ronny was called in for a job interview at Carrows, a chain restaurant that served $9.99 sirloin steak and shrimp. He called me up, asking for help. I loaned him a crisp white dress shirt, which I had purchased at a discount store when I worked as a server at a steak house during my undergraduate years. I convinced Ronny to wear fitted khakis, rather than his customary baggy jeans. He agreed, on the condition that he would wear his white Nike Air Force Ones, a popular basketball shoe at the time. These shoes had been in and out of style in the urban setting since the early 1980s. By 2002, a famous rapper, Nelly, created a popular song named "Air Force Ones," and famous basketball players such as Kobe Bryant wore these shoes during games. Black and Latino youths in Oakland sometimes even wore them to more formal events such as high school proms, quinceaneras, and weddings.

I asked Ronny why he insisted on wearing these shoes in a professional setting. He replied, "Because professionals wear them."

Many of the boys I worked with in my research believed they had a clear sense of what courteous, professional, and "good" behavior was. Despite their attempts to present themselves with good manners and good morals, their idea of professional behavior did not match mainstream ideas of professional behavior. This in turn created what I refer to as *misrecognition*. When the boys displayed a genuine interest in "going legit," getting a job, or doing well in school, adults often could not recognize their positive attempts and therefore criminalized them.

The boys had grown up in an environment which had deprived them of the social and cultural capital they needed to progress in school and the labor market. Therefore, they developed their own alternative social and cultural capital, which they used to survive poverty, persist in a violent and punitive social ecology, prevent violence, avoid incarceration, and attempt to fit into mainstream institutions. Education scholar Tara Yosso develops a framework for understanding and using the capital marginalized communities develop—what she calls *community cultural wealth.* She argues that marginalized communities have always generated community cultural wealth that's allowed them to survive and resist. Sociologist Martín Sánchez-Jankowski has recently discussed poor people's ability to organize their social world and maintain social order as "persistence." According to Sánchez-Jankowski, contrary to the popular academic belief that poor people live in a disorganized world where they have a limited capacity to generate "collective efficacy" (the ability of a community to solve its own social problems), the urban poor shape their behaviors around making sense of and creating social order within a marginal context. *Organic capital,* then, is the creative response the boys in this study developed in the midst of blocked opportunity and criminalization. Despite being well-intentioned, though, these efforts were often not well received by mainstream institutions.

Ronny's story is indicative of how many of the boys attempted to tap into mainstream institutions but failed. As they encountered rejection, they returned to the resilience and survival strategies that they had developed in their neighborhoods. I continued to prepare Ronny for his interview, helping him develop "acceptable" cultural capital. We prepared with mock questions: "Why do you want to work for us?" I asked him. He responded, "I am a hard worker." "That's a good start," I said. "How about expanding that and telling them that you're also a team player and that you enjoy the restaurant atmosphere?" Ronny nodded. The day of the interview, I

walked into the restaurant separately from Ronny. To calm his nerves I told him, "You look great, man. This job is yours!" He looked sharp: a professionally dressed, athletically built, charismatic, tall, African American young man with a charming dimple every time he smiled. I was certain he would get the job. I sat down for lunch at a booth, in an attempt to observe Ronny being interviewed. I looked at the menu and, with a knot in my gut, nervous for Ronny, ordered what I knew would eventually give me a worse stomach ache: a Mile-High Chipotle Southwest Burger. I sat about twenty feet away from the table where Ronny sat with a manager.

Ronny tried to use his charisma to connect with the manager, but she kept her distance and did not look at Ronny, seemingly uninterested in what he had to say. At the end of the interview, Ronny stood abruptly and walked away from the manager, with no handshake or smile. He went outside. I ordered my burger to go, paid my bill, and met him in the parking lot. As I headed to the door, I turned to look in the manager's direction, and she was greeting a White male youth. She smiled, gave him her hand, and offered him a place to sit. Ronny's first contact with her was not this friendly. I walked outside to meet Ronny, who sat on the hood of my car.

I asked for a debriefing. He told me that he had a good feeling and that the manager had seemed to like him. I asked him to walk me through the interview. He had followed the plan flawlessly. I was proud of him. "You followed the plan. You did a great job," I told him. "Why didn't you shake her hand when you left?" I asked. "'Cause," Ronny replied. "Why not?" I scolded. "Because it was a white lady. You not supposed to shake a white lady's hand. They be scared of a nigga. They think I'ma try to take their shit or fuck 'em. I just said thanks and walked out." Ronny did not get the job.

Ronny did all he could to land the job, but the limited resources at his disposal for showing respect may have kept him from getting the position. In this case, he believed that not shaking the manager's hand would show respect; instead, Ronny may have been perceived as a rude kid not able to hold employment in a restaurant environment. I asked Ronny to tell me how he learned about not shaking white women's hands. He told me that his white female teachers had asked him to keep his distance, white women on the street would clasp their purses when they saw him walking by, and white female store clerks would nervously watch him when he walked into an establishment. Ronny had been socialized from a young age to overcompensate around white women to show he was not attempting to harm or disrespect them. This behavior may have been a result of the stereotyped expectations of black men as criminals and sexual aggressors, deeply rooted in American culture.

Ronny applied for multiple jobs. After about a dozen applications and three failed interviews, he became discouraged. He reported being asked by other managers about his "drug habits" and "criminal background." Ronny decided to abandon the job-search process and instead invested $20 in pirated DVDs; a few hours later, he'd made $50 from the illegally copied movies. He reinvested the $50 in a backpack full of pirated DVDs, and after a few weeks, Ronny had made enough to buy a few new pairs of glossy Air Force Ones. However, the six to ten hours he spent in front of the grocery store, waiting for customers for his DVDs, made him a measly $20 or $30 a day—certainly not worth the risk of getting arrested for a federal offense.

Still, Ronny, like many of the other boys, preferred to take on the risk of incarceration and the low wages that this underground entrepreneurship granted him in order to avoid the stigma, shame, and feeling of failure that the job-application process produced for him. Misrecognition of genuine attempts to do well in school, the labor market, or their probation program led to frustration—and to producing alternatives in which the boys' organic capital could be put to productive use.

RESISTANCE IDENTITIES

In feeling excluded from a network of positive credentials, education, and employment opportunities, young people develop creative responses that provide them with the necessary tools to survive in an environment where they have been left behind and where they are consistently criminalized. *Resistance identities*, according to sociologist Manuel Castells, are those created by subordinated populations in response to oppression. These identities operate by "excluding the excluder." Some, like the boys I studied, develop practices that seem to embrace criminality as a means of contesting a system that sees them as criminals. Similarly, sociologist Richard Quinney argues that poor people engage in crimes such as theft as "acts of survival" in an economic system in which their well-being is not fulfilled by other collective means. He further argues that some poor and working-class people engage in "crimes of resistance," such as sabotaging workplace equipment and destroying public property, as a form of protest against their economic conditions.

The young men in this study constantly participated in everyday acts of resistance that baffled teachers, police officers, and community-center workers. From the perspective of the adults, these transgressions and small crimes were ridiculous: the risk of being caught was high and the benefit derived from the deviant act was minuscule. This frustration led adults to abandon empathy for the boys and to apply the toughest sanctions on them. "If they're going to act like idiots, I am going to have to give them the axe," explained one of the gang task-force officers.

Many of the adults I interviewed believed the boys' defiance was "stupid." Sarcastic remarks often followed when a youth purposely broke a simple rule, leading him to be ostracized, kicked out of class, or even arrested. Why would the boys break the simplest of rules knowing there would be grave consequences? For the boys, though, breaking the rules was resisting a system that seemed stacked against them. In many ways, criminality was one of the few resources the boys could use in response to criminalization.

THE STOLEN BAG OF CHIPS

One fall afternoon, I met with fifteen-year-old Flaco, a Latino gang-associated young man from east Oakland. We joined three of his friends as they walked to their usual after-school hang out, Walnut Park. They decided to make a stop at Sam's Liquor Store. I walked in with them, noticing a sign that read, "Only two kids allowed in store at one time." I realized they were breaking the store rule by entering in a group of four and pretended to walk in separately to see how the store clerk would respond to their transgression. I stood in the back of the store as Flaco walked up the candy-bar aisle—keeping a good distance between himself and the Snickers, Twix, and Skittles, to show the clerk, who was already staring him down, that he was not attempting to steal. He grabbed a candy bar, held it far away from his body, walked a few steps, and placed it on the counter. Many of the boys in this study often maintained their distance in the candy or soda aisles at stores to show they were not attempting to steal. Store clerks in the neighborhoods I studied were always apprehensive of customers: they watched people from the moment they walked in, had surveillance cameras set up, and one clerk had taped up pictures of himself holding an AK-47.

The clerk at Sam's may have been concerned that too many kids in his store meant that he could not keep an eye on all of them.

A balding, middle-aged, Asian American male, the clerk pointed to the door and yelled, "Only two kids allowed in the store at a time!" The three youths in line to pay for their items looked at the clerk and at each other. Mike, closest to the entrance, responded, "We ain't doing shit." The clerk replied, "I am going to call the police!" Mike grabbed a twenty-five-cent bag of Fritos Flamin' Hot chips, lifted it up in front of the clerk's face, and said, "You see this? I was gonna pay for it, but now I ain't paying for shit, stupid mothafucka." He rushed out of the store with the bag of chips, as the clerk called the police. The rest of the youngsters dropped the snacks they were in line to purchase and ran out. I walked up to the store clerk and gave him a quarter for Mike, who had stolen the chips. Infuriated, the clerk said, "It's too late. The police are on their way to get the robbers."

I was not able to track down the boys until a few days later. When I ran into Flaco, he informed me that the police had arrested Mike that day for stealing the twenty-five-cent bag of chips. After interviewing the boys and observing the store clerk's interactions with them in the days and weeks after this event, I found that Mike's "irrational" behavior had actually changed the way the store clerk interacted with the boys. The boys believed the clerk had begun to treat them with more respect—he avoided provoking negative interactions with the boys, even if it meant allowing a few more youths into the store than policy allowed. While even Mike's peers believed that his actions were "crazy," they also acknowledged that something significant had changed. For example, Flaco thought Mike had overreacted, but because of Mike, Flaco felt respected by the store clerk the next time he went in the store: "Mike fucked up. He was acting hyphy [crazy] that day. He should have paid the guy. . . . But because of what he did, me and my dogs go into the sto', and the guy don't say shit. We all go in like five deep—like 'what?'—and dude don't say shit no more."

When I asked Mike why he had stolen the bag of chips, he responded, "That fool was trippin'. He should've come correct. I was gonna pay him. You saw, I had the money in my hand. . . . That fool knows not to fuck with us anymore. . . . I did get taken in for that, but it don't matter. They gave me probation and shit. I'll just keep it cool now since that fool will keep it cool now too." In Mike's worldview, fighting for dignity at the cost of giving up his freedom had paid off. Though Mike's actions resulted in his commitment to the criminal justice system, he was very aware of this risk when he stole the bag of chips. He had grown frustrated at the treatment he had received at school, by police, and then at the store. This frustration, and a deep desire to feel respected, led Mike to willfully expose himself to incarceration. In the end, Mike lost his freedom, coming under the supervision of the criminal justice system. Nonetheless, Mike gained a sense of dignity for himself and his peers.

I also asked Mike, "Why didn't you steal something more expensive?" He told me that he thought about it, but, in the moment, he didn't care what he took. He wanted to prove a point to the clerk: "Not to fuck with me." It wasn't about saving a quarter, accumulating the most valuable commodity he could get his hands on, or stealing because he was poor and wanted to eat a bag of chips. Although he may have had a desire for any or all of the above, he stole the chips to redeem himself for being shamed and feeling disrespected. In the end, despite facing further punishment, Mike and his friends felt that their actions were not in vain; they had won a small battle in a war they were so tired of losing. Authority figures expected the boys to follow their rules, and the boys expressed a deep desire "to be left alone" and remain free; one of the only resources they had to feel respected

within the system was to actively engage in behaviors that defied the rules of the game. This, in turn, led to further misrecognition and criminalization.

DEFIANCE AS RESISTANCE

Defiance constituted a temporary success to the boys. Watching interactions between the boys and authority figures was often like watching a life-sized game of chess, with a rook strategically moving in response to a queen's movement. A police officer would get out of his car, the boys would posture, an officer would grab a young man, his friends would prepare to run; an officer would humiliate one of the boys, and the boy would respond by not cooperating or by cursing back. As one side moved to repress, the other moved to resist. The boys were almost always captured and eliminated from the chess board, but not before they had encroached on the opponent's territory, changing, if even subtly, the game.

Mike and Ronny were searching for something beyond immediate gratification. They did not want to follow the rules to gain social rewards like a good grade, a legitimate bag of chips, completing a probation program, or becoming a "normal" citizen. Instead, the boys chose a road that at first seemed futile and ignorant, a self-defeating path that led them into more trouble but eventually provided them with a sense of agency and dignity against criminalization.

In mocking the system, these young people gained a sense of empowerment. However, these same strategies added fuel to the criminalization fire. Many realized that they were actively stoking that fire, but they believed it was worth the negative consequences. Maintaining a sense of dignity—feeling accepted and respected—was a central struggle. The boys consciously chose to fight for their dignity, even if it meant risking their freedom.

CRIMES OF RESISTANCE

Many of the young men self-consciously "acted stupid" as a strategy to discredit the significance of a system which had excluded and punished them. These deviant politics garnered attention from the youth control complex, frustrating its agents: the police, school personnel, and others. This frustration led to more punishment, which led to a deeper crisis of control in the community. In the end, it was this crisis of control, when institutions were not able to provide a sufficient amount of social order, the young men consciously perceived to be a successful result of their defiance. As Flaco put it, "They trying to regulate me, right? So if they can't regulate me, then that means they not doing their job. So my job is to not—what's that word?—confirm [conform]."

The boys consistently chose to act "bad" in circumstances in which adults expected them to act "good." Almost all the acts that led to an arrest for violating probation were committed as conscious acts of resistance, in the boys' accounts, they knew they were facing severe consequences but decided to break the rules to make a point. This may have been their way of resisting what they perceived to be unfair treatment and punishment. These transgressions served as a resource for feeling empowered and for gaining redress for the humiliation, stigma, and punishment they encountered even when they were being "good." Because they reported that they committed their transgressions as a way of "getting back at the system," as Ronny explained, I am calling these acts *deviant politics*, by which I mean the political actions—the resistance—that youth labeled by society as "deviant" use to respond to punishment that they ubiquitously encounter.

Boys who resisted often suffered real and drastic consequences. Sometimes, they did not even realize that they were resisting. Often, they were simply, as they called it, "getting stupid," meaning that they acted "bad" for the sake of being "bad." These kinds of practices had few long-term positive outcomes for any of the boys in the study.

Breaking the rules meant resisting a system; criminality was one of the few resources the boys could use in response to criminalization.

In an environment in which there were few formal avenues for expressing dissent, which the boys believed to be extremely repressive, they developed forms of resistance they believed could change, even if only temporarily, the outcome of their treatment. The boys believed they had gained redress for the punitive social control they had encountered by adopting a subculture of resistance based on fooling the system. Their crimes of resistance, which made no sense to the system, were fully recognizable to those who had been misrecognized and criminalized.

PART VI

THE SOCIAL PRODUCTION OF REALITY

If [people] define situations as real, they are real in their consequences.

—W. I. Thomas and Dorothy Thomas (1928), *The Child in America*

[People] make their own history, but they do not make it just as they please; they do not make it under circumstances chosen by themselves, but under circumstances directly encountered, given and transmitted from the past. The tradition of all the dead generations weighs like a nightmare on the brain of the living.

—Karl Marx (1852/1963), *The 18th Brumaire of Louis Bonaparte*

BUILDING AND BREACHING REALITY

Jodi O'Brien

STORIES WE LIVE BY

Writer and philosopher Antonin Artaud once remarked that humans are beasts with stories on their backs. Interactional routines and the coherent realities through which these routines take on meaning can be analyzed as stories. We use these stories to organize and give meaning to our lives. Stories have an organizational logic to them. They are contextual realities that provide the scripts for defining the situation and the identities appropriate to the situation. One question you might ask is what the connection is between socialization and *performance scripts,* as described in Part III and Part V, and *stories* or *realities.* Think of scripts as possible lines of action that can take place in a particular type of story. Types of stories are referred to as *genres.* For instance, you are probably familiar with the differences between the horror genre and the romance genre. There are many different scripts that can be written within the horror genre, but you recognize each of them as a manifestation of the particular genre because it has familiar characters, plots, and story lines.

Similarly, social realities can be recognized in the ways in which people share expectations about the story line, the types of characters, and associated behaviors and feelings. These story lines, or realities, are often taken for granted until someone steps out of character or violates expected routines. These disruptions may cause us to stop and momentarily reflect on the expected story line. We then respond to the disruptions in ways that end up either changing the routine or reinforcing it.

One of the most common (but also most taken-for-granted) realities or stories in contemporary U.S. culture comes in the form of a romance genre. According to this story, our main life quest is to find our "true mate," form a union together, produce biological offspring, and live happily ever after. Even persons who have chosen not to pursue this quest are implicated in the story to the extent that they are constantly asked by others to justify or make sense of their nonparticipation. This story is so prevalent that we tend to think it is "natural" for all humans to want to do this, even though the emergence of heterosexual romantic love as a basis for family organization is a relatively recent historical development.

The prevalence of this marriage cultural reality, or story, is revealed in the fact that persons who are of marrying age but who are not married are expected to give accounts.

In other words, they are expected to provide an explanation for why they are not partici-pating in the cultural story as expected. Some accounts are more acceptable than others. Explaining that you have chosen to devote your life to becoming a celibate priest or nun is acceptable. Announcing that you are gay may not be entirely culturally desirable, but it makes sense in this particular context and is acceptable as an explanation. Although, with the legalization of same-gender marriage, even gay men and lesbians are expected to pur-sue marriage as the ultimate relationship goal. It is less acceptable, especially for women, to simply say, "Marriage doesn't interest me." Such a response is likely to raise suspicion among friends and family. "What is wrong with that girl?" they might wonder. They may even begin to speculate that "she is hiding something." Simply not wanting to participate is a behavior that disrupts the taken-for-granted expectation that "everyone wants to get married." Being a priest or being gay is an individual deviation from the expectation that *makes sense* and also reinforces the general expectation: "If he weren't a priest, he would probably be married." Conversely, having no interest at all in the cultural practice of mar-riage is a *breach* or disruption that leads people to press for more of an explanation, an explanation that makes sense within the existing story line that dictates that everyone must be interested in marriage.

When people feel compelled either to go along with a cultural practice or to provide a "reasonable" explanation for their deviation, the practice can be said to be *normative* or even *compulsory*. In contemporary U.S. culture, most socialized individuals feel com-pelled either to consider marriage or to provide themselves and others with an explana-tion for their nonparticipation. It's important to understand that both the act of marrying and the act of providing explanations are "performances" that highlight and reinforce the significance of marriage as a cultural practice.

Other "compulsory" practices include being employed. One of the most common ways that strangers in the United States begin conversations with one another about their own stories is through the question "What do you do?" Presumably, this is one of those questions that everyone understands. Even young children learn early how to respond to the question "What does your daddy or mommy do?" If you take the question "What do you do?" literally, you could have a lot of fun with people by responding in ways that do not assume the ques-tion is connected to employment: "I do yoga," "I do a lot of lunches," "I do my daily prayers," and so on. If you did this, chances are people would look at you as if you were a bit crazy.

Think of other cultural expectations that are taken for granted and considered "just something everyone knows." Consider the underlying cultural stories that hold these expectations together, for instance, the idea that self-worth is reflected in type of employ-ment. Recall the discussion of the *generalized other* in Part III. Cultural stories are reflected in the stories we tell ourselves about who and what we can and should be. Whenever you find yourself judging or assessing yourself in terms of a "should," you are in conversation with external expectations that you have internalized into your own self-story.

This section of the book explores the way in which people collectively participate in writing, rewriting, and performing various cultural routines or stories. If you view human behavior as a form of living through story, it may be easier to comprehend how and why people disregard or reinterpret contradictory evidence and behave in a way that results in self-fulfilling expectations. Cognitively, we tend to pay attention to things that resonate with the situational story that is unfolding in any given moment. Behaviors and experiences that disrupt the story line tend to be ignored or explained away. By acting as if nothing unusual is going on, we are able to maintain the impression that everything is going as expected. In this way, realities become self-sealing. Either we find some way to incorporate our experiences into mutually understood stories, or we disregard the experiences as much as possible. This amazing feat of collective reality making is described in detail in this essay.

MAKING SENSE

Humans are meaning makers. We make sense of our experiences by naming them. The way in which we define experiences and situations carries with it cues for how we should feel and behave. An aspect of meaning making that is important to the process of constructing realities is the way in which humans create *theories*. We don't just assign meaning to situations; the meaning holds an underlying logic and coherency, a working theory for what is going on. When things don't go as expected, we search our stockpile of working theories for the situation and make sense of things accordingly. For example, if you have a friend who is always late, then you probably have a working theory to apply when he doesn't show up to meet you at the movies as planned. "That's typical," you say to yourself, shrugging it off. And the situation is resolved. Your friend may call you later to apologize ("I'm so sorry; I got held up"). This apology reinforces the general working story (you did have a date, and that carries certain expectations) and makes sense of the disruption of the general working story. Imagine instead that you believed you had made appointments with several different people for various things, but none of them showed up. And no one called to apologize or explain. Later, you encounter one of these people, and the person acts as if nothing occurred, saying nothing about having stood you up. At this point, you would probably be confused and begin to wonder what was going on. You would think back and try to apply a working theory to make sense of this breach in expectations. It would probably continue to nag at you until you were able to make sense of the situation in a way that was consistent with your general expectations—people make appointments and follow through. Eventually, someone might explain to you that in this particular subculture, people say things all the time such as "let's do lunch," but never actually mean it. "Ah," you might say to yourself, "now I get it. People here are just rude." By deciding that people are "rude," you have reinforced your original cultural expectations and also found a way to make sense of the breach.

All human interaction is grounded in story lines for what is going on and underlying theories for making sense of things when they don't go as expected. These working theories are a central aspect of social realities. Even something as simple as "Hi, how's it going?" is an acknowledgment routine that reflects very specific cultural expectations and underlying theories. If you speak the greeting to someone and she doesn't respond, you have a working theory for why. The theory might include the possibilities "she didn't see me," "she's distracted," or perhaps even "she's annoyed with me." However, it's not likely that you would wonder if, perhaps today, you're invisible. This explanation is simply not part of your working theory.

An unquestioned assumption in the greeting ritual is that people can see one another. Similar to the assumption that people can see you if you're in their presence, there is an assumption that people can hear you. When someone doesn't respond immediately to a statement "obviously" directed at him, we file through several explanations, including "he's just being a jerk," before we hit on the possibility that "hey, maybe he can't hear me." Deaf people report that this is a common experience in encounters with hearing people. When people finally get the attention of a deaf person, they tend to be annoyed because it has taken awhile to realize what otherwise might seem obvious: This person can't hear me. Instead they've been operating with assumptions that include "the person is purposely ignoring me, is rude," and so on. Working theories, like other ways of making sense, are also a combination of individual experience and cultural information about how to make sense of those experiences. One of the features of socially constructed realities is that we have working theories that enable us to generate a vast number of explanations for situations that don't make sense, but even these theories are a product of social interaction.

Another feature of socially constructed realities is that they contain a great deal of information that "everyone just knows." However, taken literally, these *background expectations* may seem strange and contradictory when viewed out of context. In the acknowledgment routine described above, most people know that in response to this greeting, they are not supposed to actually go into detail about "how it's going." The actual words spoken are completely incongruent with the expected response. Someone who does answer elaborately might be considered a little "off." In contrast, many people who are new to U.S. culture find this greeting routine perplexing: Why would you ask someone how they are and then not stop to hear the answer?

COMMON SENSE AND BACKGROUND EXPECTATIONS

This basic "what everyone knows" knowledge of reality is called *common sense*. Common sense is a set of shared cultural rules or background expectations for making sense of the world. These rules are so well established and taken for granted that they often require no justification. To the question "How did you know that?" or "Why did you do that?" one can reply simply, "It's just common sense." These rules are the bedrock of cultural knowledge; they seem obviously true.

One of the most powerful ways of demonstrating that reality is a social construction is to show the limitations and arbitrariness of common sense, either by pointing out inconsistencies or by contrasting one culture's common sense to another's. One very popular counterculture book in the 1960s was written by two sociologists, Peter Berger and Thomas

Luckmann (1966). In this book, *The Social Construction of Reality,* Berger and Luckmann describe the ways in which people create organizing systems with the intent of making their lives orderly and predictable. Eventually, they forget they are the creators of these systems, and, thus reified, the systems take on a life of their own. What were once useful recipes for living become calcified into "commonsense" beliefs that "everyone knows."

There are several profound implications of commonsense or socially constructed realities. Self-fulfilling prophecies and the (re)creation of the cultural status quo are two that are worth extensive discussion. Before turning to those implications, let's look in detail at some of the ways in which people actively work together, usually unknowingly, to create and re-create the stories and theories that we use for making sense.

A Theory of Reality

Ethnomethodology is a research area in sociology that explores the folk methods (ethno methods) that people use to construct systems of meaning and reality. Ethnomethodologists make visible the often invisible or unseen features of reality construction. Hugh Mehan and Houston Wood are two such ethnomethodologists. They have assembled a framework for analyzing collective reality construction. As part of this framework, they have identified five features that underlie all cultural realities (Reading 36). These five key features of reality are reflexive, coherent, interactional, fragile, and permeable. You can read about each of the features in the reading, but let's look at a few examples here.

Reflexive

Realities are *reflexive.* This means that all realities contain self-sealing beliefs—unquestioned beliefs that cannot be proved wrong. For example, if you place your pencil on your desk while you go for a snack and cannot find the pencil when you return, you will assume that you somehow misplaced it. If it reappears where you left it, you will assume that you just overlooked it the first time. In many cultures, people hold an unquestioned belief regarding the immobility of inanimate objects, so it's unlikely that you would entertain the notion that your pencil left by itself and then returned. In other words, your working theory of reality does not include the possibility that inanimate objects move around on their own. This is just something everyone knows.

One of the interesting things about realities is that they often contain contradictions and inconsistencies. For instance, imagine a small child who fears monsters under her bed. Her parents might attempt to calm her by saying there are no such things as monsters, that they're not real. "But I can *see* them," she might insist. "I know they're real." Later, she may come down with the flu and ask what is making her so ill. "Germs," a parent might say. "Germs are little bugs that live inside you and make you sick, but you can't see them." How confusing is this information?! Tiny things that you can't see but that live in you and make you sick versus huge monsters you know you can see but apparently, or so you're told, are not real. All realities contain a series of working theories about how to deal with contradictory information.

These working theories are called *secondary elaborations*. In response to information that may appear to contradict a taken-for-granted assumption, we explain away the contradiction with a secondary elaboration: "That girl actually answered the 'How's it going?' question because she's so weird. Everyone knows that you don't really answer that question."

Consider this illustration: Do you watch the 5-day weather forecast? "How often do you watch it?", a newcomer to weather forecasting might ask. "Only once every 5 days?" Presumably, a 5-day forecast will give useful weather information for the next 5 days. Right? "No!" you exclaim. "You need to watch it every day." The newcomer looks at you, puzzled. "Because the forecast changes," you continue. Now the newcomer is really confused. Why watch a "forecast" if you already know it will not be accurate? You watch weather forecasts because you want to know what the weather will be, but you also recognize that the predictions are often inaccurate. So you watch the forecast again to see how it has changed. Does the frequent inaccuracy of the predictions make you doubt the reality that we can forecast the weather? No. Instead of questioning the validity of forecasting the weather, you probably explain away the inaccuracies as human error or the inadequacy of current meteorological technology. What you are not likely to do is question the taken-for-granted assumption that there is a pattern to nature and that, with the right theories and technology, we can know this pattern and make predictions based on it. In other words, you are not likely to assume that the weather is actually random. An unquestioned belief of modern Western thought is that there is order in nature. The cultural enterprise of predicting weather is based on this assumption.

In one famous (and also controversial) study, a psychiatrist, David Rosenhan (1973), conducted a casual but effective experiment intended to determine whether the sane can be reliably distinguished from the insane. His hypothesis was that psychiatric practitioners were so entrenched in their own system of diagnosing patients that they would assume *anyone* who came for treatment was insane. Rosenhan sent several students to psychiatric admitting rooms and instructed them to say they were hearing voices but otherwise to show no symptoms of abnormality. All of the student posers were evaluated and judged to be in need of psychiatric hospitalization. Rosenhan concluded that psychiatric staff operate in a context in which they *expect* patients to be insane, so they interpret the behavior of any person presumed to be a patient, even the behavior of "normal" researchers, as insane.

Unquestioned beliefs are often more easily noticed when examining a culture different from our own. In many cases, others' beliefs are described as superstitious or magical. However, Mehan and Wood demonstrate that any culture, including ours, is filled with unquestioned beliefs. When challenged with contradictions and inconsistencies, we reflexively "seal up" the contradiction with a secondary elaboration. This leads Mehan and Wood to conclude that all people are equally superstitious. People continue to hold certain unquestioned beliefs in the face of contradictory evidence.

Coherent

A second feature of realities is that they have an order and structure to them; realities are *coherent*. Even realities that seem nonsensical and anarchical to outsiders reveal their own order and logic when carefully examined. Coherency is an outcome of the apparent human need to make order out of chaos. If things are orderly, then they are predictable. If you actually had to contemplate and question everything in your environment anew every day, you'd never make it out of the house. One interesting aspect of human life is that we create systems of order and theories for making sense, and then forget how they originated and tend instead to believe that they reflect a general or real pattern.

Noncontingencies

Psychologists have conducted a series of intriguing studies called *noncontingency* experiments. *Noncontingent* means that there is no connection between an outcome and something else in the environment. For instance, you may have a headache right now, but you know it is not contingent on (not connected to) having stubbed your toe earlier. Humans create working theories by formulating connections between what they perceive to be the cause and effect. If I drink too much, I am likely to be hungover; feeling hungover is contingent on drinking too much. Getting into graduate school is contingent on getting good grades.

Noncontingency experiments reveal some very interesting things about the construction of coherency. One is that we form *superstitious* or *neurotic* theories. A horse that receives a mild electric shock in its foot at the same time that a bell is rung will continue to raise its foot every time the bell rings even after the shocks have ceased. The horse associates the shock (and corresponding urge to lift its foot) with the bell, even though the shock is not connected to the bell. Similarly, humans who experience a strong emotion, such as shock or fear due to a particular event, may continue to experience that emotion in similar situations, even if the threat is no longer present. For example, someone who has been traumatized by a dog bite may panic in the presence of all dogs. This associative-emotive pattern is sometimes referred to as a *phobia*.

There is an experiment in which a group of students was asked to develop a system for identifying "sick" versus "healthy" cells. It turns out that this is not a very difficult task if you already know the theory. However, if you don't have a working theory, you have to rely on trial and error. Students were shown pictures and with each picture they were asked to push a button indicating sick or healthy. Lights on their panels then lit up indicating either a wrong choice or a right choice. Based on this information, the students studied the pictures, trying to come up with a working hypothesis (for example, on the sick cells, "the nucleus looks broken"). When another picture was flashed, they could try out their hypothesis. The indicator lights letting them know their guesses were right or wrong provided the feedback they needed to revise and refine their working theories. Given correct feedback, cell identification turned out to be a simple task for most students. All of these students emerged from the task with a theory, and their theories were very similar. They'd created a coherent way of cataloging the cells based on trial and error and feedback.

The interesting finding concerned another group that was participating in the same experiment, with one small difference—they were being given random feedback. In other words, their "right" and "wrong" buttons had no connection to their guesses. They, too, were trying to develop a theory of cell identification based on trial and error and feedback, but in this case the feedback was not contingent on their guesses. Were they able to devise a theory? Yes! Not only did they develop theories, but the theories were very elaborate and complex. In an insightful conclusion, the researchers invited the student groups to talk with each other about their theories. The contingency group had very simple theories (based on the fact that they had received correct feedback), and when they questioned the noncontingency group about their more complicated theories, these students provided responses that were so compelling that the former group began to doubt their own theories and wonder if they were "missing something."

This experiment, and others like it, reveals several fascinating features of reality construction. Most significantly, we are able and inclined to create coherent theories out of even *random* information. It never occurred to the noncontingency group that there was no connection between their answers and the random "feedback" they received. Further, when they were informed of this later, several of them insisted that, regardless of the randomness, their theories reflected correct assessments.

As you ponder this material, consider some of the ways in which you get the feedback that enables you to create coherent theories in your own life. It's a useful "reality check" to examine your sources of information, especially whether these are connected to outcomes in the ways that you believe them to be.

"It Makes Sense to Us!"

In discussing coherency, Mehan and Wood are particularly interested in the ways in which realities that may seem preposterous to outsiders are quite ordinary and plausible to insiders. Regardless of the ways in which a system of belief and expectations arose (that is, in spite of the noncontingencies and inconsistencies), it appears coherent to those who share the system of understanding. Persons of different religious or political persuasions often try to "poke holes" in one another's beliefs by pointing out what seem to be "obvious" contradictions. From an ethnomethodological perspective this is a fruitless exercise and serves only to demonstrate the extent to which all belief systems have a coherency that includes secondary elaborations, or ways for explaining away inconsistencies. When the feature of *reflexivity* is added to *coherency,* we begin to see just how firmly entrenched belief systems can be. Challenges in the form of contradictions may actually serve to strengthen the original belief, especially as a person articulates the secondary elaborations that extend the coherency to cover all possible disruptions.

Interactional and Fragile

The process of creating and maintaining realities is ongoing and *interactional.* As noted in the example about greetings, we work together to create even the simplest realities such as the belief that we are seen by others as distinct and notable subjects. Because realities are based on ongoing interactions, they are at risk of performance breakdowns (recall the discussion in Part V). In this way, realities are *fragile*. We rely on one another to perform the expected roles and routines that make up significant cultural stories. One of the reasons that grand ceremonies, such as weddings, are a source of so much stress is because the participants are dependent on the actions of others for the event to go off well. This is why there are rehearsals for important events. We recognize that these ceremonies require us to perform roles that are highly significant, but for which people don't have much first-hand experience.

Cultural realities actually break down much more than people acknowledge. In our day-to-day lives, we encounter numerous disruptions that can bring smooth interactions to an embarrassed halt. The reflexive and coherent features of reality are reflected in the ways in which people work together to repair these disruptions. *Tact* is one interactional strategy for repairing disrupted routines. Accounts are another. As was discussed in Part V, these strategies reflect a consensus about what the expected routine should be and a willingness to help restore it to a working definition. When disruptions in the expected routine occur, people often have no idea what to do next. They simply don't have a script for the situation. Such situations occur more frequently than we tend to realize. However, we're inclined to overlook the fragility of reality maintenance, in part because we have strategies for continuing on as if nothing unusual is happening.

Breaching

Imagine you attend a dinner party given by a friend, and you invite your girlfriend, who has never met the friend, to join you. Upon your arrival, your host takes your coats and says pleasantly, "Make yourself at home." Your girlfriend replies, "Thank you, I will," and proceeds to take off her shoes and socks, turn on the television, and put her feet on the coffee table. Your friend is likely to look at you for an explanation of this seemingly bizarre behavior. You can only shrug and look on in dismay. Your shrug and look of dismay are cues to your friend that you share his view of reality. The girlfriend is behaving strangely and has violated the expected interaction rules for polite company behavior. Imagine further that you approach your girlfriend and ask what's going on. She replies, "He said I could make myself at home." In response to this, you try to explain that he didn't really mean for her to act like she was in her own home. She gives you a wilting look that suggests you're the crazy one and turns up the television.

In an article titled "A Conception of and Experiments With 'Trust' as a Condition of Concerted Stable Actions" (Reading 37), one of the founders of ethnomethodology, Harold Garfinkel, describes social *breaching experiments*. Garfinkel achieved great fame and notoriety with the breaching experiments he and his students conducted at the University of California, Los Angeles (UCLA) in the 1960s. Breaching involves making the underlying structure of reality explicit by acting in a manner that is inconsistent with the taken-for-granted rules of interaction that maintain the reality. When reality is breached, interaction often comes to a confused halt. Garfinkel describes a variety of breaching experiments as well as people's reactions to these experiments. According to him, we enter into interactional moments trusting that others share our expectations and definitions of reality. It is this trust that enables us to engage in stable, coherent, and meaningful interactions.

The situation described above is a breach. In this case, the woman has breached the expectation that certain phrases are intended as polite and are not meant literally. The host trusts his guests to know the appropriate visitor behavior. Otherwise, he would not have made a statement such as "Make yourself at home." This example is based on an actual breach conducted by one of my students. She had put off doing the assignment until the last minute and didn't know what to do. As she explained later in her written paper, when the host said, "Make yourself at home," she recalled reading in Garfinkel about taking statements literally and decided to give it a try. She actually went so far the evening of the party as to take a shower at her host's home.

Breaches reveal just how fragile and interactional (and meaningful) cultural realities are. Confronted with a breach, observers usually try first to ignore it (the *nothing unusual* bias). We do this whenever we walk away from people on the street who strike us as "off." If it is not possible to ignore the breach, such as someone in an elevator asking you to examine the cut on her arm (another breach carried out by one of my students), people look to others to reaffirm that the breacher is "weird." This usually takes the form of strangers looking at one another, smiling knowingly, and perhaps rolling their eyes. This subtle communication is an effective interactional strategy for signaling that "normal people know the routine, and this person is not normal." Another strategy when confronted with a breach that cannot easily be ignored is to treat it as a joke. If the other person (the breacher) also laughs, then the expected reality is quickly restored, and all participants can sigh in the relief of knowing that they all share the same expectations of the situation.

In the breaching experiments designed by Garfinkel, students conducting breaches were instructed not to let the person repair the breach by treating it as a joke or something that could be ignored. When people do not find interactional support for repairing the situation, they tend to become agitated, in some cases even angry. They look for information that will help them make sense of the situation in ways that are consistent with their working definition of it. If they cannot do so, they become flustered and confused. The boyfriend of the woman who "made herself at home" was furious with her for days afterward. From his perspective, she had violated his trust by not behaving as expected and by making him look bad in front of his friends. This response, which is very understandable, illustrates just how much we depend on others to maintain basic definitions of reality, such as "this is just a nice, friendly party." Her behavior resulted in a cascade of consequences that toppled several aspects of the taken-for-granted reality of the occasion and who these friends were to one another.

In another example, students devised a breach in which they "shopped" from others' carts in a grocery store. The taken-for-granted routine is that once you have placed an item in your cart, it belongs to you. The students who performed this breach matter-of-factly took items from the carts of others. When questioned, they responded simply that the item in the cart had been more convenient to reach than the one on the shelf. When assumptions are breached, people look for a reasonable explanation—something that reaffirms the underlying assumptions. "Oh, I'm sorry, I thought that was my cart" is an example of a reasonable explanation for taking something from someone else's cart. But to act as if there is nothing wrong with doing so confuses other shoppers and causes them to question, just for a moment, the reality of the situation.

In another breaching experiment, a student cheerfully asked a McDonald's clerk for a Whopper, a menu item at rival Burger King. Rather than saying, "We don't carry that," the McDonald's clerk asked the student to repeat the order. When the request for a Whopper was repeated, the clerk looked around to see if fellow employees had heard this "bizarre" request. In other words, he searched for interactional corroboration of his reality that "everyone knows" the McDonald's menu, and anyone who doesn't is obviously weird. Something as simple as a sideways glance and raised eyebrows from a coworker can indicate that one's reality is intact and that the momentary experience is merely an aberration that can be ignored. In this case, however, the students were particularly tenacious in testing reactions to breaching. After the first person breached the fast-food-order routine, another classmate stepped up and ordered a slice of pizza, which, of course, McDonald's restaurants don't serve.

Permeable

The fifth feature described by Mehan and Wood is that realities are *permeable*. We are constantly moving between different realities. In doing so, we alter our attitudes and behavior to bring them into line with the expectations of the reality of the moment. People who participate in nudist communities, for example, successfully maintain the reality while on their holidays that nudity is healthy and a source of family fun that is not associated with sexuality. They then return easily to work life, where it is commonly known that public nudity is not acceptable.

If the conditions are right, one can even move into a radically different reality. For example, soldiers move between a reality in which they are trained to kill other humans and another in which killing is defined as murder. The permeability of realities implies that we carry a variety of scripts for various routines, including routines that may seem contradictory, as well as rules and beliefs for bridging the gaps between the realities. In order to make a successful transition between the reality systems of war and civil society, soldiers have to learn and accept a cultural story that designates some people as "the enemy" and others as "those who need protection." One (among many) of the tragedies of war is the fragility of this particular system of belief. Hospitals and social service agencies are filled with men and women who find it difficult to maintain such distinct realities. Their psyches and spirits have broken down as a consequence. Soldiers who fought in Vietnam returned to a civil society that did not necessarily share the reality of the "enemy" these soldiers had been trained to fight and kill. One way to look at the post-Vietnam experience for veterans is to consider that they did not receive interactional support from the society they thought they had been protecting. This lack of support made it difficult for many of these veterans to maintain the belief that the killing they had done in one reality was indeed honorable.

CAVEAT REGARDING BREACHING EXPERIMENTS

Occasionally, students using previous editions of this text have raised the concern that breaching experiments are a violation of social trust. This concern indicates an excellent insight regarding the theories of Goffman (1959; discussed in Part V) and Garfinkel. Both note that social order is based on trust and that it occurs in the form of expected interaction routines. We *trust* one another to know the routines and to follow them through. In this way, we are able to carry on interactions with one another without the fear of being hurt or violated. I cannot speak directly for Goffman or Garfinkel, but the following is my own response to students and instructors who have concerns about breaching experiments.

Recall that one of the lessons in Part II is the extent to which we all participate in acts of categorization (stereotyping) that we may not be aware of. Much of our behavior is *mindless*. Similarly, many of our interaction routines are mindless and taken for granted. I would never advocate the senseless disruption of another person's routine or status quo just for the sake of doing it. However, breaching experiments, handled with care and sensitivity, can be a way to raise consciousness and to invite others to think critically about their own participation in mindless routines. It's important to note that there are many forms of breaching, and you do not have to involve someone else directly if this feels wrong or uncomfortable. Just thinking up the experiments can be a great exercise in mindfulness. If you do decide to implicate others, consider situations in which the others are also likely to be able to learn something useful from the encounter. Breaching is not the equivalent of being mean or cruel. Most of the students in my classes who experiment with breaching discover that once people settle down and recover from the breach, they are often eager to discuss and learn from the experiment.

The important feature is that persons performing these experiments take the time to debrief their subjects and to engage with them in a discussion of what occurred. This can be an opportunity to practice *interpersonal ethics*—that is, to use the situation to gain greater understanding among all parties involved. Remember, the point is to define and make explicit routines that reflect taken-for-granted assumptions about reality—not to hurt someone or make them needlessly uncomfortable. The best breaching experiments are those in which the person doing them is able to recognize her or his own participation in a taken-for-granted status quo.

BELIEVING MAKES IT SO: SELF-FULFILLING PROPHECIES

Imagine an elementary school teacher who is told by school personnel that one group of children in his classroom are "gifted" and likely to be high achievers. Imagine another classroom where a teacher is told that some of her students have tested as "underachievers." An experiment similar to this scenario was conducted in the 1970s by Robert Rosenthal

and Lenore Jacobson (1974). Rosenthal and Jacobson wanted to study the effects of preconceived beliefs about intelligence on the performance of schoolchildren. The study took
place in an elementary school. The teachers in Grades 1–6 were led to believe that a previously administered aptitude test indicated that some of the students in each class were
likely to show significant academic improvement over the course of the year. In fact, the
researchers had simply identified "gifted" students randomly. However, by the end of the
year, students who were seen as gifted and expected by their teachers to improve significantly had indeed improved (as measured by a standard IQ test). Rosenthal and Jacobson's
study became famous and is known as the "Pygmalion in the Classroom" study.

Several aspects of the study are noteworthy, and the findings have been supported by
many related studies done by other researchers. However, in recent years, this form of
research has been criticized, both because of the use of standard IQ tests to measure student improvement and especially because of the ethical implications of labeling the students as "overachievers" or "underachievers." Paradoxically, without the research
documenting the effects of labeling and self-fulfilling prophecies, the current ethical
concerns wouldn't have been noted. Without this research, which today we do consider
unethical, we wouldn't be aware of the potentially damaging effects of labeling expectations held by people in positions of authority.

Rosenthal and Jacobson hypothesized that student performance was shaped, in part, by
the way the teachers *treated* students. Subsequent studies of teacher behavior in the classroom indicate that teachers respond differently to students they perceive to be especially
bright. They take more time with these students, encourage them to work on more complicated problems, and invite them to participate and share more with other students. In
contrast, teachers are likely to "give up" quickly on students whom they perceive to be
underachievers. Obviously, the beliefs and actions of elementary school teachers are not
the only factors that influence student performance, but the research of Rosenthal and
Jacobson highlights one important element that has been repeatedly shown to be significant in influencing performance: the power of beliefs to shape behavior.

A *self-fulfilling prophecy* is an event that becomes true because we act in a way that
brings about our initial expectations. In this case, if teachers perceive a child to be especially bright, the belief may set in motion a related set of actions that serves to make the
expectation true. The teacher may treat the child differently, which may give the child more
chances to develop academic skills. The child, upon recognizing that she is being treated as
if she were very bright, may adjust her behavior to try to live up to that expectation. She
may begin doing more homework, asking more questions, and generally behaving as if she
were gifted. These actions are likely to result in increased performance over time.

Self-Fulfilling Prophecies and Interactional Expectations

Children (as well as adults) who are exposed to high-performance expectations and
repeatedly told that they are capable of meeting these expectations as well as being given
the means to do so are likely to meet the expectations. This is similar to the process of
possible selves discussed in an essay in Part IV. As described in the work of Nurius and

Markus (1986), *possible selves* involves the internal practice of envisioning a particular outcome and then engaging in the behavior that brings about the envisioned outcome. When others express expectations for us, and especially when they model those expectations through emotional and behavioral cues, our internal or *possible self* process is triggered, and the result is likely to be self-fulfilling.

Conversely, people can become stuck in mental loops of despair in which they conjure conversations and experiences that trigger a chain of negative expectations and the assumption that things are likely to turn out badly. Psychologist Paul Watzlawick (1984) tells us that this kind of negative-expectation thinking can also result in self-fulfilling outcomes (Reading 38). He uses the example of a couple in which the husband believes that his wife nags and the wife believes that her husband is withdrawn. These beliefs lead each to imagine that the other is going to behave as expected (nag/withdraw). When they encounter one another, each sees what he or she expects to see and is therefore poised to react in such a way that the expectations are made real. For instance, the husband, anticipating that his wife is going to nag him, comes home grumpy and withdrawn. This reinforces her perception ("He's withdrawn"), and she picks up with her nagging. It's an ongoing cycle that is difficult to break because each person perceives the other in terms of preconceived expectations. The expectations are *confirmed* by the other person's reactions, and thus each person feels justified in her or his initial impressions of the other. "She *really is* a nag." "He *really is* withdrawn." Both are quick to see and feel confirmed by the behavior of the other, but neither sees how her or his initial expectations may have actually triggered that behavior.

Self-fulfilling prophecies illustrate a key point made throughout this book: Often, what is important is not what is factually correct, but rather what is defined as real. People's actions are based on their *definitions* of what is real. That is, we respond not to the direct event but to our interpretation of it. This is especially true in interactional dynamics; people behave in ways that correspond to our expectations of them. As one old adage says, treat people like kings and they will behave like kings; treat them like rogues and they will behave like rogues.

Although the saying may seem simple, the process is a bit more complicated and involves threading together the lessons learned from previous sections. In Part II, the power of language is emphasized, expressed in the form of concepts and categories that trigger feelings, expectations, and scripts for action. These categories and scripts are especially significant when we internalize them as self-concepts and guide and judge our behavior accordingly. When you put it all together, you see that your own or others' beliefs function as expectations that trigger categorical—often mindless—responses. In turn, these responses reinforce the original categorical ideas or beliefs. Recall Reading 20 (Part IV), "A Theory of Genius," in which the author points out that children pick up on our expectations for them in the form of *reflected appraisals*. These appraisals convey beliefs or expectations about the children's ability to learn. For instance, we expect children to be able to learn to talk, even though this is actually a profoundly complicated task. Rather than shame a child when she makes a mistake, we praise her as if she were a genius and, accordingly, she masters the difficult task of language acquisition. Unfortunately, we're often not as patient or hopeful in our expectations for the acquisition of other skills such as learning a musical instrument or a sport. As a result, the child may pick up on this expectation of failure, experience shame, and give up, thus making the initial expectation self-fulfilling.

An important message in Watzlawick's article is that, by becoming aware of self-fulfilling prophecies, we will be better able to recognize and resist potentially damaging outcomes brought about by our own beliefs (and subsequent behavior in line with these beliefs). For instance, imagine what might happen in the earlier example of husband and wife if one or the other were to intervene in her or his own preconceived expectations and think something radically different, such as "My partner is so loving and supportive." How might these altered expectations result in a different reflected appraisal. If you look into the "looking glass" of another and expect to see love and support instead of nagging and resentment, what do you suppose might happen over time?

Self-Fulfilling Expectations and Stereotypes

Socially held beliefs about the characteristics of groups of people—in other words, stereotypes—often result in self-fulfilling outcomes. Another psychologist, Mark Snyder, studies the relationship between stereotypes and attraction. Snyder has conducted experiments that demonstrate that the stereotypes about attractive versus unattractive people can be self-fulfilling. In one such study, participants speak on the phone with someone they perceive to be either "traditionally attractive" or "unattractive" based on pictures they've been shown. When speaking with a presumably attractive individual, participants tend to be more upbeat and friendly. This behavior induces similar responses in the person on the phone such that they are likely to be very friendly and outgoing. Participants usually conclude that the attractive people are also more friendly. Snyder points out that this stereotypical belief may be self-fulfilling, because we are likely to treat attractive people as if they are friendly and outgoing and we give them more opportunity to act this way. In so doing, we elicit a friendly response.

Several scholars have applied this line of reasoning to the study of stereotyping and prejudice in employment settings. Despite civil and legal advancements in support of equal opportunity in employment, hiring patterns suggest that racial minorities are not hired at rates commensurate with their levels of education and expertise. One observed pattern is *homophily*—birds of a feather flock together; employers prefer to hire people most like themselves, people they feel a connection with. This social connectivity often falls along economic, gender, and racial lines. Conversely, even when they do not consider themselves to be prejudiced, White employers are typically ill at ease in the presence of racial minorities, particularly Black applicants. The probable effects of self-fulfilling prejudice are very difficult to isolate in interactional settings, but scholars agree, for the most part, that these behaviors are present and have significant impact on employment interactions such as hiring interviews. In a carefully devised experiment to capture these effects, psychologist Carol Word and her colleagues examined the nonverbal behavior of employers in job interviews (Reading 39). They tracked small but important cues such as leaning in toward the candidate, nodding or smiling in affirmation of comments, and so forth. Their hypothesis was that these subtle behaviors convey comfort and confidence in the candidate and, in turn, induce the candidate to behave in ways that demonstrate comfort and confidence—in other words, they perform better in the interview when they are expected to perform better. Ward found notable differences between the ways hiring managers behaved with Black and White candidates. They were much more friendly and solicitous of the White candidates, who were then perceived to be performing more competently in the interview. In short, the unconscious prejudicial expectations that Whites will perform better were fulfilled in the interaction as a result of the hiring managers' own behavior toward the candidates.

Together, the features of reality yield a theory explaining why people pursue certain lines of action without noticing alternatives (reflexivity) and how these routines eventually take on the status of cultural stories or belief systems that are assumed to be natural and real. Through ongoing interaction, we reinforce these belief systems and bring about preconceived outcomes by acting on our preconceived beliefs. Stereotypes are especially powerful in this process. Even disruptions and deviations reinforce the original belief or stereotype to the extent that we use secondary elaborations and behaviors to repair the breach and explain away inconsistencies. This theory is a powerful tool for understanding the maintenance of the status quo as a product of everyday beliefs and interaction. It provides an explanation for the persistence of social patterns and the behaviors that sustain those patterns, even among people who may think they are opposed to the status quo.

THE SOCIAL CONSTRUCTION OF THE STATUS QUO

Some cultural stories and routines are better established than others—that is, a large percentage of the population is likely to take them for granted and consider them as a source of authority for organizing social life. Well-established cultural practices that have widely recognized authority can be called *cultural institutions*. These institutions and practices constitute a cultural status quo. How are these institutional beliefs and practices enacted and maintained over time? This is the question we look at in this section. The theory of reality as a social construction can be used to address this question. What alternatives might exist and how might the situation be defined and approached differently if others were in charge of the cultural definition of the situation?

One of the most well-established and least questioned institutions in this country is the medical profession. Medicine is one of the relatively undisputed sources of authority regarding what constitutes "acceptable" behavior. Those who exhibit unusual or inappropriate behaviors are often referred for medical treatment. Both the determined cause and treatment of these behaviors are part of the body of organized knowledge that constitutes medicine. One feature of this form of knowledge is that certain types of actions and feelings are considered "natural." Deviations from the natural patterns are considered "pathological."

Medicalization

Sociologists Peter Conrad and Joseph Schneider (1992) have written extensively about the medicalization of behavior. They use the term *medicalization* to refer to behavior that has been defined as a medical problem or illness and, as such, mandates the medical profession to provide some type of treatment for it. Our culture has a pervasive tendency to define everything from depression to alcoholism as a physiological disease. One behavior Conrad and Schneider examined closely is *hyperkinesis*, or hyperactivity. In this study, they explored the emergence of a medical name (hyperkinesis) for hyperactivity in children—behavior that is considered distracting and "out of control" in everyday interactions. Hyperkinesis is particularly interesting because it exhibits none of the usual physiological correlates of disease (for example, fever, bacteria, viruses, changes in blood chemistry), and the symptomatic behaviors—rebelliousness, frustration, excitability—seem to have as much to do with social protest as with organic disease. Conrad and Schneider's thesis is that the increasingly high rates of diagnosed cases of hyperkinesis may indicate a social problem rather than individual behavioral disorders. This is a very controversial statement, but it's worth considering the point that parents and educators tend to look first at the child who appears to be disrupting the classroom status quo, rather than examining the underlying patterns of contemporary education. Such an examination might reveal factors such as extreme boredom, behavioral expectations that are not conducive to learning in small children, and so forth. Culturally, however, we tend to assume the infallibility of medicine and its ability to make the symptoms disappear, rather than examine underlying social patterns.

Conrad and Schneider (1992) also have written extensively on the medicalization of deviant behaviors. For example, all cultures have people who are perceived to be "mad"—that is, people who violate behavioral boundaries that are maintained by the majority. Beliefs about what these people should be called, who should deal with them, and how they should be handled differ remarkably, however. Certain cultures see their "mad" as divinely inspired. In these cultures, madness is attributed to spiritual possession rather than natural pathology. For example, in ancient Hebrew, the term for *madness* is defined variously as "to rave," "to act beside oneself," and "to behave like a prophet." "Mad" people were considered to be so filled with spirits that they could not harness themselves to the chains of worldly conduct. Prophets and the mad were both "raving lunatics" who were thought to be outside society. In terms of "madness," think about what social definitions distinguished one from the other.

One social-psychological alternative to the medical model of madness and other forms of asocial conduct is based on the theory that those people who are unusually bright and creative experience an overload of contradictions when they try to meet standard expectations for behavior. These people are thought to be responding to a very complex and contradictory set of *generalized others*, reacting rapidly to strong creative passions and urges. This complex creativity manifests as a resistance to socialization. Further, those who have the necessary interpersonal skills and material resources may avoid medical labeling and may become significant contributors in areas such as the arts. Because of their contributions, their "inappropriate" behavior is sometimes labeled "eccentric" rather than "mentally ill."

If you are interested in exploring this topic more, you might begin with some of the writings of one of the framers of this alternative perspective, Thomas Szasz. In a 1971 article, Szasz describes an extreme, even horrific, example of the medicalization of a "deviant" behavior. This historical case, reported in a prestigious medical journal in 1851, concerned a disease manifest among slaves. The primary symptom of the ominous-sounding disorder called *drapetomania* was running away from plantations!

Despite the increasing cultural awareness of the limitations and misapplications of the medical model of deviance, many medical practitioners continue to treat "conditions" such as transgender experience, same-gender sexual attraction, and "female emotion" as symptoms of pathology. There are still respected scientists who use the medical model to claim that certain people may be more inclined to "social pathology" than others based on racial ethnicity. Medicine is a powerful and influential cultural institution that has done much to improve our quality of life, but it also warrants careful scrutiny. Be aware of its limitations and untold stories.

We often think of science as neutral, but scientific inquiry is also based on preconceived notions or assumptions. These assumptions are sometimes called "pre-theories" and are rarely questioned. When they are questioned, it often leads to major scientific shifts. Think back on the nature/nurture essay at the beginning of the book (Part I). The slash indicates a supposed split or dichotomy between nature and nurture. For many decades the question has been nature *or* nurture and, depending on what field scientists were in, they were likely to be trained to see human behavior in terms of one or the other. In 2010, philosopher of science Evelyn Fox Keller published a book called *The Mirage of Space Between Nature and Nurture*. In this book she examines the history of how nature and nurture became opposites. This oppositional characterization is a cultural story and not a reflection of how bodies, brains, and behavior actually work. Scientists are now taking up the idea of the interconnectedness between nature and nurture. Fields such as "epigenetics" focus on the myriad external factors to DNA that turn genes "on" and "off." Most biologists would now say that nature provides a particular DNA sequence, but how it gets "read" by the body and is related to subsequent behavior depends on environmental factors that can range from what your grandmother ate before you were born to your immediate sociocultural environment. This view has shifted scientific inquiry and resulted in new models, especially regarding questions such as gender expression and sexual orientation, both of which are regarded as distinctly human constructs. For instance, in the 20th century the dominant model of sex differentiation in the brain was that genetic sex (XX or XY) caused differentiation in the gonads, which then secreted hormones that result in sex differences. This linear model reflected the pre-theory that there are only two sexes. But as this assumption has come to be questioned by taking into consideration contradictory evidence, the science has shifted. Twenty-first century biology makes a distinction between gonadal and non-gonadal sex differences (i.e., genetic and epigenetic), which results in at least four theoretical sex types. In other words, all cultural truths, even those grounded in the supposed rigor of science, are based on unexamined beliefs that reflect a particular status quo.

The media is another influential social institution with tremendous power to define situations in ways that either question or reinforce taken-for-granted cultural stories. Sociologist David Altheide investigates the ways in which media coverage of the Iraq War constructs a particular reality about "terror" and the "enemy." Similar to the work of Conrad and Schneider, Altheide demonstrates the power of a cultural institution, in this case the news media, to define right and wrong, good and evil, and so forth, and to tell a particular story about war in a way that reinforces socially constructed theories about U.S. "goodness." As people begin to take this cultural reality for granted, they find it easier to explain away the consequences of war, such as "collateral damage" and the proliferation of increased surveillance of ordinary citizens. Government activities that, in another context, would seem atrocious and unacceptable begin to seem reasonable when considered in the context of a media-constructed "culture of terrorism."

Science, medicine, and the media are useful areas for investigating cultural stories that shape the everyday status quo in ways that we often take for granted, even though these realities have a significant impact on our lives. Additional institutional sources of cultural realities include religion, education, and law. Each of these areas can be fruitfully analyzed using the tools from this section to reveal underlying cultural ideals and practices that have a powerful influence on what we think is real and right and good. One example of the interplay between cultural knowledge systems, social institutions, and individual lives is sociologist Victor Ray's study of veterans suffering from posttraumatic stress as a result of their war experiences. In "Coming Home to Friendly Fire" (Reading 40), Ray notes that, although there is general social sympathy toward the suffering of veterans, few seek the medical and therapeutic services available to them. Ray is curious about why this is and discovers that the prevailing norms of masculinity and war dissuade men from seeking help. His examination reveals that the "organizational culture of the military systematically inhibits veterans from seeking treatment." One of the guiding organizational principles of the military is *force readiness*. Soldiers must be combat-ready at all times—this is what makes them soldiers. This grounding assumption is at odds with trauma. In combination with larger cultural expectations of masculinity, the additional expectations of the soldier include an ability to just "shake off" the horrors of combat. Mental health professionals are increasingly aware of the long-term debilitating effects of war and have advocated for improved services for veterans. But these efforts are trumped by the more closely experienced expectations of military culture in which fellow soldiers and commanding officers treat veterans as "weaklings" and "troublemakers" if they pursue the mental health services available to them.

The Maintenance of Social Hierarchies

One aspect of the cultural status quo that deserves special attention is the maintenance of social hierarchies, or differences and inequalities. *Differences and inequalities* are a prevailing feature of most cultures, but the basis on which they are constructed differs from culture to culture. For instance, in some societies, religious tradition is the basis for extreme prejudice or privilege, whereas in the United States, social class, gender, race/ethnicity, age, and sexual orientation tend to be bases of prejudicial difference and inequality. The social sciences are filled with theories that attempt to explain the dynamics of prejudice. As you will see, the material in this book provides an especially useful set of tools for making sense of how we categorize people and then, through the processes of social construction discussed in this section, reinforce and maintain these patterns of discrimination—even when we may not intend to. Let's take socioeconomic class as an example.

Social class is a powerful influence in U.S. culture, but part of the script or routine connected to social class is the expectation that we should pretend it doesn't matter. This makes it particularly difficult to disrupt the underlying patterns of discrimination. Candace Perin (1988) is an anthropologist who did her dissertation field research in the suburbs of Minneapolis. Instead of going to a foreign country, she decided that the suburbs were rich with cultural practices worth studying from an anthropological perspective. Her book on the subject, *Belonging in America,* is an insightful examination of the day-to-day routines of suburbanites who attempt to maintain an image of middle-class wealth, prosperity, and the impression that "everything is always fine." One central suburban expectation is that it is "impolite" to directly confront neighbors about infractions and trespasses. As Perin points out, crabgrass does not respect property boundaries; if your neighbor does not maintain a crabgrass-free lawn, it's likely that some of the stuff will creep onto yours. Neighbors engage in all kinds of roundabout ways of trying to address these infractions without actually confronting the neighbor directly. Larger infractions— garbage cans left at the curb too long, rusty cars left sitting around for a period of time— are reported to the police. Perin noted that the majority of the calls received by police in the greater Minneapolis region during her months of fieldwork were from anonymous suburban callers "tattling" on their neighbors. Perin concludes that the interaction routines in the suburbs preserve the impression that all is rosy and well and conflict free. Meanwhile, suburbanites use many "backdoor" strategies to resolve conflict. This perpetuates an image of the suburbs as safe and problem free and may also explain some of the differences in urban versus suburban tolerance for conflict in group interaction (suburbanites are typically seen as conflict-avoidant).

One additional example illustrates the perpetuation of middle-class norms in mixed-class settings. Most people are aware of middle-class expectations, regardless of their own economic background. Students and faculty from working-class backgrounds can tell many stories about situations in which they have felt out of place with other students and faculty from middle-class backgrounds. Colleagues may suggest social gatherings that are beyond the price range of some of the members of the group, or they may engage in a lot of social conversation about the price of real estate in the area, their mortgages, and other class-related issues such as fancy vacation destinations and restaurants. What's interesting is that in such instances, people from working-class backgrounds rarely say anything that might indicate that they are unfamiliar or uncomfortable with the discussion. There is a tacit agreement to let the conversation continue on its own terms. Once in a while, someone may say, "I wouldn't know about that, I've never been able to afford to eat in such places." This usually brings the conversation to an awkward halt, leaving the speaker feeling as if he or she sticks out. Those whose taken-for-granted class reality has just been disrupted may, in theory, be aware of the class differences—some of us even teach this material—but in the interactional moment may just feel resentful about the awkwardness. The class norm "nice people don't talk about money" operates to maintain a cultural status quo in which profound class differences are never brought to the social stage.

Another reading in this section looks at the socially constructed process of inequality in detail. In Reading 41, sociologist Cecilia Ridgeway describes a theory that she has developed to explain the perpetuation of gender inequality in employment. Despite many formal legal changes in the past three decades that have made it unlawful to discriminate against women in employment, women still lag significantly behind men in promotions and raises. Ridgeway explains this lag as a manifestation of a particular status quo in which both men and women *perceive* women as being less competent than men in certain employment situations. According to prevailing cultural scripts and stereotypes, women just aren't as effective as men. This perception results in management decisions that may make the expectation self-fulfilling. This interactional explanation is an important contribution to understanding how gender inequality is perpetuated even when people intend to be fair.

Contradictions, Conflict, and Change

> *These conflicts which break forth are not between the ideal and reality, but between two different ideals, that of yesterday and that of today, that which has the authority of tradition and that which has the hope of the future.*
>
> —Émile Durkheim (1915/1965)

Boundaries depict differences in the beliefs, interests, and relative power *among* individuals and *among* groups. Trespasses and transgressions make evident the contradictions *within* ourselves and our groups. Émile Durkheim, one of the founders of sociology, wrote that in the act of defining deviance, a culture (or individual) defines and reinforces its own moral boundaries. Karl Marx represents society as an ongoing struggle between those who control the means of production and those who do not. Society is not the victor of one or another of these struggling groups; it is an expression of the continuous conflict between them. Social institutions and practices reflect the contradictions between the haves and the have-nots.

This final section of the book presents the thesis that contradictions and transgressions make people continually aware of what the boundaries are. Wrestling with these contradictions is the dynamic force of self and society.

Cultural production, like self-production, is a dialectical process of definition. Within groups and societies, people struggle over what significant symbols mean and who has the authority to project public definitions. The struggle over frames of meaning organizes people's lives. In this struggle to create definitions, cultural institutions are a resource—a source of privilege for some and an obstacle for others. Various institutions—family, government, religion, and the economy, for example—can wield great influence in the creation or maintenance of socially shared definitions. This influence may be unintended, or it may be consciously directed toward supporting a particular status quo. Again, however, power is an issue. Not everyone is equally able to participate in the construction of meaning. Some people's beliefs and interests are given more legitimacy than those of others.

Hegemonic practices of inequality persist because people play out the scripts expected of them—even when they may be privately opposed to these practices. People participate in practices of domination and inequality for a variety of reasons. For one, they may not realize the extent to which they contribute to the maintenance of particular definitions of the situation (hence the popular bumper sticker "Question authority"). Or, as is often the case, they may not have the resources necessary to break the chains of the existing reality. This complicity in oppression is what Marx refers to when he says that the "tradition of the dead generations weighs like a *nightmare* on the brain of the living." Prevailing realities suggest certain lines of action and forestall others. The possibility for change is in the conception of alternative lines of interaction. Alexis de Tocqueville once observed, "A grievance can be endured so long as it seems beyond redress, but it becomes intolerable once the possibility of removing it crosses people's minds." To be realized, however, even the most eloquent theories must be acted out. Change must be performed on the social stage.

In a well-known essay called "Talking Back," the writer and activist bell hooks considers what happens when an oppressed person refuses to engage in expected forms of deference (Reading 44). Oppression is a construction that requires the cooperation of many social actors—those doing the oppressing and those being oppressed. According to hooks, we choose to either join in the construction of oppression or withdraw our support. She points out that we can all actively work to breach realities that work against our interests. Even if our resistance is only small, sometimes we find ways to talk back.

CONCLUSIONS

The quotation from Karl Marx (1852/1963) at the beginning of this essay suggests that people make their own history, but that they do so within the confines of the circumstances they encounter from others. When he spoke of "circumstances encountered from the past," Marx had in mind the economic conditions—the "mode of production"—that shaped the existence of a group of people. But the idea can be extended to the broader systems of belief that groups of people use to structure and make sense of their shared reality. The definitions that people use to organize and direct their own lives are generally based on, in Marx's terms, "the traditions of the dead generations."

As we discussed in Part II, language-based knowledge systems shape our perceptions. Hence, although several definitions of a situation may be possible, people actually work within a system of beliefs inherited from social ancestors. "Commonsense" stories and theories provide us with a means of making sense of our lives. These stories and theories are often useful and meaningful. However, commonsense theories can also limit certain lines of action and confirm arbitrary "truths" that hinder our capacity to make alternative or new sense of a situation. In this regard, it can be said that these traditions "weigh like a nightmare" on our existence. In acting out these traditions of thought uncritically, we both create and re-create the circumstances of the past.

The social construction of reality is perhaps the most central and profound topic treated in this book. The phrase deserves careful attention. Note first the claim that reality is a *construction*. This idea in itself can seem counterintuitive or even nonsensical. Surely reality is simply the objective world that exists "out there," the subject of study of our sciences. But the alternative claim is that reality is malleable. Different groups, different cultures, or different historical epochs may hold completely different (even diametrically opposed) beliefs about what is "real," what is "obviously true," what is "good," and what is "desired." The second noteworthy element in the title is that reality is a *social* construction. That is, the created realities are the product, not of isolated individuals, but of relationships, communities, groups, institutions, and entire cultures.

Reality can be an amazingly malleable thing, but there are limits to how reality can be constructed. These limits include existing patterns of interaction and the taken-for-granted assumptions that underlie realities. Most of the time, expected definitions of the situation will prevail, because most of us know the routine and either follow it mindlessly or cannot risk deviation. Power, in a symbolic interactionist sense, is the ability to define a situation in a particular way and to have others act in accordance with this definition. Reality may be a social construction, but we are not all equal participants in this construction.

Stories are a useful epistemology through which to understand how collective life comes to have recognizable patterns. Realities, like stories, do not exist unless people tell them to themselves and to others. Some realities, like some stories, are more comprehensible to the group than are others. Certain stories, and ways of telling them, are considered more or less acceptable. As you ponder the material in this part of the book, ask yourself what story line underlies each of the different realities described. What sort of meaning is attached to persons, situations, and events in each of these stories? Who has the power to write and rewrite stories? How conscious are you of the stories that constitute your realities? The concept of stories illustrates how realities continue and how they change.

REFERENCES AND SUGGESTIONS FOR FURTHER READING

Berger, P., & Luckmann, T. (1966). *The social construction of reality*. Garden City, NY: Doubleday.

Conrad, P., & Schneider, J. (1992). *Deviance and medicalization: From badness to sickness.* Philadelphia. PA: Temple University Press.

Coupland, D. (1991). *Generation X*. New York, NY: St. Martin's Press.

Durkheim, E. (1965). *The cultural logic of collective representations*. New York, NY: Free Press. (Original work published 1915)

Goffman, E. (1959). *The presentation of self in everyday life*. Garden City, NY: Doubleday.

Marx, K. (1963). *The 18th Brumaire of Louis Bonaparte*. New York, NY: International Publishing Company. (Original work published 1852)

Nurius, P., & Markus, H. (1986). Possible selves. *American Psychologist, 41,* 954–969.

Perin, C. (1988). *Belonging in America.* Madison: University of Wisconsin Press.

Pollner, M., & Goode, D. (1990). Ethnomethodology and person-centering practices. *Person-Centered Review, 5,* 213–220.

Rosenhan, D. (1973). On being sane in insane places. *Science, 179,* 250–258.

Rosenthal, R., & Jacobson, L. (1974). Pygmalion in the classroom. In Z. Rubin (Ed.), *Doing unto others* (pp. 41–47). Englewood Cliffs, NJ: Prentice Hall.

Szasz, T. (1971). The sane slave: An historical note on medical diagnosis as justificatory rhetoric. *American Journal of Psychotherapy, 25,* 228–239.

Thomas, W. I., & Thomas, D. (1928). *The child in America.* New York, NY: Knopf.

Watzlawick, P. (Ed.). (1984). *The invented reality.* New York, NY: Norton.

A THEORY OF REALITY

This section focuses on the ways in which people create and maintain shared systems of belief. These belief systems or paradigms can be thought of as cultural stories that focus our attention, shape our perspectives, and provide guidelines about what is "real" and important. Culturally shared realities also provide the basis for making decisions and deciding what is true and right and good. Most inhabitants of a particular reality tend to think that their reality is the only "true" or "real" worldview. Humans have numerous strategies for maintaining belief in particular cultural realities, despite considerable experience that seems to threaten the infallibility of the reality. This is why, despite advances in technology and other developments, human societies change relatively slowly and require major paradigm shifts for doing so. The readings in this section provide examples of the ways in which humans maintain their cultural realities.

In "Five Features of Reality," Mehan and Wood describe five processes that combine to form socially shared systems of belief. Together, these features enable us to maintain dominant systems of belief even when faced with contradictory experiences. As you read the remaining articles in Part VI, consider how each of the five features is illustrated.

Harold Garfinkel's work is well known in sociology. The title of "A Conception of and Experiments With 'Trust' sounds technical, but the ideas presented here are far less complicated than one would expect. Garfinkel proposes that much of social action is based on shared and taken-for-granted expectations. We use a lot of social shorthand in our encounters with one another. We're able to do this because we share common beliefs about how the world works, and we trust others to do their part to maintain these beliefs. Garfinkel and his students at UCLA performed social experiments designed to demonstrate that realities actually require a great deal of interactional work and can be easily broken if one party breaches the expectations of the situation.

READING QUESTIONS

1. Find examples of each of the five features of reality in the essay for Part VI. Make a list of your own examples of each of the five features.

2. Discuss the experiments described in Garfinkel's article and identify exactly what interactional expectation was breached in each one. Garfinkel states that people often respond to breaching with anger. Consider how this is connected to his use of trust.

3. Think up other examples of breaching experiments that you could do. Do you find it easy or difficult to come up with ideas? How would you feel about doing a breaching experiment? What does this tell you about how the status quo is maintained?

4. Some students think that breaching experiments are unethical. Explain why they might think so. What does this indicate about social norms and how they are maintained?

5. Based on their theories, where would Goffman (see Part V) and Garfinkel say "society" is located?

36

Five Features of Reality

Hugh Mehan and Houston Wood

(1975)

REALITY AS A REFLEXIVE ACTIVITY

When the Azande of Africa are faced with important decisions, decisions about where to build their houses, or whom to marry, or whether the sick will live, for example, they consult an oracle. They prepare for these consultations by following a strictly prescribed ritual. First, a substance is gathered from the bark of a certain type of tree. Then this substance is prepared in a special way during a seancelike ceremony. The Azande then pose the question in a form that permits a simple yes or no answer, and feed the substance to a small chicken. The Azande decide beforehand whether the death of the chicken will signal an affirmative or negative response, and so they always receive an unequivocal answer to their questions.

For monumental decisions, the Azande add a second step. They feed the substance to a second chicken, asking the same question but reversing the import of the chicken's death. If in the first consultation sparing the chicken's life meant the oracle had said yes, in the second reading the oracle must now kill the chicken to once more reply in the affirmative and be consistent with its first response.

Our Western scientific knowledge tells us that the tree bark used by the Azande contains a poisonous substance that kills some chickens. The Azande have no knowledge of the tree's poisonous

qualities. They do not believe the tree plays a part in the oracular ceremony. The ritual that comes between the gathering of the bark and the administration of the substance to a fowl transforms the tree into an oracle. The bark is but a vessel for the oracle to enter. As the ritual is completed the oracle takes possession of the substance. The fact that it was once a part of a tree is irrelevant. Chickens then live or die, not because of the properties of the tree, but because the oracle "hears like a person and settles cases like a king" (Evans-Pritchard, 1937, p. 321).

The Westerner sees insuperable difficulties in maintaining such beliefs when the oracle contradicts itself. Knowing the oracle's bark is "really" poison, we wonder what happens when, for example, the first and second administration of the oracle produces first a positive and then a negative answer. Or, suppose someone else consults the oracle about the same question, and contradictory answers occur? What if the oracle is contradicted by later events? The house site approved by the oracle, for example, may promptly be flooded; or the wife the oracle selected may die or be a shrew. How is it possible for the Azande to continue to believe in oracles in the face of so many evident contradictions to this faith?

What I have called contradictions are not contradictions for the Azande. They are only contradictions because these events are being viewed from the reality of Western science. Westerners look at oracular practices to determine if in fact there is an oracle. The Azande *know* that an oracle exists. That is their beginning premise. All that subsequently happens they experience from that beginning assumption.

The Azande belief in oracles is much like the mathematician's belief in certain axioms. Gasking (1955) has described such unquestioned and unquestionable axioms as *incorrigible propositions:*

> An incorrigible proposition is one which you would never admit to be false whatever happens: it therefore does not tell you what happens. . . . The truth of an incorrigible proposition . . . is compatible with any and every conceivable state of affairs. (For example: whatever is your experience on counting, it is still true that 7 + 5 = 12.) (p. 432)

The incorrigible faith in the oracle is "compatible with any and every conceivable state of affairs." It is not so much a faith about a fact in the world as a faith in the facticity of the world itself. It is the same as the faith many of us have that 7 + 5 always equals 12 (cf. Polanyi, 1958, pp. 190–193, 257–261).

Just as Gasking suggests we explain away empirical experiences that deny this mathematical truth, the Azande too have available to them what Evans-Pritchard (1937) calls "secondary elaborations of belief" (p. 330). They explain the failure of the oracle by retaining the unquestioned absolute reality of oracles. When events occurred that revealed the inadequacy of the mystical faith in oracles, Evans-Pritchard tried to make the Azande understand these failures as he did. They only laughed, or met his arguments:

> sometimes by point-blank assertions, sometimes by one of the evasive secondary elaborations of belief . . . sometimes by polite pity, but always by an entanglement of linguistic obstacles, for one cannot well express in its language objections not formulated by a culture. (p. 319)

Evans-Pritchard goes on to write:

> Let the reader consider any argument that would utterly demolish all Zande claims for the power of the oracle. If it were translated into Zande modes of thought it would serve to support their entire structure of belief. For their mystical notions are eminently coherent, being interrelated by a network of logical ties, and are so ordered that they never too crudely contradict sensory experience, but, instead, experience seems to justify them. *The Zande is immersed in a sea of mystical notions, and if he speaks about his poison oracle he must speak in a mystical idiom* [italics added]. (pp. 319–320)

Seeming contradictions are explained away by saying such things as a taboo must have been breached, or that sorcerers, witches, ghosts, or gods must have intervened. These "mystical" notions reaffirm the reality of a world in which oracles are a basic feature. Failures do not challenge the oracle. They are elaborated in such a way that they provide evidence for the constant success of oracles. Beginning with the incorrigible belief in oracles, all events *reflexively* become evidence for that belief.[1]

The mathematician, as Gasking suggests, uses a similar process:

> But it does lay it down, so to speak, that if on counting 7 + 5 you do get 11, you are to describe what has happened in some such way as this: Either "I have made a mistake in my counting" or "Someone has played a practical joke and abstracted one of the objects when I was not looking" or "Two of the objects have coalesced" or "One of the objects has disappeared," etc. (Gasking, 1955; quoted in Pollner, 1973, pp. 15–16)

Consider the analogous case of a Western scientist using chloroform to asphyxiate butterflies. The incorrigible idiom called chemistry tells the scientist, among other things, that substances have certain constant properties. Chloroform of a certain volume and mix is capable of killing butterflies. One evening the scientist administers the chloroform as usual, and is dismayed to see the animal continue to flutter about.

Here is a contradiction of the scientist's reality, just as oracle use sometimes produces contradictions. Like the Azande, scientists have many secondary elaborations of belief they can bring to bear on such occurrences, short of rejecting the Western causal belief. Instead of rejecting chemistry they can explain the poison's failure by such things as "faulty manufacturing," "mislabeling," "sabotage," or "practical joke." Whatever the conclusion, it would continue to reaffirm the causal premise of science. This reaffirmation reflexively supports the reality that produced the poison's unexpected failure in the first place.

The use of contradictions to reaffirm incorrigible propositions can be observed in other branches of science. In the Ptolemaic system of astronomy, the sun was seen as a planet of the earth. When astronomers looked at the sun, they saw it as an orb circling the earth. When the Copernican system arose as an alternative to this view, it offered little new empirical data. Instead, it described the old "facts" in a different way. A shift of vision was required for people to see the sun as a star, not a planet of the earth.

Seeing the sun as a star and seeing it as a planet circling the earth are merely alternatives. There is no a priori warrant for believing that either empirical determination is necessarily superior to the other.

How is a choice between equally compelling empirical determinations made? The convert to the Copernican system could have said: "I used to see a planet, but now I see a star" (cf. Kuhn, 1970, p. 115). But to talk that way is to allow the belief that an object can be both a star and a planet at the same time. Such a belief is not allowed in Western science. So, instead, the Copernican concludes that the sun was a star all along. By so concluding, the astronomer exhibits an incorrigible proposition of Western thought, the *object constancy assumption.*[2] This is the belief that objects remain the same over time, across viewings from different positions and people. When presented with seemingly contradictory empirical determinations, the convert to Copernicanism does not consider that the sun changes through time. Instead he says: "I once took the sun to be a planet, but I was mistaken." The "discovery" of the sun as a star does not challenge the object constancy belief any more than an oracular "failure" challenges the ultimate reality of Azande belief.

The reaffirmation of incorrigible propositions is not limited to mystical and scientific ways of knowing. This reflexive work operates in commonsense reasoning as well. Each time you search for an object you knew was "right there" the same reflexive process is operating. Say, for example, you find a missing pen in a place you know you searched before. Although the evidence indicates that the pen was first absent and then present, that conclusion is not reached. To do so would challenge the incorrigibility of the object constancy belief. Instead, secondary elaborations—"I must have overlooked it," "I must not have looked there"—are invoked to retain the integrity of the object constancy proposition.

Without an object constancy assumption, there would be no problems about alternative determinations. But, with this assumption as an incorrigible proposition, the person faced with alternative seeings must choose one and only one as real. In choosing one, the other is automatically revealed as false. The falsehood of the rejected alternative may be explained in various ways. It may be due to a defective sensory apparatus, or a cognitive bias, or idiosyncratic psychological dynamics. We explain the inconstancy of the experienced object by saying that inconstancy is a product of the experiencing, not a feature of the object itself.[3]

Once an alternative seeing is explained away, the accepted explanation provides evidence for the object constancy assumption that made the explanation necessary in the first place. By demanding that we dismiss one of two equally valid empirical determinations, the object constancy assumption leads to a body of work that validates that assumption. The work then justifies itself afterward, in the world it has created. This self-preservative reflexive process is common to oracular, scientific, and common sense reasoning.

So far I have approached the reflexive feature of realities as if it were a form of reasoning. But reflexivity is not only a facet of reasoning. It is a recurrent fact of everyday social life. For example, *talk itself is reflexive* (cf. Garfinkel, 1967; Cicourel, 1973). An utterance not only delivers some particular information, it also creates a world in which information itself can appear.

Zimmerman (1973, p. 25) provides a means for understanding the reflexivity of talk at the level of a single word. He presents three identical shapes:

The first and third differ from the second: They each contain single words. These words interact with the box in which they appear so as to change the nature of that box. In so doing, they reflexively illumine themselves. For example, the word "projection," appearing in some other setting, would not mean what it does here. For me it means that I am to see the back panel and the word "projection" as illustrative of a projection. The word "projection" does not merely appear in the scene reporting on that scene. It creates the scene in which it appears as a reasonable object.

Similarly, the word "indentation" not only takes its meaning from the context in which it appears, it reflexively creates that very context. It creates a reality in which it may stand as a part of that reality.

These examples only hint at the reflexivity of talk. . . . Actual conversations are more complex than single words. The social context in which talk occurs, while analogous to one of these static boxes, is enormously ambiguous and potentially infinitely referential. Nonetheless, conversation operates like the printed "projection" and "indentation." An analysis of greetings can be used to show how talk partially constitutes the context and then comes to be seen as independent of it.[4]

To say "hello" both creates and sustains a world in which persons acknowledge . . . (1) [that] they sometimes can see one another; [and] (2) a world in which it is possible for persons to signal to each other, and (3) expect to be signaled back to, by (4) some others but not all of them. This is a partial and only illustrative list of some of the things a greeting accomplishes. Without the superstitious use of greetings, no world in which greetings are possible "objects" would arise. A greeting creates "room" for itself. But once such verbal behaviors are regularly done, a world is built up that can take their use for granted (cf. Sacks, Schegloff, & Jefferson, 1974).

When we say "hello" and the other replies with the expected counter greeting, the reflexive work of our initial utterance is masked. If the other scowls and walks on, then we are reminded that we were attempting to create a scene of greetings and that we failed. Rather than treat this as evidence that greetings are not "real," however, the rejected greeter ordinarily turns it into an occasion for affirming the reality of greetings. He formulates "secondary elaborations" of belief about greetings. He says, "He didn't hear me," "She is not feeling well," "It doesn't matter anyway."

Reflexivity provides grounds for absolute faith in the validity of knowledge. The Azande takes the truth of the oracle for granted, the scientist assumes the facticity of science, the layman accepts the tenets of common sense. The incorrigible propositions of a reality serve as criteria to judge other ways of knowing. Using his absolute faith in the oracle, the Azande dismisses Evans-Pritchard's Western science contradictions. Evans-Pritchard, steeped in the efficacy of science, dismissed the oracle as superstitious. An absolute faith in the incorrigibility of one's own knowledge enables believers to repel contrary evidence. This suggests that all people are equally superstitious.

REALITY AS A COHERENT BODY OF KNOWLEDGE

The phenomenon of reflexivity is a feature of every reality. It interacts with the coherence, interactional, fragility, and permeability features I describe in the rest of this chapter. These five features are incorrigible propositions of the reality of ethnomethodology. They appear as facts of the external world due to the ethnomethodologist's unquestioned assumption that they constitute the world. In other words, these features themselves exhibit reflexivity.

This reflexive loop constitutes the interior structure of ethnomethodology. This will become clearer as I describe the second feature of realities, their exhibition of a coherent body of knowledge. To illustrate this feature I will extrapolate from the work of Zimmerman and Wieder (n.d.), who investigated the life of a number of self-named "freaks," frequent drug users within America's counterculture. Both freaks and their academic ethnographers (e.g., Reich, 1970; Roszak 1969) describe freaks as radical opponents of the straight culture from which they sprang. As Zimmerman and Wieder (n.d.) write:

> From the standpoint of the "straight" members of society, freaks are deliberately irrational. . . . They disavow an interest in efficiency, making long-range plans, and concerns about costs of property (etc.) which are valued by the straight members of American society and are understood by them as indicators of rationality. (p. 103)

On first appearance, here is a reality that seems anarchical. Nonetheless, Zimmerman and Wieder found that

> when it comes to those activities most highly valued by freaks, such as taking drugs, making love, and other "cheap thrills," there is an elaborately developed body of lore. Freaks and others use that knowledge of taking drugs, making love, etc., reasonably, deliberately, planfully, projecting various consequences, predicting outcomes, conceiving of the possibilities of action in more or less clear and distinct ways, and choosing between two or more means of reaching the same end. (pp. 102–103)

The most vivid illustration that freaks use a coherent body of knowledge comes from Zimmerman's and Wieder's discoveries about the place of drugs in the everyday freak life. At first glance such drug use appears irrational. Yet, among freaks, taking drugs "is something as ordinary and unremarkable as their parents regard taking or offering a cup of coffee" (p. 57). Freak behavior is not a function of the freaks' ignorance of chemical and medical "facts" about drugs. The freaks studied knew chemical and medical facts well. They organized these facts into a different, yet coherent corpus of knowledge.

One of the team's research assistants, Peter Suczek, was able to systematize the freaks' knowledge of drugs into a taxonomic schemata (see Table 1).

What the freak calls "dope," the chemist calls "psychotropic drugs." Within the family of dope, freaks distinguish "mind-expanding" and "body" dope. Freaks further subdivide each of these species. In addition, freaks share a common body of knowledge informing them of the practicalities surrounding the use of each type of dope. All knowledge of dope use is grounded in the incorrigible proposition that dope is to be used. One must, of course, know how to use it.

Table 1   The Folk Pharmacology for Dope

Types of Dope	Subcategories
Mind-expanding dope	(Untitled)
	"grass" (marijuana)
	"hash" (hashish)
	"LSD" or "acid"
	(lysergic acid)
	Psychedelics
	mescaline
	synthetic
	organic
	natural, peyote
	psilocybin
	synthetic
	organic
	natural, mushrooms
	"DMT"
	miscellaneous
	(e.g., Angel's Dust)
Body dope	"speed" (amphetamines)
	"downers" (barbiturates)
	"tranks" (tranquilizers)
	"coke" (cocaine)
	"shit" (heroin)

Source: Zimmerman and Wieder (n.d.), p. 107.

Zimmerman and Wieder (n.d.) found the following knowledge about "psychedelic mind-expanding dope" to be common among freaks:

> The folk pharmacology of psychedelic drugs may be characterized as a method whereby drug users rationally assess choices among kinds of drugs, choices among instances of the same kind of drug, the choice to ingest or not, the time of the act of ingestion relative to the state of one's physiology and relative to the state of one's psyche, the timing relative to social and practical demands, the appropriateness of the setting for having a psychedelic experience, the size of the dose, and the effectiveness and risk of mixing drugs. (p. 118)

Freaks share similar knowledge for the rest of the taxonomy. Being a freak means living within the auspices of such knowledge and using it according to a plan, as the chemist uses his. Both the freaks' and the scientists' realities are concerned with "the facts." Though the facts differ, each reality reflexively proves its facts as absolute.

Consider how the freak assembles the knowledge he uses. He is not loath to borrow from the discoveries of science. But before accepting what the scientist says, he first tests scientific "facts" against the auspices of his own incorrigible propositions. He does not use the scientists' findings to determine the danger of the drug, but rather to indicate the particular dosage, setting, etc., under which a drug is to be taken.

Scientific drug researchers frequently attend to the experiences of freaks in a comparable way. They incorporate the facts that freaks report about dope into their coherent idiom. The two then are like independent teams of investigators working on the same phenomenon with different purposes. They are like artists and botanists who share a common interest in the vegetable kingdom, but who employ different incorrigibles.

The freak's knowledge, like all knowledge, is sustained through reflexive interactional work. For example, the knowledge contained in the drug taxonomy (Table 1) sometimes "fails," that is, it produces not a "high" but a "bummer." The incorrigible propositions of freak pharmacology are not then questioned. Instead, these propositions are invoked to explain the bummer's occurrence. "For example," Zimmerman and Wieder (n.d.) write:

> A "bad trip" may be explained in such terms as the following: it was a bad time and place to drop; my head wasn't ready for it; or it was bad acid or

mescaline, meaning that it was cut with something impure or that it was some other drug altogether. (p. 118)

The reflexive use of the freak taxonomy recalls my previous discussion of the Azande. When the oracle seemed to contradict itself, the contradiction became but one more occasion for proving the oracular way of knowing. The reality of oracles is appealed to in explaining the failure of the oracle, just as the reality of freak pharmacology is used to explain a bad trip. It would be as futile for a chemist to explain the bad trip scientifically to a freak as it was for Evans-Pritchard to try to convince the Azande that failures of the oracle demonstrated their unreality.

The coherence of knowledge is a reflexive consequence of the researcher's attention. Zimmerman and Wieder, in the best social science tradition, employed many methods to construct the freak's taxonomy. Freaks were interviewed by sociology graduate students and by their peers. These interviewers provided accounts of their own drug experiences as well. Additional freaks not acquainted with the purposes of the research were paid to keep personal diaries of their day-to-day experiences. Zimmerman and Wieder used a portion of this massive data to construct the freak taxonomy, then tested its validity against further portions of the data.

Such systematizations are always the researcher's construction (Wallace, 1972). To claim that any reality, including the researcher's own, exhibits a coherent body of knowledge is but to claim that coherence can be found *upon analysis*. The coherence located in a reality is found there by the ethnomethodologist's interactional work. The coherence feature, like all features of realities, operates as an incorrigible proposition, reflexively sustained.

Consider the analogous work of linguists (e.g., Chomsky, 1965). Within language-using communities, linguists discover the "rules of grammar." Although the linguist empirically establishes these grammatical rules, speaker-hearers of that language cannot list them. Rules can be located in their talk, upon analysis, but language users cannot describe them.

Similarly, freaks could not supply the taxonomy Zimmerman and Wieder claim they "really" know. It was found upon analysis. It is an imposition of the researcher's logic upon the freak's logic.

Castañeda's (1968, 1971) attempts to explain the reality of Yaqui sorcery further illustrates the reflexity of analysis. In his initial report, *The Teachings of Don Juan*, Castañeda (1968) begins with a detailed ethnography of his experiences of his encounter with a Yaqui sorcerer, Don Juan. In this reality it is common for time to stop, for men to turn into animals and animals into men, for animals and men to converse with one another, and for great distances to be covered while the body remains still.

In the final section of his report, Castañeda systematizes his experiences with the sorcerer. He presents a coherent body of knowledge undergirding Don Juan's teachings. Thus Castañeda, like Zimmerman and Wieder, organizes a "nonordinary" reality into a coherent system of knowledge.

In a second book Castañeda (1971) describes Don Juan's reaction to his systematization of a peyote session, a "mitote." Castañeda told Don Juan he had discovered that mitotes are a "result of a subtle and complex system of cueing." He writes:

It took me close to two hours to read and explain to Don Juan the scheme I had constructed. I ended by begging him to tell me in his own words what were the exact procedures for reaching agreement.

When I had finished he frowned. I thought he must have found my explanation challenging; he appeared to be involved in deep deliberation.

After a reasonable silence I asked him what he thought about my idea.

My question made him suddenly turn his frown into a smile and then into roaring laughter. I tried to laugh too and asked nervously what was so funny.

"You're deranged!" he exclaimed. "Why should anyone be bothered with cueing at such an important time as a mitote? Do you think one ever fools around with Mescalito?"

I thought for a moment that he was being evasive; he was not really answering my question.

"Why should anyone cue?" Don Juan asked stubbornly. "You have been in mitotes. You should know that no one told you how to feel, or what to do; no one except Mescalito himself."

I insisted that such an explanation was not possible and begged him again to tell me how the agreement was reached.

"I know why you have come," Don Juan said in a mysterious tone. "I can't help you in your endeavor because there is no system of cueing."

"But how can all those persons agree about Mescalito's presence?"

"They agree because they *see,*" Don Juan said dramatically, and then added casually, "Why don't you attend another mitote and see for yourself?" (pp. 37–38)

Don Juan finds Castañeda's account ridiculous. This rejection is not evidence that Castañeda's attempt at systematization is incorrect. It indicates that the investigator reflexively organizes the realities he investigates. All realities may *upon analysis* exhibit a coherent system of knowledge, but knowledge of this coherence is not necessarily part of the awareness of its members.

Features emerging "upon analysis" is a particular instance of reflexivity. These features exist only within the reflexive work of those researchers who make them exist. This does not deny their reality. There is no need to pursue the chimera of a presuppositionless inquiry. Because all realities are ultimately superstitious the reflexive location of reflexivity is not a problem within ethnomethodological studies. Rather, it provides them with their most intriguing phenomenon.

My discussion of these first two features of realities also shows that any one feature is separate from the other only upon analysis. In my description of reflexivity, I was forced to assume the existence of a coherent body of knowledge. Similarly, in the present discussion I could not speak about the existence of coherent systems of knowledge without introducing the caveat of "upon analysis," an implicit reference to reflexivity. This situation will continue as I discuss the remaining three features. Though I attempt to keep them separate from one another, I will only be partially successful, since the five are inextricably intertwined. Nevertheless, I will continue to talk of them as five separate features, not as one. I acknowledge that this talk is more heuristic than literal—it provides a ladder with five steps that may be climbed and then thrown away (cf. Wittgenstein, 1921/1961).

Reality as Interactional Activity

Realities are also dependent upon ceaseless social interactional work. Wood's study of a mental hospital illustrates the reality of this reality work. He discovered that psychiatric attendants shared a body of knowledge. Wood's (1968) analysis of the attendants' interaction with the patients uncovered labels like: "baby," "child," "epileptic," "mean old man," "alcoholic," "lost soul," "good patient," "depressive," "sociopath," and "nigger" (p. 36). Though borrowed from psychiatry, these terms constitute a corpus of knowledge which reflects the attendants' own practical nursing concerns. These terms can be arranged in a systematic taxonomy (see Table 2). Each is shown to differ from the others according to four parameters of nursing problems.

Wood's study explored how the attendants used this taxonomy to construct meanings for the mental patients' behavior. One explanation of label use is called a "matching procedure." The matching model of labeling patient behavior is essentially a psychological theory. It treats behavior as a private, internal state, not influenced by social dimensions. The matching model assumes the patients' behavior has obvious features. Trained personnel monitor and automatically apply the appropriate label to patients' behavior.

Wood presents five case histories that show that labels are not applied by a simple matching process. They are molded in the day-to-day interaction of the attendants with one another and with the patients. The labeling of patients is a social activity, not a psychological one.

Wood (1968, pp. 51–91) describes the labeling history of patient Jimmy Lee Jackson. Over the course of his three-month hospitalization, Jackson held the same official psychiatric label, that of "psychoneurotic reaction, depressive type." However, the ward attendants saw Jackson within the web of their own practical circumstances.

For them, at one time he was a "nigger," at another a "depressive," and at yet another a "sociopath." These seeings reflected a deep change in the meaning Jackson had for the attendants. When he was seen as a "nigger," for example, it meant that the attendants considered he was "lazy, and . . . without morals or scruples and . . . that the patient is cunning and will attempt to ingratiate himself with the attendants in order to get attention and 'use' them for his own ends" (p. 52). When Jackson became a depressive type, all these negative attributes were withdrawn. The change in attribution, Wood shows, cannot be explained by a matching procedure. The attendants' social interactional work produced the change, independent of Jackson's behavior. This suggests that realities are fundamentally interactional activities.

One evening Jackson was suffering from a toothache. Unable to secure medical attention, he ran his arm through a window pane in one of the ward's locked doors. He suffered a severe laceration of his forearm which required stitches. When the attendants who were on duty during

Table 2 The Meaning of the Labels

Psychiatric Attendant Label	Nursing Trouble				
	Work	Cleanliness	Supervisory	Miscellaneous	Frequency × 60
Mean old man	yes	yes	yes	yes	2
Baby	yes	yes	yes	—	20
Child	yes	yes	—	yes	4
Nigger	yes	—	yes	yes	1
Epileptic	—	yes	—	yes	4
Sociopath	yes	—	—	yes	3
Depressive	—	—	—	yes	2
Alcoholic	—	—	yes	—	8
Lost soul	yes	—	—	—	12
Good patient	—	—	—	—	6

Source: Wood (1968), p. 45.

this episode returned to work the following afternoon, they discovered that the preceding morning shift had decided that Jackson had attempted suicide. Jackson was no longer presented to them as a nigger. The morning shift found that persons who had not even witnessed the event had given it a meaning they themselves had never considered. Nevertheless, the evening shift accepted the validity of this label change.

The label change indexed a far larger change. Jackson's past history on the ward was reinterpreted. He now was accorded different treatment by attendants on all shifts. He was listened to sympathetically, given whatever he requested, and no longer exhorted to do more ward work. All the attendants came to believe that he had always been a depressive and that they had always seen him as such.

A few weeks later Jackson became yet another person, a "sociopath." The attendants no longer accepted that he was capable of a suicide attempt. The new label was once again applied retrospectively. Not only was Jackson believed to be incapable of committing suicide now, he was thought to have always been incapable of it. The attendants agreed that the window-breaking incident had been a "fake" or "con"—just the sort of thing a sociopath would do. Attendants who had praised Jackson as a hard worker when he was labeled a depressive now pointed to this same work as proof he was a "conniver." Requests for attention and medicine that had been promptly fulfilled for the depressive Jackson were now ignored for the sociopath Jackson, or used as occasions to attack him verbally.

Yet, as Wood describes Jackson, he remained constant despite these changes in attendant behavior. He did the same amount of work and sought the same amount of attention and medicine whether he was labeled a nigger or a depressive or a sociopath. What Jackson was at any time was determined by the reality work of the attendants.

In the final pages of his study, Wood (1968) further illustrates the power of interactional work to create an external world:

> The evening that he [Jackson] cut his arm, I, like the PAs [psychiatric attendants], was overcome by the blood and did not reflect on its "larger" meaning concerning his proper label. The next day, when I heard all of the morning shift PAs refer to his action as a suicide attempt, I too labeled Jackson a "depressive" and the cut arm as a suicide attempt. When the label changed in future weeks I was working as a PA on the ward up to 12 hours a day. It was only two months later when I had left the ward, as I reviewed my notes and my memory, that I recognized the "peculiar" label changes that had occurred. While I was on the ward, it had not seemed strange to think that cutting an arm in a window was a serious attempt to kill oneself. Only as an "outsider" did I come to think that Jackson had "really" stayed the same through his three label changes. (pp. 137–138)

As Wood says, Jackson could never have a meaning apart from *some* social context. Meanings unfold only within an unending sequence of practical actions.[5]

The *matching* theory of label use assumes a correspondence theory of signs (cf. Garfinkel, 1952, pp. 91ff.; Wieder, 1970). This theory of signs has three analytically separate elements: ideas that exist in the head, signs that appear in symbolic representations, and objects and events that appear in the world. Meaning is the relation among these elements. Signs can stand on behalf of the ideas in the head or refer to objects in the world. This theory of signs implies that signs stand in a point-by-point relation to thoughts in one's mind or objects in the world. Meanings are stable across time and space. They are not dependent upon the concrete participants or upon the specific scenes in which they appear.

Wood's study indicates that labels are not applied in accordance with correspondence principles. Instead, labels are *indexical expressions*. Meanings are situationally determined. They are dependent upon the concrete context in which they appear. The participants' interactional activity structured the indexical meaning of the labels used on the ward. The relationship of the participants to the object, the setting in which events occur, and the circumstances surrounding a definition determine the meaning of labels and of objects.

The interactional feature indicates that realities do not possess symbols, like so many tools in a box. A reality and its signs are "mutually determinative" (Wieder, 1973, p. 216). Alone, neither expresses sense. Intertwining through the course of indexical interaction, they form a life.

The Fragility of Realities

Every reality depends upon (1) ceaseless reflexive use of (2) a body of knowledge in (3) interaction. Every reality is also fragile. Suppression of the activities that the first three features describe disrupts the reality. Every reality is equally capable of dissolution. The presence of this fragility feature of realities has been demonstrated by studies called "incongruity procedures" or "breaching experiments."

In one of the simplest of these, Garfinkel used 67 students as "experimenters." These students engaged a total of 253 "subjects" in a game of tick-tack-toe. When the figure necessary for the game was drawn, the experimenters requested the subject to make the first move. After the subject made his mark, the experimenter took his turn. Rather than simply marking another cell, the experimenter erased the subject's mark and moved it to another cell. Continuing as if this were expected behavior, the experimenter then placed his own mark in one of the now empty cells. The experimenters reported that their action produced extreme

bewilderment and confusion in the subjects. The reality of the game, which before the experimenter's move seemed stable and external, suddenly fell apart. For a moment the subjects exhibited an "amnesia for social structure" (Garfinkel, 1963, p. 189).

This fragility feature is even more evident in everyday life, where the rules are not explicit. People interact without listing the rules of conduct. Continued reference is made to this knowledge nonetheless. This referencing is not ordinarily available as long as the reality work continues normally. When the reality is disrupted, the interactional activity structuring the reality becomes visible. This is what occurred in the tick-tack-toe game. A usually unnoticed feature of the game is a "rule" prohibiting erasing an opponent's mark. When this unspoken "rule" is broken, it makes its first public appearance. If we were aware of the fragility of our realities, they would not seem real.

Thus Garfinkel (1963) found that when the "incongruity-inducing procedures" developed in games

> were applied in "real life" situations, it was unnerving to find the seemingly endless variety of events that lent themselves to the production of really nasty surprises. These events ranged from . . . standing very, very close to a person while otherwise maintaining an innocuous conversation, to others . . . like saying "hello" at the termination of a conversation. . . . Both procedures elicited anxiety, indignation, strong feelings on the part of the experimenter and subject alike of humiliation and regret, demands by the subjects for explanations, and so on. (p. 198)

Another of the procedures Garfinkel developed was to send student experimenters into stores and restaurants where they were told to "mistake" customers for salespersons and waiters. . . . (see Reading 31, this volume, for details of one such experiment).

The breaching experiments were subsequently refined, such that:

> The person [subject] could not turn the situation into a play, a joke, an experiment, a deception, and the like . . . ; that he have insufficient time to work through a redefinition of his real circumstances; and that he be deprived of consensual support for an alternative definition of social reality. (Garfinkel, 1964; in 1967, p. 58)

This meant that subjects were not allowed to reflexively turn the disruption into a revalidation of their realities. The incorrigible propositions of their social knowledge were not adequate for the present circumstances. They were removed from the supporting interactional activity that they possessed before the breach occurred.

These refinements had the positive consequence of increasing the bewilderment of the subjects, who became more and more like desocialized schizophrenics, persons completely devoid of any social reality. These refinements produced a negative consequence. They were immoral. Once subjects had experienced the fragility, they could not continue taking the stability of realities for granted. No amount of "cooling out" could restore the subject's faith.

But what is too cruel to impose on others can be tried upon oneself. . . .

THE PERMEABILITY OF REALITIES

Because the reflexive use of social knowledge is fragile and interaction dependent, one reality may be altered, and another may be assumed. Cases where a person passes from one reality to another, dramatically different, reality vividly displays this permeability feature.

Tobias Schneebaum, a painter who lives periodically in New York, provides an example of a radical shift in realities in his book, *Keep the River on Your Right* (1969). Schneebaum entered the jungles of Peru in 1955 in pursuit of his art. During the trip the book describes, he gradually lost interest in painterly studies. He found himself drawn deeper and deeper into the jungle. Unlike a professional anthropologist, he carried no plans to write about his travels. In fact, the slim volume from which I draw the following discussion was not written until 13 years after his return.

He happened upon the Akaramas, a stone age tribe that had never seen a white man. They accepted him quickly, gave him a new name, "Habe," meaning "ignorant one," and began teaching him to be as they were.

Schneebaum learned to sleep in "bundles" with the other men, piled on top of one another for warmth and comfort. He learned to hunt and fish with stone age tools. He learned the Akaramas' language and their ritual of telling stories of their hunts and hikes, the telling taking longer than the doing. He learned to go without clothing, and to touch casually the genitals of his companions in play.

When one of the men in Schneebaum's compartment is dying of dysentery, crying out at his excretions of blood and pain, the "others laugh and he laughs too" (p. 109). As this man lies among them whimpering and crying in their sleeping pile at night, Schneebaum writes: "Not Michii or Baaldore or Ihuene or Reindude seemed to have him on their minds. It was as if he were not there among us or as if he had already gone to some other forest" (p. 129). When he dies, he is immediately forgotten. Such is the normal perception of death within the Akarama reality. As Schneebaum describes another incident: "There were two pregnant women whom I noticed one day with flatter bellies and no babies on their backs, but there was no sign of grief, no service . . ." (p. 109).

Gradually, Schneebaum absorbed even these ways and a new sense of time. At one point he left the Akaramas to visit the mission from which he had embarked. He was startled to find that seven months had passed, not the three or four he had supposed. As he was more and more permeated by the stone age reality, he began to feel that his "own world, whatever, wherever it was, no longer was anywhere in existence" (p. 69). As the sense of his old reality disappears, he says, "My fears were not so much for the future . . . but for my knowledge. I was removing my own reflection" (pp. 64–65).

One day, a day like many others, he rises to begin a hunting expedition with his sleeping companions. This day, however, they go much farther than ever before. They paint themselves in a new way and repeat new chants. Finally they reach a strange village. In they swoop, Schneebaum too, shouting their sacred words and killing all the men they can catch, disemboweling and beheading them on the spot. They burn all the huts, kidnap the women and children. They then hike to their own village, without pause, through an entire night. At home, a new dance is begun. The meat of the men they have murdered and brought back with them is cooked. As a new movement of the dance begins, this meat is gleefully eaten. Exhausted at last, they stumble together on the ground. Then the last of the meat is put to ceremonious use:

We sat or lay around the fires, eating, moaning the tones of the chant, swaying forward and back, moving from the hip, forward and back. Calm and silence settled over us, all men. Four got up, one picked a heart from the embers, and they walked into the forest. Small groups of others arose, selected a piece of meat, and disappeared in other directions. We three were alone until Ihuene, Baaldore, and Reindude were in front of us, Reindude cupping in his hand the heart from the being we had carried from so far away, the heart of he who had lived in the hut we had entered to kill. We stretched out flat upon the ground, lined up, our shoulders touching. Michii looked up at the moon and showed it to the heart. He bit into it as if it were an apple,

taking a large bite, almost half the heart, and chewed down several times, spit into a hand, separated the meat into six sections and placed some into the mouths of each of us. We chewed and swallowed. He did the same with the other half of the heart. He turned Darinimbiak onto his stomach, lifted his hips so that he crouched on all fours. Darinimbiak growled, Mayaarii-ha! Michii growled, Mayaari-ha!, bent down to lay himself upon Darinimbiak's back and entered him. (pp. 106–107)

Mass murder, destruction of an entire village, theft of all valuable goods, cannibalism, the ritual eating of the heart before publicly displayed homosexual acts—these are some of the acts Schneebaum participated in. He could not have done them his first day in the jungle. But after his gradual adoption of the Akarama reality, they had become natural. It would have been as immoral for him to refuse to join his brothers in the raid and its victory celebration as it would be immoral for him to commit these same acts within a Western community. His reality had changed. The moral facts were different.

Schneebaum's experience suggests that even radically different realities can be penetrated.[6] We would not have this account, however, if the stone age reality had completely obliterated Schneebaum's Western reality. He would still be with the tribe. The more he permeated the Akaramas' reality, the more suspect his old reality became. The more he fell under the spell of the absolutism of his new reality, the more fragile his old reality became. Like the cannibals, Schneebaum says: "My days are days no longer. Time had no thoughts to trouble me, and everything is like nothing and nothing is like everything. For if a day passes, it registers nowhere, and it might be a week, it might be a month. There is no difference" (p. 174).

As the vision of his old reality receded, Schneebaum experienced its fragility. He knew he must leave soon, or there would be no reality to return to. He describes his departure:

A time alone, only a few weeks ago, with the jungle alive and vibrant around me, and Michii and Baaldore gone with all the other men to hunt, I saw within myself too many seeds that would grow a fungus around my brain, encasing it with mold that could penetrate and smooth the convolutions and there I would remain, not he who had travelled and arrived, not the me who had crossed the mountains in a search, but another me living only in ease and pleasure, no longer able to scrawl out words on paper or think beyond a moment. And days later, I took myself up from our hut, and I walked on again alone without a word to any of my friends and family, but left when all again were gone and I walked through my jungle. . . . (p. 182)

The Akaramas would not miss him. They would not even notice his absence. For them, there were no separate beings. Schneebaum felt their reality obliterating "the me who had crossed the mountains in a search." Schneebaum was attached to this "me," and so he left.

In the previous section, I listed three conditions necessary for successful breaches: There can be no place to escape. There can be no time to escape. There can be no one to provide counter evidence. The same conditions are required to move between realities. That is, as Castañeda's (1968, 1971, 1972) work suggests, in order to permeate realities, one must first have the old reality breached. Castañeda has named this necessity the establishment "of a certainty of a minimal possibility," that another reality actually exists (personal communication). Successful breaches must establish that another reality is available for entry. Thus, as Don Juan attempted to make Castañeda a man of knowledge, he first spent years trying to crack Castañeda's absolute faith in the reality of Western rationalism.

Castañeda's work suggests many relations between the fragility and permeability features. It is not my purpose to explore the relations of the five features in this book. But I want to emphasize that such relations can be supposed to exist.

I relied on the "exotic" case of a person passing from a Western to a stone age reality to display the permeability feature of realities. However, any two subsequent interactional encounters could have been used for this purpose. All such passages are of equal theoretic import. Passages between a movie and freeway driving, between a person's reality before and after psychotherapy, between a "straight" acquiring membership in the reality of drug freaks, or before and after becoming a competent religious healer, are all the same. The differences are "merely" methodological, not theoretical. Studying each passage, I would concentrate on how the reflexive, knowledge, interactional, and fragility features affect the shift.

All realities are permeable. Ethnomethodology is a reality. This book is an attempt to breach the reader's present reality by introducing him to the "certainty of a minimal possibility" that another reality exists.

ON THE CONCEPT OF REALITY

Many ethnomethodologists rely on Schutz's concept of reality (e.g., 1962, 1964, 1966). . . . My use of "reality" contrasts with Schutz's view. For Schutz (e.g., 1962, pp. 208ff.), the reality of everyday life is the *one* paramount reality. Schutz says that this paramount reality consists of a number of presuppositions or assumptions, which include the assumption of a tacit, taken for granted world; an assumed practical interest in that world; and an assumption that the world is intersubjective (e.g., 1962, p. 23). Schutz argues that other realities exist, but that they derive from the paramount reality. For example, he discusses the realities of "scientific theorizing" and of "fantasy." These realities appear when some of the basic assumptions of the paramount reality are temporarily suspended. The paramount reality of everyday life has an elastic quality for Schutz. After excursions into other realities, we snap back into the everyday.

My view of realities is different. I do not wish to call one or another reality paramount. It is my contention that every reality is equally real. No single reality contains more of the truth than any other. From the perspective of Western everyday life, Western everyday life will appear paramount, just as Schutz maintains. But from the perspective of scientific theorizing or dreaming, or meditating, each of these realities will appear just as paramount. Because every reality exhibits the absolutist tendency I mentioned earlier, there is no way to look from the window of one reality at others without seeing yourself. Schutz seems to be a victim of this absolutist prejudice. As a Western man living his life in the Western daily experience, he assumed that this life was the touchstone of all realities.

My concept of reality, then, has more in common with Wittgenstein (1953) than with Schutz. Wittgenstein (e.g., 1953, pp. 61, 179) recognizes that human life exhibits an empirical multitude of activities. He calls these activities language games. Language games are forever being invented and modified and discarded. The fluidity of language activities do not permit rigorous description. Analysts can discover that at any time a number of language games are associated with one another. This association, too, is not amenable to rigorous description. Instead, language games exhibit "family resemblances." One can recognize certain games going together. But one could no more articulate *the* criteria for this resemblance than one could predict the physical characteristics of some unseen member of a familiar extended family. Wittgenstein (1953, pp. 119, 123) calls a collection of language games bound together by a family resemblance, a *form of life*.[7] Forms of life resemble what I call "realities." Realities are far more fluid than Schutz's terms

"finite" and "province" suggest. Forms of life are always forms of life forming.[8] Realities are always realities becoming.

NOTES

1. See Pollner's (1970, 1973) discussions of the reflexive reasoning of the Azande and Polanyi's (1958, pp. 287–294) examination of the same materials. In the Apostolic Church of John Marangue, illness is not bodily malfunction, it is sin. Sin is curable not by medicine, but by confessional healing. When evangelists' attempts to heal church members were not accompanied by recovery, Jules-Rosette (1973, p. 167) reports that church members did not lose their faith in the confessional process. They looked to other "causes" of the "failure." They said things like: Other persons must have been implicated in the sin, and untrue confession must have been given. Once again, contradictions that could potentially challenge a basic faith do not, as the basic faith itself is not questioned.

2. See Gurwitsch (1966) for a more technical discussion of the object constancy assumption. . . .

3. The . . . planet-star example [is] adapted from Pollner (1973). Much of this discussion of reflexivity derives from Pollner's thinking on these matters.

4. Riel (1972) illustrates how talk reflexively constitutes the context it then seems to independently reference. Trying to make a certain point, she reports turning away from an inadequate sentence she had written to explore notes and texts again. Forty-five minutes later she wrote the now-perfect sentence, only to discover it was exactly the same sentence she had rejected before.

5. Cicourel (1968) examines the interactional work that accomplishes external objects in greater detail. He shows that juvenile delinquents and crime rates are constituted by the social activities of law enforcement personnel.

6. For an account of a reality shift in the other direction, from the stone age to industrial Western society, see Kroeber's *Ishi in Two Worlds* (1961). Again the transition was never total, but this was a

result of a political decision on the part of the author's husband. As Ishi's official keeper, he wished to keep him primitive for his own and anthropology's benefit.

7. Blum (1970) has previously explored the importance of Wittgenstein's notion of "form of life" for social science.

8. This phrase, like much of this chapter, has been adapted from the unpublished lectures of Pollner. For Pollner's published writings see Zimmerman and Pollner, 1970; and Pollner, 1970, 1973, 1974.

References

Blum, A. (1970). Theorizing. In J. D. Douglas (Ed.), *Understanding everyday life.* Chicago: Aldine.

Castañeda, C. (1968). *The teachings of Don Juan.* Berkeley: University of California Press.

Castañeda, C. (1971). *A separate reality.* New York: Simon & Schuster.

Castañeda, C. (1972). *A journey to Iztlan.* New York: Simon & Schuster.

Chomsky, N. (1965). *Aspects of the theory of syntax.* Cambridge: MIT Press.

Cicourel, A. V. (1968). *The social organization of juvenile justice.* New York: John Wiley.

Cicourel, A. V. (1973). *Cognitive sociology.* London: Macmillan.

Evans-Pritchard, E. E. (1937). *Witchcraft, oracles and magic among the Azande.* London: Oxford University Press.

Garfinkel, H. (1952). *Perception of the other.* Unpublished Ph.D. dissertation, Harvard University.

Garfinkel, H. (1963). A conception of and experiments with "trust" as a condition of concerted stable actions. In O. J. Harvey (Ed.), *Motivation and social interaction.* New York: Ronald.

Garfinkel, H. (1964). Studies of the routine grounds of everyday activities. *Social Problems, 11,* 225–250 (Chapter 2 in Garfinkel, 1967).

Garfinkel, H. (1967). *Studies in ethnomethodology.* Englewood Cliffs, NJ: Prentice Hall.

Gasking, D. (1955). Mathematics and the world. In A. Flew (Ed.), *Logic and language.* Garden City, NY: Doubleday.

Gurwitsch, A. (1966). *Studies in phenomenology and psychology.* Evanston, IL: Northwestern University Press.

Jules-Rosette, B. (1973). *Ritual context and social action.* Unpublished Ph.D. dissertation. Harvard University.

Kroeber, T. (1961). *Ishi in two worlds.* Berkeley: University of California Press.

Kuhn, T. S. (1970). *The structure of scientific revolutions.* Chicago: University of Chicago Press.

Polanyi, M. (1958). *Personal knowledge.* Chicago: University of Chicago Press.

Pollner, M. (1970). *On the foundations of mundane reason.* Unpublished Ph.D. dissertation. University of California, Santa Barbara.

Pollner, M. (1973). *The very coinage of your brain: The resolution of reality disjunctures.* Unpublished manuscript.

Pollner, M. (1974). Mundane reasoning. *Philosophy of social sciences, 4*(1), 35–54.

Reich, C. A. (1970). *The greening of America.* New York: Random House.

Riel, M. M. (1972). *The interpretive process.* Paper presented to a seminar led by Paul Filmer, University of California, San Diego.

Roszak, T. (1969). *The making of a counter culture.* Garden City, NY: Doubleday.

Sacks, H., Schegloff, E., & Jefferson, G. (1974). A simplest systematics for the analysis of turn taking in conversation. *Language, 50,* 696–735.

Schneebaum, T. (1969). *Keep the river on your right.* New York: Grove.

Schutz, A. (1962). *Collected papers I: The problem of social reality.* The Hague: Martinus Nijhoff.

Schutz, A. (1964). *Collected papers II: Studies in social theory.* The Hague: Martinus Nijhoff.

Schutz, A. (1966). *Collected papers III: Studies in phenomenological philosophy.* The Hague: Martinus Nijhoff.

Wallace, H. T. (1972). *Culture and social being.* Unpublished master's thesis, University of California, Santa Barbara.

Wieder, D. L. (1970). Meaning by rule. In J. D. Douglas (Ed.), *Understanding everyday life.* Chicago: Aldine.

Wieder, D. L. (1973). *Language and social reality.* The Hague: Mouton.

Wittgenstein, L. (1953). *Philosophical investigations.* London: Basil Blackwell & Mott.

Wittgenstein, L. (1961). *Tractatus logico-philosophicus.* London: Basil Blackwell & Mott. (Original work published in 1921)

Wood, H. (1968). *The labelling process on a mental hospital ward.* Unpublished master's thesis. University of California, Santa Barbara.

Zimmerman, D. H. (1973). Preface. In D. L. Wieder, *Language and social reality.* The Hague: Mouton.

Zimmerman, D. H., & Pollner, M. (1970). The everyday world as a phenomenon. In J. D. Douglas (Ed.), *Understanding everyday life.* Chicago: Aldine.

Zimmerman, D. H., & Wieder, D. L. (n.d.). *The social bases for illegal behavior in the student community: First year report.* San Francisco and Santa Barbara: Scientific Analysis Corporation.

A THEORY OF REALITY

37

A Conception of and Experiments With "Trust" as a Condition of Concerted Stable Actions

Harold Garfinkel

(1963)

SOME PRELIMINARY TRIALS AND FINDINGS

Since each of the presuppositions that make up the attitude of daily life assigns an expected feature to the actor's environment, it should be possible to induce experimentally a breach of these expectancies by deliberately modifying scenic events so as to disappoint these attributions. By definition, surprise is possible with respect to each of these expected features. The nastiness of surprise should vary directly with the extent to which the actor complies with the constitutive order of events of everyday life as a scheme for assigning witnessed appearances their status of events in a perceivedly normal environment.

Procedures were used to see if a breach of these presuppositions would produce anomic effects and increase disorganization. These procedures must be thought of as demonstrations rather than as experiments. "Experimenters" were upper division students in the author's courses. Their training consisted of little more than verbal instructions about how to proceed. The demonstrations were done as class assignments and were unsupervised. Students reported their results in anecdotal fashion with no controls beyond the fact that they were urged to avoid interpretation in favor of writing down what was actually said and done, staying as close as possible to a chronological account.

Because the procedures nevertheless produced massive effects, I feel they are worth reporting. Obviously, however, caution must be exercised in assessing the findings.

Demonstration 1:
Breaching the Congruency of Relevances

This expectancy consists of the following. The person expects, expects that the other person does the same, and expects that as he expects it of the other the other expects the like of him that the differences in their perspectives that originate in their particular individual biographies are irrelevant for the purposes at hand of each and that both have selected and interpreted the actually and potentially common objects in an "empirically identical" manner that is sufficient for the purposes at hand. Thus, for example, in talking about "matters just known in common" persons will discuss them using a course of utterances that are governed by the expectation that the other person *will* understand. The speaker expects that the other person will assign to his remarks the sense intended by the speaker and expects that thereby the other person will permit the speaker the assumption that both know what he is talking about without any requirement of a checkout. Thus the sensible character of the matter that is being discussed is settled by a fiat assignment that each expects to make, and expects the other to make in reciprocal fashion, that as a condition of his right to decide without interference that he knows what he is talking about and that what he is talking about is so, each will have furnished whatever unstated understandings are required. Much therefore that is being talked about is not mentioned, although each

expects that the adequate sense of the matter being talked about is settled. The more so is this the case, the more is the exchange one of commonplace remarks among persons who "know" each other.

Students were instructed to engage an acquaintance or friend in an ordinary conversation and, without indicating that what the experimenter was saying was in any way out of the ordinary, to insist that the person clarify the sense of his commonplace remarks. Twenty-three students reported twenty-five instances of such encounters. The following are typical excerpts from their accounts.

Case 1. The subject was telling the experimenter, a member of the subject's car pool, about having had a flat tire while going to work the previous day.

(S): "I had a flat tire."

(E): "What do you mean, you had a flat tire?"

She appeared momentarily stunned. Then she answered in a hostile way: "What do you mean? What do you mean? A flat tire is a flat tire. That is what I meant. Nothing special. What a crazy question!"

Case 2. (S): "Hi, Ray. How is your girl friend feeling?"

(E): "What do you mean, how is she feeling? Do you mean physical or mental?"

(S): "I mean how is she feeling? What's the matter with you?" (He looked peeved.)

(E): "Nothing. Just explain a little clearer, what do you mean?"

(S): "Skip it. How are your Med School applications coming?"

(E): "What do you mean, 'How are they?'"

(S): "You know what I mean."

(E): "I really don't."

(S): "What's the matter with you? Are you sick?"

Case 3. On Friday night my husband and I were watching television. My husband remarked that he was tired. I asked, "How are you tired? Physically, mentally, or just bored?"

(S): "I don't know, I guess physically, mainly."

(E): "You mean that your muscles ache, or your bones?"

(S): "I guess so. Don't be so technical."

(S): (After more watching) "All these old movies have the same kind of old iron bedstead in them."

(E): "What do you mean? Do you mean all old movies, or some of them, or just the ones you have seen?"

(S): "What's the matter with you? You know what I mean."

(E): "I wish you would be more specific."

(S): "You know what I mean! Drop dead!"

Case 4. During a conversation (with the male *E's* fiancee) the *E* questioned the meaning of various words used by the subject. For the first minute and a half the subject responded to the questions as if they were legitimate inquiries. Then she responded with "Why are you asking me these questions?" and repeated this two or three times after each question. She became nervous and jittery, her face and hand movements . . . uncontrolled. She appeared bewildered and complained that I was making her nervous and demanded that I "Stop it!" . . . The subject picked up a magazine and covered her face. She put down the magazine and pretended to be engrossed. When asked why she was looking at the magazine, she closed her mouth and refused any further remarks.

Case 5. My friend said to me, "Hurry or we will be late." I asked him what did he mean by late and from what point of view did it have reference. There was a look of perplexity and cynicism on his face. "Why are you asking me such silly questions? Surely I don't have to explain such a statement. What is wrong with you today? Why should I have to stop to analyze such a statement. Everyone understands my statements and you should be no exception."

Case 6. The victim waved his hand cheerily.

(S): "How are you?"

(E): "How am I in regard to what? My health, my finance, my school work, my peace of mind, my . . ."

(S): (Red in the face and suddenly out of control.) "Look! I was just trying to be polite. Frankly, I don't give a damn how you are."

Case 7. My friend and I were talking about a man whose overbearing attitude annoyed us. My friend expressed his feeling.

(S): "I'm sick of him."

(E): Would you explain what is wrong with you that you are sick?"

(S): "Are you kidding me? You know what I mean."

(E): "Please explain your ailment."

(S): (He listened to me with a puzzled look.) "What came over you? We never talk this way, do we?" . . .

Case 8. Apparently as a casual afterthought, my husband mentioned Friday night, "Did you remember to drop off my shirts today?"

Taking nothing for granted, I replied, "I remember that you said something about it this morning. What shirts did you mean, and what did you mean by having them 'dropped' off?" He looked puzzled, as though I must have answered some other question than the one asked.

Instead of making the explanation he seemed to be waiting for, I persisted, "I thought your shirts were all in pretty good shape; why not keep them a little longer?" I had the uncomfortable feeling I had overplayed the part.

He no longer looked puzzled, but indignant. He repeated, "A little longer! What do you mean, and what have you done with my shirts?"

I acted indignant too. I asked, "What shirts? You have sport shirts, plain shirts, wool shirts, regular shirts, and dirty shirts. I'm no mind reader. What exactly did you want?"

My husband again looked confused, as though he was trying to justify my behavior. He seemed simultaneously to be on the defensive and offensive. He assumed a very patient, tolerant air, and said, "Now, let's start all over again. Did you drop off my shirts today?"

I replied, "I heard you before. It's your meaning I wish was more clear. As far as I am concerned dropping off your shirts—whichever shirts you mean—could mean giving them to the Goodwill, leaving them at the cleaners, at the laundromat, or throwing them out. I never know what you mean with those vague statements."

He reflected on what I said, then changed the entire perspective by acting as though we were playing a game, that it was all a joke. He seemed to enjoy the joke. He ruined my approach by assuming the role I thought was mine. He then said, "Well, let's take this step by step with 'yes' or 'no' answers. Did you see the dirty shirts I left on the kitchenette, yes or no?"

I could see no way to complicate his question, so felt forced to answer "Yes." In the same fashion, he asked if I picked up the shirts; if I put them in the car; if I left them at the laundry;

and if I did all these things that day, Friday. My answers were "Yes."

The experiment, it seemed to me, had been cut short by his reducing all the parts of his previous question to their simplest terms, which were given to me as if I were a child unable to handle any complex questions, problems, or situations.

Demonstration 2: Breaching the Interchangeability of Standpoints

In order to breach the presupposed interchangeability of standpoints, students were asked to enter a store, to select a customer, and to treat the customer as a clerk while giving no recognition that the subject was any other person than the experimenter took him to be and without giving any indication that the experimenter's treatment was anything other than perfectly reasonable and legitimate.

Case 1. One evening, while shopping at Sears with a friend, I (male) found myself next to a woman shopping at the copper-clad pan section. The store was busy . . . and clerks were hard to find. The woman was just a couple of feet away and my friend was behind me. Pointing to a tea kettle, I asked the woman if she did not think the price was rather high. I asked in a friendly tone. . . . She looked at me and then at the kettle and said "Yes." I then said I was going to take it anyway. She said, "Oh," and started to move sideways away from me. I quickly asked her if she was not going to wrap it for me and take my cash. Still moving slowly away and glancing first at me, then at the kettle, then at the other pans farther away from me, she said the clerk was "over there" pointing off somewhere. In a harsh tone, I asked if she was not going to wait on me. She said, "No, No, I'm not the saleslady. There she is." I said that I knew that the extra help was inexperienced, but there was no reason not to wait on a customer. "Just wait on me. I'll be patient." With that, she flushed with anger and walked rapidly away, looking back once as if to ask if it could really be true.

The following three protocols are the work of a forty-year-old female graduate student in clinical psychology.

Case 2. We went to V's book store, noted not so much for its fine merchandise and its wide range of stock as it is in certain circles for the fact that the clerks are male homosexuals. I approached a gentleman who was browsing at a table stacked neatly with books.

(E): "I'm in a hurry. Would you get a copy of *Sociopathic Behavior* by Lemert, please?"

(S): (Looked *E* up and down, drew himself very straight, slowly laid the book down, stepped back slightly, then leaned forward and in a low voice said) "I'm interested in sociopathic behavior, too. That's why I'm here. I study the fellows here by pretending to be . . ."

(E): (Interrupting) "I'm not particularly interested in whether you are or are only pretending to be. Please just get the book I asked for."

(S): (Looked shocked. More than surprised, believe me. Stepped around the display table, deliberately placed his hands on the books, leaned forward and shouted) "I don't have such a book. I'm not a clerk! I'm—Well!" (Stalked out of the store.)

Case 3. When we entered I. Magnin's there was one woman who was fingering a sweater, the only piece of merchandise to be seen in the shop. I surmised that the clerk must be in the stockroom.

(E): "That is a lovely shade, but I'm looking for one a little lighter. Do you have one in cashmere?"

(S): "I really don't know, you see I'm . . ."

(E): (Interrupting) "Oh, you are new here? I don't mind waiting while you look for what I want."

(S): "Indeed I shall not!"

(E): "But aren't you here to *serve* customers?"

(S): "I'm not! I'm here to . . ."

(E): (Interrupts) "This is hardly the place for such an attitude. Now please show me a cashmere sweater a shade or two lighter than this one."

(The clerk entered.)

(S): (To clerk) "My dear, this—(pointed her face toward *E*)—*person* insists on being shown a sweater. Please take care of her while I compose myself. I want to be certain this (sweater) will do, and she (pointed her face again at *E*) is so *insistent*." (*S* carried the sweater with her, walked haughtily to a large upholstered chair, sat in it, brushed her gloved hands free from imaginary dirt, jerked her shoulders, fluffed her suit jacket, and glared at *E*).

Case 4. While visiting with a friend in Pasadena, I told him about this being-taken-for-the-clerk experiment. The friend is a Professor Emeritus of Mathematics at the California Institute of Technology and the successful author of many books, some technical, some fictional, and he is most satirical in his contemplations of his fellow man. He begged to be allowed to accompany me and to aid me in the selection of scenes. . . . We went first to have luncheon at the Atheneum, which caters to the students, faculty, and guests of Cal Tech. While we were still in the lobby, my host pointed out a gentleman who was standing in the large drawing room near the entrance to the dining room and said, "Go to it. There's a good subject for you." He stepped aside to watch. I walked toward the man very deliberately and proceeded as follows. (I will use *E* to designate myself; *S*, the subject.)

(E): "I should like a table on the west side, a quiet spot, if you please. And what is on the menu?"

(S): (Turned toward *E* but looked past and in the direction of the foyer) said, "Eh, ah, madam, I'm sure." (looked past *E* again, looked at a pocket watch, replaced it, and looked toward the dining room).

(E): "Surely luncheon hours are not over. What do you recommend I order today?"

(S): "I don't know. You see, I'm waiting . . ."

(E): (Interrupted with) "Please don't keep me standing here while you wait. Kindly show me to a table."

(S): "But Madam,—" (started to edge away from door, and back into the lounge in a slightly curving direction around *E*)

(E): "My good man—" (At this *S*'s face flushed, his eyes rounded and opened wide.)

(S): "But—you—I—oh dear!" (He seemed to wilt.)

(E): (Took *S*'s arm in hand and propelled him toward the dining room door, slightly ahead of herself.)

(S): (Walked slowly but stopped just within the room, turned around and for the first time looked directly and very appraisingly at *E*, took out the watch, looked at it, held it to his ear, replaced it, and muttered) "Oh dear."

(E): "It will take only a minute for you to show me to a table and take my order. Then you can return to wait for your customers. After all, I am a guest and a customer, too."

(S): (Stiffened slightly, walked jerkily toward the nearest empty table, held a chair for *E* to be seated, bowed slightly, muttered "My pleasure," hurried toward the door, stopped, turned, looked back at *E* with a blank facial expression.)

At this point *E*'s host walked up to *S*, greeted him, shook hands, and propelled him toward *E*'s table. *S* stopped a few steps from the table, looked directly at, then through *E*, and started to walk back toward the door. Host told him *E* was the young lady whom he had invited to join them at lunch (then introduced me to one of the big names in the physics world, a pillar of the institution!). *S* seated himself reluctantly and perched rigidly on his chair, obviously uncomfortable. *E* smiled, made light and polite inquiries about his work, mentioned various functions attended which had honored him, then complacently remarked that it was a shame *E* had not met him personally before now, so that she should not have mistaken him for the maître-d'. The host chattered about his long-time friendship with me, while *S* fidgeted and looked again at his pocket watch, wiped his forehead with a table napkin, looked at *E* but avoided meeting her eyes. When the host mentioned that *E* is studying sociology at UCLA, *S* suddenly burst into loud laughter, realized that everyone in the room was looking in the direction of our table, abruptly became quiet, then said to *E* "You mistook me for the maître-d', didn't you?"

(E): "Deliberately, sir."

(S): "Why deliberately?"

(E): "You have just been used as the unsuspecting subject in an experiment."

(S): "Diabolic. But clever, I must say (To our host) I haven't been so shaken since _____ denounced my theory _____ of _____ in 19 _____. And the wild thoughts that ran through my mind! Call the receptionist from the lobby, go to the men's room, turn this woman to the first person that comes along. Damn these early diners, there's nobody coming in at this time. Time is standing still, or my watch has stopped. I will talk to _____ about this, make sure it doesn't happen to 'somebody'. Damn a persistent woman. I'm not her 'good man!' I'm Dr. _____, and not to be pushed around. This can't be happening. If I do take her to that damned table she wants, I can get away from her, and I'll just take it easy until I can. I remember _____ (hereditary psychopath, wife of one of the 'family' of the institution) maybe if I do what *this* one wants she will not make any more trouble than this. I wonder if she is 'off.' She certainly looks normal. Wonder how you can really tell?"

*Demonstration 3: Breaching
the Expectancy That a Knowledge of
a Relationship of Interaction Is a Commonly
Entertained Scheme of Communication*

Schutz proposed that from the member's point of view, an event of conduct, like a move in a game, consists of an event-in-a-social-order. Thus, for the member, its recognizably real character is furnished by attending its occurrence with respect to a corpus of socially sanctioned knowledge of the social relationships that the member uses and assumes that others use as the same scheme of expression and interpretation.

It was decided to breach this expectancy by having students treat a situation as something that it "obviously" and "really" was not. Students were instructed to spend from fifteen minutes to an hour in their own homes acting as if they were boarders. They were instructed to conduct themselves in a circumspect and polite fashion: to avoid getting personal; to use formal address; to speak only when they were spoken to.

In nine of forty-nine cases students either refused to do the assignment (five cases) or the try was "unsuccessful" (four cases). Four of the "no try" students said they were afraid to do it; a fifth said she preferred to avoid the risk of exciting her mother who had a heart condition. In two of the "unsuccessful" cases the family treated it as a joke from the beginning and refused, despite the continuing actions of the student experimenter, to change. A third family took the view that something of an undisclosed sort was the matter, but what it might be was of no concern to them. In the fourth family the father and mother remarked that the daughter was being "extra nice" and undoubtedly wanted something that she would shortly reveal.

In the remaining four-fifths of the cases family members were stupefied, vigorously sought to make the strange actions intelligible, and to restore the situation to normal appearances. Reports were filled with accounts of astonishment, bewilderment, shock, anxiety, embarrassment, and anger as well as with charges by various family members that the student was mean, inconsiderate, selfish, nasty, and impolite. Family members demanded explanations: "What's the matter?" "What's gotten into you?" "Did you get fired?" "Are you sick?" "What are you being so superior about?" "Why are you mad?" "Are you out of your mind or are you just stupid?" One student acutely embarrassed his mother in front of her friends by asking if she minded if he had a snack from the refrigerator. "Mind if you have a little snack? You've been eating little snacks around here for years without asking me. What's gotten into you?" One mother, infuriated when her daughter spoke to her only when she was spoken to, began to shriek in angry denunciation of the daughter for her disrespect and insubordination and refused to be calmed by the student's sister. A father berated his daughter for being insufficiently concerned for the welfare of others and for acting like a spoiled child.

Occasionally family members would first treat the student's action as a cue for a joint comedy routine which was soon replaced by irritation and exasperated anger at the student for not knowing "when enough was enough." Family members mocked the "politeness" of the students—"Certainly Mr. Dinerberg!"—or charged the student with acting like a wise guy and generally reproved the "politeness" with sarcasm.

Explanations were sought in terms of understandable and previous motives of the student: the accusation that the student was covering up something important that the family should know; that the student was working too hard in school; that the student was ill; that there had been "another fight" with a fiancée.

Unacknowledged explanations were followed by withdrawal of the offended member, attempted isolation of the culprit, retaliation, and denunciation. "Don't bother with him, he's in one of his moods again." "Pay no attention but just wait until he asks me for something." "You're cutting me, okay. I'll cut you and then some." "Why must you always create friction in our family harmony?" A father followed his son into the bedroom. "Your mother is right. You don't look well and you're not talking sense. You had better get another job that doesn't require such late hours." To this the student replied that he appreciated his consideration, but that he felt fine and only wanted a little privacy. The father

responded in high rage, "I don't want any more of *that* out of *you*. And if you can't treat your mother decently, you'd better move out!"

There were no cases in which the situation was not restorable upon the student's explanation. Nevertheless, for the most part, family members were not amused and only rarely did they find the experience instructive, as the student argued that it was supposed to have been. After hearing the explanation, a sister replied coldly on behalf of a family of four, "Please, no more of these experiments. We're not rats you know." Occasionally an explanation was accepted and still it added offense. In several cases students reported that the explanation left them, their families, or both wondering how much of what the student had said was "in character" and how much the student "really meant."

Students found the assignment difficult to complete because of not being treated as if they were in the role that they are attempting to play and of being confronted with situations to which they did not know how a boarder would respond.

There were several entirely unexpected results. (1) Although many students reported extensive rehearsals in imagination, very few of those that did it mentioned anticipatory fears or embarrassment. (2) Although unanticipated and nasty developments frequently occurred, in only one case did a student report serious regrets. (3) Very few students reported heartfelt relief when the hour was over. They were much more likely to report a partial relief. They frequently reported that in response to the anger of others they became angry in return and slipped easily into subjectively recognizable feelings and actions.

Demonstration 4: Breaching the Grasp of "What Anyone Knows" to Be Correct Grounds of Action of a Real Social World

Among the possibilities that a premedical student could treat as correct grounds for his further inferences and actions about such matters as how a medical school intake interview is conducted or how an applicant's conduct is related to his chances of admission, certain ones (e.g., that deferring to the interviewer's interests is a condition for making a favorable impression) he treats as matters that he is required to know and act upon as a condition of his competence as a premedical candidate. He expects others like him to know and act upon the same things; and he expects that as he expects others to know and act upon them, the others in turn expect the like of him.

A procedure was designed to breach the constitutive expectancies attached to "what-any-competent-premedical-candidate-knows" while satisfying the three conditions under which their breach would presumably produce confusion.

Twenty-eight premedical students of the University of California in Los Angeles were run individually through a three-hour experimental interview. As part of the solicitation of subjects, as well as the beginning of the interview, *E* identified himself as a representative of an Eastern medical school who was attempting to learn why the medical school intake interview was such a stressful situation. It was hoped that identifying *E* as a person with medical school ties would minimize the chance that students would "leave the field" once the accent breaching procedure began. How the other two conditions of (a) managing a redefinition in insufficient time and (b) not being able to count on consensual support for an alternative definition of social reality were met will be apparent in the following description.

During the first hour of the interview, the student furnished the facts-of-life about interviews for admission to medical school by answering for the "representative" such questions as "What sources of information about a candidate are available to medical schools?" "What can a medical school learn about a candidate from these sources?" "What kind of a man are the medical schools looking for?" "What should a good candidate do in the interview?" "What should he avoid?" With this much completed, the student was told that the "representative's" research interests had been satisfied. The student was asked if he would care to hear a recording of an actual interview. All students wanted very much to hear the recording.

The recording was a faked one between a "medical school interviewer" and an "applicant." The applicant was depicted as being a boor; his language was ungrammatical and filled with colloquialisms; he was evasive; he contradicted the interviewer; he bragged; he ran down other schools and professions; he insisted on knowing how he had done in the interview and so on.

Detailed assessments by the student of the recorded applicant were obtained immediately after the recording was finished. The following edited assessment is representative:

> I didn't like it. I didn't like his attitude. I didn't like anything about him. Everything he said grated the wrong way. I didn't like his smoking. The way he kept saying "Yeah-h!" He didn't show that he realized that the interviewer had his future in his hands. I didn't like the vague way he answered questions. I didn't like the way he pressed at the end of the interview. He was disrespectful. His motives were too obvious. He made a mess of it. He finished with a bang to say the least. . . . His answers to questions were stupid. I felt that the interviewer was telling him that he wasn't going to get in. I didn't like the interview. I felt it was too informal. To a degree it's good if it's natural but . . . the interview is not something to breeze through. It's just not the place for chit-chat. He had fairly good grades but . . . he's not interested in things outside of school and didn't say what he did *in* school. Then he didn't *do* very much— outside of this lab. I didn't like the man at all. I never met an applicant like that! "My pal"—Just one of these little chats. I never met anybody *like* that. Wrong-way Corrigan.

The student was then given information from the applicant's "official record." This information was deliberately contrived to contradict the principal points in the student's assessment. For example, if the student said that the applicant must have come from a lower-class family, he was told that the applicant's father was vice president of a firm that manufactured pneumatic doors for trains and buses. If the applicant had been thought to be ignorant, he was described as having excelled in courses like The Poetry of Milton and Dramas of Shakespeare. If the student said the applicant did not know how to get along with people, then the applicant was pictured as having worked as a voluntary solicitor for Sydenham Hospital in New York City and had raised $32,000 from thirty "big givers." The belief that the applicant was stupid and would not do well in a scientific field was met by citing A grades in organic and physical chemistry and graduate level performance in an undergraduate research course.

The Ss wanted very much to know what "the others" thought of the applicant, and had he been admitted? The "others" had been previously and casually identified by the "representative" as "Dr. Gardner, the medical school interviewer," "six psychiatrically trained members of the admissions committee who heard only the recorded interview," and "other students I talked to."

The S was told that the applicant had been admitted and was living up to the promise that the medical school interviewer and the "six psychiatrists" had found and expressed in the following recommendation of the applicant's characterological fitness.

Dr. Gardner, the medical school interviewer, wrote, "A well-bred, polite young man, poised, affable, and self-confident. Capable of independent thinking. Interests of a rather specialized character. Marked intellectual curiosity. Alert and free of emotional disturbances. Marked maturity of manner and outlook. Meets others easily. Strongly motivated toward a medical career. Definite ideas of what he wants to achieve which are held in good perspective. Unquestioned sincerity and integrity. Expressed himself easily and well. Recommend favorable consideration." The six psychiatric members of the admissions committee agreed in all essentials.

Concerning the views of "other students," S was told that he was, for example, the thirtieth student I had seen; that twenty-eight before him were in entire agreement with the medical school interviewer's assessment; and that the remaining two had been slightly uncertain but at the first bit of information had seen him just as the others had.

Following this, Ss were invited to listen to the record a second time, after which they were asked to assess the applicant again.

Results. Twenty-five of the twenty-eight subjects were taken in. The following does not apply to the three who were convinced there was a deception. Two of these are discussed at the conclusion of this section.

Incongruous materials, presented to S in the order indicated, were performance information, and characterological information. Performance information dealt with the applicant's activities, grades, family background, courses, charity work, and the like. Characterological information consisted of character assessments of him by the "medical school interviewers," the "six psychiatrically trained members of the admissions committee," and the "other students."

Subjects managed incongruities of performance data with vigorous attempts to make it factually compatible with their original assessments. For example, when they said that the applicant sounded like a lower-class person, they were told that his father was vice president of a national corporation that manufactured pneumatic doors for trains and buses. Here are some typical replies:

"He should have made the point that he *could* count on money."

"That explains why he said he had to work. Probably his father made him work. That would make a lot of his moans unjustified in the sense that things were really not so bad."

"What does that have to do with values?!"

"You could tell from his answers. You could tell that he was used to having his own way."

"That's something the interviewer knew that *I* didn't know."

"Then he's an out and out liar!"

When *Ss* said that the applicant was self-ish and could not get along with people, they were told that he had worked as a volunteer for Sydenham Hospital and had raised $32,000 from thirty "big givers."

"He seems to be a good salesman. So possibly he's missing his profession. I'd say *definitely* he's missing his profession!"

"They probably contributed because of the charity and not because they were solicited."

"Pretty good. Swell. Did he know them personally?"

"It's very fashionable to work, for example, during the war for Bundles for Britain. So that doesn't—definitely!—show altruistic motives at all. He is a person who is subject to fashion and I'm very critical of that sort of thing.

"He's so forceful he might have shamed them into giving."

"People who are wealthy—his father would naturally see those people—big contributions—they could give a lot of money and not know what they're giving it for."

That he had a straight A average in physical science courses began to draw bewilderment.

"He took quite a variety of courses . . . I'm baffled.—Probably the interview wasn't a very good mirror of his character."

"He did seem to take some odd courses. They seem to be fairly normal. Not normal—but—it doesn't strike me one way or the other."

"Well! I think you can analyze it this way. In psychological terms. See—one possible way—now I may be all *wet* but this is the way I look at *that*. He probably suffered from an inferiority complex and that's an overcompensation for his inferiority complex. His *great* marks—his *good* marks are a compensation for his failure—in social dealings perhaps, I don't know."

"Woops! And only third alternate at Georgia. (Deep sigh) I can see why he'd feel resentment about not being admitted to Phi Bet."

(Long silence) "Well! From what—that leads me to think he's a grind or something like that."

Attempts to resolve the incongruities produced by the character assessment of "Gardner" and "the other six judges" were much less frequent than normalizing attempts with performance information. Open expressions of bewilderment and anxiety interspersed with silent ruminations were characteristic.

(Laugh) "Golly!" (Silence) "I'd think it would be the other way around."—(Very subdued) "Maybe I'm all wro—My orientation is all off. I'm completely baffled."

"Not polite. Self-confident he certainly was. But not polite—I don't know. Either the interviewer was a little crazy or else I am." (Long pause) "That's rather shocking. It makes me have doubts about my own thinking. Perhaps my values in life are wrong. I don't know."

(Whistles) "I—I didn't think he sounded well bred at all. That whole tone of voice!!—I—Perhaps you noticed though, when he said 'You should have said in the first place' before he took it with a smile.—But even so! No, no I can't see that. 'You should have said that before.' Maybe he was being funny though. Exercising a—No! To me it sounded impertinent!"

"Ugh—Well, that certainly puts a different slant on my conception of interviews. Gee—that—confuses me all the more."

"Well—(laugh)—Hhh!—Ugh! Well, maybe he looked like a nice boy. He did—he did get his point across.—Perhaps—seeing the person would make a big difference.—Or perhaps I would never make a good interviewer." (Reflectively and almost inaudibly) "They didn't mention any of the things I mentioned." (HG: Eh?) (Louder) "They didn't mention any of the things I mentioned and so I feel like a complete failure."

Soon after the performance data produced its consternation, an occasional request would be made: "What did the other students make of him?" Only after Gardner's assessment, and the responses to it had been made were the opinions of the "other students" given. In some cases the subject was told "34 out of 35 before you," in others 43 out of 45, 19 out of 20, 51 out of 52. All the numbers were large. For 18 of the 25 students the delivery hardly varied from the following verbatim protocols:

[34 out of 35] I don't know.—I still stick to my original convictions. I—I—Can you tell *me* what—I saw wrong. Maybe—I—I had the wrong idea—the wrong attitude all along. (Can you tell me? I'm interested that there should be such a disparity.) Definitely.—I—think—it would be definitely the other way—I can't make sense of it. I'm completely baffled, believe me.—I—I don't understand how I could have been so wrong. Maybe my ideas—my evaluations of people are—just twisted. I mean maybe I had the wrong—maybe my sense of values—is—off—or—different—from the other 33. But I don't think that's the case—because usually—and in all modesty I say this—I—I can judge people. I mean in class, in organizations I belong to—I usually judge them right. So therefore I don't understand at *all* how I could have been so wrong. I don't think I was under any stress or strain—here—tonight but—I don't understand it.

[43 out of 45] [Laugh] I don't know what to say now.—I'm troubled by my inability to judge the guy better than that. [Subdued] I shall sleep tonight, certainly—[Very subdued] but it certainly bothers me.—Sorry that I didn't— *Well!* One question that arises—I may be wrong—(Can you see how they might have seen him?) No. No, I can't see it, no.—Sure with all that background material, yes, but I don't see how Gardner did it without it. Well, I guess that makes Gardner, Gardner, and me, me. (The other 45 students didn't have the background material.) Yeah, yeah, yeah. I mean I'm not denying it at all. I mean for myself, there's no sense saying—Of course! With their background they would be accepted, especially the second man, good God!—Okay, what else?

[23 out of 25] [Softly] Maybe I'm tired. (HG, "Eh?") [Burst of laughter.] Maybe I didn't get enough sleep last night.—Uhh!—Well—I might not have been looking for the things that the other men were looking for.—I wasn't—Huh!—It puts me at a loss, really.

[9 out of 10] So I'm alone in my judgment. I don't know, sir! I don't know, sir!!—I can't explain it. It's senseless.—I tried to be impartial at the beginning. I admit I was prejudiced immediately.

[51 out of 52] You mean that 51 others stuck to their guns, too? (Stuck to their guns in the sense that they saw him just as the judges saw him.) Uh huh. [Deep sigh] I still don't—Yeah! I see. But just listening I don't think he was a—very good chance. But in light of his other things I feel that the interview was not—showing—the real—him.—Hhh!

[36 out of 37] I would go back on my former opinion but I wouldn't go back too far. I just don't see it.—Why should I have these different standards? Were my opinions more or less in agreement on the first man? (No.) That leads me to think.—That's funny. Unless you got 36 unusual people. I can't understand it. Maybe it's my personality. (Does it make any difference?) It *does* make a difference if I assume they're correct. What I consider is proper, they don't.—It's my attitude—Still in all a man of that sort would alienate me. A wise guy type to be avoided. Of course you can talk like that with other fellows—but in an interview? . . . Now I'm more confused than I was at the beginning of the entire interview. I think I ought to go home and look in the mirror and talk to myself. Do you have any ideas? (Why? Does it disturb you?) Yes it *does* disturb me! It makes me think my abilities to judge people and values are way off from normal. It's not a healthy situation. (What difference does it make?) If I act the way I act it seems to me that I'm just putting my head in the lion's mouth. I did have preconceptions but they're shattered all to hell. It makes me wonder about myself. Why should I have these different standards? It all points to me.

Of the twenty-five *S*s who were taken in, seven were unable to resolve the incongruity of having been wrong about such an obvious matter and were unable to "see" the alternative. Their suffering was dramatic and unrelieved. Five more resolved it with the view that the medical school had accepted a good man; five others with the view that it had accepted a boor. Although they changed, they nevertheless did not abandon their former views. For them Gardner's view could be seen "in general," but the grasp lacked convincingness. When attention was drawn to particulars, the general picture would evaporate. These *S*s were willing to entertain and use the "general" picture, but they suffered whenever indigestible particulars of the same portrait came into view. Subscription to the "general" picture was accompanied by a recitation of characteristics that were not only the opposite of those in the original view but were intensified by superlative adjectives like "supremely" poised, "very" natural, "most" confident, "very" calm. Further, they saw the new features through a new appreciation of the way the medical examiner had been listening. They saw, for example, that the examiner was smiling when the applicant had forgotten to offer him a cigarette.

Three more *S*s were convinced that there was deception and acted on the conviction through the interview. They showed no disturbance. Two of these showed acute suffering as soon as it appeared that the interview was finished, and they were being dismissed with no acknowledgment of a deception. Three others inadvertently suffered in silence and confounded *E*. Without

any indication to *E*, they regarded the interview as an experimental one in which they were being asked to solve some problems and therefore were being asked to do as well as possible and to make no changes in their opinions, for only then would they be contributing to the study. They were difficult for me to understand during the interview because they displayed marked anxiety, yet their remarks were bland and were not addressed to the matters that were provoking it. Finally three more *S*s contrasted with the others. One of these insisted that the character assessments were semantically ambiguous and because there was insufficient information a "high correlation opinion" was not possible. A second, and the only one in the entire series, found, according to his account, the second portrait as convincing as the original one. When the deception was revealed, he was disturbed that he could have been as convinced as he was. The third one, in the face of everything, showed only slight disturbance of very short duration. However, he alone among the subjects had already been interviewed for medical school, had excellent contacts, despite a grade point average of less than C he estimated his chances of admission as fair, and finally he expressed his preference for a career in the diplomatic service over a career in medicine.

As a final observation, twenty-two of the twenty-eight *S*s expressed marked relief—ten of them with explosive expressions—when I disclosed the deception. Unanimously they said that the news of the deception permitted them to return to their former views. Seven *S*s had to be convinced that there had been a deception. When the deception was revealed, they asked what they were to believe. Was I telling them that there had been a deception in order to make them feel better? No pains were spared, and whatever truth or lies that had to be told were told in order to establish the truth that there had been a deception.

SELF-FULFILLING PROPHECIES

Self-fulfilling prophecies are events that come true because of actions taken based on the belief that the event is real. For instance, if many people believe a gas shortage is going to occur and they all rush to get gas at the same time, they may, in fact, cause a gas shortage. Self-fulfilling prophecies illustrate the features of reality that Mehan and Wood call *reflexive* and *interactional*. Understanding self-fulfilling prophecies can be very useful for determining how to intervene in behavioral loops that seem to be self-perpetuating. This process also helps explain the power of labels and preconceived expectations for bringing about the actions that seem to justify the original stereotype.

In his article "Self-Fulfilling Prophecies," Paul Watzlawick develops the definition of the self-fulfilling process and gives several examples of how it works. Each of these examples highlights the reflexivity and interactional features of reality. People form beliefs and expectations and then behave in a way that generates an interactional chain of events that fulfills their expectations. This reaffirms the initial belief and further entrenches it.

Psychologist Carol Word and her colleagues examine the nonverbal behavior of hiring managers in employment interviews and note that the managers' nonverbal cues suggest more comfort with White candidates than Black candidates. The authors conclude that these behavioral cues may become self-fulfilling in that White candidates are expected to perform better and given the opportunity to do so.

READING QUESTIONS

1. Watzlawick gives examples of self-fulfilling prophecies at both the individual and collective levels. Discuss examples of contemporary world politics that can be explained in terms of self-fulfilling prophecies.

2. Make a list of behavioral stereotypes, and consider how these stereotypes might become real and persistent as a result of self-fulfilling interactional expectations.

3. If someone has a preconceived notion and acts in a way that makes it real in the outcome, will the person ever know that it was her or his own behavior that caused the expected outcome? Does it matter? What feature of reality does this process describe?

SELF-FULFILLING PROPHECIES

38

Self-Fulfilling Prophecies

Paul Watzlawick

(1984)

A self-fulfilling prophecy is an assumption or prediction that, purely as a result of having been made, causes the expected or predicted event to occur and thus confirms its own "accuracy." For example, if someone assumes, for whatever reason, that he is not respected, he will, because of this assumption, act in such a hostile, overly sensitive, suspicious manner that he brings about that very contempt in others which "proves" again and again his firmly entrenched conviction. This mechanism may be commonplace and well known, but it is based upon a number of facts that are by no means part of our everyday thinking and which have a profound significance for our view of reality.

In our traditional cause-and-effect thinking we usually see event *B* as the result of a preceding, causal event (*A*)—which in turn has, of course, its own causes, just as the occurrence of *B* produces its own sequel of events. In the sequence *A* → *B, A* is therefore the cause and *B* its effect. The causality is *linear* and *B* follows *A* in the course of time. Accordingly, in this causality model, *B* can have no effect on *A*, because this would mean a reversal of the flow of time: The present (*B*) would have to exert a backward effect on the past (*A*).

Matters stand differently in the following example: In March 1979, when the newspapers in California began to publish sensational pronouncements of an impending, severe gasoline shortage, California motorists stormed the gas stations to fill up their tanks and to keep them as full as possible. This filling up of 12 million gasoline tanks (which up to this time had on the average been 75% empty) depleted the enormous reserves and so brought about the predicted shortage practically overnight. The endeavor to keep the fuel containers as full as possible (instead of getting gas when the tank was almost empty, as had been done before) resulted in endless lines and hours of waiting time at the gas stations, and increased the panic. After the excitement died down, it turned out that the allotment of gasoline to the state of California had hardly been reduced at all.

Here the customary cause-and-effect thinking breaks down. The shortage would never have occurred if the media had not predicted it. In other words, an event that had not yet taken place (i.e., an event in the future) created an effect in the present (the storming of the gas stations), which in turn caused the predicted event to become reality. In this sense it was the future—not the past—that determined the present.

The objection could be raised that all of this is neither astonishing nor unheard of. Are not almost all human decisions and actions largely dependent on the evaluation of their probable effects, advantages, and dangers (or at least should they not be)? Does not the future therefore always play a part in the present? Significant as these questions may be, they do not seem to make much sense here. Whoever tries, usually on the basis of earlier experience, to evaluate the future effect of his decision normally intends the best possible outcome. The specific action tries to take the future into consideration, and subsequently proves to be true or false, correct or incorrect; but it does not have to have any influence whatever on the course of events. However, an action that results from a self-fulfilling prophecy itself produces the requisite conditions for the occurrence of the expected event, and in this sense *creates* a reality which would not have arisen without it. The action that is at first neither true nor false produces a fact, and with it its own "truth."

Here are examples of both perspectives: If someone begins to suffer from headaches, sneezes, and shivers, he will, on the basis of past experience, assume that he is coming down with a cold; and if his diagnosis is correct, he can, with aspirin, hot drinks, and bedrest, favorably influence the (future) course of the illness by these means in the present. By doing so, he has correctly grasped a causal sequence that had at first been totally independent of him, and exerted a partial influence on it.

A fundamentally different sequence results from the practice of collecting taxes in certain countries. Since the revenue agency assumes a priori that no citizen will ever truthfully declare his income, the tax rate is dictated more or less arbitrarily. The revenue offices rely largely on the information of their assessment agents, who take into consideration such vague factors as a person's standard of living, his real estate property, the fur coats of his wife, the make of his car, and so forth. To the income, "ascertained" in this way, there is then added a certain percentage that is supposed to make up for any undeclared income, because—as we said—it is assumed a priori that the taxpayer cheats. This assumption,

however, produces the situation in which a truthful declaration of income becomes unacceptable even for an honest taxpayer, and in which dishonesty is practically made a necessity if one wants to escape unfair taxes. Again an assumption believed to be true creates the assumed reality, and again it is irrelevant whether the assumption was originally true or false. And so we see that the difference lies in the fact that, in the example of the head cold, a development that is already taking place in the present is acted upon as best as is possible, and its course is influenced in this way in the present; whereas in the examples of the gasoline shortage and the income tax the course of events is induced by the very measures which are undertaken as a (supposed) reaction to the expected event in question. Therefore what is supposed to be a *reaction* (the effect) turns out to be an action (the cause); the "solution" produces the problem; the prophecy of the event causes the event of the prophecy.

This singular reversal of cause and effect is particularly obvious in interpersonal conflicts, where the phenomenon of the so-called *punctuation* of a sequence of events is invariably present. Making use of an example that has already been employed elsewhere (Watzlawick, Bavelas, & Jackson, 1967, pp. 56–58), we will imagine a married couple struggling with a conflict that they both assume to be basically the other's fault, while their own behavior is seen only as a *reaction* to that of their partner. The woman complains that her husband is withdrawing from her, which he admits, but because he sees his silence or his leaving the room as the only possible reaction to her constant nagging and criticizing. For her this reasoning is a total distortion of the facts: His behavior is the *cause* of her criticism and her anger. Both partners are referring to the same interpersonal reality but assign to it a diametrically opposed causality. The diagram, Figure 1, may illustrate this discrepancy, although it postulates—unavoidably but wrongly—a starting point that does not really exist, because the behavior pattern between the two people has been repeating itself for a long time, and the question of who started it has long since become meaningless.

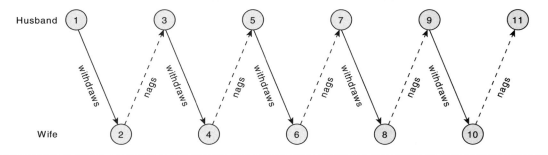

Figure 1

The arrows with the solid lines represent the behavior of the husband ("withdraws"), and the dotted lines that of the wife ("nags"). The husband dissects ("punctuates") the whole of the pattern into the triads 2–3–4, 4–5–6, 6–7–8, and so on, and so sees the interpersonal reality as one in which his wife nags (cause) and he *therefore* withdraws from her (effect). From her point of view, however, it is his cold passivity (cause) that causes her nagging (effect); she criticizes him *because* he withdraws from her, and therefore punctuates the pattern into the triads 1–2–3, 3–4–5, 5–6–7, and so on. With this opposed punctuation, both have literally brought about two contradictory realities and—what is perhaps even more important—two self-fulfilling prophecies. The two modes of behavior, which are seen subjectively as a reaction to the behavior of the partner, cause this very behavior in the other and "therefore" justify one's own behavior.

It goes without saying that self-fulfilling prophecies in an interpersonal context can also be used deliberately and with a specific intent. The dangers of this practice will be discussed later on. As an example here let me only mention the well-known method of former matchmakers in patriarchal societies, who had the thankless task of awakening a mutual interest in two young people, who possibly cared nothing for each other, because their families had decided that for financial reasons, social standing, or other similarly impersonal motives, the two would make a good couple. The matchmaker's usual procedure was to talk with the young man alone and ask him whether he had not noticed how the girl was always secretly watching him. Similarly, he would tell the girl that the boy was constantly looking at her when her head was turned. This prophecy, disguised as a fact, was often quickly fulfilled. Skilled diplomats also know this procedure as a negotiating technique.[1]

Everyday experience teaches us that only few prophecies are self-fulfilling, and the above examples should explain why: Only when a prophecy is believed, that is, only when it is seen as a fact that has, so to speak, already happened in the future, can it have a tangible effect on the present and thereby fulfill itself. Where this element of belief or conviction is absent, this effect will be absent as well. To inquire how the construction or acceptance of such a prophecy comes to be would go far beyond the scope of this essay. (An extensive study of the social, psychological, and physiological effects of self-fulfilling prophecies was published in 1974 by Jones.) Too numerous and various are the factors involved—from the realities one fabricates for oneself during the course of the so-called noncontingent reward experiments (Watzlawick, 1976, pp. 45–54) . . . , to such oddities as the (perhaps unverified, but not improbable) assertion that since Bernadette had a vision of the Virgin Mary in February of 1858, only pilgrims, but not a single inhabitant of Lourdes, found a miraculous cure there.

Of this story one can say, *se non è vero, è ben trovato,*[2] since it helps to build a bridge from our previous, somewhat trivial reflections to manifestations of self-fulfilling prophecies that have a deeper human as well as scientific significance.

The oracle had prophesied that Oedipus would kill his father and marry his mother. Horrified by this prediction, which he undoubtedly believed to be true, Oedipus tries to protect himself from the impending doom, but the precautionary measures themselves lead to the seemingly inescapable fulfillment of the oracle's dictum. As is known, Freud used this myth as a metaphor for the incestuous attraction for the opposite sex inherent in every child, and the consequent fear of retaliation on the part of the parent of the same sex; and he saw in this key constellation, the Oedipus conflict, the fundamental cause of later neurotic developments. In his autobiography the philosopher Karl Popper (1974) refers back to a self-fulfilling prophecy that he had already described two decades earlier and which he called the Oedipus *effect:*

> One of the ideas I had discussed in *The Poverty* [*of Historicism*] was the influence of a prediction upon the event predicted. I had called this the "Oedipus effect," because the oracle played a most important role in the sequence of events which led to the fulfillment of its prophecy. (It was also an allusion to the psychoanalysts, who had been strangely blind to this interesting fact, even though Freud himself admitted that the very dreams dreamt by patients were often coloured by the theories of their analysts; Freud called them "obliging dreams.")

Again we have the reversal of cause and effect, past and future; but here it is all the more critical and decisive because psychoanalysis is a theory of human behavior that hinges on the assumption of a linear causality, in which the past determines the present. And Popper points to the significance of this reversal by explicating further:

> For a time I thought that the existence of the Oedipus effect distinguished the social from the natural sciences. But in biology too—even in molecular biology—expectations often play a role in bringing about what has been expected.

Similar quotations, referring to the effect of such "unscientific" factors as simple expectations and assumptions in the sciences, could be collated in abundance—[*The Invented Reality*] is itself intended as such a contribution. In this connection one might recall, for instance, Einstein's remark in a talk with Heisenberg: "It is the theory that determines what we can observe." And in 1958 Heisenberg himself says, "We have to remember that what we observe is not nature in itself, but nature exposed to our method of questioning." And more radical still, the philosopher of science Feyerabend (1978): "Not conservative, but anticipatory suppositions guide research."

Some of the most carefully documented and elegant investigations of self-fulfilling prophecies in the area of human communication are associated with the name of the psychologist Robert Rosenthal of Harvard University. Of particular interest here is his (1968) book with the appropriate title *Pygmalion in the Classroom,* in which he describes the results of his so-called Oak School experiments. They concerned a primary school with 18 women teachers and over 650 students [see Reading 38]. The self-fulfilling prophecy was induced in the members of the faculty at the beginning of a certain school year by giving the students an intelligence test whereby the teachers were told that the test could not only determine intelligence quotients, but could also identify those 20% of the students who would make rapid and above-average intellectual progress in the coming school year. After the intelligence test had been administered, but before the teachers had met their new students for the first time, they received the names (indiscriminately picked from the student list) of those students who supposedly, on the basis of the test, could be expected with certainty to perform unusually well. The difference between these children and the others thus existed solely in the heads of their particular teacher. The same intelligence test was repeated at the end of the school year for all students and showed *real* above-average increases in the intelligence quotients and achievements of these "special" students, and the reports of the faculty proved furthermore that these children distinguished themselves from their fellow students by their behavior, intellectual curiosity, friendliness, and so on.

Saint Augustine thanked God that he was not responsible for his dreams. Nowadays we do not have this comfort. Rosenthal's experiment is only one, although an especially clear example of how deeply and incisively our fellow human beings are affected by our expectations, prejudices, superstitions, and wishful thinking—all purely mental constructions, often without the slightest glimmer of actuality—and how these discoveries erode our comfortable conviction of the surpassing importance of heredity and innate characteristics. For it hardly needs to be expressly emphasized that these constructions can have negative as well as positive effects. We are not only responsible for our dreams, but also for the reality created by our hopes and thoughts.

It would, however, be a mistake to assume that self-fulfilling prophecies are restricted to human beings. Their effects reach deeper, into prehuman stages of development, and are in this sense even more alarming. Even before Rosenthal carried out his Oak School experiment, he reported in a book published in 1966 a similar experiment with rats that was repeated and confirmed by many scholars in the following years. Twelve participants in a laboratory course in experimental psychology were given a lecture on certain studies that purported to prove that good or bad test achievements of rats (for instance, in learning experiments in labyrinth cages) can become innate by selective breeding. Six of the students then received thirty rats whose genetic constitution allegedly made them especially good, intelligent laboratory subjects, while the other six students were assigned thirty rats of whom they were told the opposite, namely, that they were animals whose hereditary factors made them unsuitable for experiments. In fact and truth, the sixty rats were all of the same kind, the one that has always been used for such purposes. All sixty animals were then trained for exactly the same learning experiment. The rats whose trainers believed them to be especially intelligent did not just do better from the very outset, but raised their achievements far above that of the "unintelligent" animals. At the end of the five-day experiment the trainers were asked to evaluate their animals subjectively, in addition to the noted results of the experiments. The students who "knew" that they were working with unintelligent animals expressed themselves accordingly, that is, negatively, in their reports, whereas their colleagues, who had experimented with rats of supposedly above-average talents, rated their charges as friendly, intelligent, ingenious, and the like, and mentioned furthermore that they had often touched the animals, petted them, and even played with them. When we consider the surpassing role rat experiments play in experimental psychology and especially in the psychology of learning, and how often inferences are drawn from them to human behavior, these inferences now seem somewhat questionable.

Rats are known to be very intelligent animals, and the students' reports suggest that in the way they handled their animals, they literally "handed" them their assumptions and expectations. But the results of another research project, reported in 1963 by the research team Cordaro and Ison, suggest that it is not only a matter of such direct influence. In this project the laboratory subjects were earthworms (planaria), who are of great interest for the student of evolution and of behavior alike, in that they are the most primitive form of life possessing the rudiments of a brain. The supposition therefore suggested itself that these worms were capable of training of the simplest kind, as, for instance, a change in direction (to the left or to the right) upon arriving at the crossbeam of a T-shaped groove arrangement. Experiments of this kind began in several American universities in the late fifties. As in the rat experiments, Cordaro and Ison caused the experimenters to believe that they were working with especially intelligent or especially incapable worms, and even here, at this primitive stage of development (which, moreover, left little room for emotional attachment), there grew from the conviction, once it was established, objectively discernible and statistically significant differences in the experimental behavior of the planaria.[3]

For the very reason that these experiments undermine our basic concepts, it is all too easy to shrug them off and return to the comfortable certainty of our accustomed routines. That, for instance, test psychologists ignore these extremely disturbing results and continue to test people and animals with unmitigated tenacity and scientific "objectivity" is only a small example of the determination with which we defend ourselves when our world view is being threatened. The fact that we are responsible to the world in its entirety and to a much higher degree than is dreamed of in our philosophy is

for the present almost unthinkable; but it can penetrate our consciousness through a better understanding of the processes of human communication—a study that will encompass many disciplines that heretofore have been either considered as being quite independent of each other or not considered at all. Rosenhan's contribution illuminates the alarming possibility that at least some so-called mental illnesses are nothing but constructions, and that the psychiatric institutions actually contribute to the constructions of those realities that are supposed to be treated therein. The chronic problem that still plagues modern psychiatry is that we have only the vaguest and most general concepts for the definition of mental health, while for the diagnosis of abnormal behavior there exist catalogs perfected to the last detail. Freud, for instance, used the concept of the ability to love and work as a basic criterion for mature emotional normalcy (a definition that does not do justice to a Hitler, on the one hand, or to the proverbial eccentricities of men of genius, on the other). The other medical specialties work with definitions of pathology that refer to certain deviations from fairly well-known normal functions of the healthy organism. Quite irrationally, in psychiatry it is just the opposite. Here pathology is considered the known factor, whereas normalcy is seen as difficult to define, if it is definable at all. This opens the floodgates to self-fulfilling diagnoses. There is a great number of very definite patterns of behavior that in the terminology of psychiatry are so tightly associated with certain diagnostic categories (again I refer to Rosenhan) that they virtually function like Pavlovian buzzers, not only in the thinking of the psychiatrist but also in the family environment of the patient. An attempt to show how certain specific forms of behavior take on the meaning of pathological manifestations on the basis of their cultural and societal significance, and how these manifestations in turn become self-fulfilling prophecies, would go beyond the scope of this essay. Of the already quite extensive literature on this topic, *The Manufacture of Madness* by Thomas Szasz (1970) is particularly notable. Suffice it to say that an essential part of the self-fulfilling effect of psychiatric diagnoses is based on our unshakable conviction that everything that has a name must *therefore* actually exist. The materializations and actualizations of psychiatric diagnoses probably originate largely from this conviction.

"Magic" diagnoses, in the actual sense of the word, have of course been known for a very long time. In his classic paper "Voodoo Death," the American physiologist Walter Cannon (1942) described a number of mysterious, sudden, and scientifically difficult to explain deaths that followed curses, evil spells, or the breaking of moral taboos. A Brazilian Indian, cursed by a medicine man, is helpless against his own emotional response to this death sentence and dies within hours. A young African hunter unknowingly kills and eats an inviolably banned wild hen. When he discovers his crime, he is overcome with despair and dies within twenty-four hours. A medicine man in the Australian bush points a bone with magic properties at a man. Believing that nothing can save him, the man sinks into lethargy and prepares to die. He is saved only at the last moment, when other members of the tribe force the witch doctor to remove the spell.

Cannon became convinced that voodoo death exists as a phenomenon,

> characteristically noted among aborigines— among human beings so primitive, so superstitious, so ignorant, that they feel themselves bewildered strangers in a hostile world. Instead of knowledge, they have fertile and unrestricted imaginations which fill their environment with all manner of evil spirits capable of affecting their lives disastrously.

At the time when Cannon wrote these lines, hundreds of thousands of human beings who were neither superstitious nor ignorant had every reason to see themselves as bewildered victims of an unimaginably hostile world. From the haunted, shadowy world of the concentration camps Viktor Frankl (1959, pp. 74–75) reports a phenomenon that corresponds to voodoo death:

> The prisoner who had lost faith in the future— his future—was doomed. With his loss of belief in the future, he also lost his spiritual hold; he let himself decline and became subject to mental and physical decay. Usually this happened quite suddenly, in the form of a crisis, the symptoms of which were familiar to the experienced camp inmate. We all feared this moment—not for ourselves, which would have been pointless, but for our friends. Usually it began with the prisoner refusing one morning to get dressed and wash or to go out on the parade grounds. No entreaties, no blows, no threats had any effect. He just lay there.

One of Frankl's fellow prisoners lost his will to live when his own prediction, seen in a dream, did not come true and thereby became a negative self-fulfillment. "I would like to tell you something, Doctor," he said to Frankl,

> I have had a strange dream. A voice told me that I could wish for something, that I should only say what I wanted to know, and all my questions would be answered. What do you think I asked? That I would like to know when the war would be over for me. You know what I mean, Doctor—for me! I wanted to know when we, when our camp, would be liberated and our sufferings come to an end.... Furtively he whispered to me, "March thirtieth."

But when the day of the prophesied liberation was near and the Allied forces were still far from the camp, things took a fateful turn for Frankl's fellow sufferer, the prisoner F.:

On March twenty-ninth, F. suddenly became ill and ran a high temperature. On March thirtieth, the day his prophecy had told him that the war and suffering would be over for him, he became delirious and lost consciousness. On March thirty-first, he was dead. He had died of typhus.

As a physician, Frankl understood that his friend died because

the expected liberation did not come and he was severely disappointed. This suddenly lowered his body's resistance against the latent typhus infection.

We admire human beings who face death calmly. Dying "decently," in a composed manner, without wrangling with the inevitable, was and is considered in most cultures an expression of wisdom and unusual maturity. All the more surprising and sobering therefore are the results of modern cancer research, which suggest that the mortality rate is higher in those patients who prepare themselves for death in a mature, serene way or who, like the concentration camp prisoner F., fall victim to a negative self-fulfilling prophecy. For those patients, however, who cling to life in a seemingly senseless, irrational, and immature way or who are convinced that they simply "cannot" or "must not" die because they have important work to do or family members to take care of, the prognosis is considerably more favorable. To the American oncologist Carl Simonton (1975), whose name is associated, above all, with the appreciation of the impact of emotional factors, now more and more recognized for their importance in the treatment of cancer, three things are of the utmost significance in this connection: the belief system of the patient, that of the patient's family, and, third, that of the attending physician. That each one of these belief systems can become a self-fulfilling prophecy seems credible in the light of what we have discussed so far. Furthermore, the studies and research reports about the susceptibility of the human

immune system to mood swings, suggestions, and visual imagery (O. Simonton & S. Simonton, 1978; Solomon, 1969) are increasing.

How much can and should a physician tell his patients, not only about the gravity of their illnesses, but also about the dangers inherent in the treatment *itself*? At least in certain countries this question is becoming more and more rhetorical. The risk of getting hit with a malpractice suit because a patient has not been informed about his disease and its treatment down to the last technical detail causes many doctors in the United States, for example, to protect themselves in a way that can have serious consequences. The protection consists in asking the patient for a written consent to treatment in which the most catastrophic possible consequences of the illness and of the measures deemed necessary by the doctor are listed in every detail. It is not hard to imagine that this creates a kind of self-fulfilling prophecy that has a paralyzing effect on the confidence and will to recover of even the most sanguine patient. Who has not read the description of even a seemingly harmless medication and then had the feeling of swallowing poison? How does the layman (or, presumably, even the professional) know that he is not going to be the fourth of the three fatalities reported to date that were inexplicably caused by a medication so far used safely by millions? But *fiat justitia, pereat mundus.*[4]

Since in the patient's eye a doctor is a kind of mediator between life and death, his utterances can easily become self-fulfilling prophecies. The astonishing degree to which this is possible is portrayed in a case reported (but unfortunately not sufficiently documented) by the American psychologist Gordon Allport (1964). What is unusual here is that a misunderstanding shifted the prophecy from **death** to life:

In a provincial Austrian hospital, a man lay gravely ill—in fact, at death's door. The medical staff had told him frankly that they could not diagnose his disease, but that if they knew the diagnosis they could probably cure him. They told him further that a famous diagnostician was soon to visit the hospital and that perhaps he could spot the trouble.

Within a few days the diagnostician arrived and proceeded to make the rounds. Coming to this man's bed, he merely glanced at the patient, murmured, "Moribundus," and went on.

Some years later, the patient called on the diagnostician and said, "I've been wanting to thank you for your diagnosis. They told me that if you could diagnose me I'd get well, and so the minute you said 'moribundus' I knew I'd recover."

Knowledge of the healing effect of positive predictions is undoubtedly just as ancient as faith in the inescapable consequences of curses and evil spells. Modern use of positive suggestions and autosuggestions ranges from the "I will recover; I feel better every day" of Emile Coué, through numerous forms of hypnotherapeutic interventions (Haley, 1973), to influencing the course of an illness—and not only cancer—by positive imagery. The extent to which such imagery that a (future) event has already taken place can reach into the physical realm is suggested by several studies according to which it is possible to increase a woman's chest measurement by an average of four to five centimeters through the use of certain self-hypnotic techniques (Staib & Logan, 1977; Willard, 1977). I mention these "successes" with all due skepticism and simply as curiosities testifying to the towering importance of the female breast in the North American erotic ethos.

Brief mention should also be made of the modern physiological and endocrinological studies that indicate more and more the possibility of stimulating the functions of the immune system of the human organism by certain experiences and that these functions are by no means completely autonomous (that is, outside conscious control), as was assumed until quite recently. Medical research is likely to make astonishing discoveries in this field in the near future. For instance, it is now known that the organism itself produces a number of morphene-like substances—the so-called endorphins (Beers, 1979)—that are analgesic and whose production is stimulated by certain emotional processes. There is thus a wide-open, unexplored territory in which the phenomenon of self-fulfilling prophecies begins to achieve scientific respectability.

Just as decisive as a doctor's suggestive comments, expectations, and convictions are the measures he takes and the remedies he administers. Of special interest here are *placebos*[5] (Benson & Epstein, 1975), those chemically inert substances that resemble certain medicines in shape, taste, or color but which have no pharmaceutical effect. We must remember that until about 100 years ago nearly all medications were practically ineffective in the modern sense. They were only slightly more elegant tinctures and powders than the ground toads, the lizard blood, the "sacred oils," or the pulverized horn of the rhinoceros of even earlier times. During my childhood, people in the rural areas of Austria still believed that a necklace of garlic would protect them from the common cold, to say nothing about the well-known success of magic in the treatment of warts. Even in our time, old "tried and true" remedies or sensational new discoveries (as, for example, Laetrile) are always being unmasked as pharmaceutically ineffective. But that is not to say that they were or are *functionally* ineffective. "One should treat as many patients as possible with the new remedies, as long as these are still working," reads the maxim of a famous physician, attributed to Trousseau, Osler, or Sydenham. Scientific interest in placebos is rapidly increasing. In his contribution to the history of the placebo effect Shapiro (1960) points out that more articles on this topic were published in scientific journals between 1954 and 1957 alone than in the first fifty years of the twentieth century. Most of these reports discuss traditional pharmaceutical effectiveness studies, in which one group of patients receives the new medication while another takes a placebo. The purpose of this well-meaning procedure is to find out whether the course of the illness of the "actually" treated patients is different from that of the placebo group. Only people whose world view is based on classical linear causal thinking (for which there is only an "objective" relationship between cause and effect) react with consternation when they realize that the patients "treated" with placebos often show a quite "inexplicable" improvement in their condition. In other words, the claim of the doctor who administers the placebo that it is an effective, newly developed medicine and the patient's willingness to believe in its effectiveness create a reality in which the assumption actually becomes a fact.

Enough examples. Self-fulfilling prophecies are phenomena that not only shake up our personal conception of reality, but which can also throw doubt on the world view of science. They all share the obviously reality-creating power of a firm belief in the "suchness" of things, a faith that can be a superstition as well as a seemingly strictly scientific theory derived from objective observation. Until recently it has been possible to categorically reject self-fulfilling prophecies as unscientific or to ascribe them to the inadequate reality adaptation of muddleheaded thinkers and romanticists, but we no longer have this convenient escape hatch open to us.

What all this means cannot yet be appraised with any certainty. The discovery that we create our own realities is comparable to the expulsion from the paradise of the presumed suchness of the world, a world in which we can certainly suffer, but for which we need only feel responsible in a very limited way (Watzlawick, 1976).

And here lies the danger. The insights of constructivism may have the highly desirable advantage of allowing for new and more effective forms of therapy (Watzlawick, 1978), but

like all remedies, they can also be abused. Advertising and propaganda are two especially repugnant examples: Both try quite deliberately to bring about attitudes, assumptions, prejudices, and the like, whose realization then seems to follow naturally and logically. Thanks to this brainwashing, the world is then seen as "thus" and therefore is "thus." In the novel *1984* (Orwell, 1949) this reality-creating propaganda language is called *Newspeak,* and Orwell explains that it "makes all other modes of thinking impossible." In a recent review of a volume of essays published in London on censorship in the People's Republic of Poland (Strzyzewski, 1977–1978), Daniel Weiss (1980) writes about this magic language:

> Compare for example the great number of adjectives, characteristic for Newspeak: Every development is nothing less than "dynamic," every plenary session of the party "historic," the masses always "proletarian workers." A sober communication scientist will find nothing but *redundance* in this inflation of mechanized epithets, drained of meaning. But after listening repeatedly, this automation is felt to have the equality of an incantation: The spoken word is no longer used to carry information, it has become the instrument of magic. (p. 66)

And finally the world simply *is thus.* How it was *made* to be this way was well known to Joseph Goebbels (1933/1976), when he lectured the managers of German radio stations on March 25, 1933:

> This is the secret of propaganda: To totally saturate the person, whom the propaganda wants to lay hold of, with the ideas of the propaganda, without him even noticing that he is being saturated. Propaganda has of course a purpose, but this purpose must be disguised with such shrewdness and virtuosity that he who is supposed to be filled with this purpose never even knows what is happening. (p. 120)

In the necessity of disguising the purpose, however, lies the possibility of overcoming it. As we have seen, the invented reality will become "actual" reality only if the invention is believed. Where the element of faith, of blind conviction, is absent, there will be no effect. With the better understanding of self-fulfilling prophecies our ability to transcend them grows. A prophecy that we know to be only a prophecy can no longer fulfill itself. The possibility of choosing differently (of being a heretic) and of disobeying always exists; whether we see it and act on it is, of course, another question. An insight from the seemingly far-removed domain of the mathematical theory of games is of interest here. Wittgenstein (1956) already pointed out in his *Remarks on the Foundations of Mathematics* that certain games can be won with a simple trick. As soon as someone calls our attention to the existence of this trick, we no longer have to continue playing naively (and continue losing). Building on these reflections, the mathematician Howard (1967) formulated his *existential axiom* which maintains that "if a person becomes 'aware' of a theory concerning his behavior, he is no longer bound by it but is free to disobey it" (p. 167). Elsewhere he also says that

> a conscious decision maker can always choose to disobey any theory predicting his behavior. We may say that he can always "transcend" such a theory. This indeed seems realistic. We suggest that among socio-economic theories, Marxian theory, for example, failed at least partly because certain ruling class members, when they became aware of the theory, saw that it was in their interest to disobey it. (1971)

And almost a hundred years before Howard, Dostoevski's underground man writes in his *Letters from the Underworld* (1913),

> As a matter of fact, if ever there shall be discovered a formula which shall exactly express our wills and whims; if ever there shall be discovered a formula which shall make it absolutely clear what those wills depend upon, and what laws they are governed by, and what means of diffusion they possess, and what tendencies they follow under given circumstances; if ever there shall be discovered a formula which shall be mathematical in its precision, well, gentlemen, whenever such a formula shall be found, man will have ceased to have a will of his own—he will have ceased even to exist. Who would care to exercise his willpower according to a table of logarithms? In such a case man would become, not a human being at all, but an organ-handle, or something of the kind. (p. 32)

But even if this kind of mathematical formulization of our lives could ever be achieved, it would in no way comprehend the complexity of our existence. The best theory is powerless in the face of an antitheory; the fulfillment of even the truest prophecy can be thwarted if we know about it beforehand. Dostoevski (1913) saw much more in the nature of man:

> Moreover, even if man *were* the keyboard of a piano, and could be convinced that the laws of nature and of mathematics had made him so, he would still decline to change. On the contrary, he would once more, out of sheer ingratitude, attempt the perpetration of something which would enable him to insist upon himself. . . . But if you were to tell me that all this could be set down in tables—I mean the chaos, and the confusion, and the curses, and all the rest of it—so that the possibility of computing everything might remain, and reason continue to rule the roost—well, in that case, I believe, man would *purposely* become a lunatic, in order to become devoid of reason, and therefore able to insist upon himself. I believe this, and I am ready to vouch for this, simply for the reason that every human act arises out of the circumstance that man is forever striving to prove to his own satisfaction that he is a man and not an organ-handle. (p. 37)

However, even the evidence of the underground man is likely to be a self-fulfilling prophecy.

NOTES

1. The following untrue story is a further illustration: In 1974, Secretary of State Kissinger, who is on one of his innumerable mediating missions in Jerusalem, is on his way back to the hotel after a private, late-evening stroll. A young Israeli stops him, introduces himself as an economist out of work, and asks Kissinger to help him find a job through his numerous connections. Kissinger is favorably impressed by the applicant and asks him whether he would like to be the vice-president of the Bank of Israel. The young man thinks of course that Kissinger is making fun of him, but the latter promises quite seriously that he will manage the matter for him. Next day Kissinger calls Baron Rothschild in Paris: "I have a charming young man here, a political economist, talented, going to be the next vice-president of the Bank of Israel. You have to meet him; he would be a jewel of a husband for your daughter." Rothschild growls something that does not sound like total rejection, whereupon Kissinger immediately calls the president of the Bank of Israel: "I have a young financial expert here, brilliant fellow, exactly the stuff to make a vice-president for your bank, and most of all—imagine *that*—he is the future son-in-law of Baron Rothschild's."

2. *Editor's note:* Italian for "If it's not true, it is well written."

3. Here I will briefly mention an interesting sequel to these experiments: For reasons irrelevant to our topic, several researchers (McConnell, Jacobson, & Humphries, 1961) studied the fascinating theory that at the planaria's primitive stage of development information stored in a worm's ribonucleic acid (RNA) could possibly be directly transferred to other worms. For this purpose they fed untrained animals their already successfully trained fellow worms. Even we laymen can imagine the sensation among experts when the training of the worms provided with such food actually turned out to be much easier and faster. The euphoria lasted for a short while until the experiments, repeated under more rigorous controls, showed themselves to be inconclusive, and serious doubts arose concerning the transferability of intelligence through ground meat. The suspicion suggests itself, but was, as far as I know, never proven, that the original results were due to self-fulfilling prophecies,

similar to those whose effects on the worms were already known. (The analogy, however, to the superstition of certain African tribes that eating a lion's heart will confer the lion's courage cannot be dismissed out of hand.)

4. *Editor's note:* Latin for "Let justice be done though the world perish."

5. Latin for "I shall please."

REFERENCES

Allport, G. W. (1964). Mental health: A generic attitude. *Journal of Religion and Health, 4,* 7–21.

Beers, R. F. (Ed.). (1979). *Mechanisms of pain and analgesic compounds.* New York: Raven.

Benson, H., & Epstein, M. D. (1975). The placebo effect: A neglected asset in the care of patients. *American Medical Association Journal, 232,* 1225–1227.

Cannon, W. B. (1942). Voodoo death. *American Anthropologist, 44,* 169–181.

Cordaro, L., & Ison, J. R. (1963). Observer bias in classical conditioning of the planaria. *Psychological Reports, 13,* 787–789.

Dostoevski, F. M. (1913). *Letters from the underworld.* New York: Dutton.

Feyerabend, P. K. (1978). *Science in a free society.* London: New Left.

Frankl, V. E. (1959). *From death camp to existentialism.* Boston: Beacon.

Goebbels, J. Quoted in Schneider, W. (1976). *Wörter machen leute. Magie und macht der sprache.* Munich: Piper.

Haley, J. (1973). *Uncommon therapy: The psychiatric techniques of Milton H. Erickson, M.D.* New York: Norton.

Heisenberg, W. (1958). *Physics and philosophy: The revolution in modern science.* New York: Harper & Row.

Howard, N. (1967). The theory of metagames. *General Systems, 2,* 167.

Howard, N. (1971). *Paradoxes of rationality, theory of metagames and political behavior.* Cambridge: MIT Press.

Jones, R. A. (1974). *Self-fulfilling prophecies: Social, psychological and physical effects of expectancies.* New York: Halsted.

McConnell, J. V., Jacobson, R., & Humphries, B. M. (1961). The effects of ingestion of conditioned planaria on the response level of naive planaria: A pilot study. *Worm Runner's Digest, 3,* 41–45.

Orwell, G. (1949). *1984.* New York: Harcourt, Brace.

Popper, K. R. (1974). *Unended quest.* La Salle, IL: Open Court.

Rosenthal, R. (1966). *Experimenter effects in behavioral research.* New York: Appleton-Century-Crofts.

Rosenthal, R., & Jacobson, L. (1968). *Pygmalion in the classroom: Teacher expectation and pupils' intellectual development.* New York: Holt, Rinehart & Winston.

Shapiro, A. K. (1960). A contribution to a history of the placebo effects. *Behavioral Science, 5,* 109–135.

Simonton, O. C., & Simonton, S. (1975). Belief systems and management of the emotional aspects of malignancy. *Journal of Transpersonal Psychology, 1,* 29–47.

Simonton, O. C., & Simonton, S. (1978). *Getting well again.* Los Angeles: J. P. Tarcher.

Solomon, G. F. (1969). Emotions, stress, the nervous system, and immunity. *Annals of the New York Academy of Sciences, 164,* 335–343.

Staib, A. R., & Logan, D. R. (1977). Hypnotic stimulation of breast growth. *American Journal of Clinical Hypnosis, 19,* 201–208.

Strzyzewski, T. (1977–1978). *Czarna ksiega cenzury PRL* (Black Book of Polish Censorship, 2 vols.). London: "Aneks."

Szasz, T. S. (1970). *The manufacture of madness: A comparative study of the Inquisition and the mental health movement.* New York: Harper & Row.

Watzlawick, P. (1976). *How real is real?* New York: Random House.

Watzlawick, P. (1978). *The language of change: Elements of therapeutic communication.* New York: Basic Books.

Watzlawick, P., Bavelas, J. B., & Jackson, D. D. (1967). *Pragmatics of human communication: A study of interactional patterns, pathologies and paradoxes.* New York: Norton.

Weiss, D. (1980). Sprache und propaganda—Der sonderfall Polen. *Neue Zürcher Zeitung, 39,* 66.

Willard, R. R. (1977). Breast enlargement through visual imagery and hypnosis. *American Journal of Clinical Hypnosis, 19,* 195–200.

Wittgenstein, L. (1956). *Remarks on the foundations of mathematics.* Oxford, UK: Blackwell.

SELF-FULFILLING PROPHECIES

39

The Nonverbal Mediation of Self-Fulfilling Prophecies in Interracial Interaction

Carol O. Word, Mark P. Zanna, and Joel Cooper

(1974)

Sociologist Robert Merton (1957), by suggesting that an originally false definition of a situation can influence the believer to act in such a way as to bring about that situation, is generally credited with focusing attention on the phenomenon of the self-fulfilling prophecy. The present investigation is concerned with such a phenomenon in face-to-face, dyadic interactions. In this context it is hypothesized that one person's attitudes and expectations about the other person may influence the believer's actions, which in turn, may induce the other person to behave in a way that confirms the original false definition. Interpersonally, this phenomenon has been documented in schools, with teachers' expectations influencing students' performances, and in psychology laboratories, with experiments' expectations influencing subjects' responses (cf. Rosenthal, 1971).

In the present study attention will be directed toward (1) possible nonverbal mediators of this effect, and (2) the reciprocal performances of the interactants. The focus, in addition, will be on the interaction of black and white Americans with a view toward examining the employment outcomes of black job applicants interviewed by whites.

WHITE-BLACK INTERACTION IN A JOB INTERVIEW SETTING

It has been demonstrated time and again that white Americans have generalized negative evaluations (e.g., stereotypes) of black Americans. Such negative evaluations, of course, represent the kind of attitudes that can initiate an interpersonal, self-fulfilling prophecy. The general hypothesis that the present study sought to investigate, therefore, was that whites interacting with blacks will emit nonverbal behaviors corresponding to negative evaluations and that blacks, in turn, will reciprocate with less immediate behaviors. If the context in which the interaction occurs involves a job interview, with the white interviewing the black, such reciprocated behavior may be interpreted as less adequate performance, thus confirming, in part, the interviewer's original attitude.

These general expectations are operationalized by two subhypotheses: First, black, as compared to white, job applicants will receive less immediate nonverbal communications from white job interviewers; second, recipients of less immediate nonverbal communications, whether black or white, will reciprocate these communications and be judged to perform less adequately in the job interview situation than recipients of more positive nonverbal communications. The first hypothesis was tested in Experiment 1, which employed naive, white job interviewers and trained white and black job applicants; the second in Experiment 2, which used naive, white job applicants and trained white job interviewers who were instructed to emit either immediate or nonimmediate cues.

EXPERIMENT 1

Method

Overview

In the context of a study on group decision-making white subjects, as representatives of a team in competition with other teams, interviewed both white and black job applicants. The applicants were trained to respond similarly in both the verbal and nonverbal channels. The interview situation itself was arranged to give the subject-interviewers the opportunity to treat their applicants differentially without the knowledge (1) that their own behavior was being monitored, or (2) that race of the applicants was the experimental variable.

Subjects (Interviewers) and Confederates (Applicants and Team Members)

Subject-interviewers were 15 white, Princeton males recruited to participate in a study of group decision-making conducted by Career Services and the Psychology Department. They were informed that the study would last approximately one hour and a half and that they would be paid $2.00 and possibly $5.00 more. One of the subjects was eliminated when he indicated that he was aware of the purpose of the study before the debriefing period. No other subject volunteered this sort of information after intensive probing, leaving an *n* of 14.

Confederate-applicants were two black and three white high school student volunteers referred by their high school counselor. Each was told that the study was concerned with cognitive functioning and that the experimenter was interested in finding out how subjects made up their minds when forced to choose between nearly identical job applicants. All confederates in both experiments were naive with respect to the hypotheses. Intensive probing following the experiment indicated that they did not become aware. The three confederates who served as the subject's "team members" and the experimenter were male Princeton volunteers.

Procedure

Upon arrival the subjects entered a room containing two confederate team members, who introduced themselves and acted friendly. Another confederate entered and acted friendly, as well. Then the experimenter entered, handed out written instructions and answered any questions.

The instructions informed subjects that the four people in the room constituted a team; that they were to compete with four other teams in planning a marketing campaign; and that they needed to select another member from four high school applicants. In order to increase incentive and concern, an additional $5.00 was promised to the team which performed best in the competition. Using a supposedly random draw, the subject was chosen to interview the applicants. He was then handed a list of 15 questions which was to serve as the interview material, told he had 45 minutes to interview all four high school students and taken to the interview room where the first confederate-applicant was already seated.

In order to measure the physical distance that the interviewer placed himself from the applicant, the experimenter upon entering the interview room, feigned to discover that there was no chair for the interviewer. Subjects were then asked to wheel in a chair from an adjoining room.

Subjects were led to believe that there would be four interviews so that the race variable would be less apparent to them. In addition, to eliminate any special effect that might occur in the first and last interview, an a priori decision was made not to analyze the data from the first "warm-up" interview and not to have a fourth interview. The "warm-up" job candidate was always white. Half the subjects then interviewed a black followed by a white applicant; the other half interviewed a white then a black candidate. After completion of the third interview, subjects were told that the fourth applicant had called to cancel his appointment. After the third interview, subjects were paid and debriefed.

Applicant Performance

Confederate-applicants were trained to act in a standard way to all interviewers. First, they devised answers to the 15 questions such that their answers, though not identical, would represent equally qualifying answers. Confederates then rehearsed these answers until two judges rated their performances to be equal. Confederates were also trained to seat themselves, shoulders parallel to the backs of their chairs (10° from vertical) and to make eye contact with the interviewer 50% of the time. A code was devised to signal confederates during their interviews if they deviated from the pose or began to reciprocate the gestures or head nods given them.

Dependent Measures

Immediacy behaviors. Four indices of psychological immediacy were assessed: (1) Physical

Distance between interviewer and interviewee, measured in inches; (2) Forward Lean, scored in 10° units, with zero representing the vertical position and positive scores representing the torso leaning toward the confederate; (3) Eye Contact, defined as the proportion of time the subject looked directly at the confederate's eyes; and (4) Shoulder Orientation, scored in units of 10° with zero representing the subject's shoulders parallel to those of the confederate and positive scores indicating a shift in either direction. Two judges, placed behind one-way mirrors, scored the immediacy behaviors.

More distance and shoulder angle represent less immediate behaviors while more foreward [sic] lean and more eye contact represent more immediate behaviors. An index of total immediacy was constructed by summing the four measures, standardized, and weighted according to the regression equation beta weights established by Mehrabian (1969). Final scores of this index represent $(-.6)$ distance $+ (.3)$ forward lean $+ (.3)$ eye contact $+ (-.1)$ shoulder orientation. Positive scores represent more immediate performances.

Related Behaviors. Two related behaviors, which indicate differential evaluations of the applicants (cf. Mehrabian, 1969), were also assessed: (1) Interview length indicates the amount of time from the point the subject entered the interview room until he announced the interview was over, in minutes. This measure was taken by the experimenter. (2) Speech Error Rate, scored by two additional judges from audiotapes, represents the sum of (a) sentence changes, (b) repetitions, (c) stutters, (d) sentence incompletions, and (e) intruding, incoherent sounds divided by the length of the interview and averaged over the two judges. Higher scores represent more speech errors per minute.

Results

Table 1   Mean Interviewer Behavior as a Function of Race of Job Application; Experiment 1

Behavior	Reliability	Blacks	Whites	t	p
Total immediacy	—	−.11	.38	2.79	< .02
Distance	.90	62.29 inches	58.43 inches	2.36	< .05
Forward lean	.68	−8.76 degrees	−6.12 degrees	1.09	n.s.
Eye contact	.80	62.71%	61.46%	< 1	n.s.
Shoulder orientation	.60	22.46 degrees	23.08 degrees	< 1	n.s.
Related behaviors					
Interview length	—	9.42 min.	12.77 min.	3.22	< .01
Speech error rate	.88	3.54 errors/min.	2.37 errors/min.	2.43	< .05

Immediacy Behaviors

The results, presented in Table 1, indicate that, overall, black job candidates received less immediate behaviors than white applicants ($t = 2.79$; $df = 13$; $p < .02$). On the average, blacks received a negative total immediacy score; whites received a positive one. This overall difference is primarily due to the fact that the white interviewers physically placed themselves further from black than white applicants ($t = 2.36$; $df = 13$; $p < .05$).

Related Behaviors

The results for interview length and speech error rate are also presented in Table 1. Here it can be seen that blacks also received less immediate behaviors. White interviewers spent 25% less time ($t = 3.22$; $df = 13$; $p < .01$) and had higher rates of speech errors ($t = 2.43$; $df = 13$; $p < .05$) with black as compared to white job candidates.

The results of the first experiment provide support for the hypothesis that black, as compared to white, job applicants receive less immediate nonverbal communications from white job interviewers. Indirectly the results also provide support for the conceptualization of blackness as a stigmatizing trait. The differences in time (evidenced by 12 of 14 interviewers), in total immediacy (evidenced by 10 of 14 interviewers), and in speech error rate (evidenced by 11 of 14 interviewers) argues for an extension of the stigma effect to include black Americans.

EXPERIMENT 2

Method

Overview

A second experiment was conducted to ascertain what effect the differences black and white applicants received in Experiment 1 would have on an applicant's job interview performance. In the context of training job interviewers, subject-applicants were interviewed by confederate-interviewers under one of two conditions. In the Immediate condition, as compared to the Nonimmediate condition, interviewers (1) sat closer to the applicant, (2) made fewer speech errors per minute, and (3) actually took longer to give their interviews. The main dependent measures were concerned with the interview performance of the applicant, both in terms of its judged adequacy for

obtaining the job and in terms of its reciprocation of immediacy behaviors.

Subjects (Job Applicants) and Confederates (Interviewers)

Thirty white male Princeton University students were recruited ostensibly to help Career Services train interviewers for an upcoming summer job operation. No subjects were eliminated from the study, leaving an *n* of 15 in each condition. The two confederate-interviewers were also white male Princeton students.

Procedure

Upon arrival each subject was given an instruction sheet which informed him that Career Services had contracted with the Psychology Department to train Princeton juniors and seniors in the techniques of job interviewing and that one of the techniques chosen included videotaping interviewers with job applicants for feedback purposes. The subject was then asked to simulate a job applicant, to be honest, and to really compete for the job, so as to give the interviewer real, lifelike practice. To make the simulation more meaningful, subjects were also informed that the applicant chosen from five interviewed that evening would receive an additional $1.50.

Subjects were taken to the interview room and asked to be seated in a large swivel chair, while the Experimenter turned on the camera. The confederate-interviewer then entered, and assumed either an immediate or nonimmediate position which will be described in more detail below. Exactly five minutes into the interviewing in both conditions, a guise was developed whose result was that the experimenter had to reclaim the chair in which the subject was sitting. The subject was then asked to take a folding chair leaning against the wall and to continue the interview. The distance from the interviewer which the subject placed his new chair was one of the study's dependent measures designed to assess reciprocated immediacy.

When the interview ended, the experimenter took the subject to another room where a second investigator, blind as to the condition of the subject, administered self-report scales and answered any questions. Subject was then paid and debriefed.

Immediacy Manipulation

Systematic nonverbal variations were introduced by specifically training confederates. Two confederate-interviewers alternated in the two conditions. In the Immediate condition, confederates sat in a chair on the side of a table. In the Nonimmediate condition, confederates sat fully behind the table. The difference in distance from the subject's chair was about four inches, representing the mean difference in distance white interviewers gave black and white applicants in Experiment 1.

In addition, the confederate-interviewers in the Immediate condition were trained to behave as precisely as possible like the subject-interviewers in Experiment 1 had acted toward white applicants. In the Nonimmediate condition, interviewers were trained to act as subject-interviewers had acted toward Blacks in Experiment 1. The factors used to simulate the immediacy behaviors found in the first experiment were speech error rate, length of interview and, as has been previously mentioned, physical distance. Eye contact, shoulder orientation and forward lean did not show significant differences in Experiment 1 and thus were held constant in Experiment 2 (with the levels set at 50% eye contact, 0° shoulder orientation and 20° forward lean).

Dependent Measures

Three classes of dependent variables were collected: (1) judges' ratings of interview performance; (2) judges' ratings of reciprocated immediacy behaviors; and (3) subjects' ratings of their post-interview mood state and attitudes toward the interviewer.

Applicant performance. Applicant interview performance and demeanor were rated by a panel of two judges from videotapes of the interviews. The videotapes were recorded at such an angle that judges viewed only the applicant, not the confederate-interviewer. The judges were merely instructed about the type of job subjects were applying for, and were asked to rate (1) the overall adequacy of each subject's performance and (2) each subject's composure on five (0–4) point scales. High scores, averaged over the judges, represent more adequate and more calm, relaxed performances, respectively.

Reciprocated immediacy behaviors. Two additional judges, placed behind one-way mirrors as in Experiment 1, recorded subjects' forward lean, eye contact, and shoulder orientation in accordance with the procedures established by Mehrabian (1969). Distance was directly measured after each interview, and represents the distance, in inches, from the middle of the interviewer-confederate's chair to the middle of the subject's chair, after the interruption. Speech errors were scored by another panel of two judges from audiotapes of the interviews, also according to Mehrabian's (1969) procedures. High scores represent more speech errors per minute.

Applicant mood and attitude toward the interviewer. After the interview, subjects filled out a series of questionnaires designed to assess their mood state and their attitudes toward the interviewer. Following Jones and Cooper (1971), subjects' moods were expected to vary as a function of immediacy conditions. The mood scale adapted from that study was employed. It consisted of six polar adjectives (e.g., happy–sad) separated by seven-point scales. Subjects were asked to respond to each pair according to "the way you feel about yourself."

Two measures of subjects' attitudes toward the interviewer were collected. First, subjects were asked to rate the friendliness of the interviewer on an 11-point scale, with zero representing an "unfriendly" and 10 representing a "friendly" interviewer, respectively. Second, in order to assess subjects' attitudes concerning the adequacy of the interviewer as an individual, they were asked to check the six adjectives best describing their interviewer from a list of 16 drawn from Gough's Adjective Checklist. Final scores represent the number of positive adjectives chosen minus the number of negative adjectives checked.

Table 2 Mean applicant responses under two conditions of interviewer immediacy; Experiment 2

Response	Reliability	Nonimmediate	Immediate	F	P
Applicant performance					
Rated performance	.66	1.44	2.22	7.96	< .01
Rated demeanor	.86	1.62	3.02	16.46	< .001
Immediacy behaviors					
Distance	—	72.73 inches	56.93 inches	9.19	< .01
Speech error rate	.74	5.01 errors/min.	3.33 errors/min.	3.40	< .10
Self reported mood and attitudes					
Mood	—	3.77	5.97	1.34	n.s.
Interviewer friendliness	—	4.33	6.60	22.91	< .001
Interviewer adequacy	—	−1.07	1.53	8.64	< .01

Results

Applicant Performance

It was predicted from an analysis of the communicative functions of nonimmediacy that applicants would be adversely affected by the receipt of nonimmediate communications. Those effects were expected to manifest themselves in less adequate job-interview performances.

Subjects in the two conditions were rated by two judges from videotapes. The main dependent measure, applicant adequacy for the job, showed striking differences as a function of immediacy conditions (see Table 2). Subjects in the Nonimmediate condition were judged significantly less adequate for the job ($F = 7.96$; $df = 1/28$; $p < .01$). Subjects in the Nonimmediate condition were also judged to be reliably less calm and composed ($F = 16.96$; $df = 1/28$; $p < .001$).

Reciprocated Immediacy Behaviors

Following Rosenfeld (1967) among others, it was expected that subjects encountering less immediate communications would reciprocate with less immediate behaviors of their own. This expectation was supported by both the measures of physical distance and speech error rate (see Table 2).

Subjects in the Immediate condition, on the average, placed their chairs eight inches closer to the interviewer after their initial chair was removed; subjects in the Nonimmediate conditions placed their chairs four inches further away from their interviewer. The mean difference between the two groups was highly significant ($F = 9.19$; $df = 1/28$; $p < .01$).

As in Experiment 1 mean comparisons for the forward lean, eye contact, and shoulder orientation measures of immediacy did not reach significance. The combination of these measures, using the weighting formula devised by Mehrabian (1969), however, was reliably different (means of −.29 and .29 in the Nonimmediate and Immediate conditions, respectively; $F = 5.44$; $df = 1/28$; $p < .05$).

The rate at which subjects made speech errors also tended to be reciprocated with subjects in the Nonimmediate condition exhibiting a higher rate than subjects in the Immediate condition ($F = 3.40$; $df = 1/28$; $p < .10$).

*Applicant Mood and
Attitude Toward the Interviewer*

It was expected that subjects receiving less immediate (i.e., less positive) communication would (1) feel less positively after their interviews, and (2) hold less positive attitudes toward the interviewer himself. These expectations were only partially supported (see Table 2). Although subjects in the Nonimmediate condition reported less positive moods than subjects in the Immediate condition, this difference was not statistically reliable.

Subjects in the less immediate condition did, however, rate their interviewers to be less friendly ($F = 22.91$; $df = 1/28$; $p < .001$) and less adequate overall ($F = 8.64$; $df = 1/28$; $p < .01$) than subjects in the more immediate condition.

Discussion

Results from the two experiments provide clear support for the two subhypotheses, and offer inferential evidence for the general notion that self-fulfilling prophecies can and do occur in interracial interactions.

The results of Experiment 1 indicated that black applicants were, in fact, treated to less immediacy than their white counterparts. Goffman's (1963) conception of blackness as a stigmatizing trait in Anglo-American society is, thus, given experimental support—insofar as that classification predicts avoidance behaviors in interactions with normals. These results may also be viewed as extending the stigma effect documented by Kleck and his associates with handicapped persons.

That the differential treatment black and white applicants received in Experiment 1 can influence the performance and attitudes of job candidates was clearly demonstrated in Experiment 2. In that experiment those applicants, treated similarly to the way Blacks were treated in Experiment 1, performed less well, reciprocated less immediacy, and found their interviewers to be less adequate. Taken together the two experiments provide evidence for the assertion that nonverbal, immediacy cues mediate, in part, the performance of an applicant in a job interview situation. Further, the experiments suggest that the model of a self-fulfilling prophecy, mediated by nonverbal cues, (1) is applicable to this setting, and (2) can account, in part, for the less adequate performances of black applicants.

Social scientists have often tended to focus their attention for such phenomena as unemployment in black communities on the dispositions of the disinherited. Such an approach has been termed "victim analysis" for its preoccupation with the wounds, defects and personalities of the victimized as an explanation for social problems. The present results suggest that analyses of black-white interactions, particularly in the area of job-seeking blacks in white society, might profit if it were assumed that the "problem" of black performance resides not entirely within the blacks, but rather within the interaction setting itself.

REFERENCES

Jones, R. E., and Cooper, J. Mediation of experimenter effects. *Journal of Personality and Social Psychology*, 1971, 20, 70–74.

Mehrabian, A. Some referents and measures of nonverbal behavior. *Behavior Research Methods and Instrumentation*, 1969, 1, 203–207.

Merton, R. K. *Social theory and social structure*. New York: Free Press, 1957.

Rosenfeld, H. M. Nonverbal reciprocation of approval: an experimental analysis. *Journal of Experimental and Social Psychology*, 1967, 3, 102–111.

Rosenthal, R. Teacher expectations. In G. S. Lesser (Ed.), *Psychology and the educational process*. Glenview, Illinois: Scott, Foresman, 1971.

THE SOCIAL PRODUCTION OF THE CULTURAL STATUS QUO

When you combine everything that you have learned from this book up to this point, you will find that you now have a basis for explaining how major social patterns are created and maintained by small and seemingly insignificant everyday beliefs and actions. An important point to realize is that all of us may be contributing to the status quo, even when we sometimes believe we don't agree with it. People don't necessarily intend to perpetuate inequality; however, preconceived ideas about social differences such as gender or ethnicity or social class may lead us to engage in behavior that inadvertently contributes to these patterns. The readings in this section provide examples of the maintenance of two kinds of *patterned* social discrimination. As you read, pay close attention to the everyday actions that perpetuate these social lines of division.

Sociologist Victor Ray describes the experiences of returning veterans who seek mental health services in "Coming Home to Friendly Fire." He finds that military culture deters veterans from seeking support for combat trauma by defining them as "weaklings" and by questioning their fitness as soldiers.

In "The Persistence of Gender Inequality in Employment Settings," sociologist Cecilia Ridgeway asks why women have not been able to move into the highest ranks of professional management, even with legal interventions such as affirmative action. She finds the answer to this puzzle in an analysis of the preconceived *status expectations* that both men and women hold about management characteristics. All else being equal, when promotion decisions are discussed in groups, people often revert to stereotypical assessments that result in a default assumption that men are better suited for certain jobs. Through their conversations and promotion decisions, the group upholds a gender status quo.

READING QUESTIONS

1. Review Ridgeway's discussion of *gender status beliefs* and make a list of other categories of status beliefs (for example, race, class). Discuss how her theory might be used to explain persistent discrimination for these other statuses.

2. Some social situations may appear isolated and private but also reflect a strongly entrenched social hierarchy. Discuss the relationship between maids and their employers. Employers often engage in behaviors in the presence of their maids that they would never engage in around "polite company." This is a form of interactional *disappearance*—the maid is expected to act as if she does not exist. Think of some other relationships in which this kind of status distancing occurs.

40

Coming Home to Friendly Fire

Victor Ray

(2013)

The U.S. Military offers veterans and active personnel a variety of mental health support services. Yet many of those who would most benefit from help choose to suffer in silence.

Andre and Kenny hit it off the night they met. They swapped stories for hours, shared dinner together, and even learned they had attended neighboring high schools. Andre wasn't on the patrol the next day when Kenny was killed—but he watched as Kenny's tank was towed back to base with the tarp-covered body inside.

He recalled: "The tank completely blew to pieces. When it hit the landmine . . . all of the ammunition stuff started going off inside, and a couple of the guys got caught inside the tank . . . the seat had embedded into [the driver's] spinal cord, and they tried to pull him out. He was screaming; they couldn't pull him out. He was . . . he burnt on fire."

Today, Andre is haunted by the image of his friend's burned corpse, which he glimpsed as the wind lifted the tarp. Before the war, he was jovial, known to clown around and deescalate neighborhood conflicts. But his wartime experiences transformed him. His ex-wife—they divorced after his deployment—noticed he'd changed too.

When he returned home, Andre attended a mental health-screening program designed to identify Post-Traumatic Stress Disorder (PTSD) among combat veterans. During the screening, he recalled, "the flood-gates just opened up. I didn't know it was bothering me that much until, you know, they had me really talking about it. And I just started crying and I couldn't stop."

A new set of troubles began. Once diagnosed with PTSD, Andre was forced to leave the military. But his civilian job, working in aviation for the federal government, required him to be a standing member of the National Guard, so he lost the job.

In the aftermath of the Vietnam War, activist anti-war veterans and psychologists developed PTSD as a formal diagnosis, eventually forcing the military and the Veterans' Administration (VA) to adopt policies to deal with psychological problems. Today, however, screening programs for the disorder can serve as a sorting mechanism, removing those deemed "damaged."

Andre experienced traumas that most of us cannot fathom. His story and those of other veterans show that policies designed to ease reintegration often hurt. Popular, well-meaning programs, such as mental health screenings, mark soldiers as trouble-makers unfit for service in a process I call "punitive empathy." While publicly, the military points to these programs as evidence that mental health issues are being taken seriously, service members who report problems have a different version of events.

Over the past year and a half, I interviewed 50 veterans about their wartime experiences and reintegration into post-military life. The ravages of combat are written on their bodies, in slumped shoulders, broken speech, and tears. In searching for meaning in their experiences, their anguish makes it clear why many veterans are reticent to talk. Some have learned that discussing war comes with a social price tag. Family and friends often don't understand, and may condemn them. Punitive empathy in the military reinforces this culture of silence.

I had expected veterans to tell me about the mental health problems associated with their service. But I was surprised that many hid their issues from the military. If the military and the general public acknowledge that combat can have life-long psychological effects, though, why do some veterans avoid getting care?

In 2007, the *Washington Post* reported that Walter Reed, the nation's premier Veterans Affairs hospital, was systematically failing. The articles chronicled a labyrinthine bureaucracy that failed to heal the physical and psychological scars of combat. Since then, a steady stream of stories has depicted a VA bogged down by the growing volume of mental health cases. Recently, the Department of Veterans Affairs' Inspector General reported that the average wait for preliminary screenings is nearly three months—at a time when the number of suicides among veterans and active duty troops now exceeds combat deaths in Afghanistan.

Explanations that focus on the VA system's inadequate facilities or capacities fail to tell the whole story. Nor can explanations that focus on the masculine culture of military and the tendency to shame those who seek out help. My interviews suggest that it's the organizational culture of the military that systematically inhibits veterans from seeking out mental health treatment.

FORCE READINESS?

Throughout the 20th century, the military has been under pressure to provide therapeutic help for its members who suffer from mental health problems. But having deployable soldiers fit for combat regardless of trauma—"force readiness," in military jargon—is a paramount internal goal.

Historically, then, the United States military has veered between ensuring the internal goal of force readiness and helping its personnel navigate psychological trauma. According to sociologist Wilbur Scott, what was known as "shell shock" during WWI was thought to afflict only "weaklings." So, when the U.S. military joined the war effort, psychiatrists were to ensure soldiers returned to combat as quickly as possible following trauma exposure. Short-term force readiness was a more immediate concern than soldiers' long-term mental health, and those complaining of severe distress risked labels like coward or malingerer.

Institutions like the U.S. military derive their legitimacy, in part, from presenting "fronts" that conform to public expectations of care for their personnel. But while Department of Defense mental health programs demonstrate the military's commitment to helping veterans, those who seek out help are often punished for doing so. Bosses, managers, or commanders frequently retaliate against those who come forward, strengthening the very institutional inequalities such programs were designed to alleviate.

Outside the media's eye, in "back stage" interactions with commanders, fellow soldiers, and the military bureaucracy, service members are vulnerable to retribution, hazing, or worse. The military's entrenched hierarchies mean that those with power have the discretion to apply policies that reinforce traditional hierarchies of race, gender, and mental health status.

So while mental health screening programs serve a public relations function, those who use the programs run the risk of stigma. Fearful of losing their jobs, veterans often hide their mental health problems or seek help outside the military. The conflict between force readiness and mental health needs is key to understanding the issues facing today's veterans.

Men who experience combat are more likely to be unemployed and disabled for the rest of their lives. In 2010, sociologist Alair Maclean showed that Vietnam combat veterans were nearly twice as likely to be unemployed in 1999 as non-combat veterans and non-veterans. Yet we know little about the organizational mechanisms shaping post-service life and work for Iraq and Afghanistan veterans.

The 2.3 million veterans who were deployed to Iraq and Afghanistan experienced a historically unprecedented cycle of service. These wars' long duration, coupled with military procedures called "stop-loss policies" that keep service members enlisted long beyond their contractual end-dates, have profoundly stressed veterans, their families, and the healthcare system. When they return, veterans must contend with limited job opportunities in a recessionary civilian labor market. Together, these factors create a situation where service members frequently return to war when they might otherwise have left the military.

Multiple deployments increase the risk of trauma exposure. Nearly 20 percent of returning vets have been diagnosed with PTSD, and rates of traumatic brain injury (TBI), depression, and military sexual trauma (MST)—harassment or assaults often perpetrated by fellow soldiers or superiors—are also high. Insurgents' asymmetrical warfare has erased traditional notions of the "front lines," as Improvised Explosive Devices (IEDs) indiscriminately strike both "support" and combat service members. And despite the formal ban on women in combat (lifted only very recently), women have been serving on the "front lines." These female service members experience higher rates of PTSD and MST than their male counterparts.

Rather than seek out treatment within the military healthcare system, many veterans and active-duty service members suffer in silence. They live with the threat of repercussions in the form of sabotaged careers, hazing through extra duty—such as when commanders force enlisted soldiers to do menial, degrading, or dangerous work—or expulsion. Military estimates of mental health disorders are therefore undercounts of the true psychological costs of conflict. Qualitative evidence of the complications of homecoming is vitally important for sociologists and policymakers to fully understand and address how the vicissitudes of combat shape veterans' lives.

The military has multiple programs in place to help with mental health issues affecting soldiers, including mandatory post-deployment mental health screenings. Psych-techs are available in the field and on base, and soldiers are often encouraged to seek care. The "front stage" of these apparently empathetic programs recognizes service members' potential problems and tries to offer solutions—bolstering the combat mission and reputation on the home front.

But the veterans I interviewed still feared retribution.

"You're Finished. You're Done."

Like many soldiers, Joe joined the military for college tuition. A black single father of two in his mid-forties, he deployed to Afghanistan and experienced anxiety disorder and severe depression after combat. Joe was aware of the military's media outreach encouraging soldiers to get mental healthcare, recalling, "they'll come on TV and talk about, 'Oh, generals go see the doctor and they talk, you know, they get help.'"

Joe's voice was tinged with disgust as he implied that this outreach was disingenuous at best. "I don't give a flying flip what they say. . . . If that comes up in your file, you're done. That next rank, you're finished. You're finished. You are done! If you are an enlisted guy . . . and it goes in your file that you went to the Gulf and you came back and you went to see somebody for major depressive disorder. . . . You won't reenlist. They won't let you. You're done." Further, Joe had little faith that his relatively high-ranking status would help him. "If you're an officer, you're especially done," he said. "I was a senior officer. So I knew that I had to protect myself." Joe's self-protection took the form of seeking care through an outside psychiatrist. For 18 months he received therapy twice a week, hiding his condition from the military to avoid repercussions.

Despite the military's front stage proclamations of support, Joe simply feared getting mental health care through the military. He describes a back stage where acknowledging a psychological disorder would harm a soldier's career. According to Joe, if commanders think a soldier's mental illness would impede the military's internal organizational goals, the mission comes first. Soldiers' concerns about reporting mental health issues are pervasive: several of the lower-ranking soldiers I interviewed explained that they feared the consequences of telling the truth about their mental health needs.

Punitive empathy also influences veterans' willingness to report sexual assault, which female service members experience at twice the rate of civilian women. Women who experience sexual assaults may avoid reporting attacks for many reasons, including worry about the military's response. The veterans I interviewed know women who were discharged after they reported such attacks.

Cherrie, for example, joined the military to escape a rough childhood and a string of bad relationships. Cherrie had tremendous family responsibilities, including helping to care for her HIV-positive mother. Despite these barriers, Cherrie had a remarkable career, earning two masters' degrees during her service. A calm and pensive Latina, she credited the military for offering her opportunities absent in civilian life. Cherrie was on leave when she went to a party at a lifelong friend's house. While there, she was drugged and sexually assaulted.

"I wanted to go to the police but I was ready to deploy. And I thought, I am not going to go to the cops because if they open up a case, I'm not going to deploy," she said. "Plus, it's going to affect my career because they are going to ask what drugs, let's do a drug test, and you can get discharged." Although a civilian had committed the assault, Cherrie believed that dealing with the military was too risky; she thought she'd be doubly victimized, forced out of her job. So instead of reporting her assault, Cherrie decided, in her words, to "push this away, and go on deployment and do what I have to do and deal with it later." This decision placed her at greater risk for mental health problems, as another deployment exposed her to further trauma: she experienced several mortar attacks while she was at work providing mental health services to active duty troops. Ironically, Cherrie is a psych-tech, screening returning vets for the very problems she is afraid to reveal to her commanders.

Since she returned from her second deployment, Cherrie continues to seek mental health-care outside the military. Among other difficulties, she blames her mental health issues for the loss of some of her G.I. Bill benefits after she withdrew from a prestigious advanced degree program.

THE MILITARY—AND BEYOND

The term "punitive empathy" explains the gap between word and deed in organizations, and it has broad implications for understanding the reproduction of institutional inequality. Organizations require conformity to operate, and those who don't fit organizational molds—because of racial, gender, or other differences—may be targeted for harassment. However, organizations do not exist in a vacuum; social pressures compel them to conform to prevailing notions of equal opportunity and compassion. For instance, the civil and women's rights movements forced organizations to adopt policies to alleviate endemic racial and gender discrimination. Despite these on-paper reforms, racial and gender inequalities persist.

As sociologist Vincent Roscigno has shown, women reporting workplace sexual harassment "are often exposed and punished" through the very anti-discrimination programs designed to remedy the harassment. Roscigno claims that, in many cases, "workplace responses to harassment are as much a part of the problem as the harassment itself," compounding problems for women workers. And diversity programs can harm people of color, according to sociologist Adia Harvey Wingfield. The backstage implementation of programs, in other words, is often at odds with the front stage goal of addressing inequality, reinforcing traditional workplace hierarchies.

In the coming years, the strain on the Veterans Affairs health care system will only grow. The number of those diagnosed with PTSD, depression, and anxiety will also increase. And, although the military has implemented hundreds of new programs designed to address these issues, a recent comprehensive report from the Institute of Medicine at the National Academy of Science acknowledges that the effectiveness of these programs is unknown.

As I write, we are approaching the thirteenth year of war in Afghanistan, and combat troops are scheduled to remain in that country until at least 2014. Troops have only recently returned home from Iraq to begin changed lives. Despite the military's front stage endorsement of its mental health programs, veterans like Joe and Cherrie still fear reprisals for seeking mental health care, so they avoid the programs designed to help them.

RECOMMENDED RESOURCES

1. Iraq and Afghanistan Veterans of America. "Women Warriors: Supporting She 'Who Has Borne the Battle,'" *Issue Report* (2009), Iava.org. Comprehensive documents about issues concerning women veterans and their transition to civilian status.

2. Maclean, Alair. "The Things They Carry: Combat, Disability, and Unemployment Among U.S. Men." *American Sociological Review* (2010) 75:563–585. This article shows that combat veterans are more likely to be disabled and experience spells of unemployment later in life.

3. Roscigno, Vincent J. *The Face of Discrimination: How Race and Gender Impact Work and Home Lives* (Rowman & Littlefield, 2007). Drawing on data from the Ohio Civil Rights Commission, this work shows how pervasively organizational discrimination shapes employees' lives.

4. Wingfield, Adia H. "Are Some Emotions Marked 'Whites Only'? Racialized Feeling Rules in Professional Workplaces." *Social Problems* (2010) 57(2):251–68. This article shows how the rules governing emotional expression vary by race and gender within workplaces.

41

The Persistence of Gender Inequality in Employment Settings

Cecilia Ridgeway

(2001)

Gender hierarchy is a system of social practices that advantages men over women in material resources, power, status, and authority. Oddly, gender hierarchy has persisted in Western societies despite profound changes in the economic arrangements on which it seems, at any given time, to be based. It has continued in one form or another despite major economic transformations such as industrialization, the movement of women into the paid labor force, and, most recently, women's entry into male-dominated occupations. What accounts for gender hierarchy's uncanny ability to reassert itself in new forms when its former economic foundations erode?

Although many factors are involved, one part of the answer lies in the way gender hierarchy in economic and other social arrangements is mediated by interactional processes that are largely taken for granted. Gender processes taking place as people interact during economic and other activities can operate as an "invisible hand" that rewrites gender inequality into new socioeconomic arrangements as they replace the earlier arrangements upon which gender hierarchy was based. To illustrate this point, I will describe some interactional processes that mediate gender inequality in paid employment and play a role in its persistence. First, however, we should consider how gender and interaction are related.

GENDER AND INTERACTION

Gender is an important part of the organization of interaction. It is striking that people are nearly incapable of interacting with each other if they cannot guess the other's sex. The television program *Saturday Night Live* illustrated this problem in its comedy sequence about "Pat," an androgynous person who wreaks confusion and havoc even in trivial, everyday encounters because the others present cannot place Pat as a man or a woman. The difficulty of dealing with a person whose gender is ambiguous suggests that gender categorization is a basic first step in the cultural rules we use for organizing interaction (West and Zimmerman 1987).

In order to interact with someone, you need some initial idea of "who" you are dealing with. You must classify the person in relation to yourself in socially meaningful ways so that you can draw on cultural knowledge about how "people like this" are likely to behave and how you should act in return. In other words, organizing interaction requires you to categorize the other as well as yourself in socially significant ways. Some of the social rules that you use for categorizing self and other must be so simplified and apparently obvious that they provide an easy means for initially defining "who" self and other are so interaction can begin at all. The cultural rules for classifying people as either male or female provide a quick initial category system—one that everyone takes for granted. Once interaction begins, definitions of self and other that are more complicated and specific to the situation can be introduced.

As research has shown, the cognitive processes by which we perceive others are hierarchically organized (Brewer 1988; Fiske and Neuberg 1990). They begin with an initial, automatic, and usually unconscious classification of the other according to a very small number of primary cultural categories and move on to more detailed typing depending on the circumstances. The evidence shows that gender is one of these primary categories in Western societies so that we automatically and unconsciously gender-categorize any specific other to whom we must relate.

In institutional settings, such as workplaces, there are often clear social scripts that define who self and other are and frame interaction (e.g., supervisor and worker). Yet gender categorization continues in these settings because the actual process of enacting a social script with a concrete other evokes habitual person perception and with it, the cultural rules that define gender as something that must be known to make sense of others. Research shows that when institutional roles become salient in the process of perceiving someone, those roles become nested within the prior understanding of that person as a man or woman and take on slightly different meanings as a result (Brewer 1988). We may be able to imagine an ungendered institutional script whereby "the student talks to the teacher" but we cannot interact with any actual students or teachers without first classifying them as male or female. The gender categorization of self and others, even in institutionally scripted settings, is a fundamental, unnoticed process that involves gender in the activities and institutional roles that people enact together.

Gender categorization in work-related encounters sets the stage for two interactional processes that contribute to and help preserve gender inequality in paid employment. Gender categorization cues gender status beliefs that can unconsciously shape people's assumptions about how competent women in the situation are compared to similar men. Gender categorization also unconsciously biases whom people compare themselves to. Comparisons, in turn, affect the rewards to which people feel entitled and the wages for which they will settle.

GENDER STATUS PROCESSES

Gender status beliefs are widely held cultural beliefs that posit one gender as generally superior and diffusely more competent than the other. Such beliefs are well established in Western societies. Gender categorization in interaction makes gender status beliefs implicitly accessible to shape actors' perceptions of one another.

In interaction, people are never just males or females without simultaneously being many other social identities (e.g., young or old, of a given ethnic group, a worker or a student). The impact of gender status beliefs (and other cultural assumptions about men and women) on people's perceptions and behaviors in a given situation depends on the relevance of gender to the situation compared to other identities that are also salient. In work settings, work-related identities are likely to be in the foreground of people's perceptions and shape behavior most powerfully. Gender often acts as a *background identity* that flavors the performance of those work identities. Research shows, however, that even when other identities are the strongest determinant of behavior, gender status beliefs are still sufficiently salient to measurably affect people's expectations and behavior under two conditions: in mixed gender settings and when gender is relevant to the purposes or context of the setting (e.g., a women's caucus group) (Berger et al., 1977; Deaux and Major 1987). This means that gender status beliefs are effectively salient in many but not all work-related interactions.

When gender status beliefs are effectively salient like this in a work setting, they have three types of effects on goal-oriented interaction that affect employment inequality. First, they cause both men and women to unconsciously expect slightly greater competence from qualified men than from similarly qualified women. These implicit expectations tend to become self-fulfilling, shaping men's and women's assertiveness and confidence in the situation, their judgments of each other's ability, their actual performances, and their influence in the setting (see Ridgeway 1993 for details).

Second, gender status beliefs, when salient, cause people to expect and feel entitled to rewards that are commensurate with their relative status and expected competence in the setting. Thus, if gender status beliefs cause people in a work setting to assume the men are more important and competent than women, both men and women in the situation will also presume that men are entitled to higher levels of rewards such as pay or "perks." Consequently, when gender status is salient, men may react negatively if they are placed on the same reward level as a similarly qualified woman. They may experience this situation as an implicit status threat.

Third, because gender status beliefs advantage men, men in interaction are less likely to notice, and more likely to discount if they do notice, information about self or other that might diminish or eliminate the effects of gender status beliefs on expectations for competence or rewards. This effect of gender status beliefs is due to the way people's interests in a situation unconsciously bias what they perceive.

The effect makes it more difficult for women in the interaction to introduce information that would alter the lower expectations held for them. For example, there is a tendency in meetings for persons to attribute interesting or new ideas to a male speaker, even if a woman was the first to raise the point. Men who are "rewarded" for having expressed the good idea do not seem to notice that a woman may have mentioned the idea first. If the woman were to try to claim credit for the idea, and thereby lay claim to her competence, it is likely that she would be regarded as being pushy or out of line.

GENDER-BIASED COMPARISONS AND REWARDS

In addition to cueing gender status beliefs, gender categorization of self and other in workplace relations affects who people compare themselves to when they evaluate their own rewards or outcomes on the job. In general, people search out information about people whom they see as similar to them in order to evaluate whether they are receiving the rewards to which they are entitled. Automatic gender categorization causes people to unconsciously compare their own rewards more closely to those of the same gender than to those of the opposite gender. If pay, perks, or other rewards are distributed unequally among men and women on the job, then the tendency to compare with same-gender others will cause men to form higher estimates of what the "going rate" is for people with their qualifications. Women, gathering more comparisons from other women, form lower estimates of the going rate for the same qualifications. Not recognizing that their estimates of what others earn on the job have been biased by their tendency to compare with same-gender others, women form lower expectations for the pay and rewards to which they are entitled than do similar men.

Such reward expectations become self-fulfilling because they affect people's willingness to settle for a given level of pay or to press for more (see Major 1989 for research on this process).

GENDER INEQUALITY IN EMPLOYMENT

Gender inequality in employment is something of a puzzle. Theoretically, competitive market forces should wipe out gender discrimination because employers who prefer men and pay higher wages to get them will be driven out of business by smarter employers who hire cheaper but equally qualified women for the same jobs. Yet gender inequality in wages and gender segregation in occupations (i.e., the tendency for men and women to work in different occupations) have stubbornly persisted and improved only slowly over decades. England (1992) argues that gender inequality persists despite the flattening effect of market forces because it is continually being created anew, even if is worn down slightly over time. A consideration of how interaction drives gender categorization in work contexts and brings in gender status and comparison processes can help explain why the work world is so relentlessly gendered. It can also help explain why such gendering persists despite ongoing economic and organizational change.

Most work-related interaction takes place in organizational contexts with established job structures and institutional rules that heavily constrain what happens. Under business-as-usual conditions, gender status and comparison-reward processes occurring in these interactions are just part of the means by which existing gender-biased job structures and practices are enacted and sustained. Interactional gender processes, however, become important in themselves, rather than merely the agents of organizational structures and rules, at the interstices of organizations and under conditions that

force change on an organization. In these transition zones where organizational structures are less clearly defined, gender categorization, status, and comparison processes play a part in shaping the interaction through which actors create new organizational rules and structural forms and map gender hierarchy into them as they do so.

Occupational arrangements and wage outcomes are mediated by interaction in many ways, whether it be face-to-face, computer-mediated (e.g., e-mail), or indirect interaction through exchanges on paper. Workers learn about jobs and evaluate them through contact with others. Employers hire workers through direct (e.g., interviews) or indirect interaction (e.g., reviewing resumes and references). On the job, performance, evaluations, task assignments, and promotions involve interactions among people in complex ways. All these mediating interactions through which the world of work is conducted are potential sites where interactional mechanisms can map gender hierarchy into the occupational patterns and wages that result.

THE SEX LABELING OF WORKERS AND JOBS

Gender inequality in employment begins with the gender labeling of workers. This point seems so obvious and natural that we don't bother to explain it. Yet why should all workers be either male workers or female workers and not just workers? Why is gender a primary descriptor of workers at all? The answer lies in the way interaction evokes gender categorization, infusing gender into the hiring processes as it mediates employers' recruitment and placement of workers. Because interaction triggers gender categorization, employers can never interview or read the resume of a gender-neutral worker. Similarly, workers cannot interact with a gender-unclassified co-worker, boss, subordinate, or client.

The taken-for-granted, unconscious gender labeling of workers begins a process that also leads to the labeling of jobs themselves as men's or women's jobs. As the economy changes and develops, jobs that have been traditionally labeled as men's or women's jobs may fade in importance and new jobs, such as computer programmer, are continually created. Theoretically, these new occupations could be gender neutral. Yet, in an example of the force of gender in the organization of work, most of these new occupations are themselves quickly labeled as either men's or women's occupations. The persistent gender labeling of new jobs continually renews the gender-segregated nature of our occupational structure.

Gender categorization in workplace interaction plays a role in the continual gender labeling of jobs by priming workers and employers alike to infuse stereotypic assumptions about gender into the institutional scripts by which a job is enacted and represented to others. Employers often begin the process by implicitly or explicitly seeking workers of a particular gender on the basis of assumptions about labor costs that are themselves suffused by the effect of gender status beliefs. Employees of one gender come to predominate in the job. Since gender categorization in interaction primes people's cultural beliefs about gender even in segregated contexts, workers and employees may use gender-stereotypic terms to justify the activities in a gender-segregated job even when those activities originally seemed gender irrelevant. Thus, electronic assembly comes to be represented as a woman's job requiring women's "attention to detail and manual dexterity." Selling securities becomes a man's job requiring masculine "aggressiveness."

As the stories and social scripts that represent a job in the media and elsewhere come to be gendered as masculine or feminine, the differential status attached to men and women spreads to the job as well. Research shows that a job or task, when labeled feminine, is viewed by both job evaluators and those in the job themselves as requiring less ability and effort and as worth less compensation than the identical job or task is when labeled masculine. Other research shows that the gender composition of a job alone has a significant impact on what it pays, as does the association of the job with stereotypically feminine tasks such as nurturance (see Ridgeway 1997 for more details). Continual gender categorization in workplace interactions reinforces the tendency to apply gender labels to activities and perpetuates gender-based evaluations of jobs and activities.

MEN AND WOMEN AS INTERESTED ACTORS IN THE WORKPLACE

The interests of those in more powerful positions in employment organizations (e.g., bosses), who are more often men, are represented more forcefully than the interests of those who are in less powerful positions (e.g., secretaries). When gender status is salient in workplace interactions it creates a number of apparently gender-interested behaviors on the part of men, whether as employers, workers, or customers. The men themselves as well as observers of both genders will tend to see men in a situation as a bit more competent and deserving of rewards than similarly qualified women. They may miss or discount information in the situation that undermines these perceptions and perceive an implicit status threat when equivalent men and women are put on the same reward level.

All these effects usually occur as a modification or biasing of behavior during the enactment of an occupational or institutional identity that is more salient in the situation than the background identity of gender. A man acting in his role as an electrical engineer or union representative, for instance, may slightly bias his treatment of other men over women, usually in an implicit way that he himself does not recognize. Only occasionally will gender be so salient in the situation that men act self-consciously to preserve their interests as men. Yet the repeated background activation of gender status over many workplace interactions, biasing behavior in subtle or more substantial degrees, produces the effect of men acting in their gender interests, even when many men feel no special loyalty to their gender.

What about women in the workplace? Don't they pursue their interests as well? Yes, but the effect of gender status beliefs in interaction handicaps their efforts. It is in women's interests to introduce into a situation added information about their skills and accomplishments that undermines status-based assumptions about their competence compared to men and the rewards that they deserve. It is often difficult to introduce such information, however, precisely because gender is usually a background identity in workplace interactions. The participants do not explicitly think of gender as part of "what is going on here." The implicitness of gender in workplace interaction complicates the task of recognizing when bias is occurring and introducing countervailing information in the real time of actual interaction. The process is difficult as well because men's own status interests tend to make them more cognitively resistant to such information.

As a result, women on the job may periodically sense that something prejudicial is happening to them, but be frustrated in their efforts to act effectively against it. They will be vulnerable to "role encapsulation" whereby others define them in their work identities in implicitly gendered terms (e.g., "too nice" or "passive") that limit their effectiveness as actors in their own interests.

EMPLOYERS' PREFERENCES FOR MALE WORKERS

Reskin and Roos (1990) argue that employers show general preferences for hiring male workers, especially for "good," well-paying jobs. There are exceptions, of course, as when employers actually prefer female workers for jobs like nursery school teacher that involve tasks that are stereotypically associated with women. For other jobs, however, Reskin and Roos suggest that employers' preferences for male workers is a key factor that maintains gender inequality in wages and access to jobs with status and authority. While competitive market forces work against such preferences, they are nevertheless maintained by institutional rules and practices that embody them and by the implicit effects of gender status on workplace relations.

When an employer's automatic gender categorization of a potential employee cues gender status beliefs, these beliefs affect the employer's judgment of the worker's potential productivity. Expectations about competence based on gender status make the male worker appear "better" than an equally qualified woman. Also, an equally competent job or test performance by the two appears to the employer to be more indicative of ability and skill in the man than in the woman (see Ridgeway 1997 for a description of this research). On the surface merit is the basis of judgment. Yet the workers' gender is connected with merit by the way employers' evaluations of workers involve interactions that are unconsciously shaped by gender status beliefs. The result is what is called "error discrimination" where two workers who would perform equally are judged to be different and paid accordingly.

Gender status beliefs operating in the workplace can contribute to this process because they bias employers' expectations for workers' performances and these expectations tend to be self-fulfilling. This tendency often produces employer experiences with male and female workers that confirm the employers' initial judgments about them. A competent performance by a woman worker appears less competent coming from her than from her male co-worker. Also, and more insidious, the pressure of an employer's low expectations for them can actually interfere with some women workers' performances. Some male workers, on the other hand, may feel buoyed by their employer's confidence in them and perform even better than they otherwise might have. Thus, the effect of an employer's status-based expectations on some men and some women can create "real" differences in the average performance and productivity of groups of similar male and female workers. When interactional gender categorization makes gender salient in the hiring process, the employer's experience of these average differences also becomes salient. The employer may react by preferring male workers across the board (statistical discrimination). This form of discrimination is especially powerful in maintaining gender inequality in the workplace because it is more resistant to the equalizing effects of market forces than are other types of discrimination (England 1992).

Why Do Women Workers Accept Lower Wages?

An employer's ability to attract and retain women workers for lower wages is also critical for maintaining gender inequality in employment. Why do women settle for less than similarly qualified men? Here, too, gender processes in interaction play a role by shaping different senses of entitlement on the part of similarly qualified men and women.

Although many women work in predominantly female jobs (e.g., nurses, secretaries, or elementary school teachers), their work performance is often evaluated through direct or indirect interaction with male supervisors, clients,

or customers. Also, their work may have become typed a stereotypically female task. In any of these situations, gender categorization during interaction will activate status beliefs affecting women workers' own performance and expectations for rewards as well as their employer's and fellow workers' expectations for them. In fact, the evidence shows that women underestimate the quality of their performances in comparison with men. This makes them susceptible to arguments that they deserve less pay.

Gender categorization in work relations also unconsciously biases women's choices of whom to seek out in order to compare the pay they are receiving and evaluate whether it is fair. As we saw, women's tendency to compare their pay more closely with other women than similar men can cause them to underestimate the going rate for work by people with given qualifications. Such underestimates of possible pay rates is a second factor that causes women to peg the compensation they deserve at lower rates than do men.

If women workers inadvertently underestimate the rewards they are entitled to, employers can more easily force them to settle for lower wages (Major 1989). If corresponding gender status and biased comparison processes cause male workers to overestimate what they deserve, then employers find it harder to force lower wages on them. Out of such processes, women inadvertently accept lower wages than men. Women's unintentional acceptance of lower pay helps sustain gender hierarchy in employment over time by moderating women's resistance to pay differences.

Women's Entrance Into Male Occupations

In recent decades, women have entered male occupations in large numbers. Yet wage inequality and the gender segregation of jobs has not declined as much as one might expect. As

Reskin and Roos point out (1990), the problem is that as women enter a male occupation in number, men often flee it so that it "turns over" to become a women's occupation. This has happened to the job of bank teller over the past couple of decades. Sometimes, when women enter a male occupation, instead of men leaving the occupation altogether, the occupation becomes reorganized so that some specialties within it are predominantly female while others are predominantly male. Thus, as women have entered medicine in recent years, pediatrics has become a women's specialty while neurosurgery has remained overwhelmingly male. Again, wage inequality and gender segregation of jobs are preserved despite women's entrance into the formerly male profession of medicine.

While many processes are behind these transformations of occupations, once again, gender processes during interaction are involved. Given employer preferences for male workers, women often gain access to men's occupations when the demand for workers in that occupation outstrips the pool of interested male workers available at an acceptable wage. As the shortage of male workers brings women into the job, gender-based status interests become increasingly salient in the workplace and may create tensions. Gender status beliefs activated by the mixed-sex context cause women's presence to subtly devalue the status and reward-worthiness of the job in the eyes of both workers and employers. Male workers may react to this perceived threat to their status and rewards with hostility toward women in the job. More men may begin to leave the job.

As women become more numerous in the job, supervisors' gender status beliefs and women workers' lower sense of entitlement exert self-fulfilling effects on women's pay and other rewards and these effects increasingly spread to the job itself. This situation makes it easier for employers to introduce organizational and technological changes to the job that further reduce the status

and rewards that it offers. Although this scenario is not inevitable, when it occurs, it often results in the job becoming a woman's job with lowered status and pay. Or the job may resegregate by specialty with lower pay and status for the female specialties.

Such transitions in occupations maintain gender hierarchy over a change in the technological and organizational structure of jobs. In the many interactions through which these transitions occur, activated gender status processes and biased reward comparisons create a complex mix of discrimination, status-based competitions of interests, differences in entitlement, and differential perceptions of alternatives. The result is a system of interdependent gender effects that are everywhere and nowhere because they develop through multiple workplace interactions, often in taken-for-granted ways. Their aggregate result is the preservation of wage inequality and the gender segregation of jobs.

CONCLUSION

Adding an interactional perspective to labor market and organizational explanations for inequality in employment helps explain why gender is such a major force in the organization of work. Hiring, job searches, placement, performance evaluation, task assignment, promotion, and dealing with customers, clients, bosses, coworkers, and subordinates all involve direct or indirect (e.g., via resumes) interaction. Interaction with a concrete other evokes primary cultural rules for making sense of self and of other, pushing actors to gender-categorize one another in each of these interactions. Gender categorization pumps gender into the interactions through which the world of work is enacted. It cues gender status beliefs and biases the choice of comparison others. The process is insidious because gender is usually an implicit background identity that acts in combination with more salient work identities and tinges their performance with gendered expectations.

In highly structured organizational work contexts, gender processes in interaction become part of the processes through which more formal structures that embody bias, such as job ladders and evaluation systems, are enacted. Gender processes in interaction contribute to the gender labeling of jobs, to the devaluation of women's jobs, to forms of gender discrimination by employers, to the construction of men as gender-interested actors, to the control of women's interest, to differences between men's and women's pay expectations, and to the processes by which women's entrance into male occupations sometimes leads to feminization of the job or resegregation by specialty.

In less bureaucratically organized work contexts, such as those at organizational interstices, in start-up companies, in newly forming professions, or in some types of works (e.g., screen writers), interpersonal processes come to the fore and are sufficient in themselves to create gender inequality in wages and gender typing of work. As they do so, interactional processes conserve gender inequality despite significant, ongoing changes in the organization of work and the economy, writing inequality into new work structures and practices as they develop.

If this inequality is to be reduced, it is vital to understand that gender inequality is maintained by structural processes and interactional processes acting together. Change will require intervention at both the structural and interactional level through policies such as affirmative action that change the interpersonal configuration of actors and, potentially, create stereotype disconfirming experiences for all.

While much has been learned about gender inequality in employment, the study of gender-based interactional processes may help to answer some of the stubborn questions that persist. These questions include the reasons why new jobs that develop as occupations change continue to acquire connotations as men's or women's jobs, how employers' apparent preferences for male workers persist even under competitive market pressures, why women's work is devalued, whether and how people act in their gender interests in employment matters, and why women accept lower wages than men for similar work.

REFERENCES

Berger, Joseph, M. Hamit Fisek, Robert Z. Norman, and Morris Zelditch, Jr. 1977. *Status Characteristics and Social Interaction.* New York: Elsevier.

Brewer, Marilynn. 1988. "A Dual Process Model of Impression Formation." Pp. 1–36 in *Advances in Social Cognition,* Vol. 1, edited by Thomas Srull and Robert Wyer. Hillsdale, NJ: Erlbaum.

Deaux, Kay, and Brenda Major. 1987. "Putting Gender Into Context: An Interactive Model of Gender-Related Behavior." *Psychological Review* 94: 369–389.

England, Paula. 1992. *Comparable Worth: Theories and Evidence.* New York: Aldine.

Fiske, Susan, and Steven Neuberg. 1990. "A Continuum of Impression Formation, From Category-Based to Individuating Processes: Influences of Information and Motivation on Attention and Interpretation." Pp. 1–73 in *Advances in Experimental Social Psychology,* edited by Mark Zanna. New York: Academic Press.

Major, Brenda. 1989. "Gender differences in Comparisons and Entitlement: Implications for Comparable Worth." *Journal of Social Issues* 45: 99–115.

Reskin, Barbara, and Patricia Roos. 1990. *Job Queues, Gender Queues: Explaining Women's Inroads into Male Occupations.* Philadelphia: Temple University Press.

Ridgeway, Cecilia L. 1993. "Gender, Status, and the Social Psychology of Expectations." Pp. 175–198 in *Theory on Gender/Feminism on Theory,* edited by Paula England. New York: Aldine.

———. 1997. "Interaction and the Conservation of Gender Inequality: Considering Employment." *American Sociological Review* 62: 218–235.

West, Candace and Don Zimmerman. 1987. "Doing Gender." *Gender and Society* 1: 125–151.

THE SOCIAL PRODUCTION OF CHANGE

The reading examples in the next-to-last section of Part VI, "The Social Production of the Cultural Status Quo," explored some of the ways in which everyday social interaction results in the persistence of the status quo. This section looks at examples of complexity and change in cultural production.

In "Discovering Truth", social psychologist Tom DeGloma explores the life-changing experiences people describe when they use phrases such as "I saw the light." These experiences involve leaving one reality for another and typically include a process of redefining one's personal truth and history.

"Take Your Good Friday to the Streets" is a selection from Pierrette Hondagneu-Sotelo's book *God's Heart Has No Borders.* Hondagneu-Sotelo spent several years talking with and observing social activists working to better the lives of Latin American immigrants in the Los Angeles area. This selection describes the complex relationship between a group of religious leaders and union organizers working together to support labor reform. The religious leaders explain their activism in terms of their beliefs about God and service to fellow human beings. Accordingly, they are able to reconcile seemingly contradictory social positions as they work toward social change.

"Talking Back" is a short essay from renowned contemporary author and scholar bell hooks. In this brief autobiographical sketch, hooks recalls an event in which it became impossible to maintain the expected social routine. She found that she simply had to "talk back."

READING QUESTIONS

1. According to Hondagneu-Sotelo, religious activists use their moral authority to influence labor reform, enabling them to be more effective than secular union organizers. Explain how moral authority works in this case.

2. Make a list of some of the central cultural shifts that have taken place in recent history. Who or what groups were largely responsible for these shifts, and how did they manage to be effective in changing the status quo?

3. Discuss one taken-for-granted belief or practice that you have reconsidered as a result of studying the material in this book.

42

Discovering "Truth"

Thomas DeGloma

I once was lost, but now am found,

Was blind, but now I see.

John Newton, "Amazing Grace"

AWAKENINGS

The first verse of the popular Christian song widely known as "Amazing Grace," partially reproduced in the epigraph above, is one of the most recognizable articulations of religious conversion in the Western world. The hymn was composed by John Newton when he was serving as an Anglican priest in Buckinghamshire, England, and published with a collection of hymns in 1779 under its original title, "Faith's Review and Expectation." It is also an autobiographical account. Prior to serving the Christian ministry, Newton worked as a slave trader. He tells us that on March 10, 1748, at the age of twenty-three, a violent storm threatened to sink the ship he worked while en route from West Africa to England. According to his own account, the young Newton cried out in deep and profound fear for his life and begged God for mercy. Nearly four weeks and several storms later, his badly damaged vessel reached land. Newton later interpreted his escape from this near-death experience as an act of divine intervention, writing, "[. . .] [T]he Lord of heaven delivered me out of deep waters. [. . .] About this time I began to know

that there is a God who hears and answers prayer. This experience, John Newton tells us, was a major moment in a more protracted awakening that ultimately led him to embrace a newfound Christian worldview and strive for a way of life grounded in Christian morality. Decades later, Newton became a vocal abolitionist, taking a stand in marked contrast to his earlier profession. It was not until this later period of his life when he began working in the priesthood that he composed "Amazing Grace." In just a few words, the poet-priest captured the tension between a life of despair marked by wretched "blasphemy and profaneness" and the joy of salvation and virtue. Using his own life story as a template, he produced a popular story model that his parishioners and the public at large could use to account for their own personal discoveries.

For centuries individuals have told stories about discovering truth in their lives. Such storytellers describe having once held false beliefs about the world and consequently having lived a significant part of their lives "blind" to reality. Simultaneously, they tell of "seeing the light" or "waking up" to discover the "truth" about themselves and the "reality" of the world in which they live. Some, like Newton, tell stories about discovering a religious "truth," typically to explain their conversion to a new faith or their rejection of a religion in which they once believed. Yet others describe discovering a political "truth" as they work to promote an ideological agenda they once actively opposed. More, some individuals account for a newfound psychological "truth," often finding causes for their psychological troubles in newly discovered childhood experiences. Others describe discovering a sexual "truth," commonly to account for their embrace of a newly acquired sexual orientation or identity. Still others describe coming to a newfound scientific "truth" that leads them to reject long-held beliefs about the universe. Despite the notable differences among their concerns, all such individuals tell autobiographical stories about awakening to a "truth" that pertains to some personally and socially significant issue.

[Here], I explore the distinctly social logic of such *awakening narratives*—stories people tell about having once been contained in a world of darkness and ignorance and subsequently awakening to an enlightened understanding of their experiences and situations. Such stories do not concern relatively mundane or minor developments in the storyteller's life. Rather, individuals tell awakening stories to explain a radical transformation of consciousness, a fundamental change in their perception of their lives and their orientation to the world around them. People tell such stories in order to account for a major change of heart and mind—to convey what Peter Berger describes as an "alternation . . . between varying and sometimes contradictory systems of meaning." As opposed to relatively localized discoveries (such as discovering the cause of an ongoing problem at work) or accounts of a particular misperception (such as realizing a friend or lover is not the person you thought they were), awakening stories involve a narrated substitution of one worldview . . . for another. Individuals use such accounts to justify their embrace of new attitudes, beliefs, perceptions, and actions. Awakening stories are quite prevalent; they pertain to many different subject matters and span a wide variety of social and historical contexts.

There are various ways that we might understand the stories people tell about discovering truth. One way would be to view awakenings as experiences in which individuals actually discover an objectively "real" yet previously hidden truth or reality.

I am not interested in measuring the objective character of truth and falsehood. Nor do I take a position on the issue of what *really* happened in an individual's life and what did not. Instead, I am interested in the ways such awakenings involve conceptions of truth that rely on and take shape around the worldview—the beliefs, values, perceptions, ideas, feelings, and moral evaluations—of the community to which one belongs. That is to say, rather than a representational view of truth (one that involves judging claims about truth based on whether or how well they represent the "real" world), I advance a social and interrelational view (one that involves treating truth as a function of the social situation or cultural vantage point of the individual making claims). I am interested in how individuals use these awakening stories to give meaning to their lives.

Contrary to the tenets of psychological individualism, I am interested in the social foundations of awakenings. I explore the ways individuals and communities draw on shared sociomental norms and deep-seated cultural and emotion codes to frame the relationship between the "true" and the "false" as they tell their seemingly personal awakening stories. Telling stories about discovering "truth" involves seeing the world through a new "community's distinctive mental lenses."

In order to fully appreciate the distinctly social significance of awakening stories, we need to be aware of three interrelated dimensions of autobiographical work—the self-reflexive, the dialogical, and the performative.

Taking these three interrelated dimensions of autobiographical work into account, we can begin to see how the stories we tell about our lives are inseparable from our experience of self and identity and our position in a web of social relationships.

THE AWAKENING-STORY FORMULA

Writing to an audience of fellow ex-Mormons, an individual who goes by the name Moonshine comments, "Like many of you, I have spent the last several years trying to make sense out of the most extraordinary experience of my life—my evolution through and beyond traditional Mormon beliefs. [. . .] [I now have] an acute awareness of the [. . .] fear and dependence the church fosters in its faithful members [. . .]. What a trip! [. . .] The cognitive dissonance I felt set in motion a chain of events that led to some painful conclusions." Using phrases like "evolution through and beyond," "a chain of events," and "What a trip!" Moonshine lays out a rudimentary temporal map of her life with just a few words. She uses the general metaphors of evolution and a journey to shape her life along a formulaic *plotline*. As she goes on to fill in more detail, her audience is already given a sense of her personal awakening. We are aware of a sharp distinction between her former mindset (defined by her "traditional Mormon beliefs") and her present worldview (as an apostate who has moved "beyond" Mormonism). From her current storytelling standpoint, Moonshine sees things very differently than she used to.

I first took interest in awakenings while studying trauma narratives. In particular, as I was researching "recovered" memories of child sexual abuse, I began to notice that the process of recovering memories involves a formulaic discovery of "truth" (in this case, the memory of abuse) and a consequent formulaic account of the narrator's "false" belief (the prior, mistaken perception that the abuse wasn't there). Such self-identified

survivors of child sexual abuse tell scripted stories about awakening to the truth about their lives. Philip's account, for example, was published in a therapeutic volume. Philip recalls, "When I was 14 my mother used to come into my bed in the early hours of the morning, arouse me sexually, and sexual intercourse would take place. Until recently (I am now 52) I thought I had dreamed those sessions, because I must have never been fully awake [. . .]. [. . .] I can't tell you how I felt when this dawned on me." Philip is telling us that what he used to believe was a dream, he now—quite suddenly at the age of fifty-two—knows was sexual abuse. As he tells us this story, he is describing his prior state of "false" consciousness ("I thought I had dreamed those sessions") while testifying to the "truth" (intercourse, sexual abuse) and radically redefining his relationship with his mother. In remarkably few words, he describes a major transformation of consciousness—a discovery of "truth" and "reality" that is accompanied by profound feelings and has significant implications for his future attitudes, behaviors, and relationships.

Philip's story is certainly very personal. His "dawning" or awakening, however, is far from unique. With regard to this particular issue, many other individuals use this psychological version of the awakening story to describe recovering memories of child sexual abuse in therapeutic or support group–like settings. However, at a transcontextual level, such stories are formally similar to stories told in other settings about different topics. For example, Eleonai "Eli" Israel, an Army National Guard specialist and member of the social movement organization Iraq Veterans Against the War, describes a major transformation of consciousness with regard to an explicitly political subject matter. Eli recounts,

Like many after September 11th I wanted to serve, again. I felt I owed something more to my country after my years of training. I trusted my president and my leadership to tell me the truth. I also trusted my own integrity. I knew that I would never willingly do anything that I knew to be immoral or wrong. [. . .] I reasoned that my actions during these missions were justified in the name of "self-defense." However, I came to realize my perception was wrong. I was in a country that I had no right to be in, violating the lives of people, and doing so without regard to the same standards of dignity and respect that we as Americans hold our own homes and our own lives to. [. . .] I have taken and/or destroyed the lives of people who were defending their families from being the "collateral damage" of the day.

Like Philip, Eli describes a significant personal discovery, a dawning in which he realized his old perceptions and beliefs were "false" while coming to understand the "true" nature of his actions, experiences, and relationships. Despite using their autobiographical stories to address very different subject matters, Moonshine, Philip, and Eli all juxtapose a past state of *cognitive constraint* (a false or deluded mental state) with a more current state of *cognitive emancipation* (a newly enlightened mental state). Their stories conform to this common social pattern and formula of storytelling.

By focusing on the formal properties shared by these three stories at the expense of their otherwise significant differences, we can begin to see how this story formula has a generic social logic that Moonshine, Philip, and Eli each use to give meaning to their lives and justify their current beliefs and perceptions. When individuals tell such a story, they make use of a strong cultural doctrine that truth emerges from the debunking of false belief and is therefore temporally situated in binary opposition to some falsehood. In other words, the properties of the story formula allow individuals to justify a major change of mind by positioning a newfound "truth" in diametric contrast to their previous mindset. They thereby emplot their life course as

a testimony to that newfound "truth." Despite their variant concerns, they each justify one way of seeing by negating another. In the process such individuals use their autobiographical accounts to corroborate particular—and often controversial—knowledge claims in the world.

The generic properties of the awakening-story formula are evident in the following example in which conservative activist David Horowitz describes realizing that his long-held Marxist worldview was in fact "false." Horowitz writes,

> One evening [. . .] I had a sudden shock of recognition. [. . .] I had always [. . .] visualized a pyramid whose apex was Marxism, which was my life's work and which provided the key to all other knowledge. [. . .] But in that very moment a previously unthinkable possibility also entered my head: The Marxist idea, to which I had devoted my entire intellectual life and work, was *false*. All around me, the room went black. In the engulfing dark, the pyramid flattened and a desert appeared in its place, cold and infinite, and myself an invisible speck within it. [. . .] For the first time in my conscious life I was looking at myself in my human nakedness, without the support of revolutionary hopes, without the faith in a revolutionary future [. . .].

Horowitz goes on to describe his realization of political "truth" as he rejects his prior, left-wing beliefs in favor of a conservative worldview. However, regardless of the particular political details of his autobiographical account, Horowitz uses a generic awakening-story formula to depict his life and engage in an ongoing social dispute over truth and meaning. The generic character of his account can be seen when we eliminate a mere four words (just over 3 percent of the selected passage) and replace them with others. The account becomes generic when the stricken words below are ignored. If we were to replace them with either *Catholicism/Catholic or conservatism/conservative*, for example, we would completely change the meaning of the story, illustrating the remarkable flexibility of the story formula.

> One evening [. . .] I had a sudden shock of recognition. [. . .] I had always [. . .] visualized a pyramid whose apex was ~~Marxism~~, which was my life's work and which provided the key to all other knowledge. [. . .] But in that very moment a previously unthinkable possibility also entered my head: The ~~Marxist~~ idea, to which I had devoted my entire intellectual life and work, was *false*. All around me, the room went black. In the engulfing dark, the pyramid flattened and a desert appeared in its place, cold and infinite, and myself an invisible speck within it. [. . .] For the first time in my conscious life I was looking at myself in my human nakedness, without the support of ~~revolutionary~~ hopes, without the faith in a ~~revolutionary~~ future [. . .].

As a result of changing just a few words, we can use Horowitz's rendition of the awakening narrative to create an entirely different meaning. By replacing the stricken words with the words *Catholicism/Catholic*, we make the story about religion as opposed to political revolution. By using the words *conservatism/conservative*, we turn the story into its ideological "opposite." The versatility of the basic story framework and the generic character of its moral and emotional symbolism are exactly what make the narrative *formulaic*. With slight changes, the narrative formula can be used to undermine and reject any one system of meaning and pave the way to justify and defend any newly acquired worldview.

Stories that follow this formulaic awakening plot involve several core components. First, storytellers account for a past state of "darkness," which usually involves conveying a sense of reaching a low point in one's life as an inevitable consequence of one's commitment to a worldview or belief system from which one is now estranged. Second, storytellers describe their experience of discovery and personal transformation. Third, storytellers account for a current state of "light" and commonly describe having found their true place in the world. Here, they "redeem the past," making up for self-ascribed failures, mistakes, and misbeliefs by casting their current worldview as a positive moral contrast to their former worldview.

THE SEMIOTIC STRUCTURE OF AWAKENING STORIES

When telling awakening stories, individuals draw from a stock of conventional metaphors to strike a moral contrast between their now-rejected and newly embraced worldviews. Generally speaking, this moral contrast is reinforced by the widespread practice of depicting "falsehood" and "truth" as situated on different *epistemic planes,* linking downward or lower with falsehood/ignorance/bad and upward or higher with truth/knowledge/good.

Each family of metaphors captures a different facet of the diametric contrast between falsehood/evil and truth/good that is central to the awakening-narrative formula. However, as Arthur W. Frank notes, an individual's reliance on "culturally conventional rhetorics" does not mean that his or her lived experiences are any less real. Rather, storytellers use these cultural codes as a framework with which to organize, define, and articulate their personal experiences while sharing their stories with others and situating themselves in the world.

Individuals who tell awakening stories use the metaphoric contrast of *asleep* versus *awake* to define the experience of "falsehood" and the discovery of "truth" from a first-person perspective.

Related to the asleep-versus-awake family of metaphors, *darkness*-versus-*light* metaphors are used to characterize various environments of falsehood and truth by people who tell awakening stories. They use "darkness" to define the contexts and conditions of cognitive constraint and "light" (including the related concepts of enlightenment, fire, illumination, elucidation, dawning, and more) to define the contexts and conditions of cognitive emancipation. Using metaphors of darkness and light, individuals who tell awakening stories account for their prior lack and more recent attainment of the social and environmental conditions necessary to see and know "truth" in the world.

When individuals use the *blindness*-versus-*sight* family of metaphors, they combine the themes inherent in the asleep/awake and darkness/light metaphoric contrasts to portray their sense of looking at the world through a new set of eyes.

Finally, people who tell awakening stories use the broad *lost*-versus-*found* family of metaphors (including various related concepts and themes) to define the experiences of *cognitive alienation* and *cognitive solidarity*. When one is lost, one is typically in an unfamiliar and perhaps threatening setting. When one has been found, one joins a space of comfort and familiarity, a home base where one is supposed to be. Storytellers often convey the experience of being "lost" by describing their isolation and loneliness or by depicting the inauthenticity of their "false" relationships. They often convey the experience of being "found" with metaphors of family and homecoming. Using this broad set of metaphoric contrasts, individuals account for their prior state of being without a "true" community and their more current state of finding a sociomental "family."

Individuals use these metaphoric contrasts to describe the process of acquiring new cognitive norms—to express a *sociomental migration* between different worldviews.

THE AWAKENER AS A SOCIAL TYPE OF STORYTELLER

The particular constellation of dialogical orientations inherent in the awakening-story formula can be used to define the awakener as a social type of storyteller.

First, the awakener takes a contentious dialogical orientation toward the proponents of a rejected worldview (one that the awakener has left in the past). This contentious and antagonistic orientation, typically imbued with feelings related to betrayal, loss, and anger, is not necessarily directed against the members of the awakener's former community (for whom the awakener may feel sympathy) but toward the cognitive authority figures and other advocates who uphold the worldview that the awakener is working to undermine. Second, the awakener takes a harmonious dialogical orientation toward the proponents of a newly embraced worldview. These include cognitive authority figures and confederates that make up a new community of like-minded others with whom the awakener expresses sentiments of solidarity, such as love, appreciation, comfort, or security. Third, the awakener takes a proselytizing dialogical orientation toward individuals in the world at large (who are often conceived to be the "sleeping" or the "blind") as the act of telling the story inherently involves an invitation to share in or sympathize with the awakening. Finally, the awakener takes a critical-deprecating dialogical orientation toward his or her past self. The awakener portrays and symbolically engages his or her past persona in order to facilitate the contentious, harmonious, and proselytizing orientations mentioned above.

By telling their stories, awakeners are both converts *and* apostates—sociomental conformists and deviants. On the one hand, like religious testimonials, their stories "provide [a] collectivity with evidence that its beliefs are efficacious."

On the other hand, their testimonies also repudiate countertestimonies and thereby undermine the beliefs and values of other groups. Thus, interest groups and thought communities spotlight their awakeners as role models that others can emulate to "see the light."

AUTOBIOGRAPHICAL COMMUNITIES

When individuals tell such awakening stories, they clue us in to deep moral and cultural fissures in the world around them. They also take a stand, using their personal testimonies to mark their place within a contested social terrain.

Generally speaking, people tell stories about their lives during various "autobiographical occasions" and in a variety of social contexts that affirm particular types of accounts and privilege "institutionally preferred themes, plots, and characters." Such institutional contexts also compel certain perceptions and enforce particular definitions of reality. Social movement meetings, therapeutic support groups, high school reunions, Alcoholics Anonymous meetings, religious rituals, and other social contexts serve as "narrative environments" where individuals adopt shared autobiographical scripts and construct personal accounts in accordance with (often unacknowledged) social norms of storytelling, cognitive conventions, and feeling rules. Participants face social pressures (from other individuals, from the group as a whole, and from the context itself) to accentuate certain details of their lives while ignoring others. Further, institutions often have homogeneous goals and work to shape personal accounts and particular types of identities so that they are in line with those goals. However, even given the impact of contextual norms, individuals are typically adept at conveying a feeling of personal experience with their stories. This is in part because "how we come to understand ourselves and narrate our experience" does not involve blind compliance to expectation but is "an artful and interactional process." Individuals creatively fashion their experiences and sentiments with socially approved scripts in order to convey personal information.

When individuals identify with an autobiographical community, they situate themselves in the world and emplot themselves in relation to various others. The autobiographical community, in turn, becomes a referential locus of situated perceptions, beliefs, values, and feelings as members share community-based cognitive, epistemic, moral, and affective frameworks for understanding the world. As Tamotsu Shibutani notes with regard to reference groups more generally, such communities shape their members' orientation to the world as "one comes to perceive the world from [the group's] standpoint." In the process, adherents use community norms to shape stories about their lives. An autobiographical community can be a formal organization (like an established religion or social movement organization) or a less formal, more diffuse reference group (like communities of ex-Mormons or self-identified survivors of child sexual abuse). In either case such communities are "autobiographical" because they privilege particular scripts and conventions that individuals use to construct stories about their lives for specific purposes.

In November 2008, Christine Bakke appeared at a public press conference in Denver, Colorado, in order to tell the story of her personal "journey" to accept her homosexuality after years of corrective therapy intended to "cure" her of her homosexual attractions. Her account was especially relevant because she was speaking to oppose the annual convention of the National Association for Research and Therapy of Homosexuality (NARTH), one of the largest and most-vocal organizations promoting "sexual reparative therapy" and advancing the view that homosexuality is a pathological condition. Like other self-identified "ex-gay survivors," Christine described once accepting the tenets of sexual reparative therapy and believing the psychological professionals who defined her homosexuality as a mental disorder while promising a therapeutic remedy. Now wholeheartedly rejecting that position and defending the authenticity of her homosexuality, Christine told the public, "I've spent the past five years in recovery from the ex-gay treatments I received. [. . .] I have also met hundreds of others negatively affected by ex-gay theories and treatments, and together we have helped each other in moving beyond this troubled time in our lives." Like the war veterans previously described, such ex-gay survivors derive their authority to define sexual reparative therapy because they once subscribed to it but, they claim, have since come to see what it "truly" means.

While sharing her personal story, Christine undermines the core vision, ideas, and values expressed by NARTH and its advocates. Like the many other members and affiliates of the "Beyond Ex-Gay" community or the "Truth Wins Out" movement, her autobiographical account reveals the contours of a cultural conflict over the "truth" concerning the nature of human sexuality. In this battle over scientific and sexual "truth," the awakening stories told by members of the gay pride community, an autobiographical community that includes ex-gay survivors like Christine, are socially situated in opposition to the awakenings of those individuals who embrace sexual reparative therapy—those who describe awakening to discover their "true" heterosexuality after years of leading a homosexual lifestyle.

In the introduction to his book *Healing Homosexuality: Case Stories of Reparative Therapy,* psychologist Joseph Nicolosi undermines the gay pride community's standpoint and articulates the sexual reparative community's position in this cultural and epistemic

conflict when he writes, "[. . .] [W]e are offering *the opposite sort of personal testimony,* that of homosexual men who have tried to accept a gay identity but were dissatisfied and then benefited from psychotherapy *to help free them* of the gender identity conflict that lies behind most homosexuality." In order to reinforce the sexual reparative community's authority in this contest, Nicolosi then deploys a collection of biographical sketches (testimony in the form of psychotherapeutic case studies) that detail the lives of individuals who have discovered the "truth" about their sexuality as they rejected homosexuality and embraced a heterosexual lifestyle. The awakening stories published in Nicolosi's collection, as well as the first-person accounts of "repaired" heterosexuals published elsewhere, are oppositionally situated in relation to the awakening stories of those who "come out" as gay as well as those who, like Christine Bakke, identify as "ex-gay survivors." Their life stories are in dialogical contrast— "counternarratives" mobilized in competition with one another in a broader autobiographical field. Despite expressing antithetical versions of truth, these dueling autobiographical communities both use the awakening-story formula to wage this cultural battle over the nature of sexuality. Further, both autobiographical communities offer the awakening stories of their members as evidence, providing autobiographical models that those who are committed to the opposing sexual orientation can (and, from each perspective, *should*) use to jump ship and switch sociomental camps.

As they tell their personal stories, awakeners establish their *sociomental standpoint* is in a community that is situated in a pluralistic and contentious world. Agents use the generic awakening formula, one that involves founding a truth claim on the declaration of "false" belief, to fit their stories within this discursive framework. In the process, they mark the social distinction between those they claim to be awake and those they deem asleep. Therefore, just as social discourses in general "both reflect and reproduce power relations that 'live' in social structures," autobiographical stories can reflect and reproduce cultural contests over the cognitive authority to define ongoing and past issues of significant moral and political concern.

THE SOCIAL PRODUCTION OF CHANGE

43

Take Your Good Friday to the Streets

Pierrette Hondagneu-Sotelo

(2008)

After decades of declining rates of unionization, a revitalized labor movement emerged in the United States at the turn of the millennial century. Unions had dedicated more than a century to organizing white male citizen workers, and, in fact, had been historically key to pushing for nativist, restrictionist policies, but they have now deliberately diversified their strategies and also the kinds of workers they include. Spearheaded by progressive leaders working at the grassroots level and in the AFL-CIO, the movement gained momentum with the rise of service-sector unions; the concerted cultivation of community allies; and a new commitment to organizing women, minorities, and immigrant workers. Less well publicized are the new mobilizations of clergy marching in the street to support these unionization efforts. Religion is a critical part of this newly revitalized style of unionism, which relies on building allies and cultivating community support. Often in clerical robes and regalia, rabbis, priests, and ministers from various denominations are marching in the streets, holding prayer vigils, engaging in civil disobedience, and visiting workers at their homes and workplaces. Through their actions, they collectively offer their moral authority and spiritual support to the struggles faced by low-wage workers, many of whom are immigrants.

How did this happen? The development of these religious support groups for workers follows on the heels of the new openness in the labor movement, but it also reflects the clergy's pent-up desire for meaningful social engagement. Religious people who had grown weary of the limitations of religious charity—and who longed to once again, or perhaps for the first time, experience participating in something like the civil rights movement—coalesced to form labor support organizations such as Clergy and Laity United for Economic Justice (CLUE) in the 1990s. Many of these clergy groups around the country are coordinated through the Chicago offices of Interfaith Worker Justice (IWJ), an organization founded by Kim Bobo in 1995. As Bobo told me, "There were a lot of folks in the religious community who had done twenty or twenty-five years of soup kitchens and shelters and were beginning to realize that this was just a complete dead end." These were religious people looking for a way to put their faith into action for social change. "We had to find," Bobo explained, "some new ways to challenge what was going on in society."

CLUE is located in Los Angeles, and it is among the strongest of the sixty religious-based labor support organizations in the country. These groups support workers by relying on religious moral authority, scripture, and a mixture of modern political persuasion techniques (such as street protests, phone calls, and delegations to authority figures) and ancient religious symbols (such as stone tablets, bitter herbs, and milk and honey). In Los Angeles and Santa Monica, CLUE has acted quite militantly in demanding economic justice for workers and the working poor. Sometimes their opponents, the managers and employees of corporations, allege that the CLUE clergy are not authentic religious leaders or that they are merely puppets of the union. For example, when CLUE members organized civil disobedience and clergy delegations at a major luxury hotel in support of service workers and their union, the hotel management circulated a flyer warning workers not to be duped by "phony priests." Leaders in CLUE were outraged and exacted an apology from the management. CLUE members also bristle at the insinuation that they were simply manufactured by the union or that they follow union orders. "We're not on their payroll," they say. Rather, they see themselves as an autonomous organization, constituted by people of deep religious faith who have embraced the cause of worker justice as their own, precisely because it is a direct expression of their religious beliefs and doctrines. For many of them, supporting the struggles of low-wage immigrant workers has become an integral part of their religious identity and practice. A CLUE board member and minister of a small congregation told me, "Faith is what you do." Many of the clergy said that the experience of participating in CLUE has brought them spiritual renewal and positive transformation.

In cities like Los Angeles, where Latino immigrant workers constitute the majority of those in the low-wage, super-exploited jobs, labor organizers of the 1980s and 1990s concentrated on a particular set of industries that seemed organizable. Consequently, much of the sparkle and success in the new labor movement comes from immigrant workers in the hotel and restaurant industry, in home health care, and in the janitorial sector. Organizations such as CLUE support the cause of economic justice broadly, but some of their biggest and most successful efforts have concentrated on union campaigns where Mexican and Central American immigrant workers predominate.

Scriptures and Protest

As one of their first direct actions in support of the hotel workers, CLUE inaugurated Java for Justice. Seemingly inspired by the lunch counter sit-ins of the civil rights movement, small groups of clergy dressed in clerical collars and ministerial garb ordered coffee at the hotel restaurants. They used these opportunities to preach about the injustices of hotel managers who refused to sign union contracts or allow for workers' demands. Reverend Dick Gillet recalls one of his first experiences with the Java for Justice campaign this way: He and about a half-dozen other clergy, several of them in clerical collars, visited the restaurant of one of the luxury hotels and ordered coffee. "We finished our drinks and coffee and stuff and then I got up," he related, "and said, 'May I have your attention?'" Speaking in as loud a voice as he could muster, he recalled saying, "I know this is a bit unusual, and certainly not my real congregation, but I would like you to know that we are here in support of the people who are waiting on you, who make your beds, who are tending to you while you are in this hotel. They need your help, and you can help them if you go downstairs to the front desk after you are through here and tell them that you personally want the hotel to sign a fair contract."

CLUE would continue to develop and refine this tactic. In 2002, after Elba Hernandez, an employee who had worked for Santa Monica's Doubletree Hotel for eleven years, was fired, allegedly for union organizing, CLUE participated in a "lunch-in" action at the hotel restaurant. Twenty-two CLUE members filtered into the hotel restaurant, and after ordering drinks and lunch, they stood up in unison, holding placards that read, "Support Your Workers' Rights." Reverend Jarvis Johnson led them in prayer and declared, "These walls of Jericho," the ones that separate rich and poor, "need to come tumbling down." The clergy activists were quickly ushered out of the building, but outside they gathered to pray while Reverend Sandy Richards read a letter of support from the Muslim Public Affairs Council's senior advisor, Maher Hathout. Letters in support of reinstating the fired worker were also sent to the hotel from bishops of the Methodist, Episcopal, and evangelical Lutheran churches. Following this event, Father Michael Gutierrez, also a CLUE member and a priest at a Santa Monica church, had a private meeting with the general manager of the hotel, a fellow Catholic. At the meeting, he expressed his dissatisfaction with the hotel management decisions, and he suggested the manager face the moral contradiction of being a Catholic and treating employees so unfairly. A few months after these actions, Elba Hernandez was reinstated with back pay.

CLUE members have used a variety of tactics to express their support for union mobilization. To show their support for workers to the public and to corporate management, they have marched in picket lines, spoken out publicly in support of the union mobilizations, and participated in several instances of civil disobedience and a well-publicized fast at USC (University of Southern California). Many clergy were also arrested at USC in their attempts to win union contracts for the food service workers. Some clergy also visited the offices of hotel and USC managers.

The battle with the Westside hotels reached a high point in April 1998 when CLUE, together with the Westside Interfaith Council and the Jewish Labor Committee, organized what would become the first annual Holy Week-Passover Procession. At that first event, sixty priests, rabbis, and ministers outfitted in robes, shawls, collars, and yarmulkes walked alongside another one hundred lay supporters and workers on that iconic boulevard of consumer dreams, glitzy Rodeo Drive in Beverly Hills. By the time the procession occurred, two of the three Beverly Hills hotels had already signed the contract with Local 11, so these hotels were publicly rewarded with symbolic offerings of milk and honey, referring to the land where Moses set the Jews free. The managers at the Summit Rodeo Hotel received bitter herbs after a brief street-side seder, symbolizing the plight of the ancient Jews. Soon after, the Summit Rodeo signed the union contract.

In all of CLUE's actions, biblical references and faith-based morality are used as justifications. One of CLUE's earliest declarations in support of the living wage cited Deuteronomy 24:14–15: "Don't withhold the wages of poor and needy laborers—including those of 'aliens.'" In the struggle at USC, CLUE relied on the biblical story of David and Goliath to call attention to how "the University of Southern California, like Goliath of old, has unleashed its enormous economic and corporate power on its own little David, the 340 Food Service and Housing working men and women members of H.E.R.E. Local 11" (Dalton 2003:44–45). And Moses and stories of exodus (e.g., "You must welcome the alien, the stranger as yourself") as well as references to Incarnation have been frequently invoked in various CLUE campaigns.

GOD'S HEART HAS NO BORDERS

"A new movement, an old commandment, or both?" This was the question printed in big bold type on the envelope of a mass mailing from the Interfaith Worker Justice during spring 2006, when millions of people marched nationwide in massive rallies in support of immigrant rights. The accompanying letter, sent to supporters nationwide, cited the Leviticus quote that is reproduced above and informed readers that many immigrant workers lost their jobs for participating in the marches. It also listed the different ways in which the IWJ participated in the "emerging social justice movement" for immigrant rights. "We must stand for all workers—both immigrant and native-born—when they fight for justice in their workplaces," declared the letter, "We are called to do it through all of our sacred traditions."

CLUE leaders also marched through the streets of Los Angeles during spring 2006. Later that year, CLUE and IWJ joined forces to help coordinate the new sanctuary movement to protect immigrant families facing orders of deportation. While CLUE continued to mobilize in favor of all low-wage workers, CLUE members also saw their mission as including immigrant workers because, as one member told me in an interview, Los Angeles "is a pretty immigrant-looking city."

Most fundamentally, the clergy leaders saw their support of low-wage workers, immigrant or U.S. born, as a direct extension of their religious faith. "We don't see religions as isolated over here and handling one thing," explained Reverend William Campbell, a minister in an African American congregation. "We see it performing in all facets of life. Jesus clearly identified with the poor," he said, and clearly that is how [Reverend Campbell] saw his mission as well. Regardless of whether they were Christian or Jewish, clergy saw their work in CLUE as rooted in scripture and ancient religious traditions.

RELIGION AT WORK

CLUE participants used religion and their position as religious leaders to better the lives of low-wage immigrant workers. In this next section, I discuss three relevant CLUE activities: providing spiritual support to workers, deploying religious symbols in public spaces to underscore a labor struggle, and exercising moral voice and persuasion in favor of the unions.

During the late 1980s and 1990s, the Latino immigrant unions in Los Angeles, such as SEIU Justice for Janitors and HERE Local 11, innovated protests that featured the dramatization of labor struggles in the streets. These involved using props like big papier-mâché figures, placing beds in the middle of a street protest to show how many beds hotel housekeepers must make in a shift, or having a person dressed as Scrooge represent a greedy employer. CLUE followed suit by boldly brandishing religious symbols far beyond the confines of their churches and temples. Material objects with roots in ancient scripture, such as stone tablets, bitter herbs, and milk and honey, played central roles in CLUE protests and processions.

Clerical dress was a key part of these public activities. For these public events, concerted organizational steps were taken to ensure that clergy arrived attired in ways that left little ambiguity about whether they were union people or ordained religious leaders. The flyer announcing the 2001 interfaith procession that occurred during Holy Week-Passover, for example, reminded the participants to bring appropriate symbols of their identities. The flyer said, "Religious Leaders: Wear Vestments; All Workers: Bring a Symbol of Your Work; and Congregations, Organizations: Bring a Banner." Procession participants complied with this request, and the outcome was visually stunning.

The participants were all costumed and carrying props, but these were not theatrical performances but rather enactments of verifiable identities and social locations. Reverend Bob Miller, a retired minister who became quite active in various union-led direct actions, recalled attending his first demonstration in support of the hotel and restaurant employees' union in 1997. There he saw a peaceful demonstration, where, he said, the workers were blocking traffic while "costumed according to whether they were a concierge, housekeeper, whatever." The idea of telegraphing one's identity, whether a worker or clergy member, appealed to him. "The workers received me so warmly," he recalled. "And I thought, Well, I'll have to buy some new shirts and collars and wear them because I want the hotel management to know that I wasn't just a union employee."

Religious garb was donned in the streets and in front of the luxury hotels, but it was not just theatrical costuming. It was used together with traditional religious practices, such as prayer, song, and scripture, and concrete, symbolic reminders of ancient texts. Together, this array of identifiably familiar practices and objects communicated the religious significance of these struggles. When the clergy offered blessings and prayers, they were momentarily transforming a secular site into a sacred place. Moments of Durkheimian collective effervescence ensued. When I asked Don Smith, a Presbyterian minister, to describe his experiences in the CLUE processions and protests, he recalled his experience at the first Holy Week-Passover events. "As you can imagine, it's a tremendous feeling of solidarity. You're there with all the workers, you're there with a whole bunch of clergy . . . you're marching down Rodeo Drive, and . . . you're having an effect. People are stopping on the street, asking, 'What is this?'" Part of the excitement comes from breaking the norms of mundane social interaction, and part of the meaning comes from the religious rituals. As Reverend Smith put it, "There is the sense that this is not usually done. What are these religious people doing out here,

dressed up? And that's what one has to do, to interrupt the status quo, to make a point." The marches, he said, were empowering and uplifting because they gave the "sense that you're making an impact."

In all of these venues, the CLUE clergy were exercising moral voice. But part of their challenge was to use their religious authority to persuade others of the urgency of economic justice. CLUE's mission, as Reverend Perez summed up, involved "bringing moral pressure to bear, pressuring political leaders and working with unions, and pushing corporations and businesses to do the right thing." To be effective, they sought venues where they might direct their moral persuasion toward particular audiences. These included targeting the leaders at their own congregations, the owners and managers of the hotels, and their own congregation members. Clergy were well-suited to this task, as they are socially recognized as moral leaders, as experts in distinguishing right from wrong. Some of them felt that it was "not fair that clergy are respected more than the workers," but none of them failed to recognize the moral credibility which their positions afforded them.

Most of the clergy did not preach about economic justice on a weekly basis, but each Labor Day there was a concerted effort to do so. This is part of a national effort begun in 1996 and coordinated by IWJ and the AFL-CIO. On Labor Day weekend across the country, participating clergy are urged to speak to their congregations about the religious commitment to economic justice, tying the importance of unions today to biblical and scriptural readings. Union members are invited as guest speakers to discuss how they mesh their religious faith and union commitments.

During Labor Day weekend 2001, about one hundred Los Angeles–area congregations participated in this program, with guest speakers appearing at about fifty. I attended two services organized by CLUE clergy. Both featured special emphasis on immigrant worker rights and, in particular, Latino immigrant labor struggles. The two services were radically different, reflecting the different sizes of the congregations, the style of worship, and the congregations' demographic composition. Both, however, were unambiguously directed at the same cause: bringing religious communities and unions together to work for immigrant worker justice. Elsewhere, other religious services at predominantly black churches were focused on honoring the struggles of bus transit and airport security workers, many of whom are African American.

The first Labor in the Pulpit service that I attended occurred at a relatively small Unitarian church in affluent Santa Monica. In this small church filled with natural light, about two hundred or two hundred fifty people, many of them elderly or middle-aged white folks, filled the pews. After welcoming remarks, the lighting of a candle within a chalice (with some difficulty because of a faulty lighter), and the singing of songs such as "This Little Light of Mine," a middle-aged congregation member hobbled to the altar. She revealed that she suffered from multiple sclerosis, and she read a beautifully rendered narrative of thanks to all of the workers who made her life possible—the taxi drivers, the concrete workers, the designers and builders of her motorized wheelchair, and the builders of ramps and rails. More songs ensued, and then small children entered with offerings of food for a food bank before gathering around the group Los Jornaleros del Norte. This is a band formed by Latino immigrant men who met in the day laborer organizing project of the Coalition for Humane Immigrant Rights in Los Angeles. Pablo Alvarado, an immigrant rights and day laborer organizer and member of the band, introduced them by saying, "All of us are immigrant workers and all of us are parents, too." And then he introduced Jose, one of the band members. With that, Jose took the microphone and explained, in Spanish and through a translator, that he was a single parent of six children in Mexico. "I would like to tell the children here," he said, directing himself to the kids who sat on the steps around the altar, "to thank God because they live with their parents. I would love to be with my children, but I cannot." While the band played one of their compositions about the plight of children "back home" with parents working in the United States, the audience bobbed their heads to the beat.

Like the testimonials offered by union workers at the CLUE breakfast meetings, these were two different social worlds coming together. Speaking in Spanish through a translator, the first speaker said, "We day laborers use this Labor Day to protest the exploitation of immigrant workers." Another cited Leviticus and denounced abusive employers who violate the laws of government and the laws of God. They played more songs, ending with a lively rendition of "Si, Se Puede" on accordion, electric piano, bass, and guitar, and the expressions on the band members' and the congregation's faces suggested genuine warmth, appreciation, and feelings of solidarity.

DENOMINATIONAL DIFFERENCES?

CLUE and IWJ brought together clergy and laity from a variety of religious faiths and traditions, but when I asked if these denominational differences played out into conflicts, nearly everyone told me no. Reverend Don Smith, who had worked in numerous interfaith groups, including explicitly immigrant rights organizations, said, "In these social ministries, you'll never find the need to kind of say that, well, 'You're Catholic, I'm Jewish, and you're Episcopal.' There's this kind of innate understanding that all religions have in common, [which] is this need to address human pain, human suffering."

Just about everyone concurred. Political progressives were less likely to be mired in denominational differences. "The majority of those who will come into CLUE are your more progressive clergypersons anyway," said one clergyman, "and because they are more progressive, they are less likely to bring in denominational garbage." In fact, some clergy found this denominational diversity and shared understanding of social justice, theology, and social action to be particularly gratifying, giving them opportunities for clerical solidarity. Reverend Altagracia Perez, a youthful thirtyish female black and Latina pastor, said, for example, that she had tired of repeatedly explaining to other neighboring Episcopal pastors that she was not the youth minister or the pastor's wife. She said she had more in common with a particular Lutheran minister (and co-CLUE participant) who pastored in the same Central Los Angeles neighborhood and was similarly bound up with problems of poverty and worker injustice than she did with pastors in suburban Episcopal churches. "We have the same kind of population, we're serving the same neighborhood, and we have a lot of the same issues," she said of the Lutheran minister. "We share a common theology." In fact, she went even further, stating, "I think that the priests, ministers, and religious leaders that see themselves as part of the call to social justice feel more connected to each other than they do to people within their own denomination." A ministry focused on social and economic justice brought diverse clergy together in ways that being ordained in the same denomination did not.

Denominational differences did come up when CLUE planned liturgical programming. During the plans for the Journey Toward Justice march in Santa Monica, there was some dispute over the incorporation of Wiccans from Santa Monica. A couple of CLUE clergy felt that an interfaith organization needed to be open and inclusive. In fact, during the discussions, these two people said that even having "clergy and laity" in the name of the organization

was regressive and exclusive, as some religions, such as Buddhism, do not have ordained clergy. Other clergy disagreed, including one clergy member who anticipated that if pagan rituals were included in the interfaith blessings, Latina women in the union would fear becoming involved with anything that smacked of *brujeria,* or witchcraft. Another person told me that union organizers had asked, "How's it going to look if we invite a witch?" Big theological discussions ensued within CLUE, with some clergy arguing that pagan traditions were part of indigenous religion and at the root of Christianity and other faith traditions while other clergy were still opposed. The resulting program reflected something of a compromise, with blessings to the four directions included in the liturgy. In general, in efforts to be inclusive, the CLUE liturgies walked a fine line, avoiding overtly Christ-centered ceremonies and yet remaining true to ancient faith traditions of the major religions, principally those of Christianity and Judaism.

SPIRITUAL RENEWAL

"CLUE doesn't realize it, but I needed them just as much as they need me." These are the words of Reverend Jarvis Johnson, and they speak to the deep gratification that many of the clergy derived from their participation with CLUE. In the struggle for economic justice and for the rights of Latino immigrant workers in Los Angeles, we have seen how important the integration of religion and religious moral voice has proved to be. Religion is critical to this burgeoning social movement, but so, too, many of the clergy said that CLUE activism was a way for them to reaffirm their faith.

No one was more effusive in this regard than Reverend Altagracia Perez, who found her CLUE involvement to be deeply transformative. She had been experiencing something of an emotional and spiritual crisis, but she was newly revitalized and inspired when she met the workers through CLUE. These mostly Latino immigrant workers "were taking risks and making sacrifices—and not just doing it, but doing it willingly and joyfully," she recalled. "And I, who had all this privilege, was doing everything begrudgingly. . . . It really shamed me. . . . It was a conversion experience for me to see that, and it invited my involvement." Although she had been active in community organizing around youth and HIV in the Bronx, she had never really experienced a seamless fit of faith and action. Becoming a faith-based activist in CLUE, she said, was "what I always dreamed of when I was in seminary. I had studied liberation theology, and . . . I was finally doing it!"

Similarly, Reverend Dick Gillet, a veteran of religiously inspired economic justice activism, also found a sort of redemption in his CLUE work. He had worked with factory workers in Puerto Rico in the 1970s, then in Los Angeles in the 1980s as part of "a very small but quite effective coalition to address massive plant closures in Los Angeles" and high unemployment [Los Angeles Coalition Against Plant Shut Downs]. But it "was not right for massive protest at that time, and the religious community, well there was just a handful of us that were involved in that." As a retired clergy, he felt renewed through CLUE, which had provided him with new experiences. "I find that in my late sixties I am learning, and I'm kind of in awe that I can learn, and I feel myself developing skills. I feel myself really rooted in this higher plan, and so it's an exciting time."

CONCLUSIONS

[W]e have seen how a group of clergy, most of them from Christian and Jewish traditions, use religious tools to promote the labor rights of Latino immigrant workers in the service industries. These clergy, many of them influenced by

strategies and experiences of clergy in the civil rights movement and of César Chávez and the UFW (United Farm Workers), enjoy access to a well-stocked religious tool box.

First, they not only come to their social activism motivated by their religious beliefs, but they are frequently verbally reasserting this to one another in meetings and forums. When I asked why they do what they do for the immigrant workers, [clergy members] frequently invoked scripture, and they spoke of the importance of faith-based sacrifice for the good of others. They said their activism around economic justice was a way to express and practice their faith. For these clerical leaders, this activism goes to the core of what it means to be a religious person.

Second, they rely on the concrete religious resources at their disposal to organize protests, meetings, and lobbying visits to the homes of workers or the offices of hotel managers and employers. Important religious-based resources include the well-honed oratory skills and charismatic talents of many of the clergy and the mundane but vital resources of church meeting halls, folding chairs, and office equipment.

[The CLUE] clergy and laity are not at all shy about using their religious authority and moral legitimacy for the cause. At this, they excel. They engage in civil disobedience, direct actions, and street protests when necessary. They are committed to nonviolence, but they will shut down the streets and avenues of Los Angeles, if necessary, and they freely use religious symbols and morality in these activities. They also use religion to directly pressure and persuade employers and managers to negotiate in good faith with the unions. In both lobbying activities and direct actions, they act as moral specialists.

CLUE members and the unions they support are media savvy and telegenic. As modern clergy, they do not wear collars and robes on all days of the week, but when doing their political work, they deliberately wear the clerical garb with the intent to persuade others of their moral authority. These religious activists are also cognizant of the need to respect religious pluralism and multiculturalism against the backdrop of re-Christianization. Therefore, they include religious rituals drawn from various religious traditions in protests, being careful not to get too denominational or exclusive. In the process, they make secular spaces momentarily sacred and imbue their movement for social change with collective corporeal activities that invoke ancient religious connections with the past.

REFERENCE

Dalton, Frederick John. 2003. *The Moral Vision of Cesar Chavez*. Maryknoll, NY: Orbis Books.

THE SOCIAL PRODUCTION OF CHANGE

44

Talking Back

bell hooks

(1989)

In the world of the southern black community I grew up in, "back talk" and "talking back" meant speaking as an equal to an authority figure. It meant daring to disagree and sometimes it just meant having an opinion. In the "old school," children were meant to be seen and not heard. My great-grandparents, grandparents, and parents were all from the old school. To make yourself heard if you were a child was to invite punishment, the back-hand lick, the slap across the face that would catch you unaware, or the feel of switches stinging your arms and legs.

To speak then when one was not spoken to was a courageous act—an act of risking and daring. And yet it was hard not to speak in warm rooms where heated discussions began at the crack of dawn, women's voices filling the air, giving orders, making threats, fussing. Black men may have excelled in the art of poetic preaching in the male-dominated church, but in the church of the home where the everyday rules of how to live and how to act were established it was black women who preached. There, black women spoke in a language so rich, so poetic, that it felt to me like being shut off from life, smothered to death if one was not allowed to participate.

It was in that world of woman talk (the men were often silent, often absent) that was born in me the craving to speak, to have a voice, and not just any voice but one that could be identified as belonging to me. To make my voice, I had to speak, to hear myself talk—and talk I did—darting in and out of grown folk's conversations and dialogues, answering questions that were not directed at me, endlessly asking questions, making speeches. Needless to say, the punishments for these acts of speech seemed endless. They were intended to silence me—the child—and more particularly the girl child. Had I been a boy they might have encouraged me to speak believing that I might someday be called to preach. There was no "calling" for talking girls, no legitimized rewarded speech. The punishments I received for "talking back" were intended to suppress all possibility that I would create my own speech. That speech was to be suppressed so the "right speech of womanhood" would emerge.

Within feminist circles, silence is often seen as the sexist "right speech of womanhood"—the sign of woman's submission to patriarchal authority. This emphasis on woman's silence may be an accurate remembering of what has taken place in the households of women from WASP backgrounds in the United States, but in black communities (and diverse ethnic communities) women have not been silent. Their voices can be heard. Certainly for black women, our struggle has not been to emerge from silence into speech but to change the nature and direction of our speech, to make a speech that compels listeners, one that is heard.

Our speech, "the right speech of womanhood," was often the soliloquy, the talking into thin air, the talking to ears that do not hear you—the talk that is simply not listened to. Unlike the black male preacher whose speech was to be heard, who was to be listened to, whose words were to be remembered, the voices of black women—giving orders, making threats, fussing—could be tuned out, could become a kind of background music, audible but not acknowledged as significant speech. Dialogue—the sharing of speech and recognition—took place not between mother and child or mother and male authority figure but among black women. I can remember watching fascinated as our mother talked with her mother, sisters, and women friends. The intimacy and intensity of their speech—the satisfaction they received from talking to one another, the pleasure, the joy. It was in this world of woman speech, loud talk, angry words, women with tongues quick and sharp, tender sweet tongues, touching our world with their words, that I made speech my birthright—and the right to voice, to authorship, a privilege I would not be denied. It was in that world and because of it that I came to dream of writing, to write.

Writing was a way to capture speech, to hold onto it, keep it close. And so I wrote down bits and pieces of conversations, confessing in cheap diaries that soon fell apart from too much handling, expressing the intensity of my sorrow, the anguish of speech—for I was always saying the wrong thing, asking the wrong questions. I could not confine my speech to the necessary corners and concerns of life. I hid these writings under my bed, in pillow stuffings, among faded underwear. When my sisters found and read them, they ridiculed and mocked me—poking fun. I felt violated, ashamed, as if the secret parts of my self had been exposed, brought into the open, and hung like newly clean laundry, out in the air for everyone to see. The fear of exposure, the fear that one's deepest emotions and innermost thoughts would be dismissed as mere nonsense, felt by so many young girls keeping diaries, holding and hiding speech, seems to me now one of the barriers that women have needed and still need to destroy so that we are no longer pushed into secrecy or silence.

Despite my feelings of violation, of exposure, I continued to speak and write, choosing my hiding places well, learning to destroy work when no safe place could be found. I was never taught absolute silence, I was taught that it was important to speak but to talk a talk that was in itself a silence. Taught to speak and yet beware of the betrayal of too much heard speech, I experienced intense confusion and deep anxiety in my efforts to speak and write. Reciting poems at Sunday afternoon church service might be rewarded. Writing a poem (when one's time could be "better" spent sweeping, ironing, learning to cook) was luxurious activity, indulged in at the expense of others. Questioning authority, raising issues that were not deemed appropriate subjects brought pain, punishments—like telling mama I wanted to die before her because I could not live without her—that was crazy talk, crazy speech, the kind that would lead you to end up in a mental institution. "Little girl," I would be told, "if you don't stop all this crazy talk and crazy acting you are going to end up right out there at Western State."

Madness, not just physical abuse, was the punishment for too much talk if you were female. Yet even as this fear of madness haunted me, hanging over my writing like a monstrous shadow, I could not stop the words, making thought, writing speech. For this terrible madness which I feared, which I was sure was the destiny of daring women born to intense speech (after all, the authorities emphasized this point daily), was not as threatening as imposed silence, as suppressed speech.

Safety and sanity were to be sacrificed if I was to experience defiant speech. Though I risked them both, deep-seated fears and anxieties characterized my childhood days. I would speak but I would not ride a bike, play hardball, or hold the gray kitten. Writing about the ways we are hurt by negative traumas in our growing-up years, psychoanalyst Alice Miller makes the point in *For Your Own Good* that it is not clear why childhood wounds become for some folk an opportunity to grow, to move forward rather than backward in the process of self-realization. Certainly, when I reflect on the trials of my growing-up years, the many punishments, I can see now that in resistance I learned to be vigilant in the nourishment of my spirit, to be tough, to courageously protect that spirit from forces that would break it.

While punishing me, my parents often spoke about the necessity of breaking my spirit. Now when I ponder the silences, the voices that are not heard, the voices of those wounded and/or oppressed individuals who do not speak or write, I contemplate the acts of persecution, torture—the terrorism that breaks spirits, that makes creativity impossible. I write these words to bear witness to the primacy of resistance struggle in any situation of domination (even within family life); to the strength and power that emerges from sustained resistance and the profound conviction that these forces can be healing, can protect us from dehumanization and despair.

These early trials, wherein I learned to stand my ground, to keep my spirit intact, came vividly to mind after I published *Ain't I a Woman* and the book was sharply and harshly criticized. While I had expected a climate of critical dialogue, I was not expecting a critical avalanche that had the power in its intensity to crush spirit, to push one into silence. Since that time I have heard stories about black women, about women of color, who write and publish (even when the work is quite successful), having nervous breakdowns, being made mad because they cannot bear the harsh responses of family, friends, and unknown critics, or becoming silent, unproductive. Surely, the absence of a humane critical response has tremendous impact on the writer from any oppressed, colonized group who endeavors to speak. For us, true speaking is not solely an expression of creative power; it is an act of resistance, a political gesture that challenges the politics of domination that would render us nameless and voiceless. As such, it is a courageous act—as such, it represents a threat. To those who wield oppressive power, that which is threatening must necessarily be wiped out, annihilated, silenced.

Recently, efforts by black women writers to call attention to our work serve to highlight both our presence and absence. Whenever I peruse women's bookstores I am struck not by the rapidly growing body of feminist writing by black women but by the paucity of available published material. Those of us who write and are published remain few in number. The context of silence is varied and multi-dimensional. Most obvious are the ways racism, sexism, and class exploitation act as agents to suppress and silence. Less obvious are the inner struggles, the efforts made to gain the necessary confidence to write, to rewrite, to fully develop craft and skill—and the extent to which such efforts fail.

Although I have wanted writing to be my life-work since childhood, it has been difficult for me to claim "writer" as part of that which identifies and shapes my everyday reality. Even after publishing books, I would often speak of wanting to be a writer as though these works did not exist. And though I would be told, "you are a writer," I was not yet ready to fully affirm this truth. Part of myself was still held captive by domineering forces of history, of familial life that had charted a map of silence, of right speech. I had not completely let go of the fear of saying the wrong thing, of being punished. Somewhere in the deep recesses of my mind, I believed I could avoid both responsibility and punishment if I did not declare myself a writer.

One of the many reasons I chose to write using the pseudonym bell hooks, a family name (mother to Sarah Oldham, grandmother to Rosa Bell Oldham, great-grandmother to me), was to construct a writer-identity that would challenge and subdue all impulses leading me away from speech into silence. I was a young girl buying bubble gum at the corner store when I first really heard the full name bell hooks: I had just "talked back" to a grown person. Even now I can recall the surprised look, the mocking tones that informed me I must be kin to bell hooks—a sharp-tongued woman, a woman who spoke her mind, a woman who was not afraid to talk back. I claimed this legacy of defiance, of will, of courage, affirming my link to female ancestors who were bold and daring in their speech. Unlike my bold and daring mother and grandmother, who were not supportive of talking back, even though they were assertive and powerful in their speech, bell hooks as I discovered, claimed, and invented her, was my ally, my support.

The initial act of talking back outside the home was empowering. It was the first of many acts of defiant speech that would make it possible for me to emerge as an independent thinker and writer. In retrospect, "talking back" became for me a rite of initiation, testing my courage, strengthening my commitment, preparing me for the days ahead—the days when writing, rejection notices, periods of silence, publication, ongoing development seem impossible but necessary.

Moving from silence into speech is for the oppressed, the colonized, the exploited, and those who stand and struggle side by side a gesture of defiance that heals, that makes new life and new growth possible. It is that act of speech, of "talking back," that is no mere gesture of empty words, that is the expression of moving from object to subject—the liberated voice.

EPILOGUE

The mind that has conceived a plan of living must never lose sight of the chaos against which that pattern was conceived.

—Ralph Ellison, *Invisible Man*

As any action or posture long continued will distort and disfigure the limbs; so the mind likewise is crippled and contracted by perpetual application to the same set of ideas.

—Samuel Johnson: *Rambler #173*

God can be shaped. God is Change.

—Octavia Butler, *Parable of the Sower*

On January 10, 2009, my close friend and longtime colleague Peter Kollock was killed instantly when he struck a tree while driving a motorcycle near his home in the Malibu hills of California. Peter and I conceived the original edition of this book together in the early 1990s when we were both eager young professors fresh out of graduate school. The impetus for the book was a request from a publisher who hoped to break free from some of the more limiting aspects of textbook production and create a line of books that would be socially relevant and engaging for students. The publisher promised us that in producing this text, we would have creative freedom. Peter and I were enthusiastic about the prospect of creating a text that deviated from some of the mind-numbing, "dumbed down" material that was available to students at the time. In thinking about how to approach the first original edition of the book, we identified one primary aim: We wanted to introduce readers to the usefulness of symbolic interactionism as a set of tools for self and social awareness. We called this awareness *mindfulness*.

In addition to being a professor of sociology, Peter was a dedicated student of Buddhism (in the tradition of the Vietnamese teacher Thich Nhat Hanh). Buddhist practices emphasize meditation and mindfulness as a means to liberation from pain and suffering. Many contemporary practices, both religious and secular, also focus on what are sometimes called *contemplative* exercises or forms of insight and meditation intended to induce greater awareness of our personal and social patterns. Common to all of these contemplative practices is the promise that by slowing down and bringing our awareness to taken-for-granted feelings, experiences, and routines, we will gain insight into the patterns that shape our daily lives. This insight enables us to make mindful choices about how we are living. In other words, we wake up to our selves and our social surroundings.

Peter and I were always fascinated with the ways in which the study of sociology in general, and symbolic interactionism in particular, is similar to these contemplative practices. In both, the focus is on gaining awareness of the internal conversations and social routines and patterns that shape our lives and our relationships with others. For us, sociology has been a practice of becoming more mindful. In the recent years before his death, Peter had extended his sociology class offerings at UCLA (where he was a professor) to include a course on mindfulness. In addition to readings and guest lectures from some of the leading contemporary scholars studying the positive effects of meditation on brain activity and creativity, Peter's syllabus included a significant amount of material derived from studies in symbolic interactionism. The class was wildly popular and always had a long waiting list. Students applying to take the class often commented that their college education was giving them a lot of information, but this information didn't necessarily include recipes or tools for how to incorporate this information into a useful and meaningful life. They also hoped the class would yield insights into how to live satisfying, balanced lives in a time that, for many people, feels increasingly chaotic and out of control.

Peter and I pondered similar questions as we considered how best to organize this text in a way that demonstrates the usefulness of symbolic interactionism as a set of tools for mindfulness. At the time of his death, Peter was working on a book he called *The Sociology of Mindfulness*. By way of conclusion, and in tribute to Peter's efforts, I offer some thoughts on symbolic interactionism as a set of tools for mindful, meaningful living.

FRACTURED SELVES

The conditions of contemporary life leave many of us feeling harried, overwhelmed, and incapable of "catching up" to ourselves. Rapid advances in electronic communication enable us to connect with others all across the globe at lightning speed. We welcome this potential for expanded social networking, but we also feel overwhelmed with the quickened pace and rising confusion of being in multiple worlds simultaneously. Most of us find ourselves occupying a variety of social positions and taking on a wide range of social identities daily. What are the consequences of this multiplicity of self? People increasingly report that they feel "fractured."

Social psychologist Kenneth Gergen (1991) talks about this contemporary experience as the *saturated self*. In Gergen's assessment, the hectic pace of everyday life leaves us "saturated" with social demands. As a result of the increasing complexity of social life, we experience ourselves as filled to overflowing with a "multiplicity of incoherent and unrelated languages of the self" (p. 6). In this flood of social stimuli, our awareness of an inner core, or beacon, is diluted. We need re-centering, but even when we do manage to find solitude, we can no longer hear ourselves. This inner deafness is exacerbated by the encroaching presence of television and other forms of media output in nearly every public space. This external hubbub is reproduced as an internal chatter that we find difficult to silence even when we are alone.

As an exercise, I ask my students to sit someplace public but not necessarily too busy and "do nothing" for 10 minutes. Joking about having an assignment to "do nothing," they happily embark to various sites to do their "homework." The subsequent essays are very revealing and suggest the difficulty in turning off the inner chatter that tells us we should always be busily engaged, or at least appear to be. Many students write that they were surprised to find that they couldn't settle down, even for 10 minutes. Several note that they felt frustrated, even angry, because they were "wasting time." Many of them are also intrigued when they realize just how strong their inner critic is and how in sync it is with the pace of contemporary life.

Arlie Hochschild (1983; see Reading 33) suggests that the *emotional labor* that we are required to engage in as we perform a variety of social roles, especially in employment, diminishes our ability to hear ourselves. Emotions can be an important source of information for making sense of our experiences. However, prolonged and uninterrupted emotion management makes it difficult for us to recognize emotional cues that may be signalling something important, such as stress, grief, anxiety, and so on. The more we ignore these cues and the less practiced we are in listening to ourselves, the more likely we are to be at the mercy of social forces, including our own unexamined, internalized social reflexes such as guilt, shame, and competition. For Hochschild, the result is "burnout" or disassociation.

Sociologists Jay Gubrium and James Holstein (2001) sum up the state of the contemporary self as "trying times and troubled selves." In their analysis, the self has become increasingly institutionalized. The idea of the *institutionalized self* offers an interesting play on words: We are not necessarily locked up in institutions (such as prisons and asylums); in fact we are technically more "free" than our ancestors due to the technological advances that allow us to roam all over the world at the touch of a finger. These same technological advances also enable many people to work from their homes, in coffee shops, and elsewhere and thereby avoid the presumably stifling environment of the office. In theory, these conditions should make us less institutionalized. However, the resulting din and speed at which we are living our lives has resulted in a chaos that, in the absence of being able to tune in internally, means we are living more from the outside in—we are much more likely to behave in response to socially instituted practices that have been (mindlessly) incorporated and now act as institutional reflexes.

An analysis of all the conditions that have given rise to this state of being is beyond the scope of this brief essay (I do hope the issues tempt you to pursue more sociology).

However, an antidote can be found in our ability for developing awareness or mindfulness of the social practices in which we participate. As a basis for this, I offer a brief review of some of the lessons of symbolic interactionism, especially as they relate to the construction of taken-for-granted social beliefs and practices. To the extent that we become aware of these practices, and of our own ability to reframe them, we become more awake, more engaged, and better able to listen to ourselves and others.

SYMBOLIC INTERACTIONISM, MEANING, AND TRUTH

What's real? How do you determine what is true and right and good? These are the questions that opened this book (see Part I). Symbolic interactionism as a form of intellectual inquiry implies that realities are multiple, shifting, contradictory, and situationally specific. Whereas some contemporary scholars focus on deconstructing cultural beliefs and practices, symbolic interactionists focus on studying how people learn and sustain culturally specific practices and beliefs through everyday patterns of interaction. If you really follow the logic of the symbolic interactionist perspective, you will note that it implies (1) interactions are always fraught with misunderstandings, miscues, misinformation, and possibly even attempts to mislead and manipulate, and (2) meaning is *always negotiated*: It is always in flux and always reflects the interactional context and the relationship between persons in the interaction.

Because symbolic interactionism implies that there is no universal meaning or "truth," the perspective has been criticized as perpetuating cynicism and social dissolution. Students of symbolic interactionism sometimes conclude that it is not worthwhile to participate in social life because, ultimately, there is no *real* meaning. The conclusion they draw is that nothing really matters. The dilemma, as they represent it to themselves, is whether to participate in social relations that are, theoretically, always in flux.

This is especially a dilemma for people who are newly aware of the complex, contradictory, and shifting aspects of social relations. However, the crisis is not so much a crisis of meaning that has been brought about by symbolic interactionist studies and critical inquiries, but a crisis that arises because people who learn these perspectives remain stuck in unquestioned or taken-for-granted beliefs that meaning is not real or authentic unless it transcends human construction. *The real dilemma is not that there is no universal meaning, but that persons fail to comprehend the significance of their own expressive and creative potential.* As a way of reframing this dilemma, consider the following story:

In the book *The Sword and the Stone*, by T. H. White (1938/1978), a wise old badger tells his young apprentice, Wart, how all the creatures of the earth came to be as they are. According to the badger, God assembled a multitude of fledgling embryos before him on the sixth day of creation and explained that He was going to hand out gifts. The embryos could each choose two or three gifts. These gifts would serve as a set of tools that would mark the creature's unique existence on earth. The embryos chattered excitedly among themselves about the possible combinations of tools each might ask for. When the time came, each embryo stepped forward and requested its gifts from God. Some asked for arms that were diggers or garden forks, some chose to use their arms as flying machines, and others asked for bodies like boats and arms that were oars. One of the lizards decided to swap its entire body for blotting paper. Still others asked to be able to use their mouths as drills or offensive weapons. Finally, it was the turn of the embryo called "human." This small, naked creature approached God and stammered shyly, "I have considered your generous offer, and I thank you for it, but I choose to stay as I am."

"Well chosen," thundered God. "In deciding to retain your embryonic form you will have use of all the gifts that mark the being of each of the other creatures. You will exist always as potential: the potential to take up and put down the tools of the other creatures, the potential to create uniforms and tools of your own design and to wear and discard them as you see fit. You have chosen wisely, human. We wish you well in your earthly journey."

An important lesson of symbolic interactionism is that humans exist as embryonic potential. We are capable of creating, taking on, and casting off various identities and cultural institutions. Our potential is limited only by our imagination and our ability to assemble the materials necessary to realize our visions. As social beings, the ability to create shared meaning is the distinctive mark of our species. However, the history of Western consciousness suggests a somewhat paradoxical acceptance of this ability. We are eager to embrace our creative potential but at the same time reluctant to recognize our own authority as social creators and the responsibility that this implies.

Imagine using this logic if you intended to build a sand castle on the beach. It will only be washed away by the tides or eroded by the wind. It's fragile and temporary, so why bother? *Why* do people build sand castles? Certainly not because they expect them to last, but rather for the sheer pleasure of doing so. The experience lingers long after the sand form has crumbled away. Why do people form friendships, get married, or invest time and energy in pursuing a vocation (such as law school or the ministry), even though they may have doubts about its permanence? Presumably, these activities are more stable than the sand castle, but are they more stable because they are "naturally" more stable or because we care enough to remain continually engaged in their ongoing creation?

This is a significant distinction and one that is at the core of symbolic interactionism with its emphasis on social interaction as a basis for creating and maintaining social routines. Symbolic interactionism provides us with the tools for exploring *why* and *how* specific social activities become stable and take on the form of social institutions that have firmly grounded social stability and corresponding social authority. In other words, according to the symbolic interactionist perspective *there are stable, predictable patterns of behavior and systems of belief*. The central focus of this perspective is not only to demonstrate the existence of these patterns, but *to show the ways in which ordinary people create and re-create them.* Just because these patterns are the result of human activity does not make them any less meaningful. The pertinent question is whether people are *mindfully engaged* in these practices or *mindlessly* rattling around in old routines and beliefs that may have lost their meaning.

The fact that we create and re-create our own systems of meaning and ideals doesn't make these beliefs and practices any less real. In fact, our ability to analyze, critique, and *change* our practices for the common good is a mark of our creative potential. Again, the pertinent point is the extent to which we are mindfully engaged in the process of social relations. When you are engaged and critically aware of the role you play in various systems of meaning, then you are also able to take responsibility for your actions and to participate in ongoing discussions about what is "right" and "good." Authority, morality, and authenticity are *embedded* in these social relations. The actual process of involvement can be seen as an enactment of morality and authenticity.

We like to think that most people who were given a choice between (1) living a life in mindless ignorance of the social processes that shape who and what we are and (2) becoming mindfully and critically aware of these processes would choose mindful awareness. This process of becoming aware can itself be an act of meaningful engagement. Through critical reflection and analysis, we learn to discern taken-for-granted beliefs and practices; through engaged, mindful participation, we contribute to the ongoing creation of a mindful existence. In the remainder of this essay I discuss two consequences of mindlessness that must be addressed in pursuit of a mindful, meaningful existence: ossification and entropy.

Ossification

We have discussed the tendency for human routines and ideas to harden, or ossify, into habits and entrenched systems of belief (see the essays for Parts V and VI). We have also discussed some of the reasons why this occurs in human relations (desire for predictability, cognitive efficiency, mindlessness). Ossified social practices (aka social institutions) are not necessarily bad. The problems arise when we forget the purpose of the initial routine or practice or fail to remain mindful about the fact that these are socially created routines. What may have served as a useful basis for achieving some particular end becomes an ideology and an end in itself. In other words, useful recipes for living become calcified as ideologies. We may persist in maintaining these ossified constructions simply because they have become permanent, hardened features of our social landscape. But at the same time, we may be contributing to the maintenance of our own prisons.

People usually know when to tear down a building that has ceased to serve any useful function and may even be a source of danger. However, we sometimes rattle around in social institutions that are cracked and crumbling simply because we fail to realize that it is within our power to step beyond the confines of these structures and build others. The point is not that all old social institutions should be torn down; it is that we should be mindful of the purposes of the social institutions that our actions (or inactions) help to perpetuate. Unfortunately, such purposes become increasingly difficult to recognize—and change becomes more difficult—the more hardened, or ossified, the institution becomes.

Consider the prevalent social routine of giving exams in U.S. universities. In a seminar for graduate students on how to teach, I ask prospective college teachers to provide a rationale for giving exams. At first, this seems like a simple task, but the seminar participants usually end up struggling once they begin to think about it. The practice of giving exams has become such an ossified element of the educational landscape that many instructors engage in the practice mindlessly. They really don't know why they do it. If exams are written and administered with a particular purpose, such as providing feedback for the student and the instructor or as an incentive to organize chunks of information, then teachers are participating in the mindful maintenance of this social institution. But to give exams simply because "that's what's always been done" is to perpetuate a potentially meaningless social routine.

Once the purpose for a particular social routine is isolated, it is possible to devise potentially more useful routes to achieve it. For example, one unfortunate outcome of the exam procedure may be the unnecessary rank ordering of students. If the purpose of exams is to motivate students to organize and articulate their knowledge, then it may be possible to create an alternative exercise that more directly serves the intended purpose and avoids the pitfalls. It is possible, however, that the purpose of exams is indeed to rank-order persons—perhaps to facilitate their entrance into a stratified institution, such as the labor market. In that case, instructors should be mindfully aware that their examination procedures serve to perpetuate social stratification and that they are performing a gate-keeping role for other social institutions.

The point is to understand how one's participation in particular cultural routines perpetuates the existence of social institutions. Here, in the exploration of ossified structures, is where the tools of deconstruction serve a useful end. Such explorations need not lead to the conclusion that the entire structure should be dismantled, however. Mindful construction instructs us to ask what purpose the social routine serves and whether we want to participate in that purpose.

Entropy

If any pattern in nature seems to play itself out in human relations, it is entropy. In nature entropy is the natural process of decay. Applied to social relationships, entropy is a tendency toward erosion. According to the laws of thermodynamics, coherent molecular systems require constant input of energy to maintain their structure. If this energy is diverted, the system (whether molecule, leaf, or earlobe) will erode or fall apart into increasingly random elements. This tendency toward randomness is entropy. Similarly, the meaning and purpose of our social relationships are constantly threatened with erosion unless participants infuse these routines with mindful energy. Failure to do so is the reason we so often find ourselves thinking, "The thrill is gone."

What are some of the activities or relationships in your life that you take for granted? Do you have a spouse or family member whom you love but "don't have enough time for"? Love and family involvement require ongoing, active participation in the ritual interactions that maintain these institutions (e.g., celebration of significant events and small gestures of acknowledgment). We can't take for granted even seemingly well-established social institutions such as "the family." These social institutions do not endure without active maintenance.

MINDFUL ENGAGEMENT

Kahlil Gibran once wrote that pain is the experience of breaking the shell that encapsulates understanding. The implication is that, in the process of stretching one's experiences, intelligence, and understanding, there will always be the pain of breaking old habits and relinquishing old ways of knowing. Mindfulness requires both critical self-examination and the courage to break step with known, predictable routines. This can be difficult. At the same time, the words of Anaïs Nin remind us that "the time came when the risk to remain tight in the bud was more painful than the risk it took to bloom."

In conclusion we offer two takeaway messages for mindful engagement: (1) be mindfully choosy about the realities that you intend to produce or reproduce, and (2) recognize that the production of any reality requires your participation. To the extent that you participate mindfully, your life will take on increased meaning and purpose.

Trudy the bag lady, introduced in Reading 2 by Jane Wagner, is a true hero from the perspective of the mindful construction of reality. She has scrutinized the social institutions in which she dwells and found them to be unacceptable. Rather than turn away in despair, she has created a rich, lively alternative reality for herself. Now, as she describes it, her days are "jam-packed and fun-filled." Trudy is both a product of the general social realities that form this society and a commentator on them. Her commentary is compelling because it is both informed and hopeful. She is neither a social robot nor a cynic. She has taken responsible control of the construction of her own reality, and she invests in this production with enthusiasm and vigor. She is an intriguing character in that, although she is a street person, we do not feel pity for her. In fact, we may even feel a bit envious of her insightful, energetic reality, mad though it may appear by conventional standards. Trudy is bursting with potential.

Our own realities can be similarly produced, whether by doing something as simple as participating wholeheartedly in small daily rituals with those you love or as revolutionary as "talking back to outrage" in the form of large-scale collective protest. The message is that it takes insight, courage, and responsibility to engage in the mindful production of reality. This is the basis of a meaningful existence.

Another aspect of mindful engagement is the realization that our realities are always interactional. This means that we are likely to encounter tension and conflict. How we engage with this conflict is significant in determining the course or the realities we are a part of.

EMBRACING CONFLICT
AND CONTRADICTION/NEPANTLERAS

Nepantla is a concept used by Gloria Anzaldúa (Part IV) to describe the experience of being in between—we know where we're coming from but aren't sure yet where we're going. In her words:

Bridges span liminal (threshold) spaces between worlds, spaces I call nepantla, a Nahuatl word meaning tierra entre medio. Transformations occur in this in-between space, an unstable, unpredictable, always-in-transition space lacking clear boundaries. . . . [L]iving in this liminal zone means being in a constant state of displacement—an uncomfortable, even alarming feeling. (Anzaldúa & Keating 2002, p. 1)

Building on her earlier concept of mestiza consciousness wherein *la mestiza* experiences internal conflict, offering the idea of *El Mundo Zurdo* or the "Left-Handed World."

El Mundo Zurdo is a visionary place where people from diverse backgrounds with diverse needs and concerns co-exist and work together to bring about revolutionary change. We are the queer groups, the people that don't belong anywhere, not in the dominant world nor completely within our own respective cultures. Combined, we cover so many oppressions. But the overwhelming oppression is that we don't fit. . . . [D]espite the many differences among us we are all interconnected . . . we are "almas fines," or "kindred spirits." (pp. 520–521)

The inhabitants of *El Mundo Zurdo* are joined through rejection of the status quo, deviation from the dominant culture, and the strategic use of difference to forge new alliances. For Anzaldúa, this form of collective awareness involves a recognition that we are "living in a place/time of nepantla: exiting from the old worldview, we have not yet created new ones to replace it. We're questioning the barriers that divide us, and . . . opening the gate to the stranger within and without" (p. 529).

This final quotation serves as a rallying point:

Conflict, with its fiery nature, can trigger transformation depending on how we respond to it. Often, delving deeply into conflict instead of fleeing from it can bring an understanding (conocimiento) that will turn things around. . . . Where others saw borders, these nepantleras saw links; where others saw abysses, they saw bridges spanning these abysses. For nepantleras, to bridge is an act of will, an act of love, an attempt toward compassion and reconciliation, and a promise to be present with the pain of others without losing themselves to it. (p. 4)

Meaningful social psychology and meaningful living both involve finding connections, revealing patterns, and striving to bridge seemingly contradictory perspectives by offering deeper, richer frameworks of understanding. When we experience the contradiction, conflict, and pain of engaging fully in our own lives, we can't help but be transformed into *nepantleras*. We disrupt the status quo, and we become uniquely practiced, through our critical engagement with the complex processes underlying the appearance of a stable social reality, in mapping complexity and journeying through difference to new frontiers.

REFERENCES

Anzaldúa, G. (1987). *Borderlands/La Frontera: The new mestiza.* San Francisco, CA: Aunt Lute Books.

Anzaldúa, G., & Keating, A. (2002). *This bridge we call home: Radical visions for transformation.* New York, NY: Routledge.

Gergen, K. (1991). *The saturated self.* New York, NY: Basic Books.

Gubrium, J., & Holstein, J. (2001). *Institutional selves: Troubled identities in a postmodern world.* New York, NY: Oxford University Press.

Hochschild, A. (1983). *The managed heart.* Berkeley: University of California Press.

White, T. S. (1978). *The sword and the stone.* New York: Laurel Leaf. (Original work published 1938)

CREDITS

NAME INDEX

SUBJECT INDEX

ABOUT THE AUTHOR

Jodi O'Brien is Professor of Sociology at Seattle University. She teaches courses in social psychology, social inequalities, gender and sexualities, religion, and social theory. She writes and lectures on the cultural politics of transgressive identities and communities. Her other books include *Everyday Inequalities* (Basil Blackwell) and *Social Prisms: Reflections on Everyday Myths and Paradoxes* (Pine Forge Press), and she is the editor of *The Encyclopedia of Gender and Society* (SAGE).